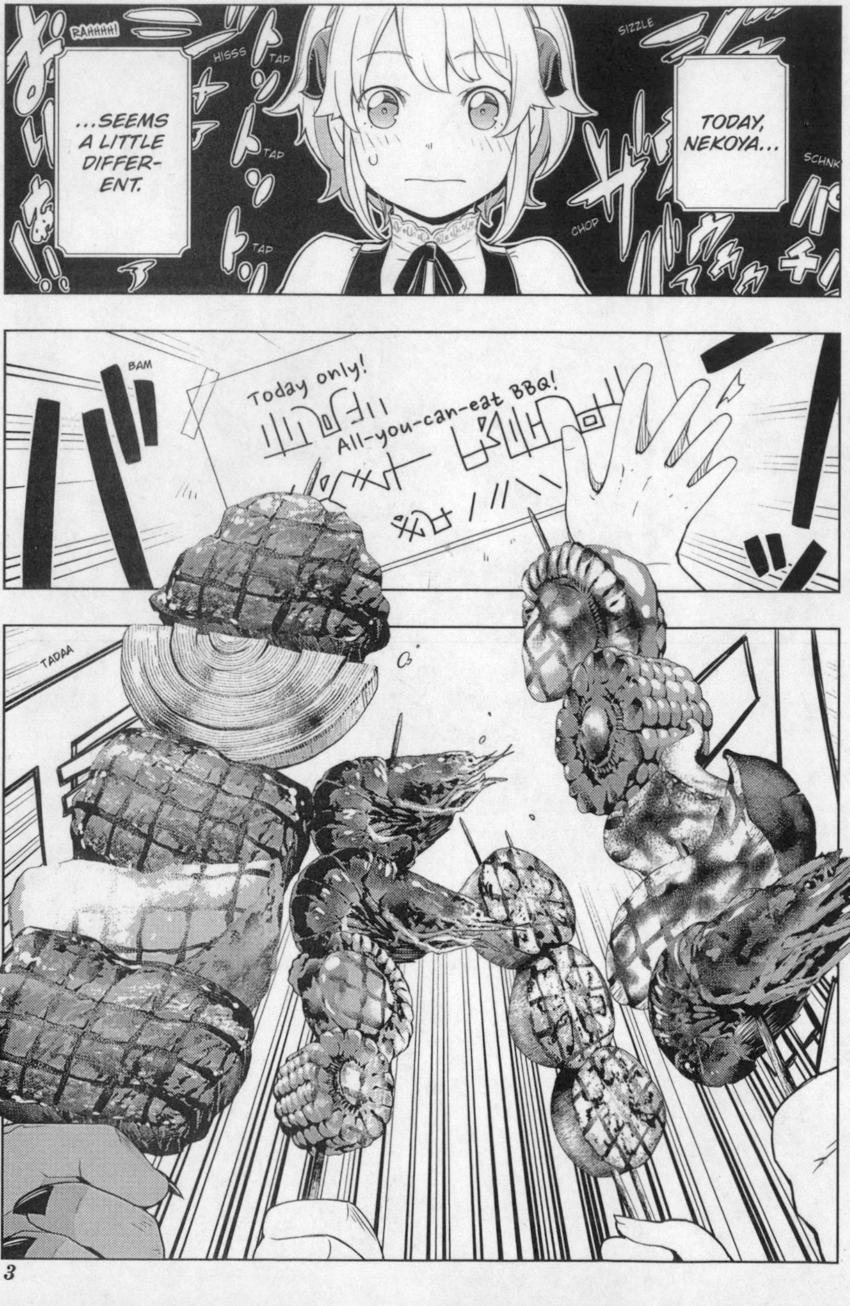
TODAY, NEKOYA...
SIZZLE
SCHNK
CHOP
TAP
TAP
TAP
HISSS
RAHHHH!
...SEEMS A LITTLE DIFFER-ENT.
BAM
Today only!
All-you-can-eat BBQ!
TADAA

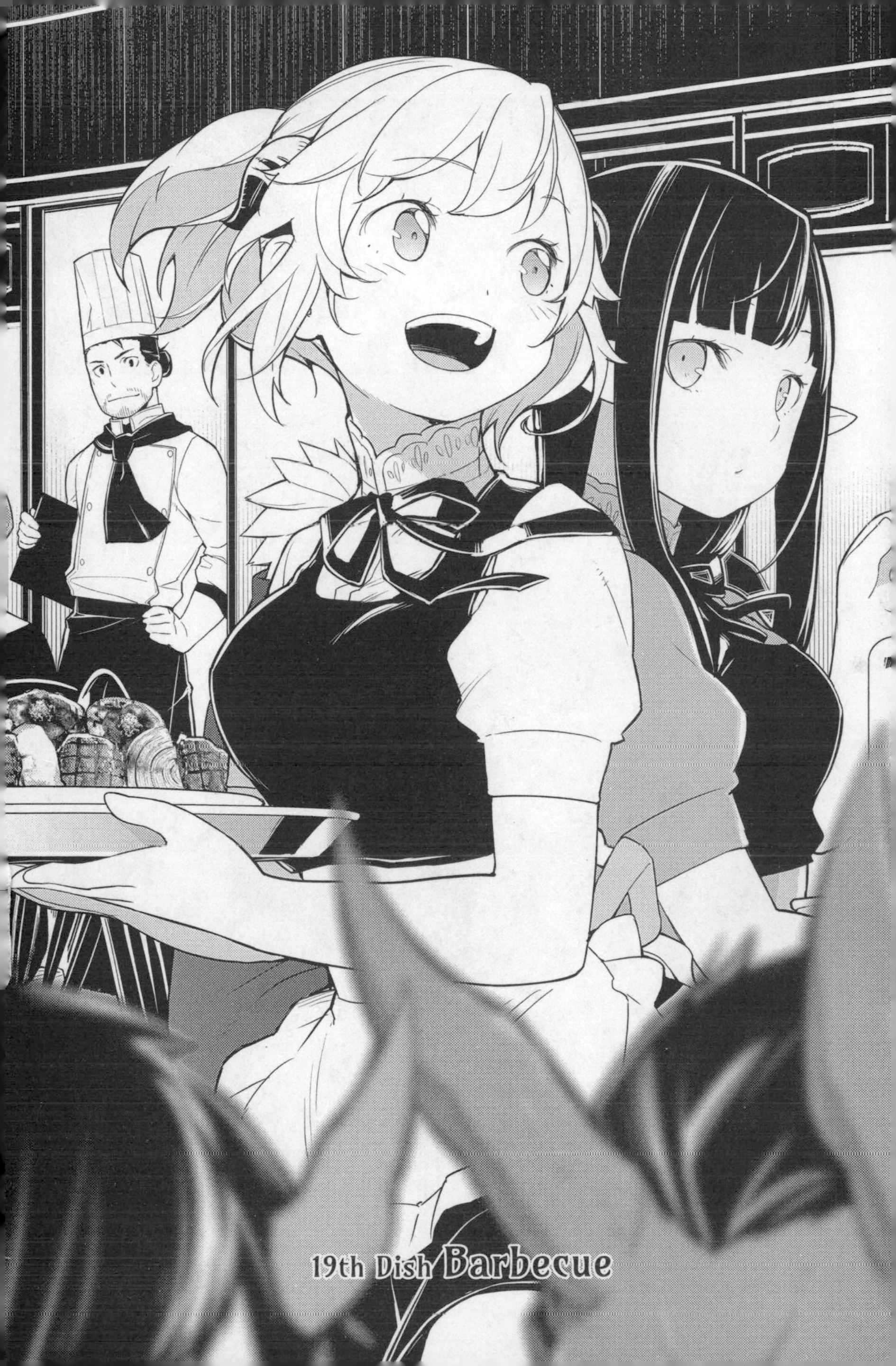
19th Dish Barbecue

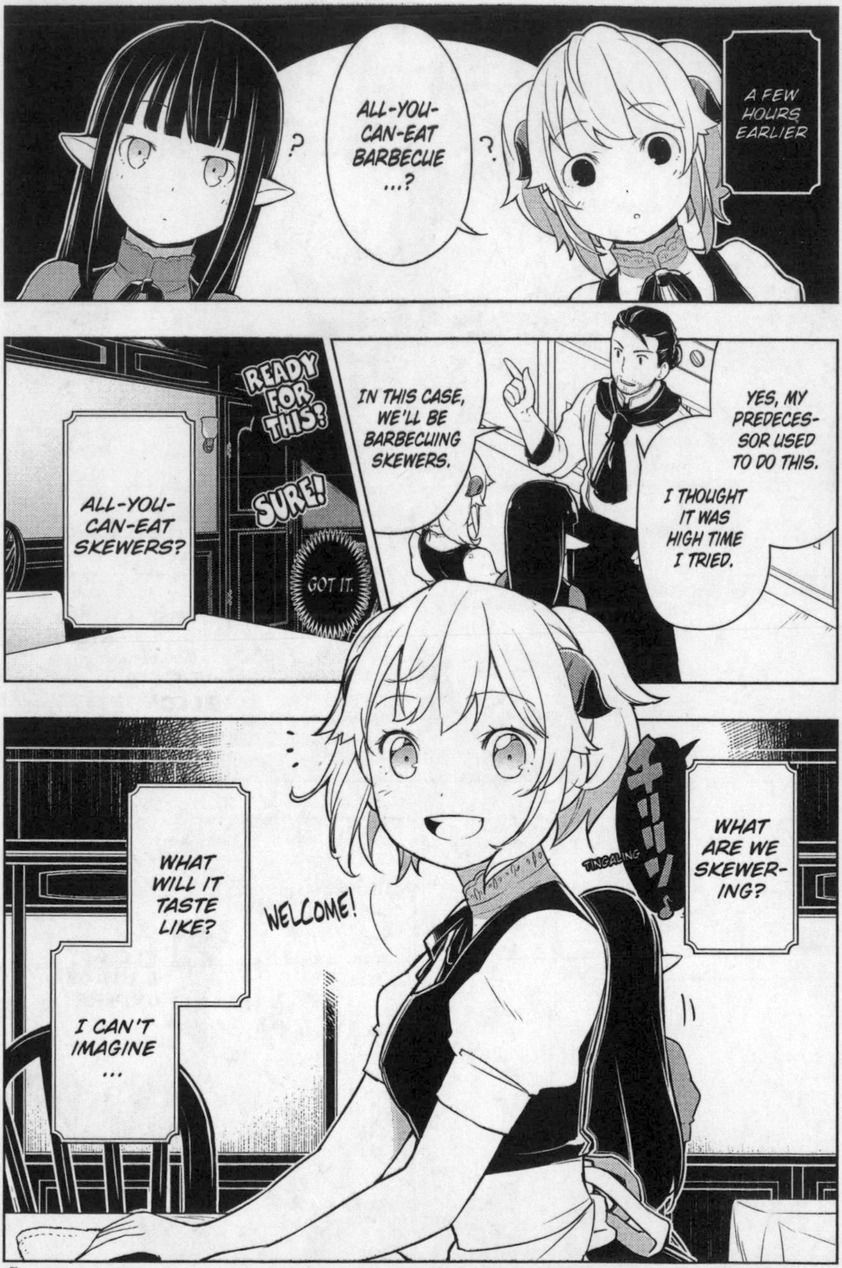
A FEW HOURS EARLIER
?
?
ALL-YOU-CAN-EAT BARBECUE ...?
YES, MY PREDECES-SOR USED TO DO THIS.
I THOUGHT IT WAS HIGH TIME I TRIED.
IN THIS CASE, WE'LL BE BARBECUING SKEWERS.
READY FOR THIS?!
SURE!
GOT IT.
ALL-YOU-CAN-EAT SKEWERS?
WHAT ARE WE SKEWER-ING?
TINGALING
WELCOME!
WHAT WILL IT TASTE LIKE?
I CAN'T IMAGINE ...

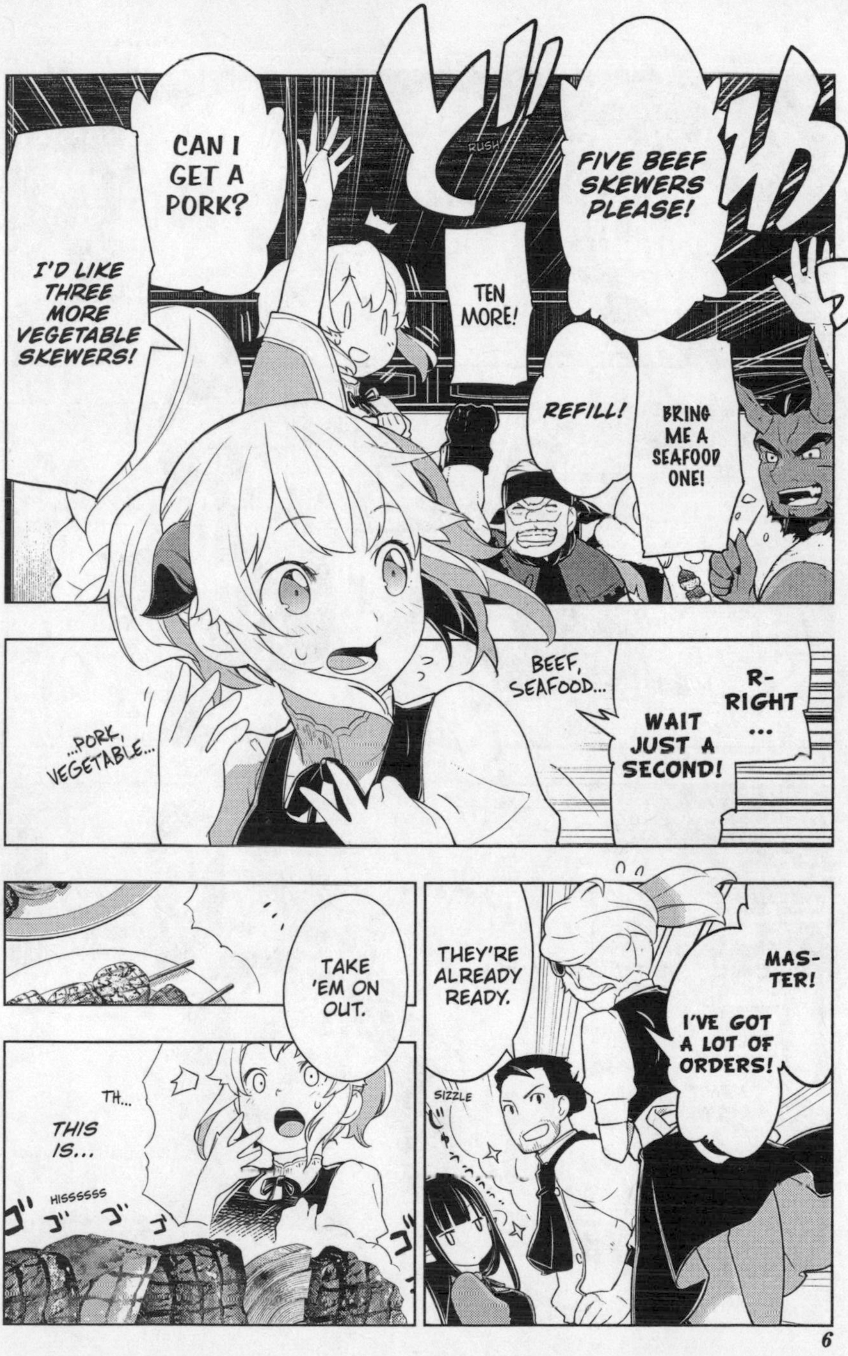
RUSH
FIVE BEEF SKEWERS PLEASE!
CAN I GET A PORK?
BRING ME A SEAFOOD ONE!
REFILL!
TEN MORE!
I'D LIKE THREE MORE VEGETABLE SKEWERS!
R-RIGHT...
WAIT JUST A SECOND!
BEEF, SEAFOOD...
...PORK, VEGETABLE...
MAS-TER!
I'VE GOT A LOT OF ORDERS!
THEY'RE ALREADY READY.
SIZZLE
TAKE 'EM ON OUT.
TH...
THIS IS...
HISSSSSS

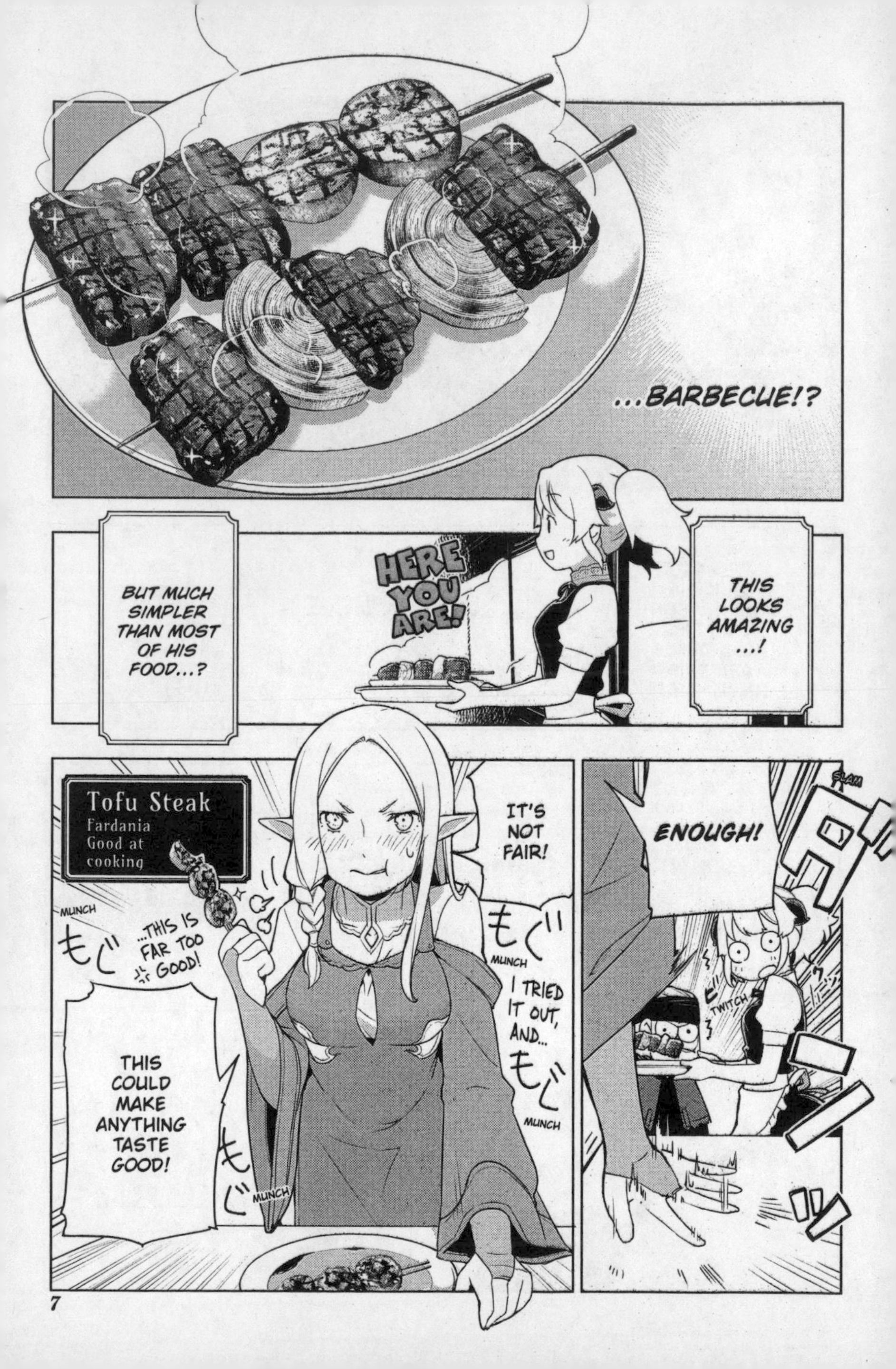
...BARBECUE!?
THIS LOOKS AMAZING ...!
HERE YOU ARE!
BUT MUCH SIMPLER THAN MOST OF HIS FOOD...?
SLAM
ENOUGH!
TWITCH
IT'S NOT FAIR!
もぐ
MUNCH
I TRIED IT OUT, AND...
もぐ
MUNCH
Tofu Steak
Fardania
Good at cooking
...THIS IS FAR TOO GOOD!
もぐ
MUNCH
THIS COULD MAKE ANYTHING TASTE GOOD!
もぐ
MUNCH

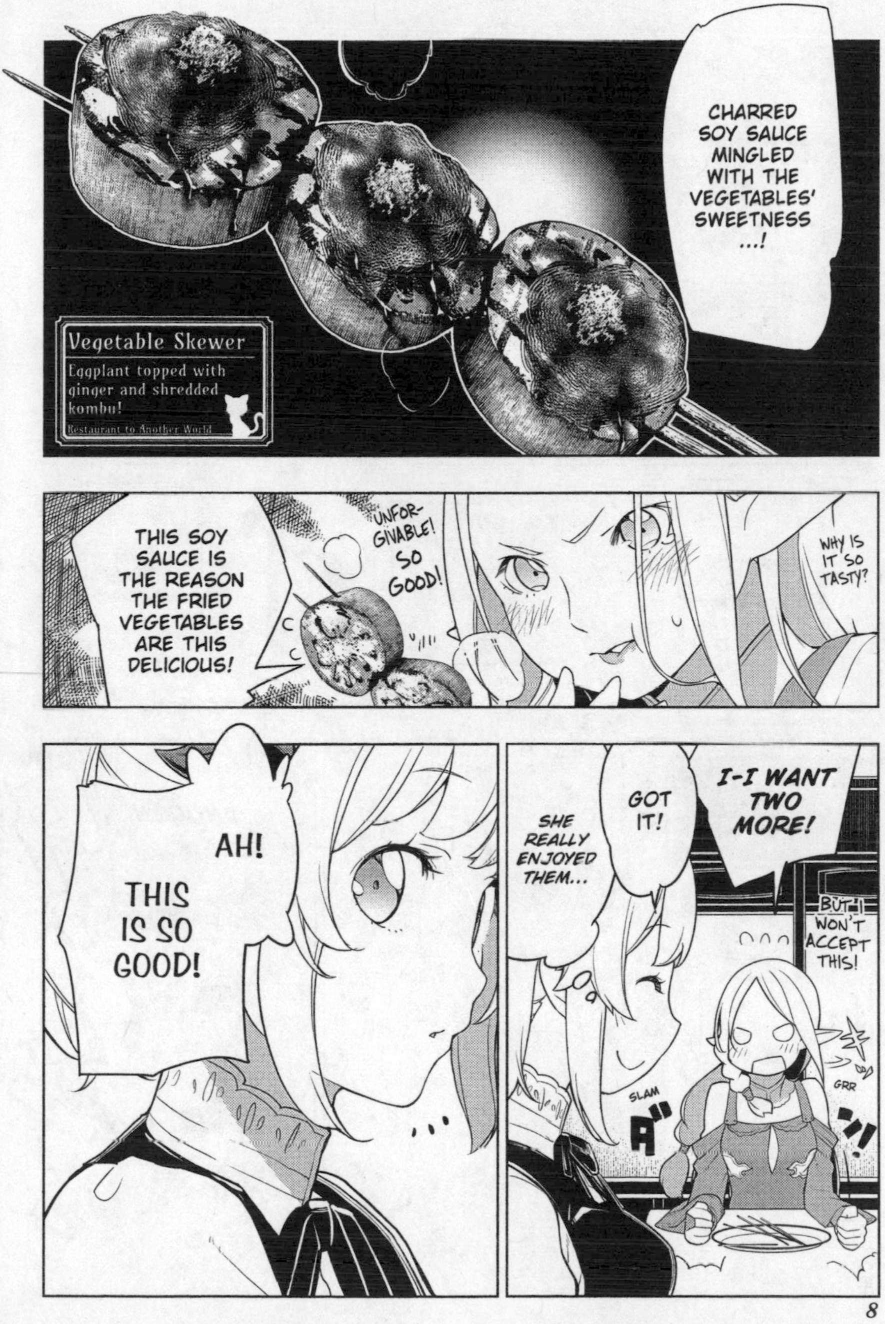
CHARRED SOY SAUCE MINGLED WITH THE VEGETABLES' SWEETNESS ...!
Vegetable Skewer
Eggplant topped with ginger and shredded kombu!
Restaurant to Another World
WHY IS IT SO TASTY?
UNFORGIVABLE! SO GOOD!
THIS SOY SAUCE IS THE REASON THE FRIED VEGETABLES ARE THIS DELICIOUS!
I-I WANT TWO MORE!
GOT IT!
SHE REALLY ENJOYED THEM...
BUT I WON'T ACCEPT THIS!
GRR
SLAM
AH!
THIS IS SO GOOD!

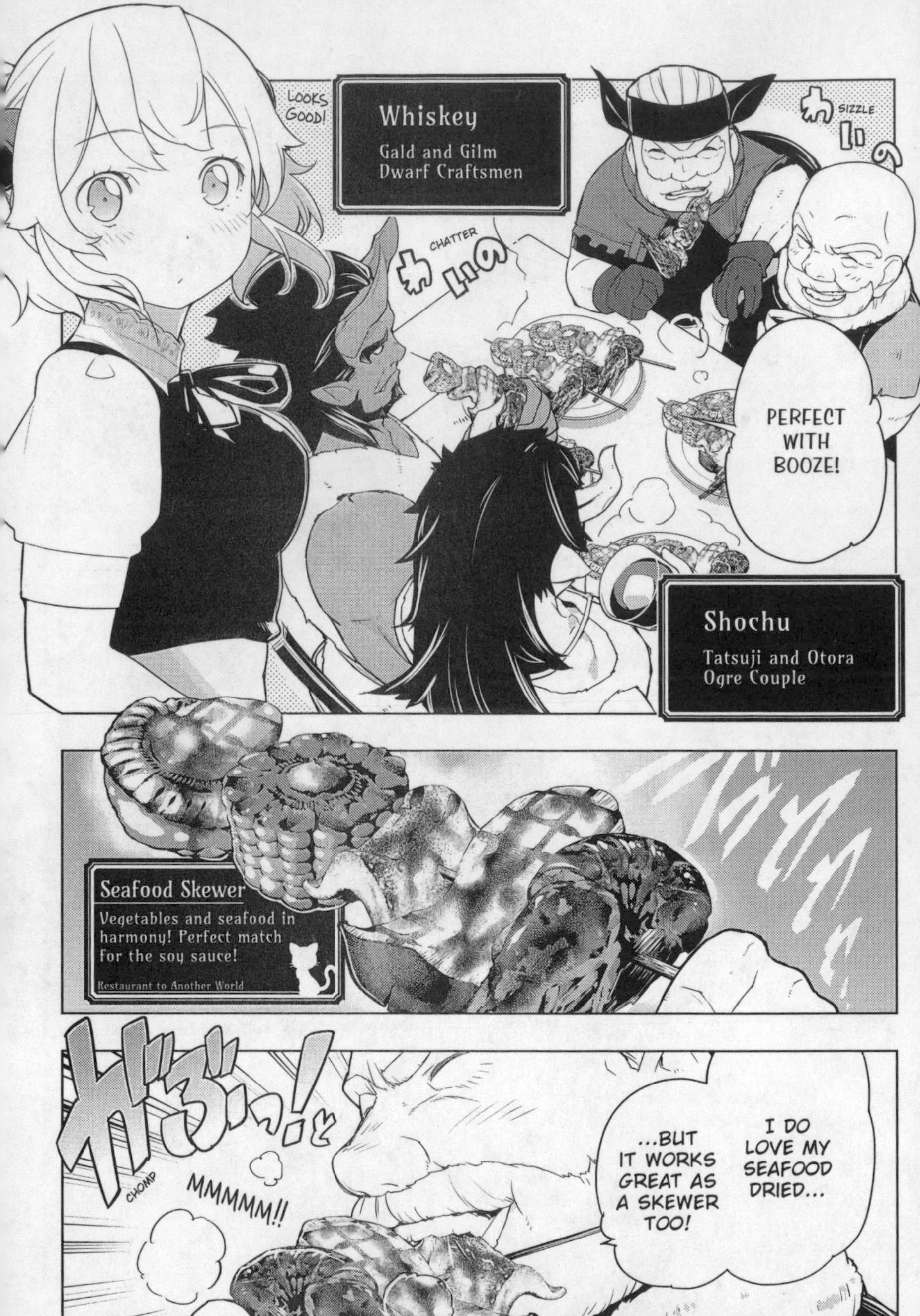
SIZZLE
Whiskey
Gald and Gilm
Dwarf Craftsmen
LOOKS GOOD!
PERFECT WITH BOOZE!
CHATTER
Shochu
Tatsuji and Otora
Ogre Couple
Seafood Skewer
Vegetables and seafood in harmony! Perfect match for the soy sauce!
Restaurant to Another World
I DO LOVE MY SEAFOOD DRIED...
...BUT IT WORKS GREAT AS A SKEWER TOO!
MMMMM!!
CHOMP

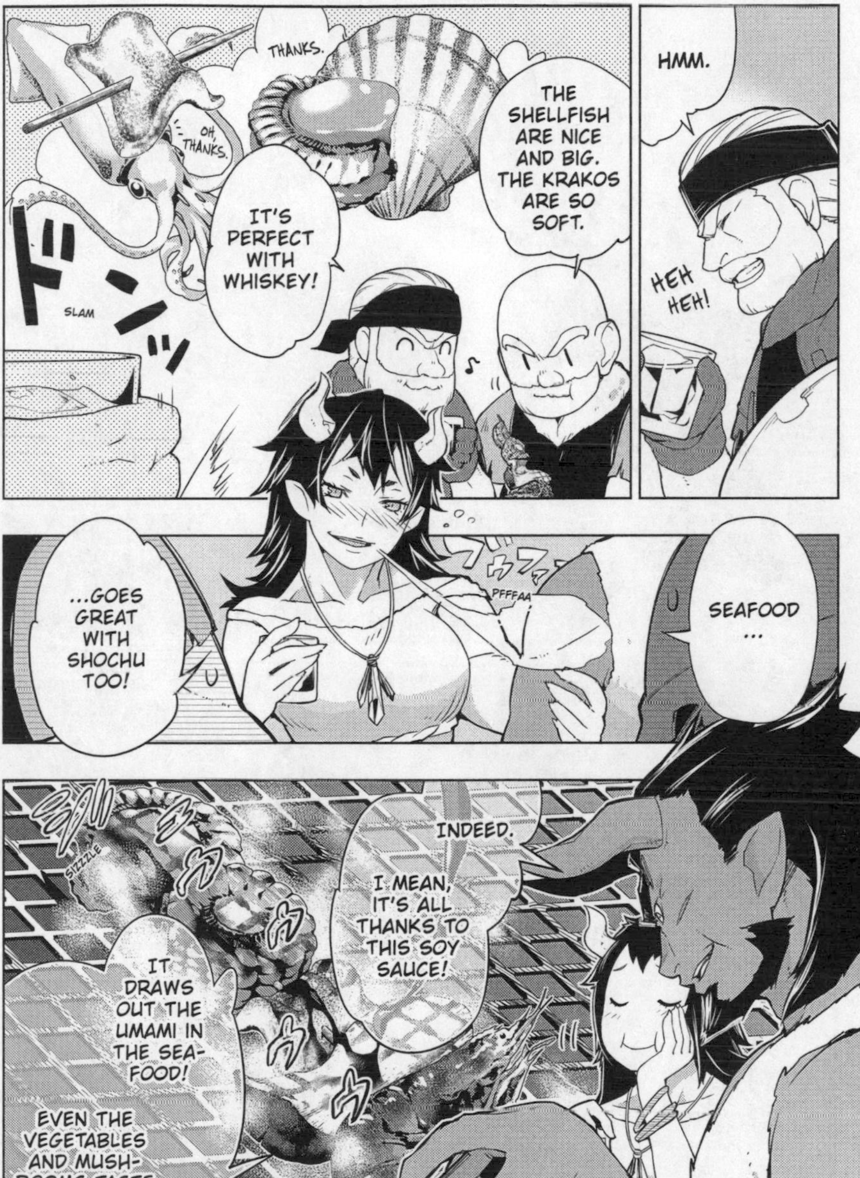
HMM.
HEH HEH!
THE SHELLFISH ARE NICE AND BIG. THE KRAKOS ARE SO SOFT.
THANKS.
IT'S PERFECT WITH WHISKEY!
OH, THANKS.
SLAM
SEAFOOD ...
PFFFAA
...GOES GREAT WITH SHOCHU TOO!
INDEED.
I MEAN, IT'S ALL THANKS TO THIS SOY SAUCE!
IT DRAWS OUT THE UMAMI IN THE SEA-FOOD!
SIZZLE
EVEN THE VEGETABLES AND MUSH-ROOMS TASTE INCREDIBLE.

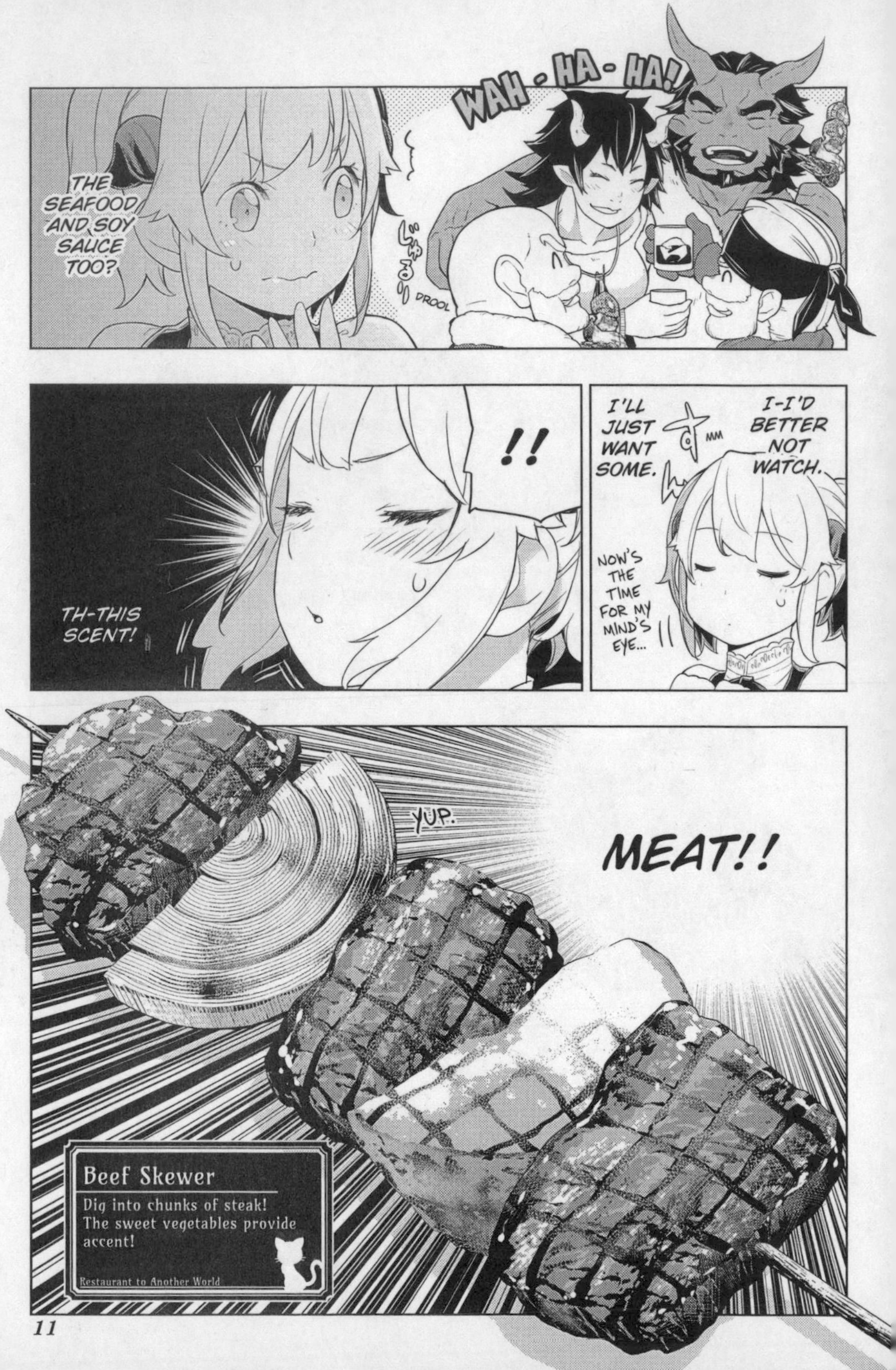
WAH-HA-HA!
じゅるっ DROOL
THE SEAFOOD AND SOY SAUCE TOO?
I-I'D BETTER NOT WATCH.
I'LL JUST WANT SOME.
すん MM
NOW'S THE TIME FOR MY MIND'S EYE...
!!
TH-THIS SCENT!
MEAT!!
YUP.
Beef Skewer
Dig into chunks of steak! The sweet vegetables provide accent!
Restaurant to Another World

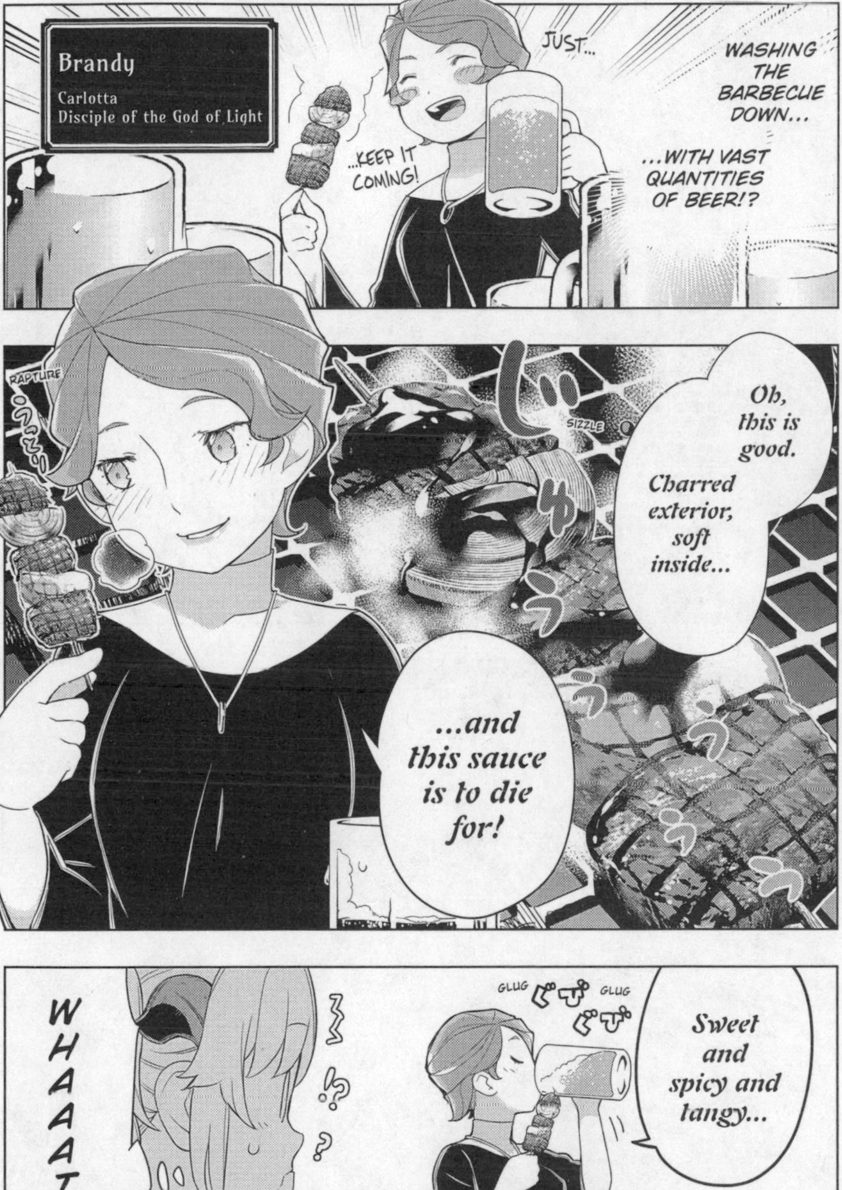
WASHING THE BARBECUE DOWN...
JUST...
...WITH VAST QUANTITIES OF BEER!?
Brandy
Carlotta
Disciple of the God of Light
...KEEP IT COMING!
Oh, this is good. Charred exterior, soft inside...
SIZZLE
...and this sauce is to die for!
RAPTURE
GLUG GLUG
Sweet and spicy and tangy...
!?
?
WHAAAAT!?

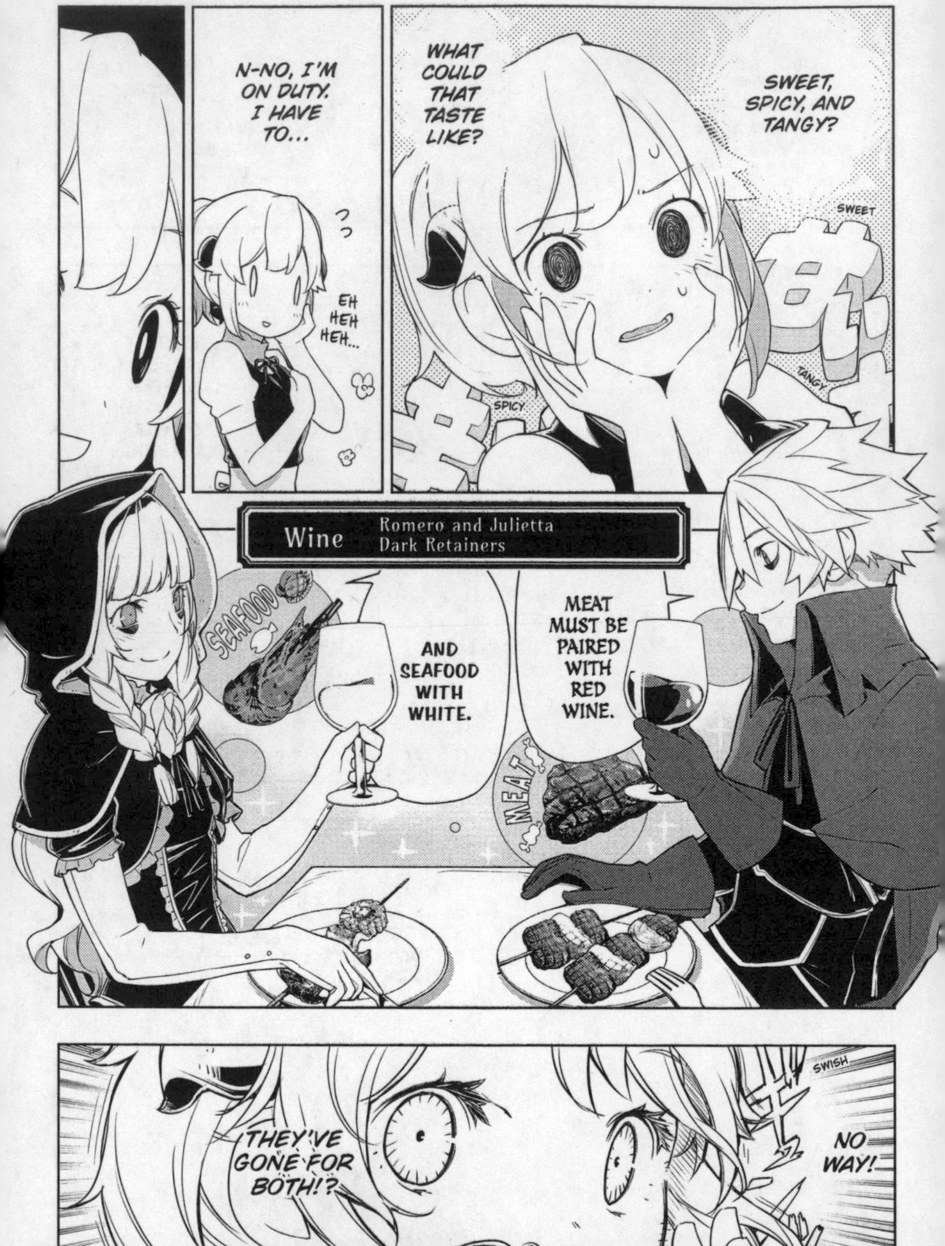
SWEET, SPICY, AND TANGY?
WHAT COULD THAT TASTE LIKE?
SWEET
TANGY
SPICY
N-NO, I'M ON DUTY. I HAVE TO...
EH HEH HEH...
Wine
Romero and Julietta
Dark Retainers
MEAT MUST BE PAIRED WITH RED WINE.
AND SEAFOOD WITH WHITE.
SEAFOOD
MEAT
SWISH
NO WAY!
THEY'VE GONE FOR BOTH!?

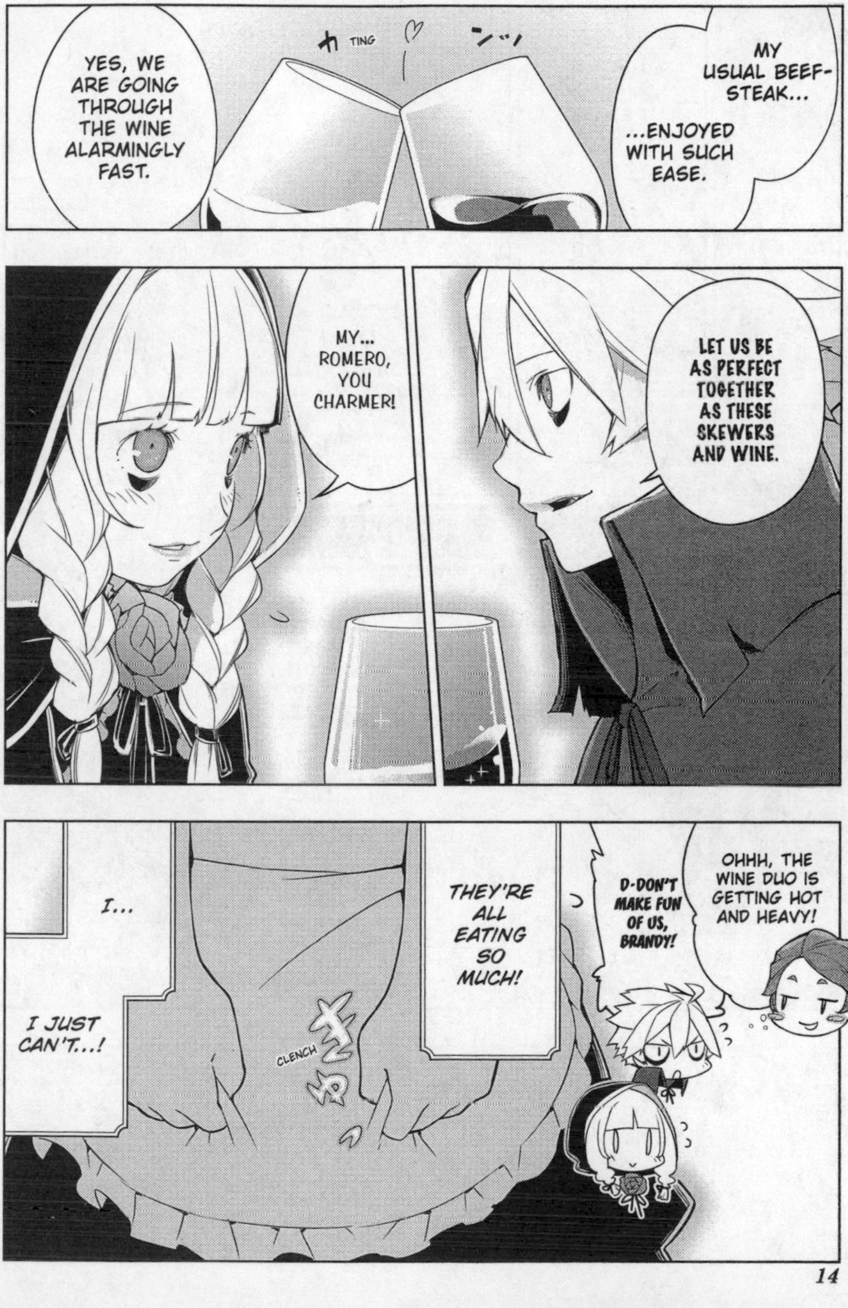
MY USUAL BEEF-STEAK...
...ENJOYED WITH SUCH EASE.
TING
YES, WE ARE GOING THROUGH THE WINE ALARMINGLY FAST.
LET US BE AS PERFECT TOGETHER AS THESE SKEWERS AND WINE.
MY... ROMERO, YOU CHARMER!
OHHH, THE WINE DUO IS GETTING HOT AND HEAVY!
D-DON'T MAKE FUN OF US, BRANDY!
THEY'RE ALL EATING SO MUCH!
CLENCH
I...
I JUST CAN'T...!

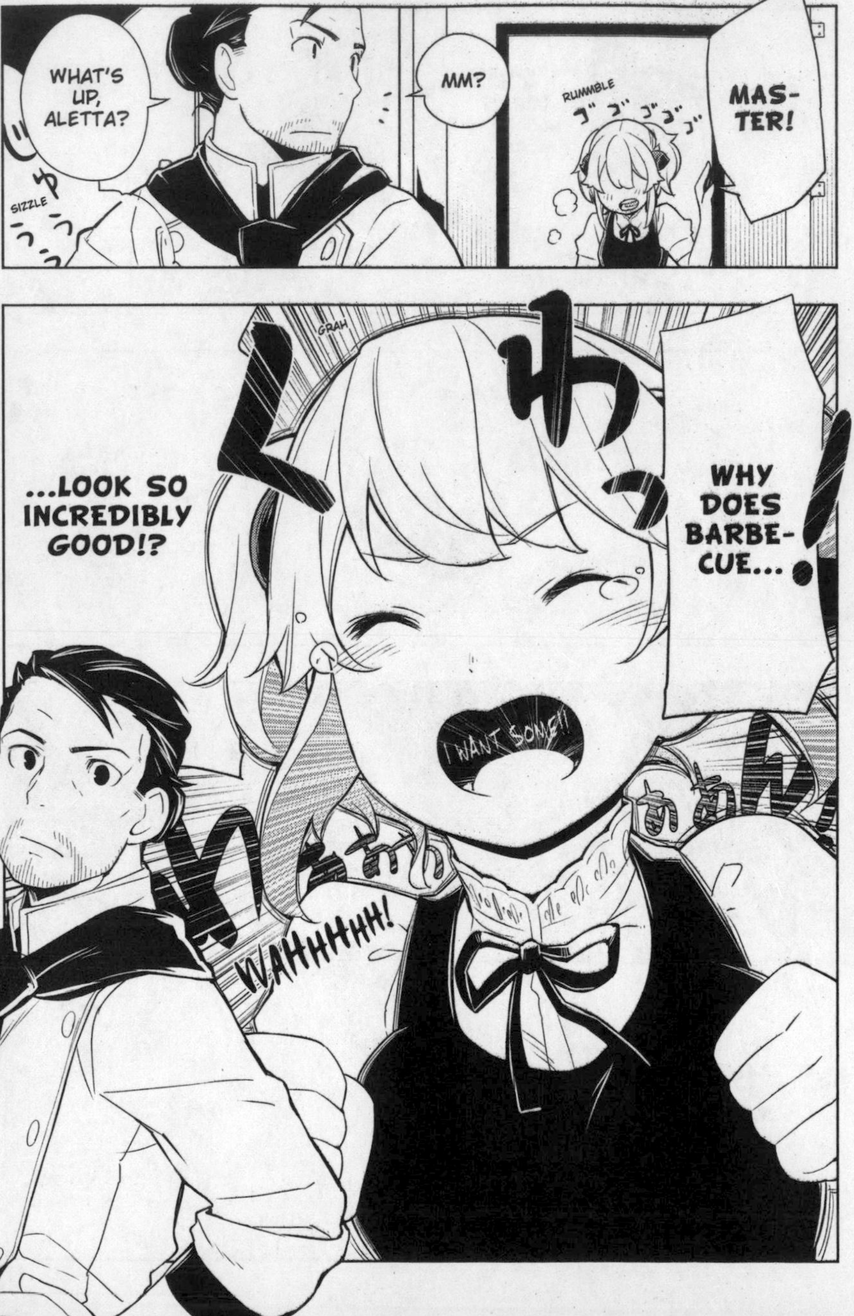
MAS-TER!
RUMMBLE
MM?
WHAT'S UP, ALETTA?
SIZZLE
WHY DOES BARBECUE...
GRAH
...LOOK SO INCREDIBLY GOOD!?
I WANT SOME!!
WAHHHHH!

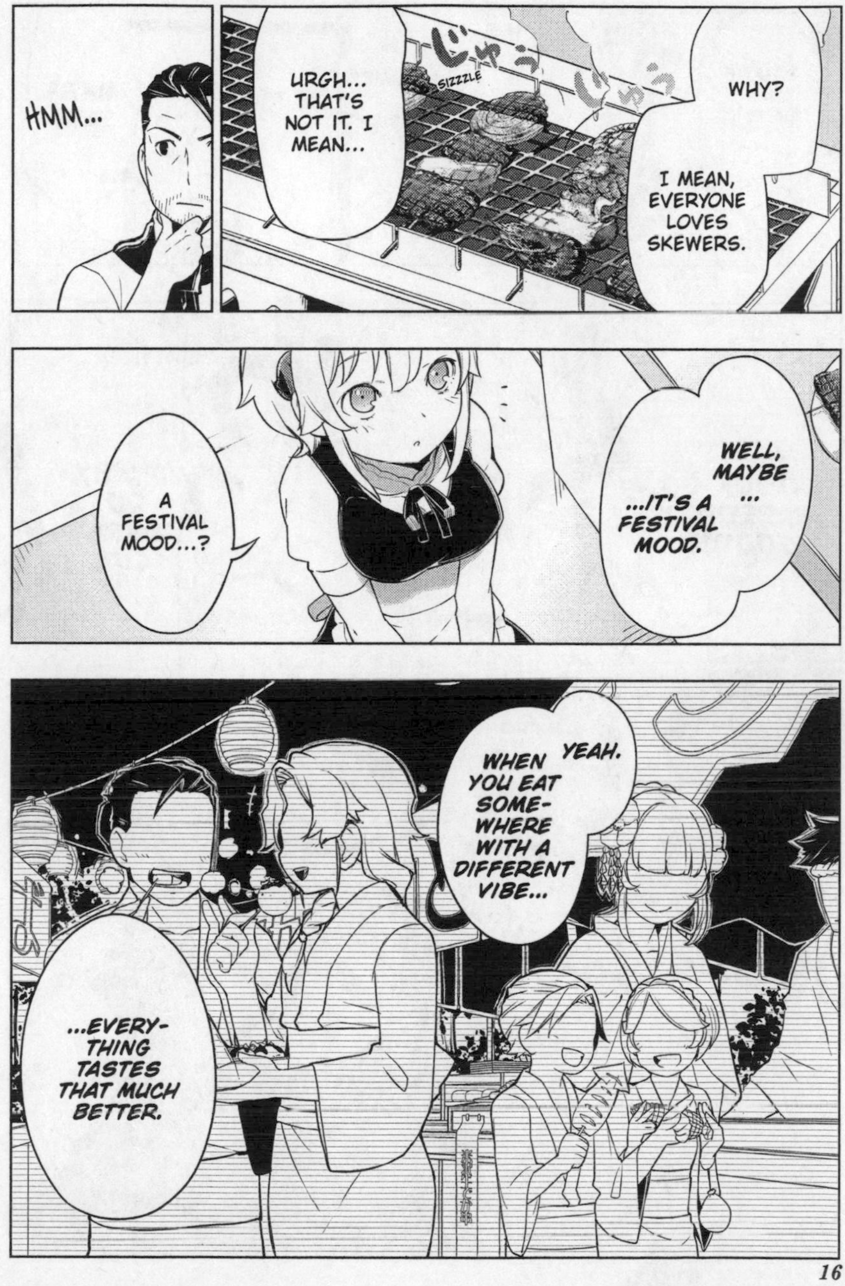
WHY?
I MEAN, EVERYONE LOVES SKEWERS.
SIZZZLE
URGH... THAT'S NOT IT. I MEAN...
HMM...
WELL, MAYBE ...
...IT'S A FESTIVAL MOOD.
A FESTIVAL MOOD...?
YEAH.
WHEN YOU EAT SOME-WHERE WITH A DIFFERENT VIBE...
...EVERY-THING TASTES THAT MUCH BETTER.

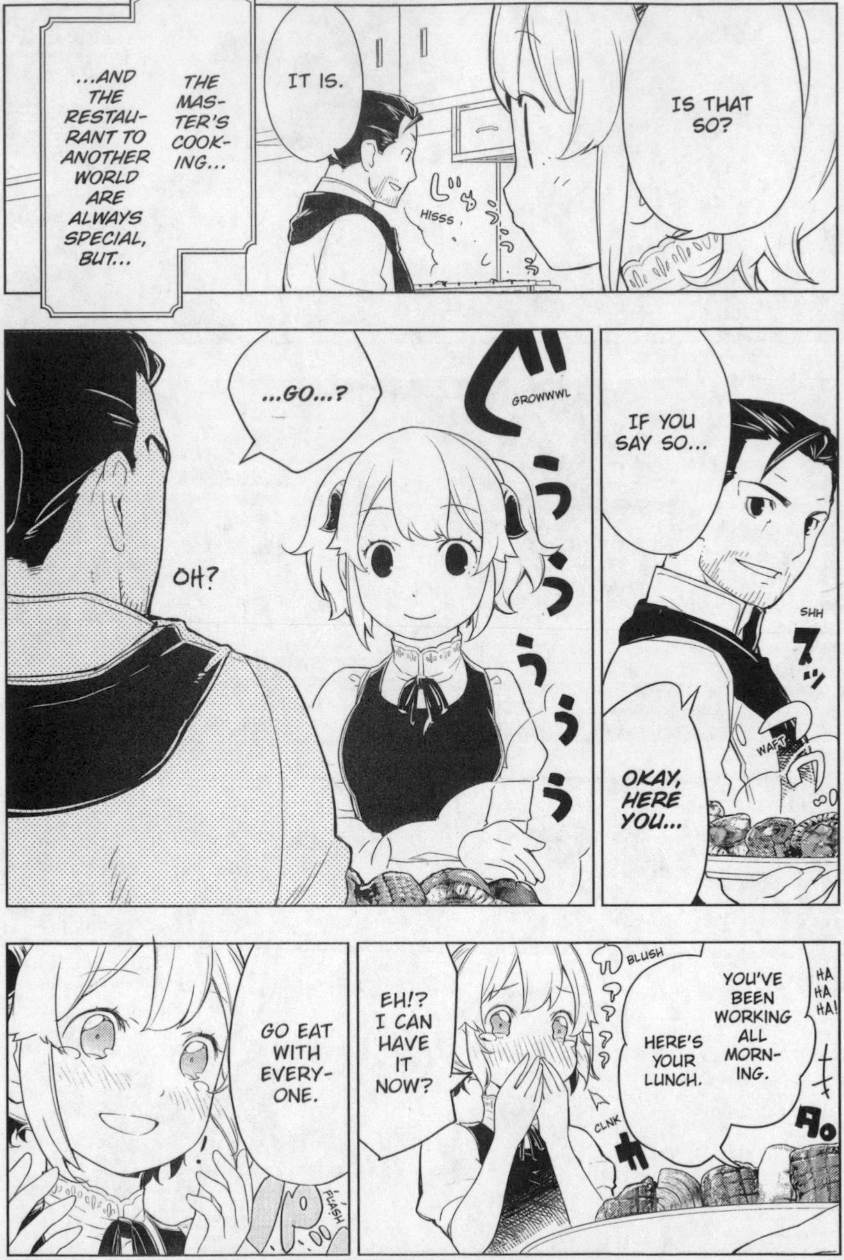
IS THAT SO?
IT IS.
HISSS
THE MASTER'S COOKING...
...AND THE RESTAURANT TO ANOTHER WORLD ARE ALWAYS SPECIAL, BUT...
IF YOU SAY SO...
SHH
WAFT
OKAY, HERE YOU...
GROWWWL
...GO...?
OH?
HA HA HA!
YOU'VE BEEN WORKING ALL MORNING.
HERE'S YOUR LUNCH.
BLUSH
CLNK
EH!? I CAN HAVE IT NOW?
GO EAT WITH EVERYONE.
FLASH

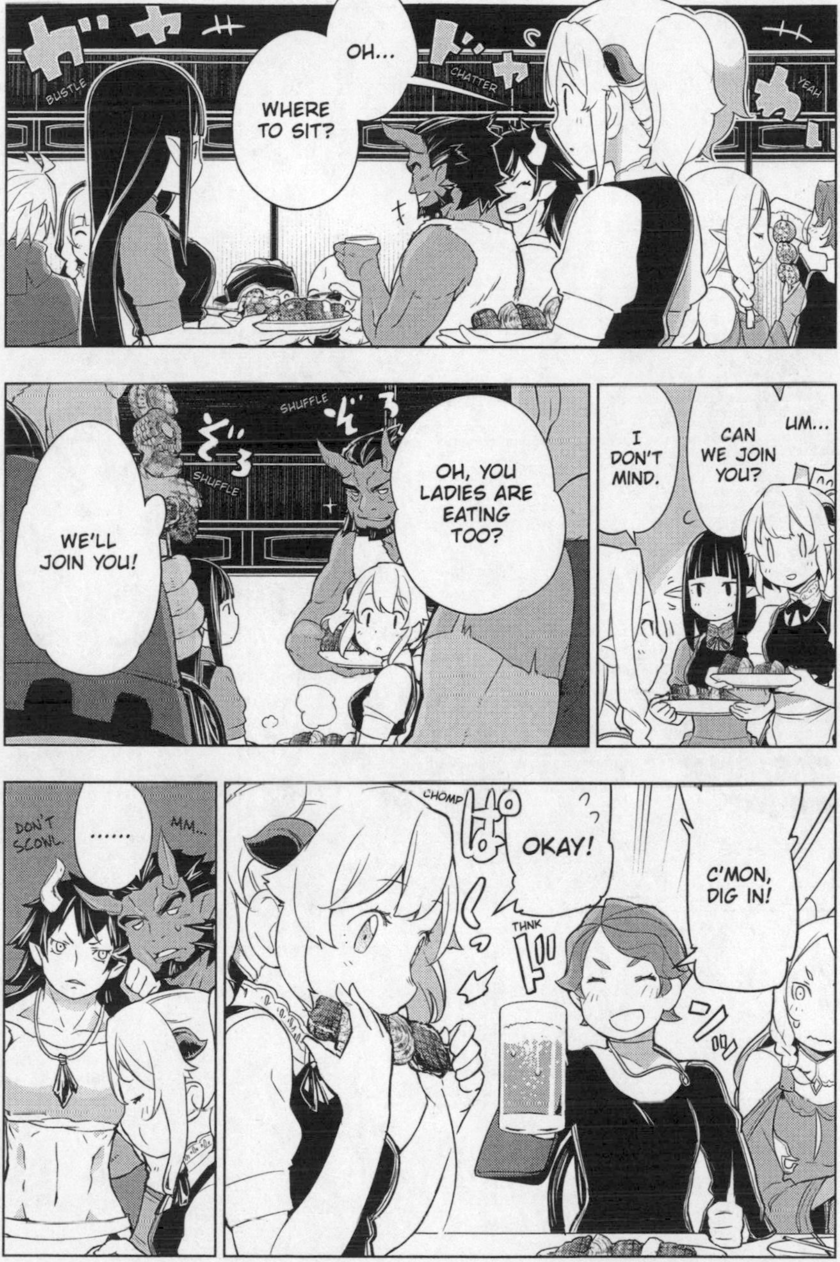
YEAH
CHATTER
OH... WHERE TO SIT?
BUSTLE
UM...
CAN WE JOIN YOU?
I DON'T MIND.
OH, YOU LADIES ARE EATING TOO?
SHUFFLE
SHUFFLE
WE'LL JOIN YOU!
C'MON, DIG IN!
OKAY!
CHOMP
THNK
MM...
......
DON'T SCOWL.

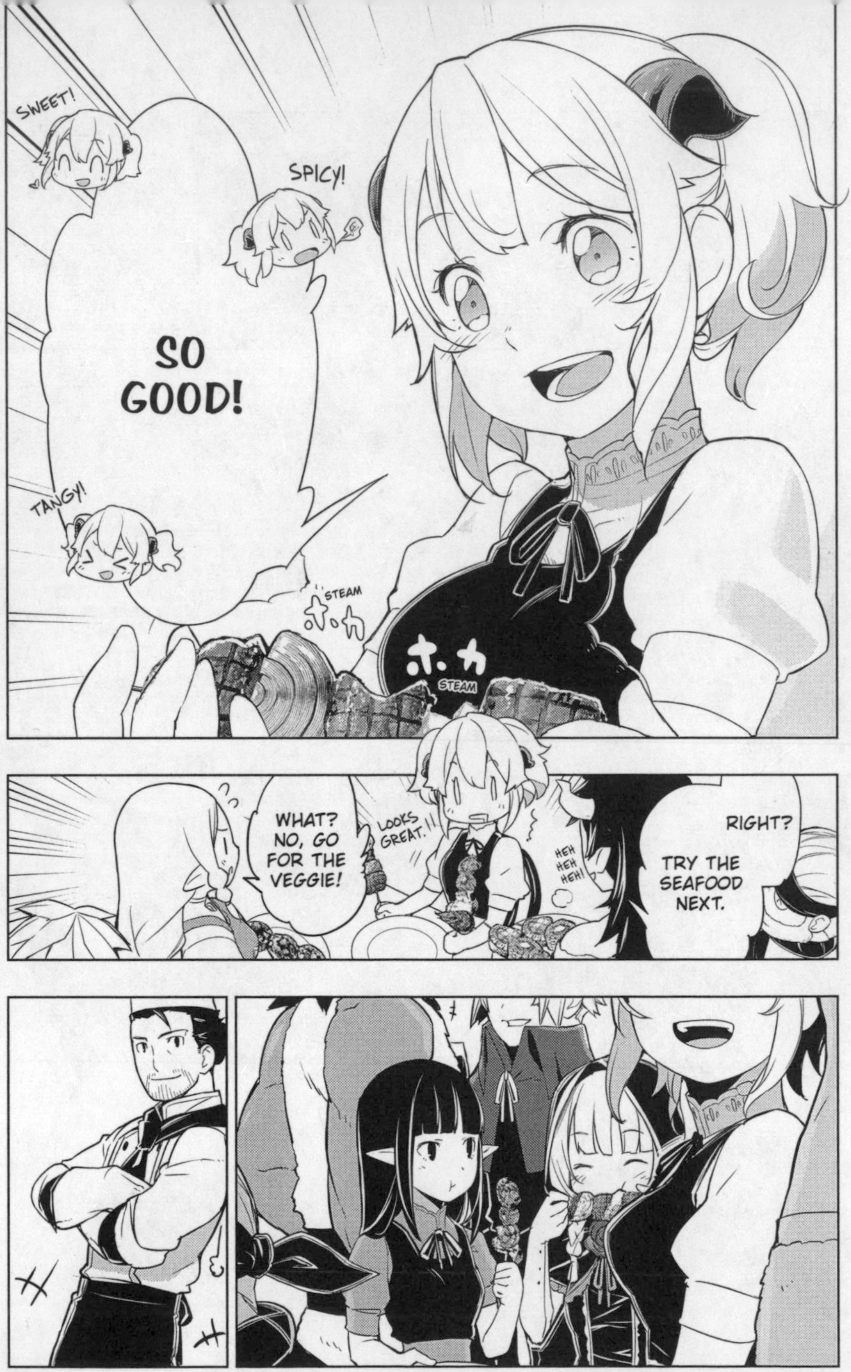
SPICY!
SWEET!
SO GOOD!
TANGY!
ホカ STEAM
ホカ STEAM
RIGHT?
TRY THE SEAFOOD NEXT.
HEH HEH HEH!
LOOKS GREAT.
WHAT? NO, GO FOR THE VEGGIE!

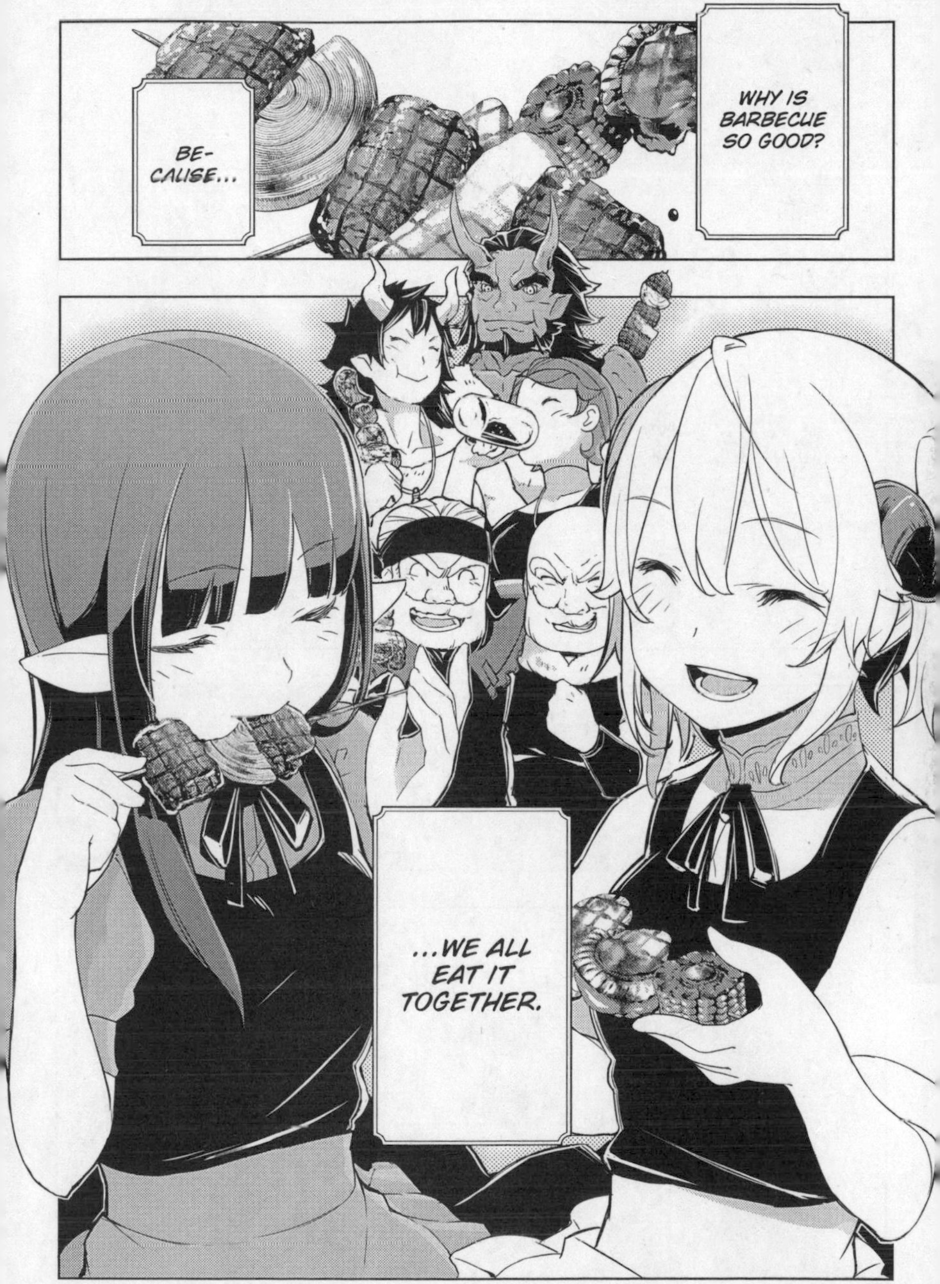
WHY IS BARBECUE SO GOOD?
BE-CAUSE...
...WE ALL EAT IT TOGETHER.

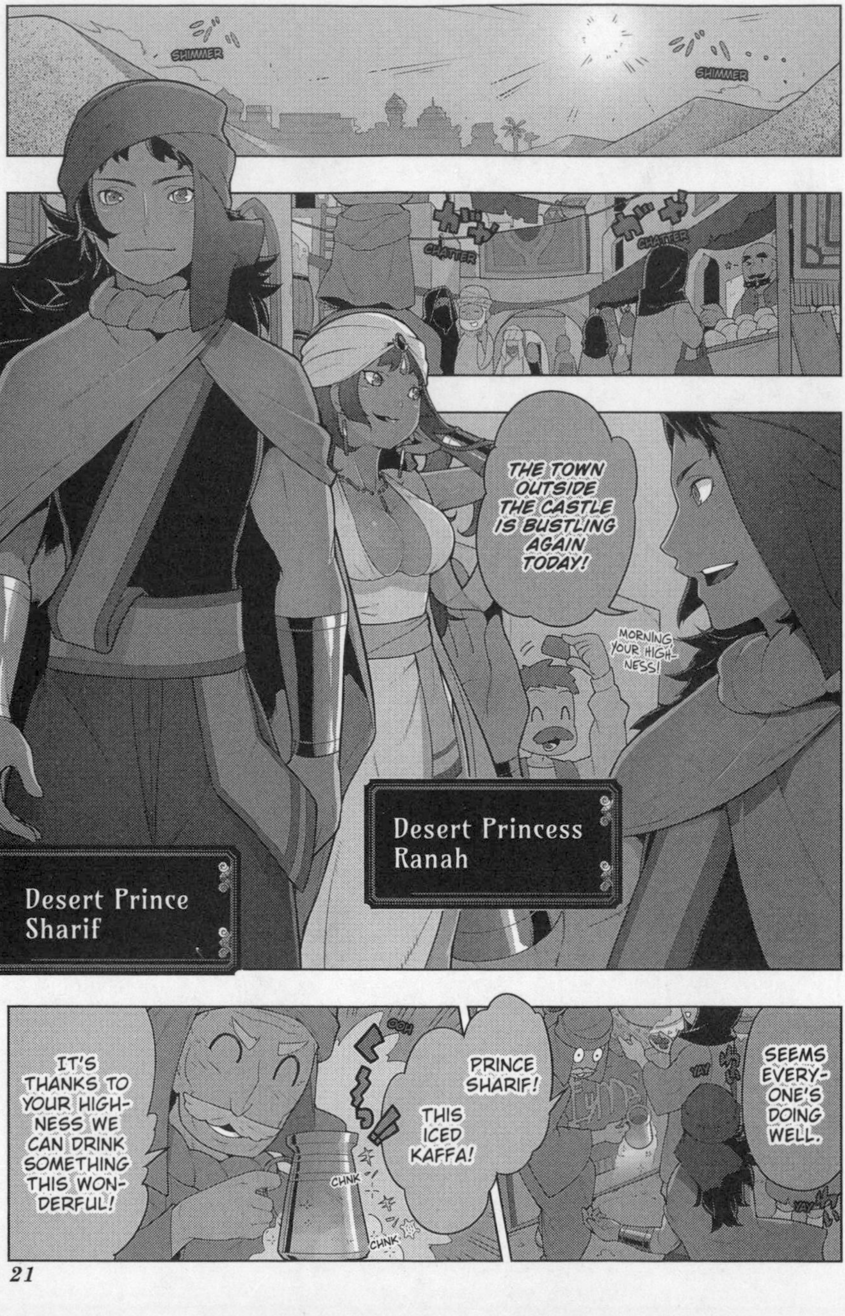
SHIMMER
SHIMMER
CHATTER
CHATTER
THE TOWN OUTSIDE THE CASTLE IS BUSTLING AGAIN TODAY!
MORNING, YOUR HIGH-NESS!
Desert Princess Ranah
Desert Prince Sharif
SEEMS EVERY-ONE'S DOING WELL.
YAY
YAY
PRINCE SHARIF!
THIS ICED KAFFA!
OOH
IT'S THANKS TO YOUR HIGH-NESS WE CAN DRINK SOMETHING THIS WON-DERFUL!
CHNK
CHNK

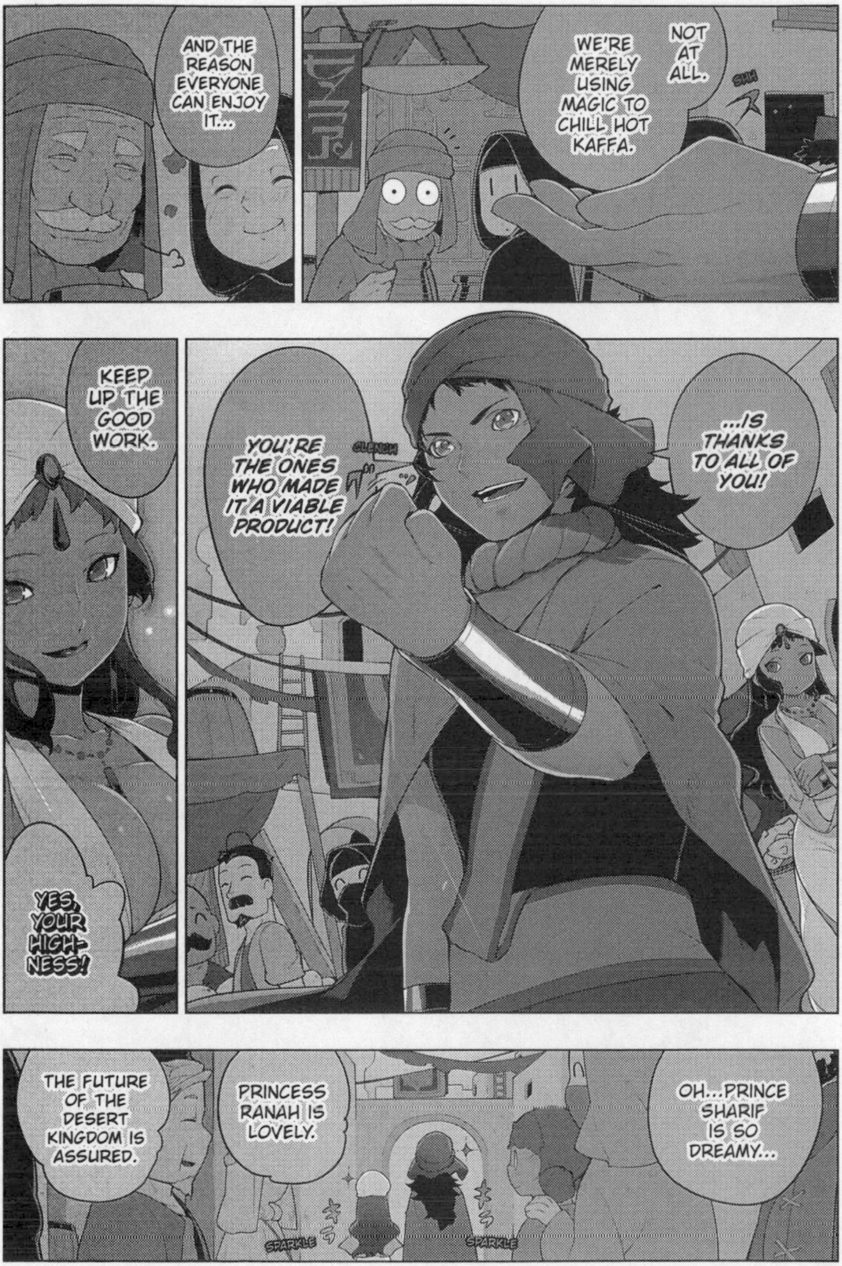
NOT AT ALL.
WE'RE MERELY USING MAGIC TO CHILL HOT KAFFA.
SHH
AND THE REASON EVERYONE CAN ENJOY IT...
...IS THANKS TO ALL OF YOU!
CLENCH
YOU'RE THE ONES WHO MADE IT A VIABLE PRODUCT!
KEEP UP THE GOOD WORK.
YES, YOUR HIGHNESS!
OH...PRINCE SHARIF IS SO DREAMY...
SPARKLE
PRINCESS RANAH IS LOVELY.
SPARKLE
THE FUTURE OF THE DESERT KINGDOM IS ASSURED.

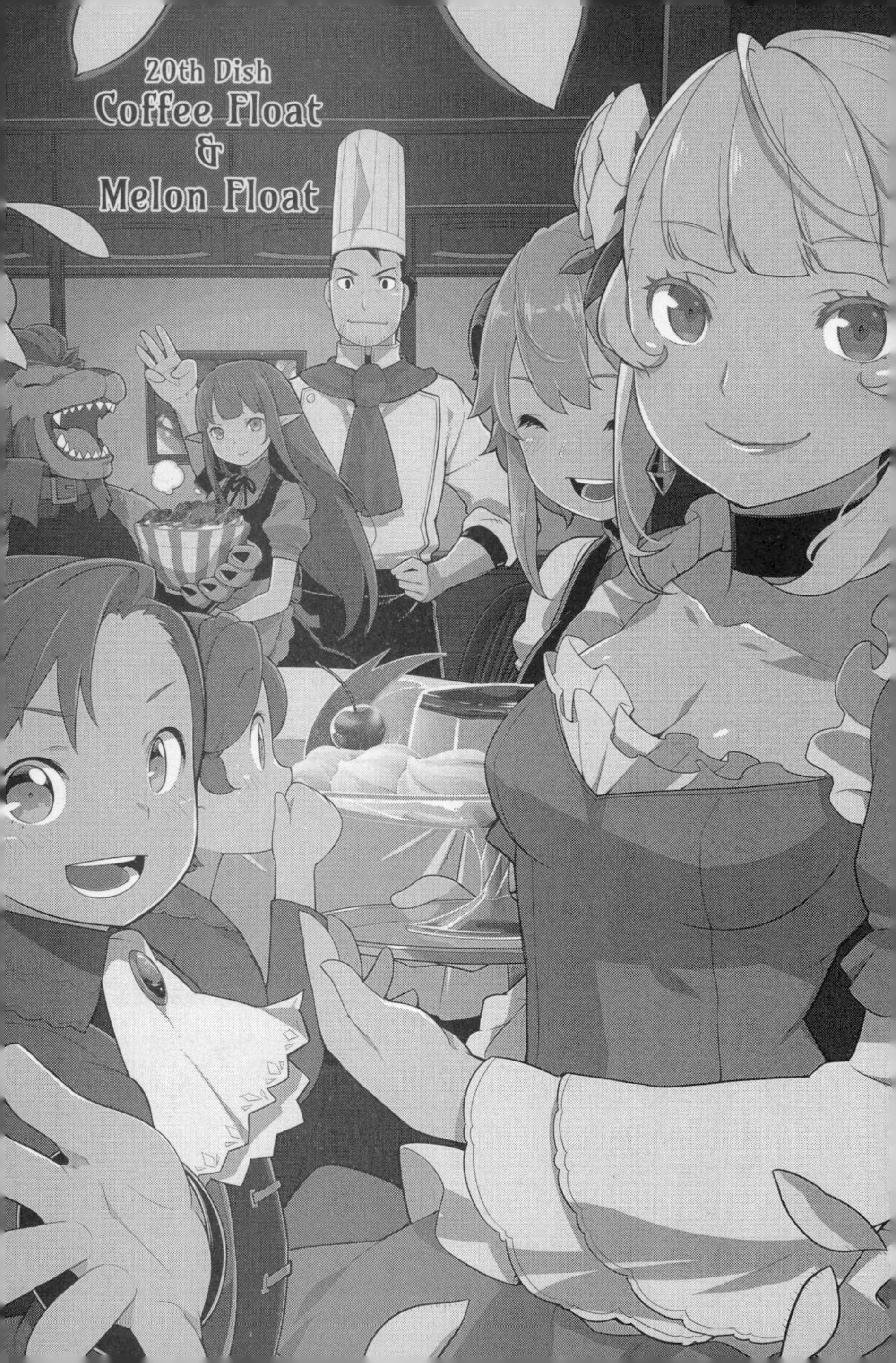
20th Dish
Coffee Float
&
Melon Float

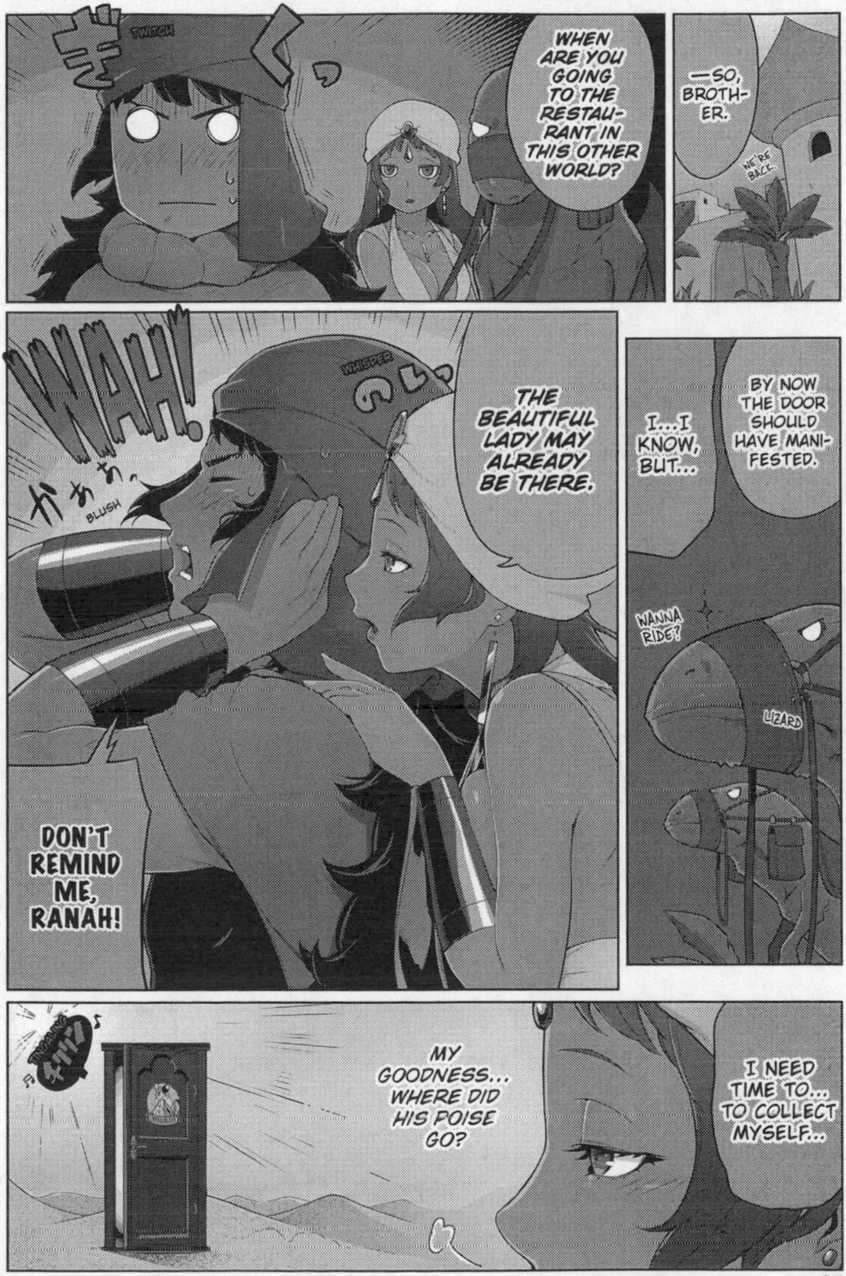
—SO, BROTHER.
WE'RE BACK.
WHEN ARE YOU GOING TO THE RESTAURANT IN THIS OTHER WORLD?
TWITCH
BY NOW THE DOOR SHOULD HAVE MANIFESTED.
I...I KNOW, BUT...
WANNA RIDE?
LIZARD
THE BEAUTIFUL LADY MAY ALREADY BE THERE.
WHISPER
WAH!
BLUSH
DON'T REMIND ME, RANAH!
I NEED TIME TO... TO COLLECT MYSELF...
MY GOODNESS... WHERE DID HIS POISE GO?
TINGALING

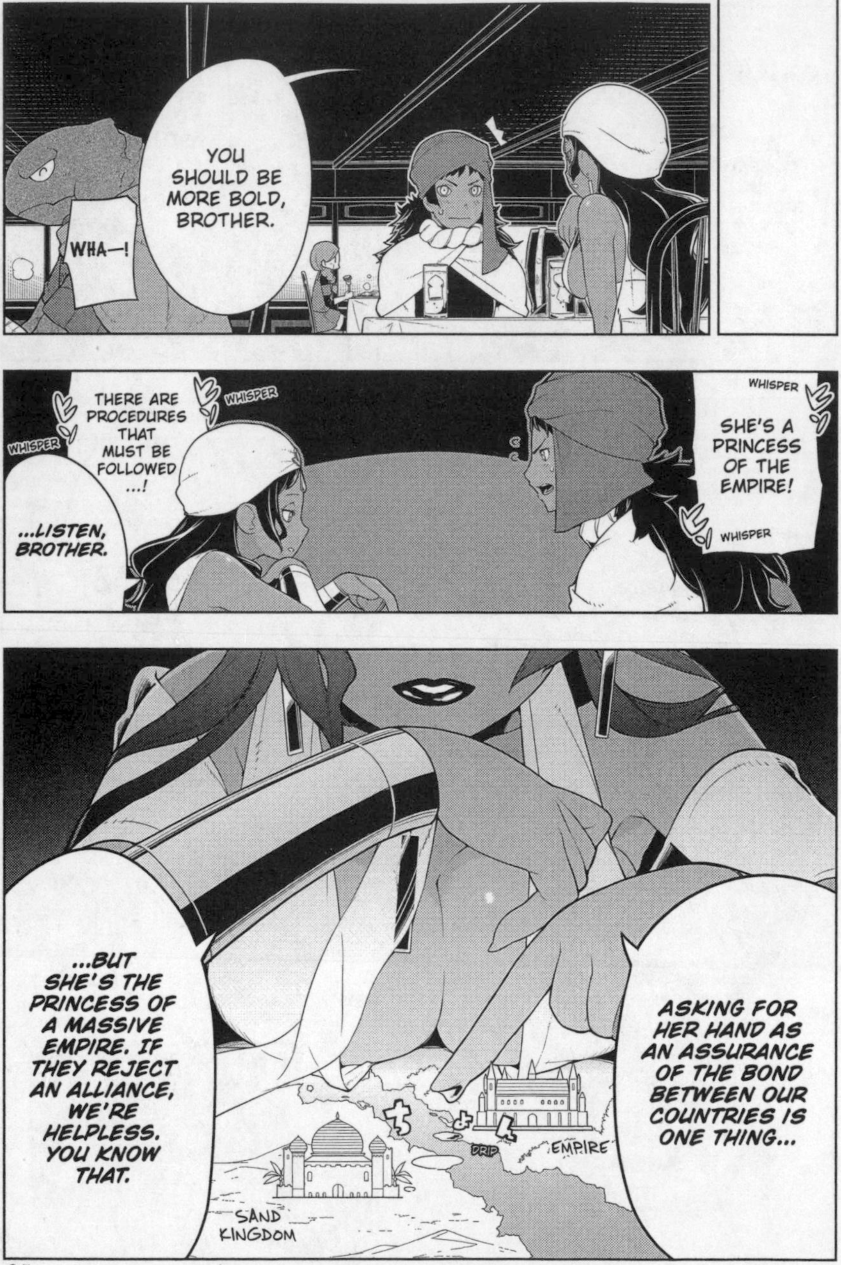
YOU SHOULD BE MORE BOLD, BROTHER.
WHA—!
WHISPER
SHE'S A PRINCESS OF THE EMPIRE!
WHISPER
WHISPER
THERE ARE PROCEDURES THAT MUST BE FOLLOWED ...!
WHISPER
...LISTEN, BROTHER.
ASKING FOR HER HAND AS AN ASSURANCE OF THE BOND BETWEEN OUR COUNTRIES IS ONE THING...
EMPIRE
DRIP
...BUT SHE'S THE PRINCESS OF A MASSIVE EMPIRE. IF THEY REJECT AN ALLIANCE, WE'RE HELPLESS. YOU KNOW THAT.
SAND KINGDOM

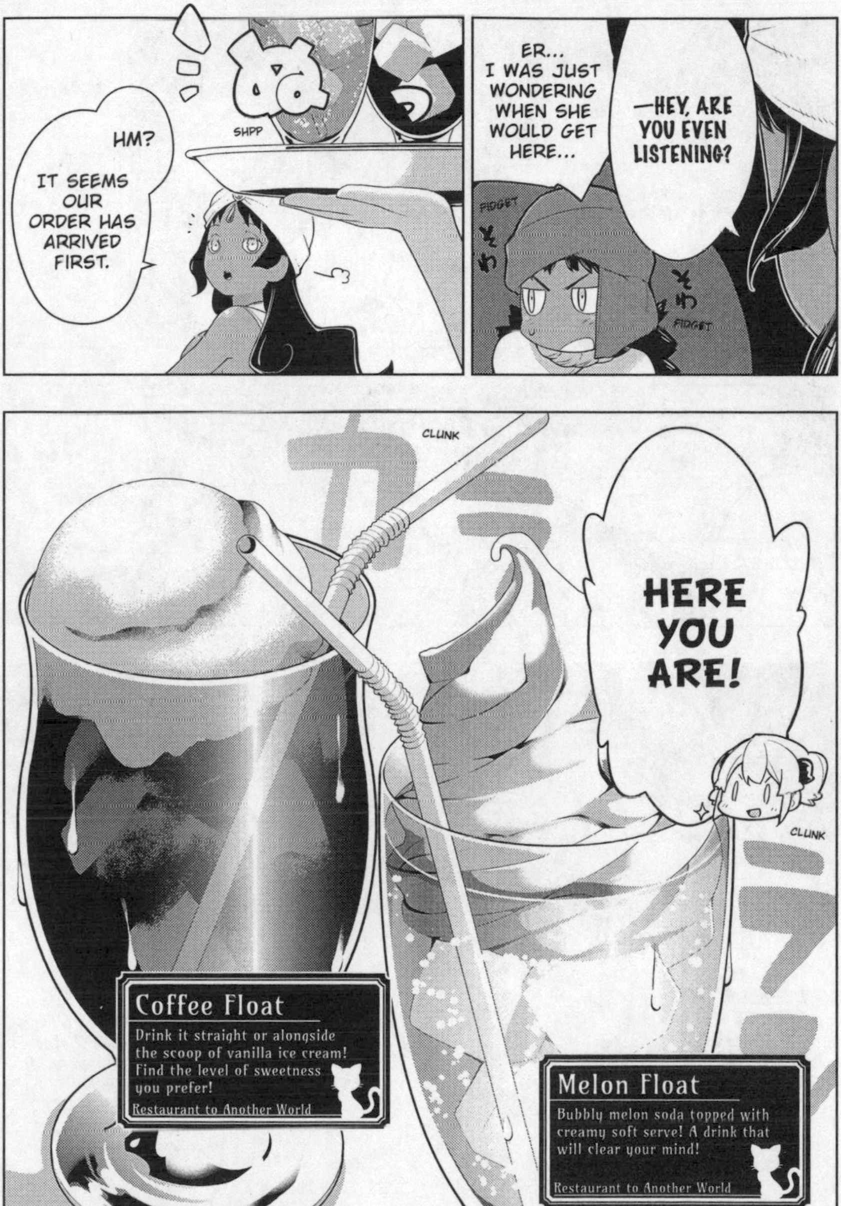
—HEY, ARE YOU EVEN LISTENING?
ER... I WAS JUST WONDERING WHEN SHE WOULD GET HERE...
FIDGET
FIDGET
SHPP
HM?
IT SEEMS OUR ORDER HAS ARRIVED FIRST.
CLUNK
HERE YOU ARE!
CLUNK
Melon Float
Bubbly melon soda topped with creamy soft serve! A drink that will clear your mind!
Restaurant to Another World
Coffee Float
Drink it straight or alongside the scoop of vanilla ice cream! Find the level of sweetness you prefer!
Restaurant to Another World

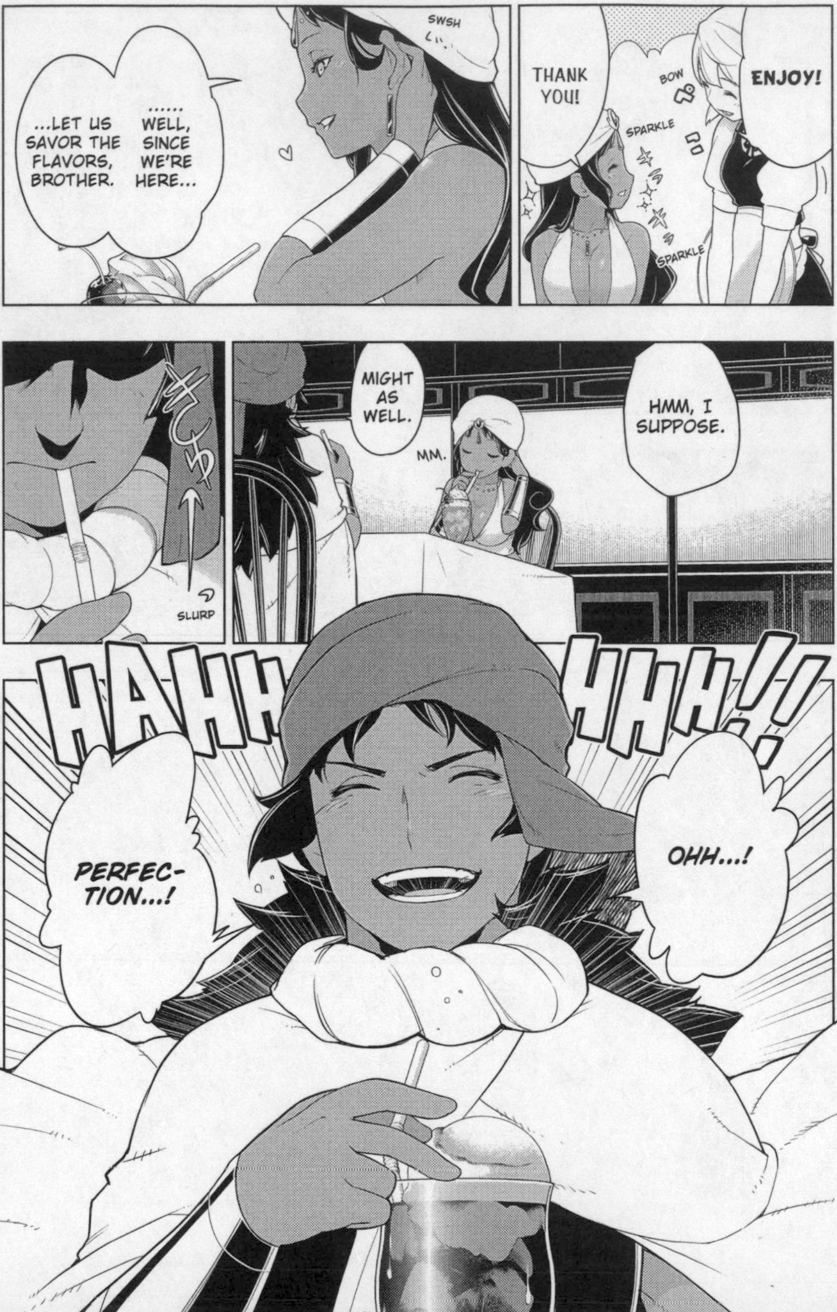
ENJOY!
BOW
THANK YOU!
SPARKLE
SPARKLE
SWSH
......WELL, SINCE WE'RE HERE...
...LET US SAVOR THE FLAVORS, BROTHER.
HMM, I SUPPOSE.
MIGHT AS WELL.
MM.
SLURP
HAHH HHHH!!
OHH...!
PERFEC-TION...!

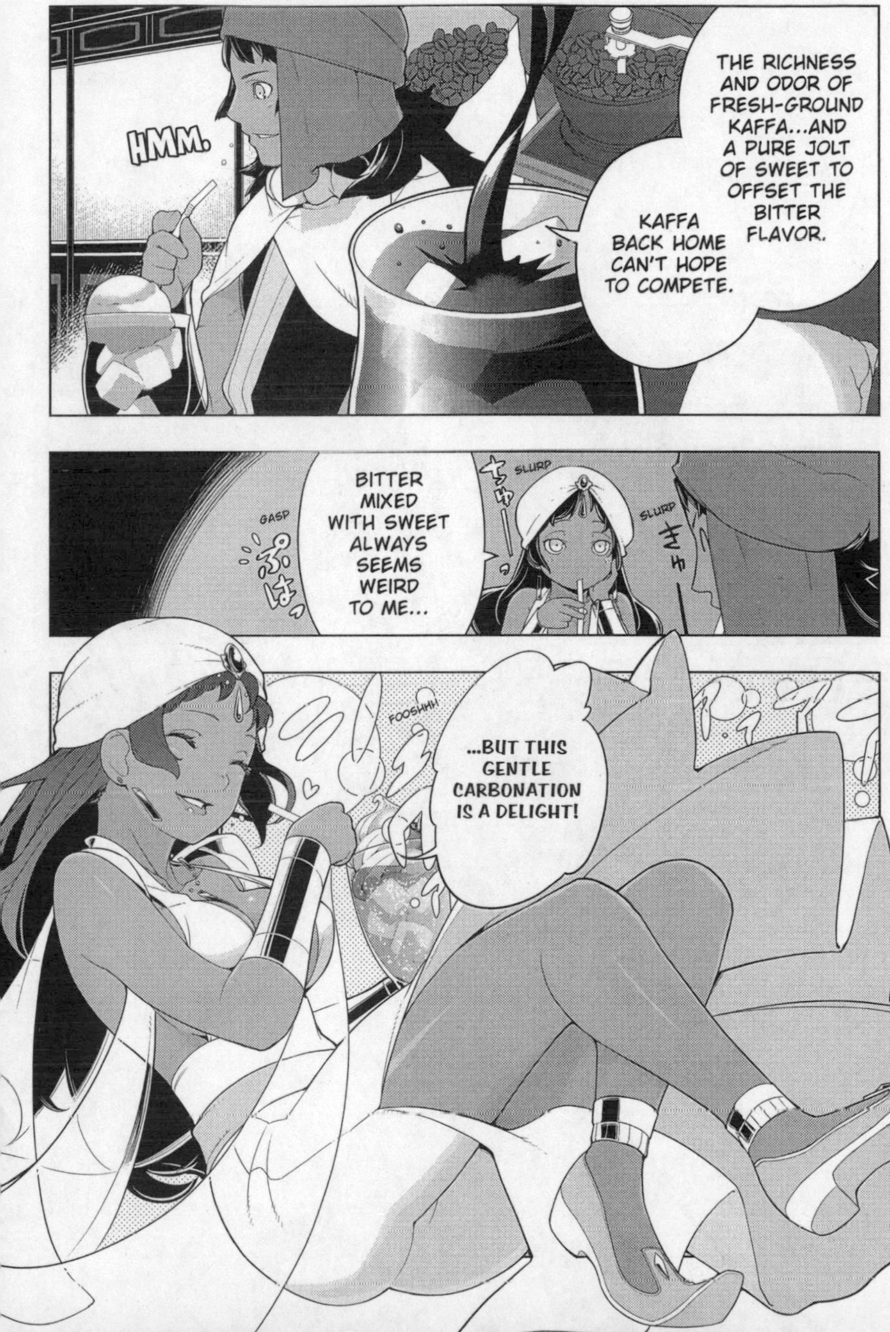
THE RICHNESS AND ODOR OF FRESH-GROUND KAFFA...AND A PURE JOLT OF SWEET TO OFFSET THE BITTER FLAVOR.
KAFFA BACK HOME CAN'T HOPE TO COMPETE.
HMM.
SLURP
SLURP
BITTER MIXED WITH SWEET ALWAYS SEEMS WEIRD TO ME...
GASP
...BUT THIS GENTLE CARBONATION IS A DELIGHT!
FOOSHHH

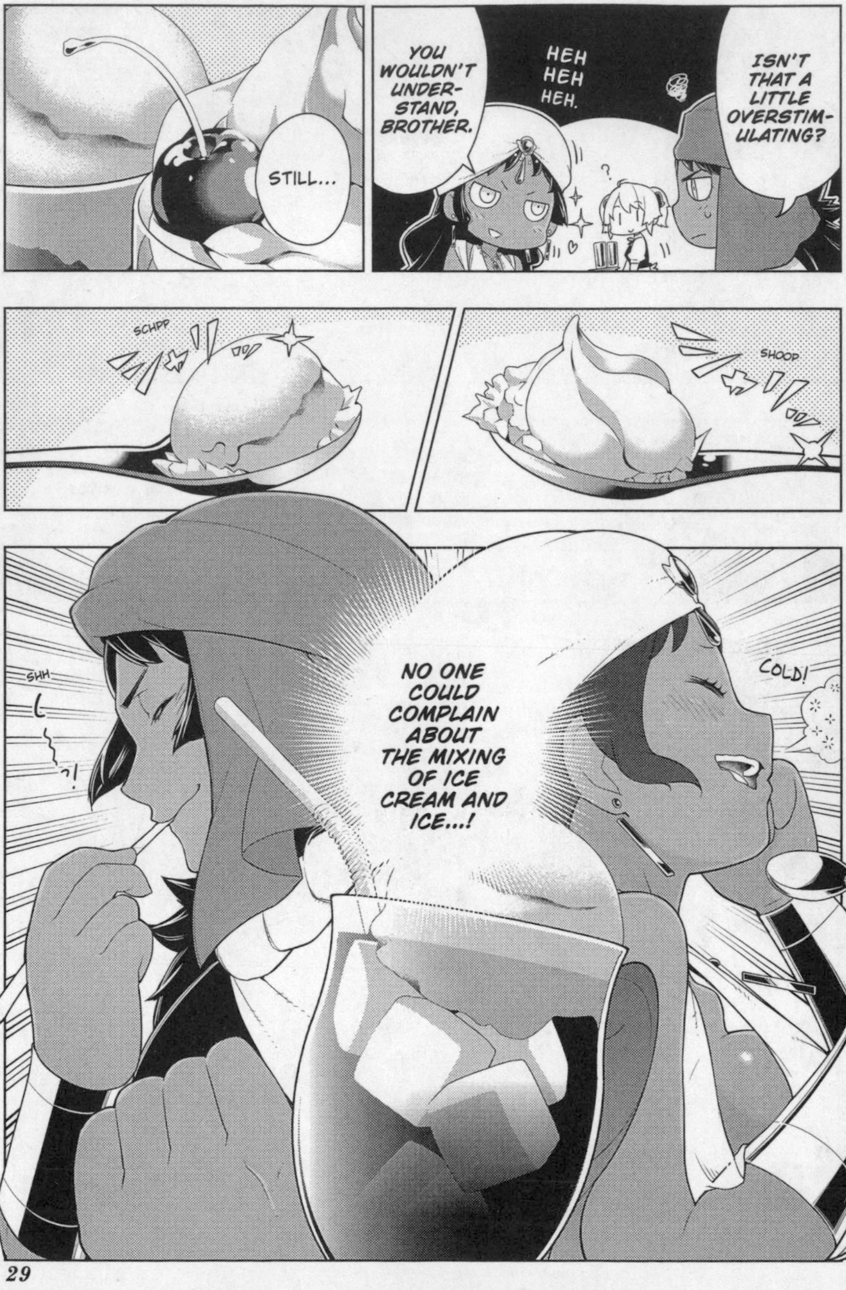
ISN'T THAT A LITTLE OVERSTIMULATING?
HEH HEH HEH.
YOU WOULDN'T UNDERSTAND, BROTHER.
STILL...
SHOOP
SCHPP
COLD!
NO ONE COULD COMPLAIN ABOUT THE MIXING OF ICE CREAM AND ICE...!
SHH
?!

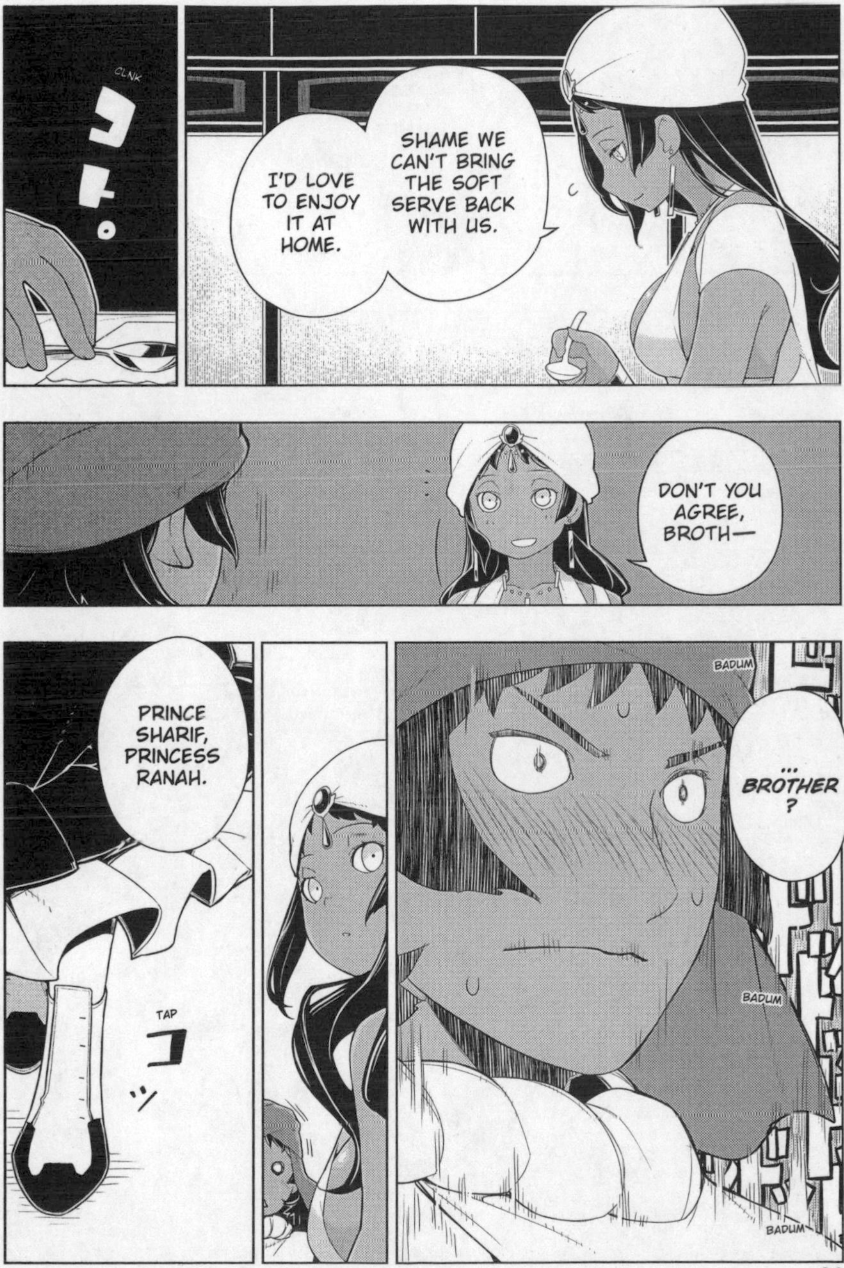
SHAME WE CAN'T BRING THE SOFT SERVE BACK WITH US.
I'D LOVE TO ENJOY IT AT HOME.
CLNK
DON'T YOU AGREE, BROTH—
BADUM
...BROTHER?
BADUM
BADUM
PRINCE SHARIF, PRINCESS RANAH.
TAP

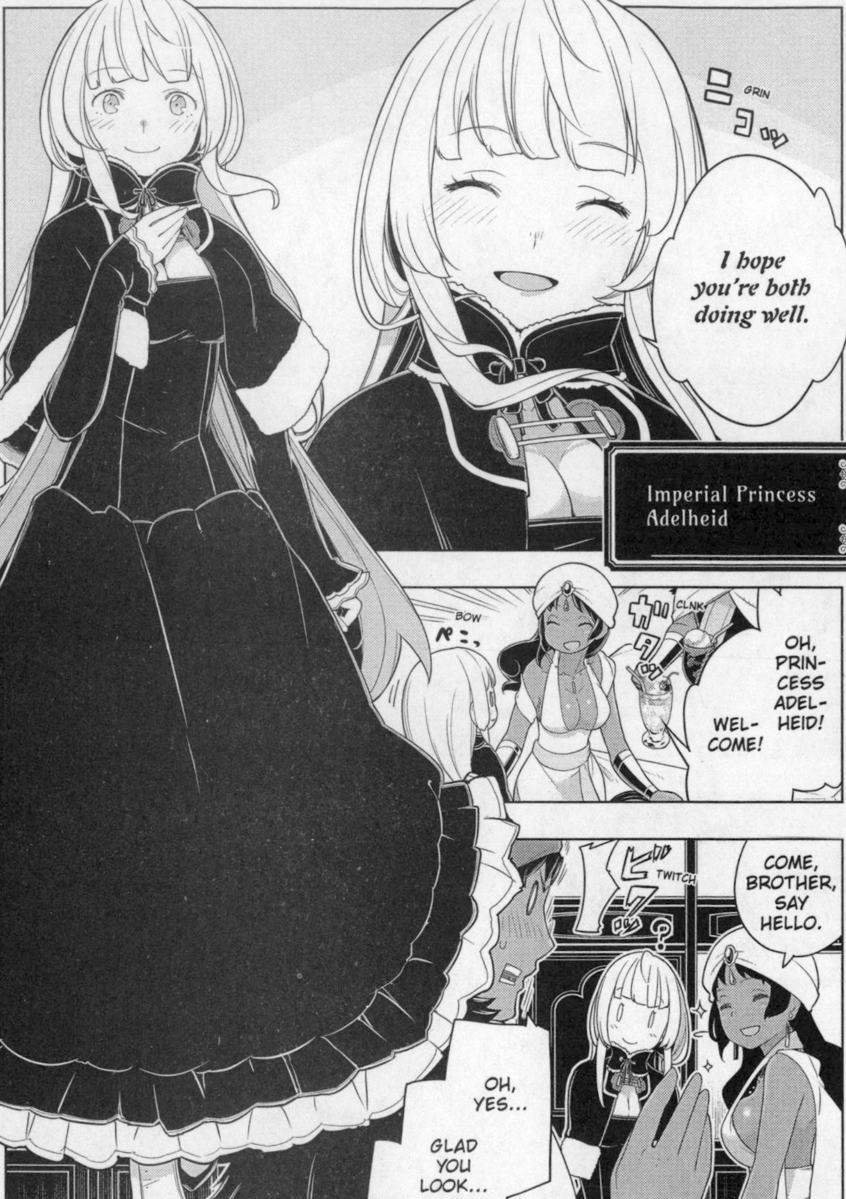
GRIN
I hope you're both doing well.
Imperial Princess Adelheid
CLNK
OH, PRINCESS ADELHEID!
WELCOME!
BOW
COME, BROTHER, SAY HELLO.
TWITCH
OH, YES...
GLAD YOU LOOK...
UM...

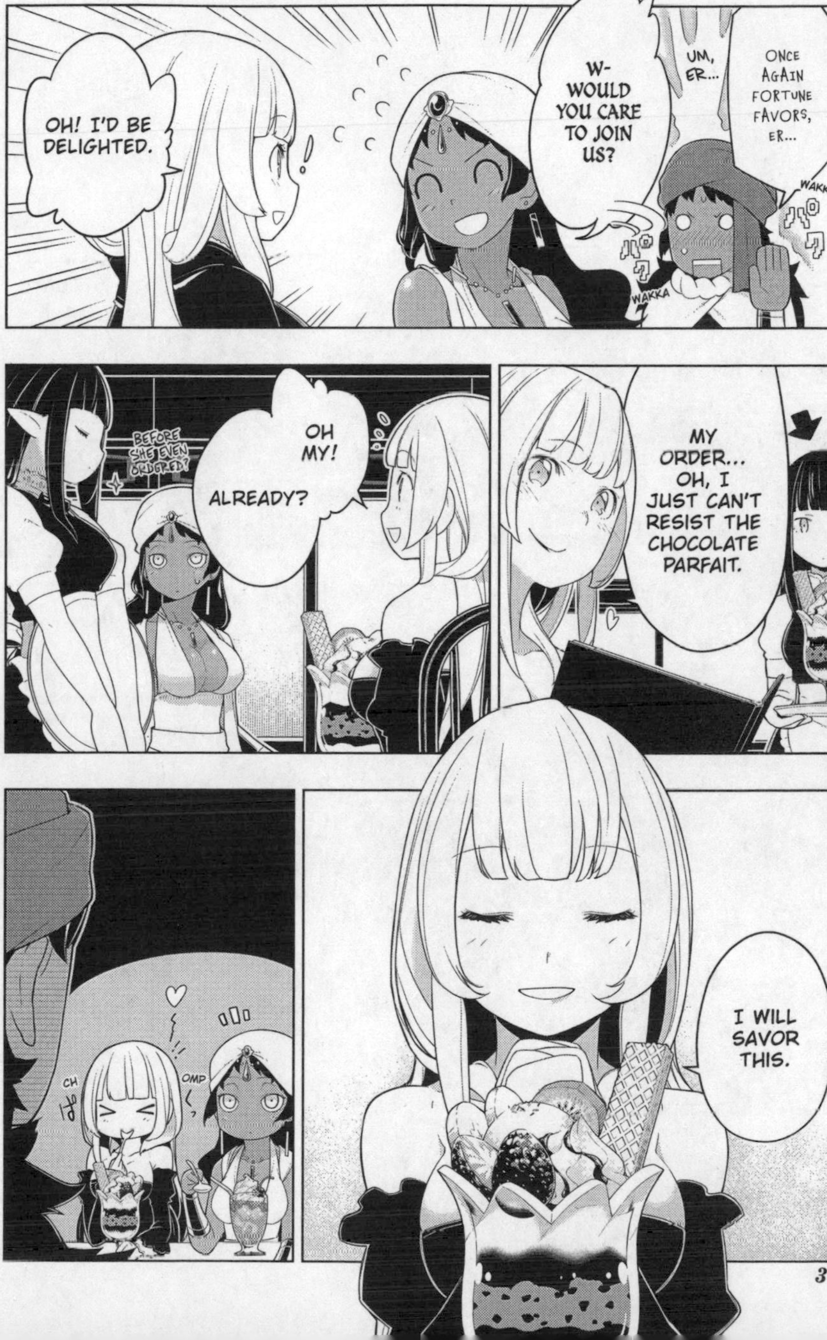
ONCE AGAIN FORTUNE FAVORS, ER...
UM, ER...
W- WOULD YOU CARE TO JOIN US?
WAKKA
WAKKA
OH! I'D BE DELIGHTED.
MY ORDER... OH, I JUST CAN'T RESIST THE CHOCOLATE PARFAIT.
OH MY!
ALREADY?
BEFORE SHE EVEN ORDERED?
I WILL SAVOR THIS.
OMP
CH

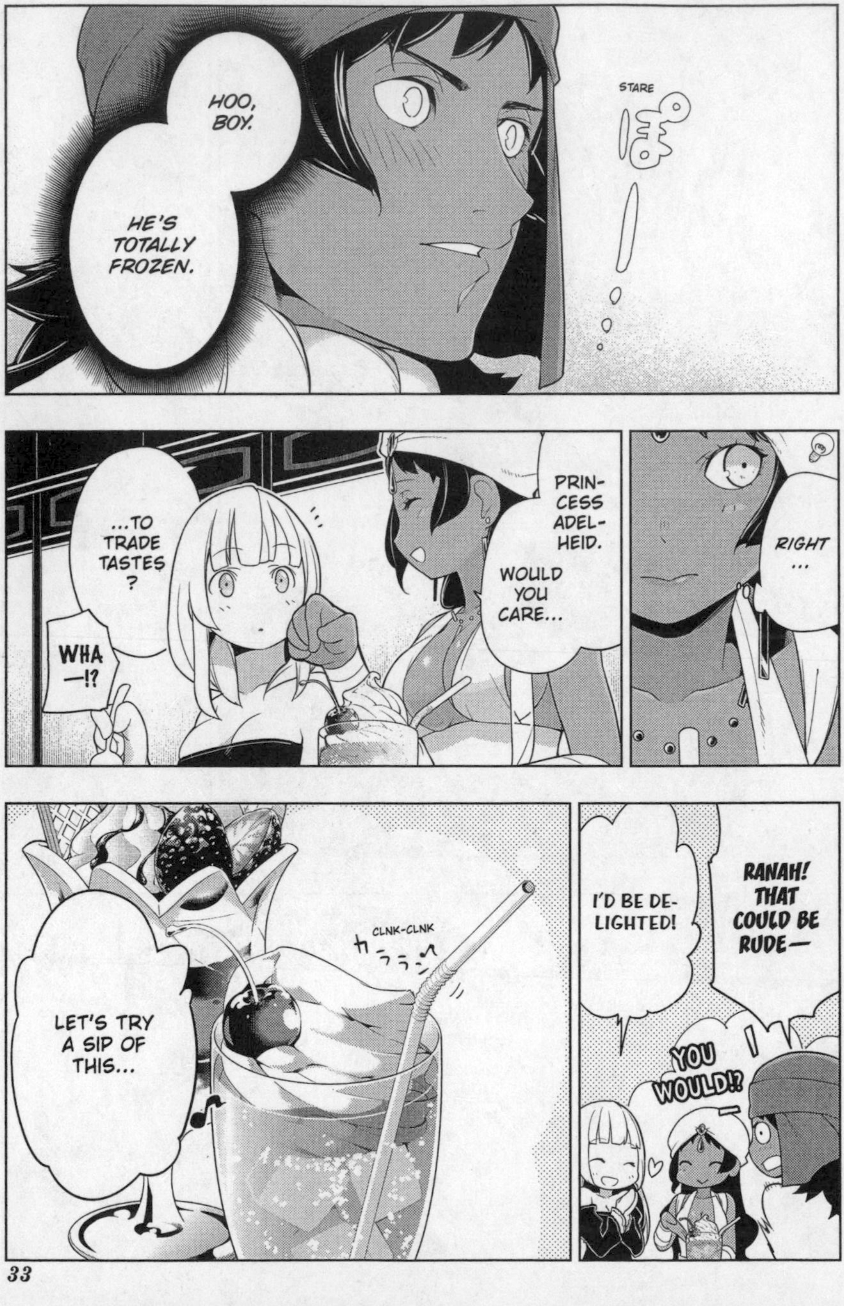
STARE
HOO, BOY.
HE'S TOTALLY FROZEN.
RIGHT...
PRINCESS ADELHEID.
WOULD YOU CARE...
...TO TRADE TASTES?
WHA—!?
RANAH! THAT COULD BE RUDE—
I'D BE DELIGHTED!
YOU WOULD!?
CLNK-CLNK
LET'S TRY A SIP OF THIS...

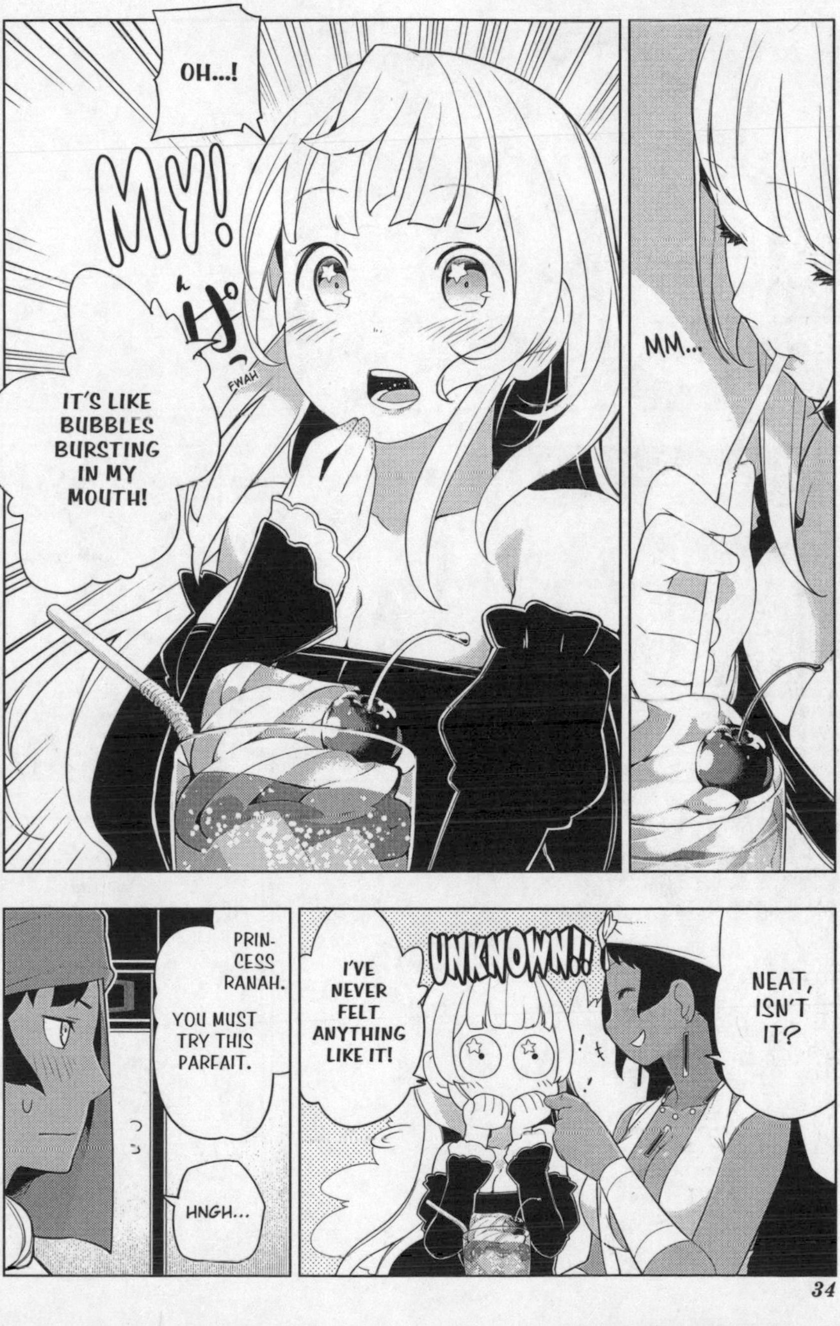
MM...
OH...!
MY!
FWAH
IT'S LIKE BUBBLES BURSTING IN MY MOUTH!
NEAT, ISN'T IT?
UNKNOWN!!
I'VE NEVER FELT ANYTHING LIKE IT!
PRIN-CESS RANAH.
YOU MUST TRY THIS PARFAIT.
HNGH...

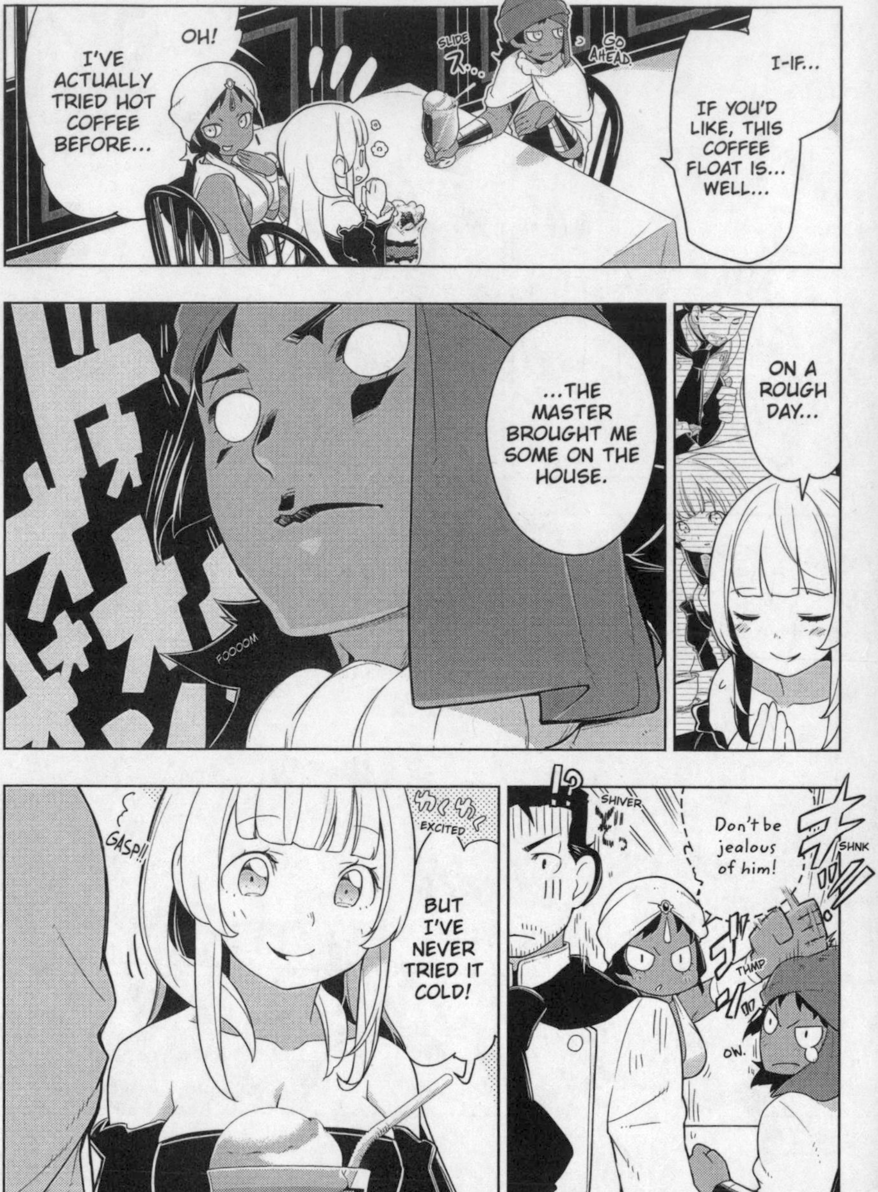
I-IF...
IF YOU'D LIKE, THIS COFFEE FLOAT IS... WELL...
GO AHEAD.
SLIDE
OH!
I'VE ACTUALLY TRIED HOT COFFEE BEFORE...
ON A ROUGH DAY...
...THE MASTER BROUGHT ME SOME ON THE HOUSE.
FOOOOM
SHNK
Don't be jealous of him!
SHIVER
THMP
OW.
EXCITED
BUT I'VE NEVER TRIED IT COLD!
GASP!!

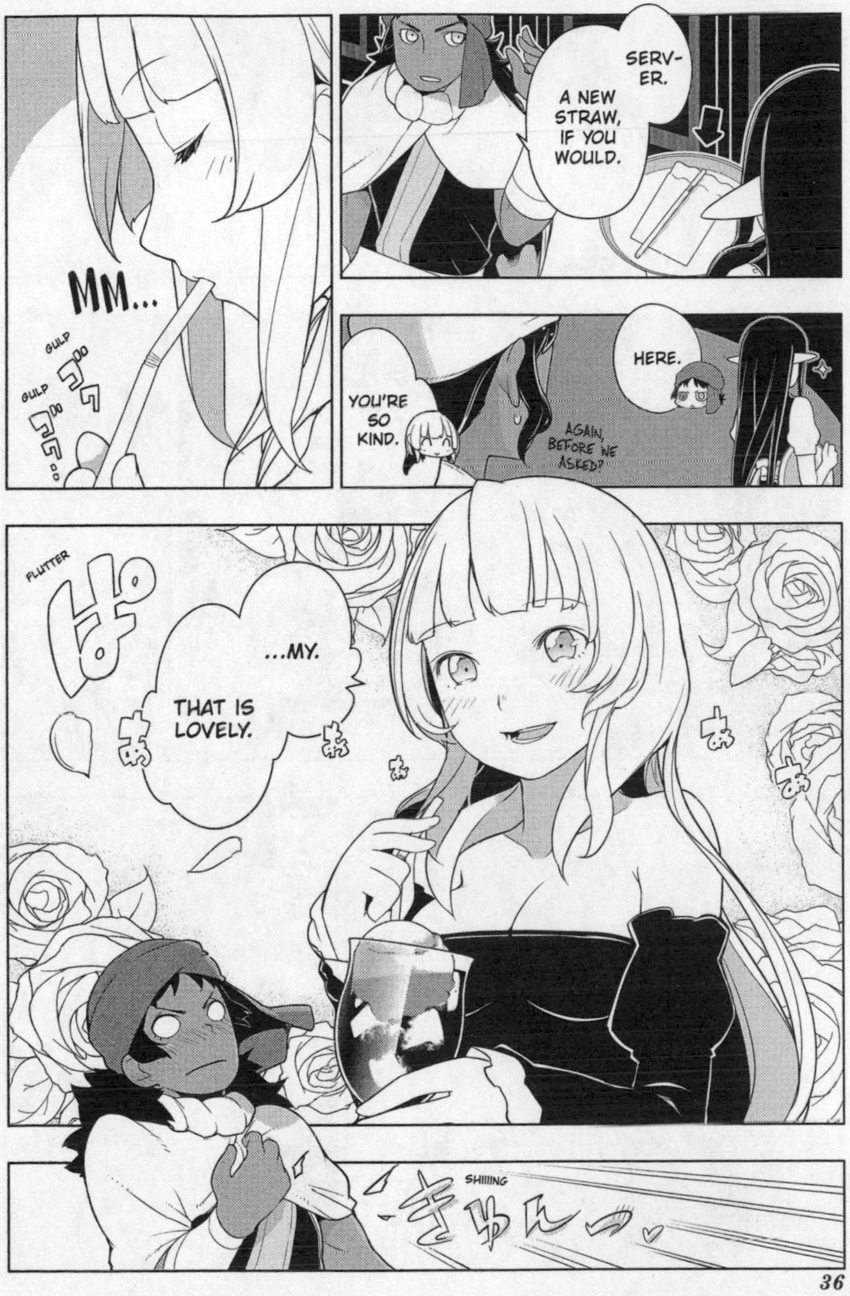
SERVER. A NEW STRAW, IF YOU WOULD.
HERE.
AGAIN, BEFORE WE ASKED?
YOU'RE SO KIND.
MM...
GULP
GULP
...MY. THAT IS LOVELY.
FLUTTER
SHIIIING

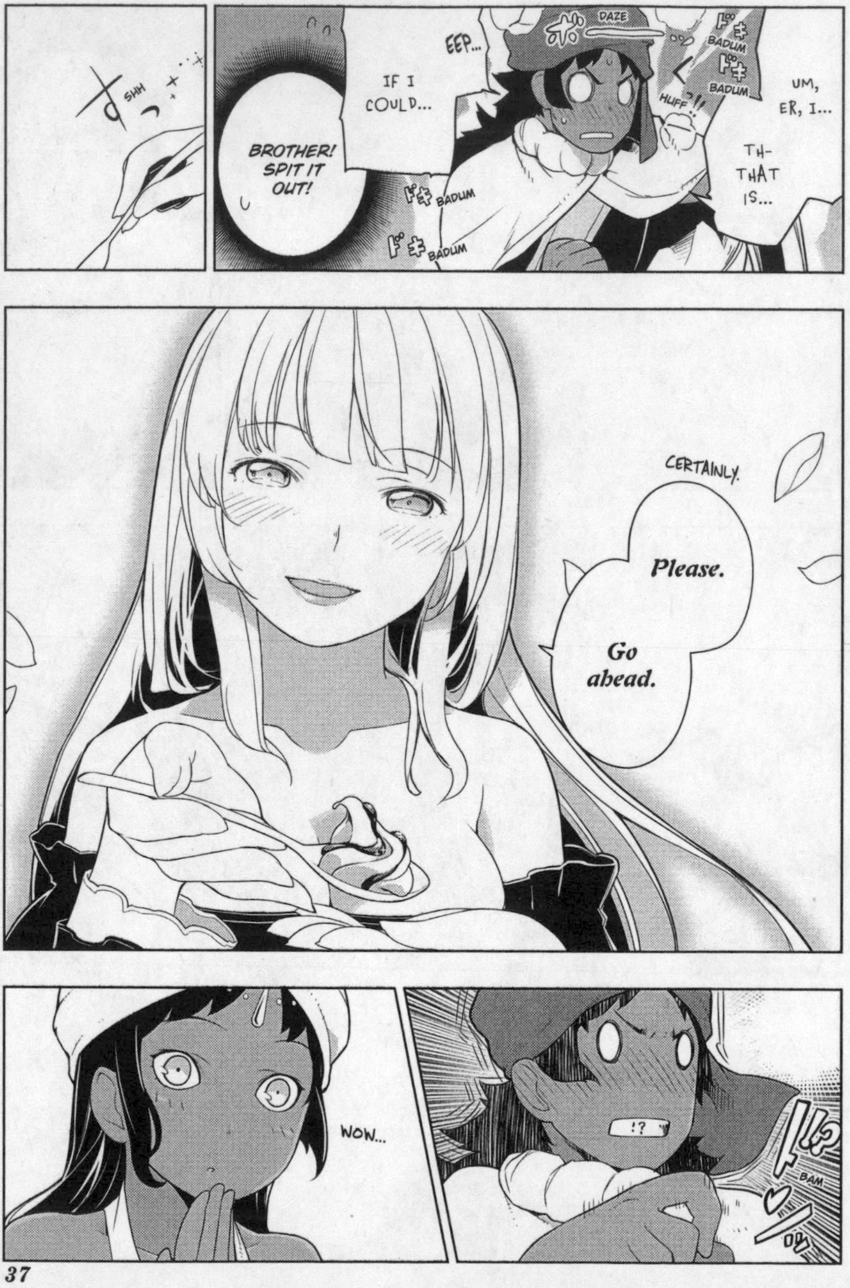
DAZE
BADUM
BADUM
UM, ER, I...
TH- THAT IS...
HUFF
EEP...
IF I COULD...
BROTHER! SPIT IT OUT!
BADUM
BADUM
SHH
CERTAINLY.
Please.
Go ahead.
!?
BAM
WOW...

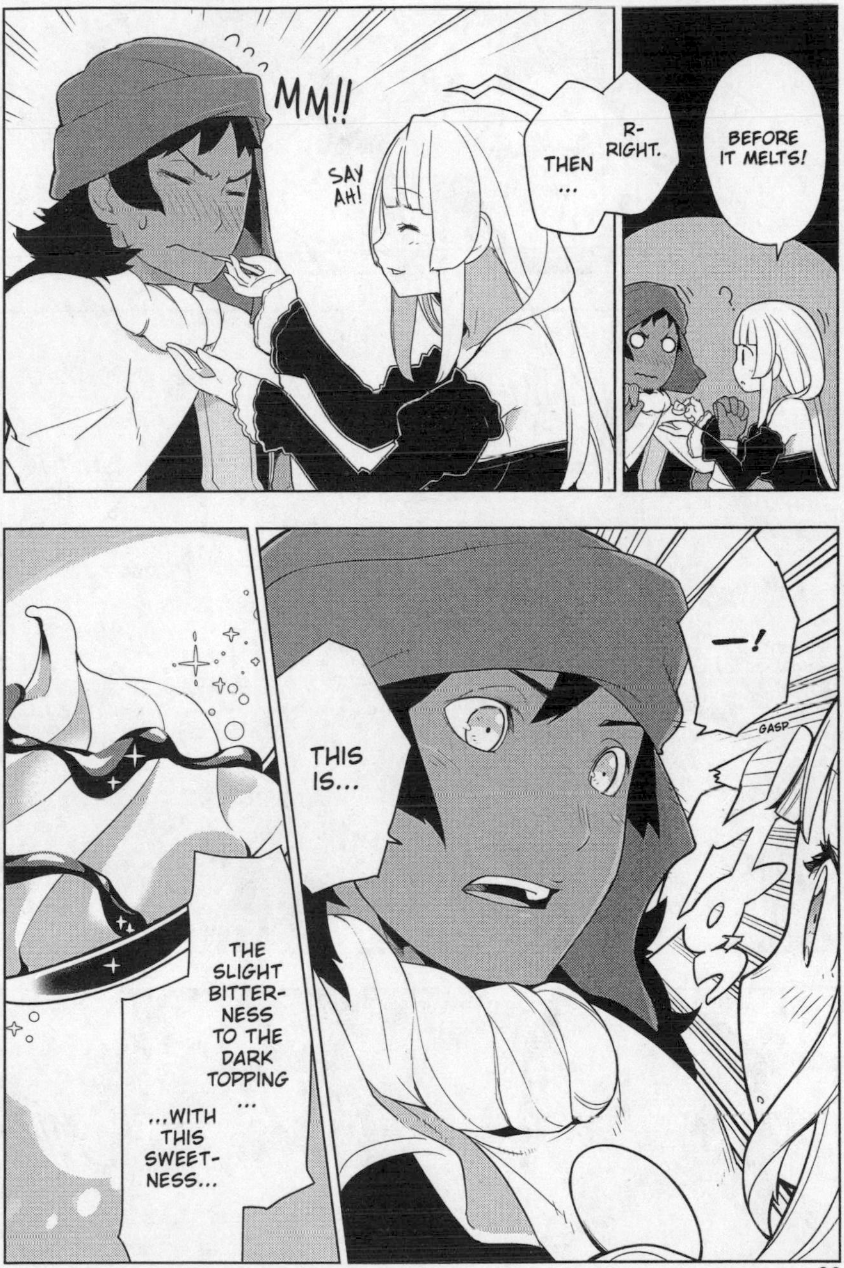
BEFORE IT MELTS!
R- RIGHT.
THEN ...
SAY AH!
MM!!
—!
GASP
THIS IS...
THE SLIGHT BITTER-NESS TO THE DARK TOPPING ...
...WITH THIS SWEET-NESS...

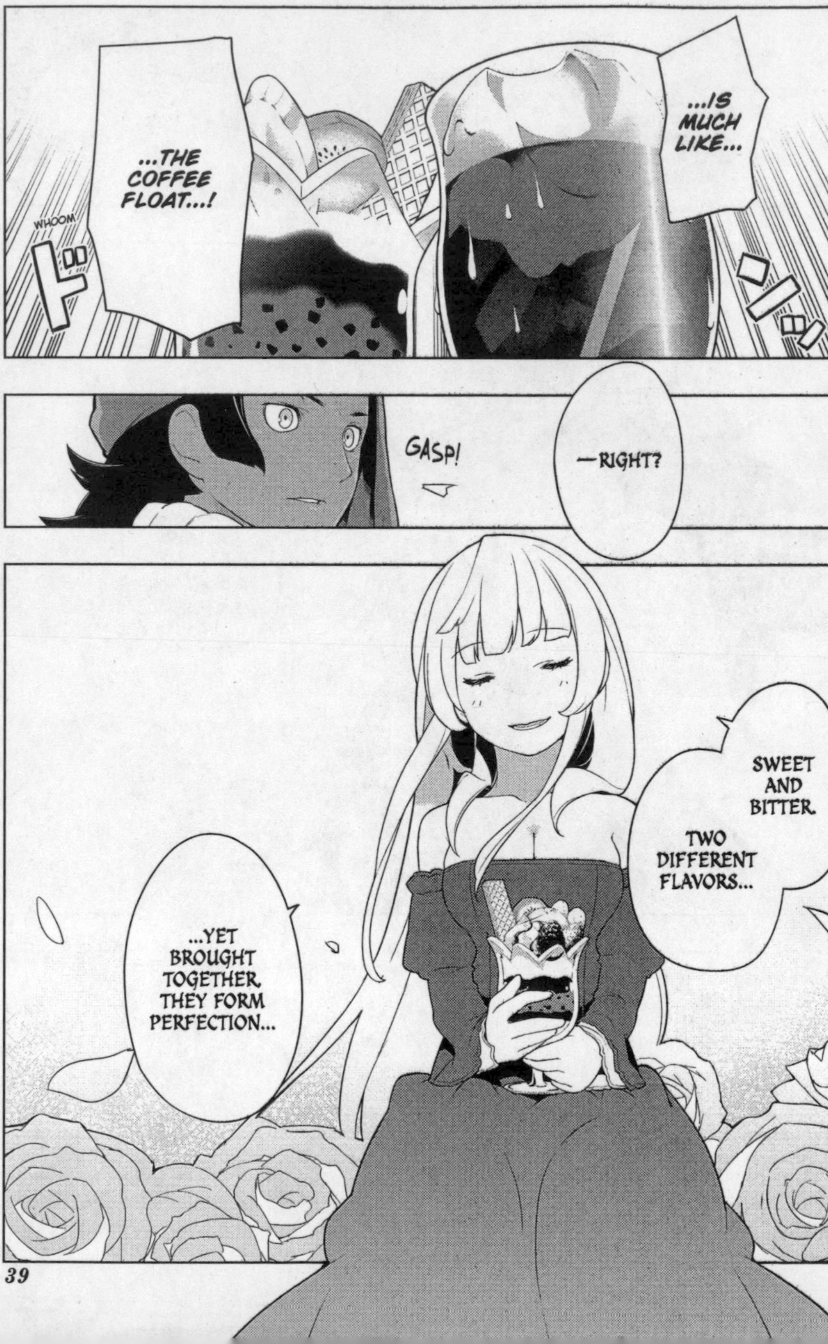
...IS MUCH LIKE...
...THE COFFEE FLOAT...!
WHOOM
—RIGHT?
GASP!
SWEET AND BITTER.
TWO DIFFERENT FLAVORS...
...YET BROUGHT TOGETHER, THEY FORM PERFECTION...

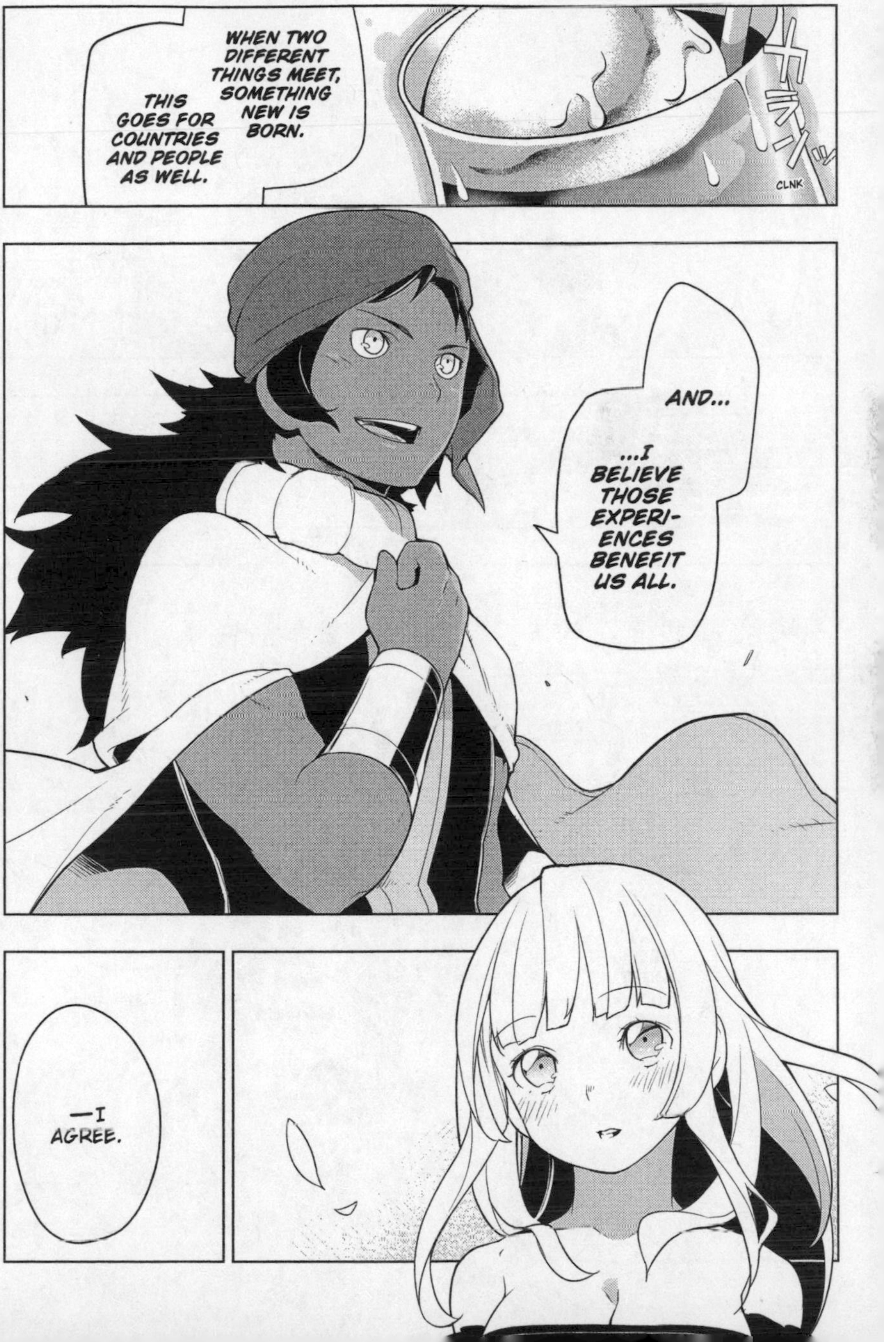
カランッ
CLNK
WHEN TWO DIFFERENT THINGS MEET, SOMETHING NEW IS BORN.
THIS GOES FOR COUNTRIES AND PEOPLE AS WELL.
AND...
...I BELIEVE THOSE EXPERI-ENCES BENEFIT US ALL.
—I AGREE.

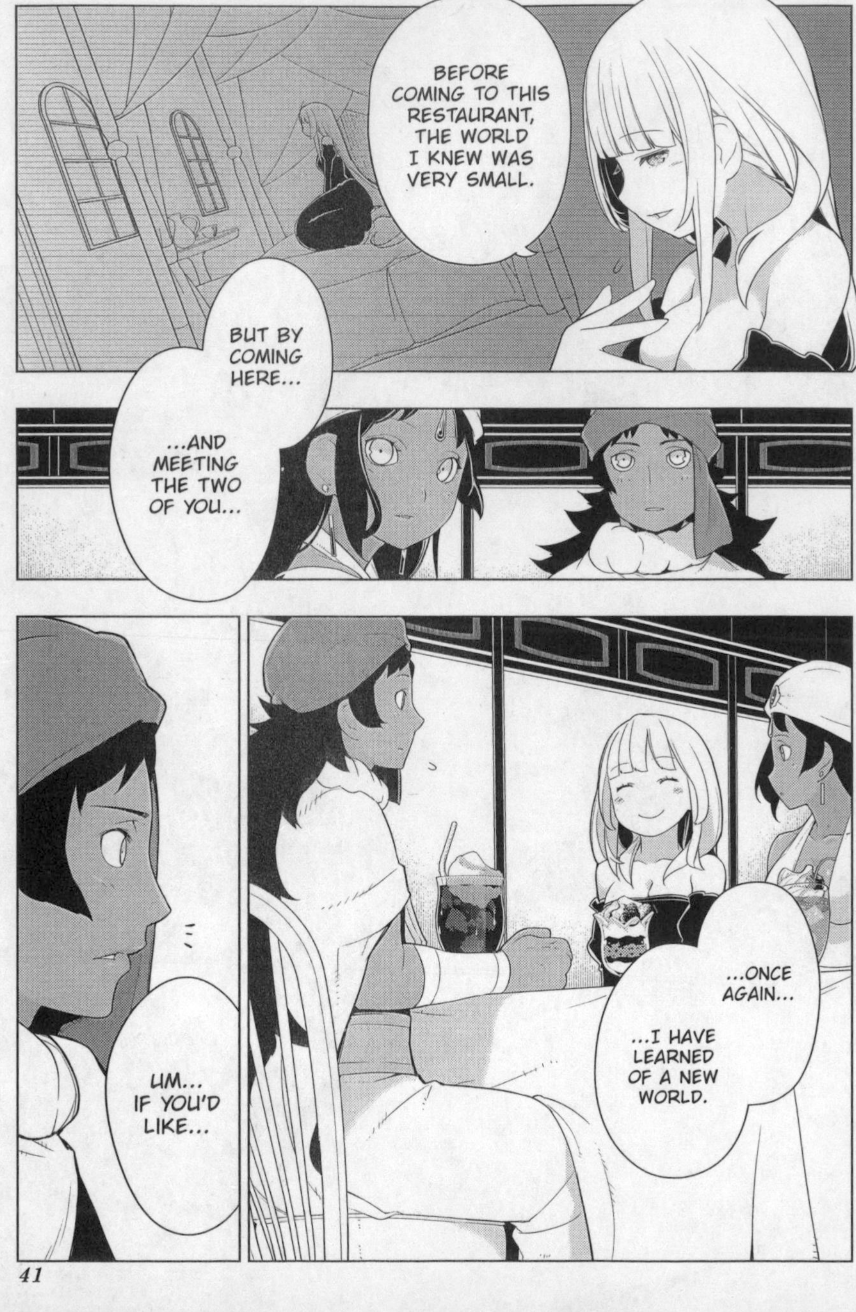
BEFORE COMING TO THIS RESTAURANT, THE WORLD I KNEW WAS VERY SMALL.
BUT BY COMING HERE...
...AND MEETING THE TWO OF YOU...
...ONCE AGAIN...
...I HAVE LEARNED OF A NEW WORLD.
UM... IF YOU'D LIKE...

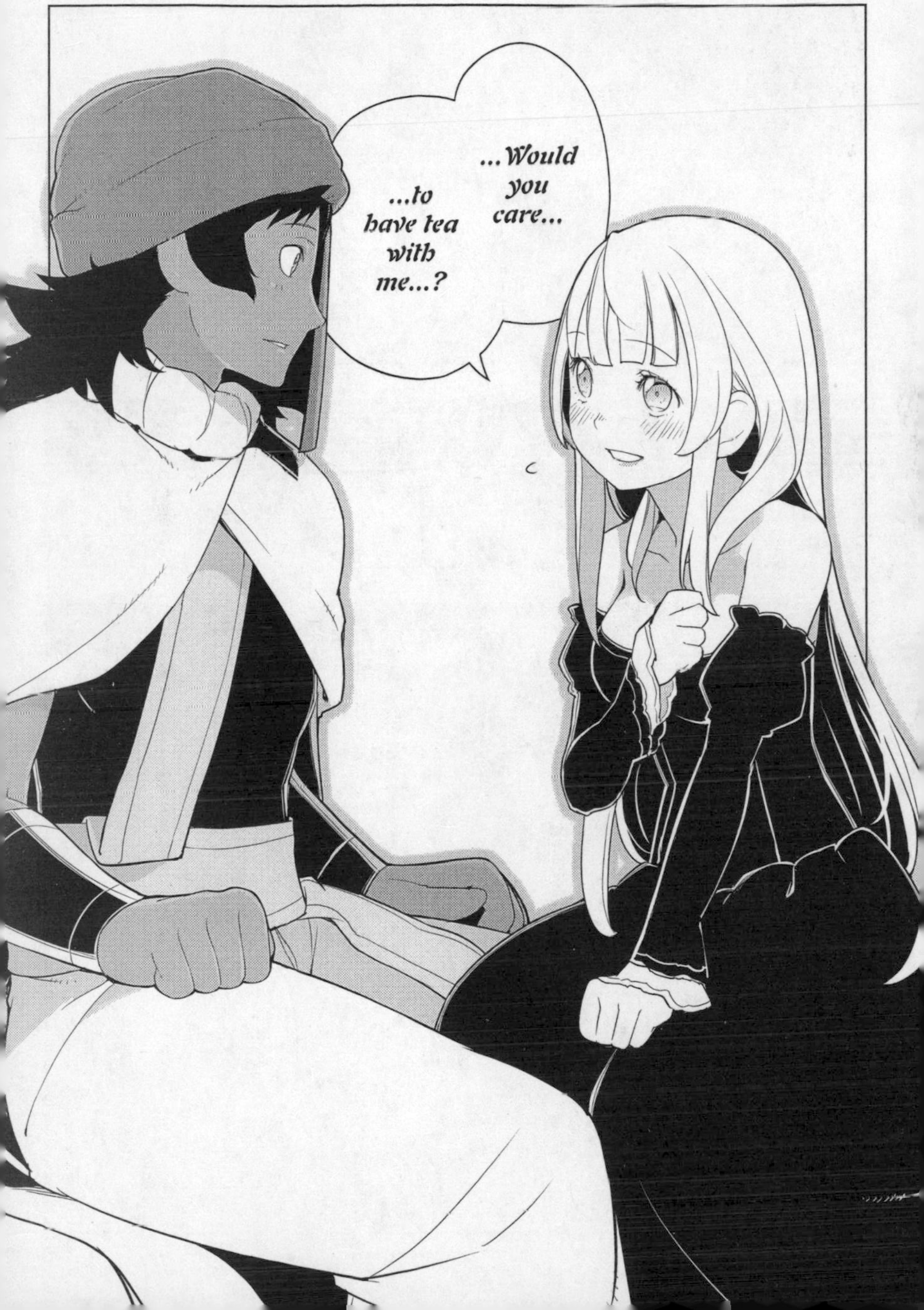
...Would you care...
...to have tea with me...?

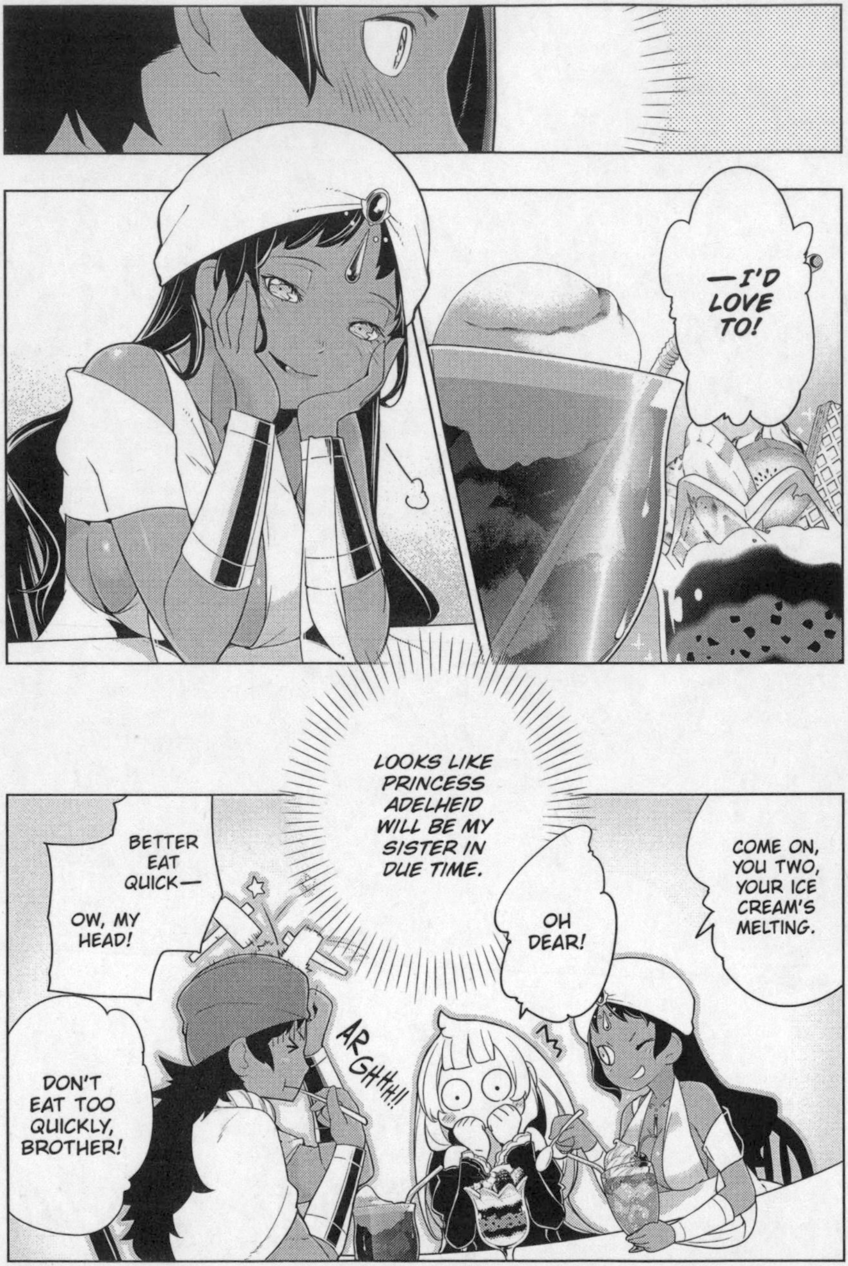
—I'D LOVE TO!
LOOKS LIKE PRINCESS ADELHEID WILL BE MY SISTER IN DUE TIME.
COME ON, YOU TWO, YOUR ICE CREAM'S MELTING.
OH DEAR!
BETTER EAT QUICK—
OW, MY HEAD!
ARGHH!!
DON'T EAT TOO QUICKLY, BROTHER!

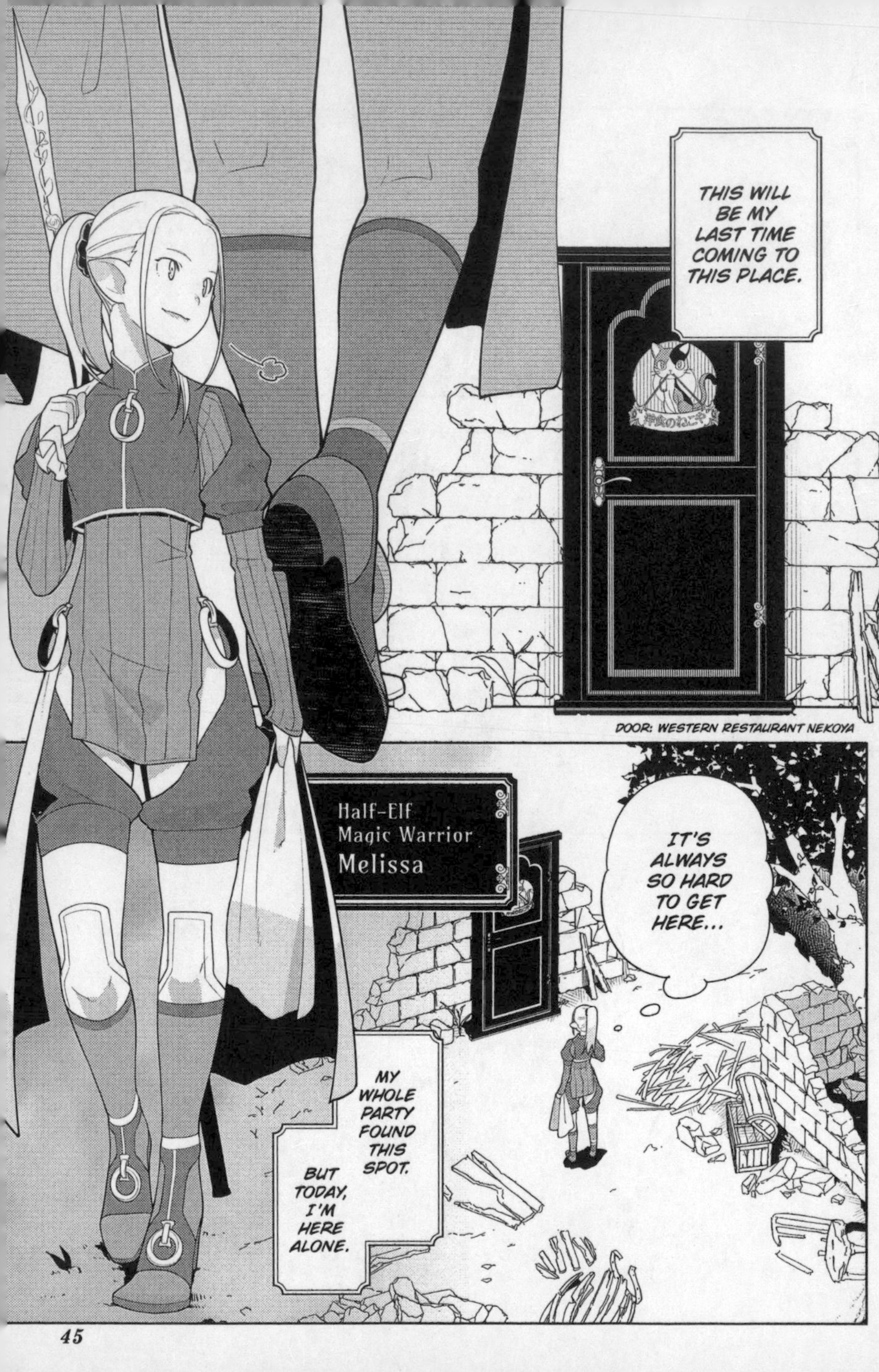
THIS WILL BE MY LAST TIME COMING TO THIS PLACE.
DOOR: WESTERN RESTAURANT NEKOYA
IT'S ALWAYS SO HARD TO GET HERE...
Half-Elf Magic Warrior Melissa
MY WHOLE PARTY FOUND THIS SPOT.
BUT TODAY, I'M HERE ALONE.

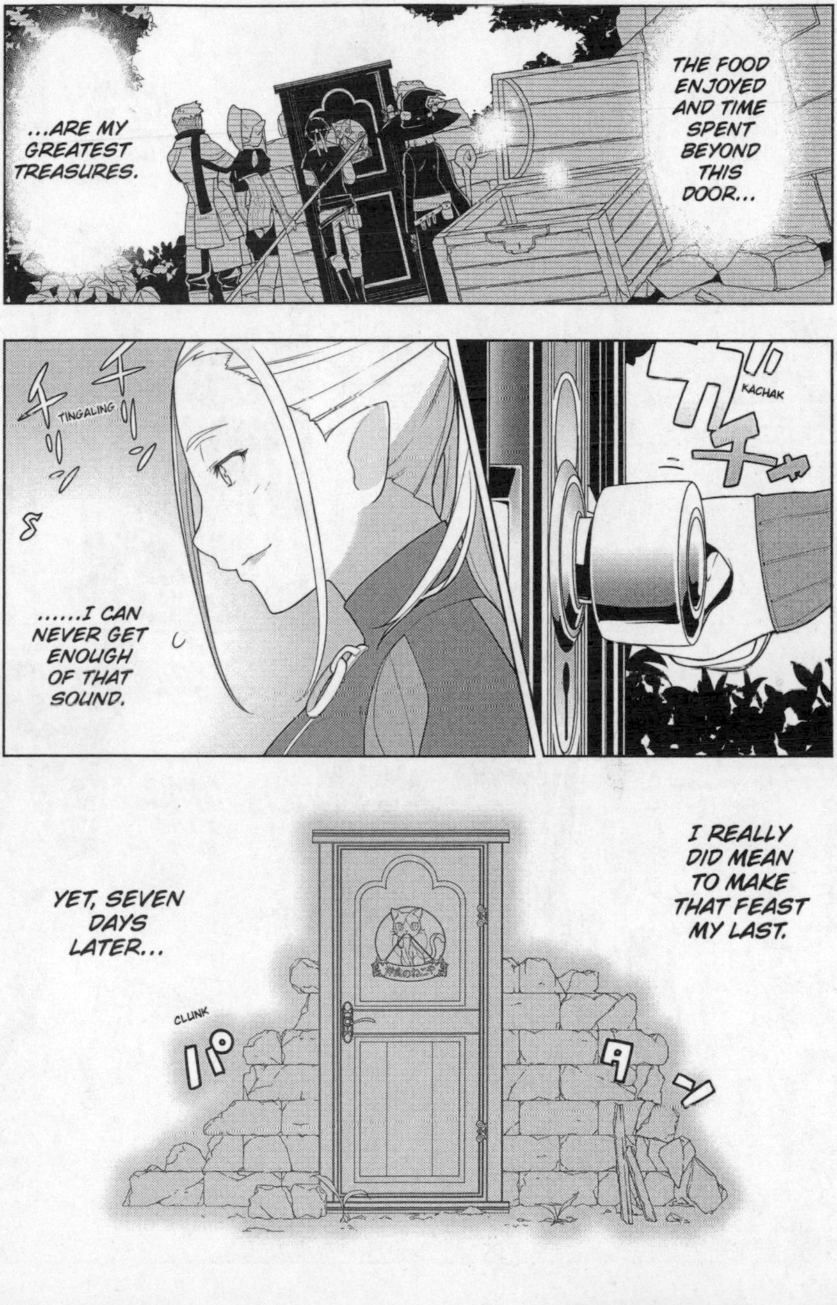
THE FOOD ENJOYED AND TIME SPENT BEYOND THIS DOOR...
...ARE MY GREATEST TREASURES.
KACHAK
TINGALING
......I CAN NEVER GET ENOUGH OF THAT SOUND.
I REALLY DID MEAN TO MAKE THAT FEAST MY LAST.
YET, SEVEN DAYS LATER...
CLUNK

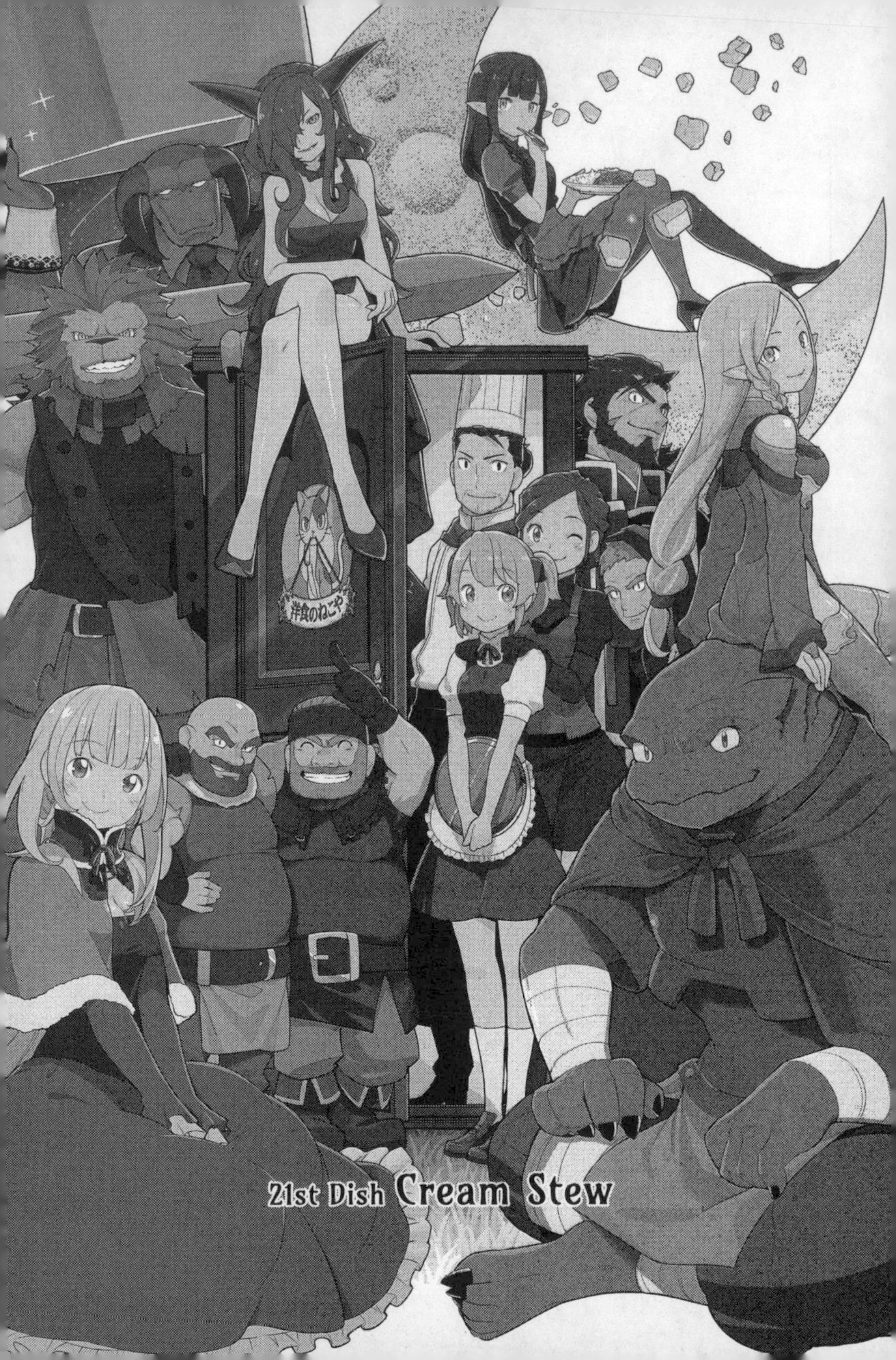
洋食のねこや

21st Dish Cream Stew

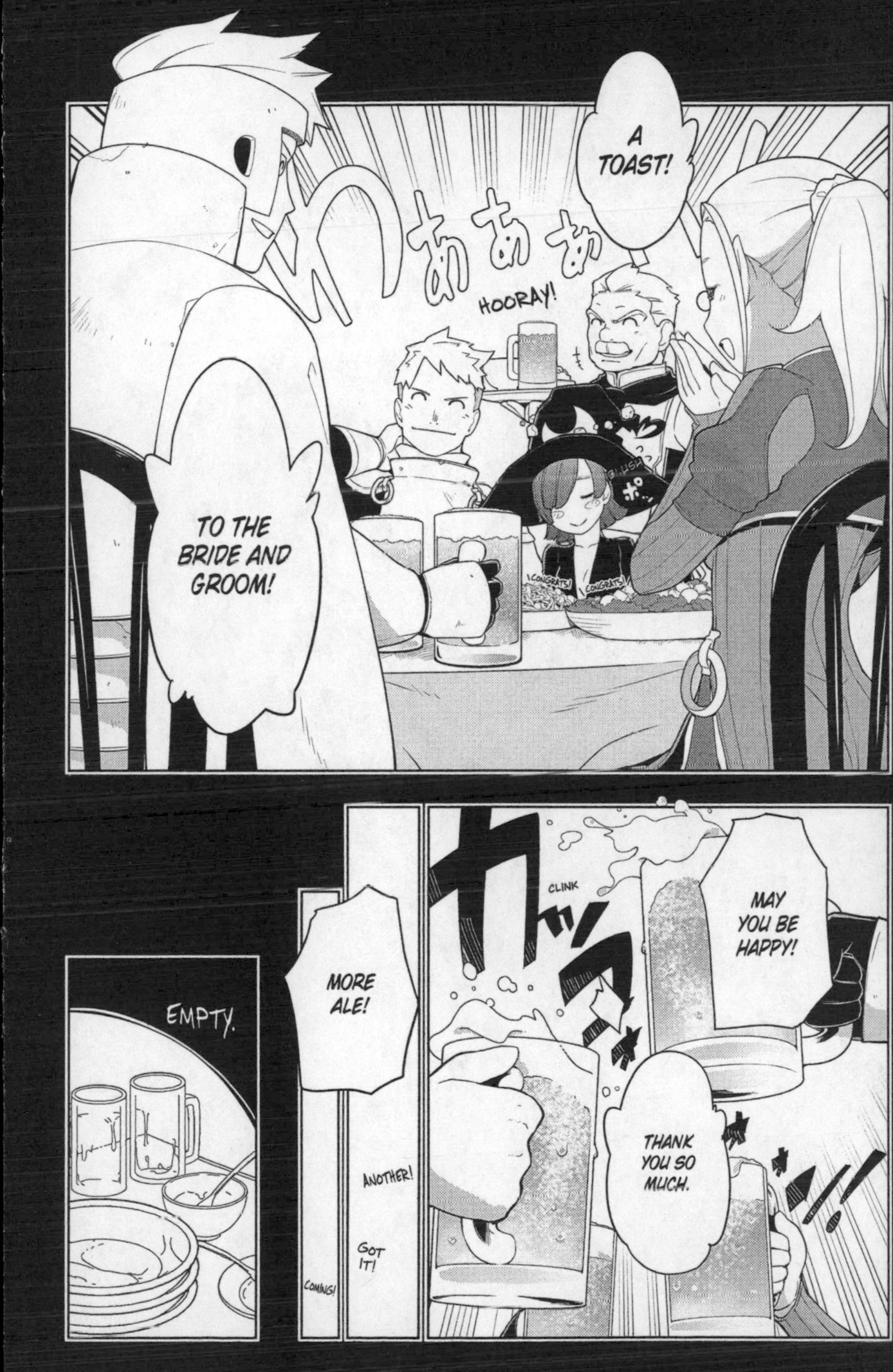
A TOAST!
HOORAY!
CONGRATS!
CONGRATS!
TO THE BRIDE AND GROOM!
MAY YOU BE HAPPY!
CLINK
THANK YOU SO MUCH.
MORE ALE!
ANOTHER!
GOT IT!
COMING!
EMPTY.

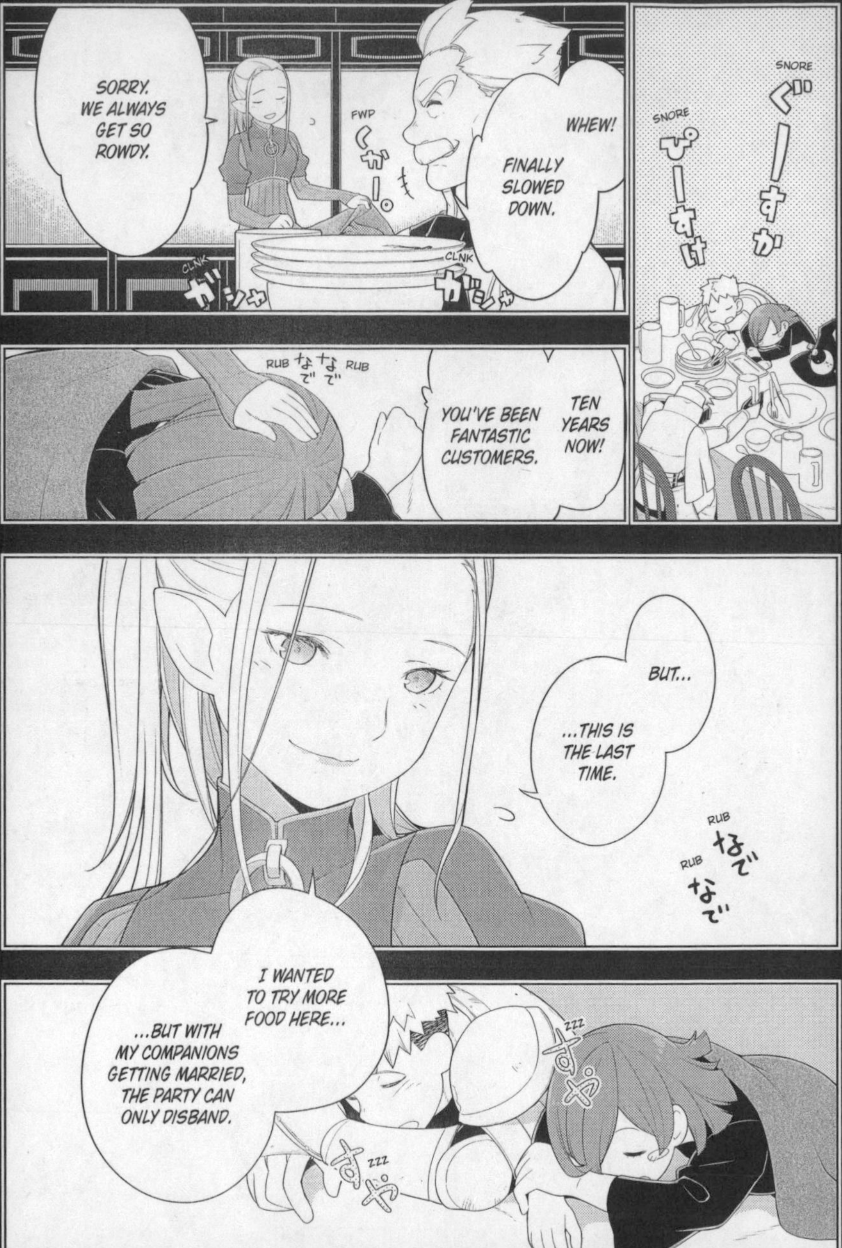
SNORE
ぐーすか
SNORE
ぴーすけ
WHEW!
FINALLY SLOWED DOWN.
CLNK
ガシャ
FWP
くかー。
SORRY. WE ALWAYS GET SO ROWDY.
CLNK
ガシャ
TEN YEARS NOW!
YOU'VE BEEN FANTASTIC CUSTOMERS.
RUB なで RUB なで
BUT...
...THIS IS THE LAST TIME.
RUB なで
RUB なで
I WANTED TO TRY MORE FOOD HERE...
...BUT WITH MY COMPANIONS GETTING MARRIED, THE PARTY CAN ONLY DISBAND.
ZZZ すや
ZZZ すや

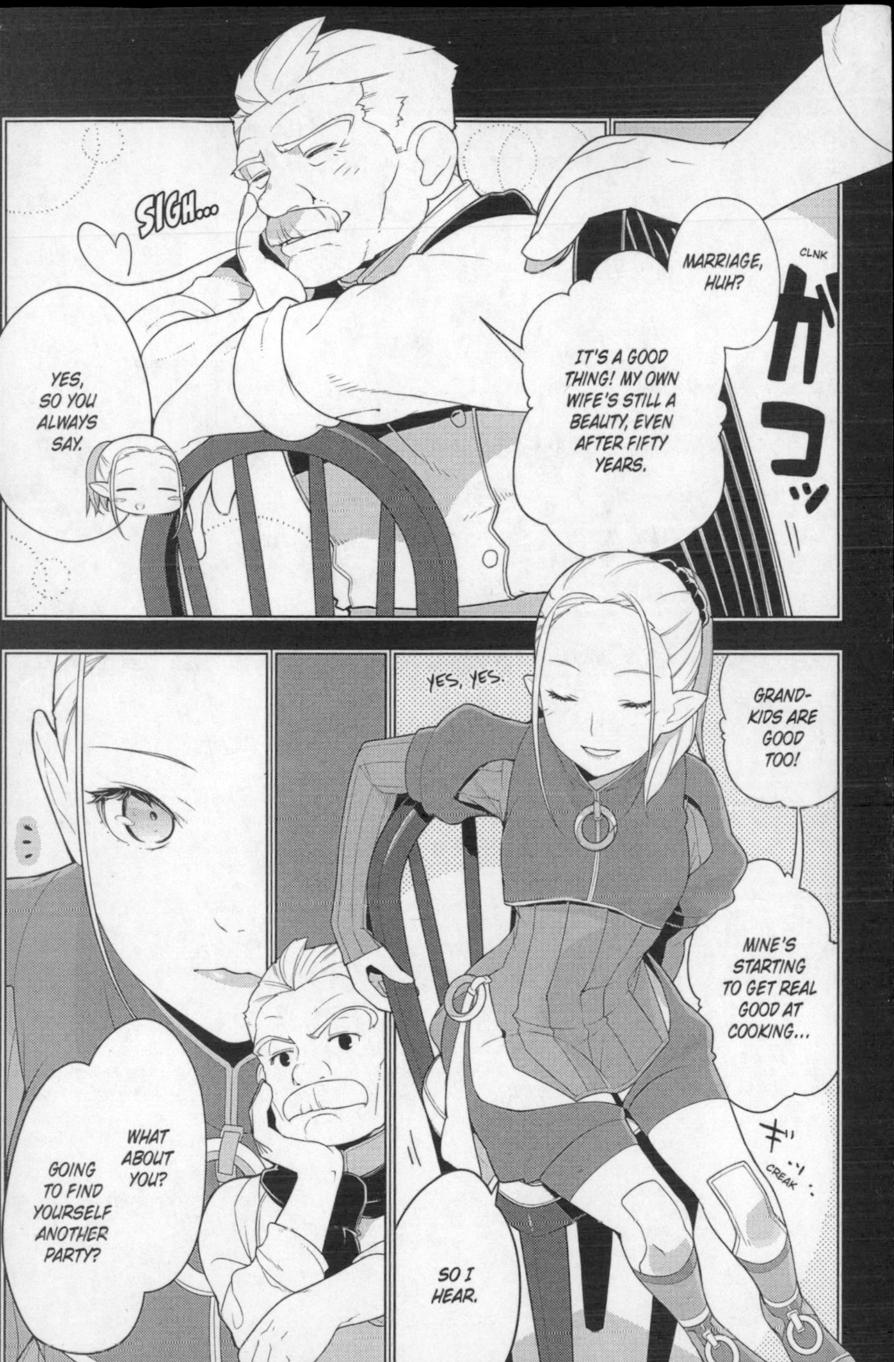
MARRIAGE, HUH?
CLNK
IT'S A GOOD THING! MY OWN WIFE'S STILL A BEAUTY, EVEN AFTER FIFTY YEARS.
SIGH...
YES, SO YOU ALWAYS SAY.
GRAND-KIDS ARE GOOD TOO!
YES, YES.
MINE'S STARTING TO GET REAL GOOD AT COOKING...
CREAK
SO I HEAR.
WHAT ABOUT YOU?
GOING TO FIND YOURSELF ANOTHER PARTY?

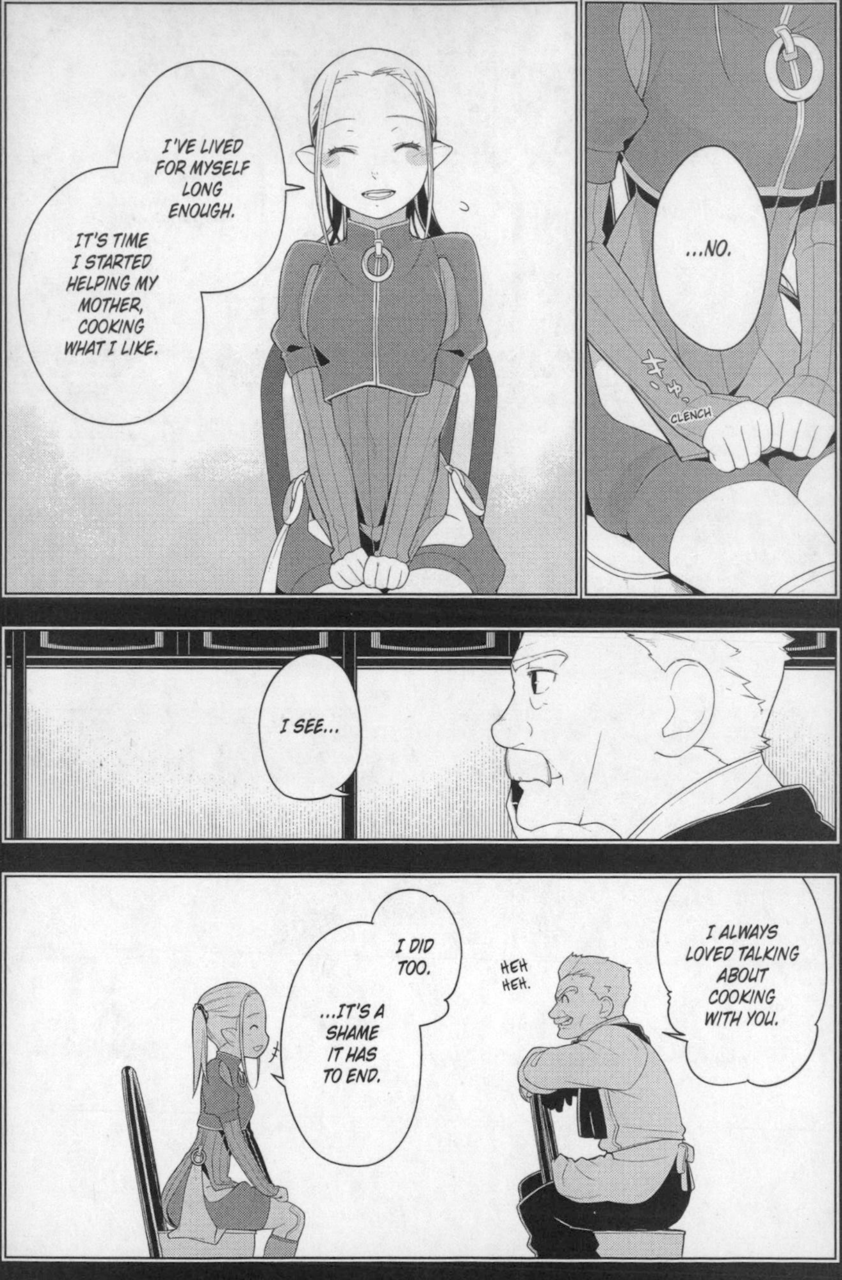
...NO.
CLENCH
I'VE LIVED FOR MYSELF LONG ENOUGH.
IT'S TIME I STARTED HELPING MY MOTHER, COOKING WHAT I LIKE.
I SEE...
I ALWAYS LOVED TALKING ABOUT COOKING WITH YOU.
HEH HEH.
I DID TOO.
...IT'S A SHAME IT HAS TO END.

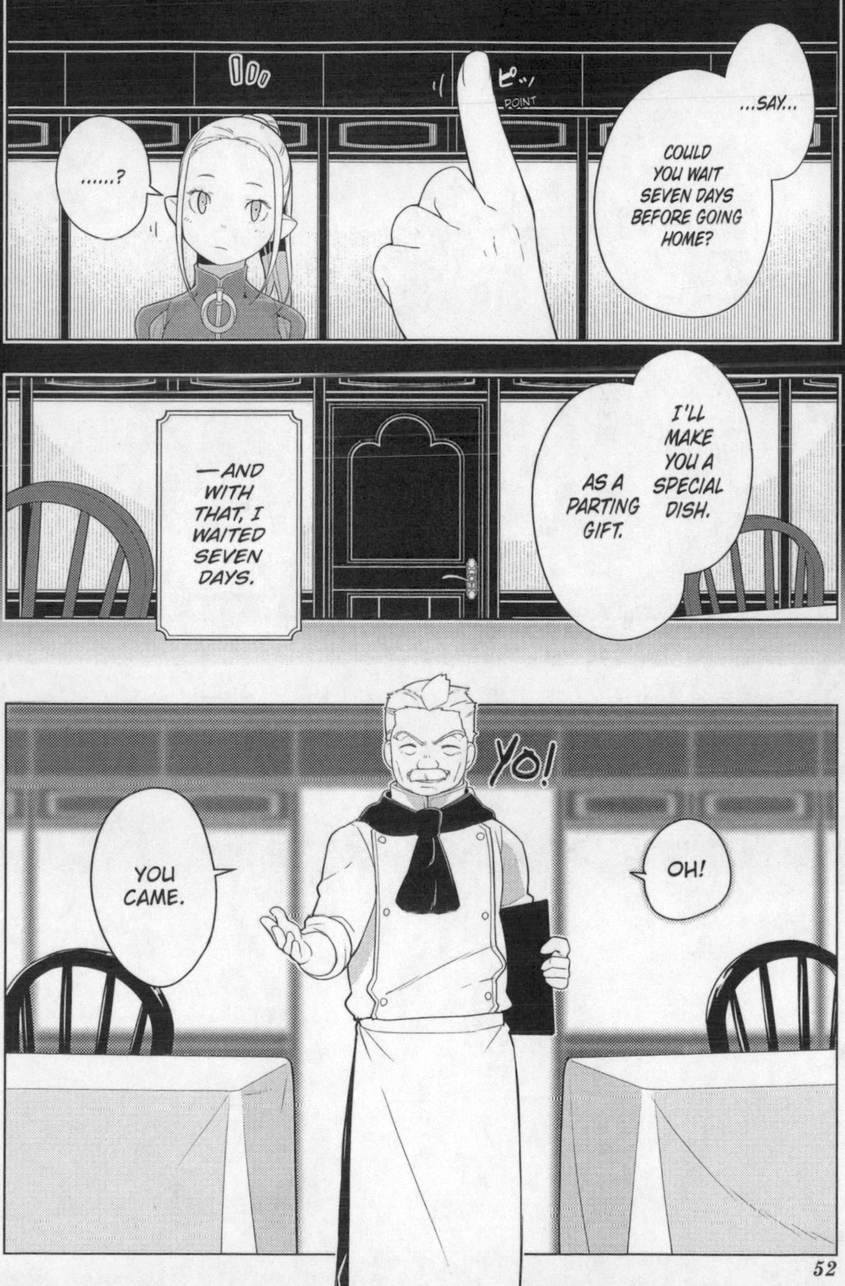
...SAY...
COULD YOU WAIT SEVEN DAYS BEFORE GOING HOME?
ピッ
POINT
......?
I'LL MAKE YOU A SPECIAL DISH.
AS A PARTING GIFT.
—AND WITH THAT, I WAITED SEVEN DAYS.
OH!
YO!
YOU CAME.

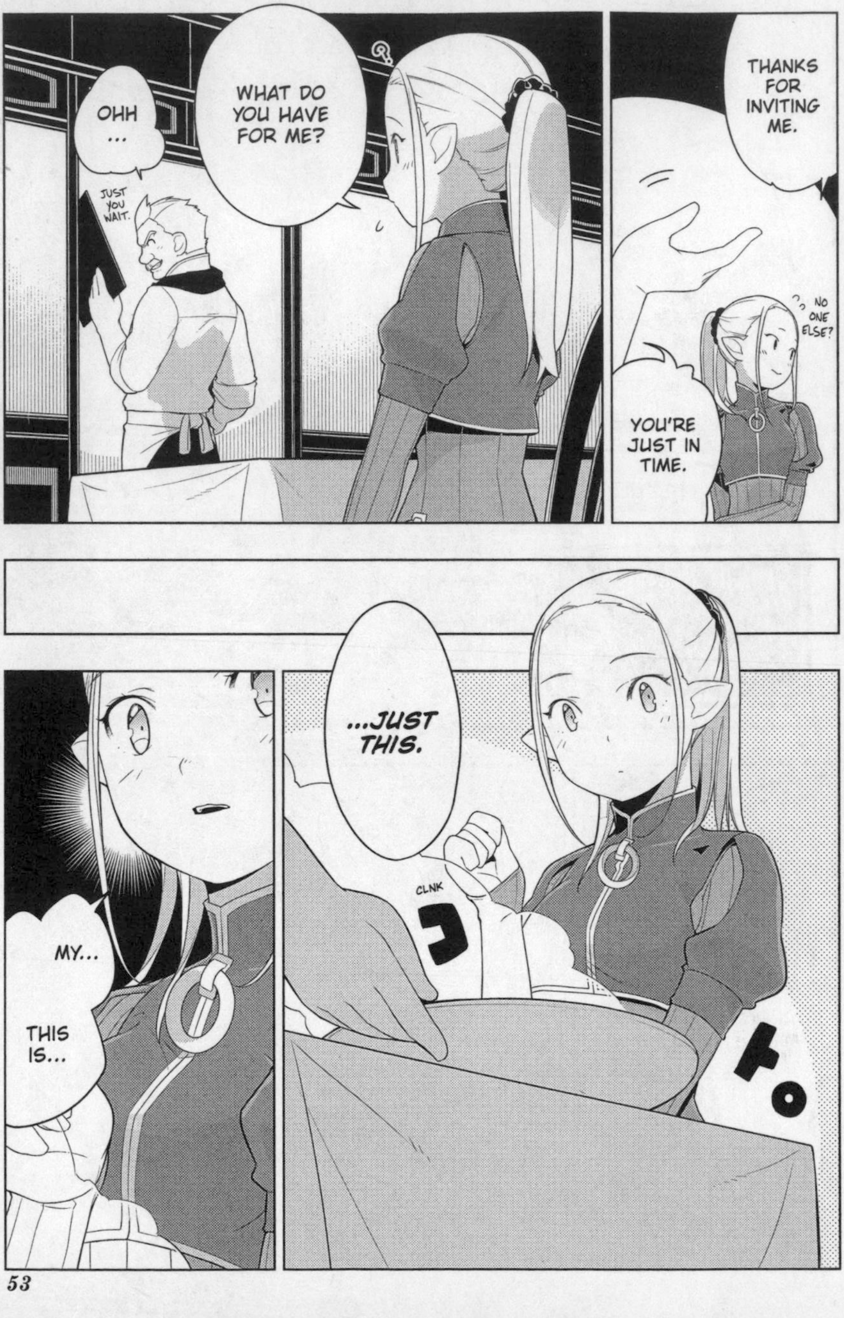
THANKS FOR INVITING ME.
NO ONE ELSE?
YOU'RE JUST IN TIME.
WHAT DO YOU HAVE FOR ME?
OHH ...
JUST YOU WAIT.
...JUST THIS.
CLNK
コト
MY...
THIS IS...

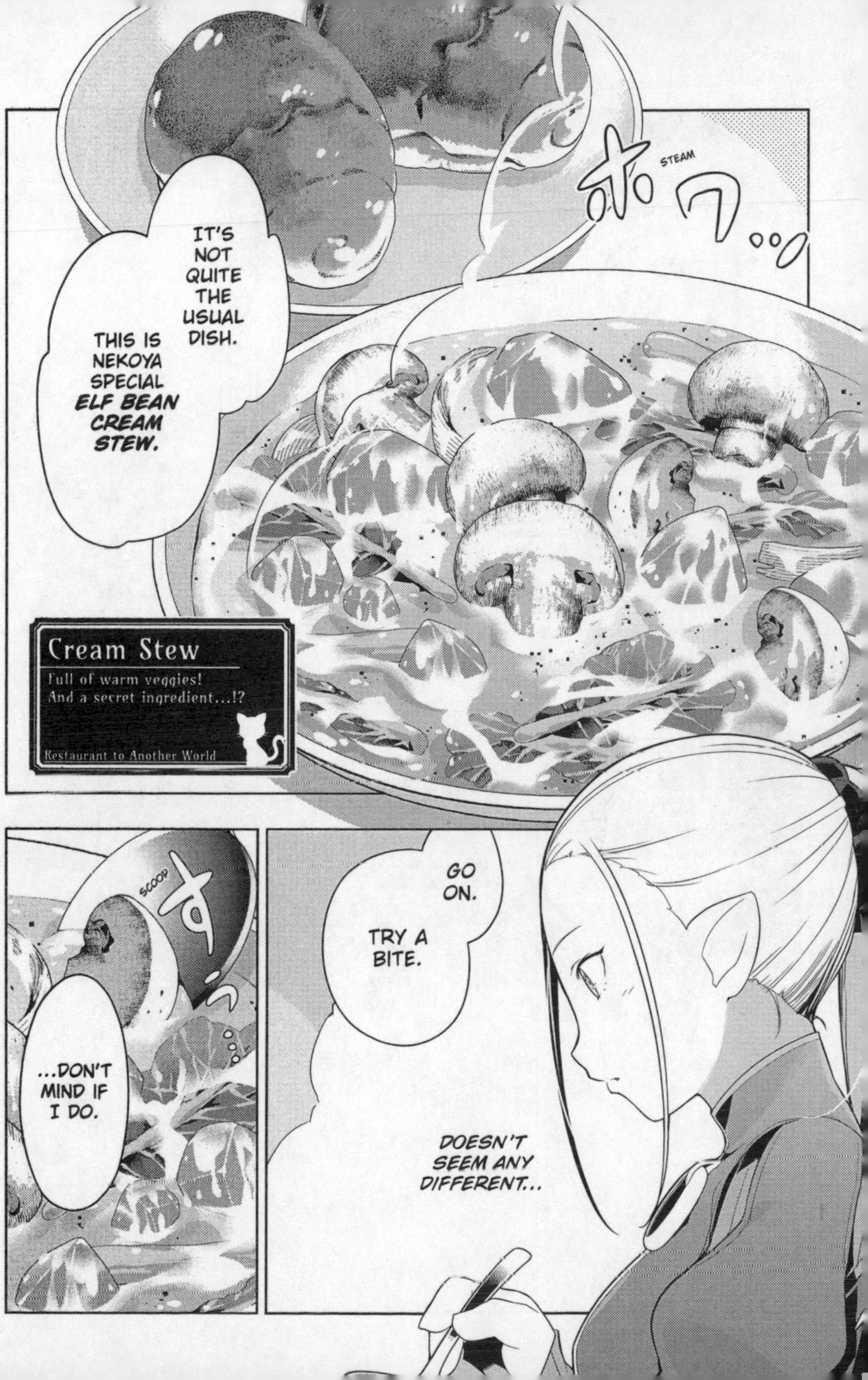
STEAM
IT'S NOT QUITE THE USUAL DISH.
THIS IS NEKOYA SPECIAL ELF BEAN CREAM STEW.
Cream Stew
Full of warm veggies! And a secret ingredient...!?
Restaurant to Another World
GO ON.
TRY A BITE.
DOESN'T SEEM ANY DIFFERENT...
SCOOP
...DON'T MIND IF I DO.

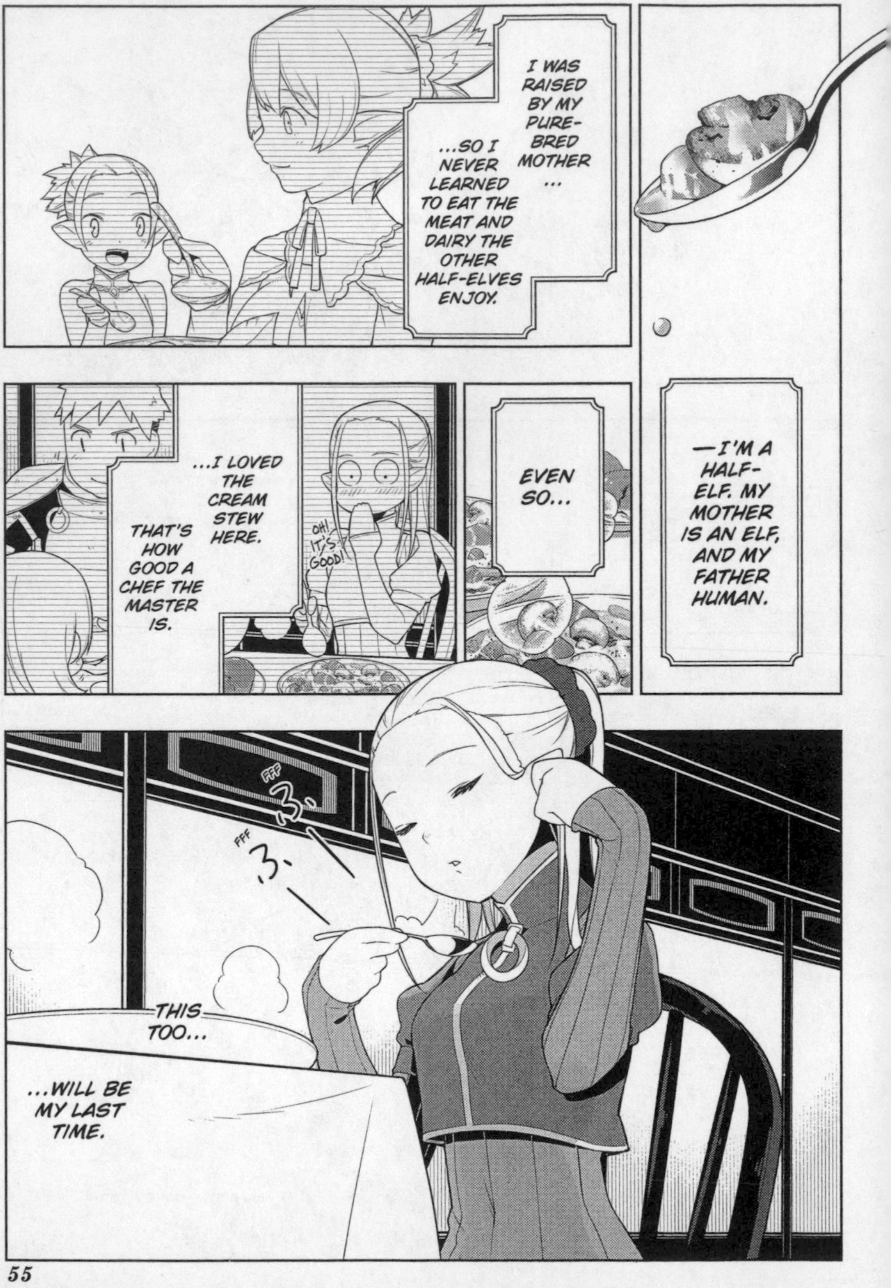
—I'M A HALF-ELF. MY MOTHER IS AN ELF, AND MY FATHER HUMAN.
I WAS RAISED BY MY PURE-BRED MOTHER...
...SO I NEVER LEARNED TO EAT THE MEAT AND DAIRY THE OTHER HALF-ELVES ENJOY.
EVEN SO...
...I LOVED THE CREAM STEW HERE.
OH! IT'S GOOD!
THAT'S HOW GOOD A CHEF THE MASTER IS.
FFF
FFF
THIS TOO...
...WILL BE MY LAST TIME.

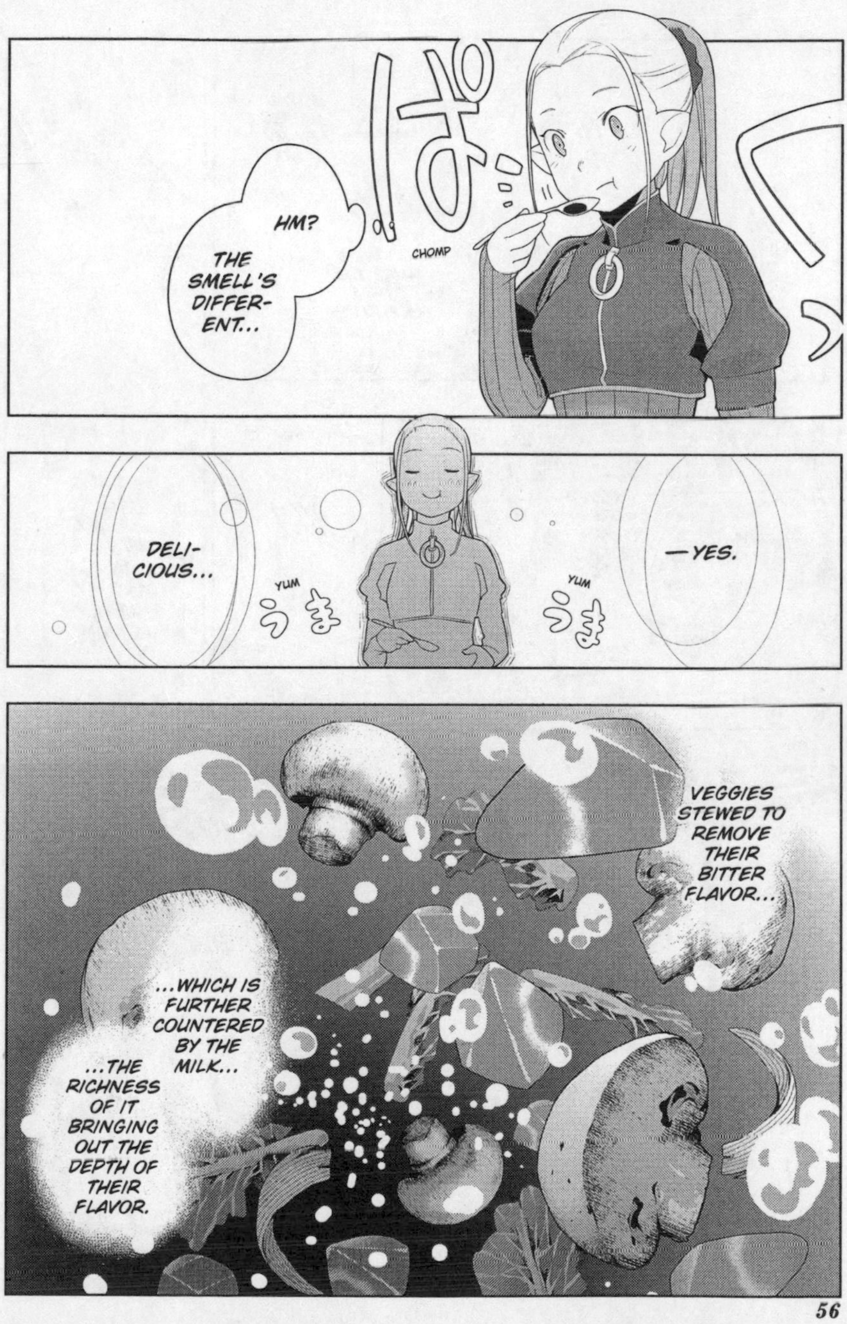
ぱくっ
CHOMP
HM?
THE SMELL'S DIFFER-ENT...
—YES.
YUM
うま
YUM
うま
DELI-CIOUS...
VEGGIES STEWED TO REMOVE THEIR BITTER FLAVOR...
...WHICH IS FURTHER COUNTERED BY THE MILK...
...THE RICHNESS OF IT BRINGING OUT THE DEPTH OF THEIR FLAVOR.

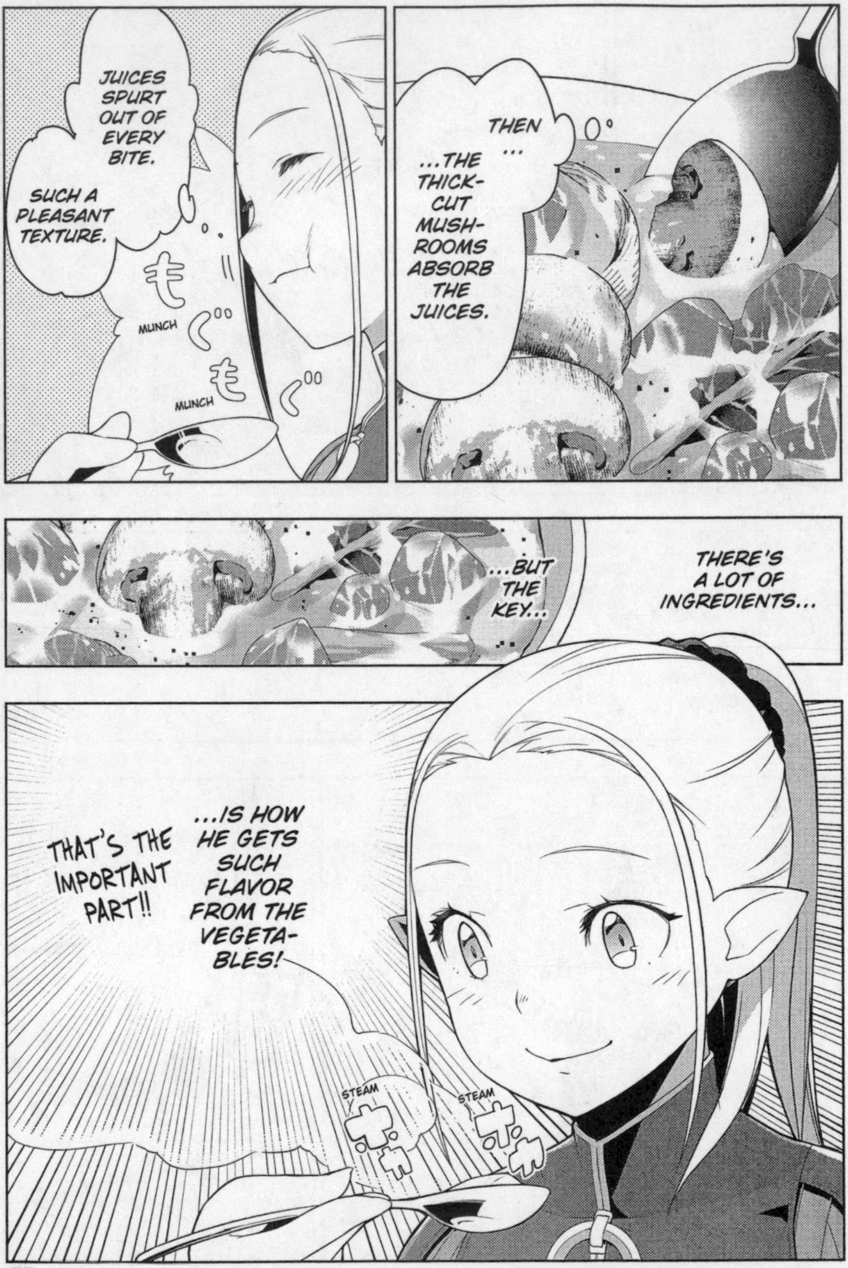

THEN ...
...THE THICK-CUT MUSH-ROOMS ABSORB THE JUICES.
JUICES SPURT OUT OF EVERY BITE.
SUCH A PLEASANT TEXTURE.
MUNCH
MUNCH
THERE'S A LOT OF INGREDIENTS...
...BUT THE KEY...
...IS HOW HE GETS SUCH FLAVOR FROM THE VEGETA-BLES!
THAT'S THE IMPORTANT PART!!
STEAM
STEAM

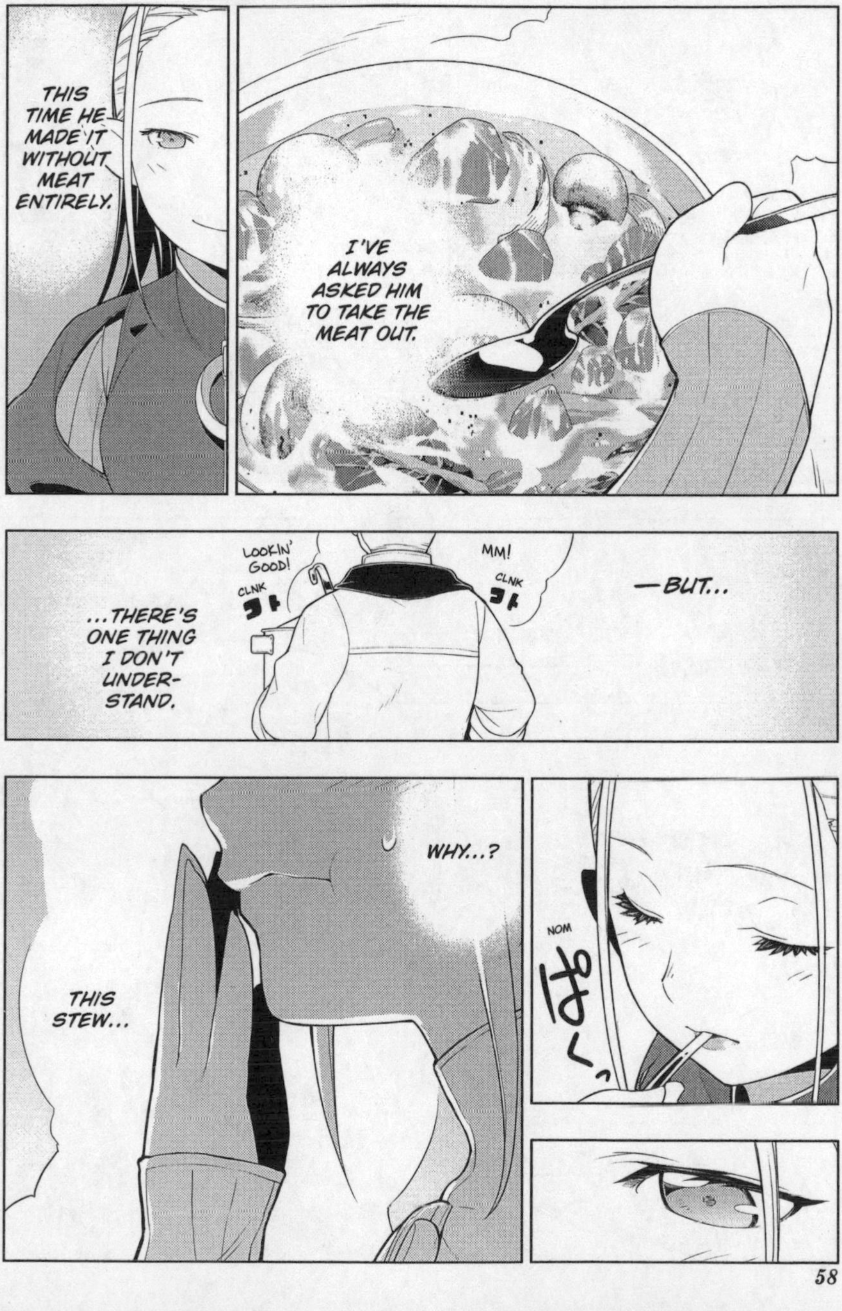
I'VE ALWAYS ASKED HIM TO TAKE THE MEAT OUT.
THIS TIME HE MADE IT WITHOUT MEAT ENTIRELY.
—BUT...
MM!
CLNK
コト
LOOKIN' GOOD!
CLNK
コト
...THERE'S ONE THING I DON'T UNDERSTAND.
NOM
ぱくっ
WHY...?
THIS STEW...

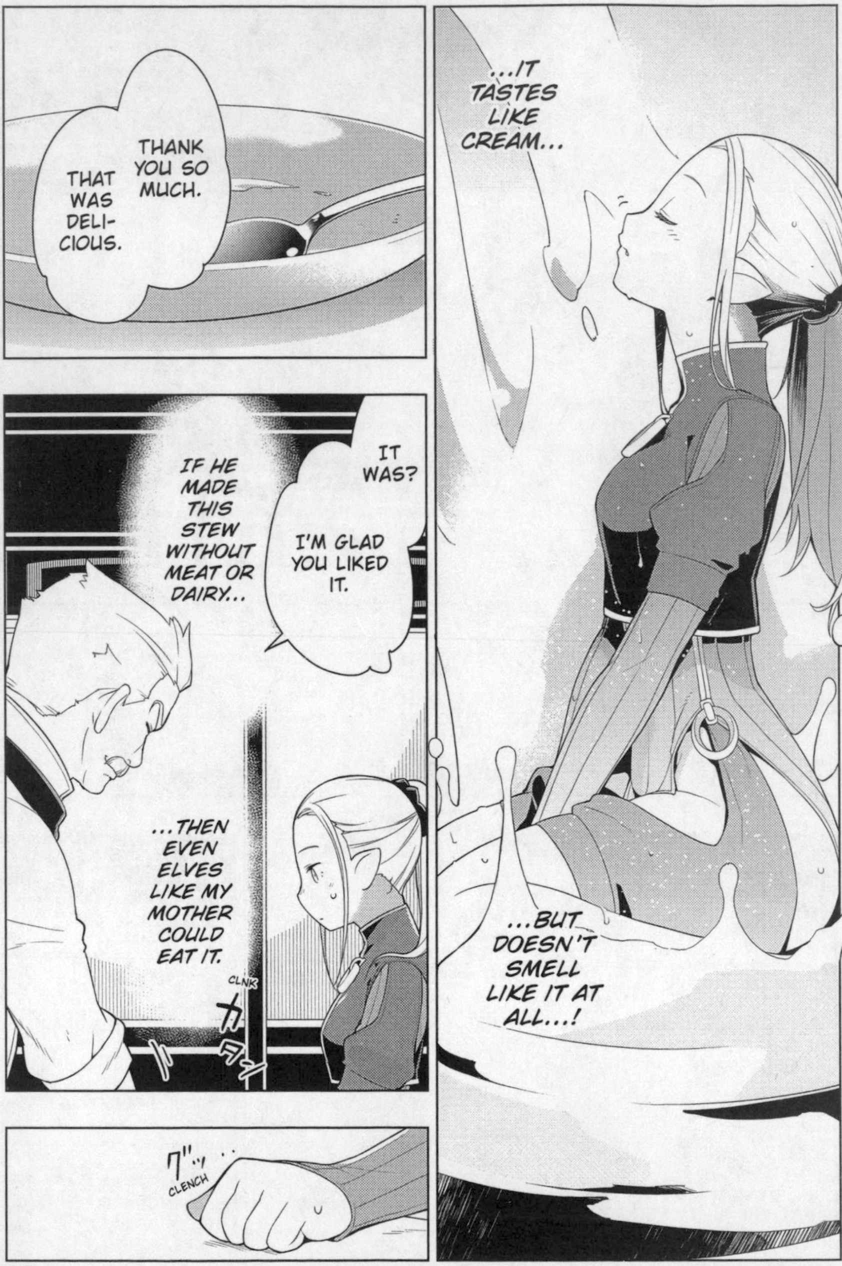
...IT TASTES LIKE CREAM...
...BUT DOESN'T SMELL LIKE IT AT ALL...!
THANK YOU SO MUCH.
THAT WAS DELICIOUS.
IT WAS?
I'M GLAD YOU LIKED IT.
IF HE MADE THIS STEW WITHOUT MEAT OR DAIRY...
...THEN EVEN ELVES LIKE MY MOTHER COULD EAT IT.
CLNK
CLENCH

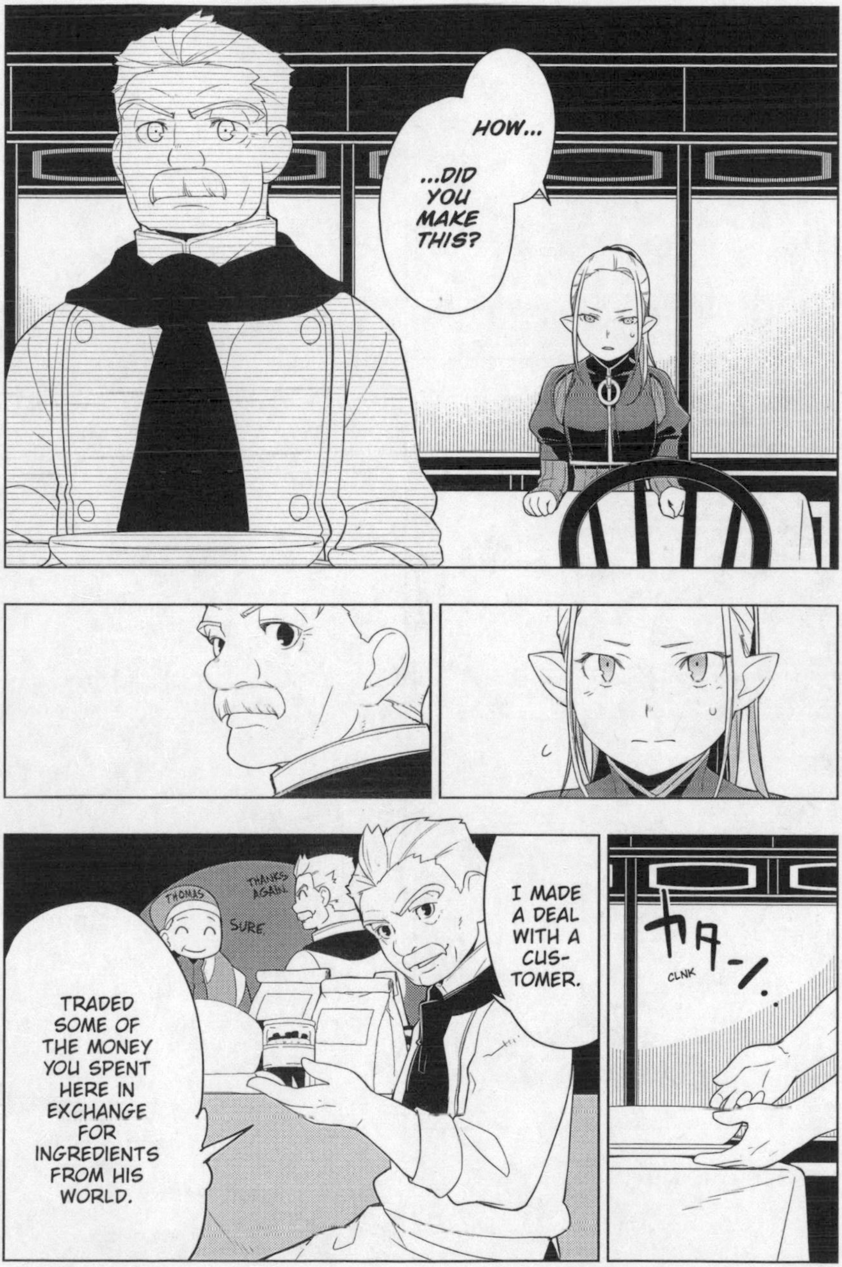
HOW...
...DID YOU MAKE THIS?
CLNK
I MADE A DEAL WITH A CUS-TOMER.
THANKS AGAIN
SURE
THOMAS
TRADED SOME OF THE MONEY YOU SPENT HERE IN EXCHANGE FOR INGREDIENTS FROM HIS WORLD.

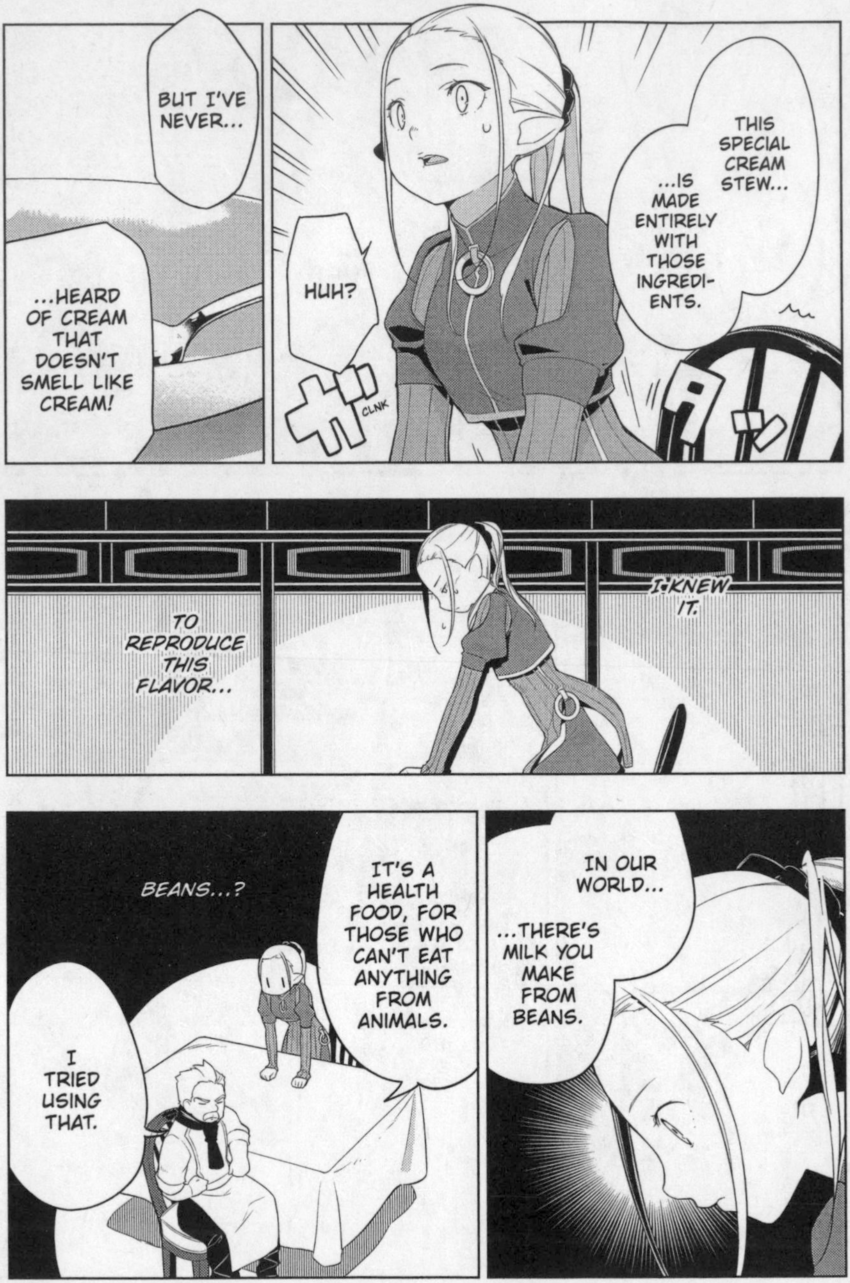
THIS SPECIAL CREAM STEW...
...IS MADE ENTIRELY WITH THOSE INGREDI-ENTS.
HUH?
CLNK
BUT I'VE NEVER...
...HEARD OF CREAM THAT DOESN'T SMELL LIKE CREAM!
I KNEW IT.
TO REPRODUCE THIS FLAVOR...
IN OUR WORLD...
...THERE'S MILK YOU MAKE FROM BEANS.
IT'S A HEALTH FOOD, FOR THOSE WHO CAN'T EAT ANYTHING FROM ANIMALS.
BEANS...?
I TRIED USING THAT.

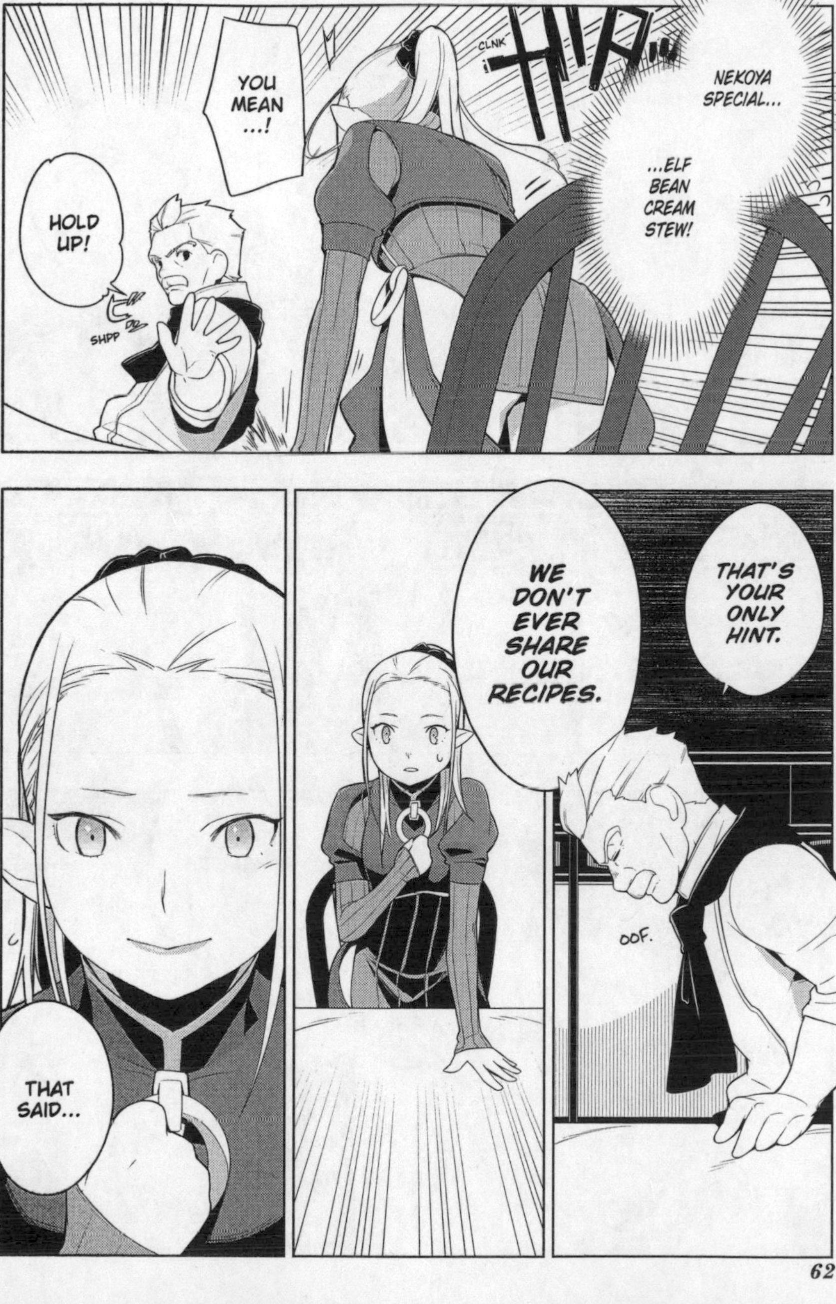
NEKOYA SPECIAL...
...ELF BEAN CREAM STEW!
CLNK
YOU MEAN ...!
HOLD UP!
SHPP
THAT'S YOUR ONLY HINT.
OOF.
WE DON'T EVER SHARE OUR RECIPES.
THAT SAID...

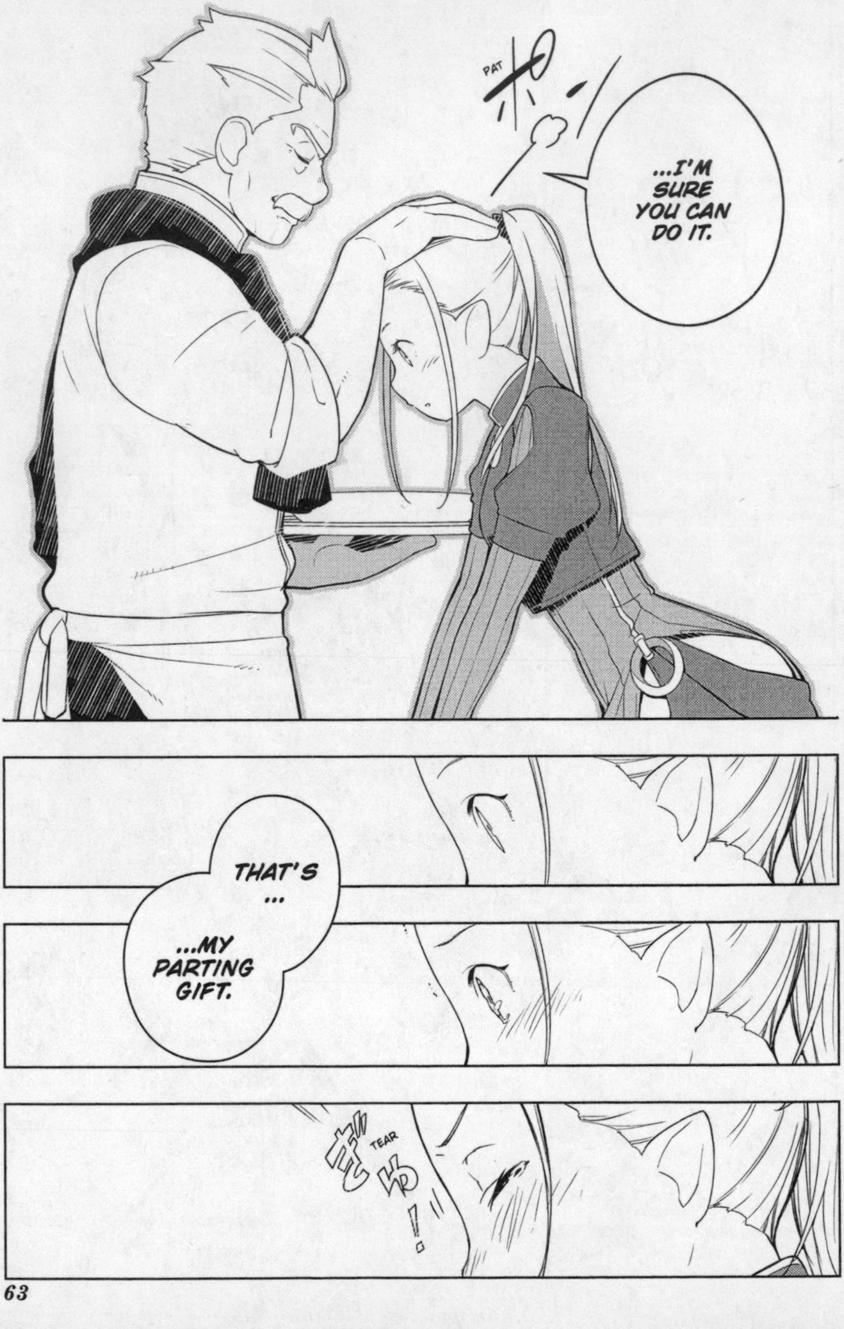
PAT
...I'M SURE YOU CAN DO IT.
THAT'S ...
...MY PARTING GIFT.
TEAR

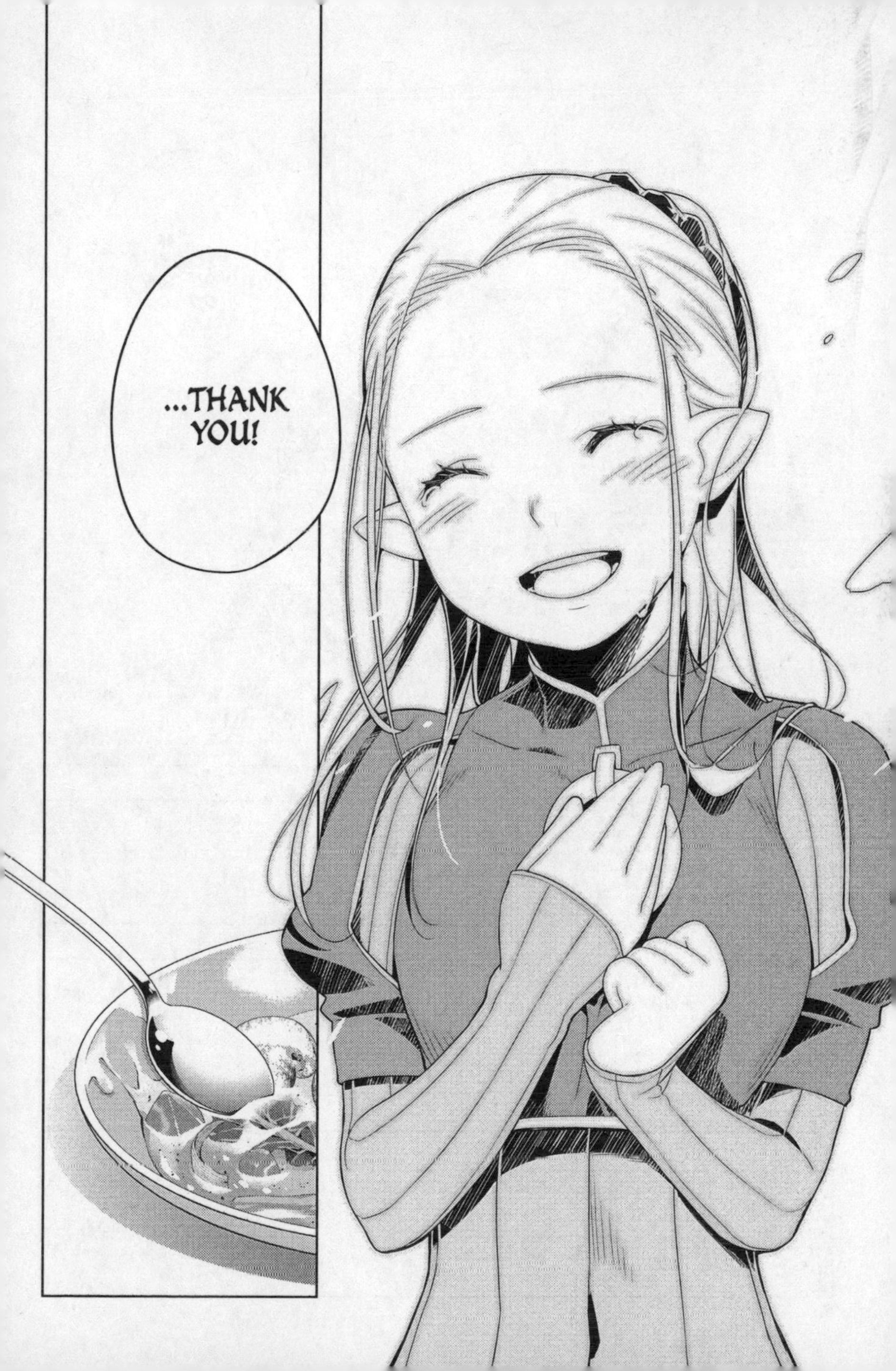
...THANK YOU!

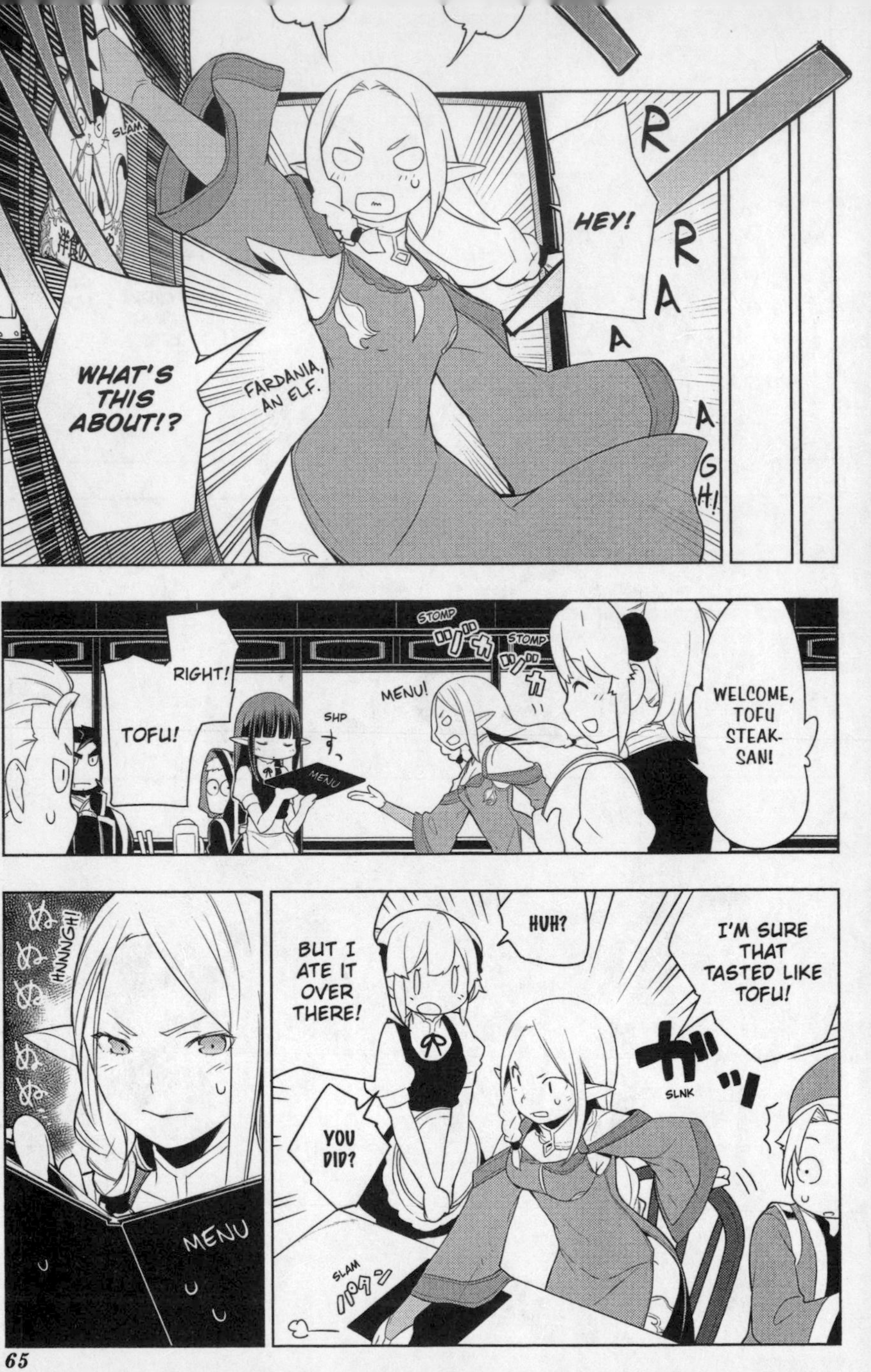
RRAAAAGH!
HEY!
FARDANIA, AN ELF.
SLAM
WHAT'S THIS ABOUT!?
WELCOME, TOFU STEAK-SAN!
STOMP
STOMP
MENU!
SHP
RIGHT!
TOFU!
MENU
I'M SURE THAT TASTED LIKE TOFU!
HUH?
SLNK
BUT I ATE IT OVER THERE!
YOU DID?
SLAM
HNNNGH!
MENU

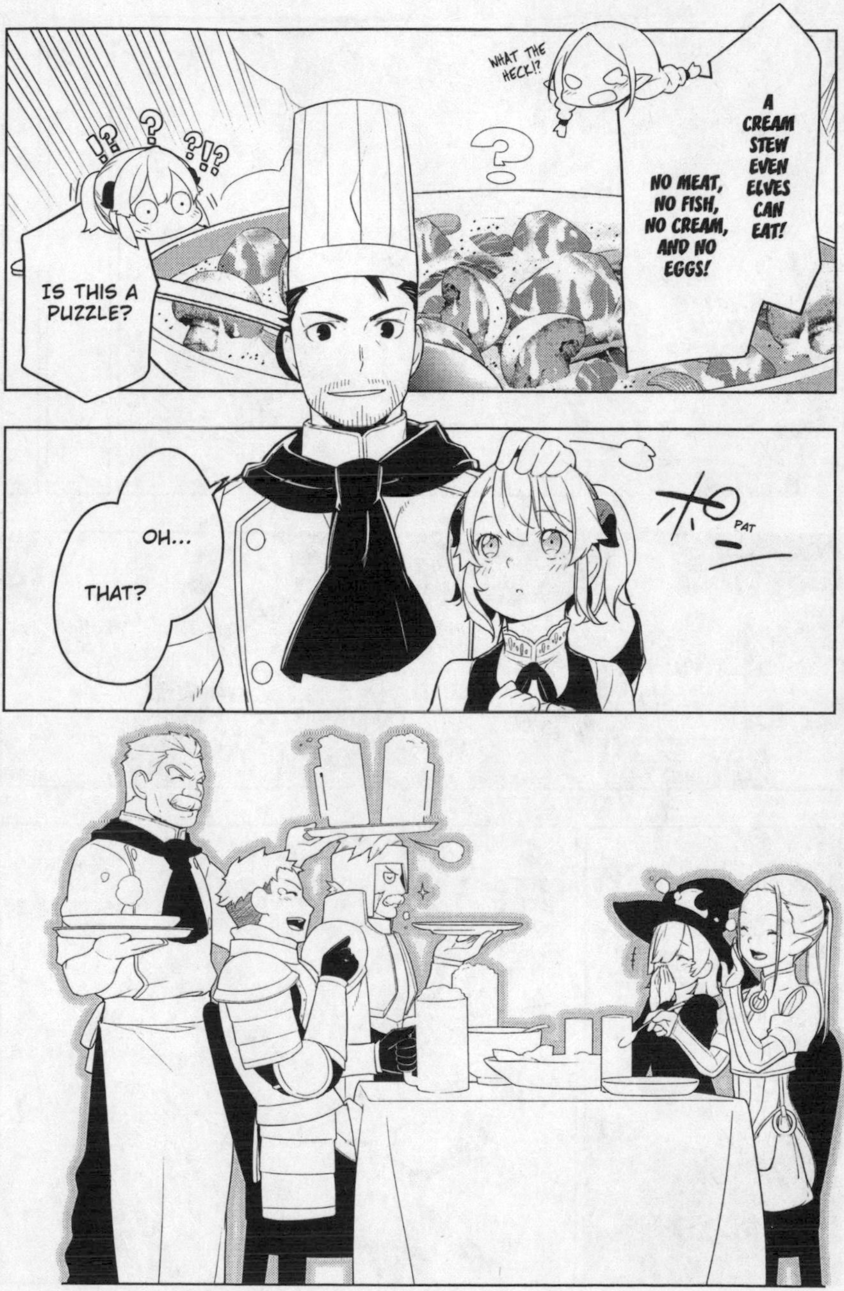
A CREAM STEW EVEN ELVES CAN EAT!
NO MEAT, NO FISH, NO CREAM, AND NO EGGS!
WHAT THE HECK!?
IS THIS A PUZZLE?
PAT
OH... THAT?

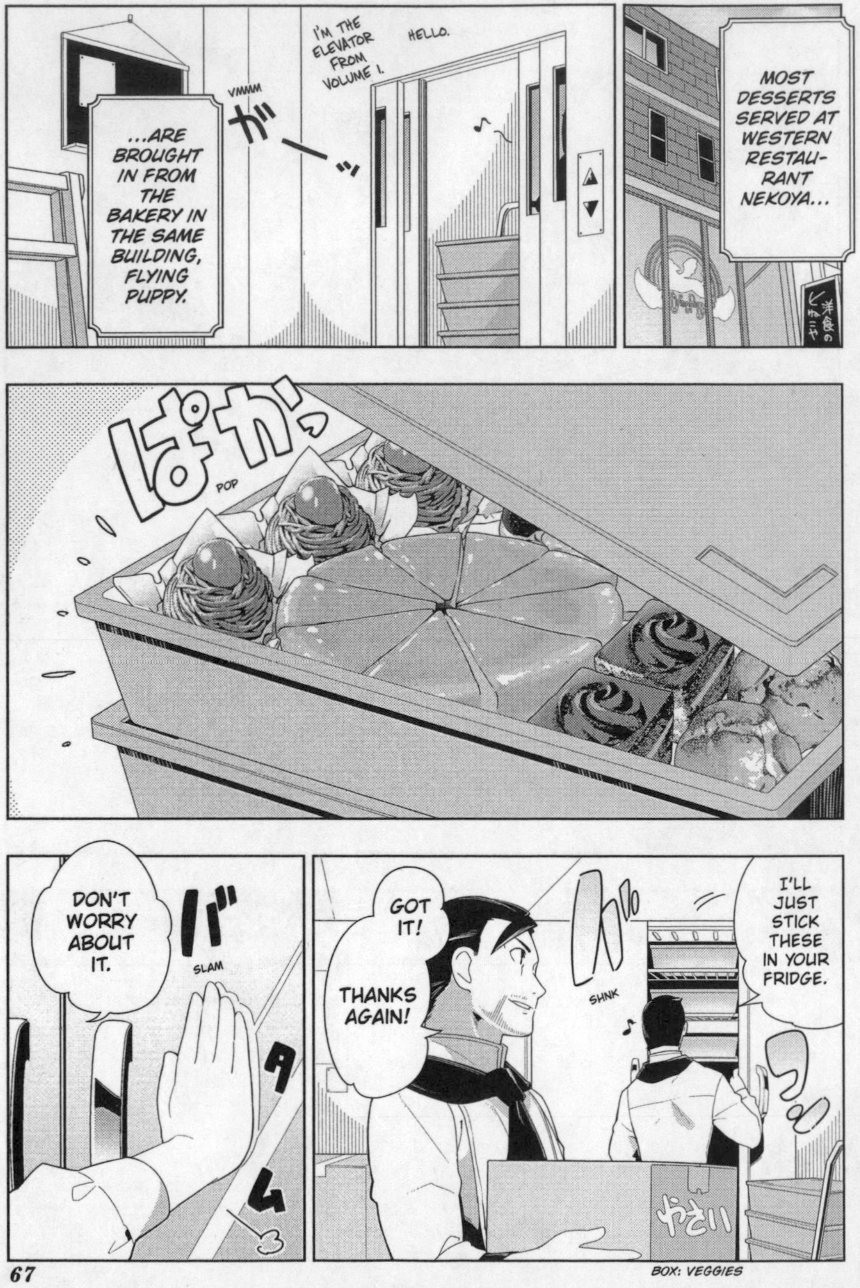
MOST DESSERTS SERVED AT WESTERN RESTAU-RANT NEKOYA...
洋食のねこや
I'M THE ELEVATOR FROM VOLUME 1.
HELLO.
ガーッ
VMMM
...ARE BROUGHT IN FROM THE BAKERY IN THE SAME BUILDING, FLYING PUPPY.
ぱかっ
POP
I'LL JUST STICK THESE IN YOUR FRIDGE.
SHNK
GOT IT!
THANKS AGAIN!
やさい
DON'T WORRY ABOUT IT.
バタム
SLAM

BOX: VEGGIES

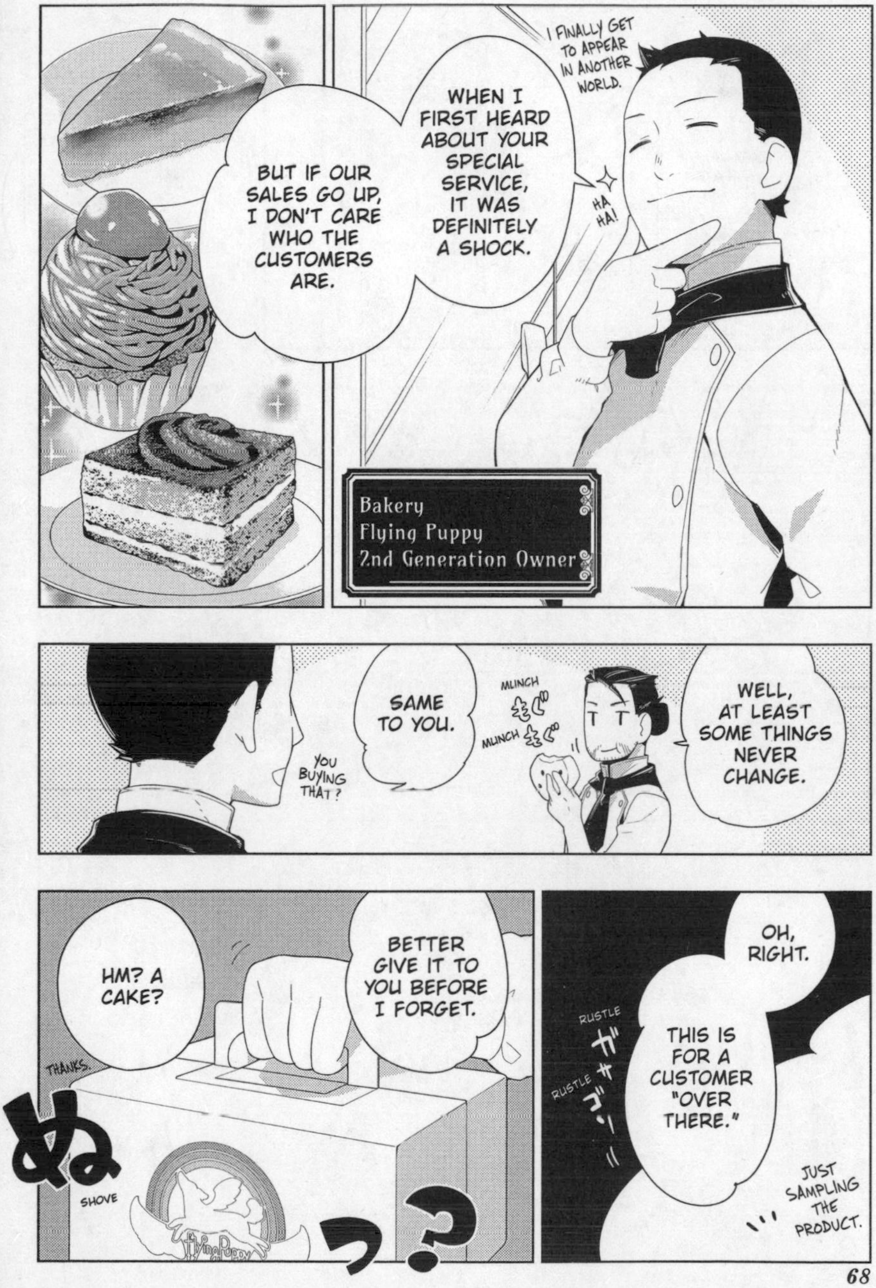
I FINALLY GET TO APPEAR IN ANOTHER WORLD.
WHEN I FIRST HEARD ABOUT YOUR SPECIAL SERVICE, IT WAS DEFINITELY A SHOCK.
HA HA!
Bakery Flying Puppy 2nd Generation Owner
BUT IF OUR SALES GO UP, I DON'T CARE WHO THE CUSTOMERS ARE.
WELL, AT LEAST SOME THINGS NEVER CHANGE.
MUNCH MUNCH
SAME TO YOU.
YOU BUYING THAT?
OH, RIGHT.
THIS IS FOR A CUSTOMER "OVER THERE."
RUSTLE RUSTLE
JUST SAMPLING THE PRODUCT.
BETTER GIVE IT TO YOU BEFORE I FORGET.
HM? A CAKE?
THANKS.
SHOVE
Flying Puppy

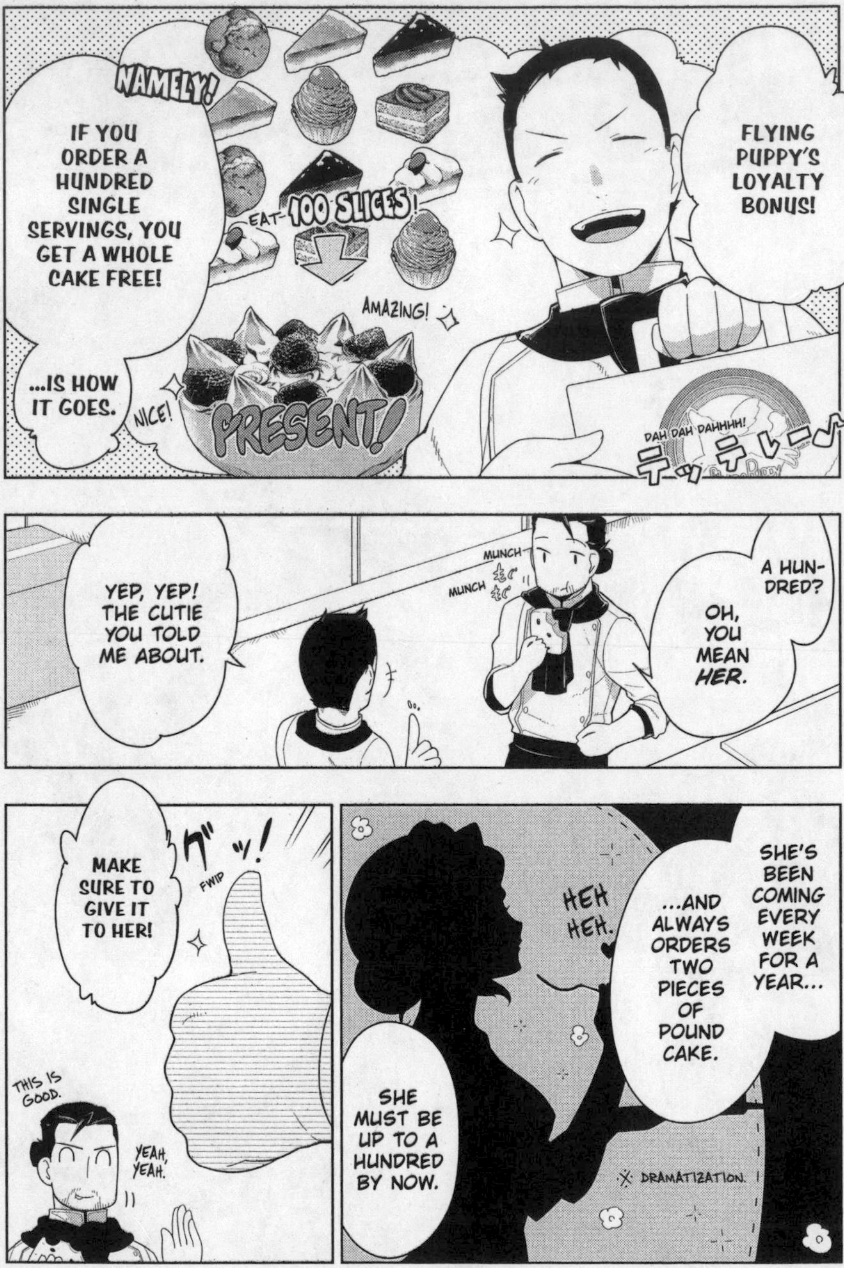
FLYING PUPPY'S LOYALTY BONUS!
NAMELY!
IF YOU ORDER A HUNDRED SINGLE SERVINGS, YOU GET A WHOLE CAKE FREE!
EAT 100 SLICES!
AMAZING!
PRESENT!
NICE!
...IS HOW IT GOES.
DAH DAH DAHHHH!
デッテレー♪
A HUNDRED?
OH, YOU MEAN HER.
MUNCH もぐ
MUNCH もぐ
YEP, YEP! THE CUTIE YOU TOLD ME ABOUT.
SHE'S BEEN COMING EVERY WEEK FOR A YEAR...
...AND ALWAYS ORDERS TWO PIECES OF POUND CAKE.
HEH HEH.
SHE MUST BE UP TO A HUNDRED BY NOW.
※ DRAMATIZATION.
MAKE SURE TO GIVE IT TO HER!
グッ!
FWIP
THIS IS GOOD.
YEAH, YEAH.

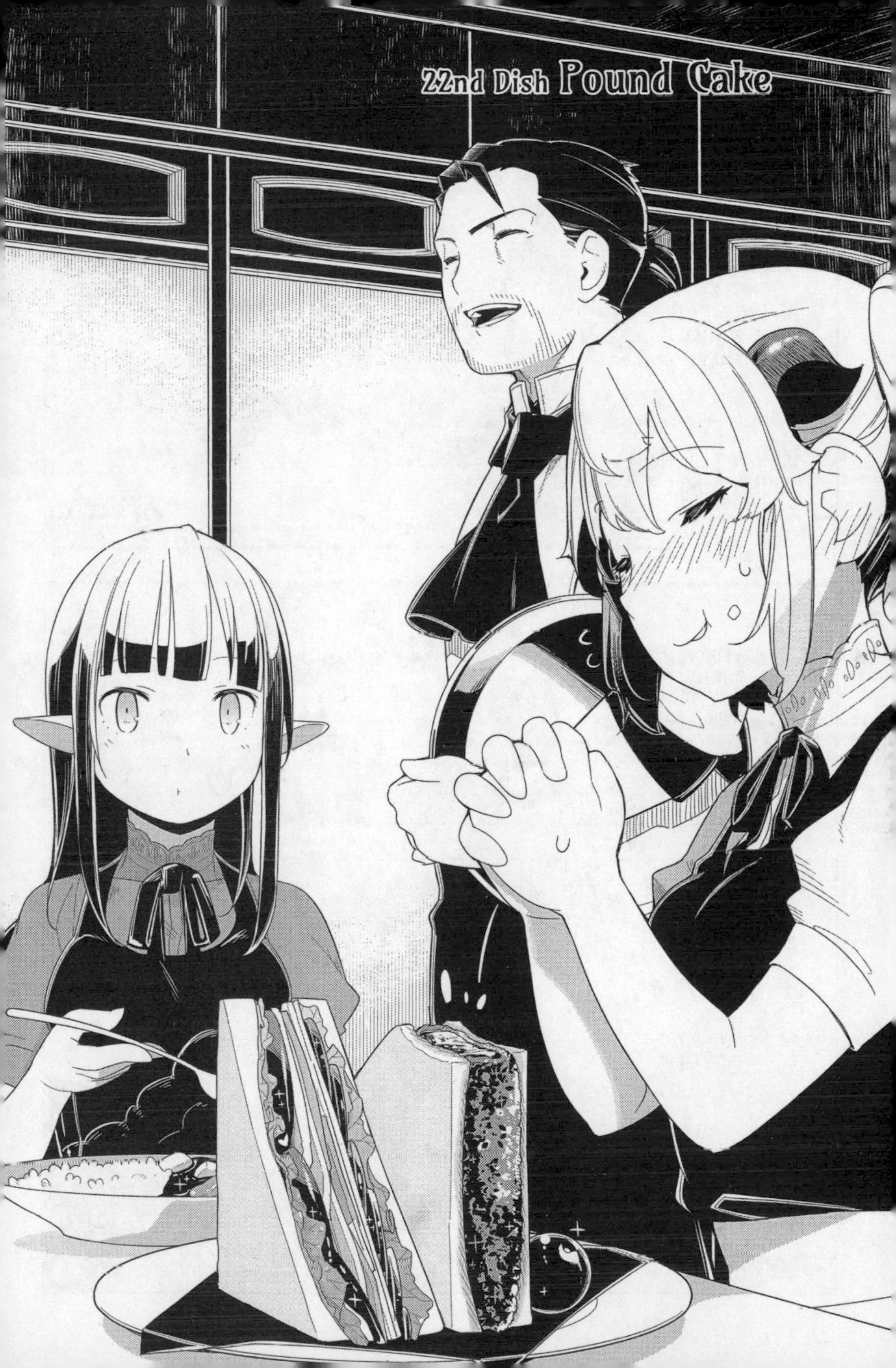
22nd Dish Pound Cake

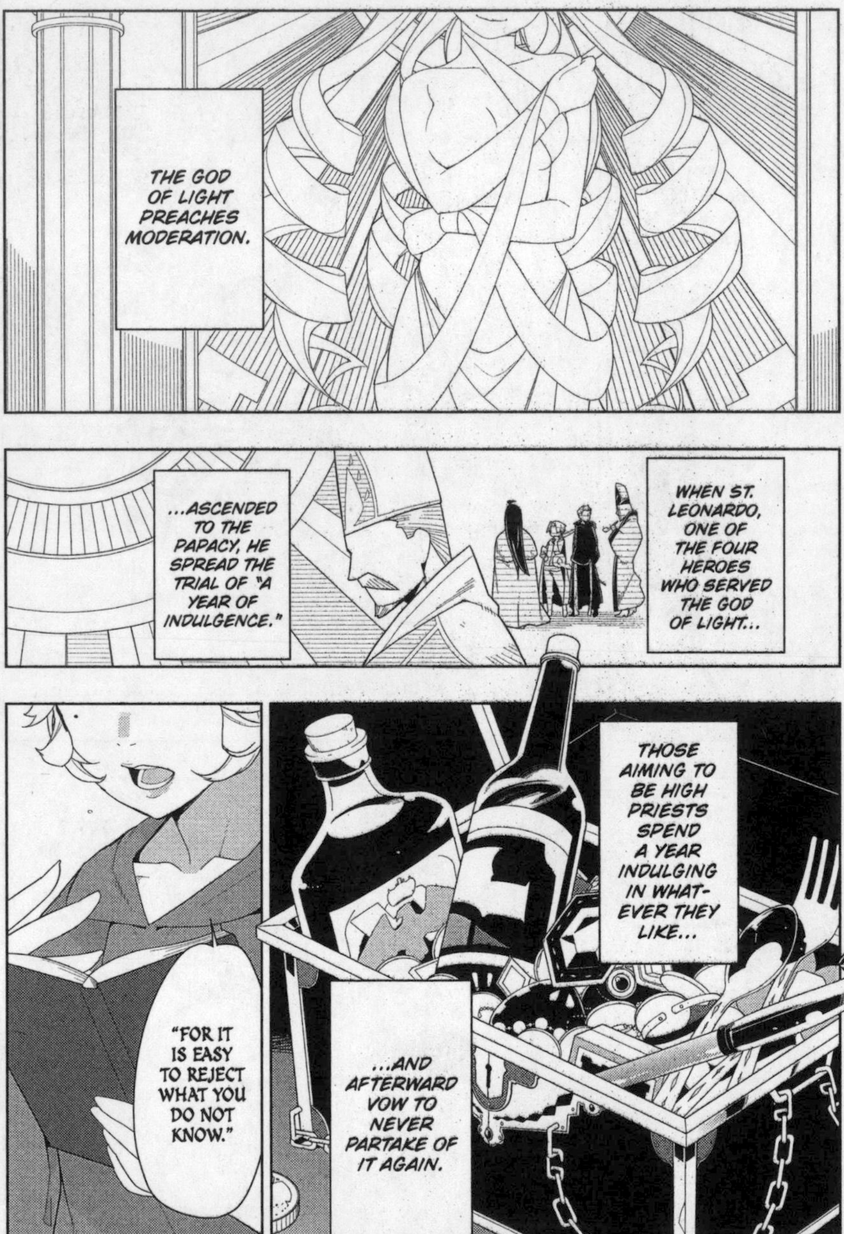
THE GOD OF LIGHT PREACHES MODERATION.
WHEN ST. LEONARDO, ONE OF THE FOUR HEROES WHO SERVED THE GOD OF LIGHT...
...ASCENDED TO THE PAPACY, HE SPREAD THE TRIAL OF "A YEAR OF INDULGENCE."
THOSE AIMING TO BE HIGH PRIESTS SPEND A YEAR INDULGING IN WHAT-EVER THEY LIKE...
...AND AFTERWARD VOW TO NEVER PARTAKE OF IT AGAIN.
"FOR IT IS EASY TO REJECT WHAT YOU DO NOT KNOW."

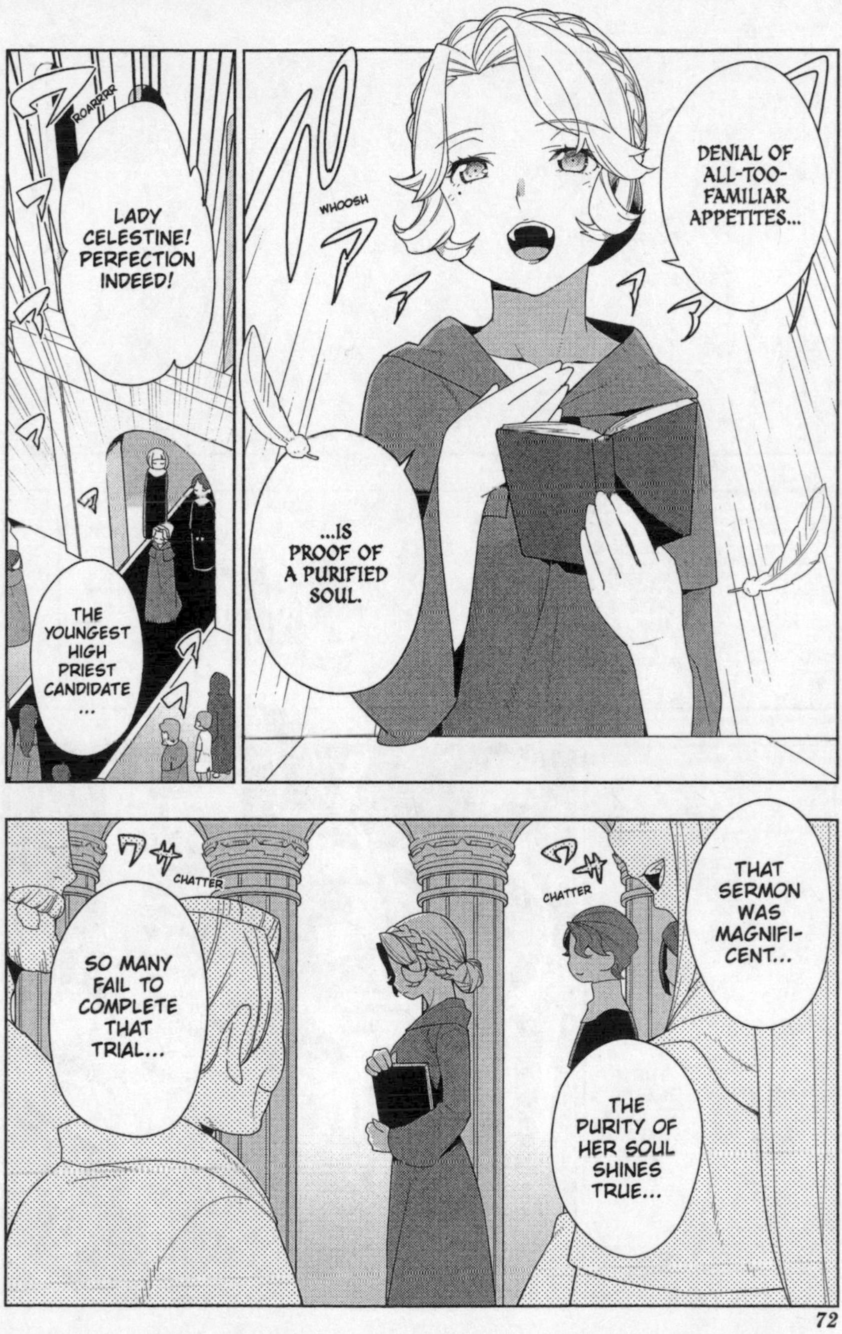

WHOOSH
DENIAL OF ALL-TOO-FAMILIAR APPETITES...
...IS PROOF OF A PURIFIED SOUL.
ROARRRR
LADY CELESTINE! PERFECTION INDEED!
THE YOUNGEST HIGH PRIEST CANDIDATE...
CHATTER
THAT SERMON WAS MAGNIFI-CENT...
THE PURITY OF HER SOUL SHINES TRUE...
CHATTER
SO MANY FAIL TO COMPLETE THAT TRIAL...

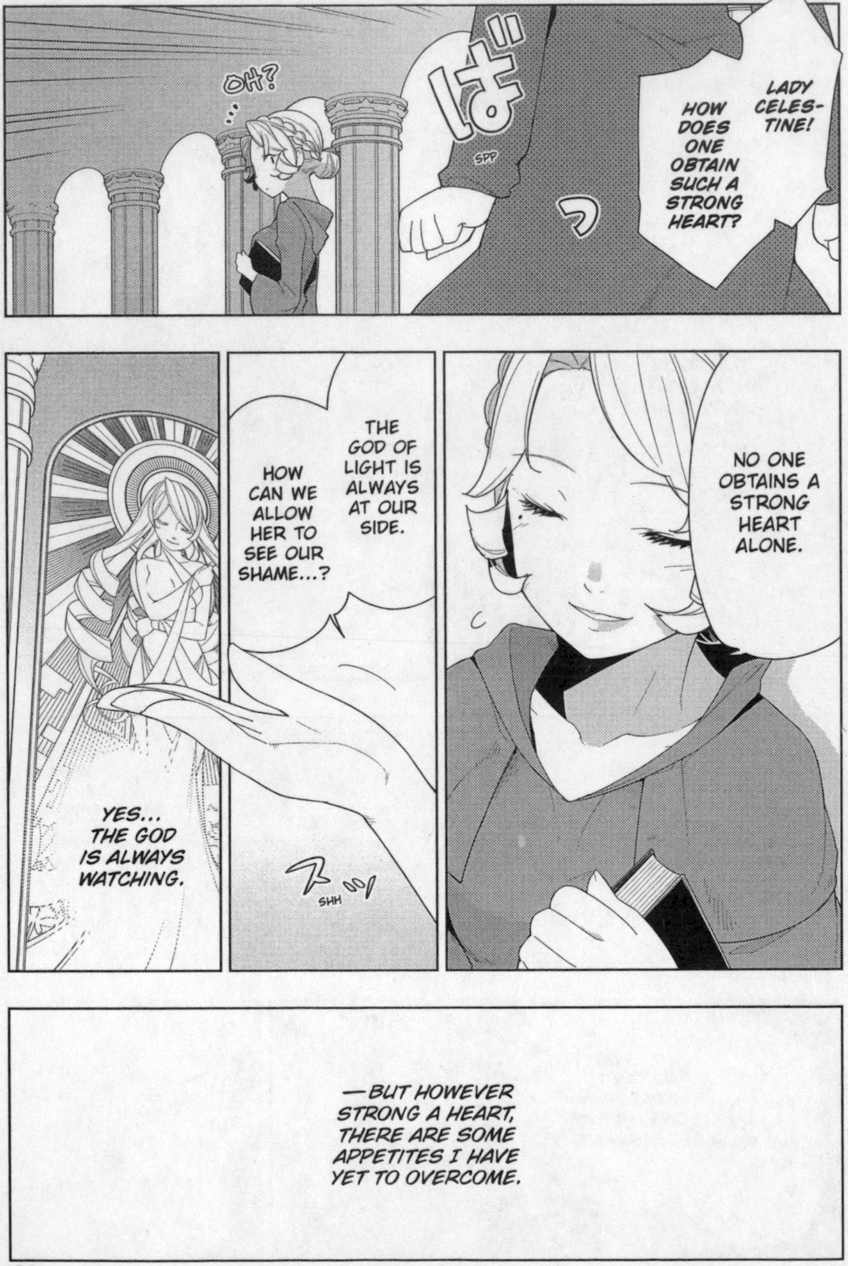
LADY CELESTINE!
HOW DOES ONE OBTAIN SUCH A STRONG HEART?
SPP
OH?
...
NO ONE OBTAINS A STRONG HEART ALONE.
THE GOD OF LIGHT IS ALWAYS AT OUR SIDE.
HOW CAN WE ALLOW HER TO SEE OUR SHAME...?
SHH
YES... THE GOD IS ALWAYS WATCHING.
—BUT HOWEVER STRONG A HEART, THERE ARE SOME APPETITES I HAVE YET TO OVERCOME.

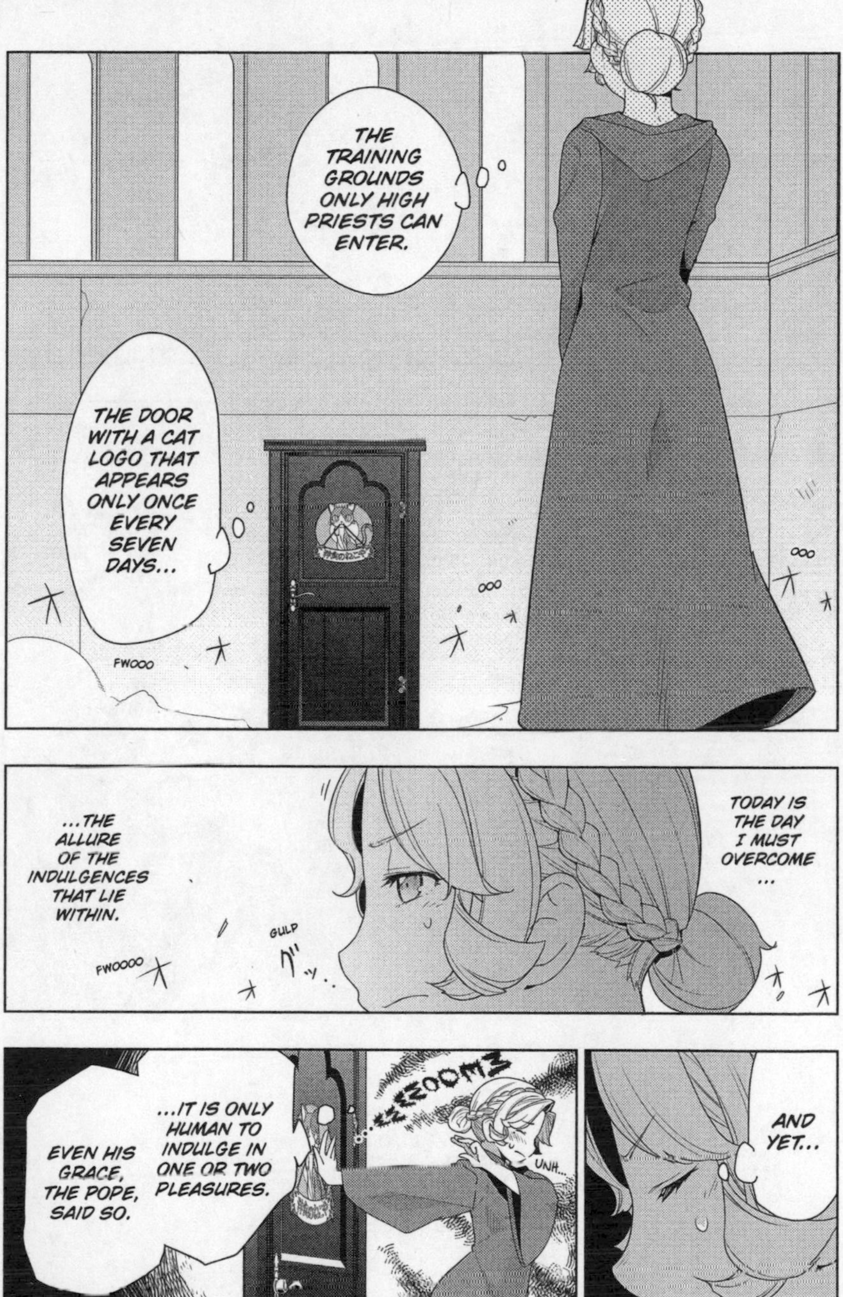
THE TRAINING GROUNDS ONLY HIGH PRIESTS CAN ENTER.
THE DOOR WITH A CAT LOGO THAT APPEARS ONLY ONCE EVERY SEVEN DAYS...
FWOOO
TODAY IS THE DAY I MUST OVERCOME ...
...THE ALLURE OF THE INDULGENCES THAT LIE WITHIN.
GULP
FWOOOO
AND YET...
UNH...
...IT IS ONLY HUMAN TO INDULGE IN ONE OR TWO PLEASURES.
EVEN HIS GRACE, THE POPE, SAID SO.

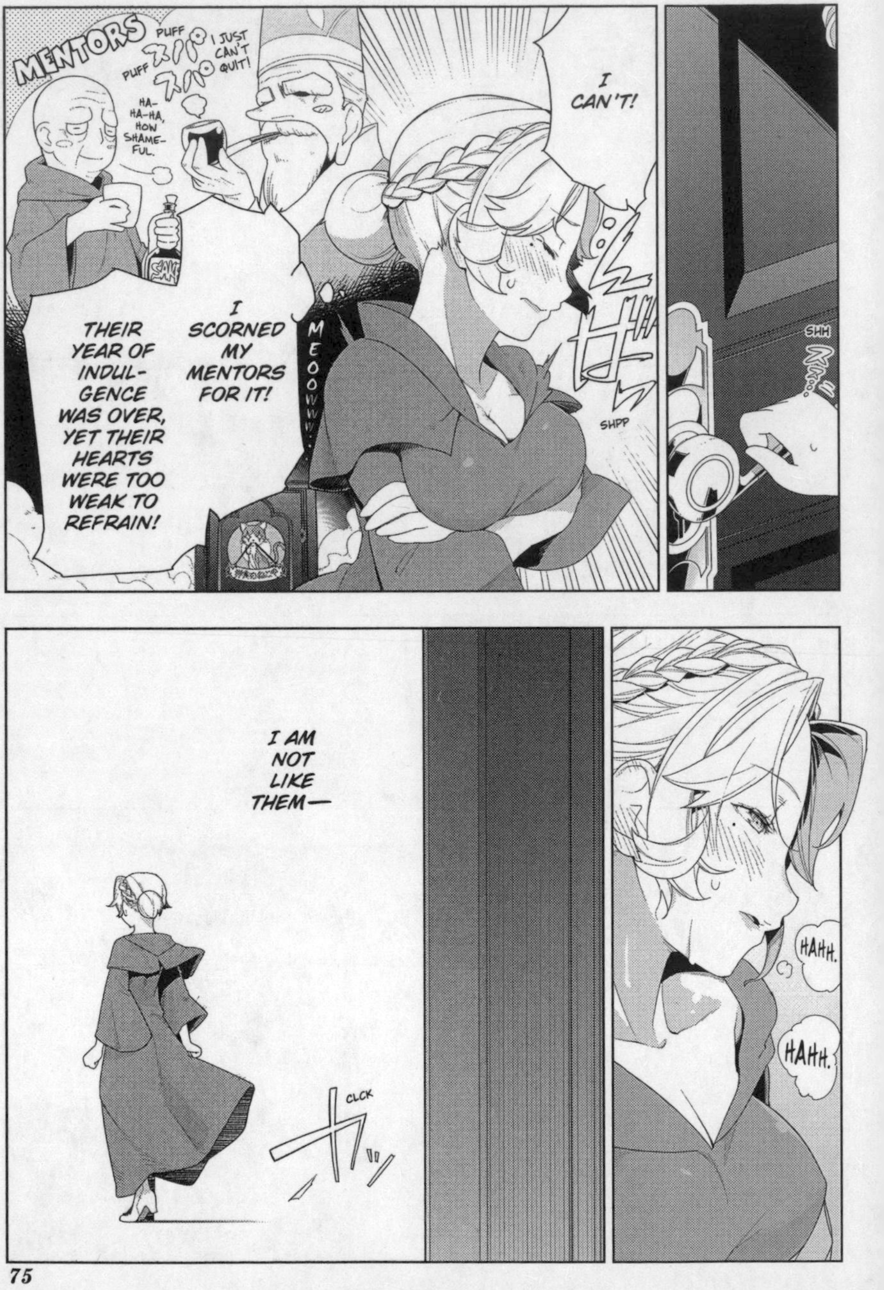
SHH
I CAN'T!
SHPP
I JUST CAN'T QUIT!
PUFF
PUFF
スパ スパ
MENTORS
HA-HA-HA, HOW SHAME-FUL.
I SCORNED MY MENTORS FOR IT!
MEOOWW...
THEIR YEAR OF INDUL-GENCE WAS OVER, YET THEIR HEARTS WERE TOO WEAK TO REFRAIN!
HAHH.
HAHH.
I AM NOT LIKE THEM—
CLCK

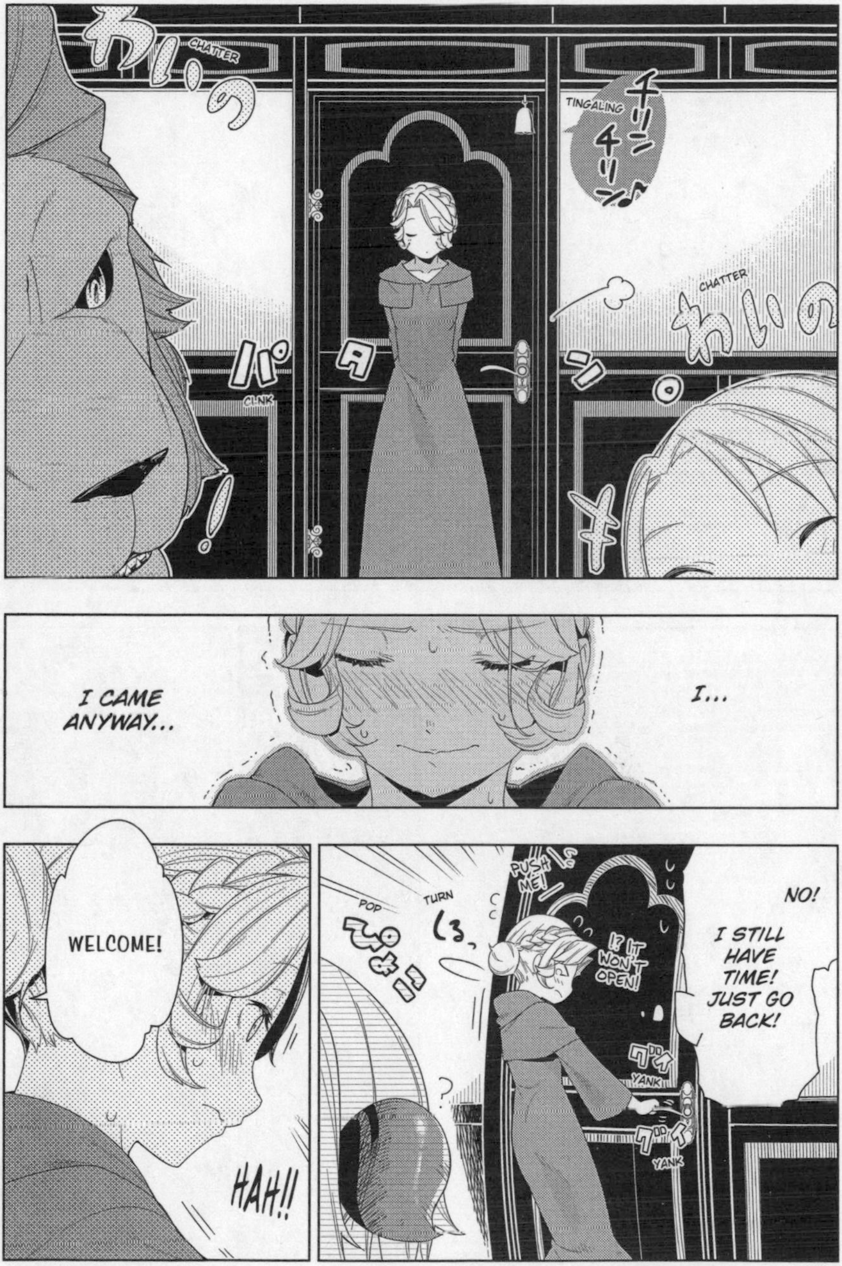

TINGALING
CHATTER
わいの
CHATTER
わいの
CLNK
I...
I CAME ANYWAY...
NO!
I STILL HAVE TIME! JUST GO BACK!
PUSH ME!
!? IT WON'T OPEN!
YANK
YANK
TURN
POP
WELCOME!
HAH!!

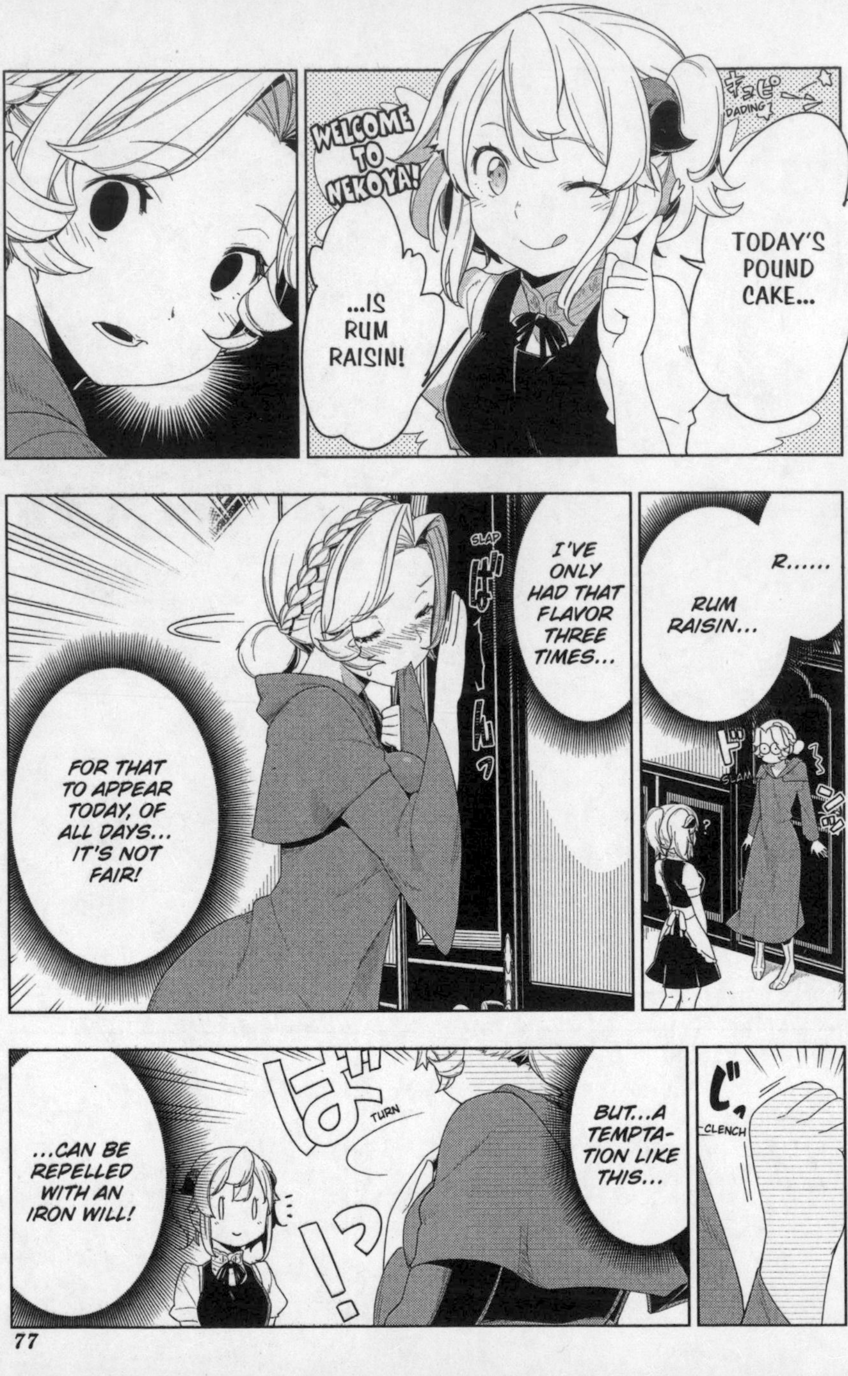
DADING
TODAY'S POUND CAKE...
WELCOME TO NEKOYA!
...IS RUM RAISIN!
R......
RUM RAISIN...
SLAM
I'VE ONLY HAD THAT FLAVOR THREE TIMES...
SLAP
FOR THAT TO APPEAR TODAY, OF ALL DAYS... IT'S NOT FAIR!
CLENCH
BUT...A TEMPTATION LIKE THIS...
TURN
...CAN BE REPELLED WITH AN IRON WILL!

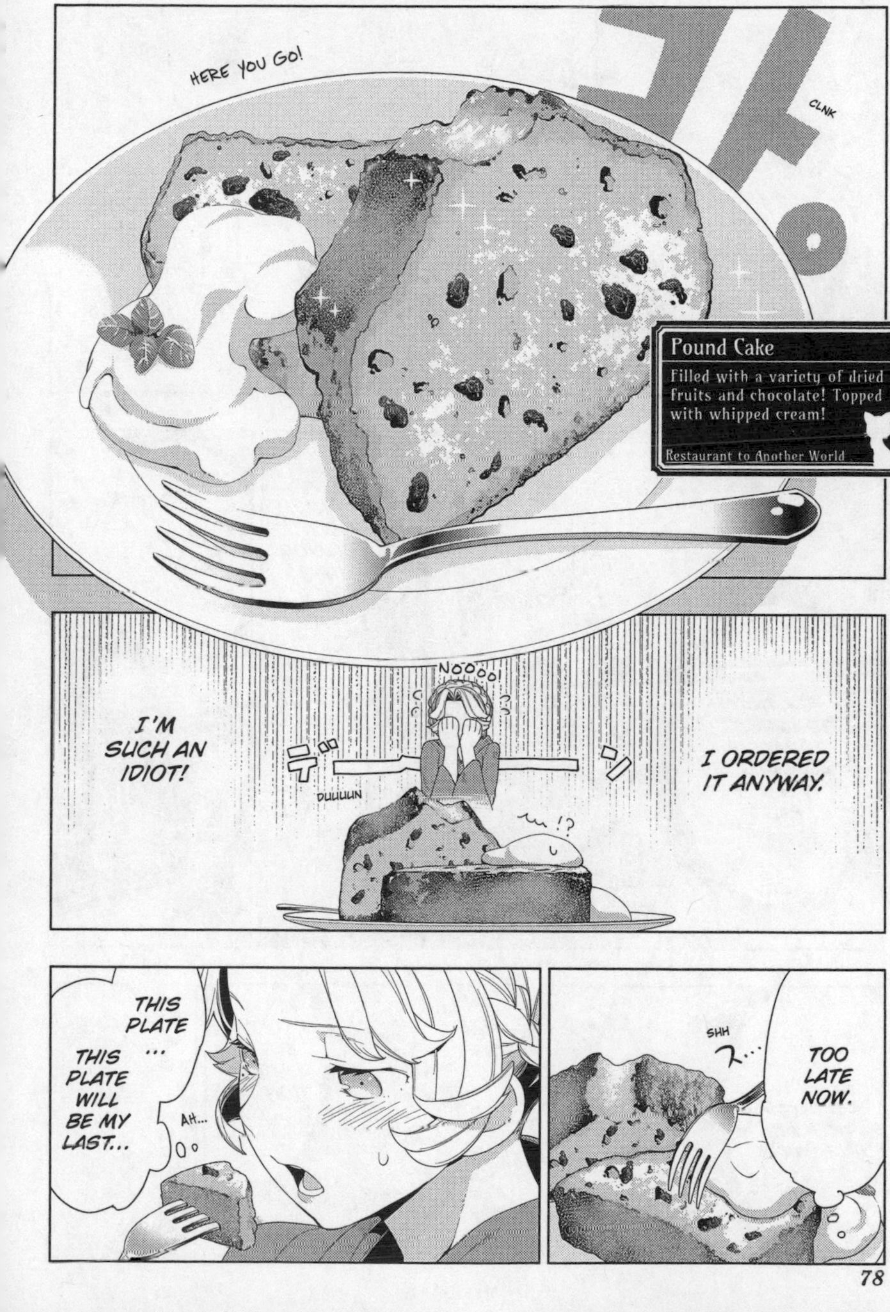
HERE YOU GO!
CLNK
Pound Cake
Filled with a variety of dried fruits and chocolate! Topped with whipped cream!
Restaurant to Another World
NOOOO!
I ORDERED IT ANYWAY.
I'M SUCH AN IDIOT!
DUUUUN
!?
SHH
TOO LATE NOW.
THIS PLATE...
THIS PLATE WILL BE MY LAST...
AH...

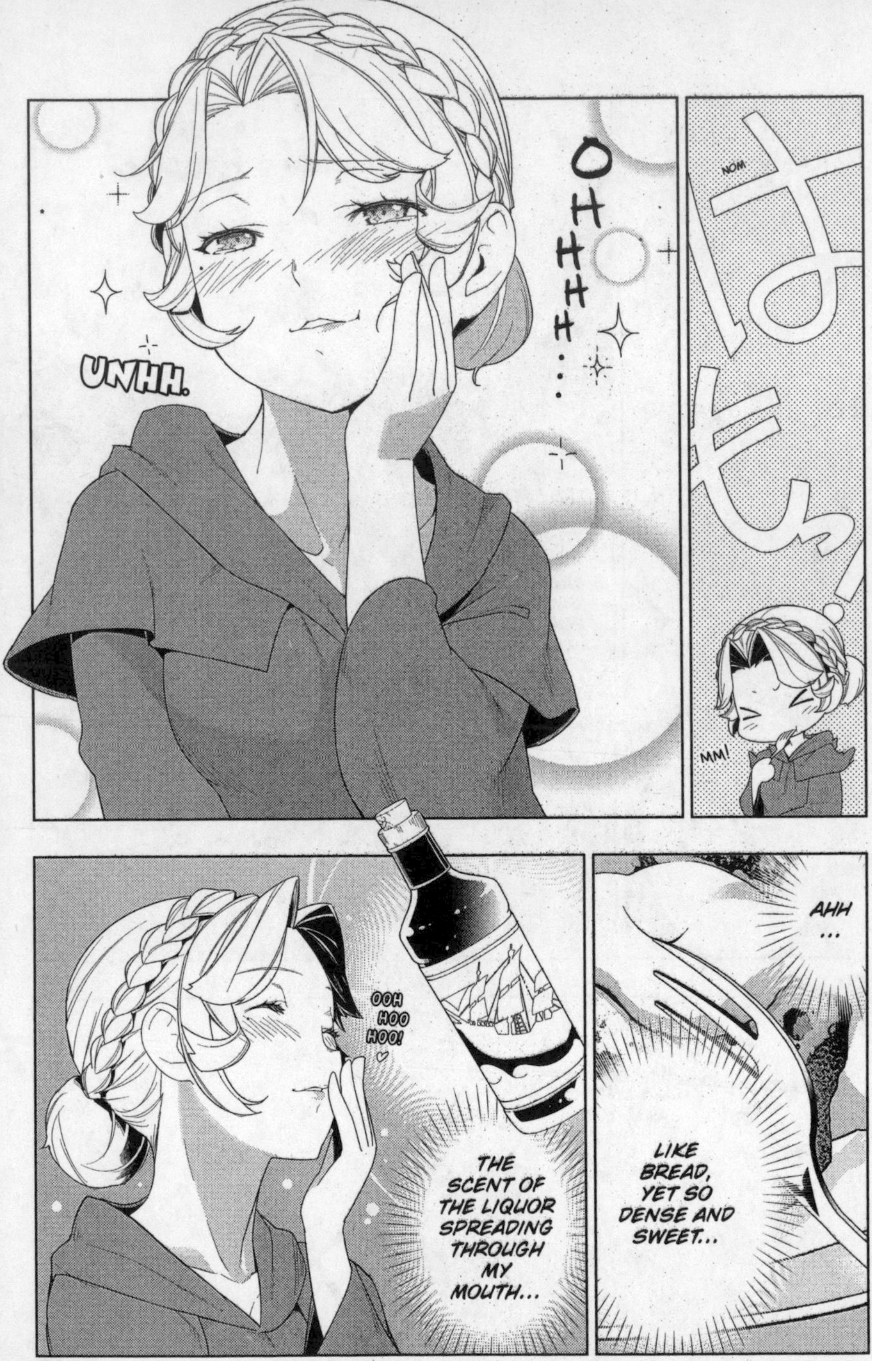

NOM
はむっ
MM!
OHHHH...
UNHH.
AHH...
LIKE BREAD, YET SO DENSE AND SWEET...
OOH HOO HOO! ♡
THE SCENT OF THE LIQUOR SPREADING THROUGH MY MOUTH...

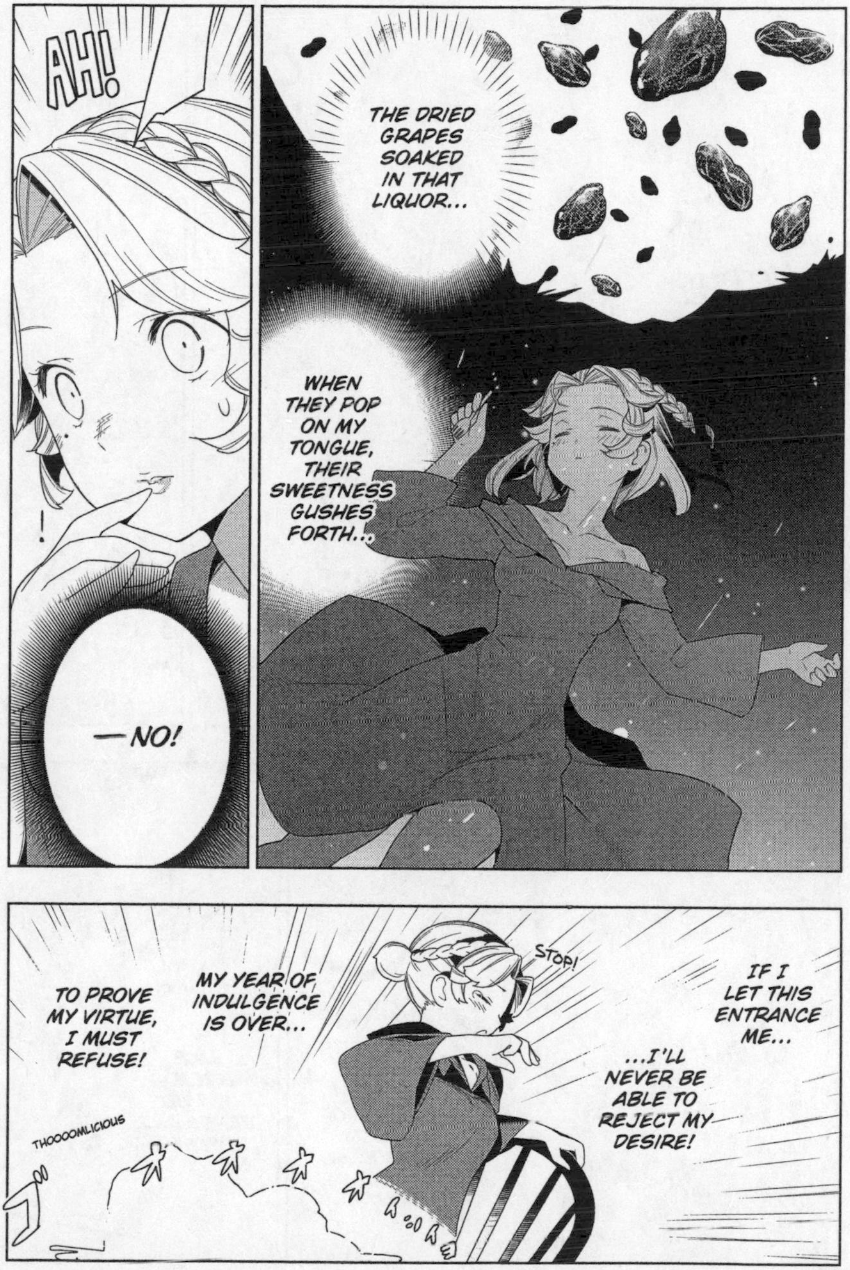
THE DRIED GRAPES SOAKED IN THAT LIQUOR...
WHEN THEY POP ON MY TONGUE, THEIR SWEETNESS GUSHES FORTH...
AH!
!
—NO!
IF I LET THIS ENTRANCE ME...
...I'LL NEVER BE ABLE TO REJECT MY DESIRE!
STOP!
MY YEAR OF INDULGENCE IS OVER...
TO PROVE MY VIRTUE, I MUST REFUSE!
THOOOOMLICIOUS

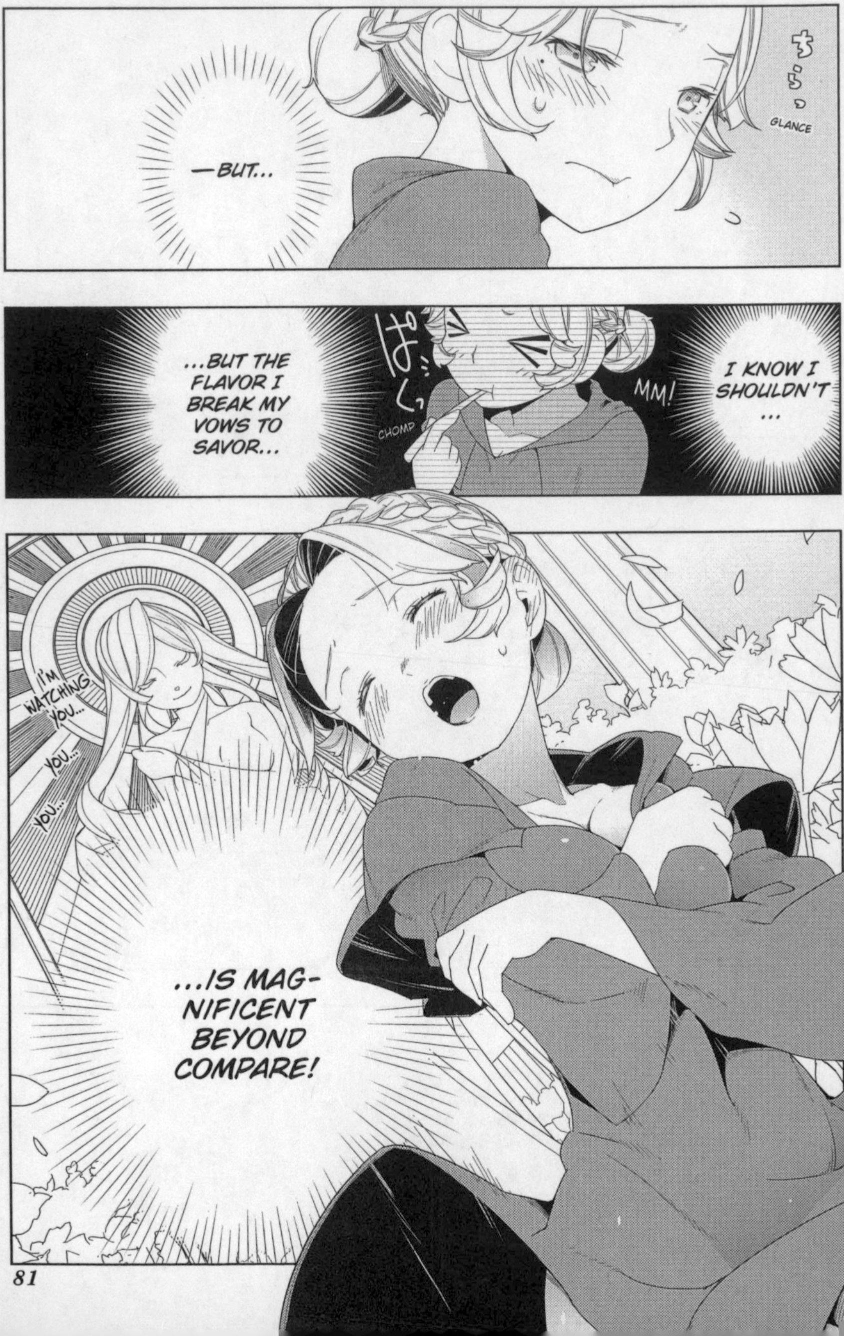
ちらっ
GLANCE
—BUT...
I KNOW I SHOULDN'T...
MM!
ぱくっ
CHOMP
...BUT THE FLAVOR I BREAK MY VOWS TO SAVOR...
...IS MAG-NIFICENT BEYOND COMPARE!
I'M WATCHING YOU...
YOU...
YOU...

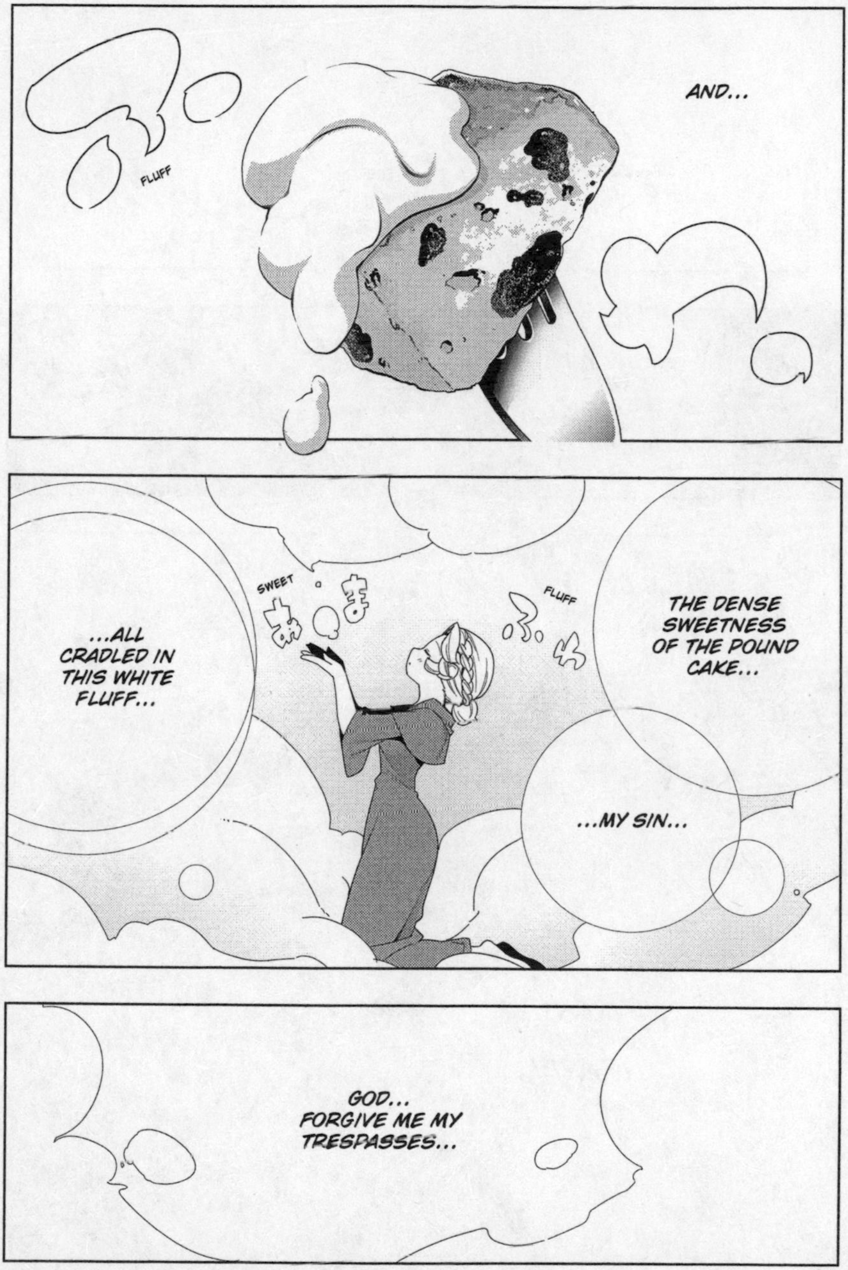
AND...
FLUFF
THE DENSE SWEETNESS OF THE POUND CAKE...
FLUFF
SWEET
...ALL CRADLED IN THIS WHITE FLUFF...
...
...MY SIN...
GOD... FORGIVE ME MY TRESPASSES...

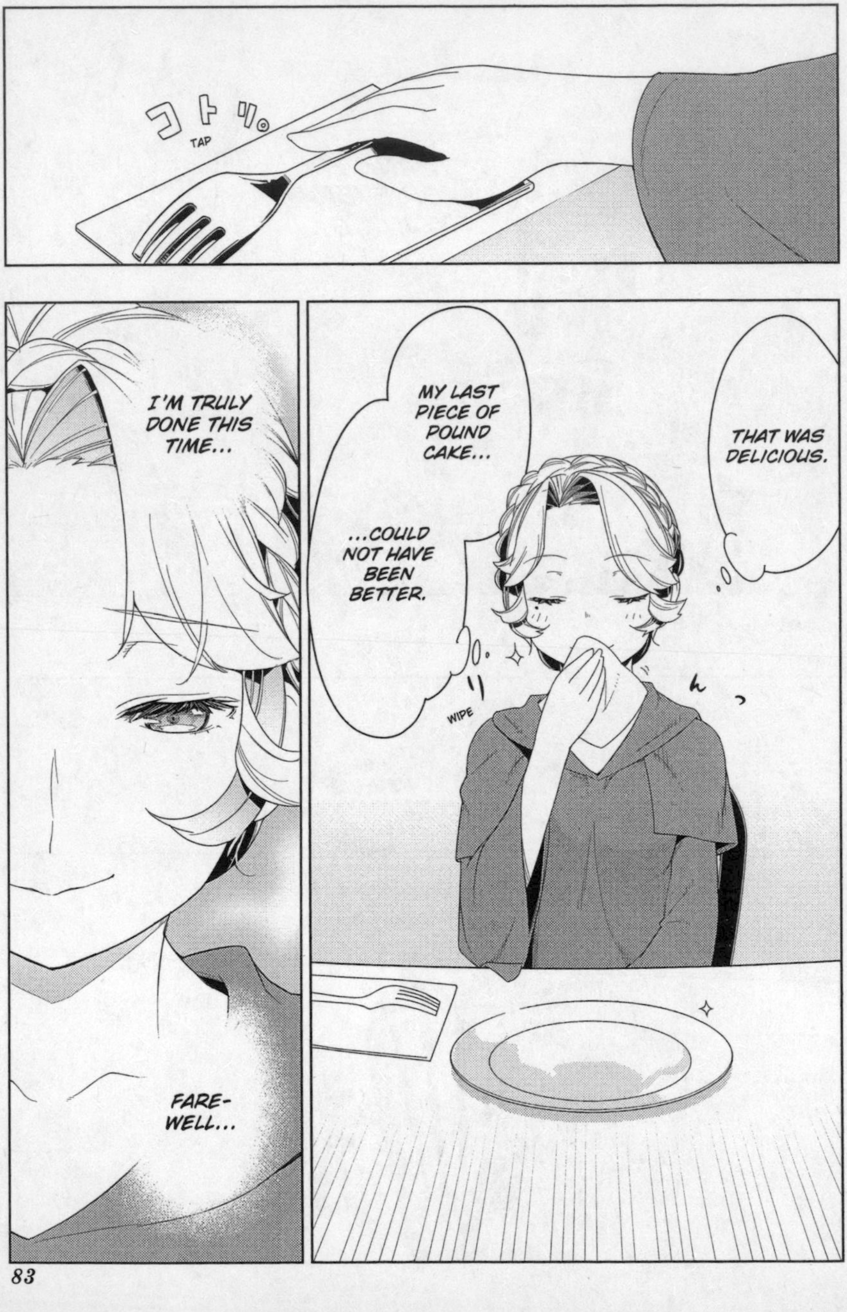
コトリ。
TAP
THAT WAS DELICIOUS.
MY LAST PIECE OF POUND CAKE...
...COULD NOT HAVE BEEN BETTER.
WIPE
I'M TRULY DONE THIS TIME...
FARE-WELL...

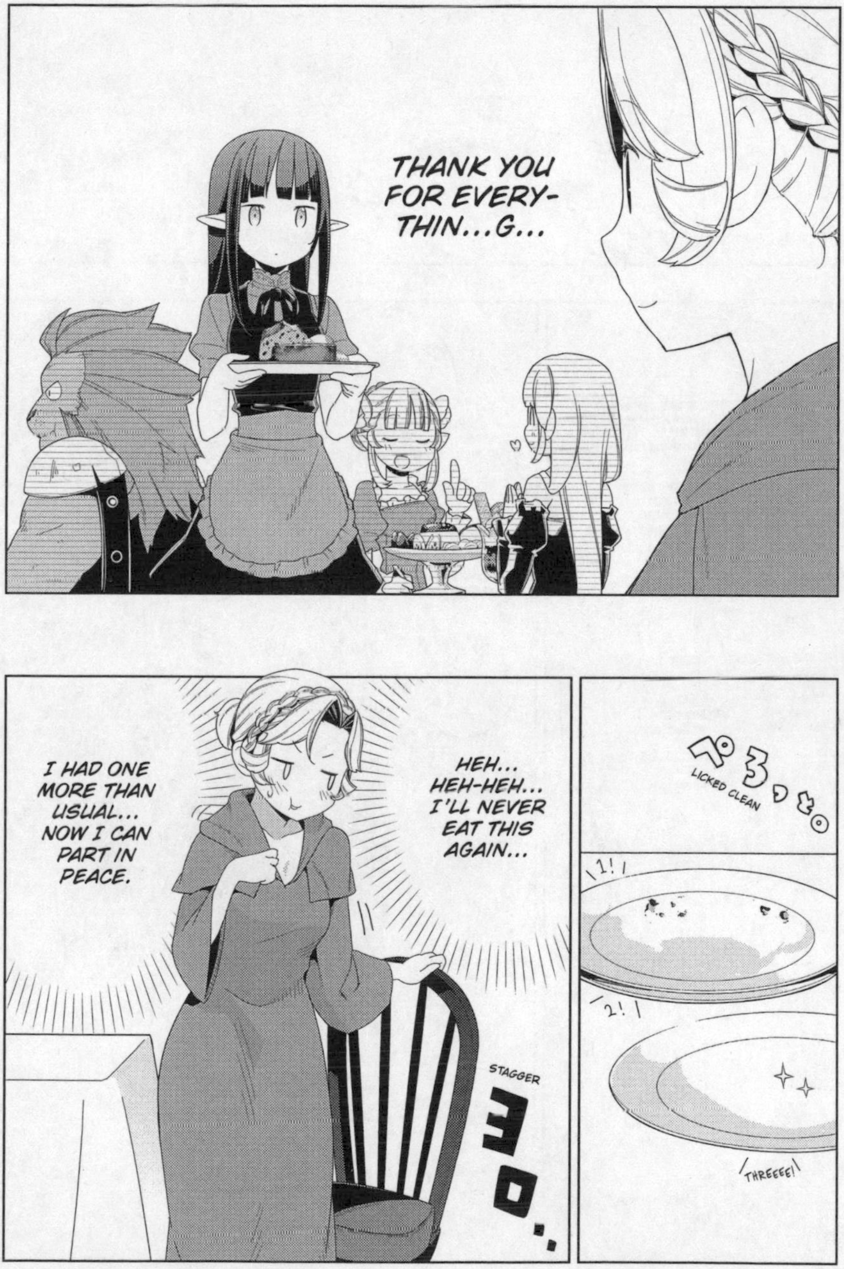
THANK YOU FOR EVERY-THIN...G...
ぺろっと
LICKED CLEAN
1!
2!
THREEEE!
HEH... HEH-HEH... I'LL NEVER EAT THIS AGAIN...
I HAD ONE MORE THAN USUAL... NOW I CAN PART IN PEACE.
STAGGER
ヨロ..

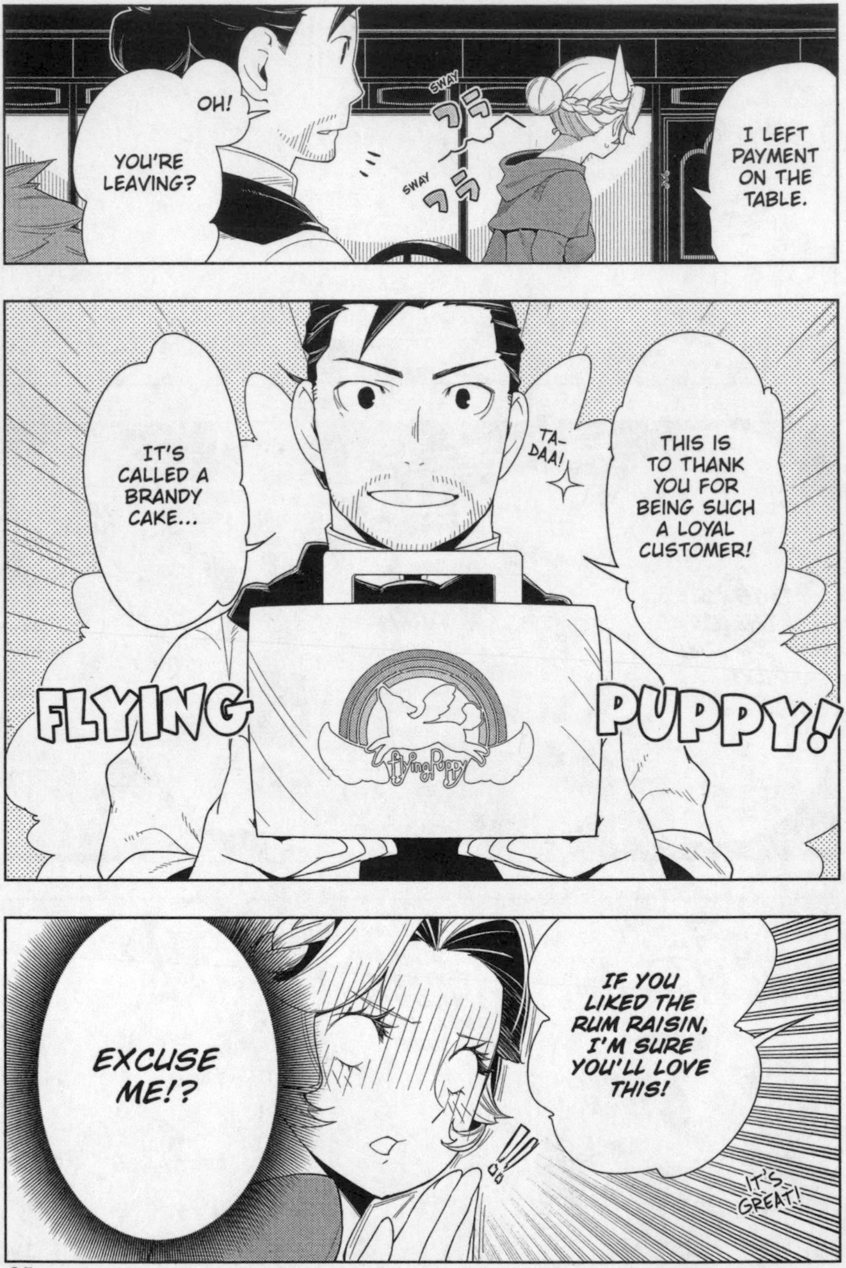

I LEFT PAYMENT ON THE TABLE.
SWAY
SWAY
OH!
YOU'RE LEAVING?
THIS IS TO THANK YOU FOR BEING SUCH A LOYAL CUSTOMER!
TA-DAA!
IT'S CALLED A BRANDY CAKE...
FLYING PUPPY!
IF YOU LIKED THE RUM RAISIN, I'M SURE YOU'LL LOVE THIS!
IT'S GREAT!
!!
EXCUSE ME!?

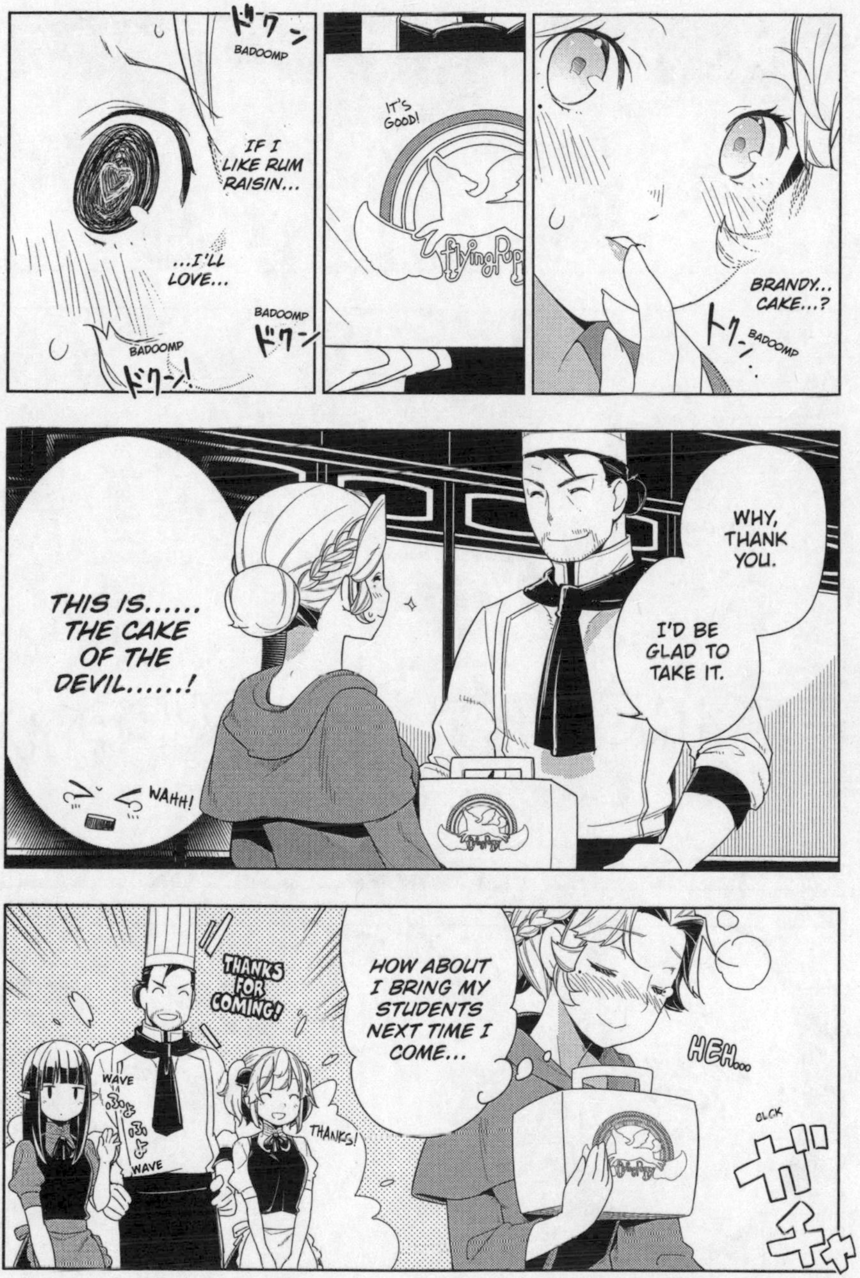
BRANDY... CAKE...?
トクン
BADOOMP
IT'S GOOD!
ドクン
BADOOMP
IF I LIKE RUM RAISIN...
...I'LL LOVE...
BADOOMP
ドクン
BADOOMP
ドクン!
WHY, THANK YOU.
I'D BE GLAD TO TAKE IT.
THIS IS...... THE CAKE OF THE DEVIL......!
WAHH!
CLCK
ガチャ
HEH...
HOW ABOUT I BRING MY STUDENTS NEXT TIME I COME...
THANKS FOR COMING!
THANKS!
WAVE
ふりふり
WAVE

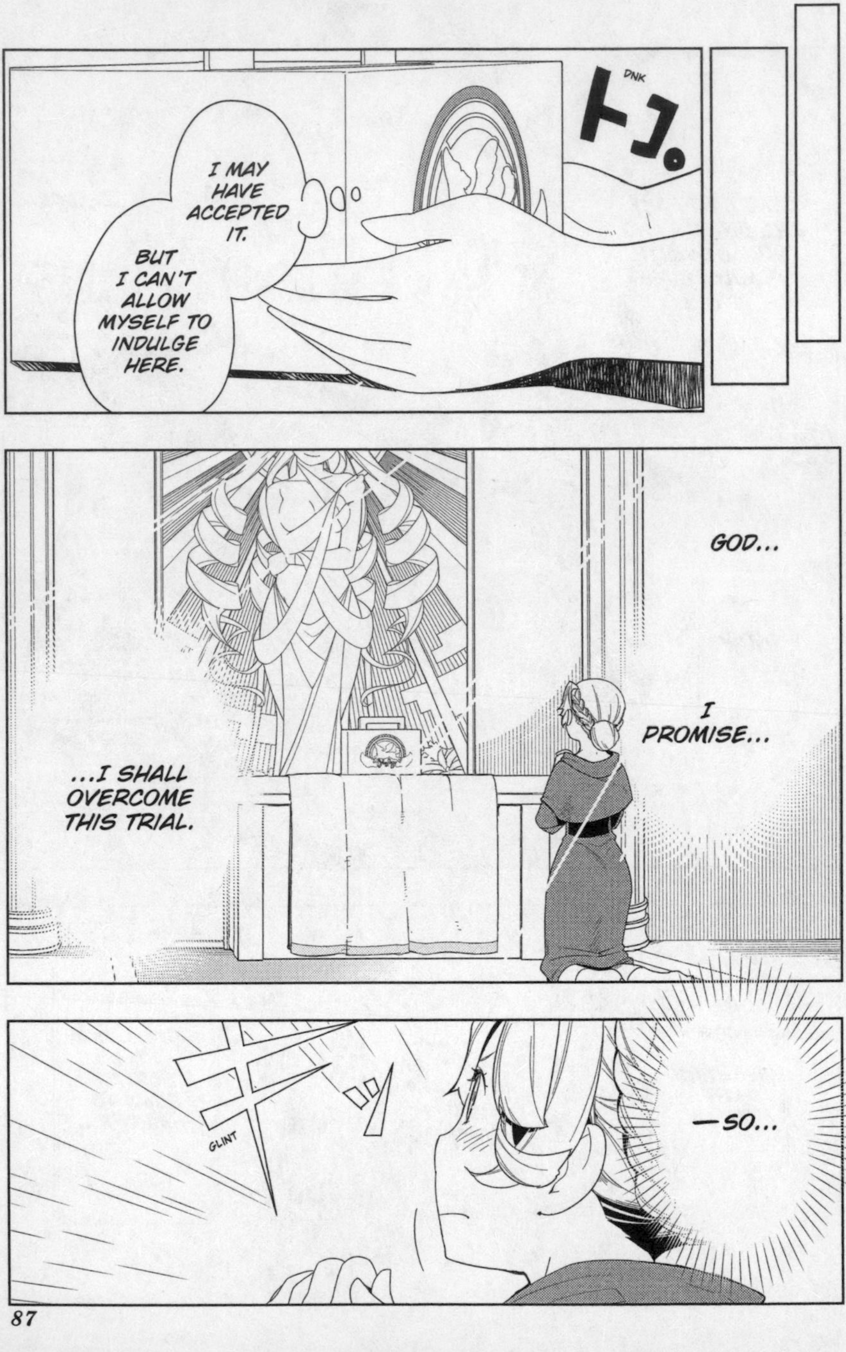
DNK
I MAY HAVE ACCEPTED IT.
BUT I CAN'T ALLOW MYSELF TO INDULGE HERE.
GOD...
I PROMISE...
...I SHALL OVERCOME THIS TRIAL.
—SO...
GLINT

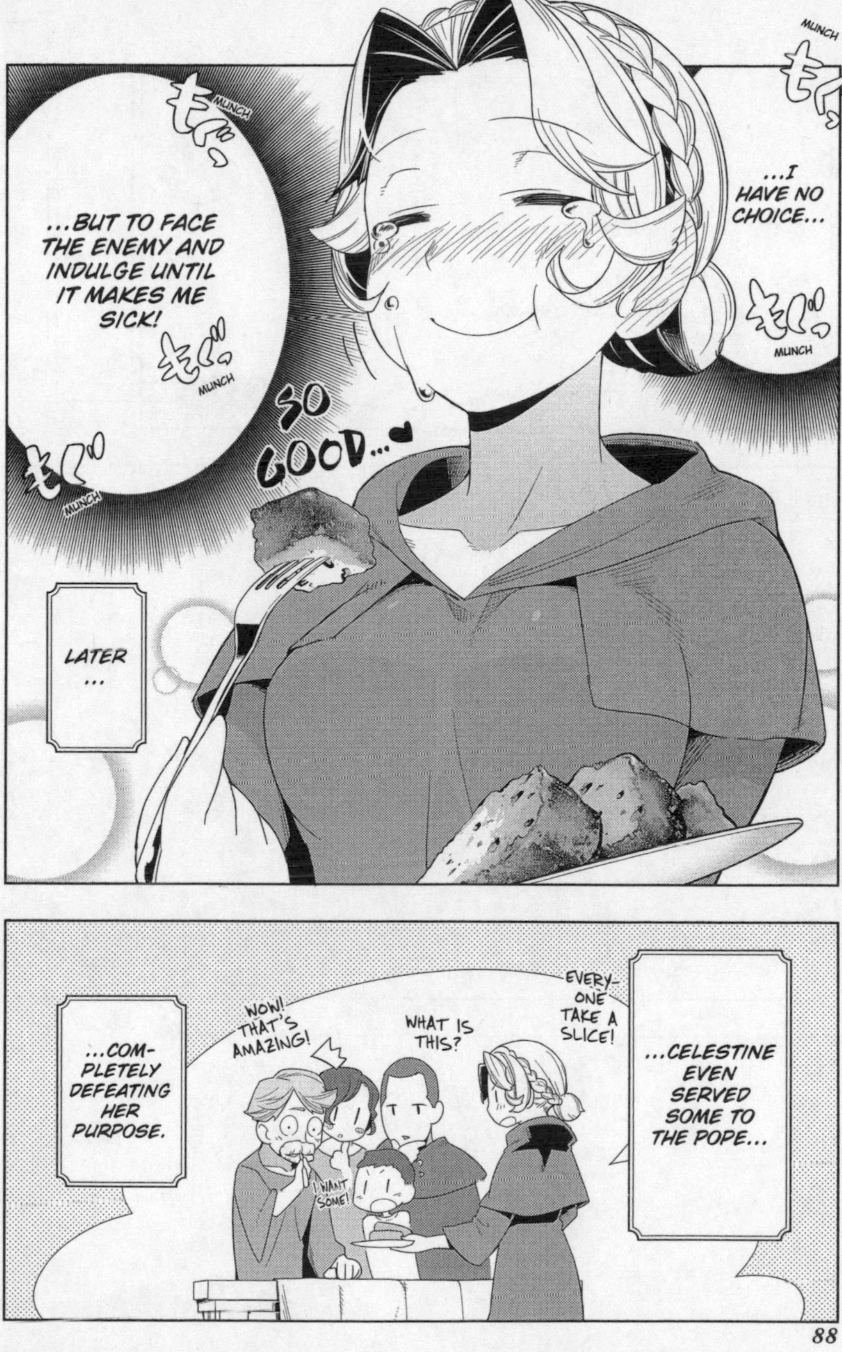
MUNCH
...I HAVE NO CHOICE...
MUNCH
...BUT TO FACE THE ENEMY AND INDULGE UNTIL IT MAKES ME SICK!
MUNCH
SO GOOD...♥
MUNCH
MUNCH
LATER...
...CELESTINE EVEN SERVED SOME TO THE POPE...
EVERY-ONE TAKE A SLICE!
WHAT IS THIS?
WOW! THAT'S AMAZING!
I WANT SOME!
...COM-PLETELY DEFEATING HER PURPOSE.

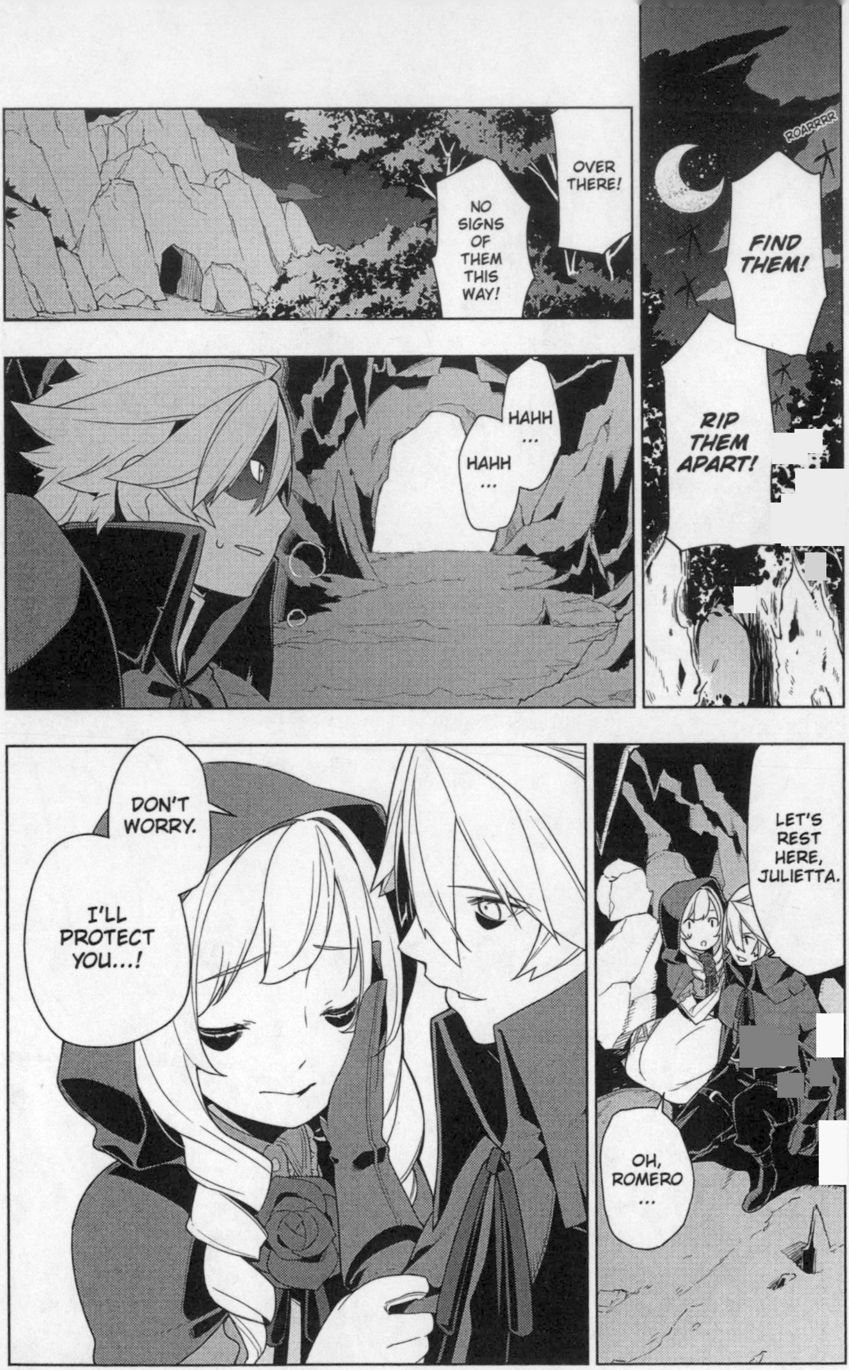
ROARRRR
FIND THEM!
RIP THEM APART!
OVER THERE!
NO SIGNS OF THEM THIS WAY!
HAHH ...
HAHH ...
LET'S REST HERE, JULIETTA.
OH, ROMERO ...
DON'T WORRY.
I'LL PROTECT YOU...!

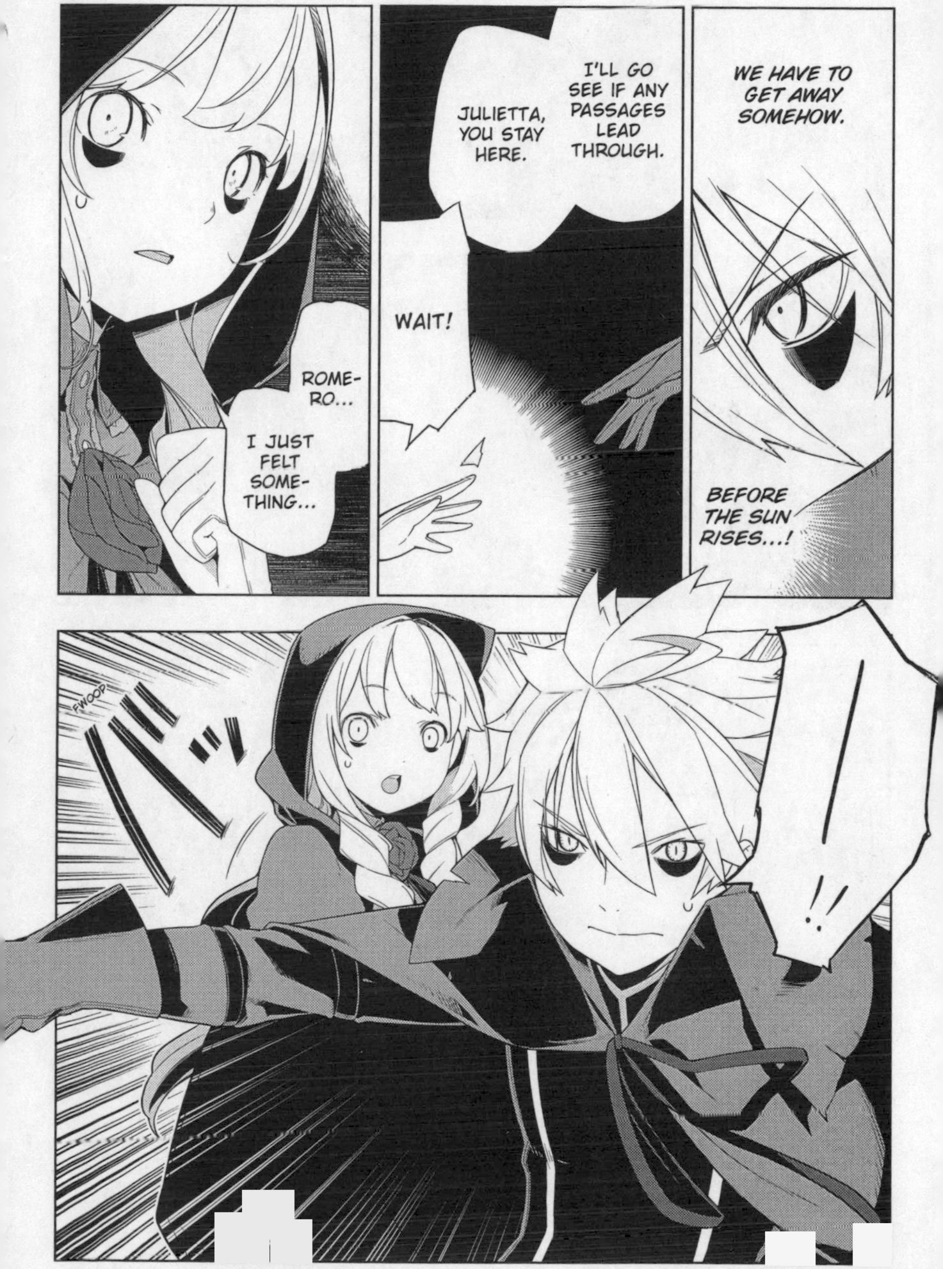
WE HAVE TO GET AWAY SOMEHOW.
BEFORE THE SUN RISES...!
I'LL GO SEE IF ANY PASSAGES LEAD THROUGH.
JULIETTA, YOU STAY HERE.
WAIT!
ROME-RO...
I JUST FELT SOME-THING...
FWOOP
!!

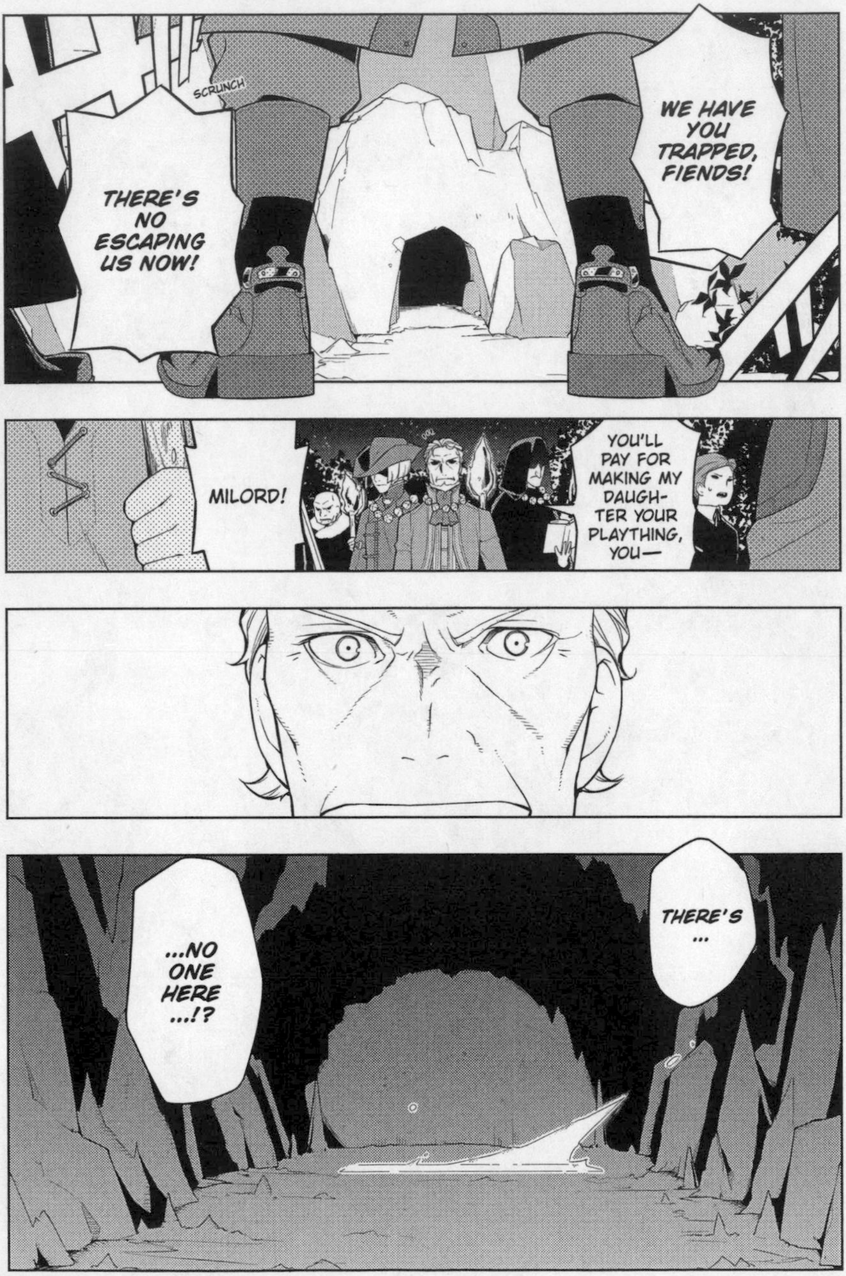
WE HAVE YOU TRAPPED, FIENDS!
SCRUNCH
THERE'S NO ESCAPING US NOW!
YOU'LL PAY FOR MAKING MY DAUGH-TER YOUR PLAYTHING, YOU—
MILORD!
THERE'S ...
...NO ONE HERE ...!?

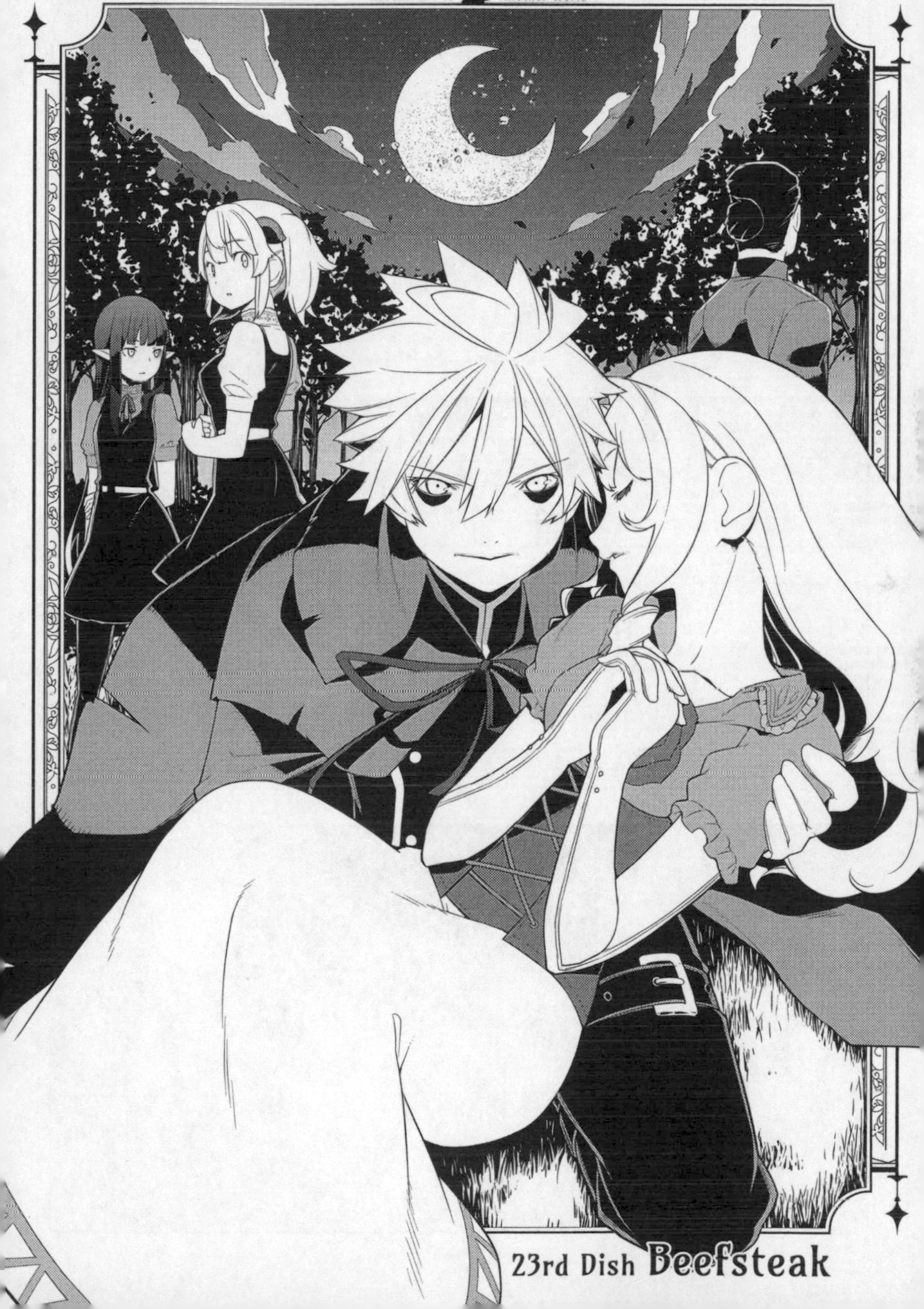
23rd Dish Beefsteak

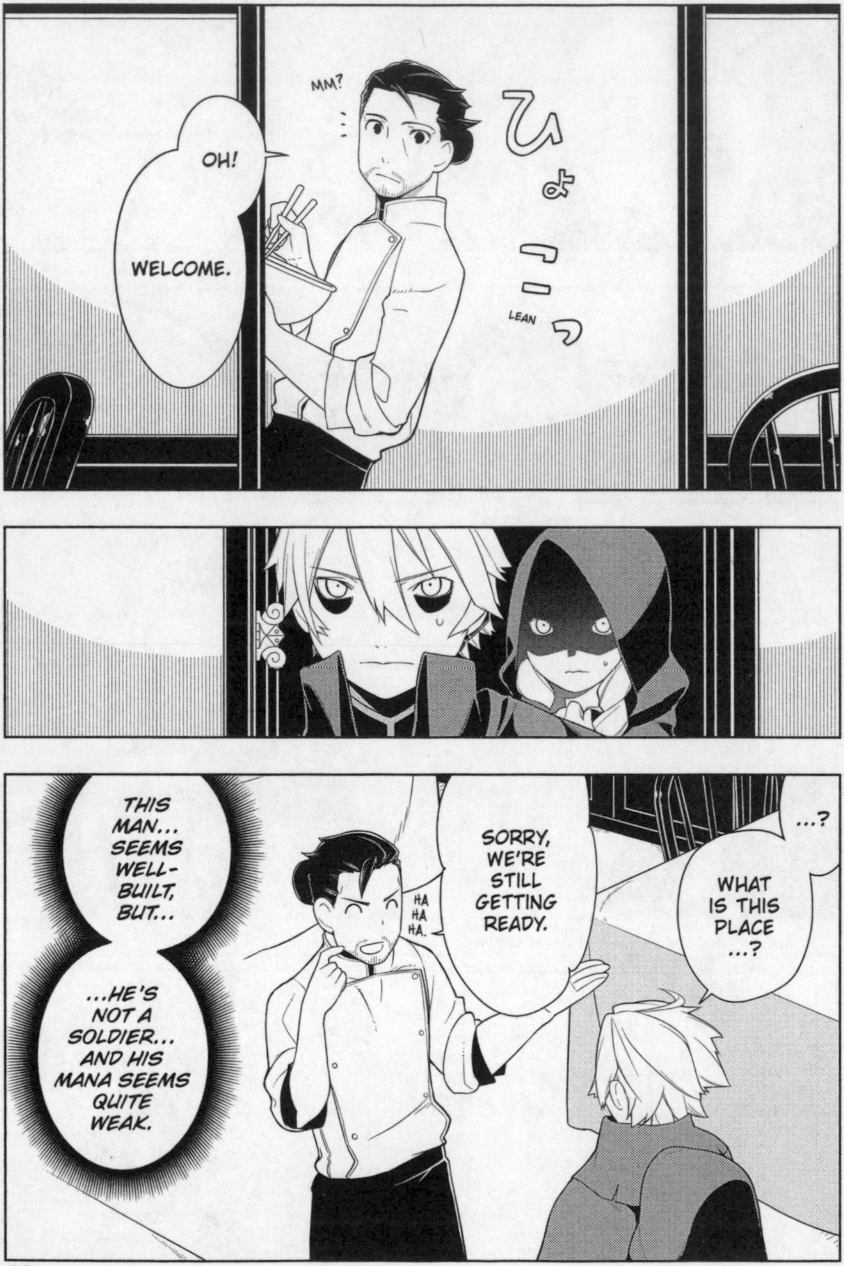
ひょこーっ
LEAN
MM?
OH!
WELCOME.
...?
WHAT IS THIS PLACE ...?
SORRY, WE'RE STILL GETTING READY.
HA HA HA.
THIS MAN... SEEMS WELL-BUILT, BUT...
...HE'S NOT A SOLDIER... AND HIS MANA SEEMS QUITE WEAK.

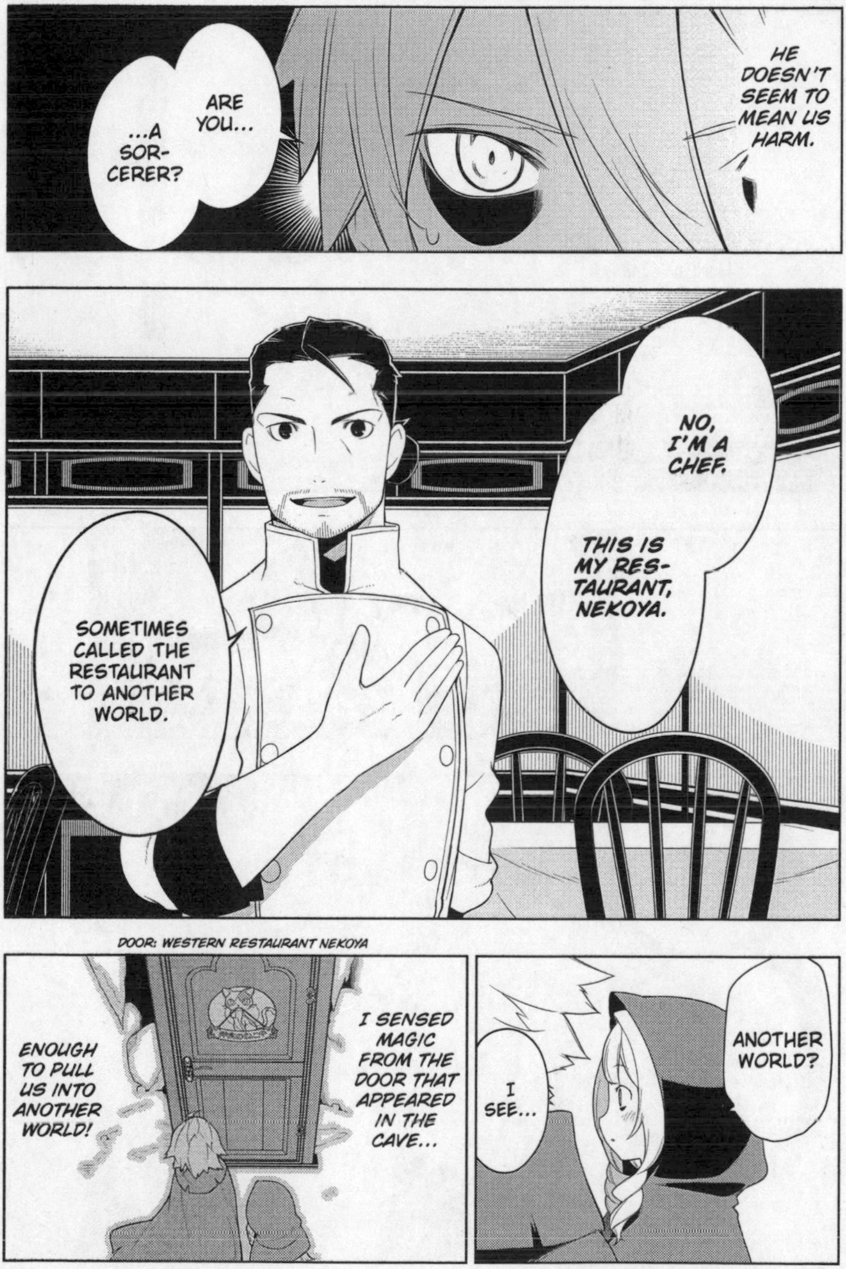
HE DOESN'T SEEM TO MEAN US HARM.
ARE YOU...
...A SORCERER?
NO, I'M A CHEF.
THIS IS MY RESTAURANT, NEKOYA.
SOMETIMES CALLED THE RESTAURANT TO ANOTHER WORLD.
ANOTHER WORLD?
I SEE...
DOOR: WESTERN RESTAURANT NEKOYA
I SENSED MAGIC FROM THE DOOR THAT APPEARED IN THE CAVE...
ENOUGH TO PULL US INTO ANOTHER WORLD!

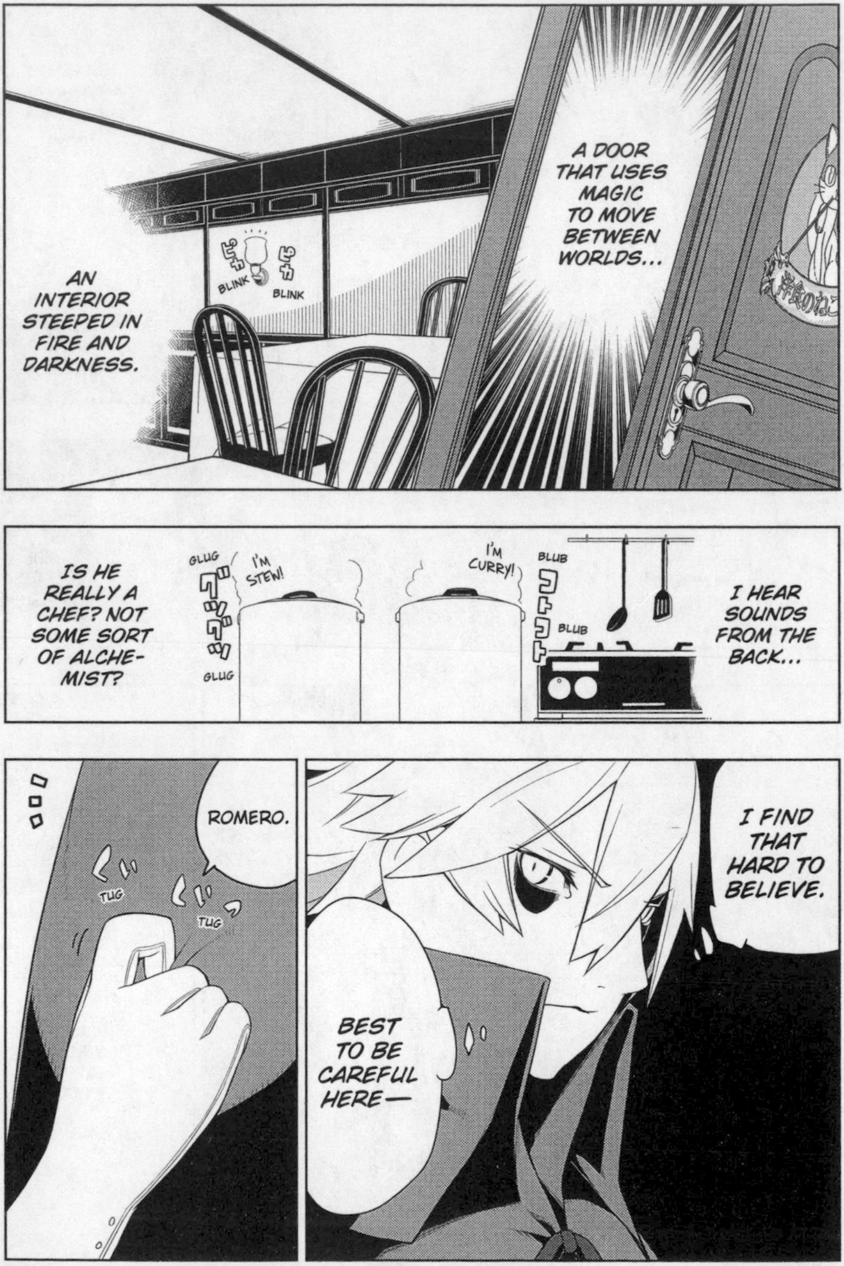
A DOOR THAT USES MAGIC TO MOVE BETWEEN WORLDS…
BLINK
BLINK
AN INTERIOR STEEPED IN FIRE AND DARKNESS.
I HEAR SOUNDS FROM THE BACK…
I'M CURRY!
BLUB
BLUB
I'M STEW!
GLUG
GLUG
IS HE REALLY A CHEF? NOT SOME SORT OF ALCHE- MIST?
I FIND THAT HARD TO BELIEVE.
BEST TO BE CAREFUL HERE—
ROMERO.
TUG
TUG

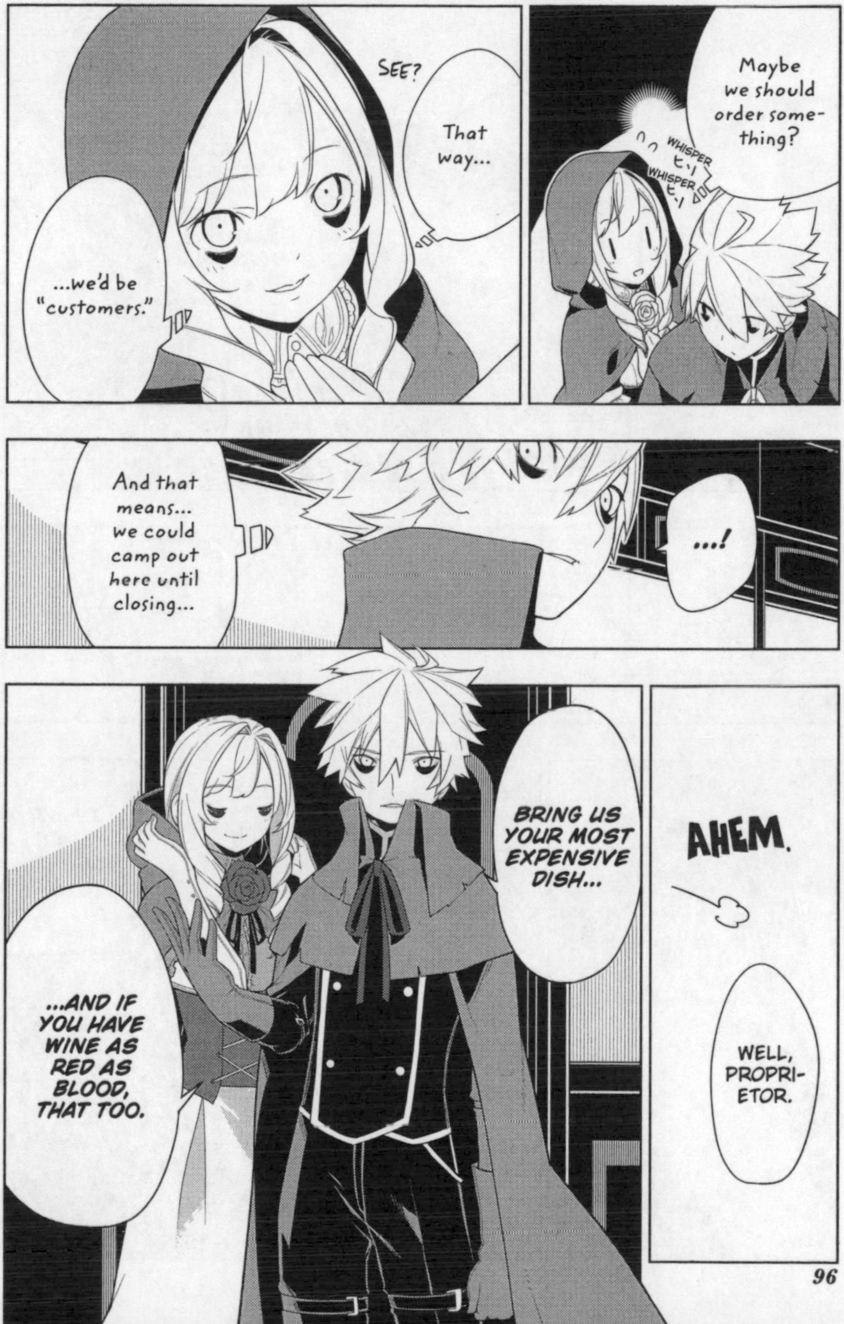
Maybe we should order some-thing?
WHISPER
ヒソ
WHISPER
ヒソ
SEE?
That way...
...we'd be "customers."
And that means... we could camp out here until closing...
...!
AHEM.
WELL, PROPRI-ETOR.
BRING US YOUR MOST EXPENSIVE DISH...
...AND IF YOU HAVE WINE AS RED AS BLOOD, THAT TOO.

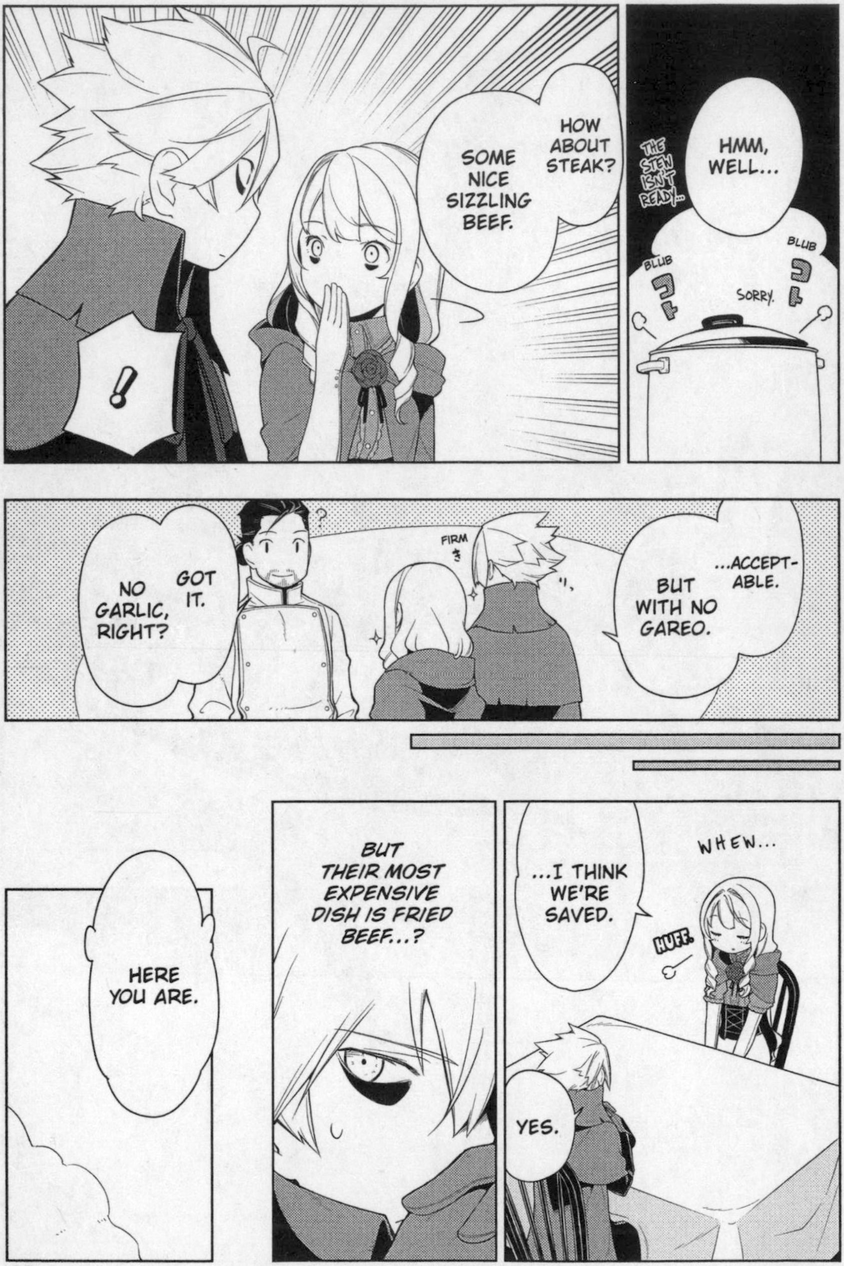
HMM, WELL...
THE STEW ISN'T READY...
BLUB
BLUB
SORRY.
HOW ABOUT STEAK?
SOME NICE SIZZLING BEEF.
...ACCEPTABLE.
BUT WITH NO GAREO.
FIRM
GOT IT.
NO GARLIC, RIGHT?
WHEW...
...I THINK WE'RE SAVED.
HUFF.
YES.
BUT THEIR MOST EXPENSIVE DISH IS FRIED BEEF...?
HERE YOU ARE.

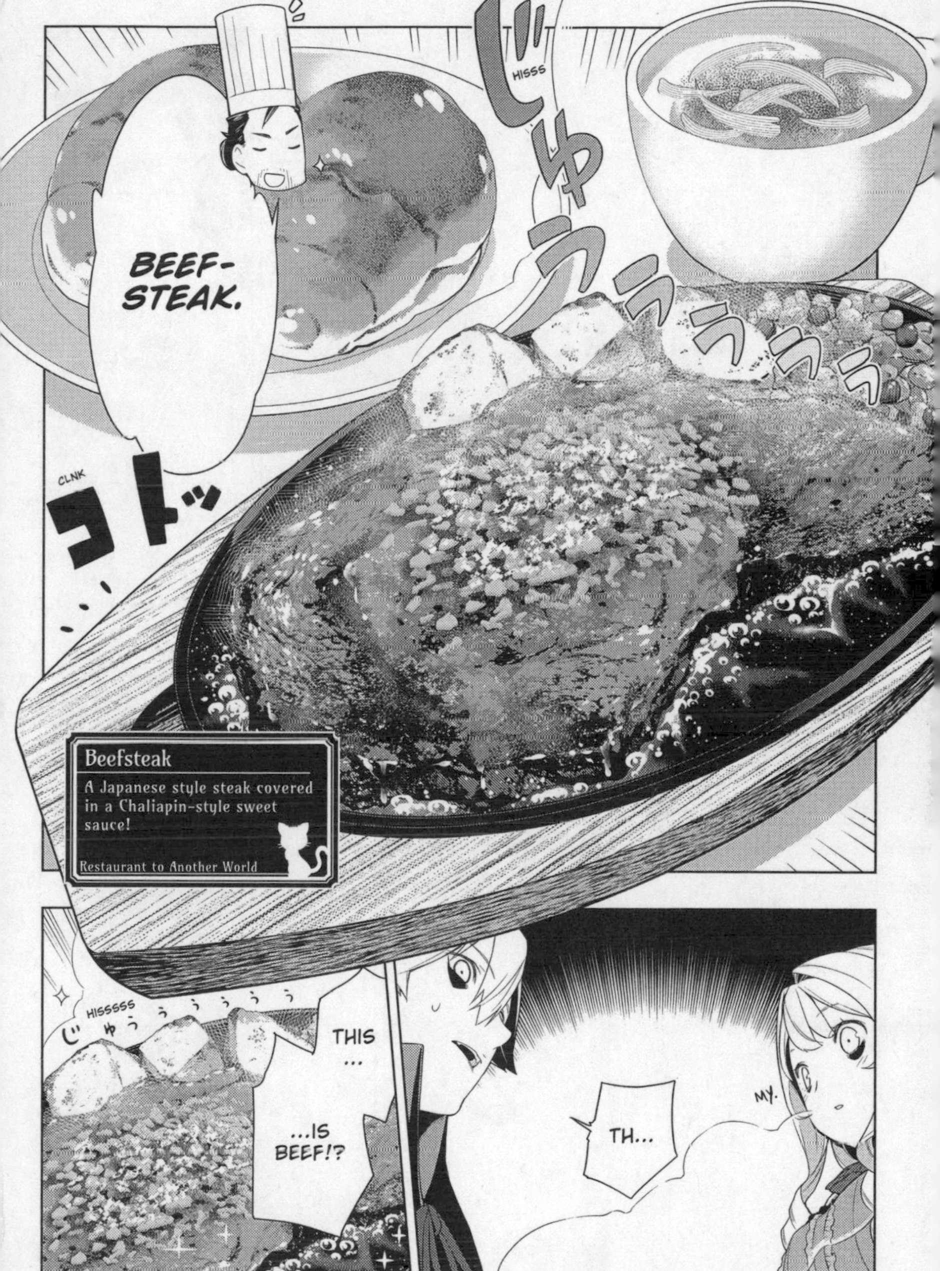
HISSS
じゅううううう
BEEF-STEAK.
CLNK
コトッ
Beefsteak
A Japanese style steak covered in a Chaliapin-style sweet sauce!
Restaurant to Another World
MY.
TH...
THIS ...
...IS BEEF!?
HISSSSS
じゅうううううう

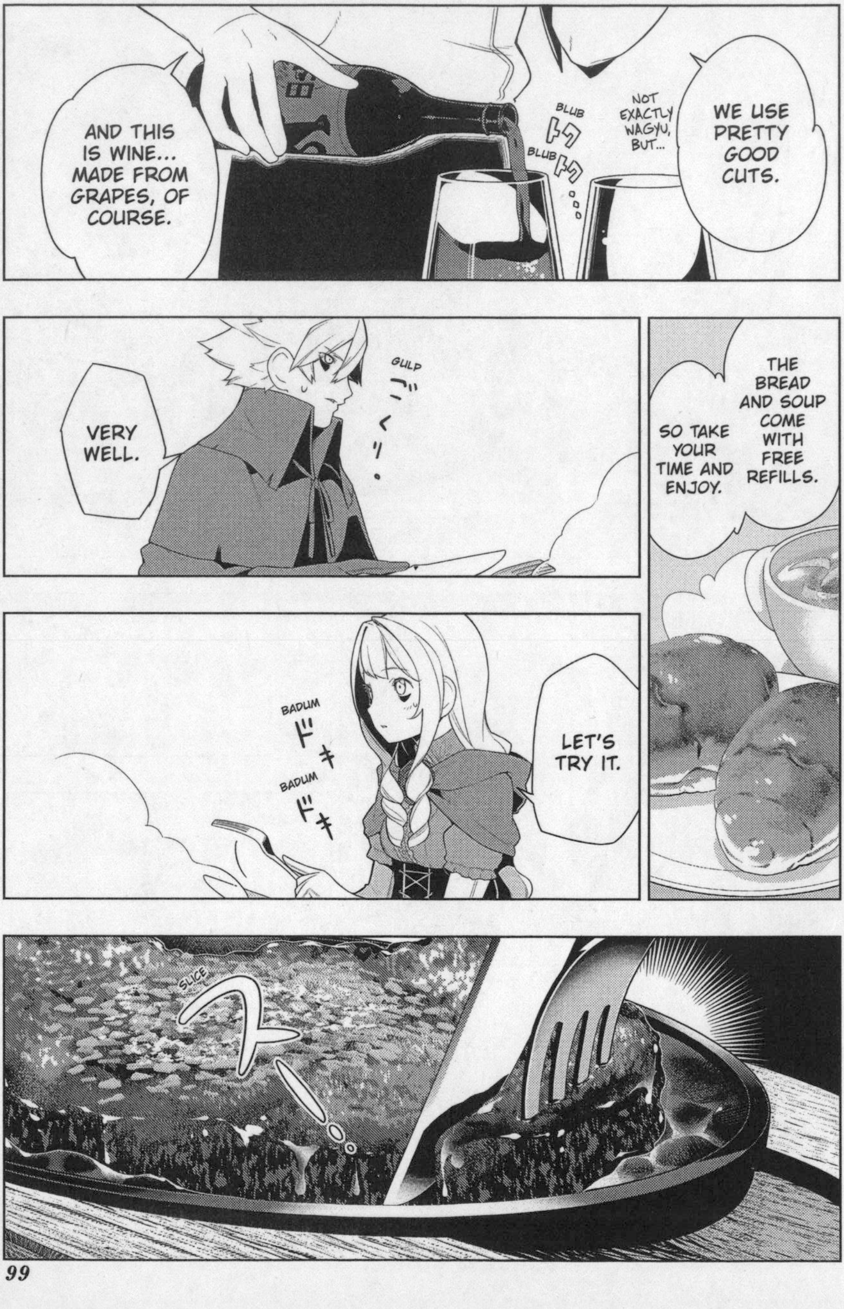
WE USE PRETTY GOOD CUTS.
NOT EXACTLY WAGYU, BUT...
BLUB
トク
BLUB
トク
AND THIS IS WINE... MADE FROM GRAPES, OF COURSE.
THE BREAD AND SOUP COME WITH FREE REFILLS.
SO TAKE YOUR TIME AND ENJOY.
GULP
ごくり。
VERY WELL.
LET'S TRY IT.
BADUM
ドキ
BADUM
ドキ
SLICE
スー…

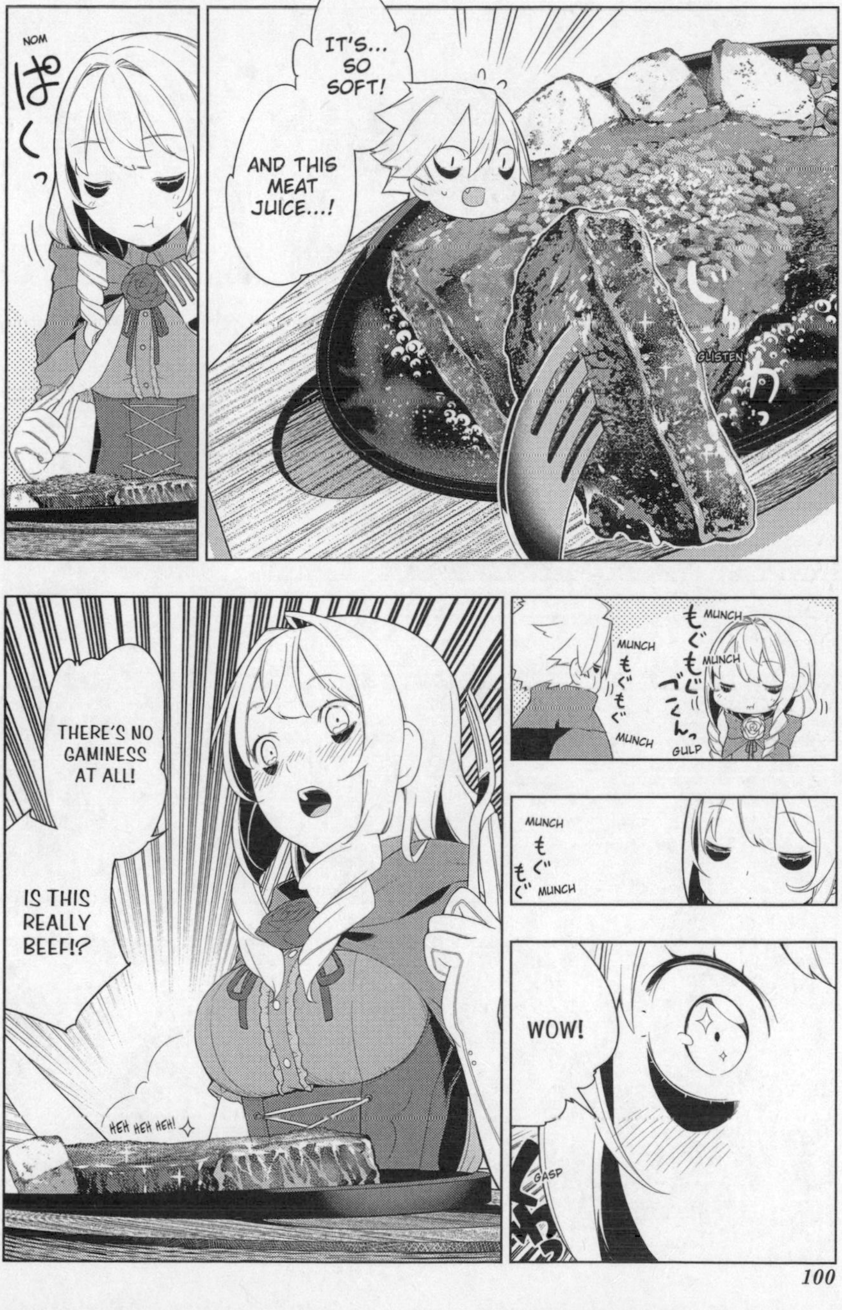
IT'S... SO SOFT!
AND THIS MEAT JUICE...!
じゅわっ
GLISTEN
NOM
ぱくっ
もぐもぐ
MUNCH
MUNCH
もぐもぐ
MUNCH
MUNCH
ごくんっ
GULP
MUNCH
もぐもぐ
MUNCH
WOW!
GASP
THERE'S NO GAMINESS AT ALL!
IS THIS REALLY BEEF!?
HEH HEH HEH!

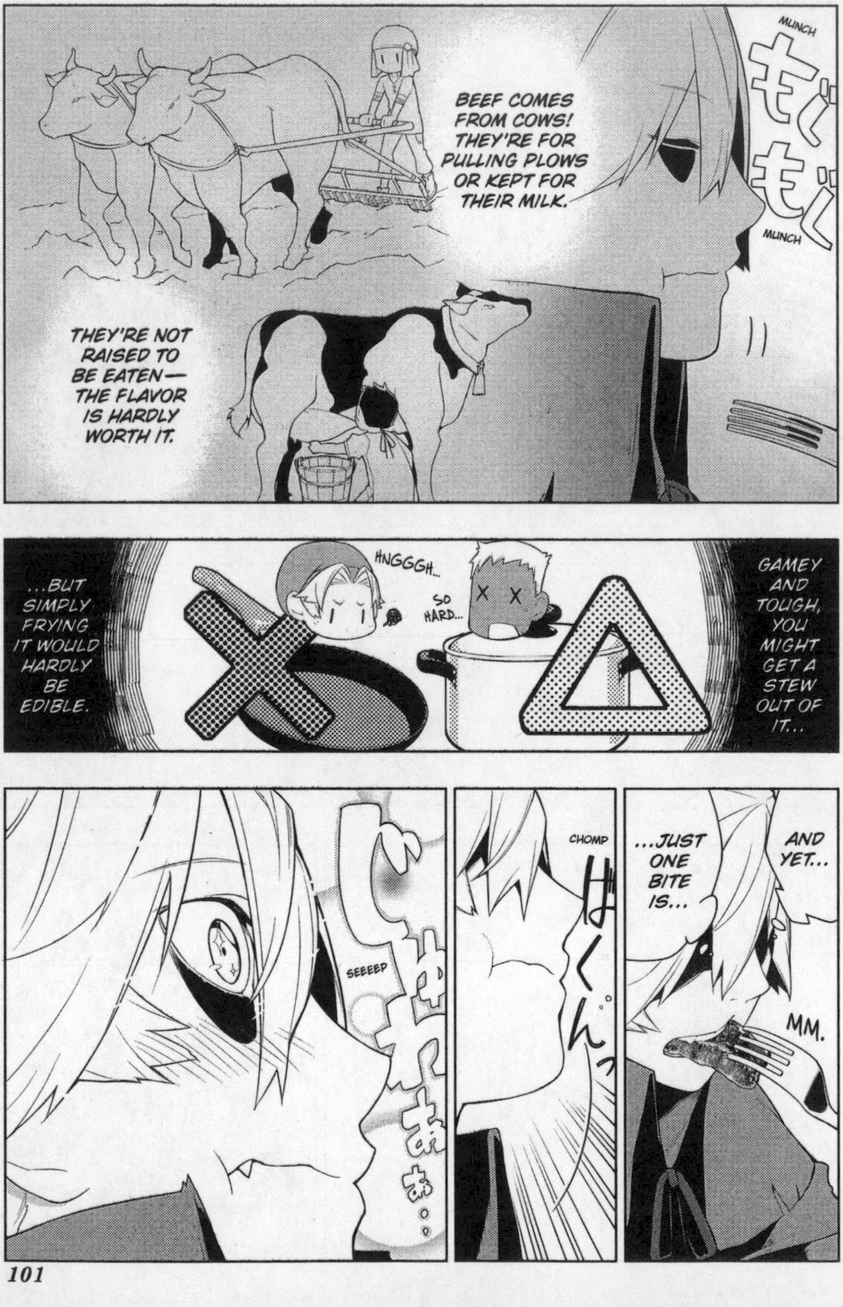

MUNCH
MUNCH
BEEF COMES FROM COWS! THEY'RE FOR PULLING PLOWS OR KEPT FOR THEIR MILK.
THEY'RE NOT RAISED TO BE EATEN—THE FLAVOR IS HARDLY WORTH IT.
GAMEY AND TOUGH, YOU MIGHT GET A STEW OUT OF IT...
HNGGGH...
SO HARD...
...BUT SIMPLY FRYING IT WOULD HARDLY BE EDIBLE.
AND YET...
...JUST ONE BITE IS...
MM.
CHOMP
SEEEEP

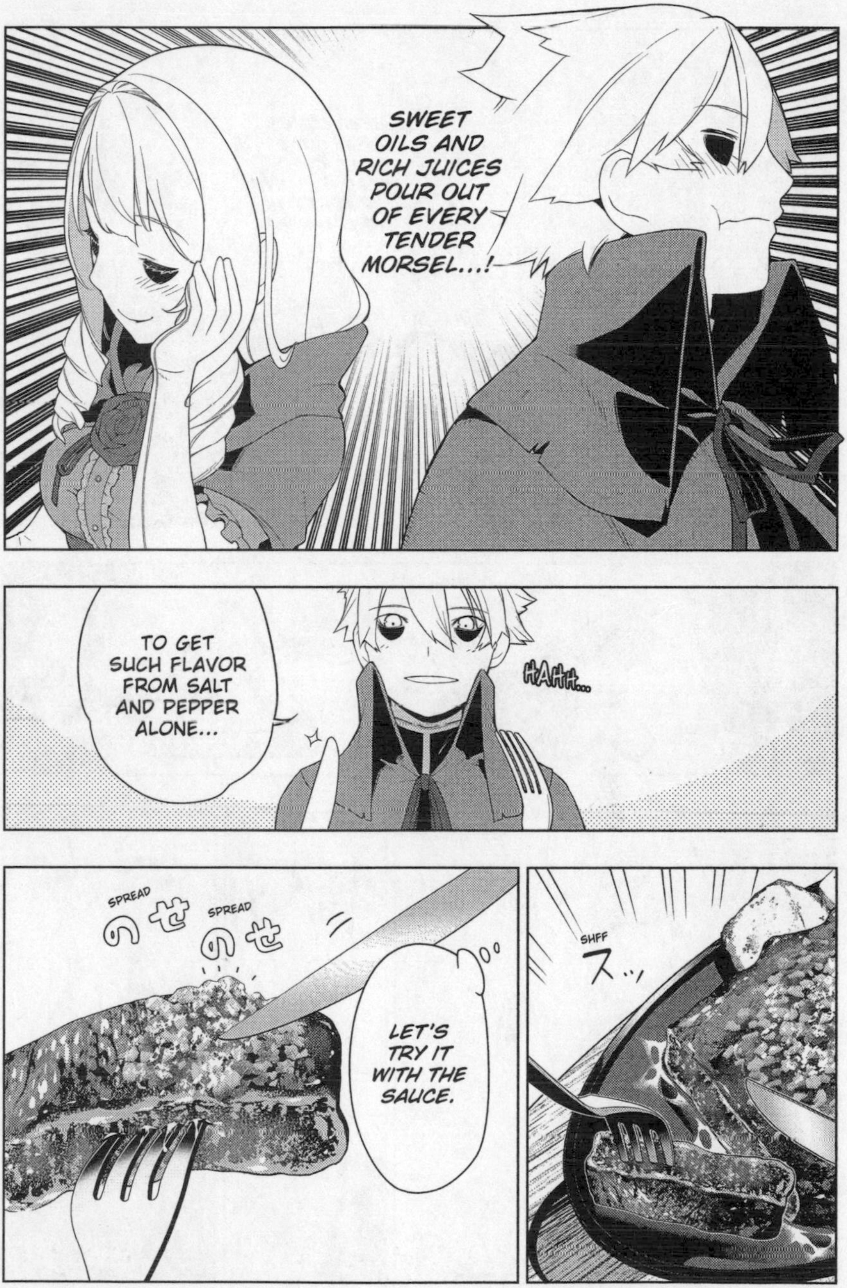
SWEET OILS AND RICH JUICES POUR OUT OF EVERY TENDER MORSEL...!
TO GET SUCH FLAVOR FROM SALT AND PEPPER ALONE...
HAHH...
SHFF
スッ
LET'S TRY IT WITH THE SAUCE.
SPREAD
のせ
SPREAD
のせ

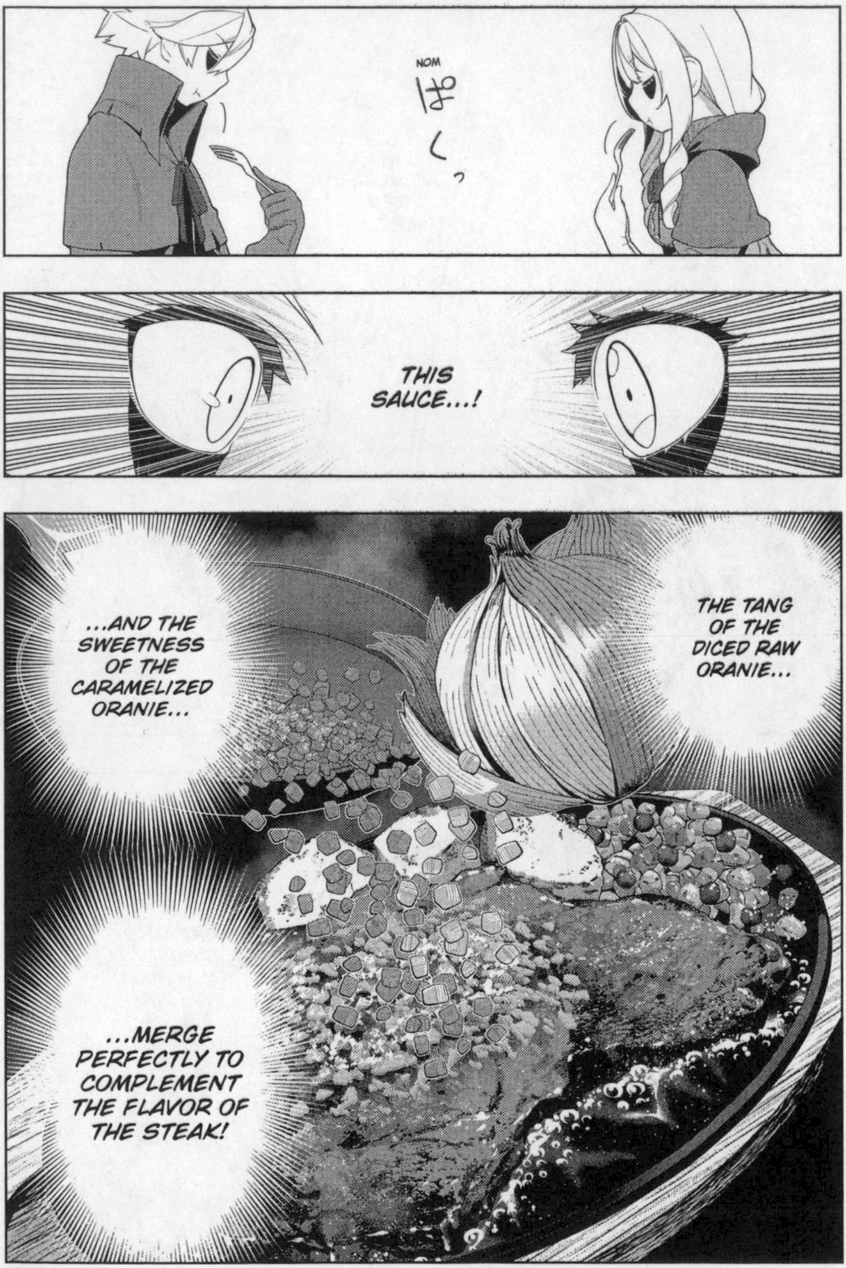
NOM
ぽくっ
THIS SAUCE...!
THE TANG OF THE DICED RAW ORANIE...
...AND THE SWEETNESS OF THE CARAMELIZED ORANIE...
...MERGE PERFECTLY TO COMPLEMENT THE FLAVOR OF THE STEAK!

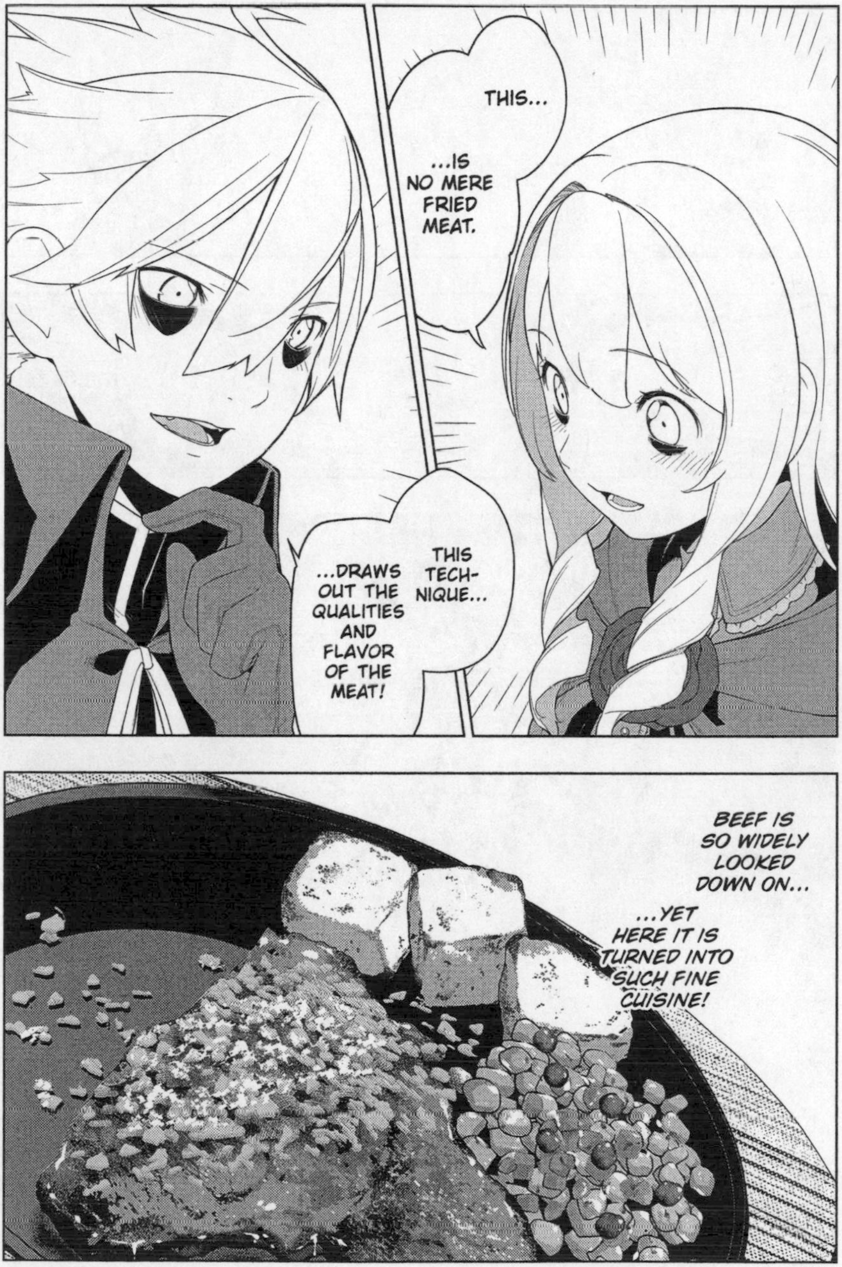
THIS...
...IS NO MERE FRIED MEAT.
THIS TECH-NIQUE...
...DRAWS OUT THE QUALITIES AND FLAVOR OF THE MEAT!
BEEF IS SO WIDELY LOOKED DOWN ON...
...YET HERE IT IS TURNED INTO SUCH FINE CUISINE!

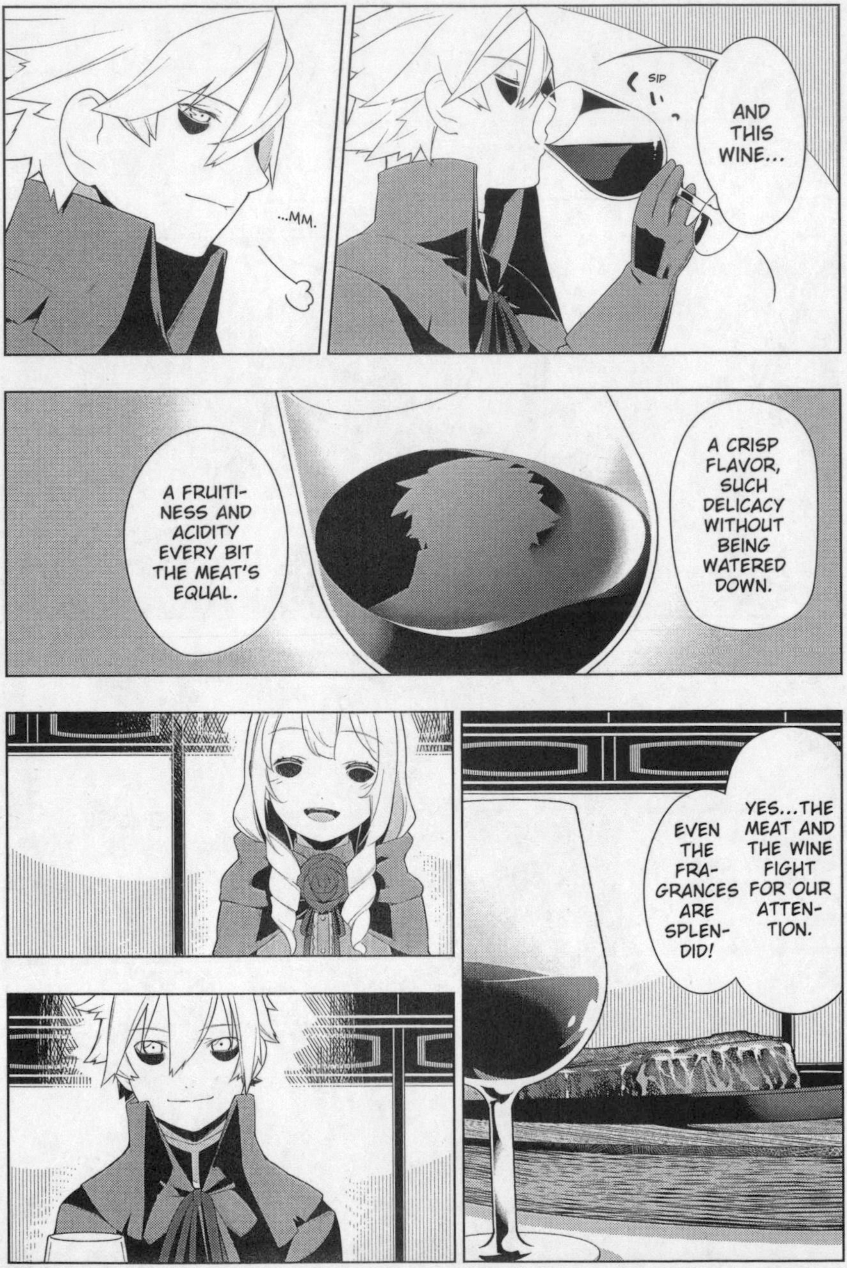
SIP
AND THIS WINE...
...MM.
A CRISP FLAVOR, SUCH DELICACY WITHOUT BEING WATERED DOWN.
A FRUITINESS AND ACIDITY EVERY BIT THE MEAT'S EQUAL.
YES...THE MEAT AND THE WINE FIGHT FOR OUR ATTENTION.
EVEN THE FRAGRANCES ARE SPLENDID!

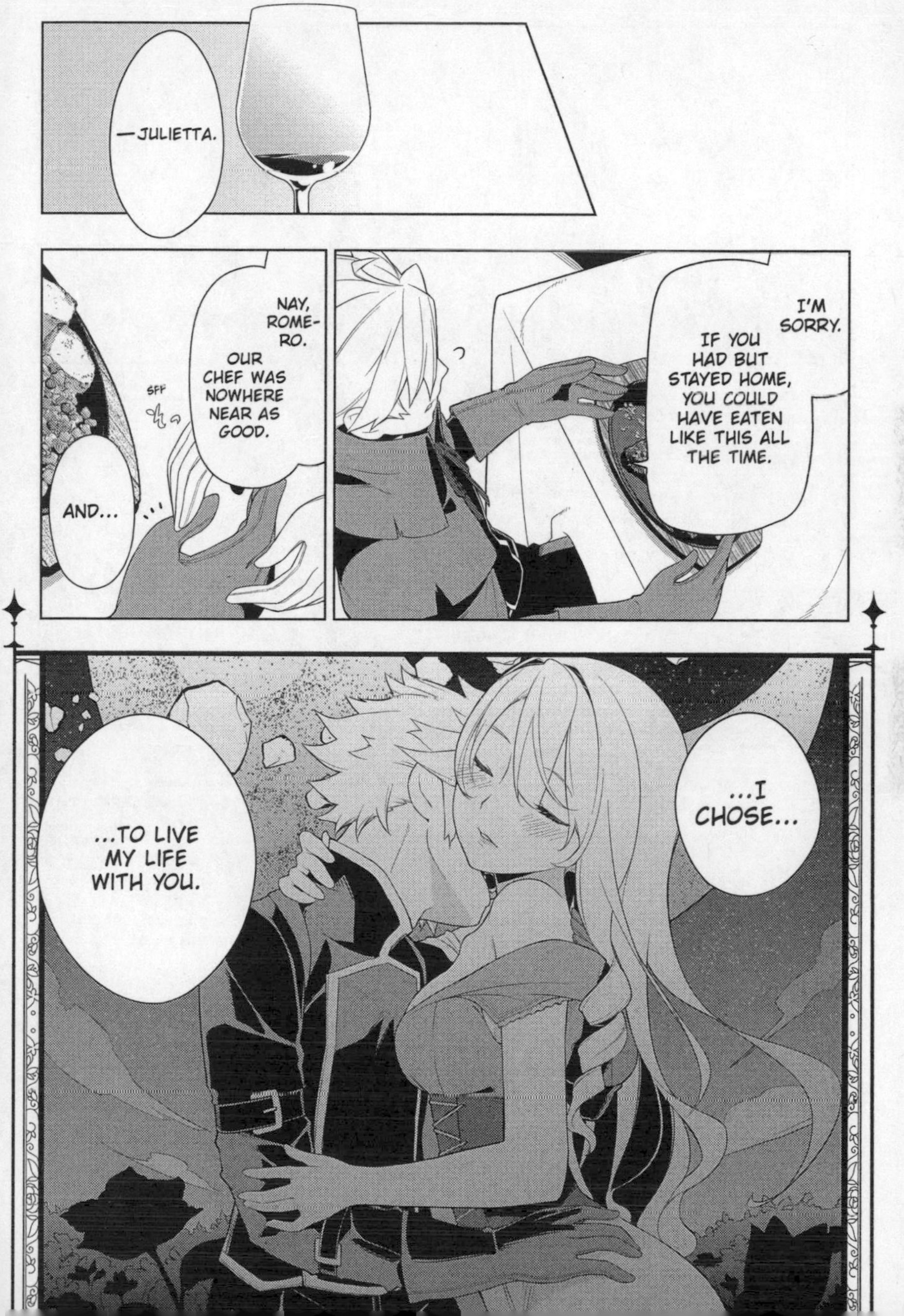
—JULIETTA.
I'M SORRY.
IF YOU HAD BUT STAYED HOME, YOU COULD HAVE EATEN LIKE THIS ALL THE TIME.
NAY, ROMERO.
OUR CHEF WAS NOWHERE NEAR AS GOOD.
SFF
AND...
...I CHOSE...
...TO LIVE MY LIFE WITH YOU.

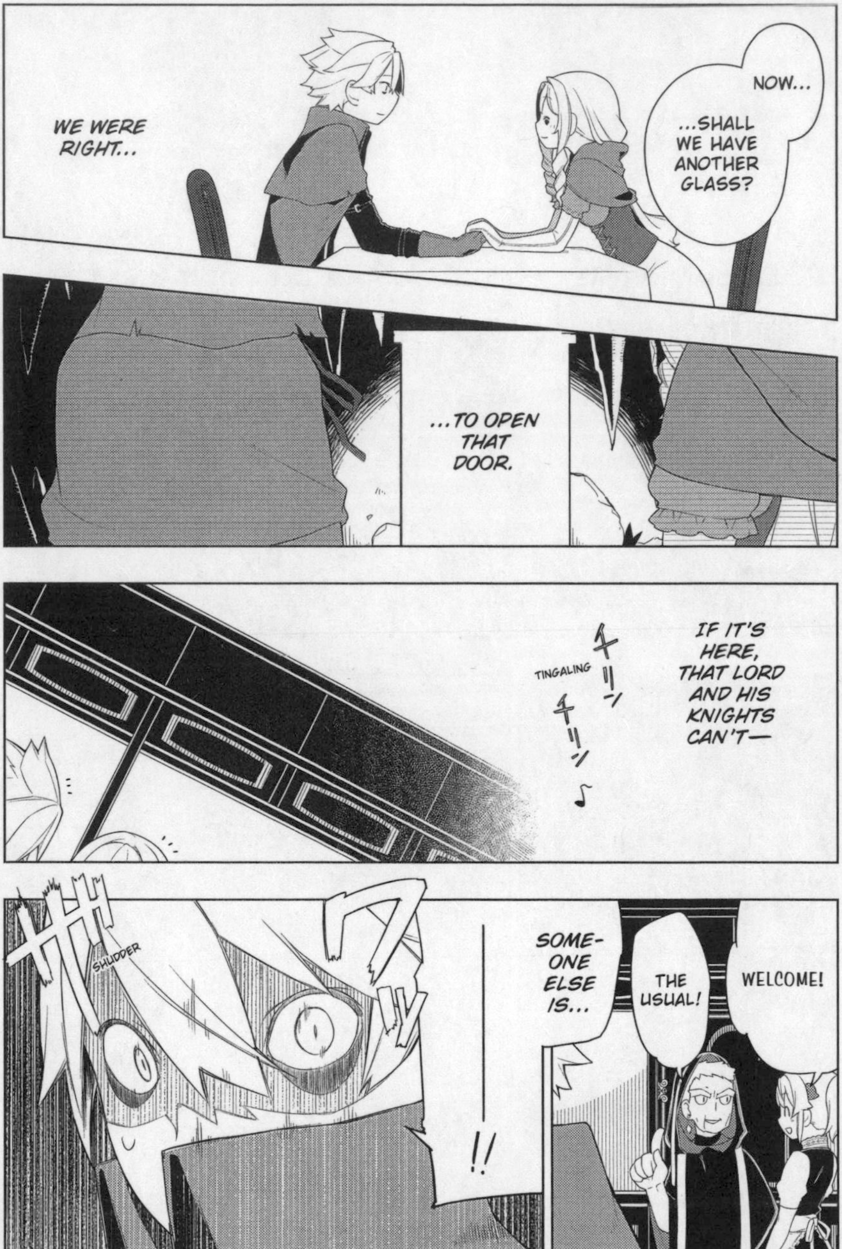
NOW...
...SHALL WE HAVE ANOTHER GLASS?
WE WERE RIGHT...
...TO OPEN THAT DOOR.
IF IT'S HERE, THAT LORD AND HIS KNIGHTS CAN'T—
TINGALING
チリン
チリン♪
WELCOME!
THE USUAL!
SOME-ONE ELSE IS...
!!
SHUDDER

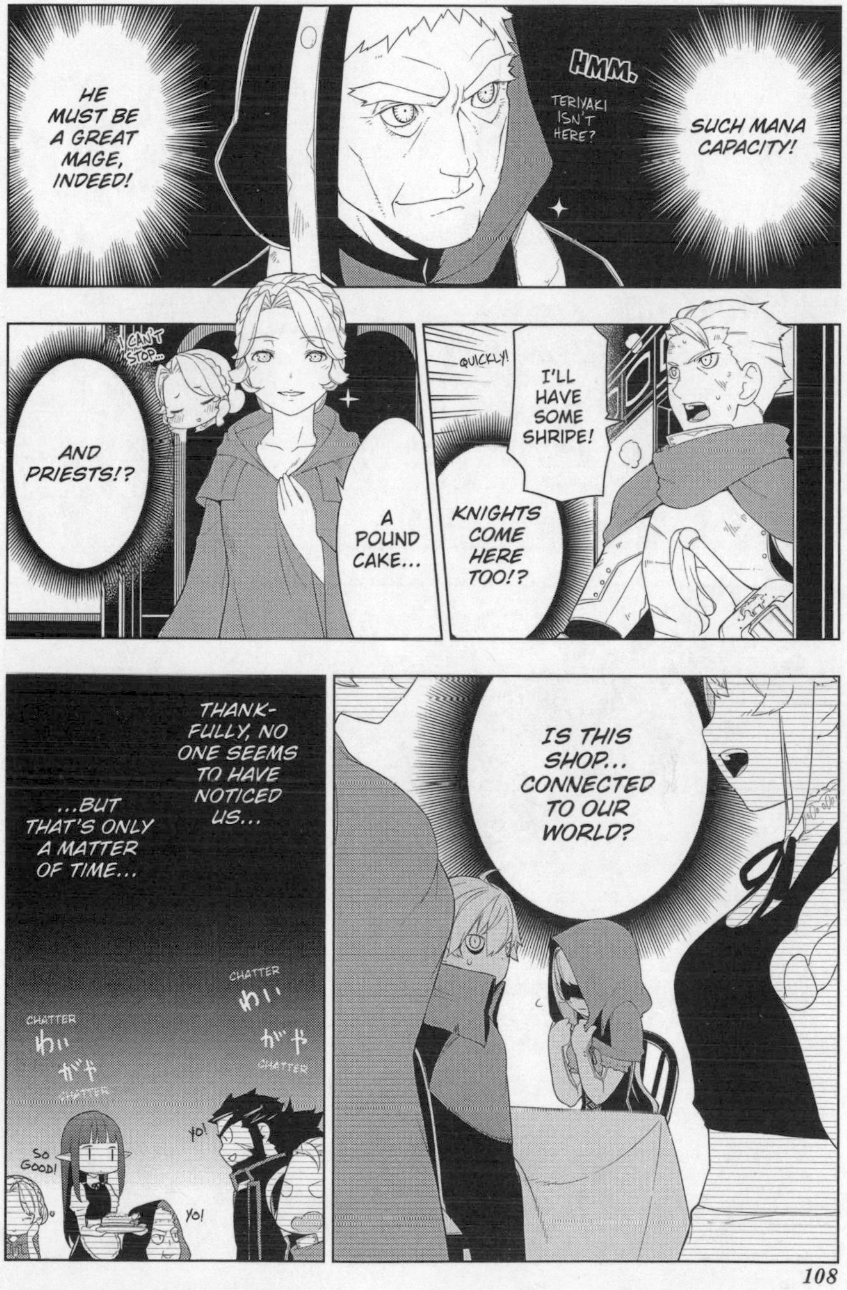
SUCH MANA CAPACITY!
HMM.
TERIYAKI ISN'T HERE?
HE MUST BE A GREAT MAGE, INDEED!
QUICKLY!
I'LL HAVE SOME SHRIPE!
KNIGHTS COME HERE TOO!?
A POUND CAKE...
I CAN'T STOP...
AND PRIESTS!?
IS THIS SHOP... CONNECTED TO OUR WORLD?
THANK-FULLY, NO ONE SEEMS TO HAVE NOTICED US...
...BUT THAT'S ONLY A MATTER OF TIME...
CHATTER
わい
がや
CHATTER
CHATTER
わい
がや
CHATTER
YO!
SO GOOD!
YO!

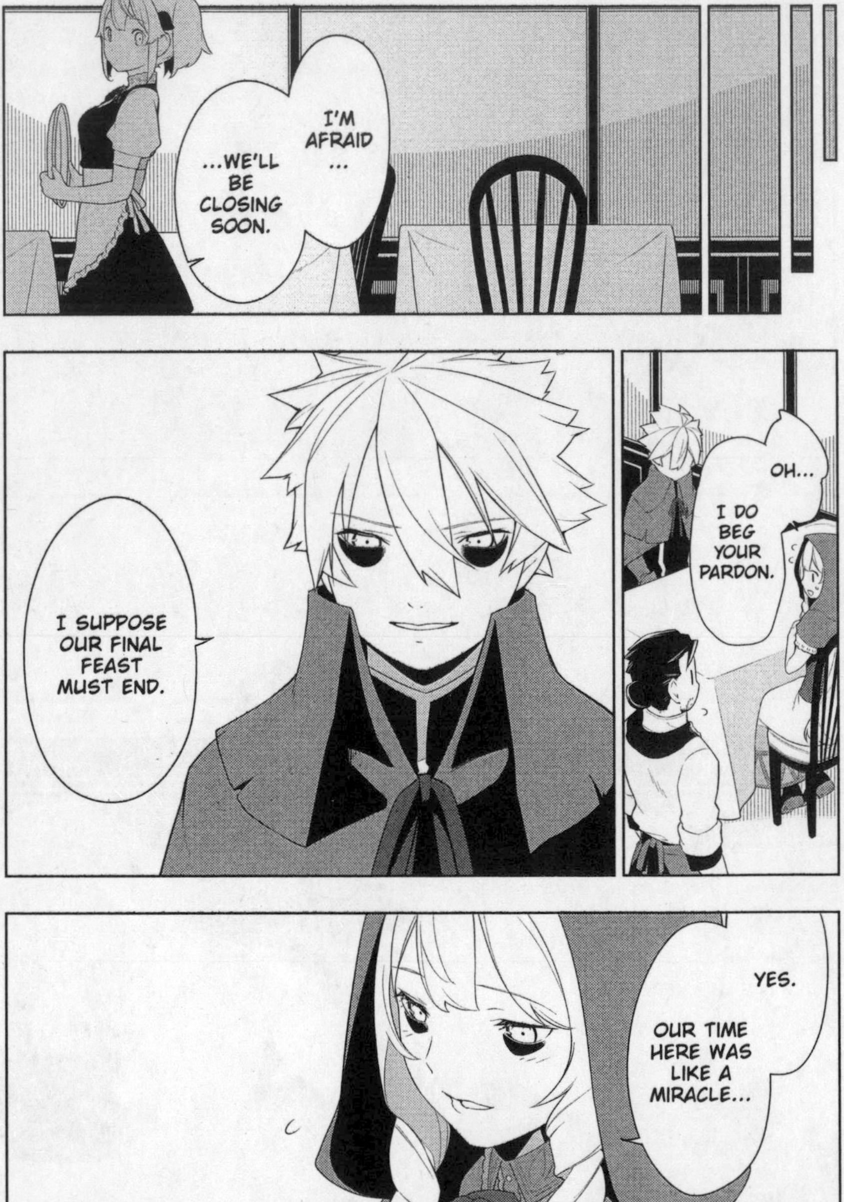
I'M AFRAID ...
...WE'LL BE CLOSING SOON.
OH... I DO BEG YOUR PARDON.
I SUPPOSE OUR FINAL FEAST MUST END.
YES. OUR TIME HERE WAS LIKE A MIRACLE...

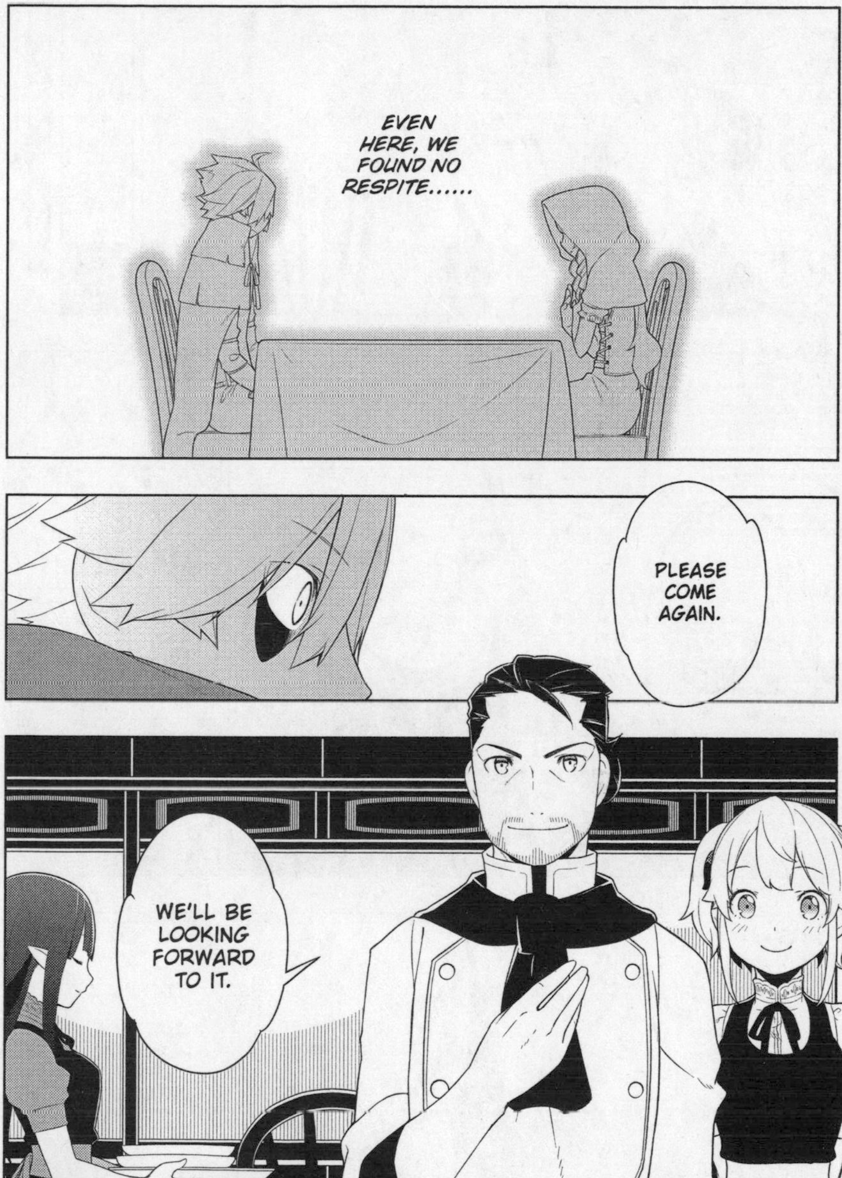
EVEN HERE, WE FOUND NO RESPITE......
PLEASE COME AGAIN.
WE'LL BE LOOKING FORWARD TO IT.

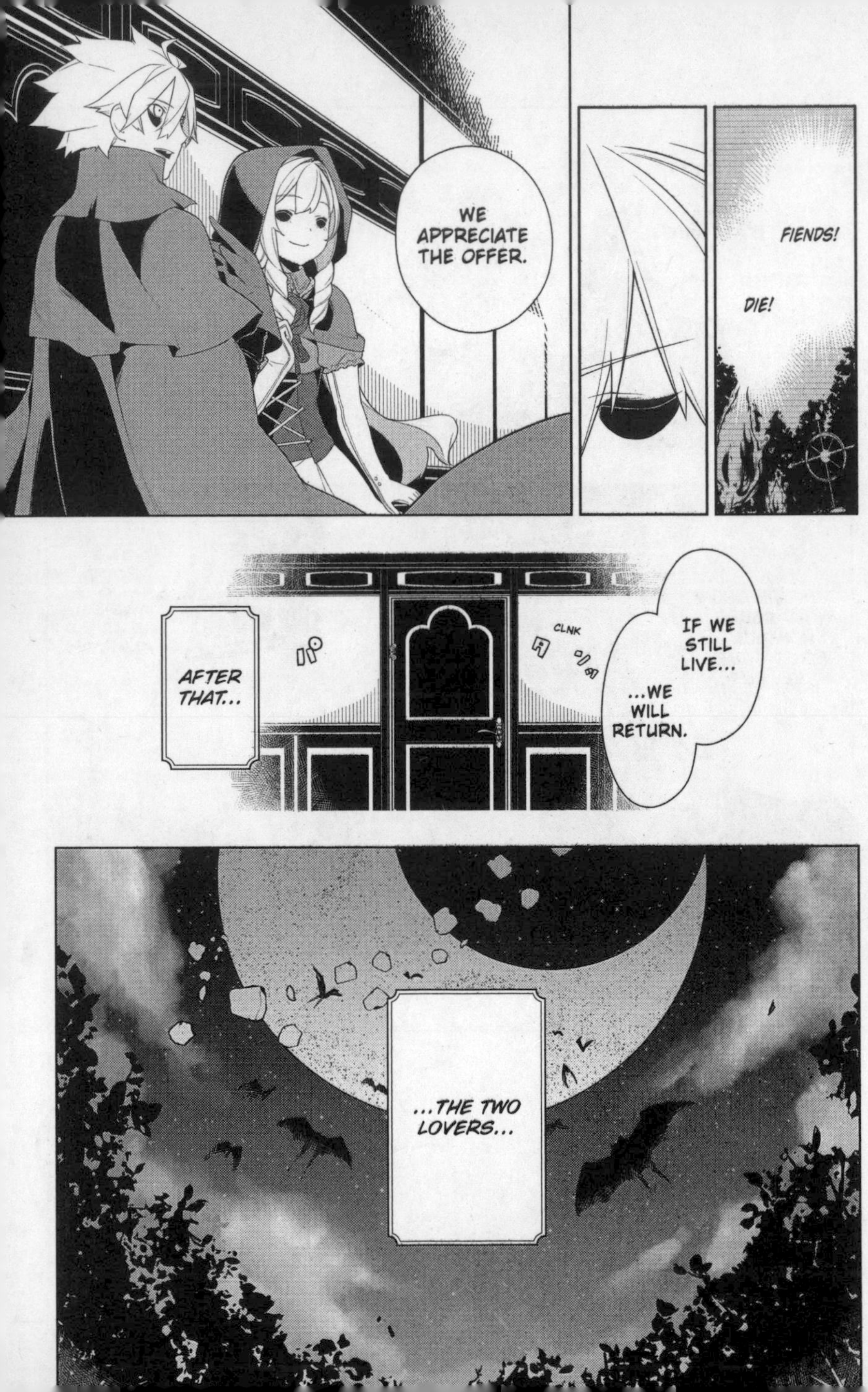
FIENDS!
DIE!
WE APPRECIATE THE OFFER.
IF WE STILL LIVE...
...WE WILL RETURN.
CLNK
AFTER THAT...
...THE TWO LOVERS...

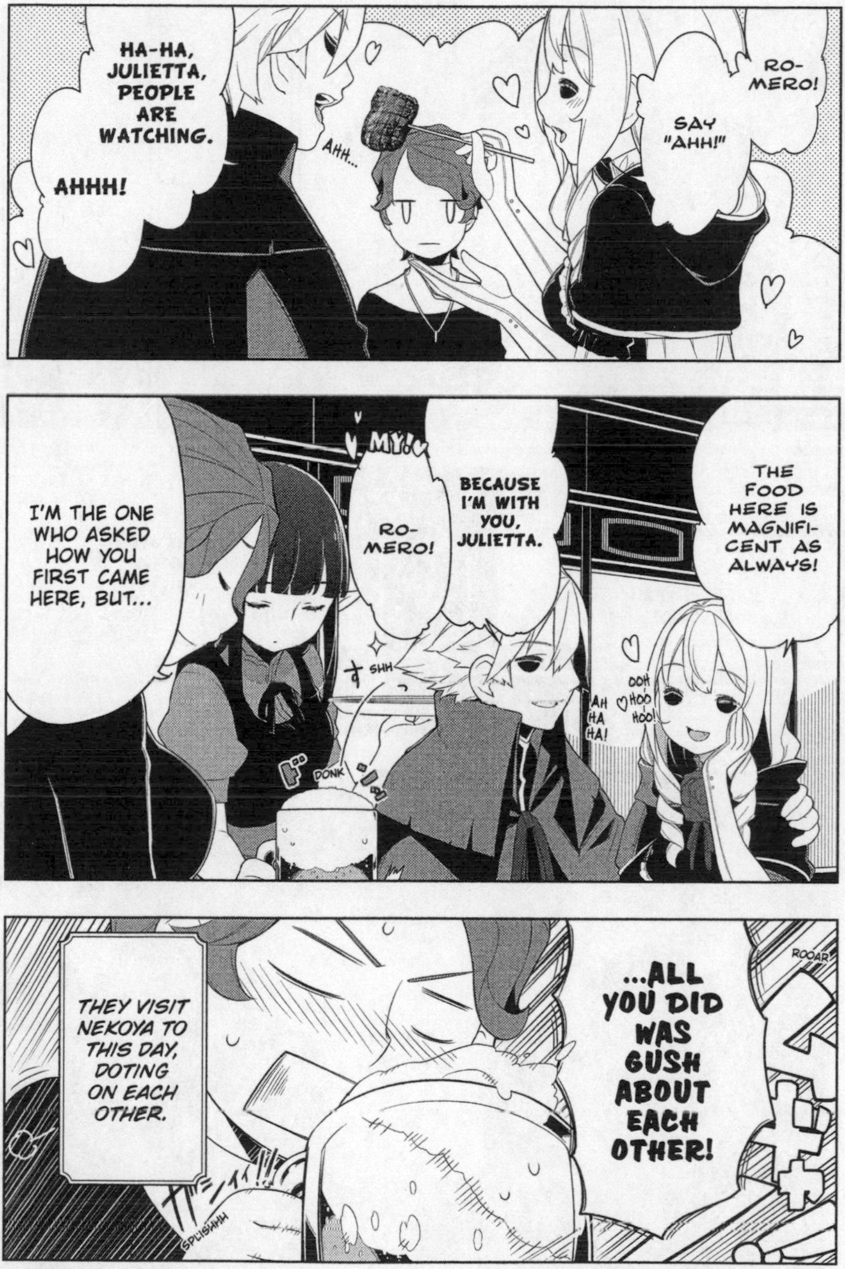
RO-MERO!
SAY "AHH!"
AHH...
HA-HA, JULIETTA, PEOPLE ARE WATCHING.
AHHH!
THE FOOD HERE IS MAGNIFICENT AS ALWAYS!
OOH HOO HOO!
AH HA HA!
BECAUSE I'M WITH YOU, JULIETTA.
RO-MERO!
MY!
SHH
DONK
I'M THE ONE WHO ASKED HOW YOU FIRST CAME HERE, BUT...
ROOAR
...ALL YOU DID WAS GUSH ABOUT EACH OTHER!
THEY VISIT NEKOYA TO THIS DAY, DOTING ON EACH OTHER.
SPLISHHH

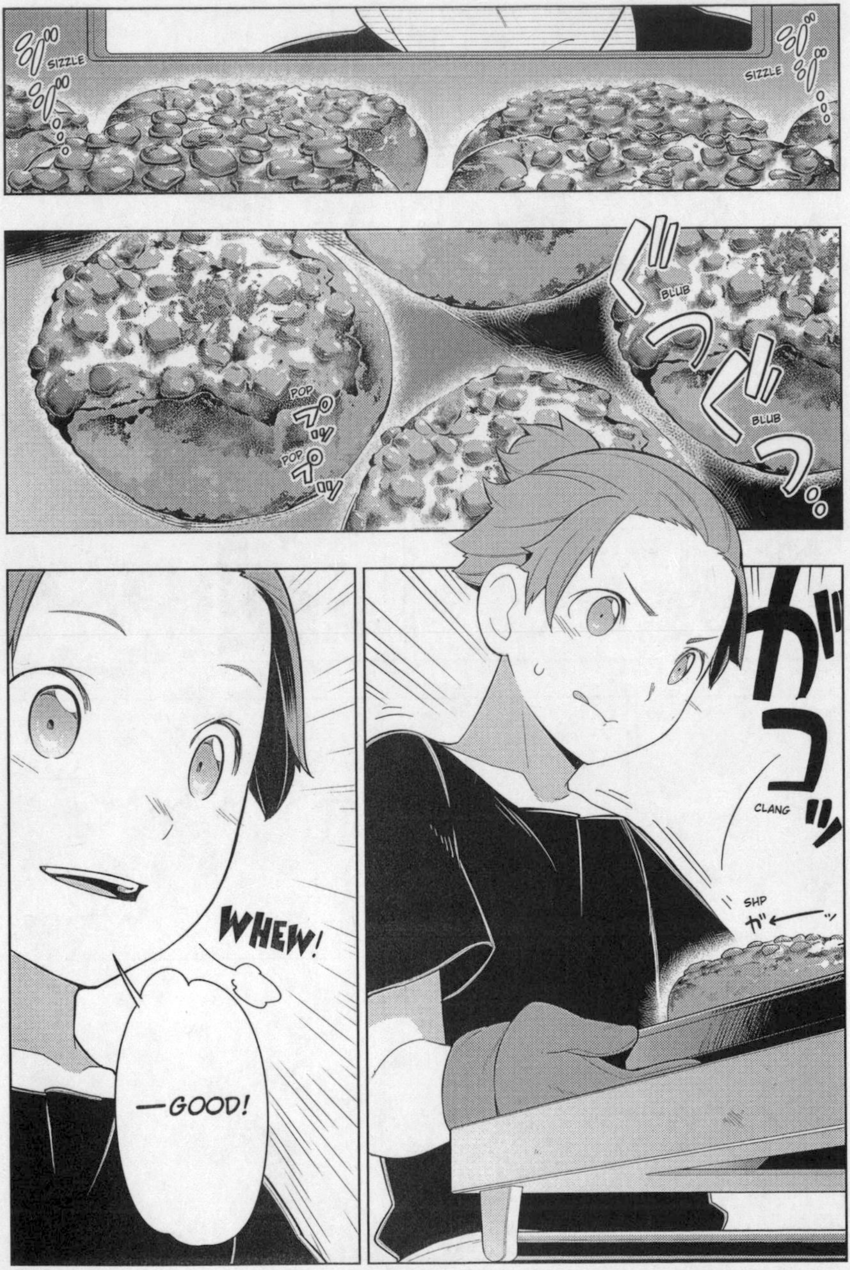
SIZZLE
SIZZLE
ぐつぐつ
BLUB
BLUB
プツ
POP
プツ
POP
がコッ
CLANG
ガッ
SHP
WHEW!
—GOOD!

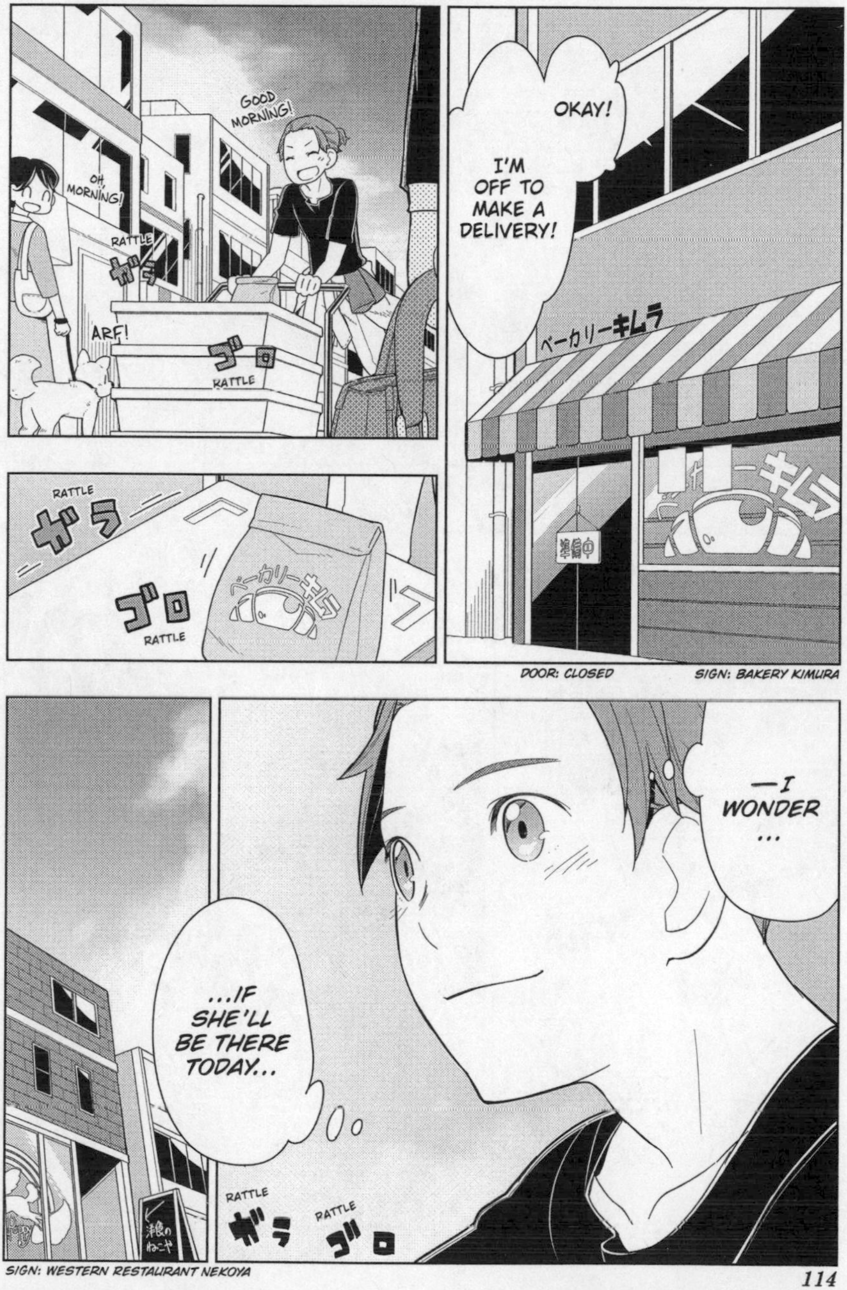
OKAY!
I'M OFF TO MAKE A DELIVERY!
ベーカリーキムラ
準備中
DOOR: CLOSED
SIGN: BAKERY KIMURA
GOOD MORNING!
OH, MORNING!
RATTLE
ガラ
ARF!
ゴロ
RATTLE
RATTLE
ガラ
ゴロ
RATTLE
ベーカリーキムラ
—I WONDER...
...IF SHE'LL BE THERE TODAY...
RATTLE
ガラ
RATTLE
ゴロ
洋食のねこや

SIGN: WESTERN RESTAURANT NEKOYA

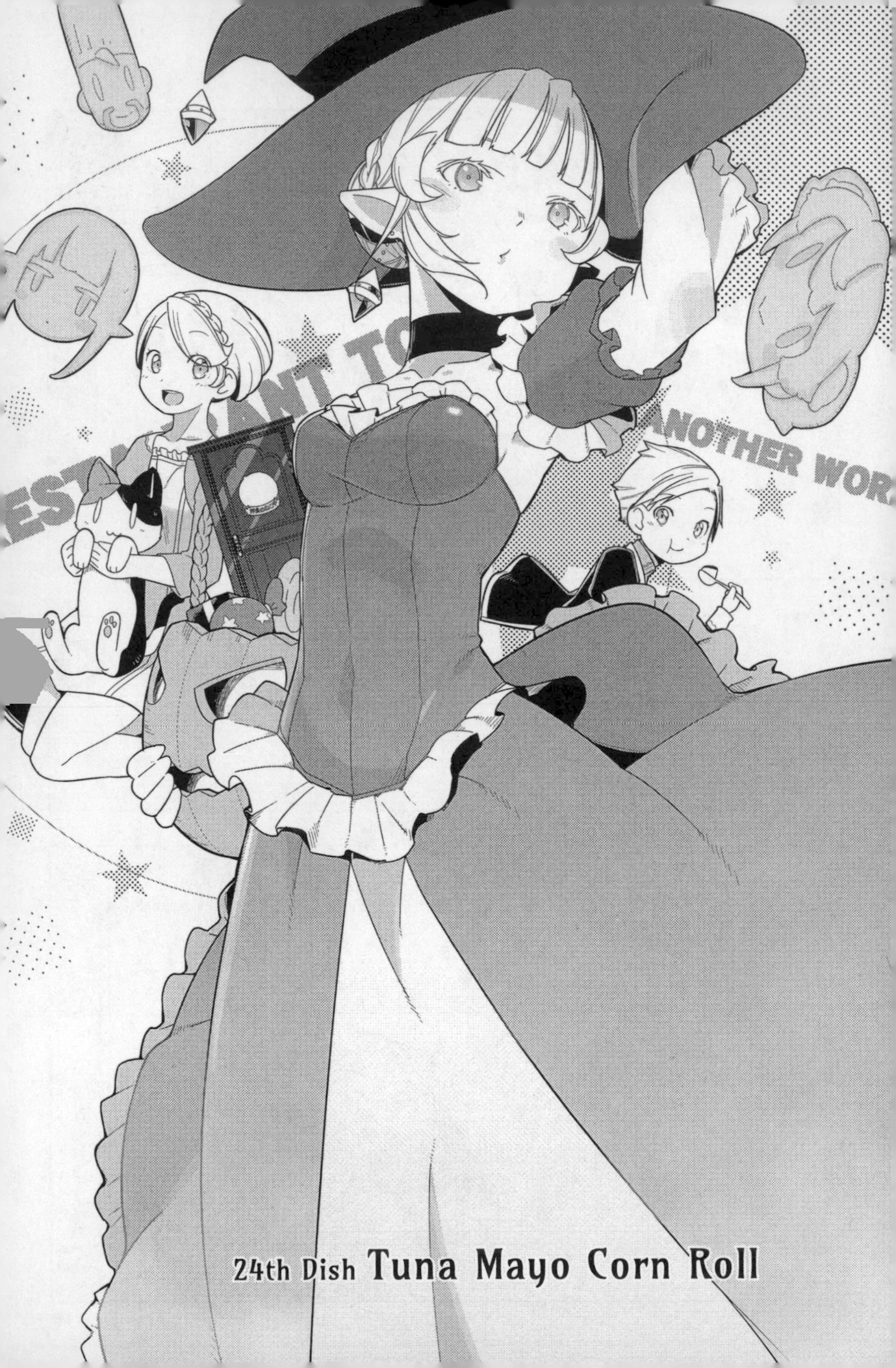

24th Dish Tuna Mayo Corn Roll

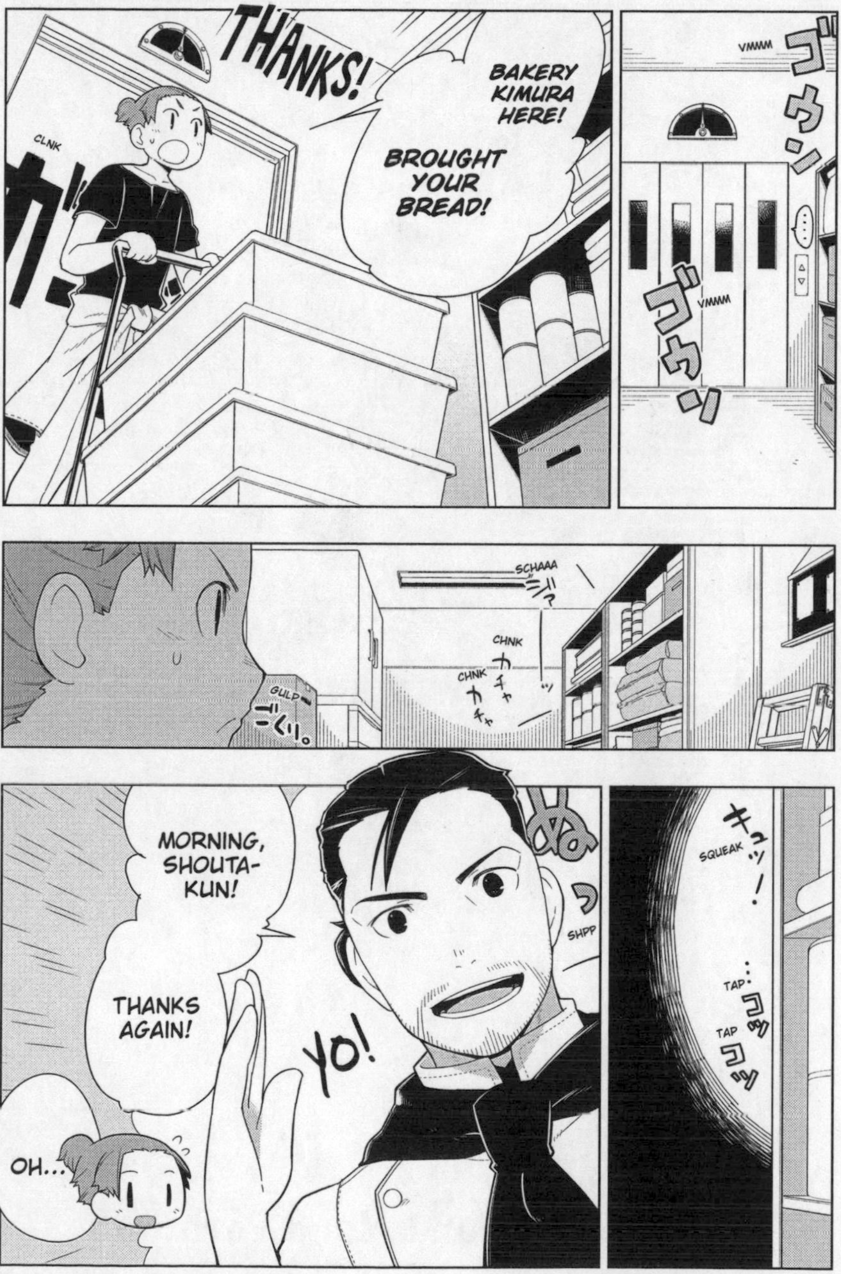
VMMM
...
VMMM
THANKS!
BAKERY KIMURA HERE!
BROUGHT YOUR BREAD!
CLNK
SCHAAA
CHNK
CHNK
GULP
SQUEAK
TAP
TAP
SHPP
YO!
MORNING, SHOUTA-KUN!
THANKS AGAIN!
OH...

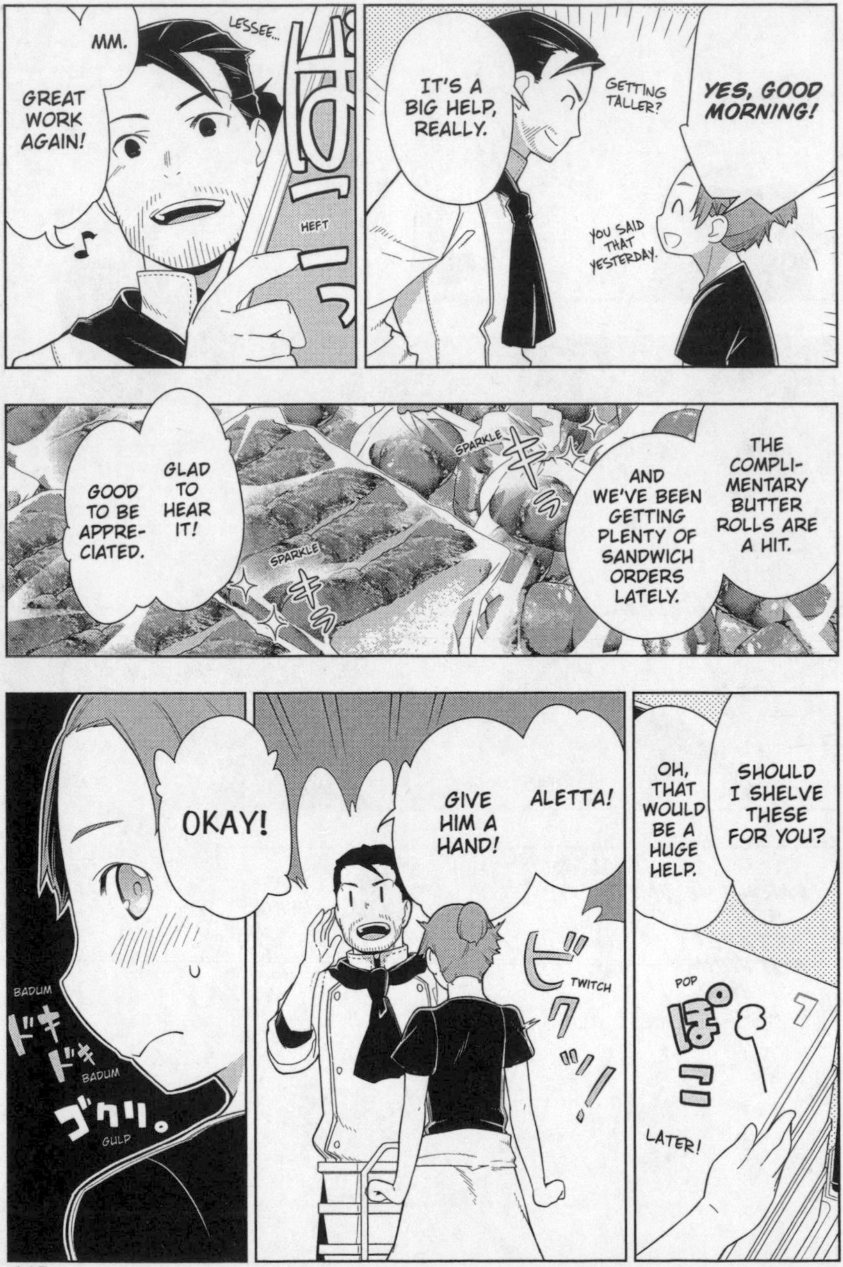
YES, GOOD MORNING!
GETTING TALLER?
IT'S A BIG HELP, REALLY.
YOU SAID THAT YESTERDAY.
LESSEE...
MM.
GREAT WORK AGAIN!
HEFT
THE COMPLIMENTARY BUTTER ROLLS ARE A HIT.
AND WE'VE BEEN GETTING PLENTY OF SANDWICH ORDERS LATELY.
SPARKLE
GLAD TO HEAR IT!
GOOD TO BE APPRECIATED.
SPARKLE
SHOULD I SHELVE THESE FOR YOU?
OH, THAT WOULD BE A HUGE HELP.
POP
LATER!
ALETTA!
GIVE HIM A HAND!
TWITCH
OKAY!
BADUM
BADUM
GULP

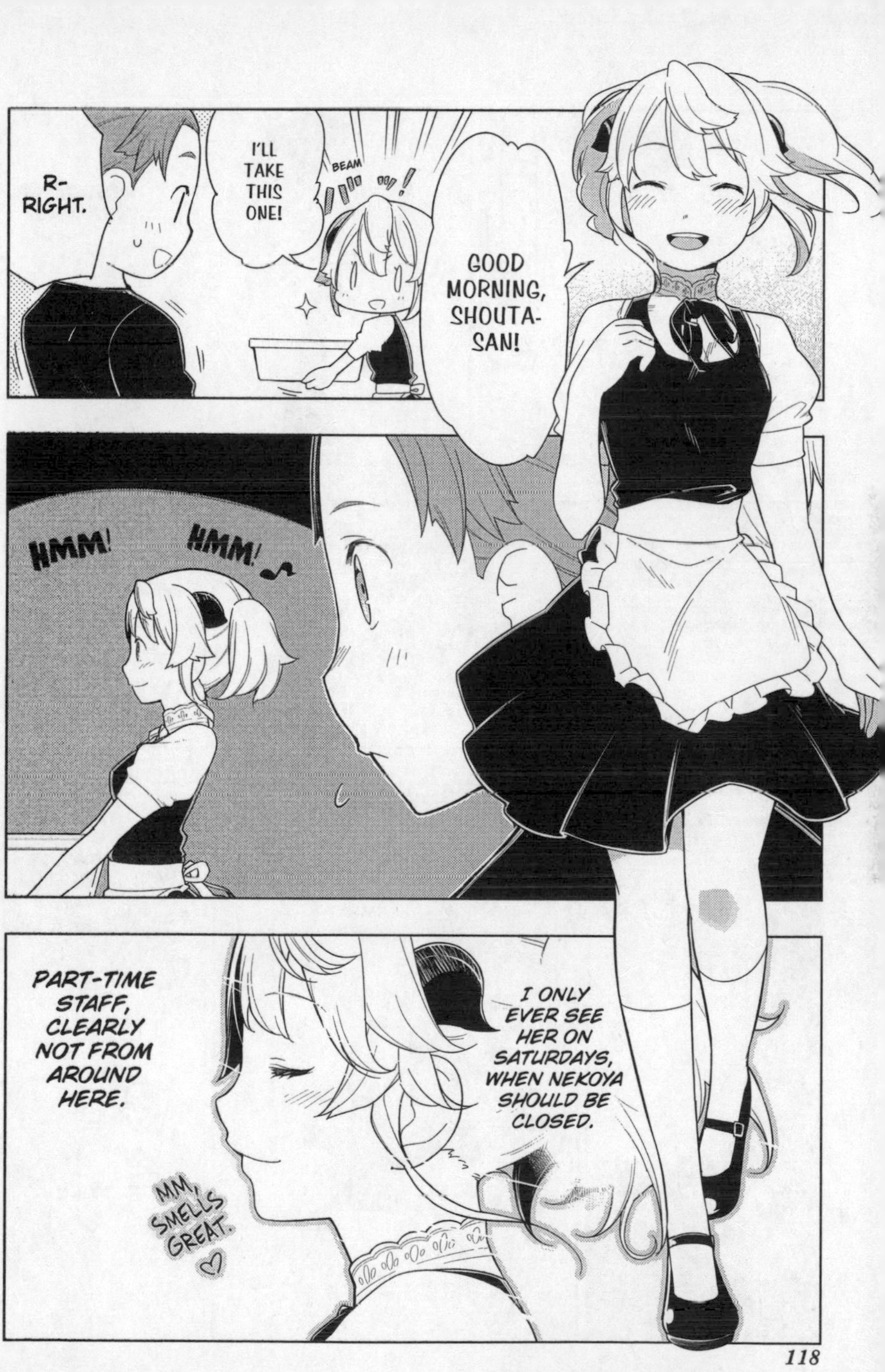
GOOD MORNING, SHOUTA-SAN!
BEAM
I'LL TAKE THIS ONE!
R-RIGHT.
HMM! HMM!
I ONLY EVER SEE HER ON SATURDAYS, WHEN NEKOYA SHOULD BE CLOSED.
PART-TIME STAFF, CLEARLY NOT FROM AROUND HERE.
MM, SMELLS GREAT.

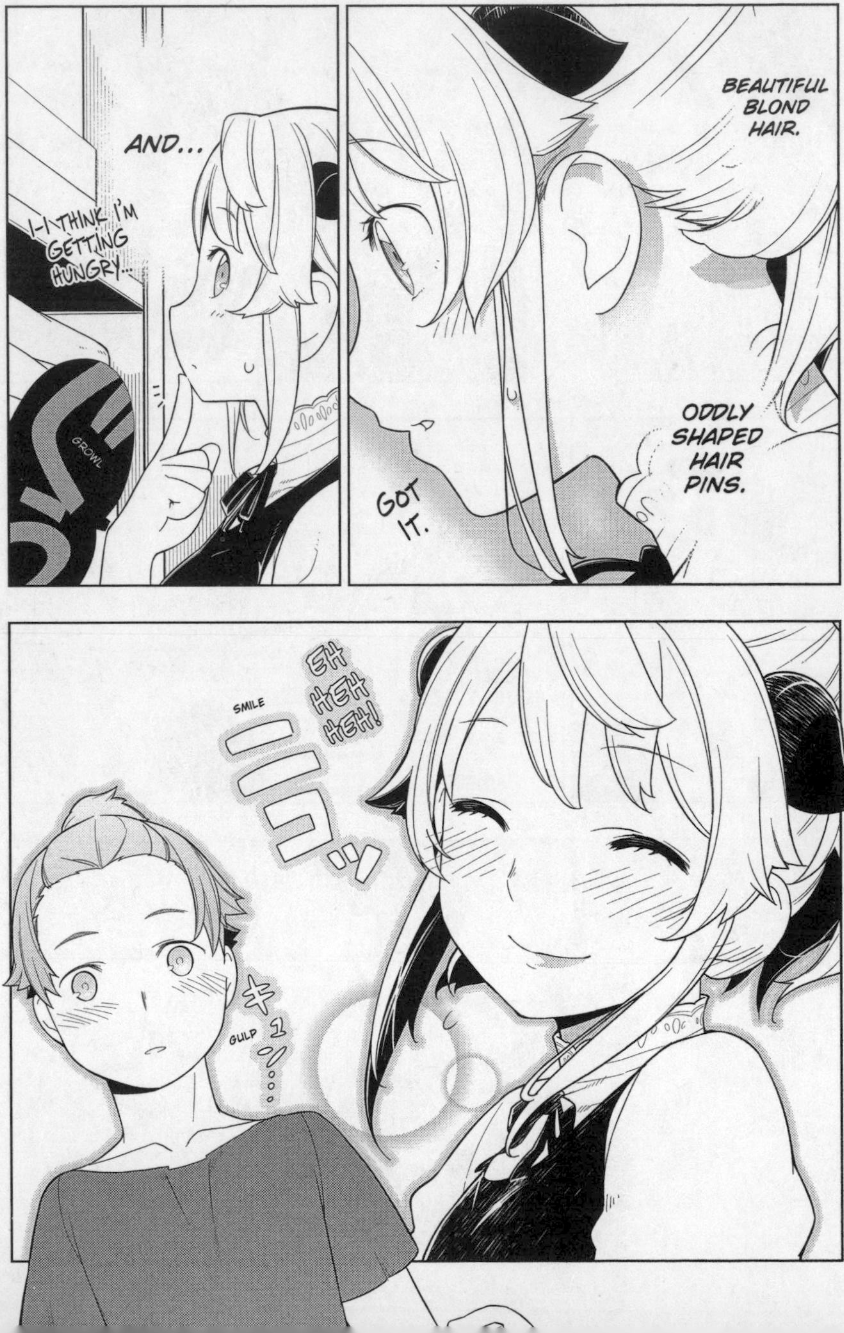
BEAUTIFUL BLOND HAIR.
ODDLY SHAPED HAIR PINS.
GOT IT.
AND...
I-I THINK I'M GETTING HUNGRY...
GROWL
EH HEH HEH!
SMILE
GULP

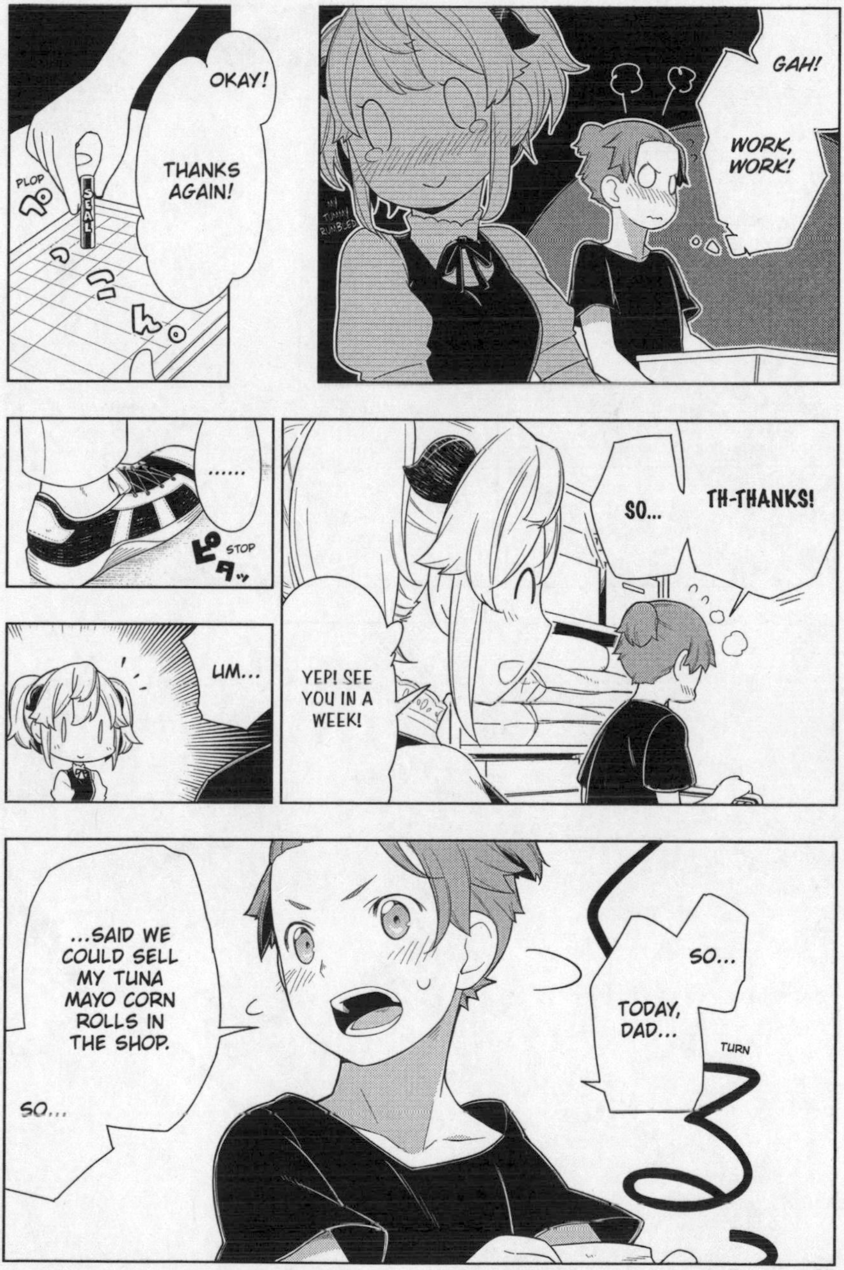
GAH!
WORK, WORK!
MY TUMMY RUMBLED
OKAY!
THANKS AGAIN!
PLOP
SEAL
SO... TH-THANKS!
YEP! SEE YOU IN A WEEK!
......
STOP
UM...
SO...
TODAY, DAD...
TURN
...SAID WE COULD SELL MY TUNA MAYO CORN ROLLS IN THE SHOP.
SO...

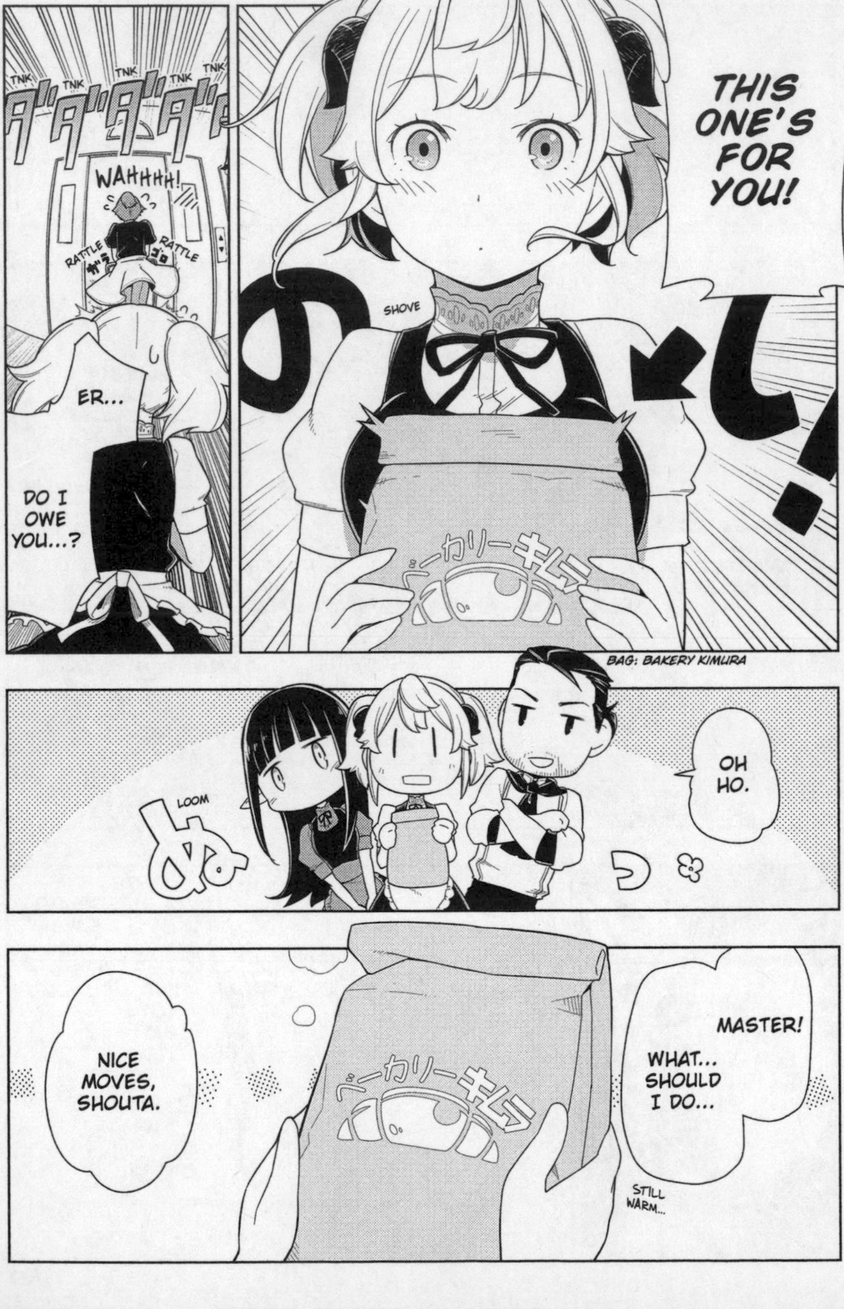
THIS ONE'S FOR YOU!
SHOVE
BAG: BAKERY KIMURA
TNK TNK TNK TNK TNK
WAHHHH!
RATTLE
RATTLE
ER...
DO I OWE YOU...?
OH HO.
LOOM
MASTER!
WHAT... SHOULD I DO...
STILL WARM...
NICE MOVES, SHOUTA.

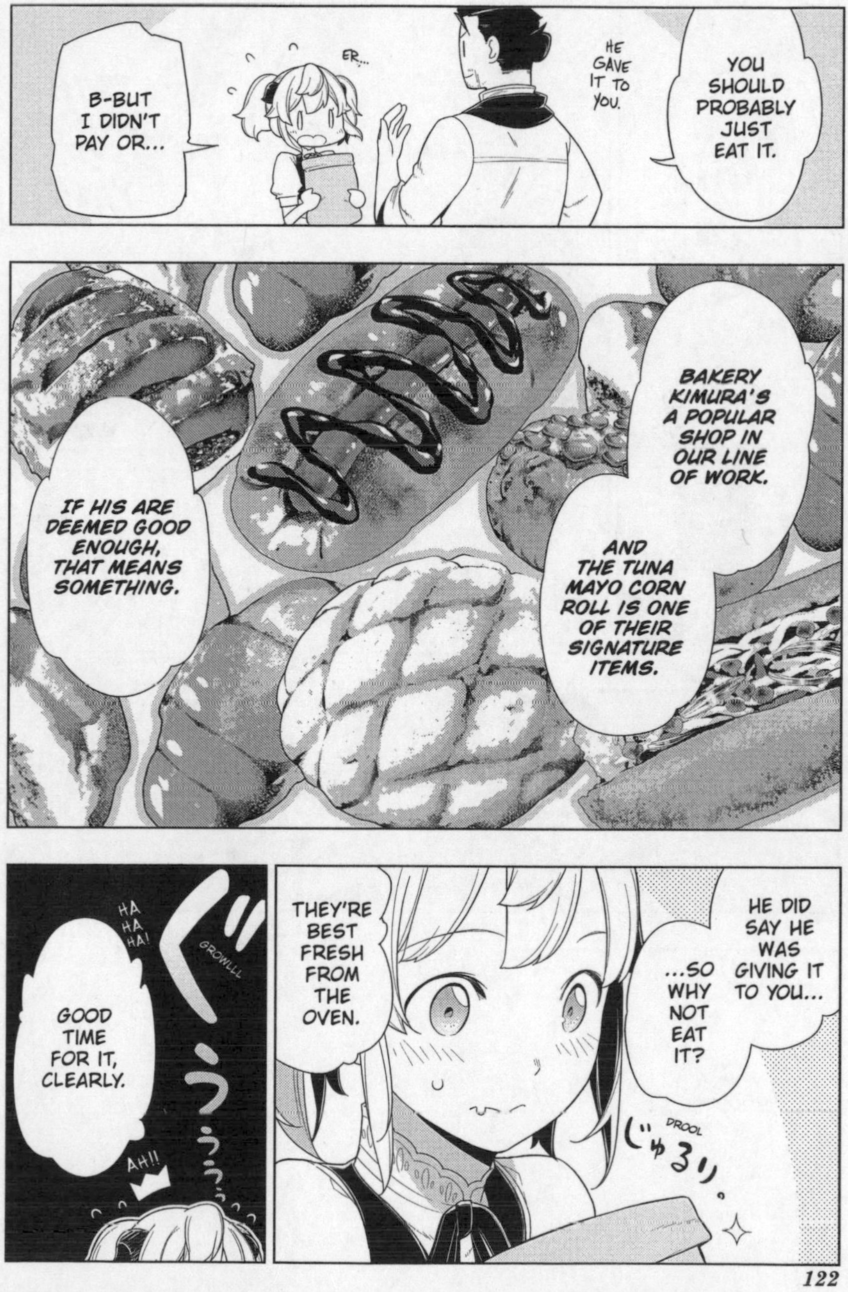
YOU SHOULD PROBABLY JUST EAT IT.
HE GAVE IT TO YOU.
ER...
B-BUT I DIDN'T PAY OR...
BAKERY KIMURA'S A POPULAR SHOP IN OUR LINE OF WORK.
AND THE TUNA MAYO CORN ROLL IS ONE OF THEIR SIGNATURE ITEMS.
IF HIS ARE DEEMED GOOD ENOUGH, THAT MEANS SOMETHING.
HE DID SAY HE WAS GIVING IT TO YOU...
...SO WHY NOT EAT IT?
THEY'RE BEST FRESH FROM THE OVEN.
DROOL
じゅるり
HA HA HA!
GROWLLL
GOOD TIME FOR IT, CLEARLY.
AH!!

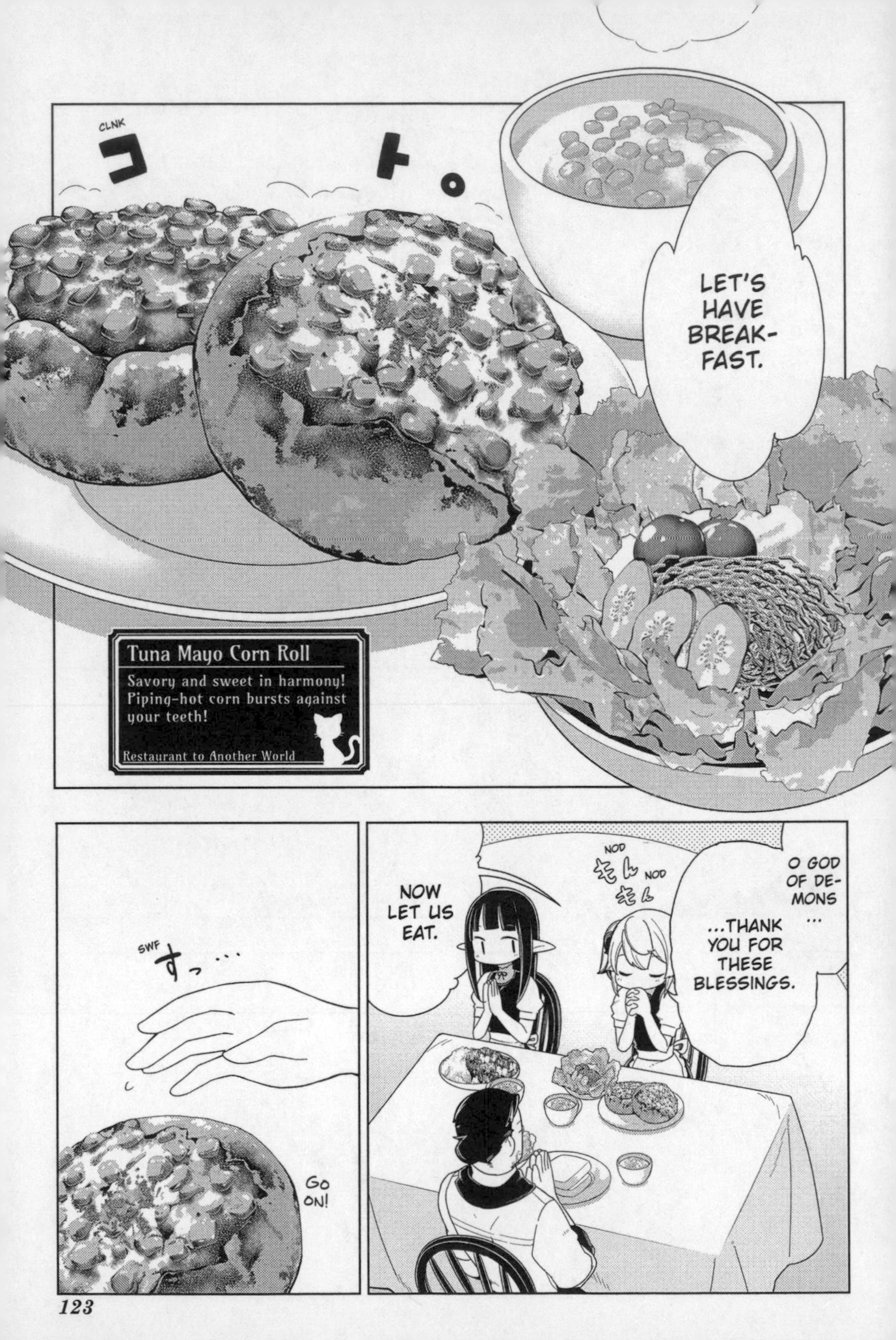
LET'S HAVE BREAK-FAST.
CLNK
コト。
Tuna Mayo Corn Roll
Savory and sweet in harmony! Piping-hot corn bursts against your teeth!
Restaurant to Another World
O GOD OF DE-MONS...
...THANK YOU FOR THESE BLESSINGS.
NOD もん NOD もん
NOW LET US EAT.
SWF す…
GO ON!

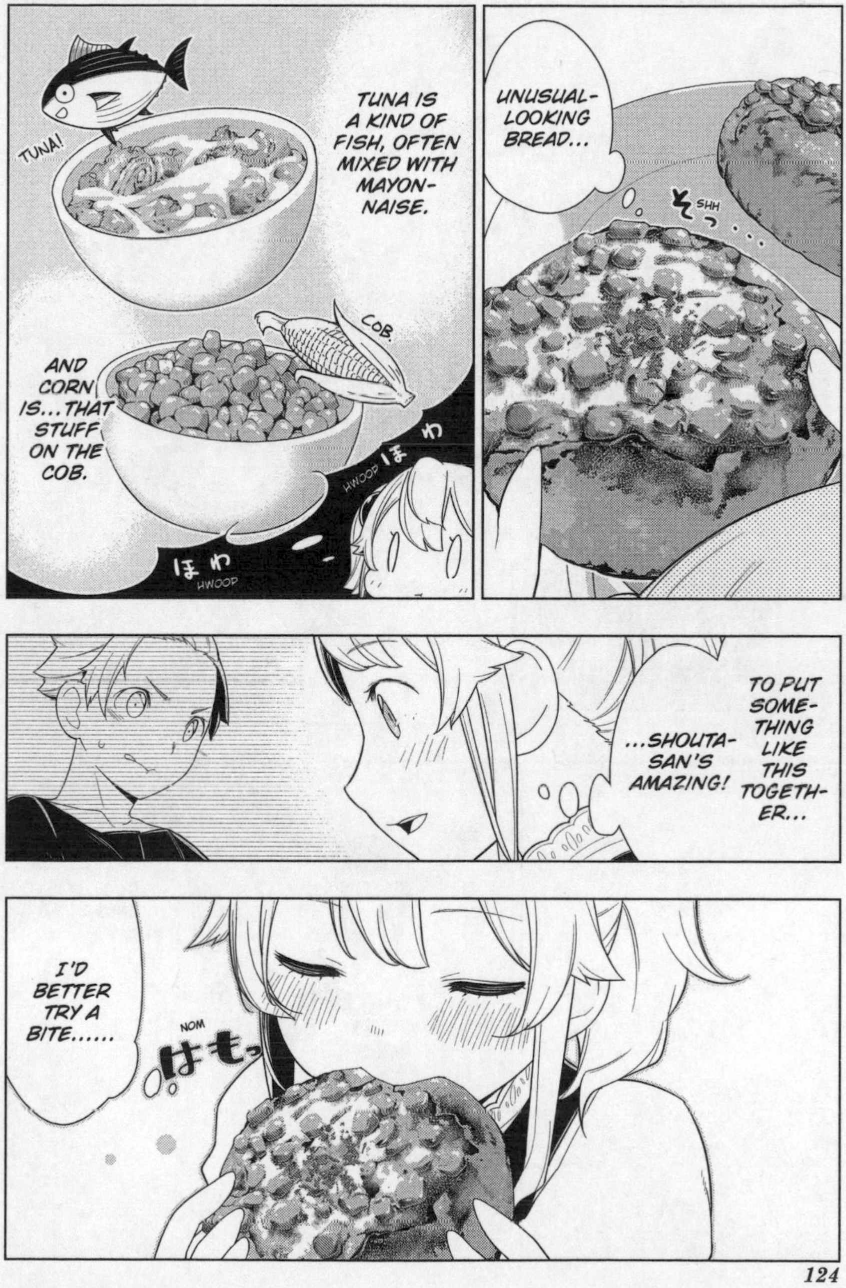
UNUSUAL-LOOKING BREAD...
そっ
SHH
TUNA IS A KIND OF FISH, OFTEN MIXED WITH MAYONNAISE.
TUNA!
AND CORN IS...THAT STUFF ON THE COB.
COB.
ほわ
HWOOP
ほわ
HWOOP
TO PUT SOMETHING LIKE THIS TOGETHER...
...SHOUTA-SAN'S AMAZING!
はもっ
NOM
I'D BETTER TRY A BITE......

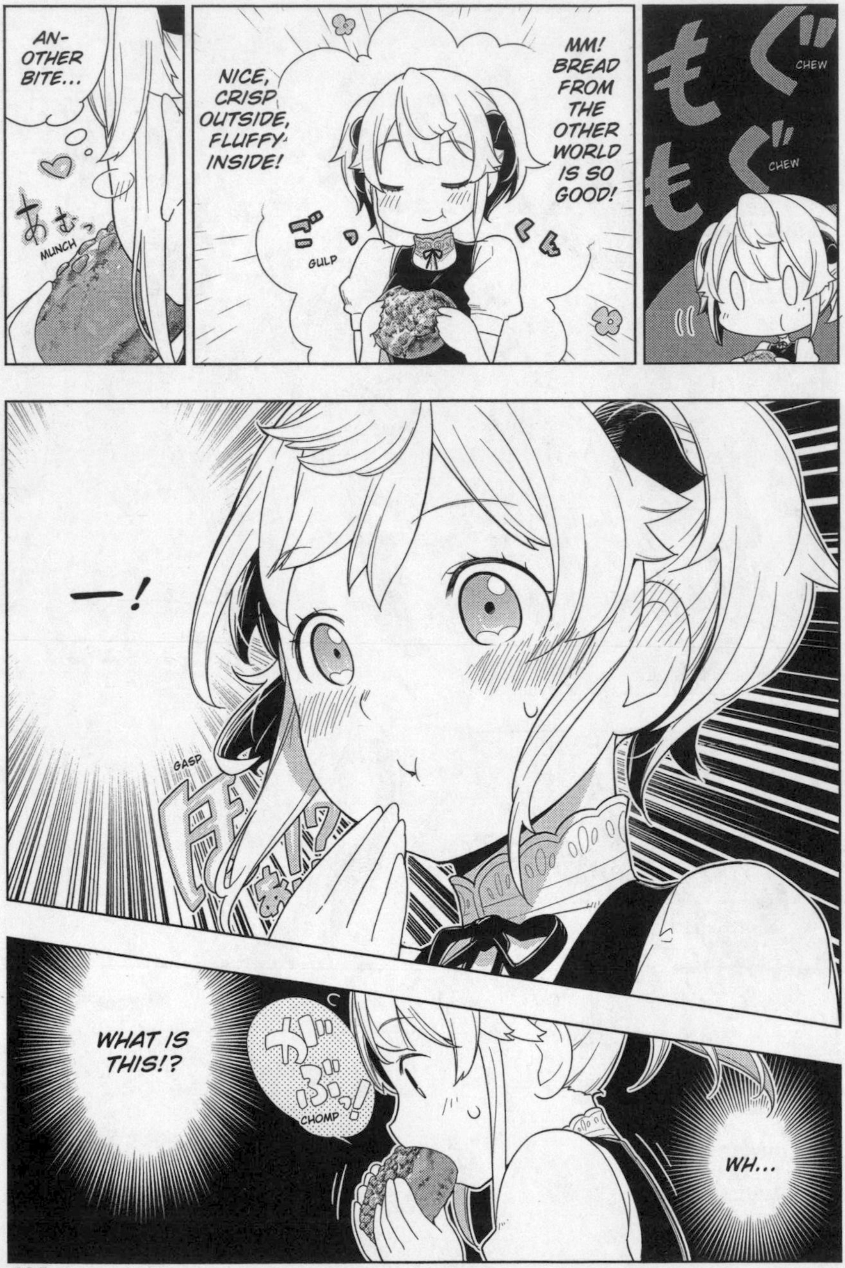
もぐもぐ
CHEW
CHEW
MM! BREAD FROM THE OTHER WORLD IS SO GOOD!
NICE, CRISP OUTSIDE, FLUFFY INSIDE!
ごっくん
GULP
AN-OTHER BITE...
あむっ
MUNCH
ーー!
GASP
WH...
WHAT IS THIS!?
CHOMP

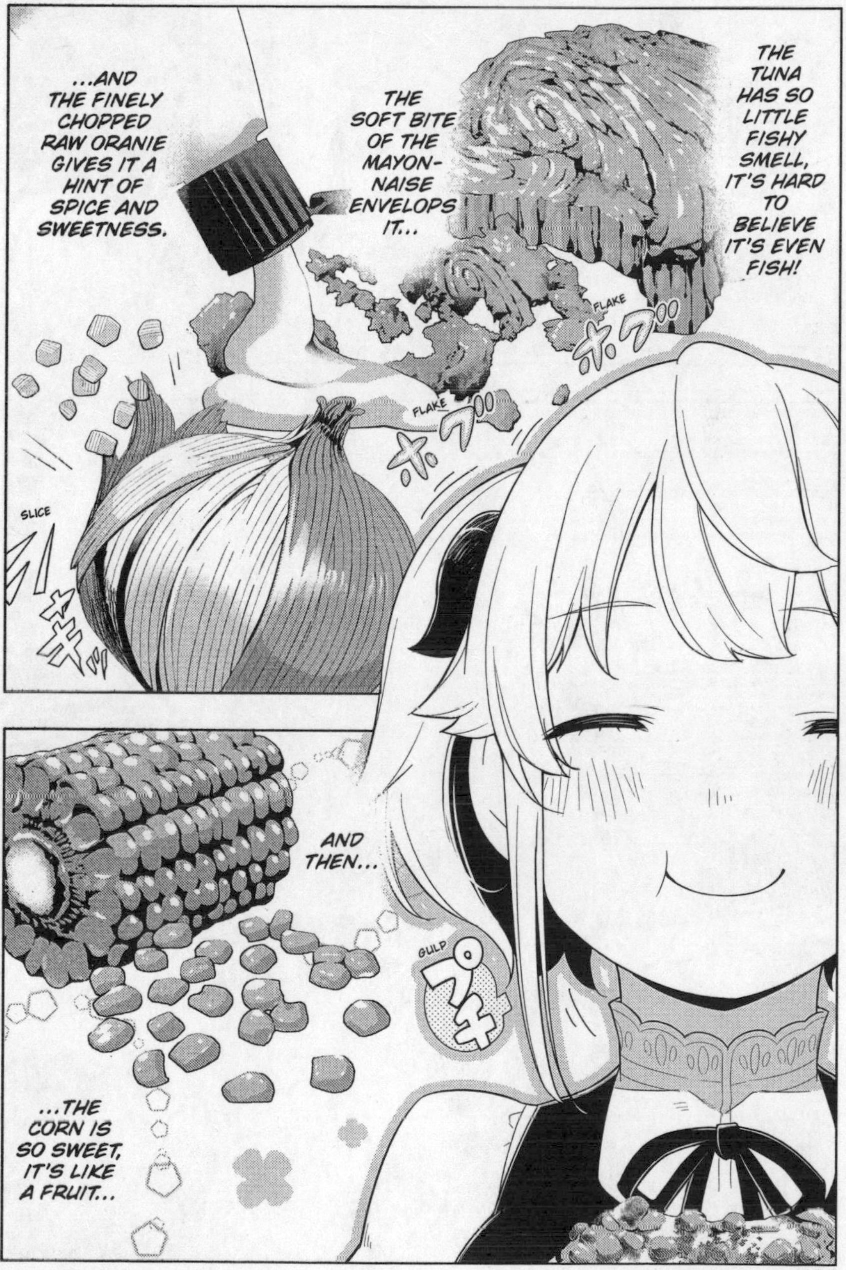
THE TUNA HAS SO LITTLE FISHY SMELL, IT'S HARD TO BELIEVE IT'S EVEN FISH!
FLAKE
THE SOFT BITE OF THE MAYON-NAISE ENVELOPS IT...
FLAKE
...AND THE FINELY CHOPPED RAW ORANIE GIVES IT A HINT OF SPICE AND SWEETNESS.
SLICE
AND THEN...
GULP
...THE CORN IS SO SWEET, IT'S LIKE A FRUIT...

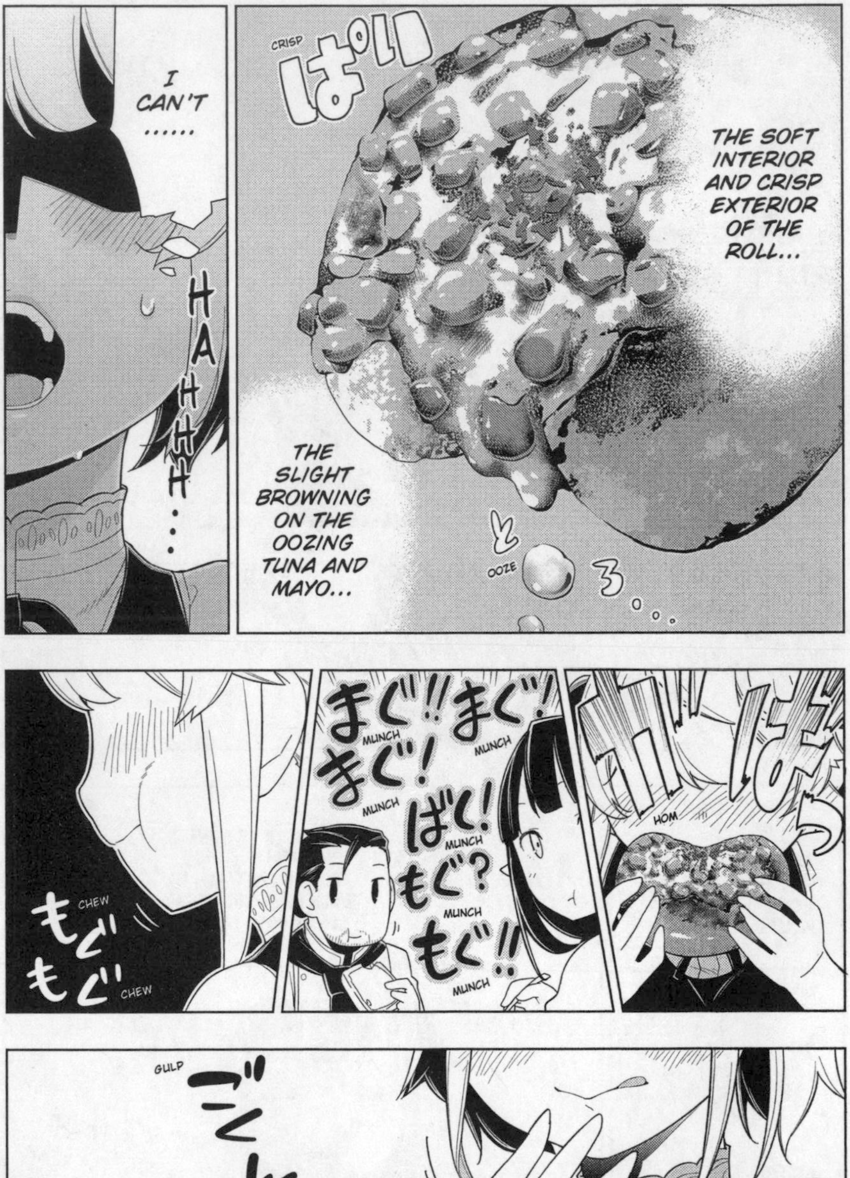
CRISP
THE SOFT INTERIOR AND CRISP EXTERIOR OF THE ROLL...
THE SLIGHT BROWNING ON THE OOZING TUNA AND MAYO...
OOZE
I CAN'T ......
HAHHHH...
HOM
まぐ!!まぐ!
MUNCH
MUNCH
まぐ!
MUNCH
ばく!
MUNCH
もぐ?
MUNCH
もぐ!!
MUNCH
もぐもぐ
CHEW
CHEW
GULP
ごくんっ

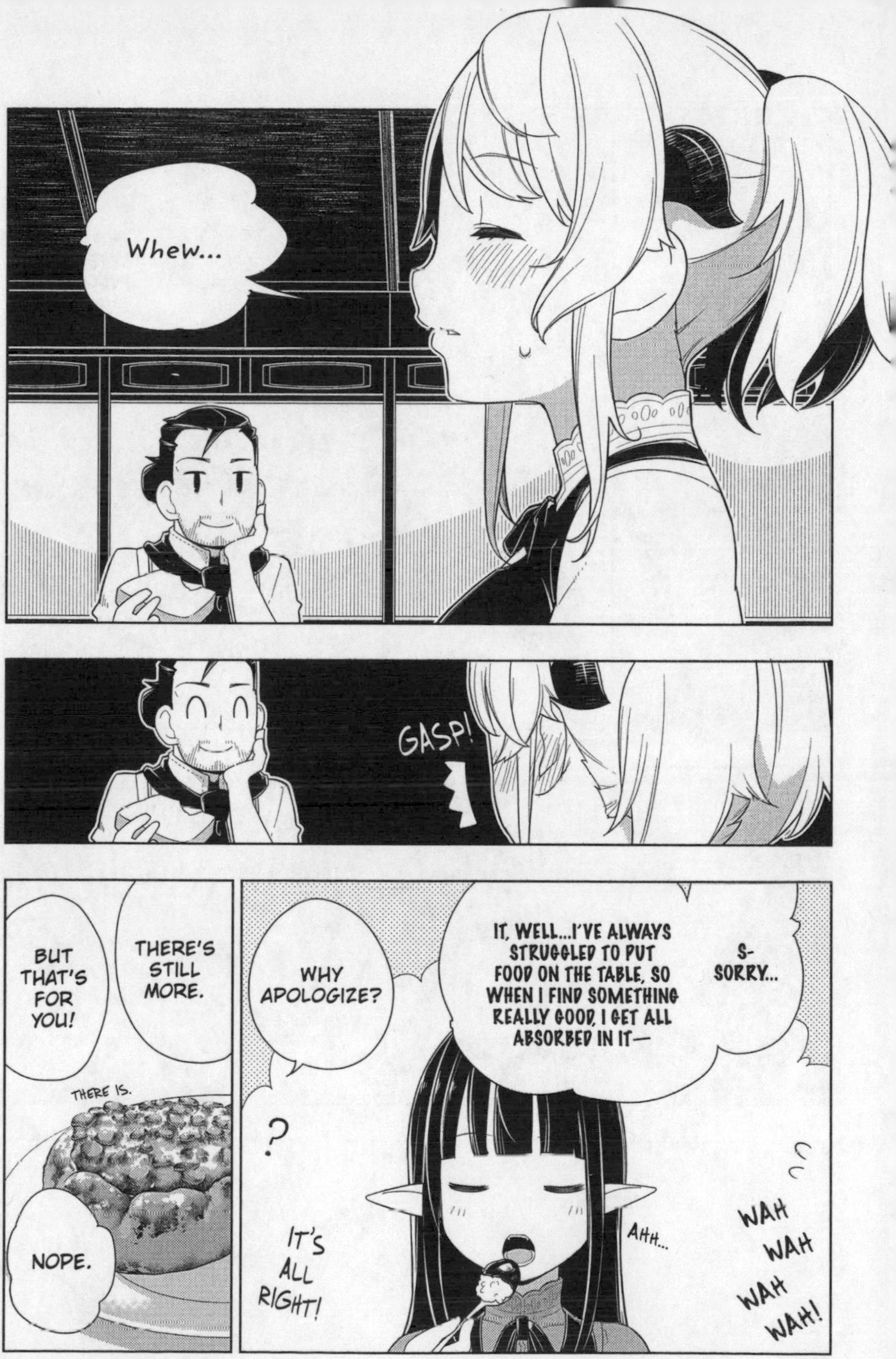
Whew...
GASP!
S-SORRY...
IT, WELL...I'VE ALWAYS STRUGGLED TO PUT FOOD ON THE TABLE, SO WHEN I FIND SOMETHING REALLY GOOD, I GET ALL ABSORBED IN IT—
WHY APOLOGIZE?
?
WAH WAH WAH WAH!
AHH...
IT'S ALL RIGHT!
THERE'S STILL MORE.
BUT THAT'S FOR YOU!
THERE IS.
NOPE.

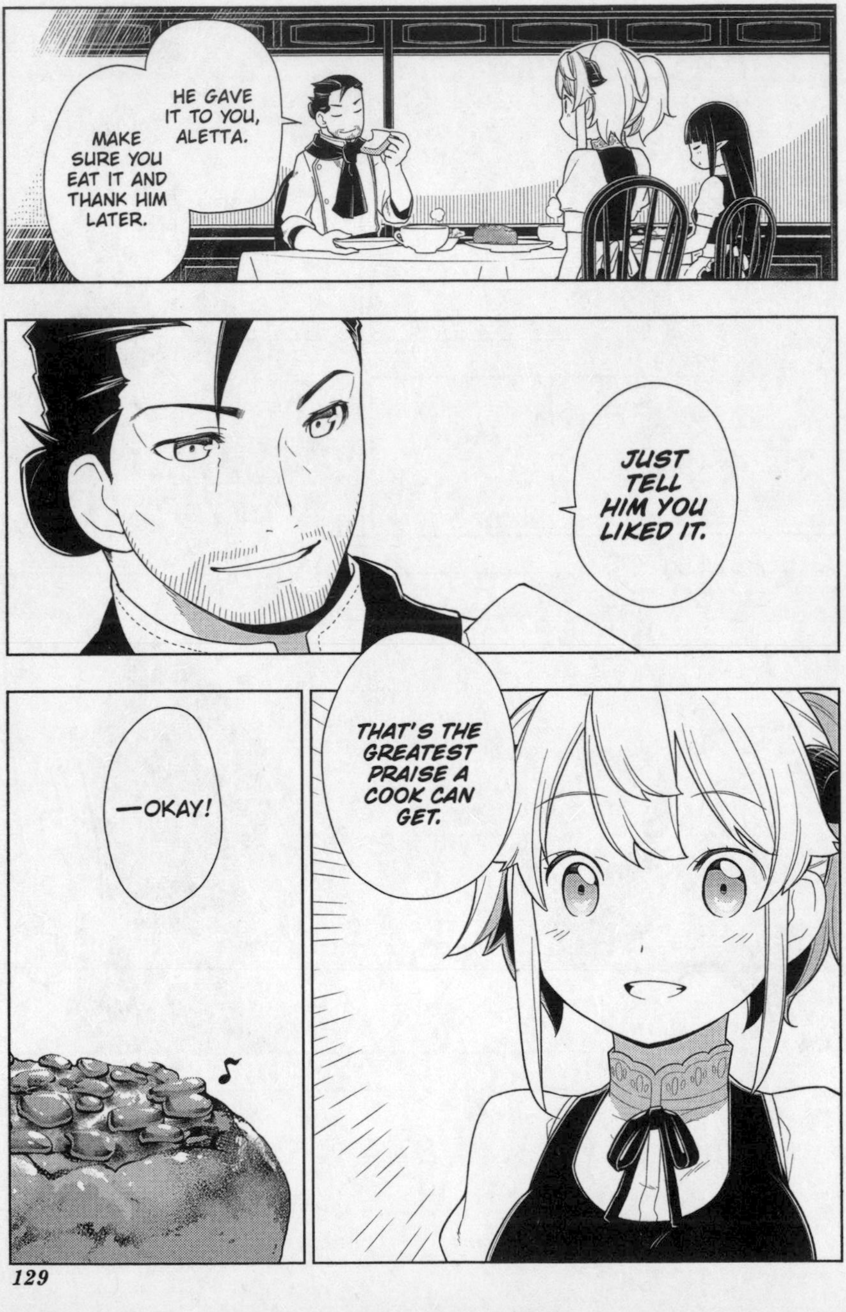
HE GAVE IT TO YOU, ALETTA.
MAKE SURE YOU EAT IT AND THANK HIM LATER.
JUST TELL HIM YOU LIKED IT.
THAT'S THE GREATEST PRAISE A COOK CAN GET.
—OKAY!
♪

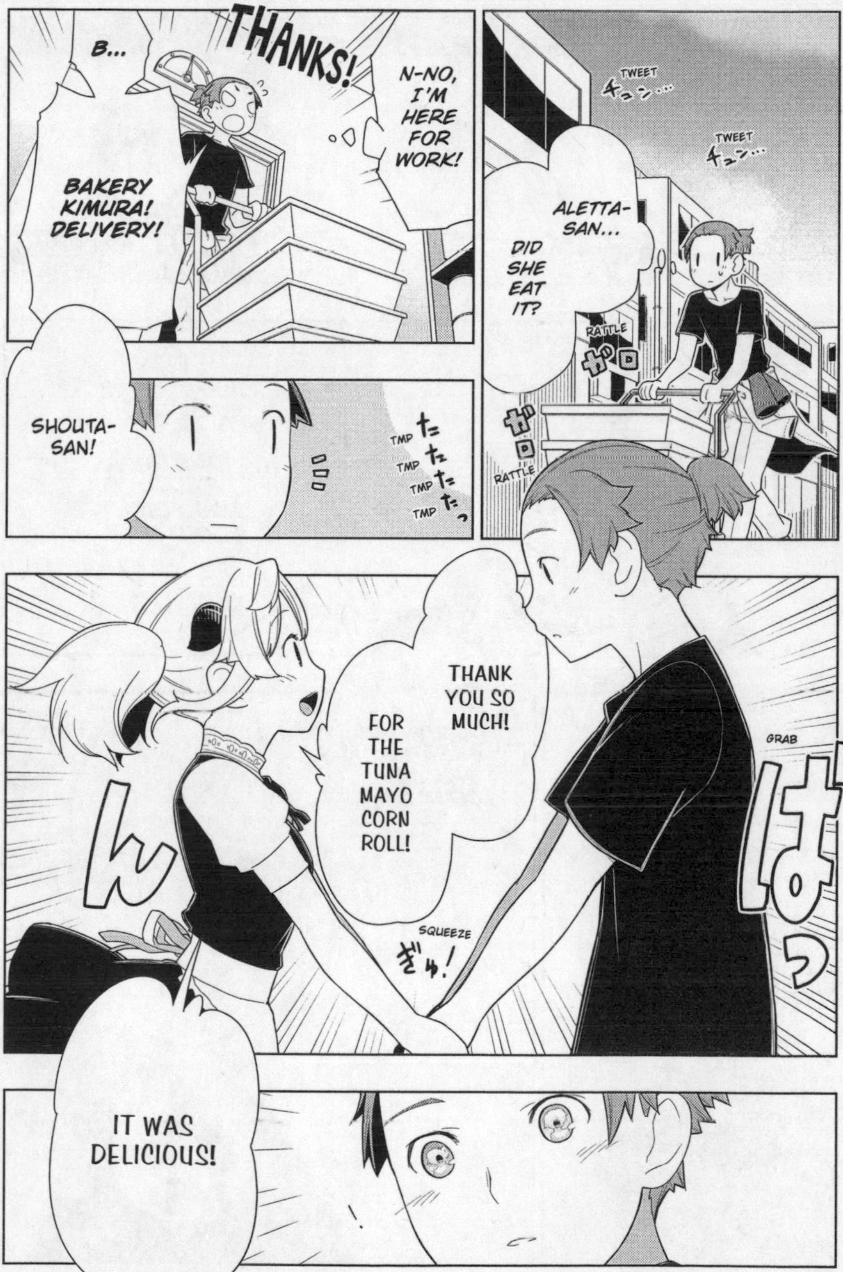
TWEET
TWEET
ALETTA-SAN...
DID SHE EAT IT?
RATTLE
RATTLE
THANKS!
N-NO, I'M HERE FOR WORK!
B...
BAKERY KIMURA! DELIVERY!
TMP
TMP
TMP
TMP
SHOUTA-SAN!
GRAB
THANK YOU SO MUCH!
FOR THE TUNA MAYO CORN ROLL!
SQUEEZE
IT WAS DELICIOUS!

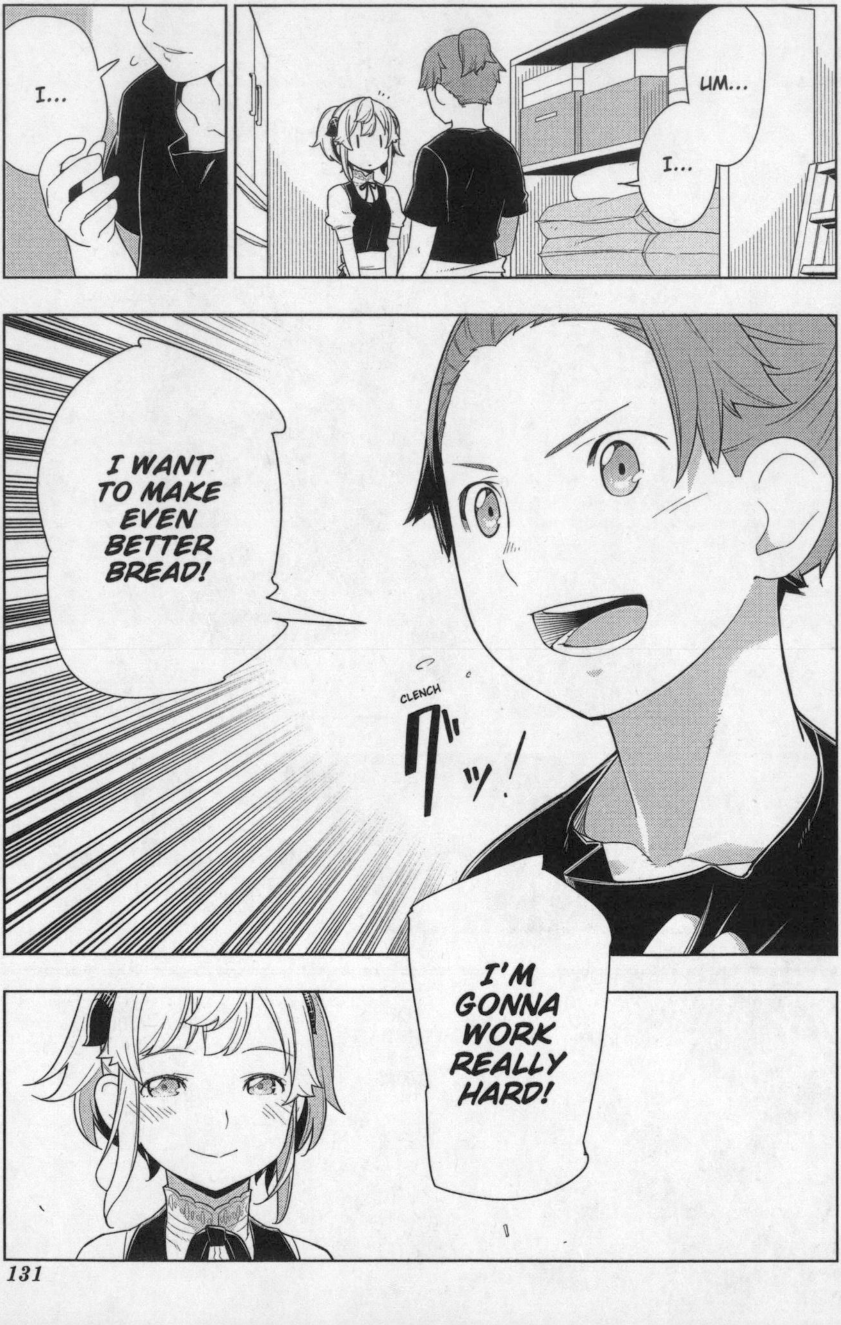
UM...
I...
I...
I WANT TO MAKE EVEN BETTER BREAD!
CLENCH
グッ!
I'M GONNA WORK REALLY HARD!

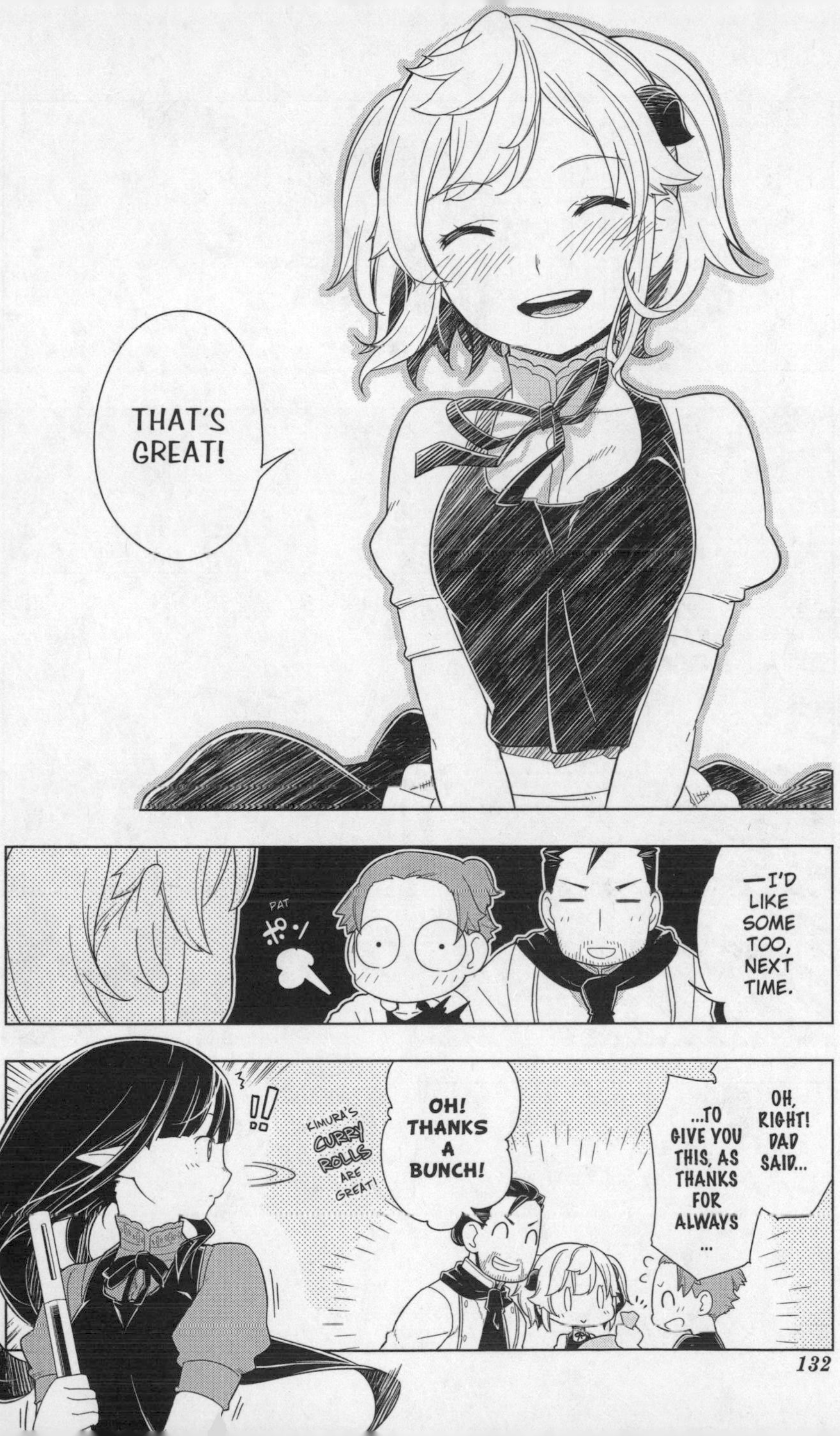
THAT'S GREAT!
—I'D LIKE SOME TOO, NEXT TIME.
PAT
OH, RIGHT! DAD SAID...
...TO GIVE YOU THIS, AS THANKS FOR ALWAYS ...
OH! THANKS A BUNCH!
KIMURA'S CURRY ROLLS ARE GREAT!
!!

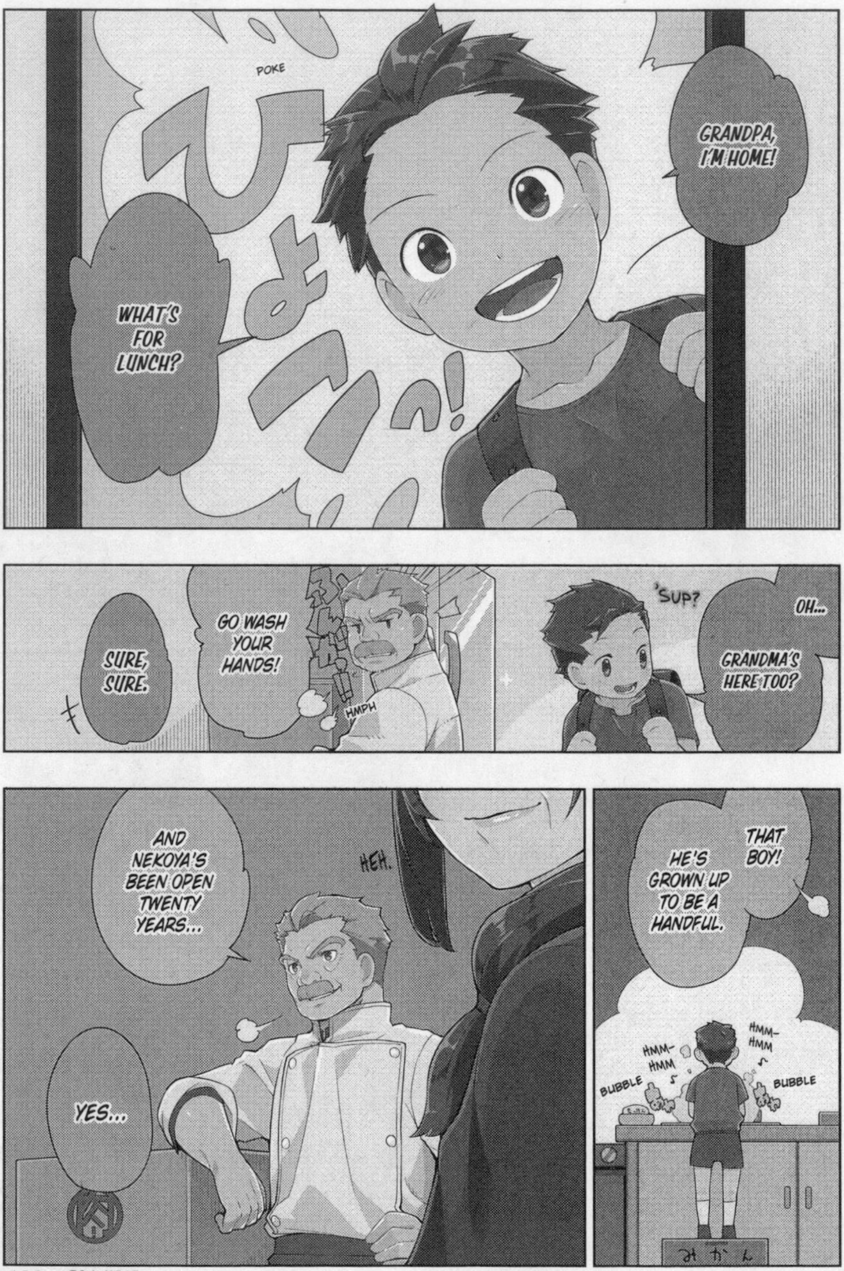
GRANDPA, I'M HOME!
POKE
WHAT'S FOR LUNCH?
OH...
GRANDMA'S HERE TOO?
'SUP?
GO WASH YOUR HANDS!
HMPH
SURE, SURE.
THAT BOY!
HE'S GROWN UP TO BE A HANDFUL.
HMM-HMM
HMM-HMM
BUBBLE
BUBBLE
HEH.
AND NEKOYA'S BEEN OPEN TWENTY YEARS...
YES...

BOX: MEAT

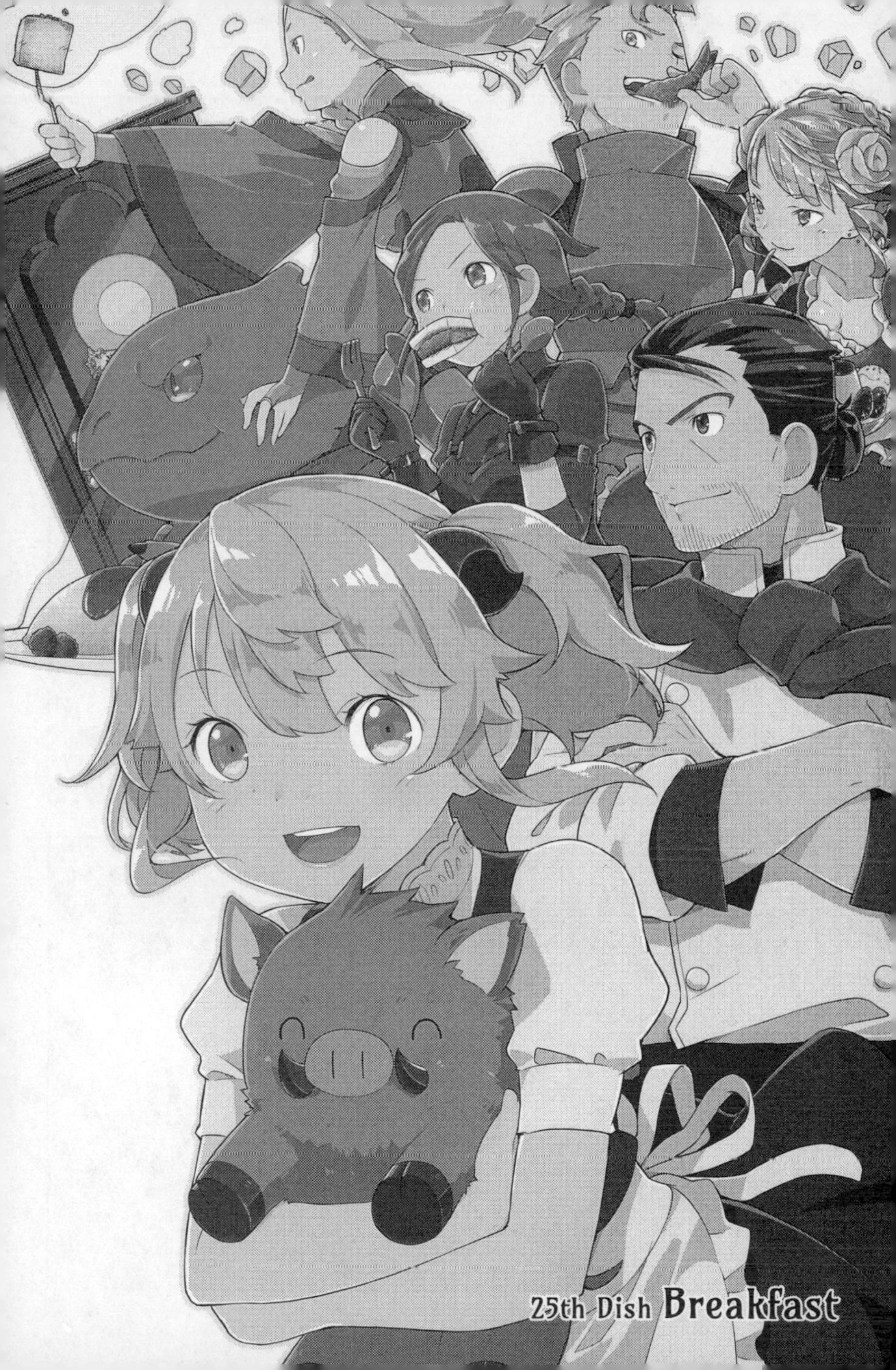
25th Dish Breakfast

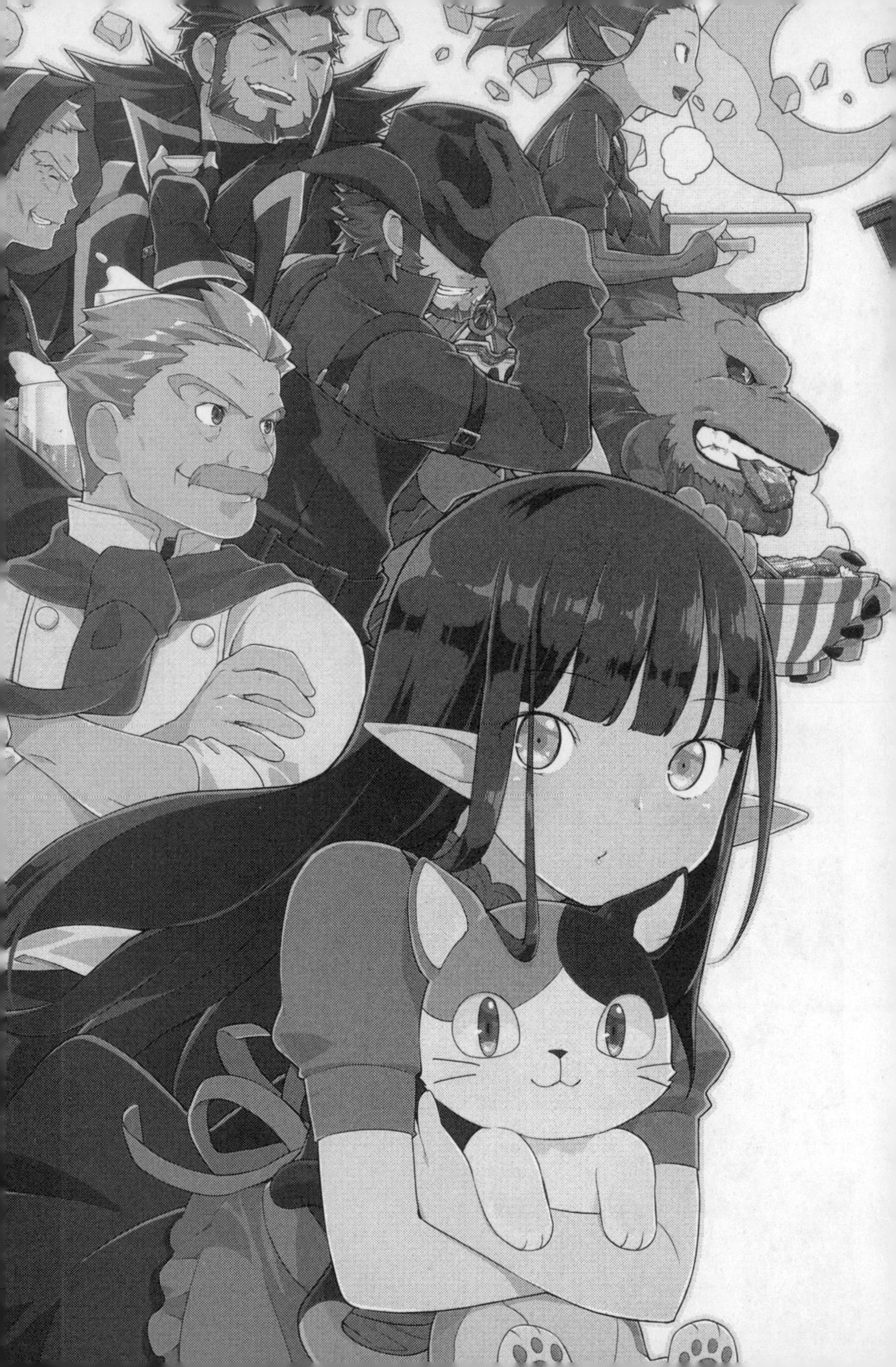

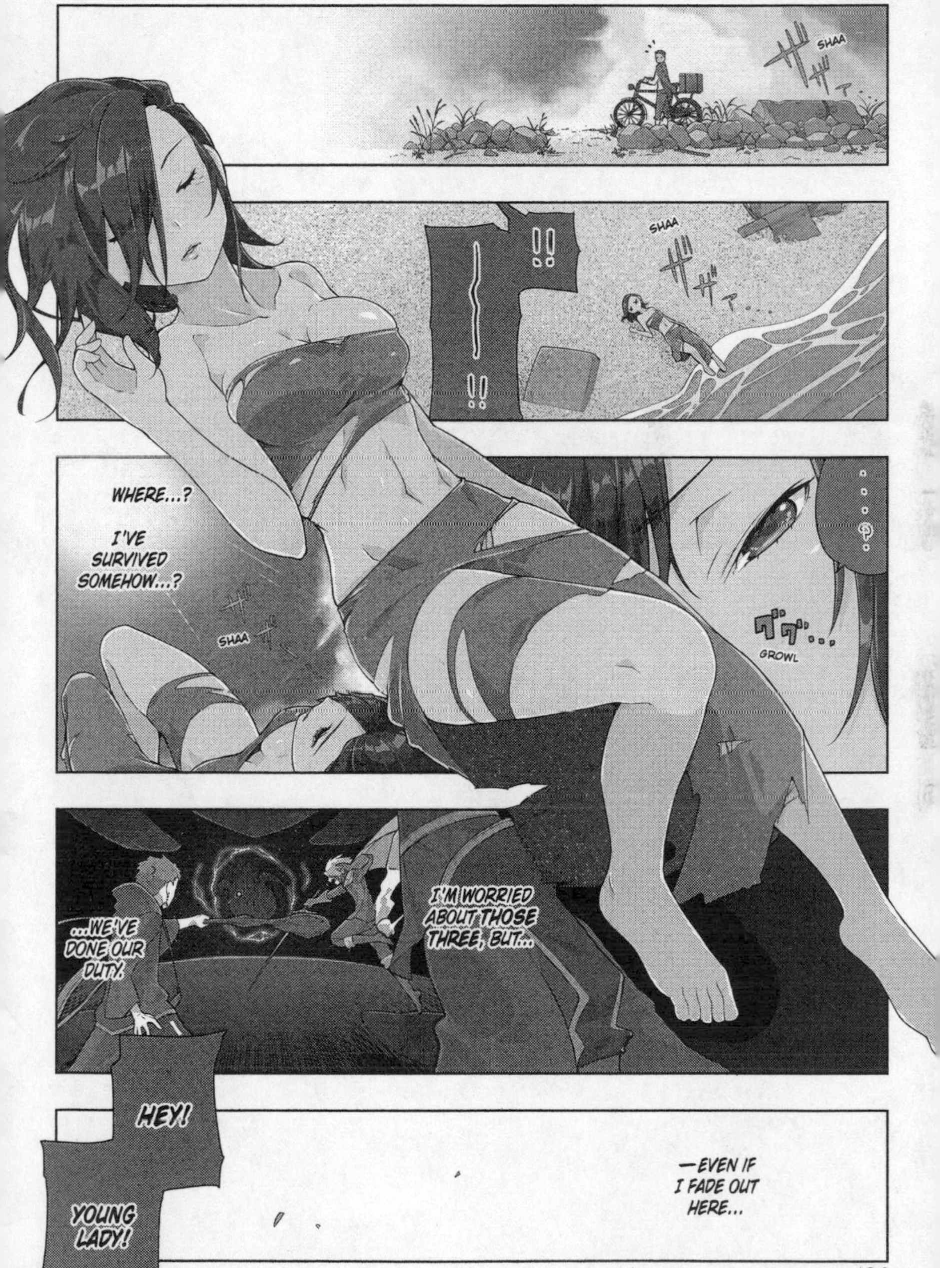
SHAA
!!
—
!!
SHAA
...?
GROWL
WHERE...?
I'VE SURVIVED SOMEHOW...?
SHAA
I'M WORRIED ABOUT THOSE THREE, BUT...
...WE'VE DONE OUR DUTY.
—EVEN IF I FADE OUT HERE...
HEY!
YOUNG LADY!

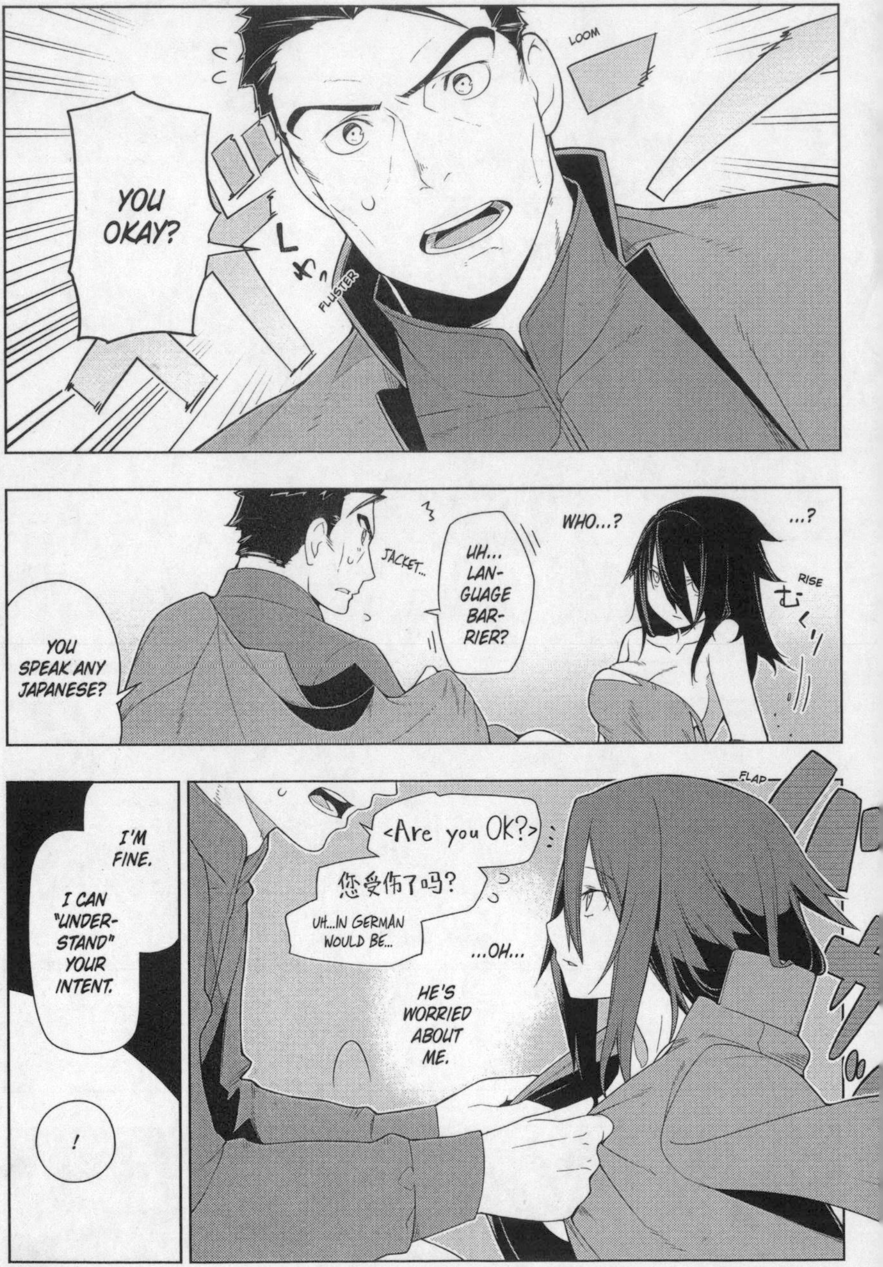
LOOM
YOU OKAY?
FLUSTER
...?
RISE
WHO...?
UH... LAN-GUAGE BAR-RIER?
JACKET...
YOU SPEAK ANY JAPANESE?
FLAP
<Are you OK?>
您受伤了吗?
UH...IN GERMAN WOULD BE...
...OH...
HE'S WORRIED ABOUT ME.
I'M FINE.
I CAN "UNDER-STAND" YOUR INTENT.
!

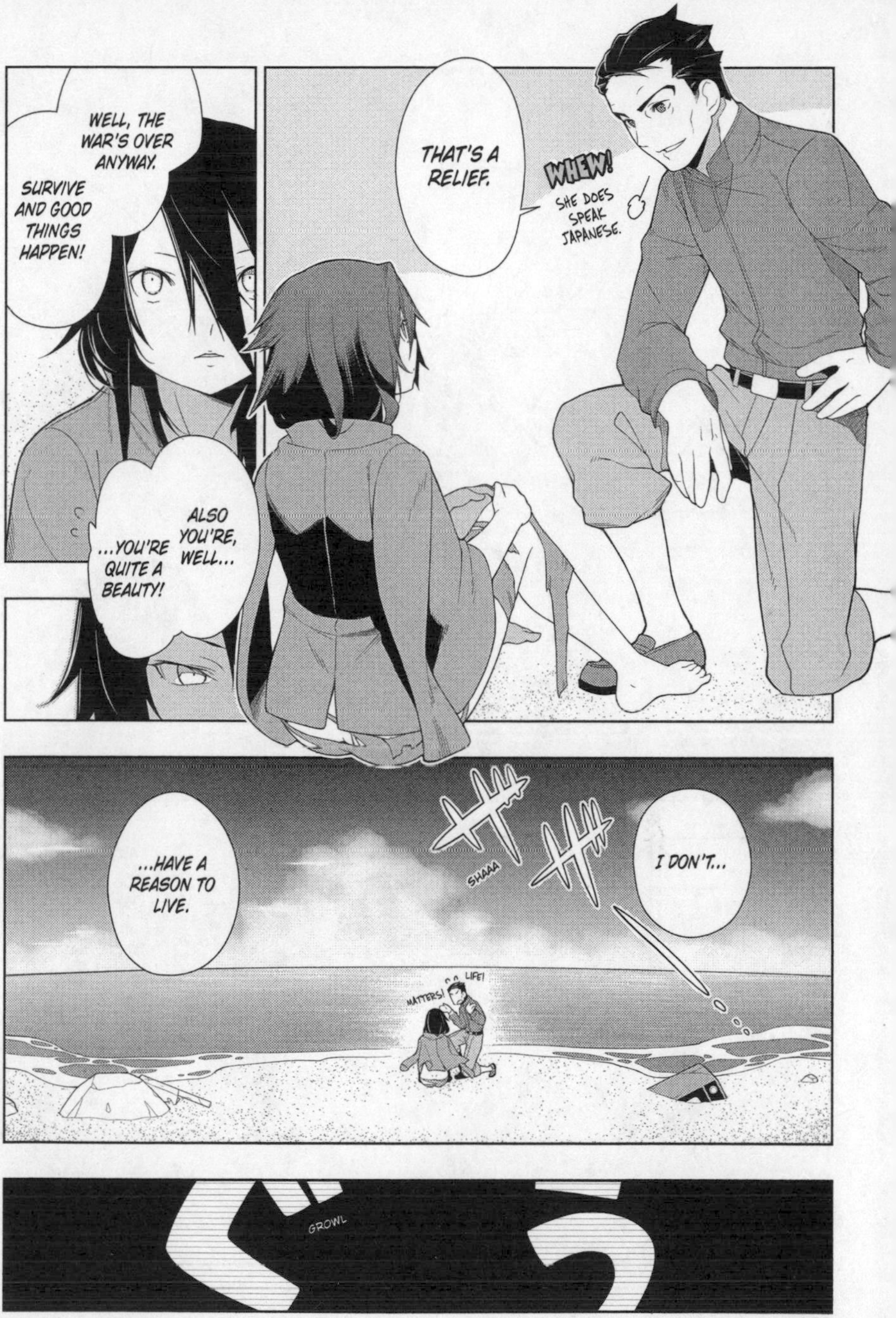
THAT'S A RELIEF.
WHEW!
SHE DOES SPEAK JAPANESE.
WELL, THE WAR'S OVER ANYWAY.
SURVIVE AND GOOD THINGS HAPPEN!
ALSO YOU'RE, WELL...
...YOU'RE QUITE A BEAUTY!
I DON'T...
SHAAA
...HAVE A REASON TO LIVE.
LIFE!
MATTERS!
GROWL

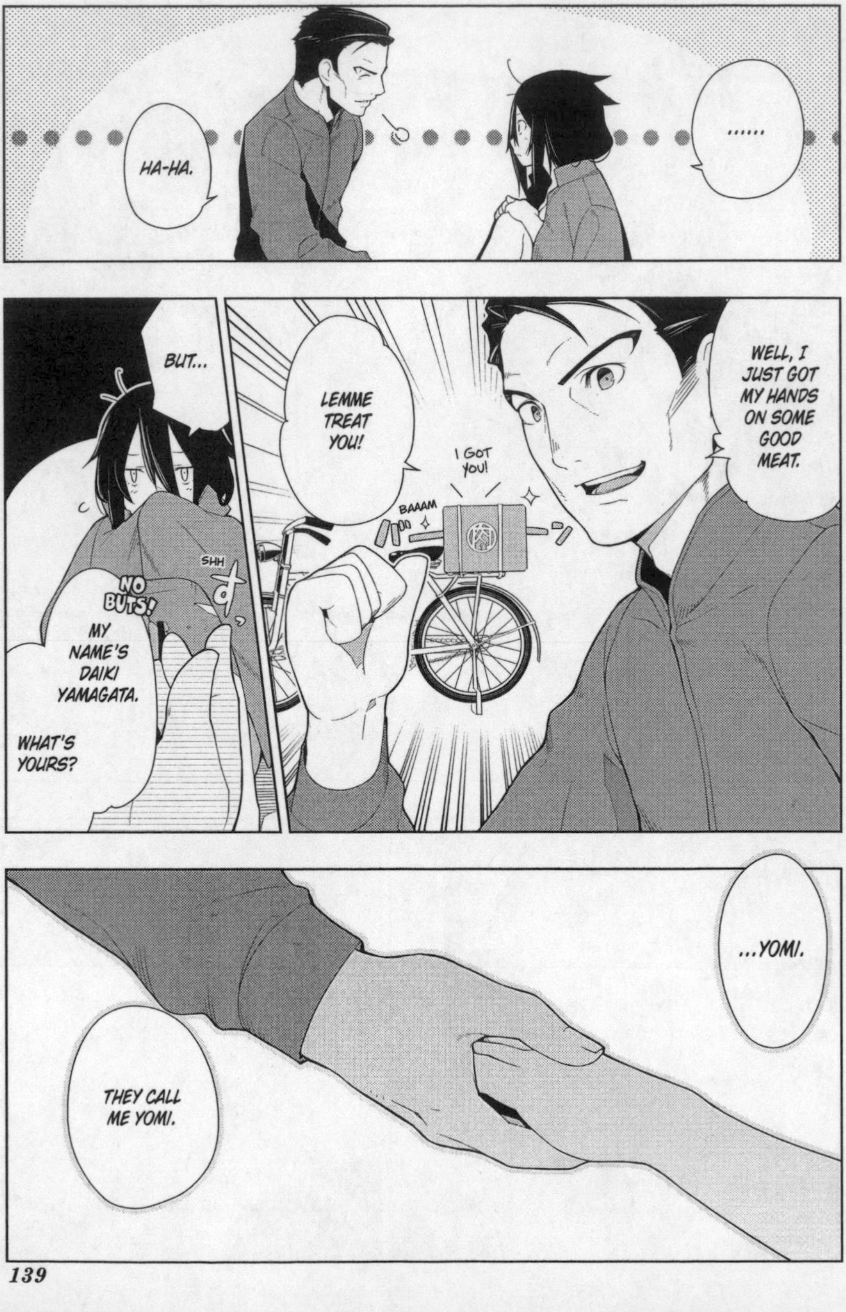
......
HA-HA.
WELL, I JUST GOT MY HANDS ON SOME GOOD MEAT.
LEMME TREAT YOU!
I GOT YOU!
BAAAM
BUT...
SHH
NO BUTS!
MY NAME'S DAIKI YAMAGATA.
WHAT'S YOURS?
...YOMI.
THEY CALL ME YOMI.

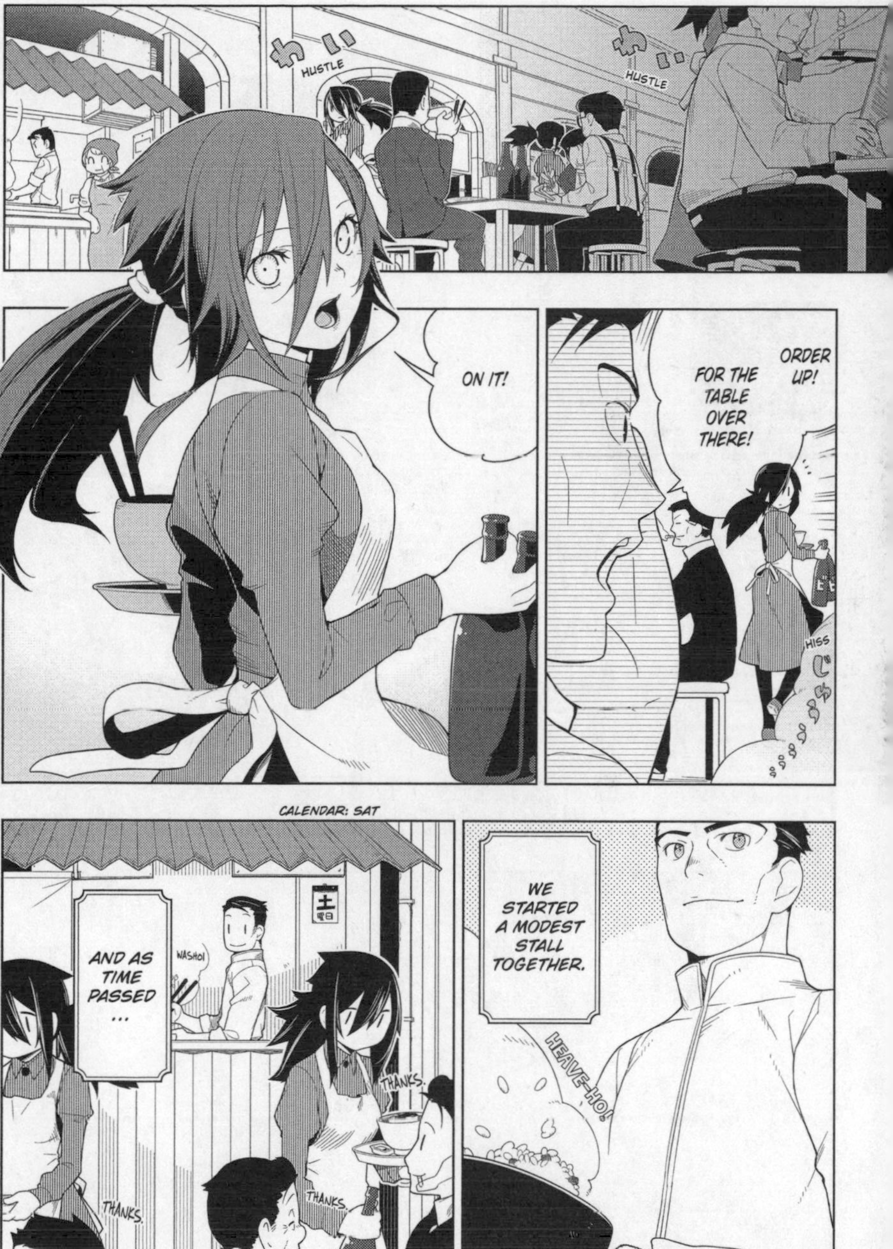
HUSTLE
HUSTLE
ORDER UP!
FOR THE TABLE OVER THERE!
HISS
ON IT!
WE STARTED A MODEST STALL TOGETHER.
HEAVE-HO!
CALENDAR: SAT
AND AS TIME PASSED...
WASHOI!
THANKS.
THANKS.
THANKS.

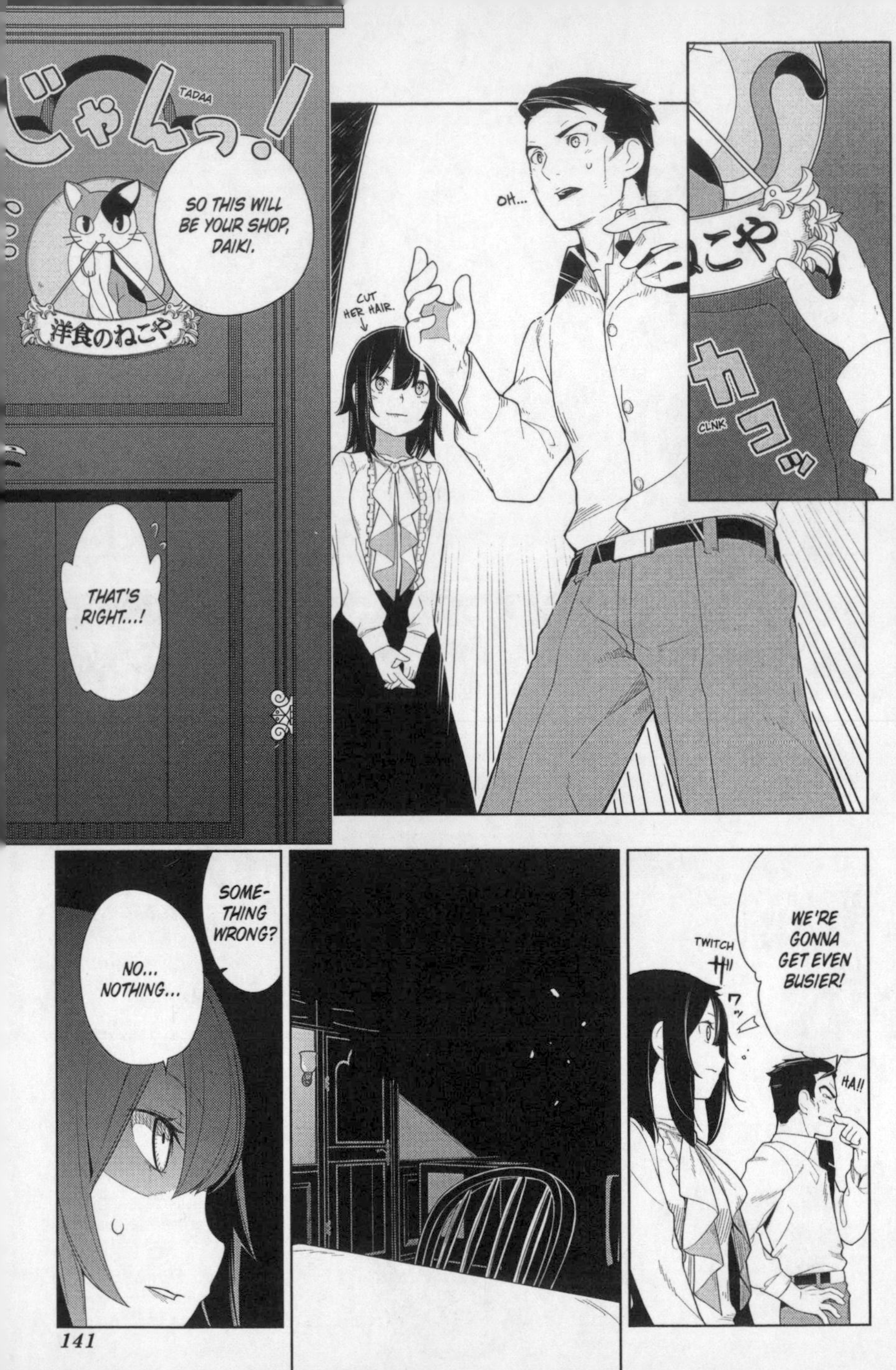
ねこや
カカッ
CLNK
OH...
CUT HER HAIR.
じゃんっ！
TADAA
洋食のねこや
SO THIS WILL BE YOUR SHOP, DAIKI.
THAT'S RIGHT...!
WE'RE GONNA GET EVEN BUSIER!
TWITCH
HA!!
SOME-THING WRONG?
NO... NOTHING...

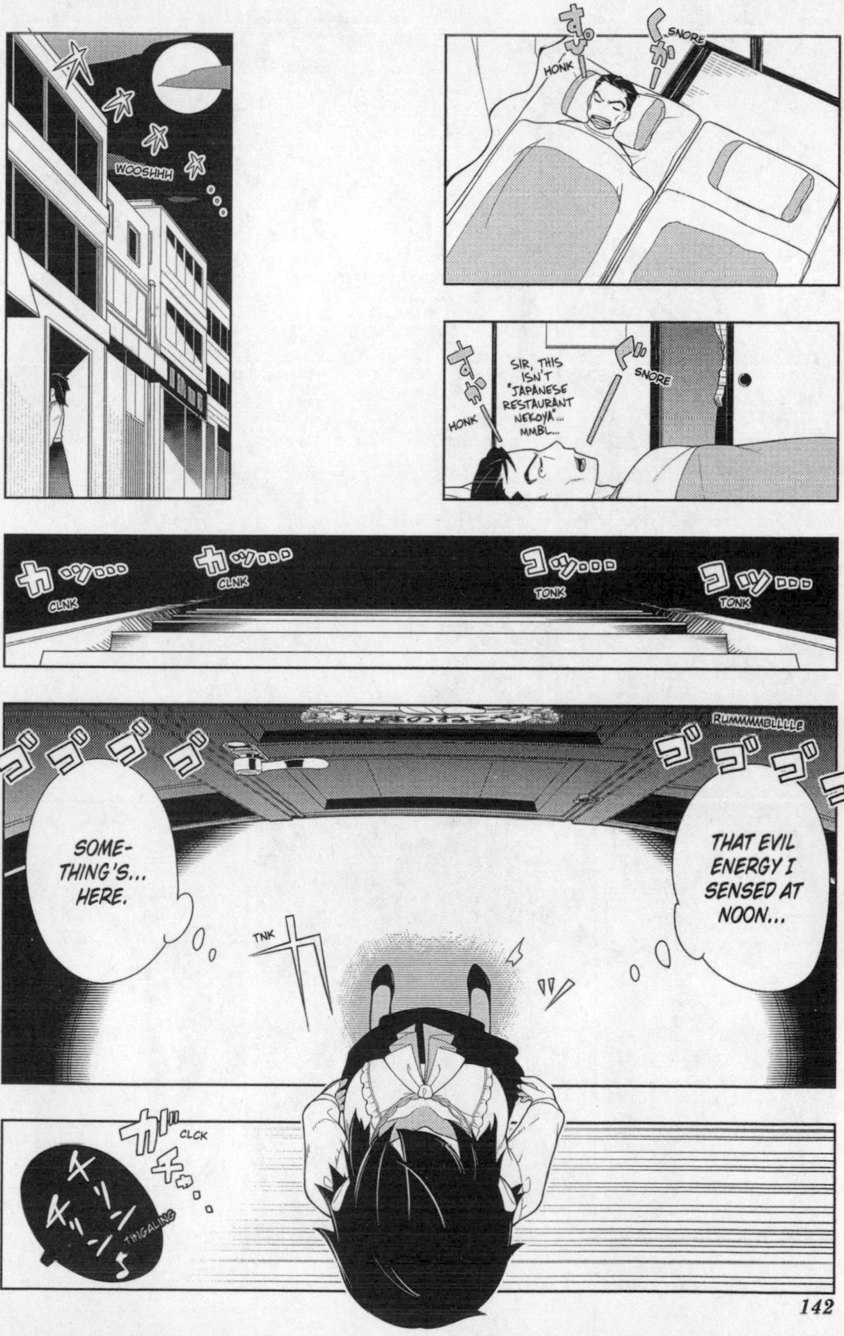
SNORE
HONK
SNORE
SIR, THIS ISN'T "JAPANESE RESTAURANT NEKOYA"... MMBL...
HONK
WOOSHHH
TONK
TONK
CLNK
CLNK
RUMMMMBLLLLE
THAT EVIL ENERGY I SENSED AT NOON...
SOME-THING'S... HERE.
TNK
CLCK
TINGALING

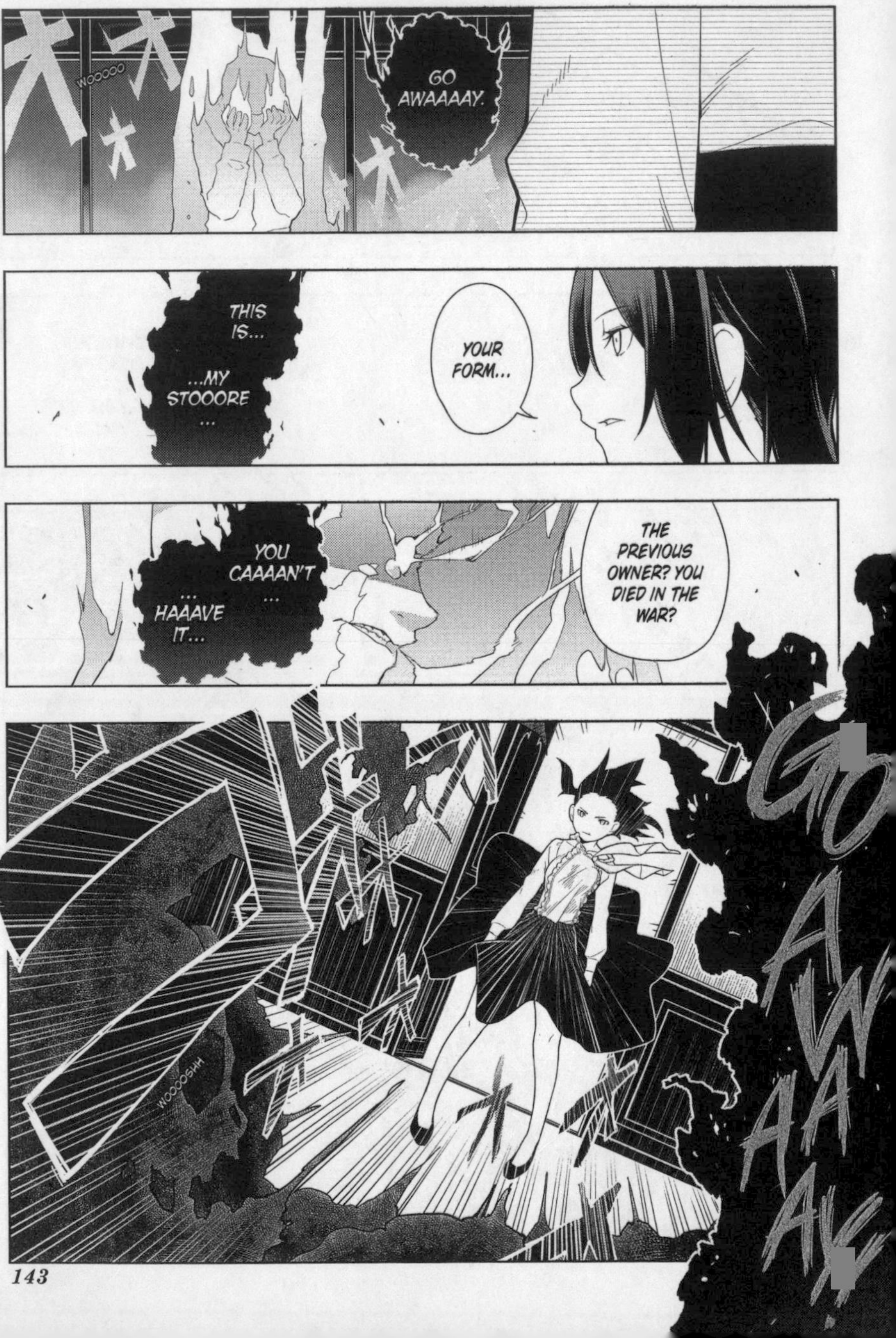
GO AWAAAAY.
WOOOOO
YOUR FORM...
THIS IS...
...MY STOOORE...
THE PREVIOUS OWNER? YOU DIED IN THE WAR?
YOU CAAAAN'T...
...HAAAVE IT...
GO AWAAAY
WOOOOSHH

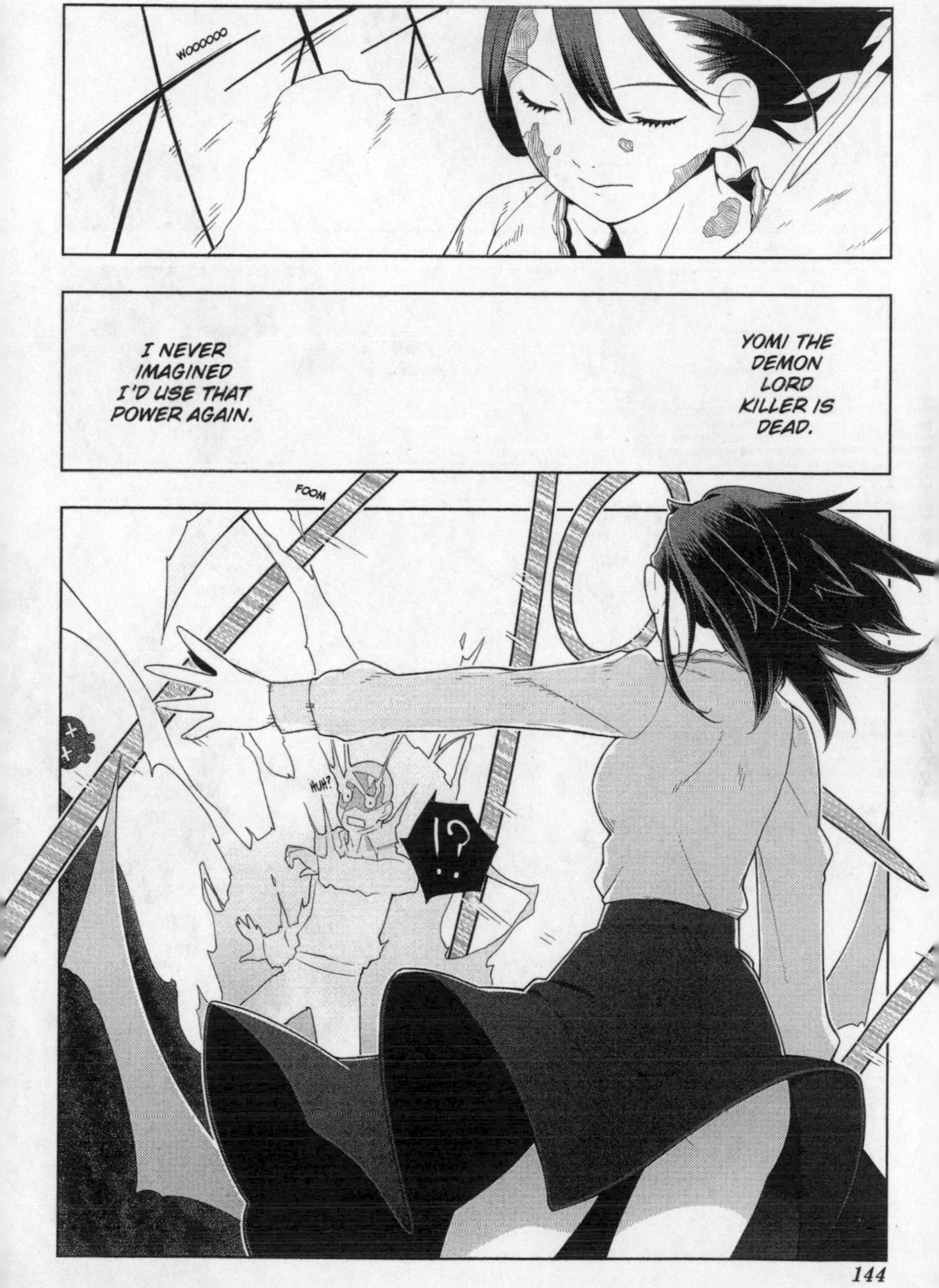
WOOOOOO
YOMI THE DEMON LORD KILLER IS DEAD.
I NEVER IMAGINED I'D USE THAT POWER AGAIN.
FOOM
!?
HUH?

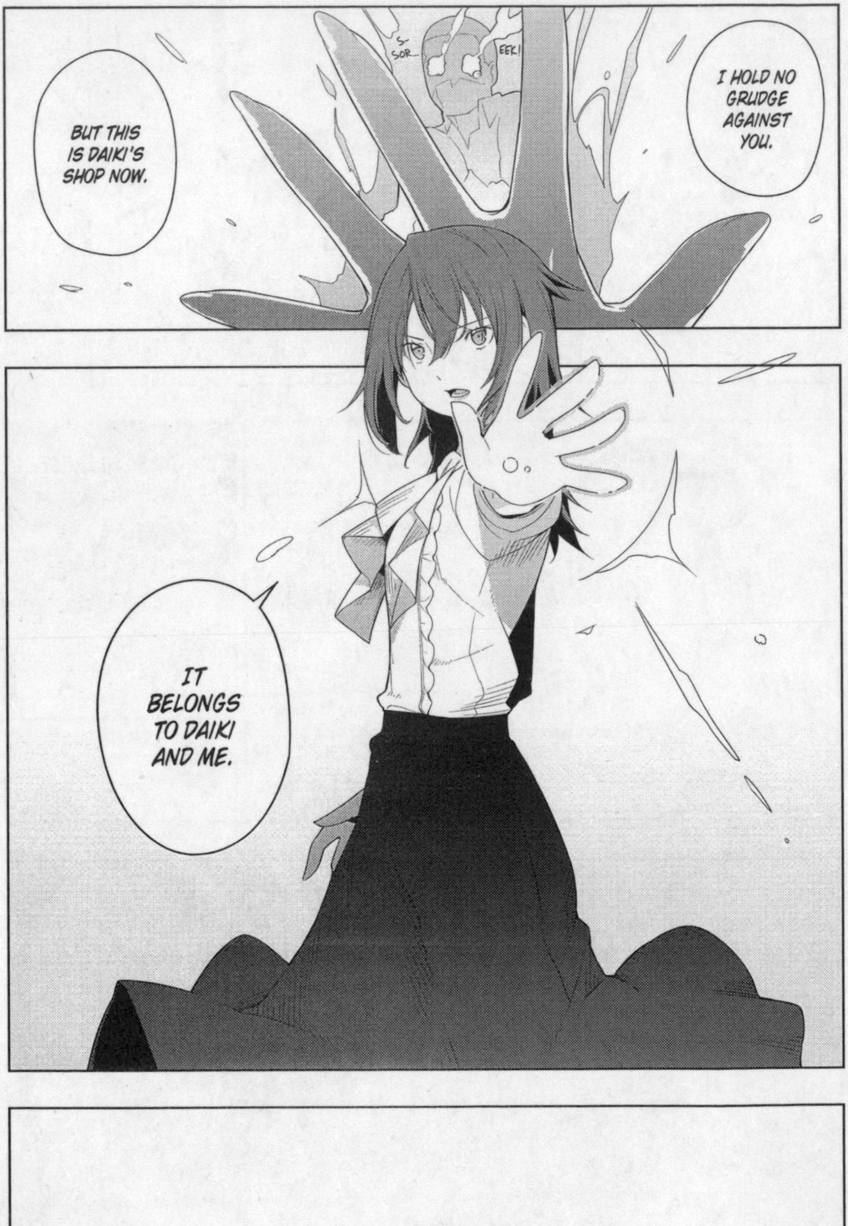
I HOLD NO GRUDGE AGAINST YOU.
EEK!
S-SOR...
BUT THIS IS DAIKI'S SHOP NOW.
IT BELONGS TO DAIKI AND ME.

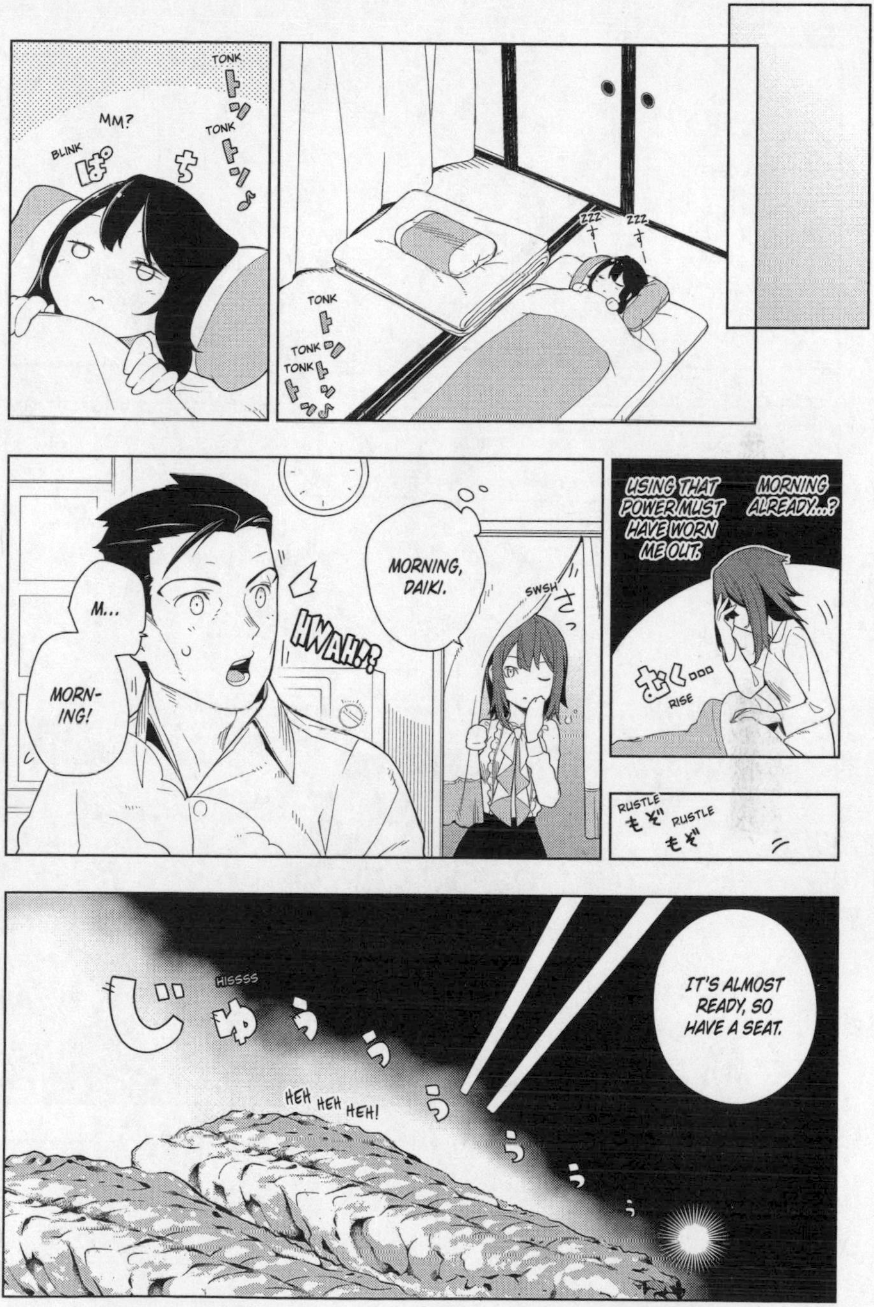
ZZZ
ZZZ
TONK
TONK
TONK
TONK
TONK
MM?
BLINK
MORNING ALREADY...?
USING THAT POWER MUST HAVE WORN ME OUT.
RISE
RUSTLE
RUSTLE
MORNING, DAIKI.
SWSH
HWAH!?
M...
MORN-ING!
IT'S ALMOST READY, SO HAVE A SEAT.
HISSSS
HEH HEH HEH!

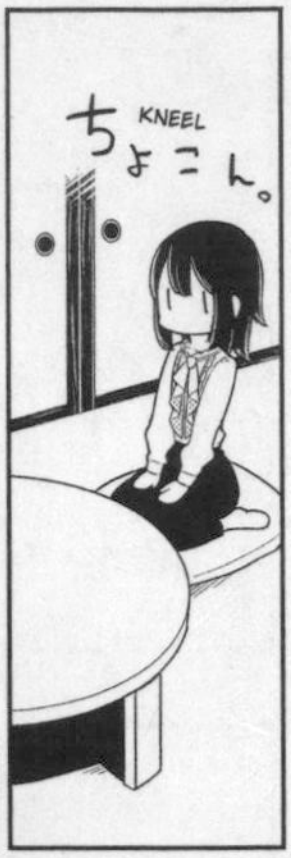
KNEEL
ちょこん。
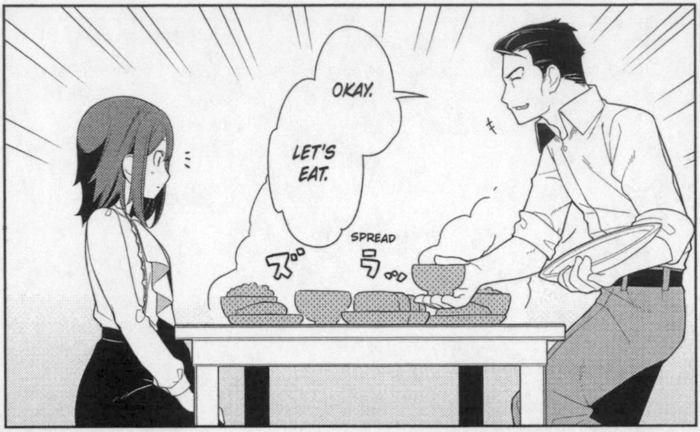
OKAY.
LET'S EAT.
SPREAD
ズラッ
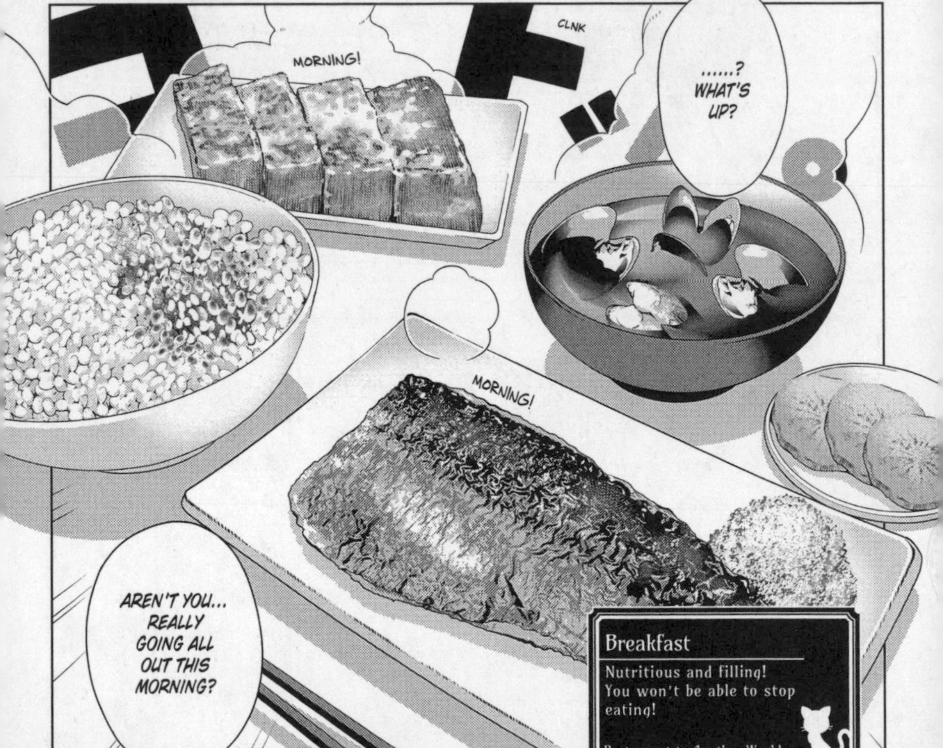
......? WHAT'S UP?
CLNK
MORNING!
MORNING!
AREN'T YOU... REALLY GOING ALL OUT THIS MORNING?
Breakfast
Nutritious and filling! You won't be able to stop eating!
Restaurant to Another World

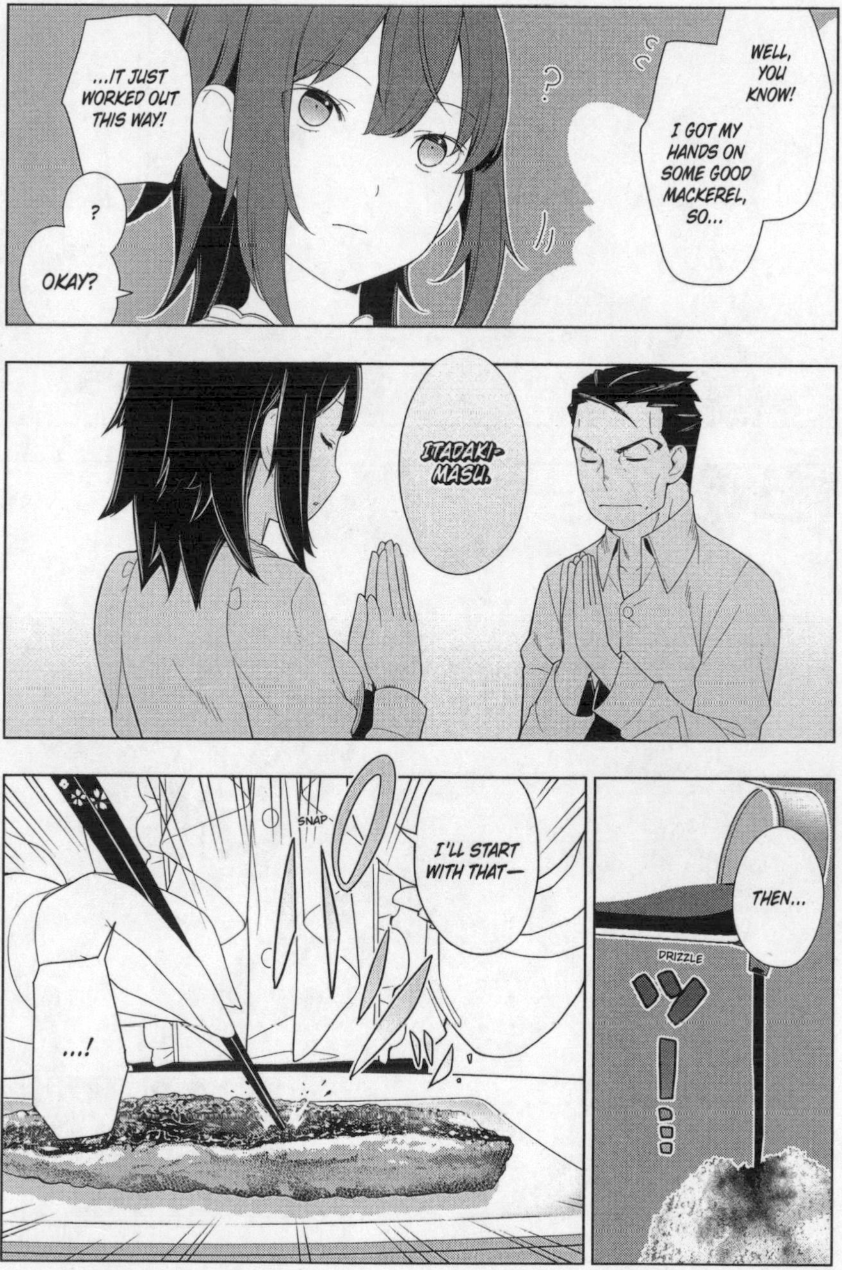
WELL, YOU KNOW!
I GOT MY HANDS ON SOME GOOD MACKEREL, SO...
...IT JUST WORKED OUT THIS WAY!
?
OKAY?
ITADAKI-MASU.
THEN...
DRIZZLE
I'LL START WITH THAT—
SNAP
...!

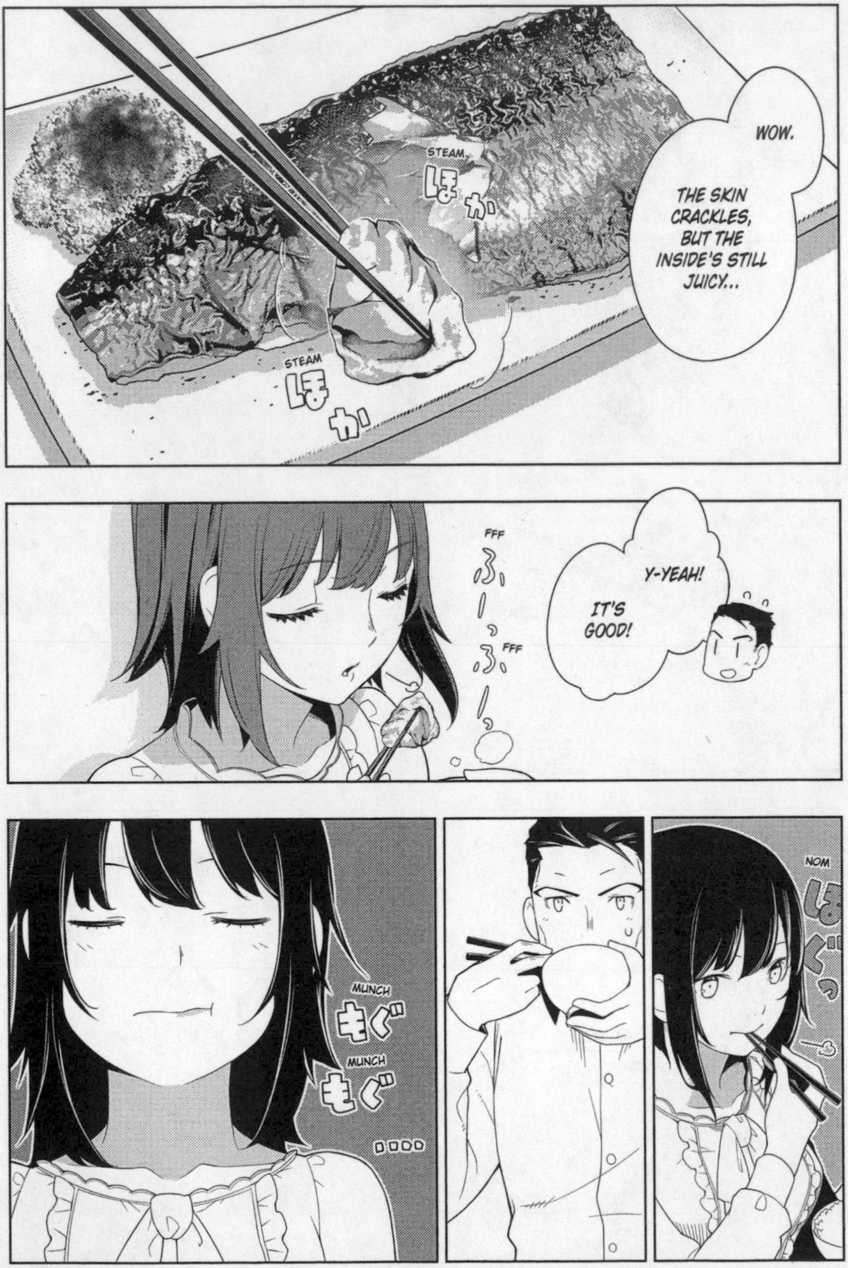
WOW.
THE SKIN CRACKLES, BUT THE INSIDE'S STILL JUICY...
STEAM
STEAM
Y-YEAH! IT'S GOOD!
FFF
FFF
NOM
MUNCH
MUNCH

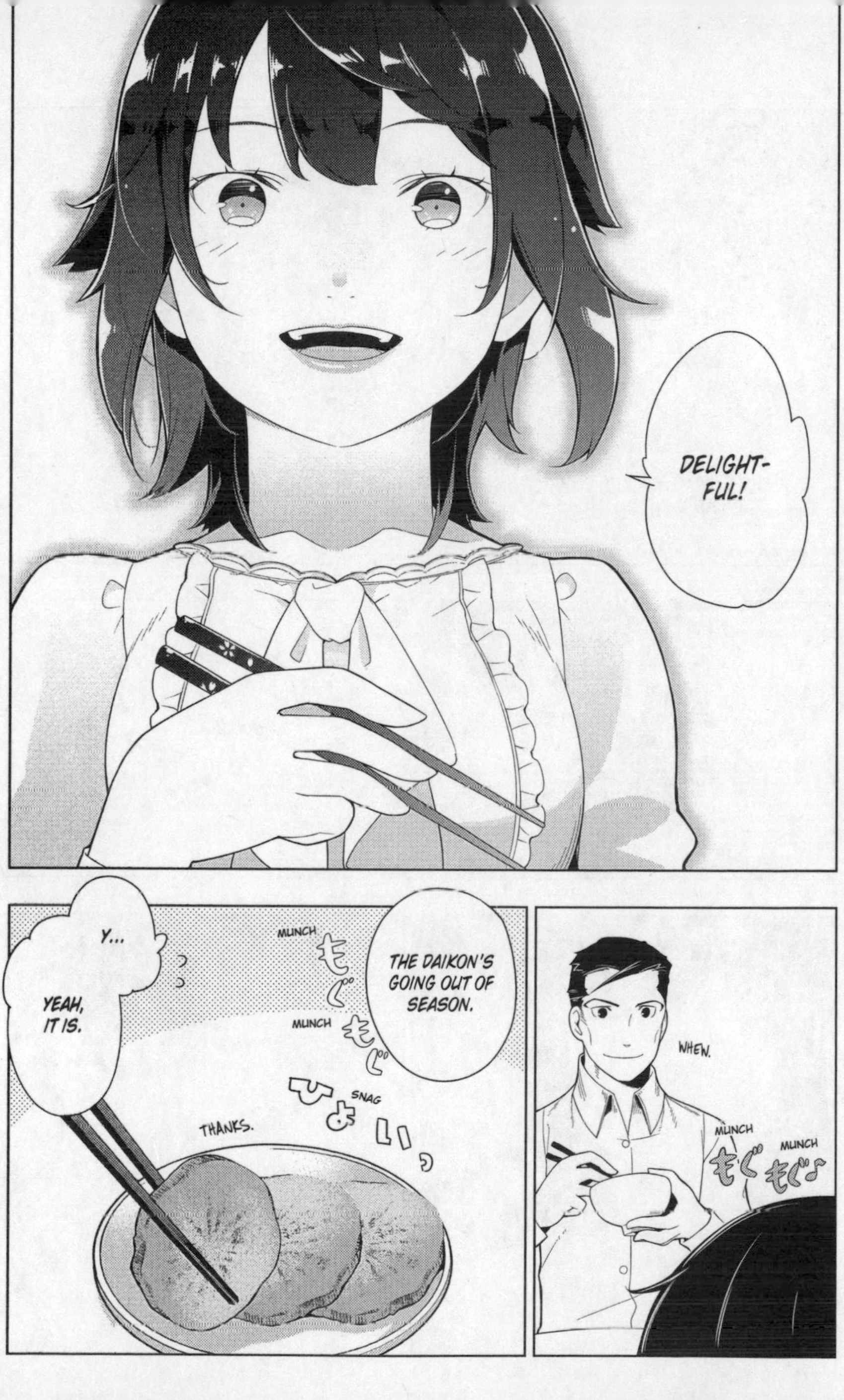
DELIGHT-FUL!
WHEW.
MUNCH MUNCH
もぐもぐ♪
THE DAIKON'S GOING OUT OF SEASON.
MUNCH
もぐ
MUNCH
もぐ
SNAG
ひょいっ
Y...
YEAH, IT IS.
THANKS.

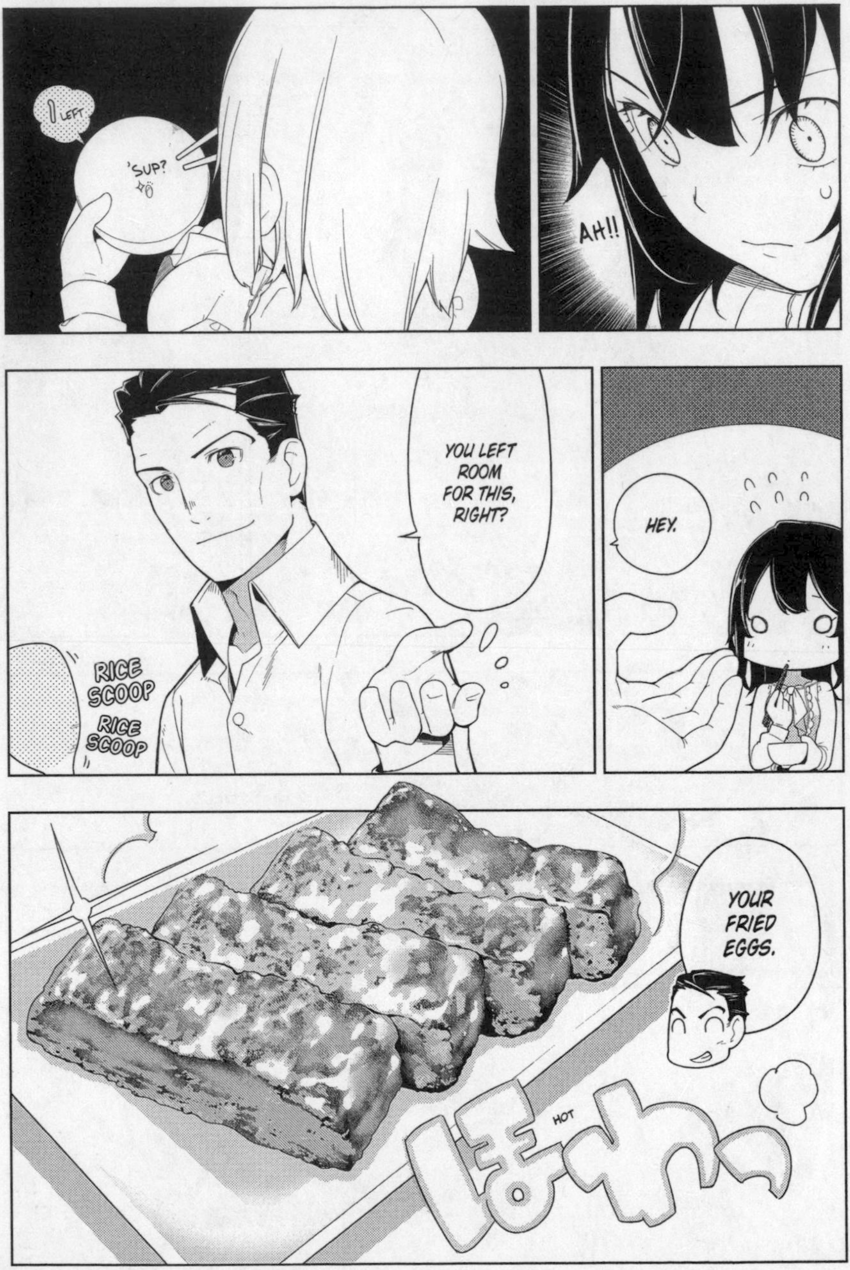
AH!!
1 LEFT.
'SUP?
HEY.
YOU LEFT ROOM FOR THIS, RIGHT?
RICE SCOOP
RICE SCOOP
YOUR FRIED EGGS.
HOT

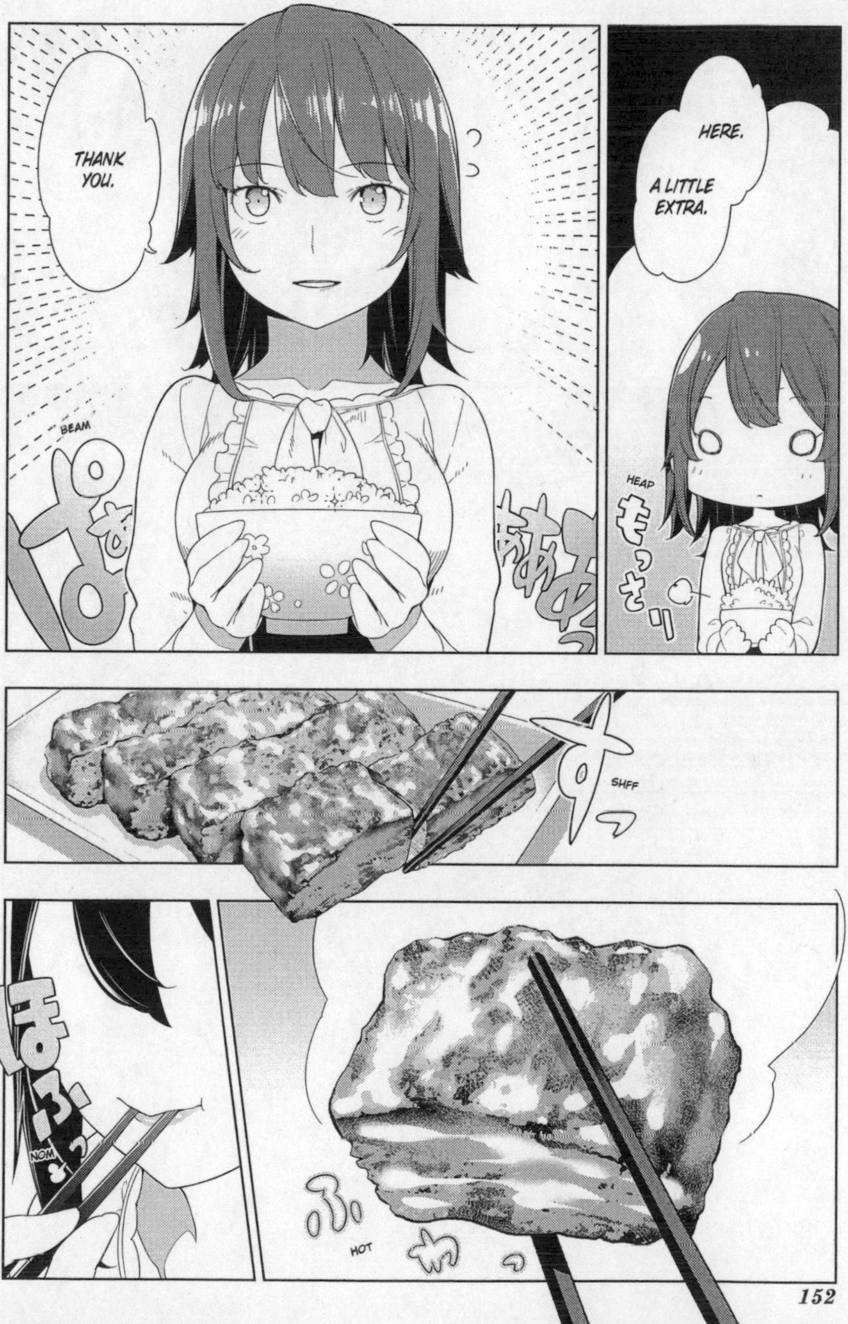
HERE.
A LITTLE EXTRA.
HEAP
もっさり
THANK YOU.
BEAM
ぱあ
あああっ
SHFF
すっ
HOT
ふわっ
NOM
ほふっ

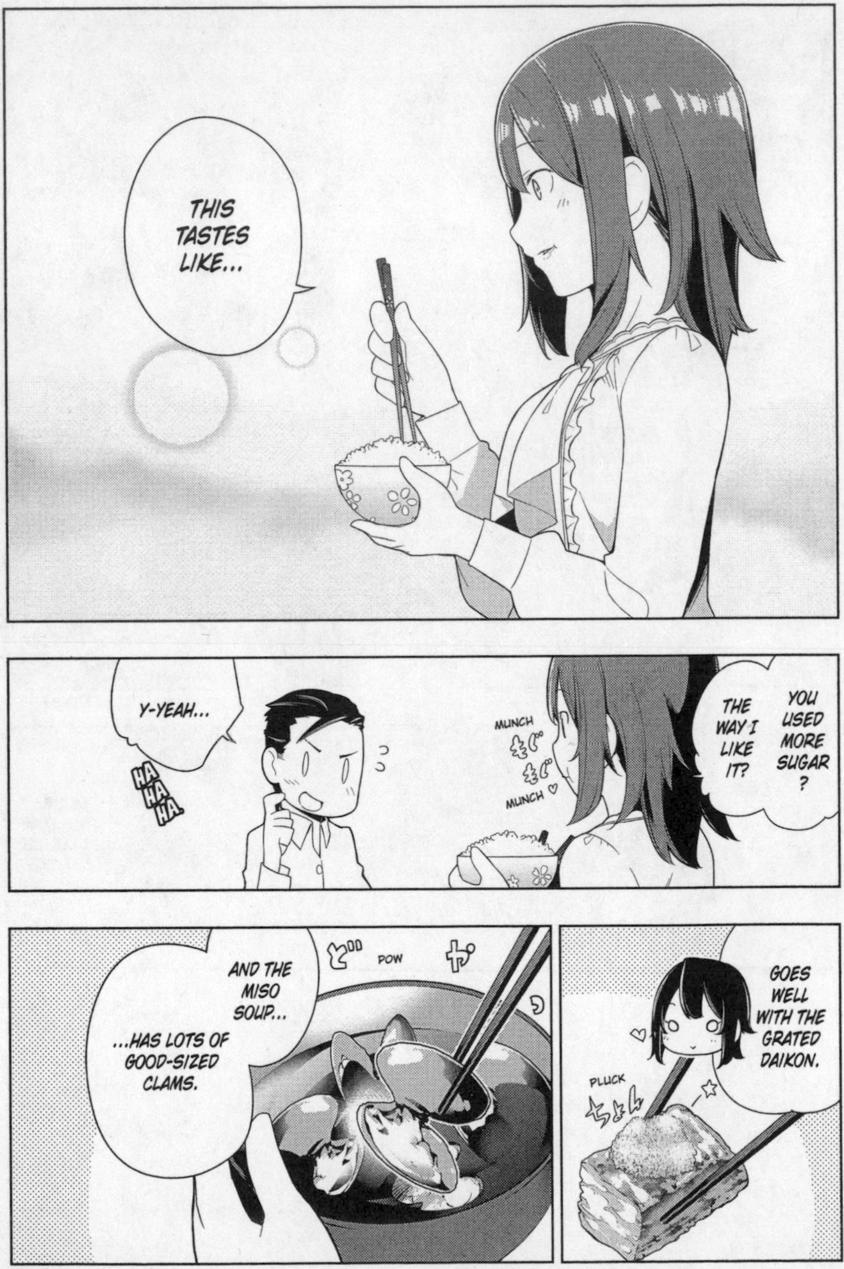
THIS TASTES LIKE...
YOU USED MORE SUGAR?
THE WAY I LIKE IT?
MUNCH もぐ
もぐ MUNCH
HA HA HA.
Y-YEAH...
GOES WELL WITH THE GRATED DAIKON.
PLUCK ちょん
POW
AND THE MISO SOUP...
...HAS LOTS OF GOOD-SIZED CLAMS.

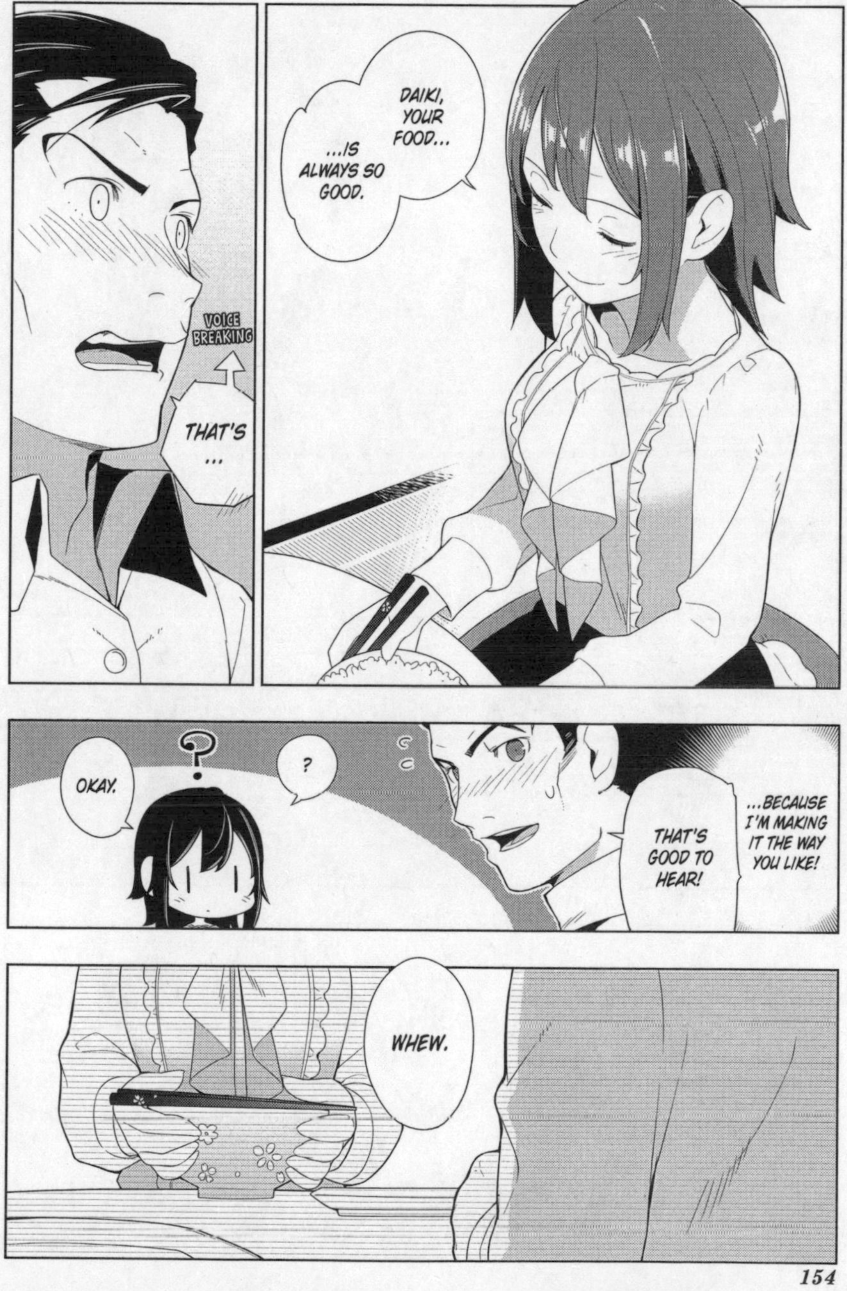
DAIKI, YOUR FOOD...
...IS ALWAYS SO GOOD.
VOICE BREAKING
THAT'S ...
...BECAUSE I'M MAKING IT THE WAY YOU LIKE!
THAT'S GOOD TO HEAR!
?
OKAY.
WHEW.

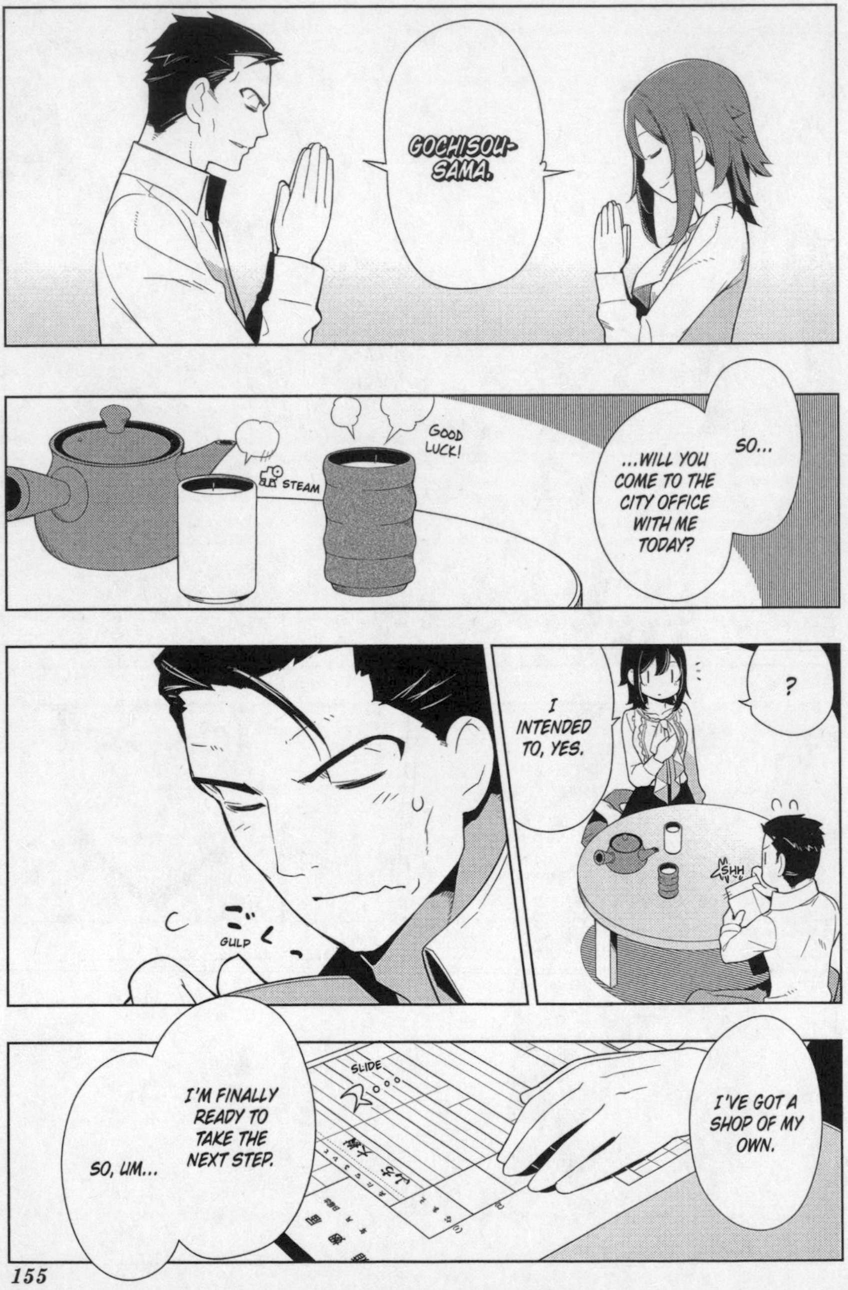
GOCHISOU-SAMA.
SO...
...WILL YOU COME TO THE CITY OFFICE WITH ME TODAY?
GOOD LUCK!
STEAM
?
I INTENDED TO, YES.
SHH
GULP
I'VE GOT A SHOP OF MY OWN.
SLIDE
I'M FINALLY READY TO TAKE THE NEXT STEP.
SO, UM...

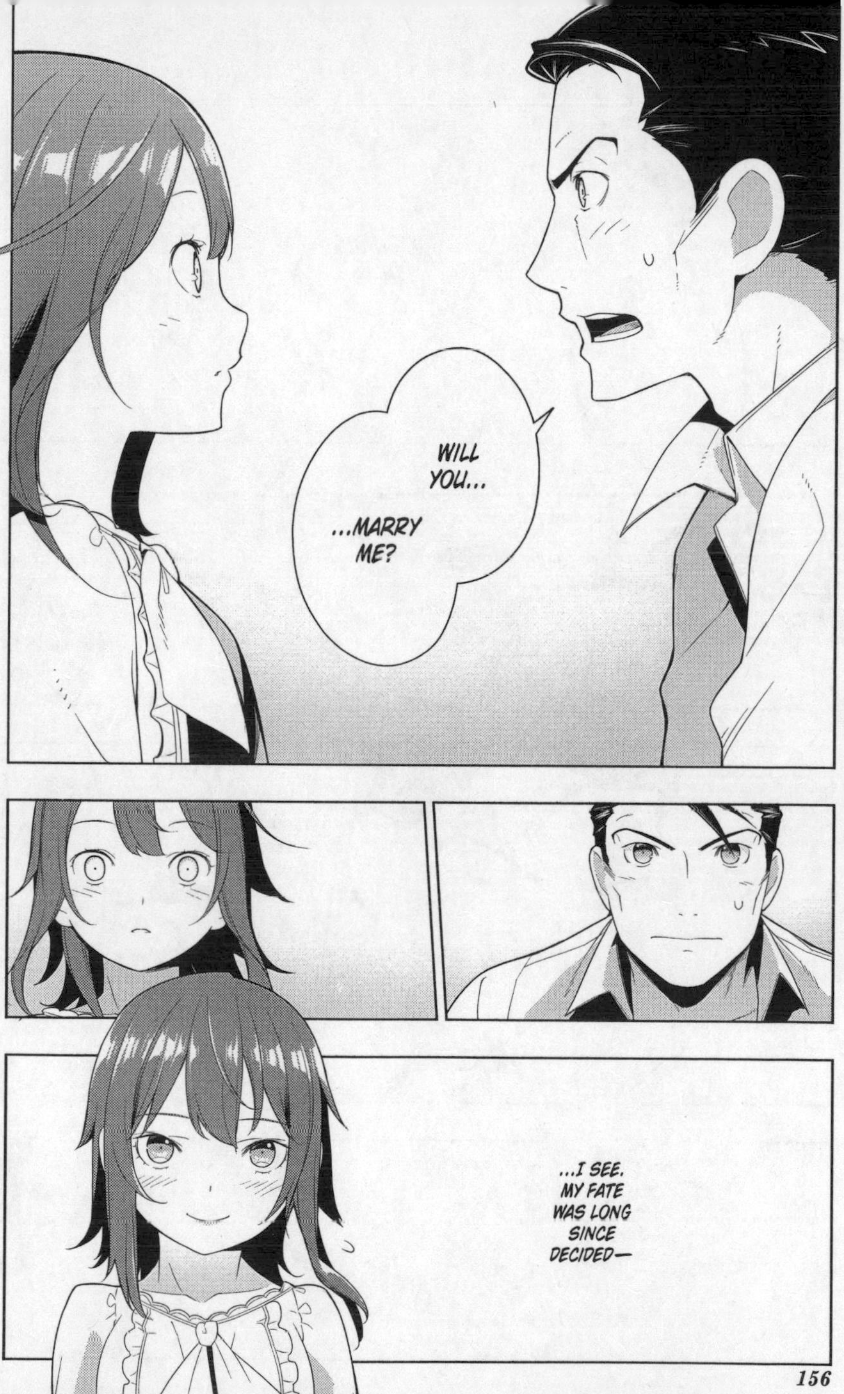
WILL YOU... ...MARRY ME?
...I SEE. MY FATE WAS LONG SINCE DECIDED—

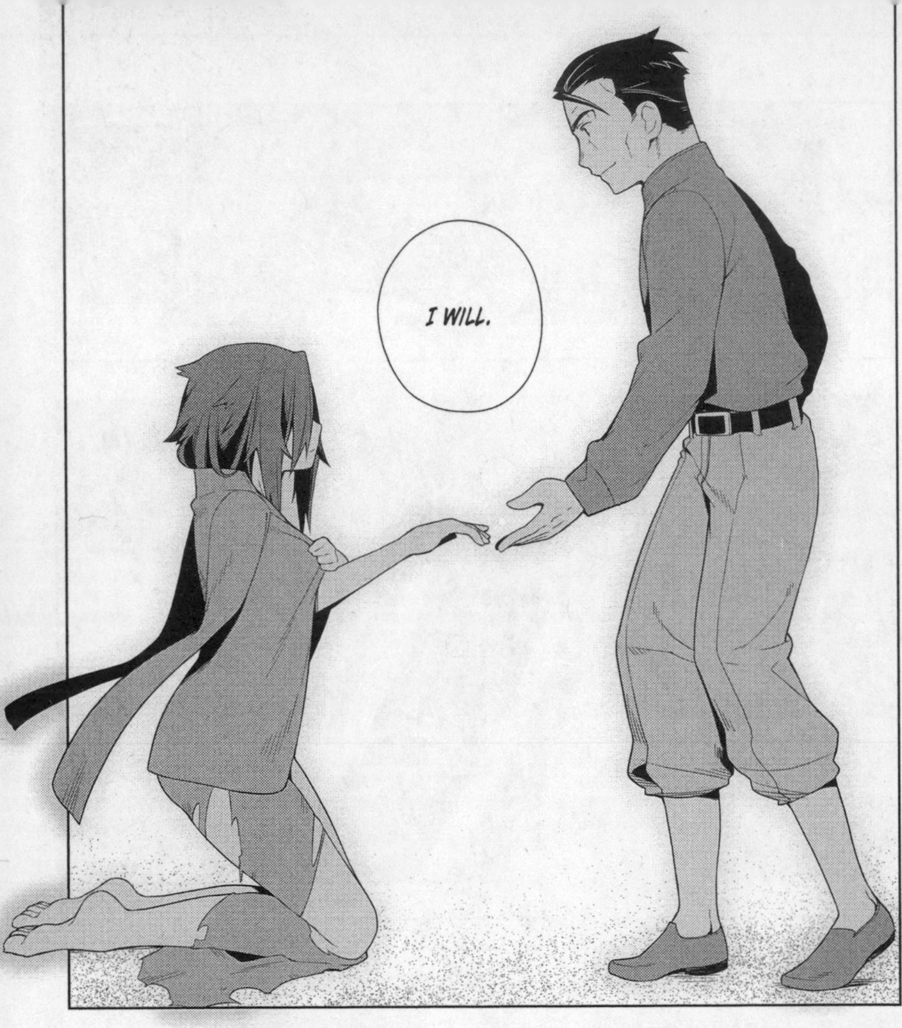
I WILL.

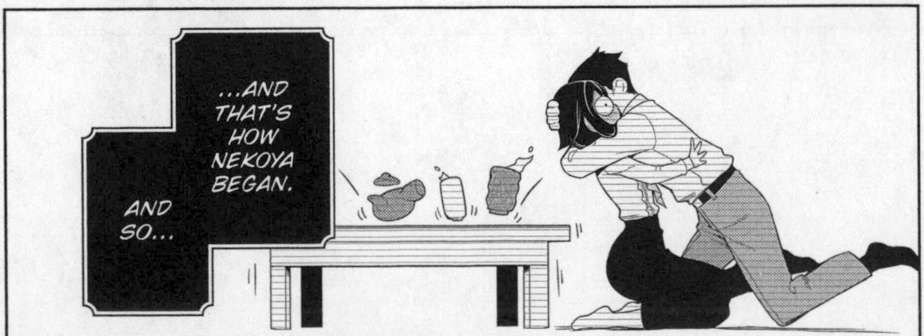
...AND THAT'S HOW NEKOYA BEGAN.
AND SO...

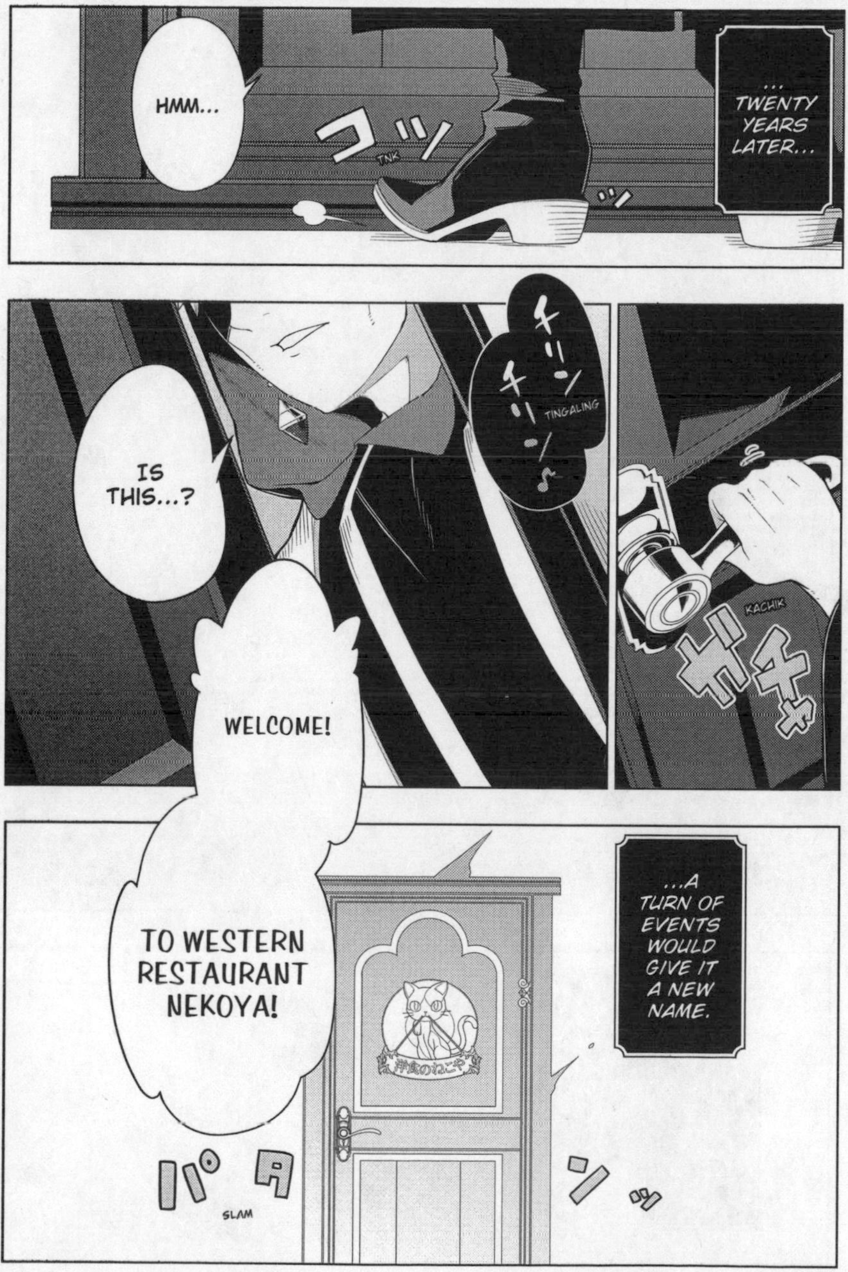
...TWENTY YEARS LATER...
コツ
TNK
HMM...
KACHIK
チリン チリン
TINGALING
IS THIS...?
WELCOME!
...A TURN OF EVENTS WOULD GIVE IT A NEW NAME.
TO WESTERN RESTAURANT NEKOYA!
洋食のねこや
SLAM

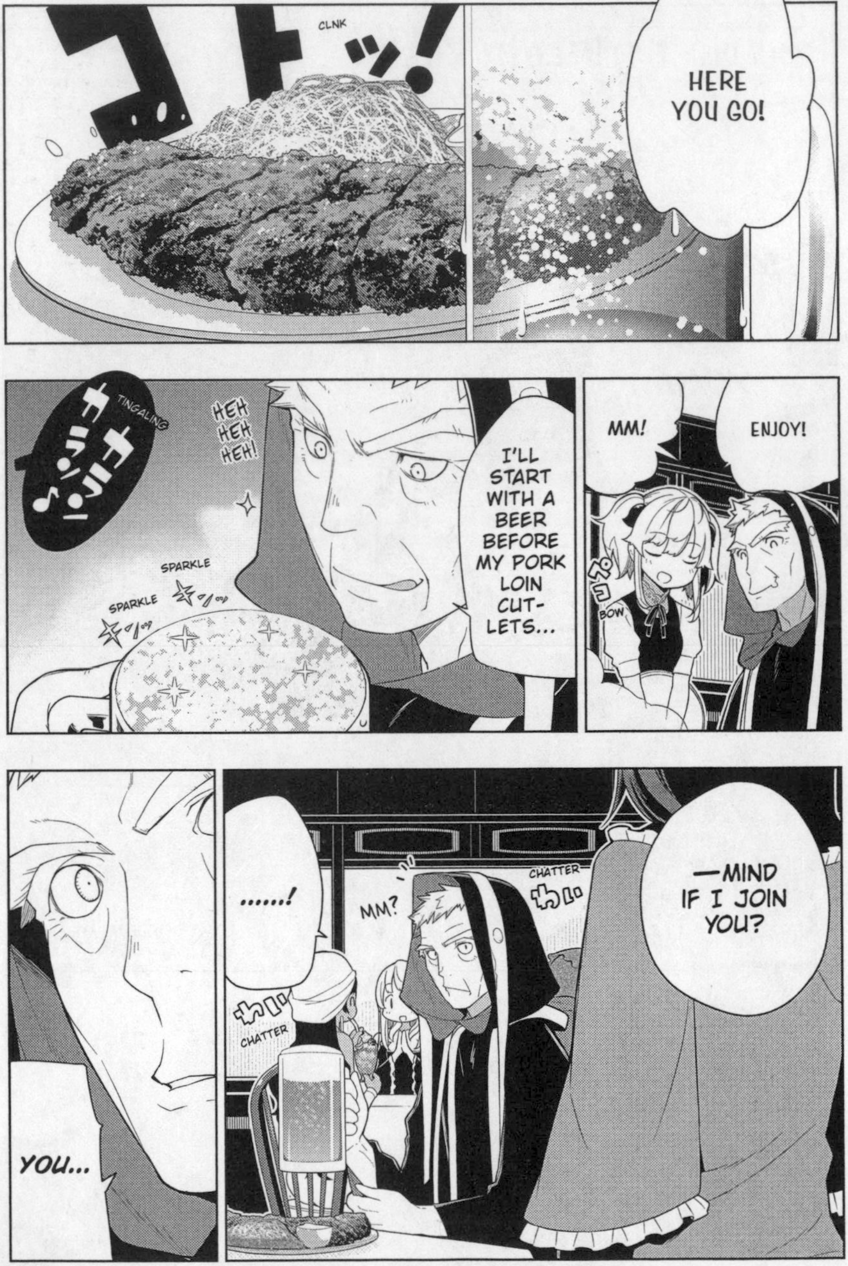
HERE YOU GO!
コトッ!
CLNK
ENJOY!
MM!
BOW
I'LL START WITH A BEER BEFORE MY PORK LOIN CUT-LETS...
HEH HEH HEH!
TINGALING
SPARKLE
SPARKLE
—MIND IF I JOIN YOU?
CHATTER
MM?
......!
CHATTER
YOU...

26th Dish Pork Loin Cutlet

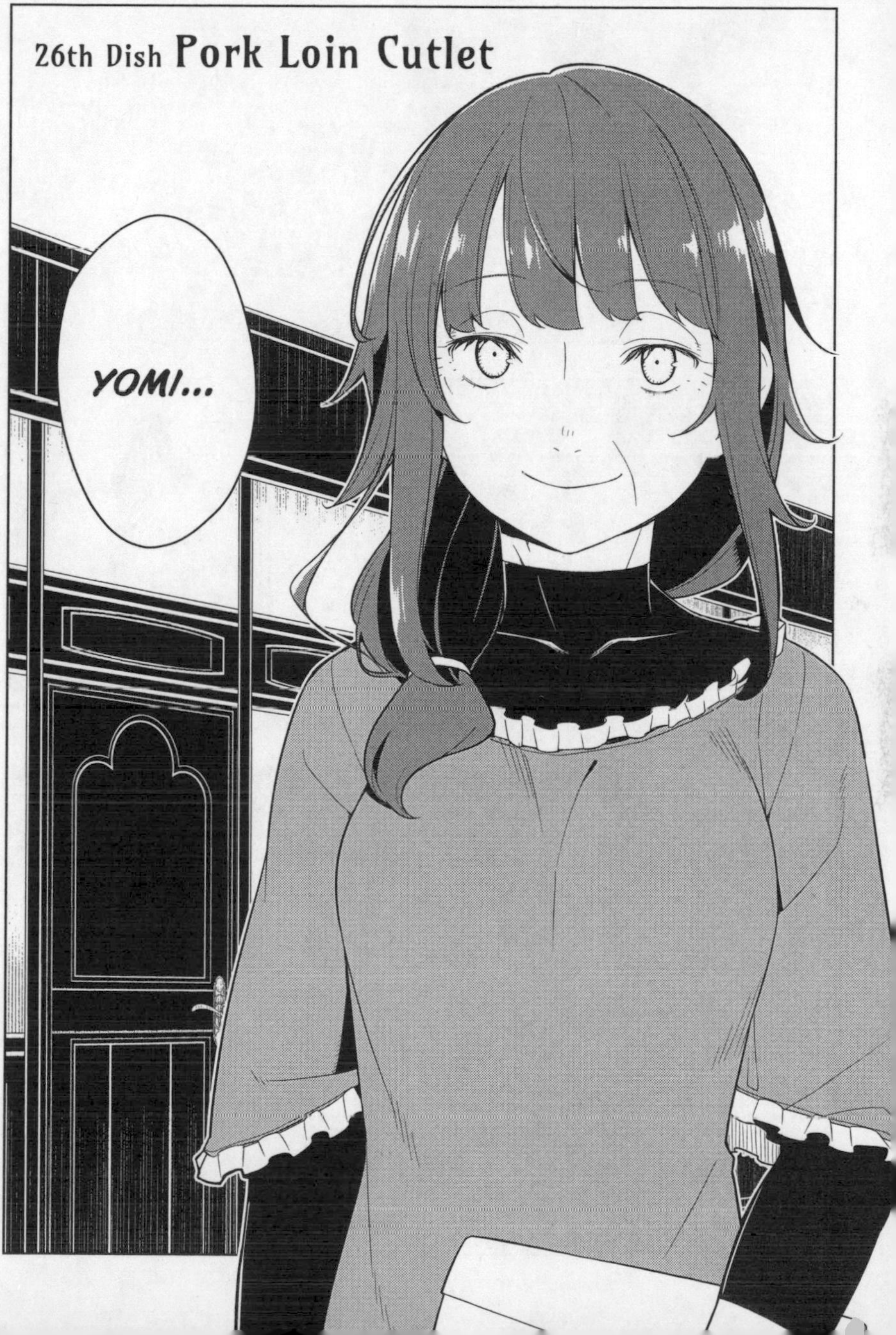
YOMI...

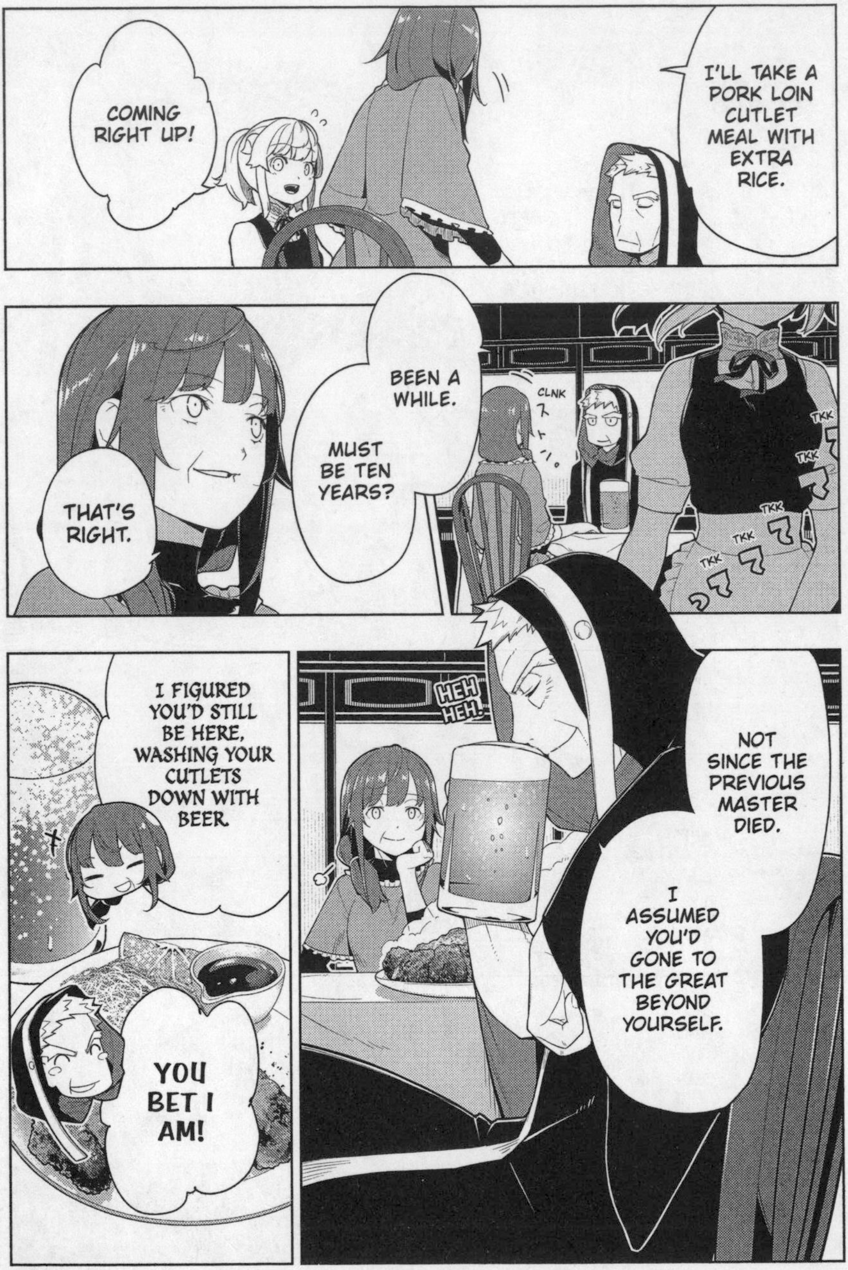
I'LL TAKE A PORK LOIN CUTLET MEAL WITH EXTRA RICE.
COMING RIGHT UP!
TKK TKK TKK TKK TKK
CLNK
BEEN A WHILE.
MUST BE TEN YEARS?
THAT'S RIGHT.
NOT SINCE THE PREVIOUS MASTER DIED.
I ASSUMED YOU'D GONE TO THE GREAT BEYOND YOURSELF.
HEH HEH!
I FIGURED YOU'D STILL BE HERE, WASHING YOUR CUTLETS DOWN WITH BEER.
YOU BET I AM!

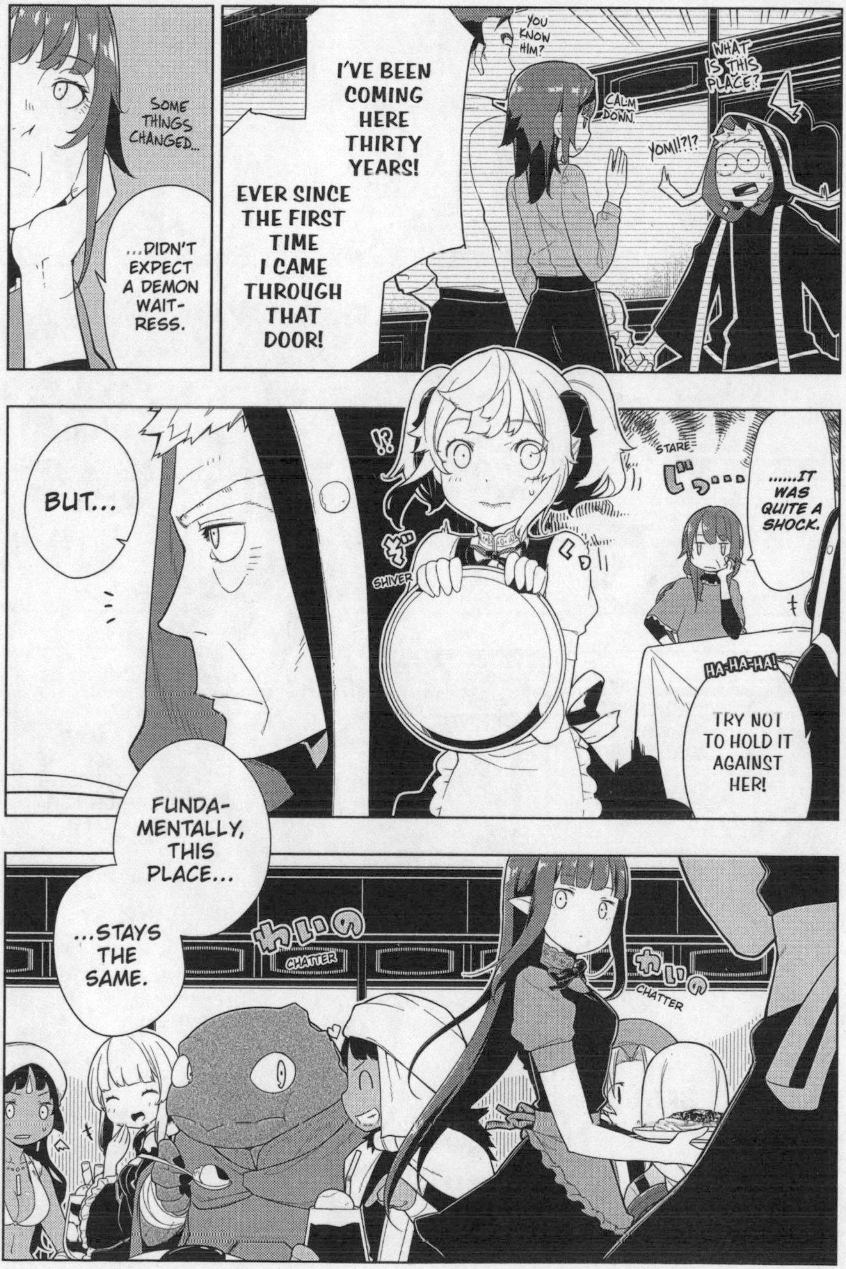
WHAT IS THIS PLACE?
YOM!!?!?
CALM DOWN.
YOU KNOW HIM?
I'VE BEEN COMING HERE THIRTY YEARS!
EVER SINCE THE FIRST TIME I CAME THROUGH THAT DOOR!
SOME THINGS CHANGED...
...DIDN'T EXPECT A DEMON WAIT-RESS.
......IT WAS QUITE A SHOCK.
STARE
HA-HA-HA!
TRY NOT TO HOLD IT AGAINST HER!
!?
SHIVER
BUT...
FUNDA-MENTALLY, THIS PLACE...
CHATTER
CHATTER
...STAYS THE SAME.

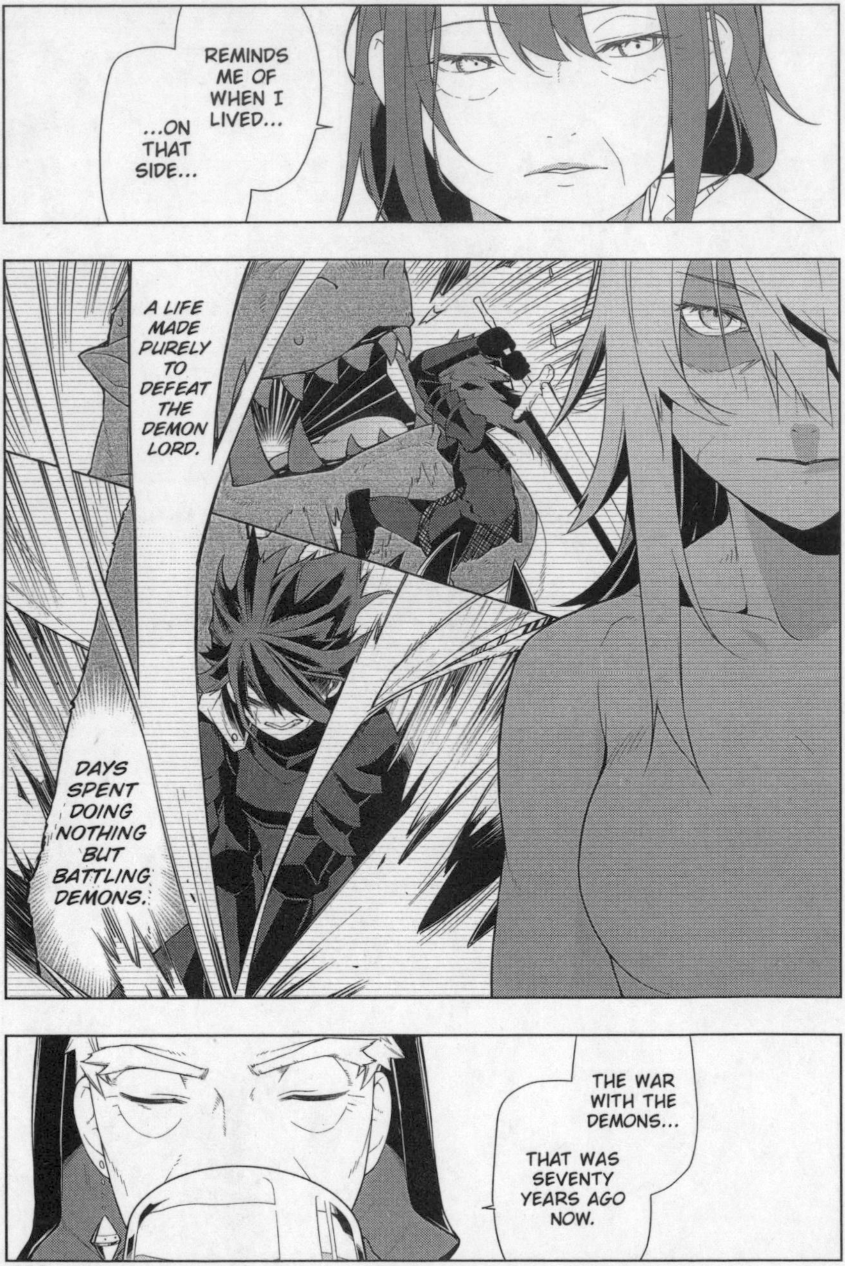
REMINDS ME OF WHEN I LIVED...
...ON THAT SIDE...
A LIFE MADE PURELY TO DEFEAT THE DEMON LORD.
DAYS SPENT DOING NOTHING BUT BATTLING DEMONS.
THE WAR WITH THE DEMONS...
THAT WAS SEVENTY YEARS AGO NOW.

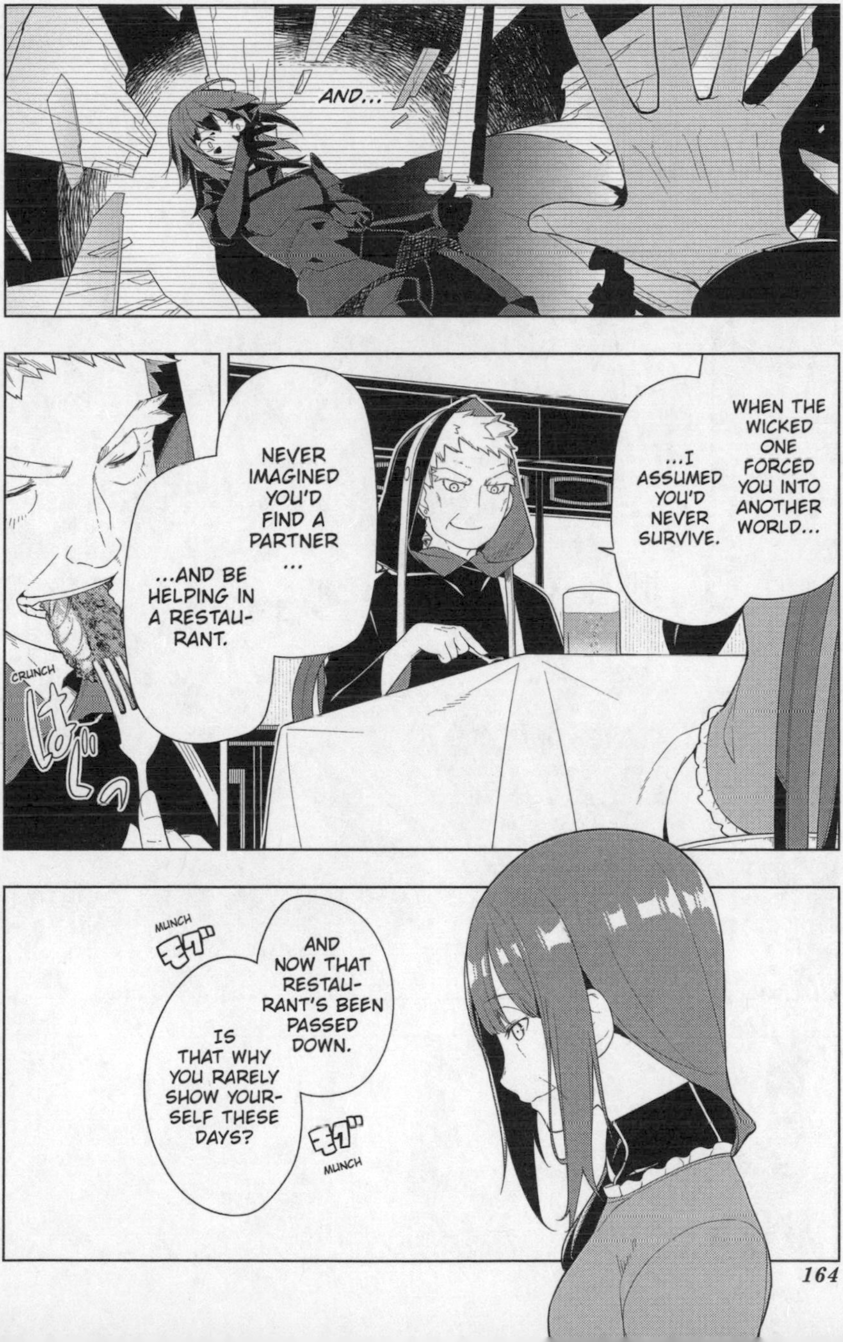
AND...
WHEN THE WICKED ONE FORCED YOU INTO ANOTHER WORLD...
...I ASSUMED YOU'D NEVER SURVIVE.
NEVER IMAGINED YOU'D FIND A PARTNER ...
...AND BE HELPING IN A RESTAURANT.
CRUNCH
MUNCH
AND NOW THAT RESTAURANT'S BEEN PASSED DOWN.
IS THAT WHY YOU RARELY SHOW YOURSELF THESE DAYS?
MUNCH

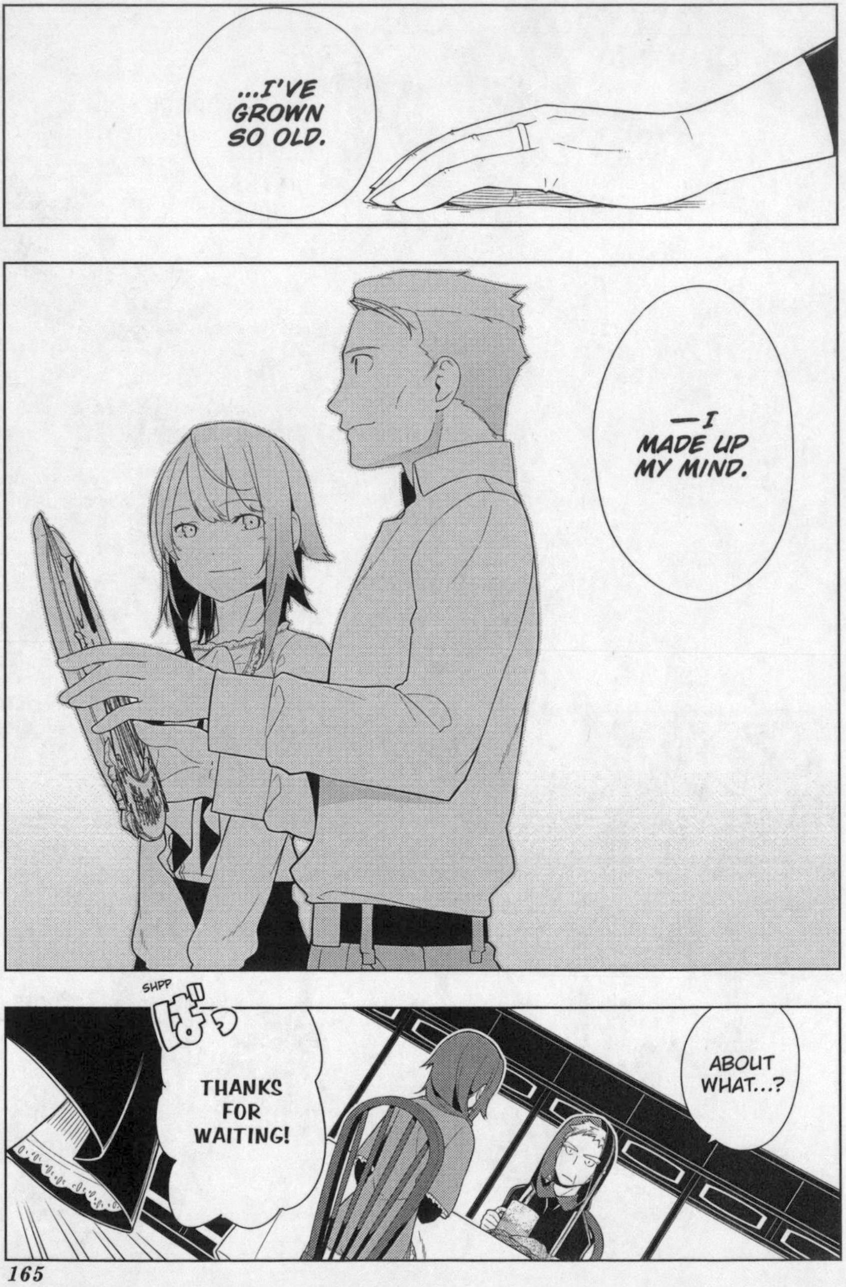
...I'VE GROWN SO OLD.
—I MADE UP MY MIND.
ABOUT WHAT...?
SHPP
ばっ
THANKS FOR WAITING!

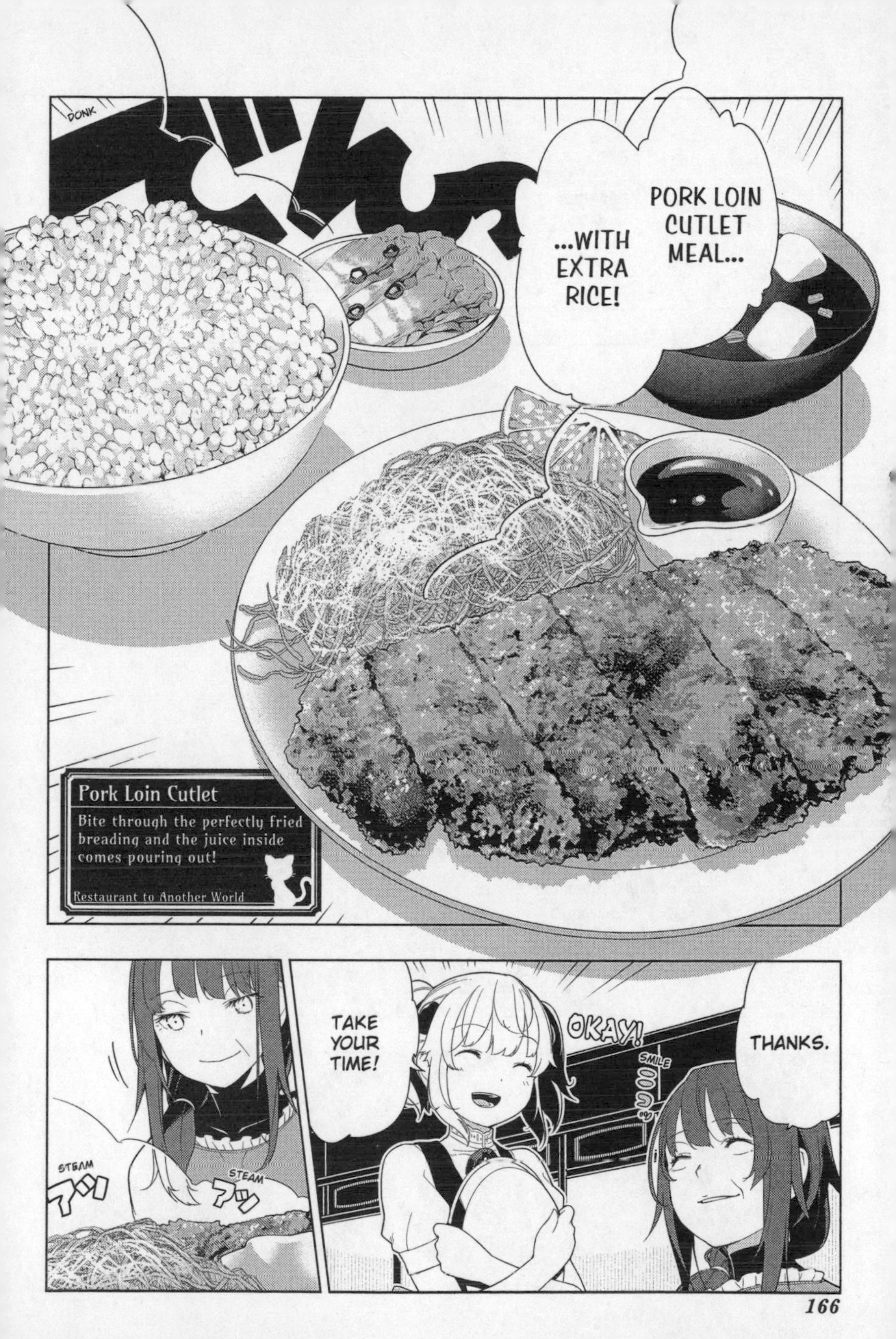
DONK
PORK LOIN CUTLET MEAL...
...WITH EXTRA RICE!
Pork Loin Cutlet
Bite through the perfectly fried breading and the juice inside comes pouring out!
Restaurant to Another World
THANKS.
SMILE
OKAY!
TAKE YOUR TIME!
STEAM
STEAM

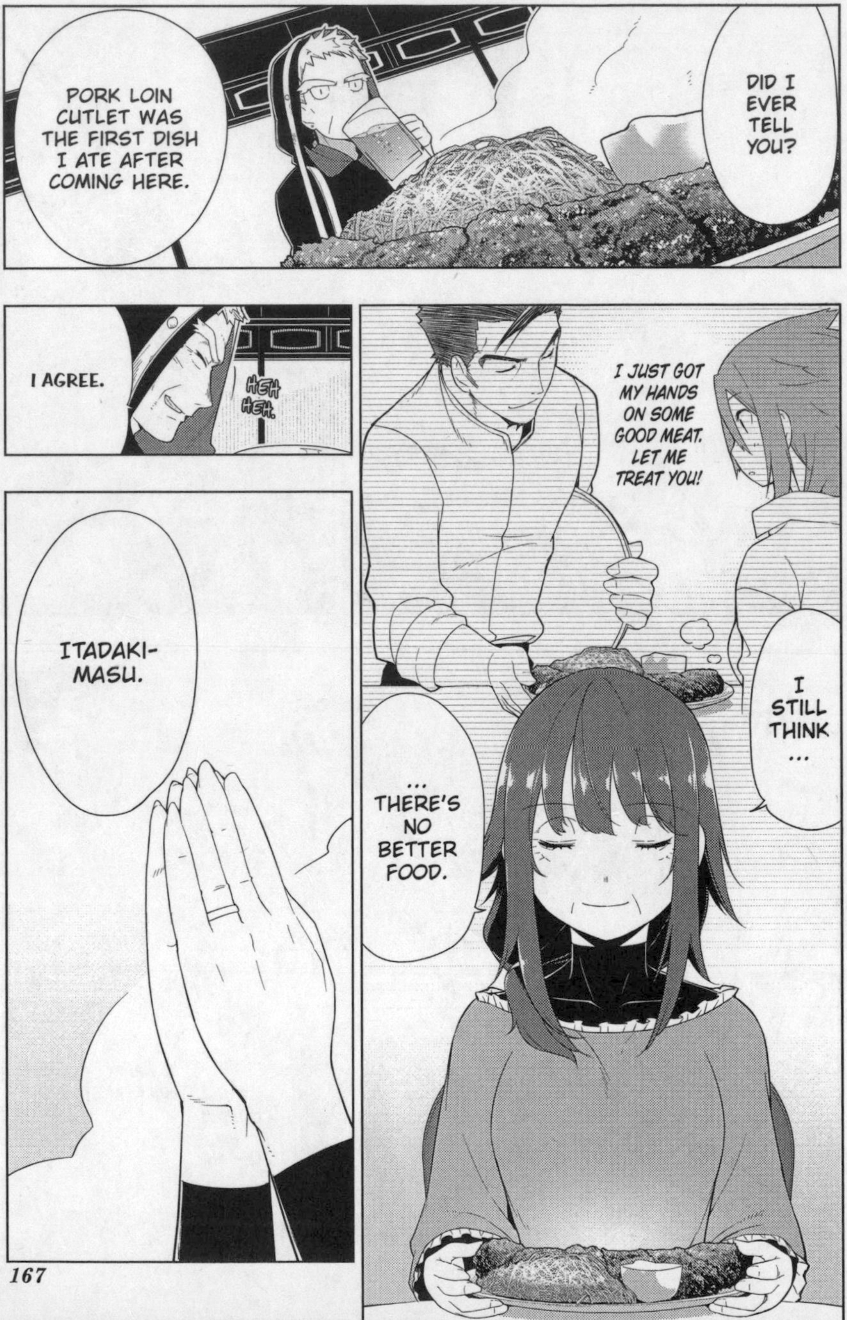
DID I EVER TELL YOU?
PORK LOIN CUTLET WAS THE FIRST DISH I ATE AFTER COMING HERE.
I JUST GOT MY HANDS ON SOME GOOD MEAT. LET ME TREAT YOU!
I STILL THINK ...
... THERE'S NO BETTER FOOD.
I AGREE.
HEH HEH.
ITADAKI-MASU.

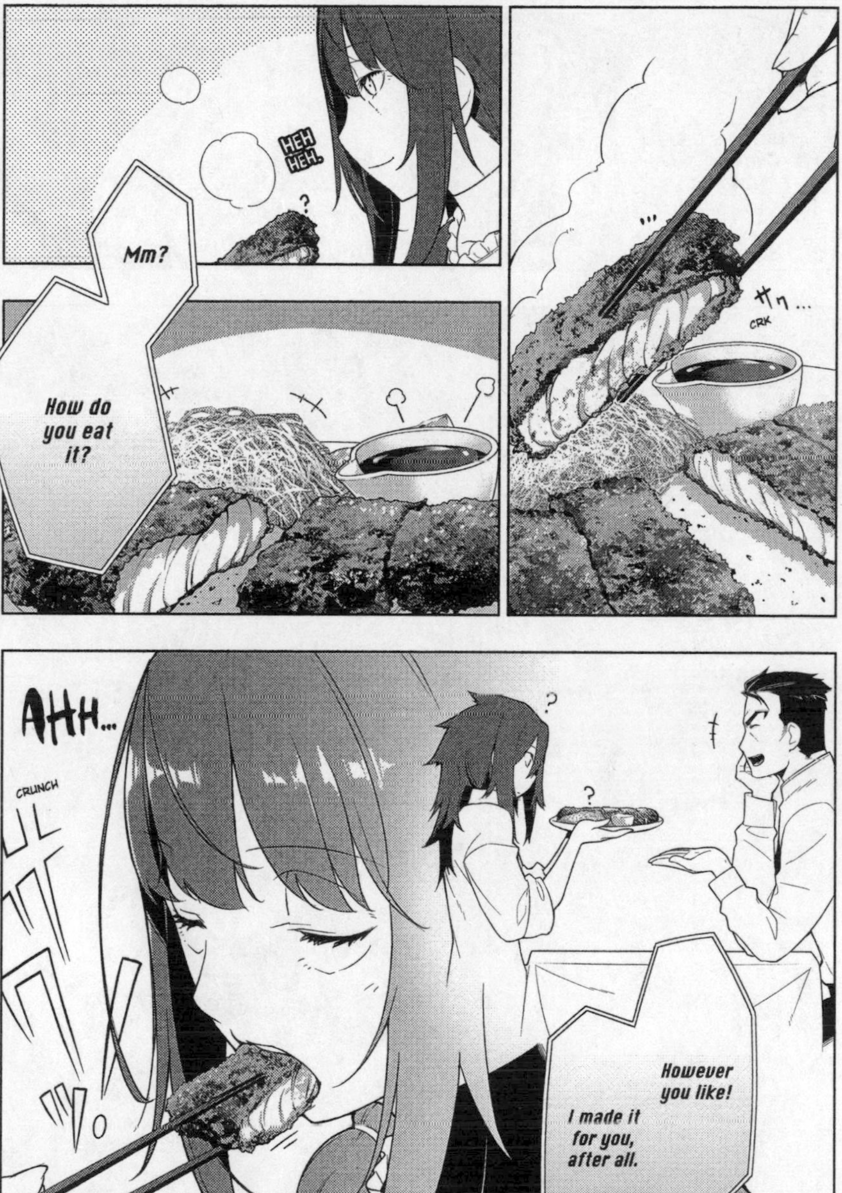
...
CRK
HEH HEH.
?
Mm?
How do you eat it?
?
?
However you like!
I made it for you, after all.
AHH...
CRUNCH

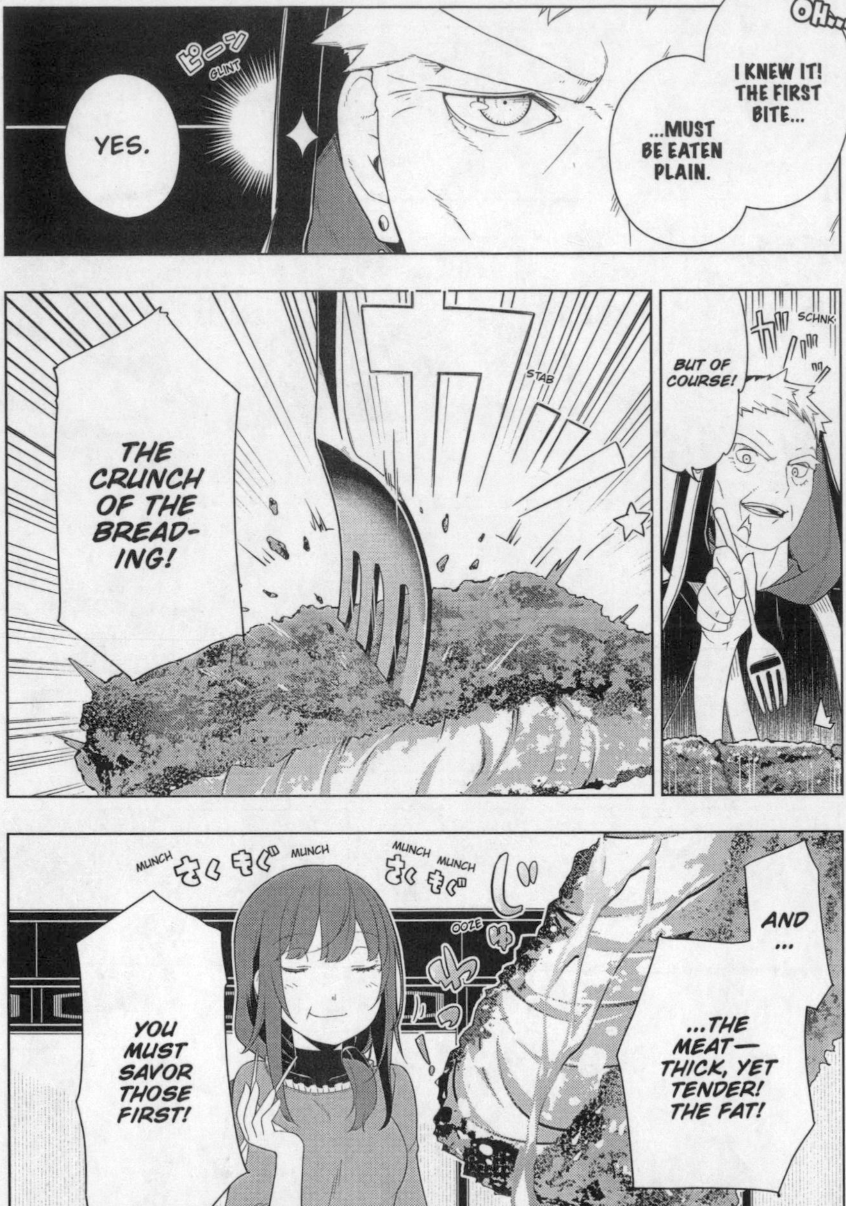
OH...
I KNEW IT! THE FIRST BITE...
...MUST BE EATEN PLAIN.
ピーン
CLINT
YES.
SCHNK
BUT OF COURSE!
STAB
THE CRUNCH OF THE BREAD-ING!
AND...
...THE MEAT—THICK, YET TENDER! THE FAT!
OOZE
MUNCH MUNCH
さくもぐ
MUNCH
MUNCH
さくもぐ
YOU MUST SAVOR THOSE FIRST!

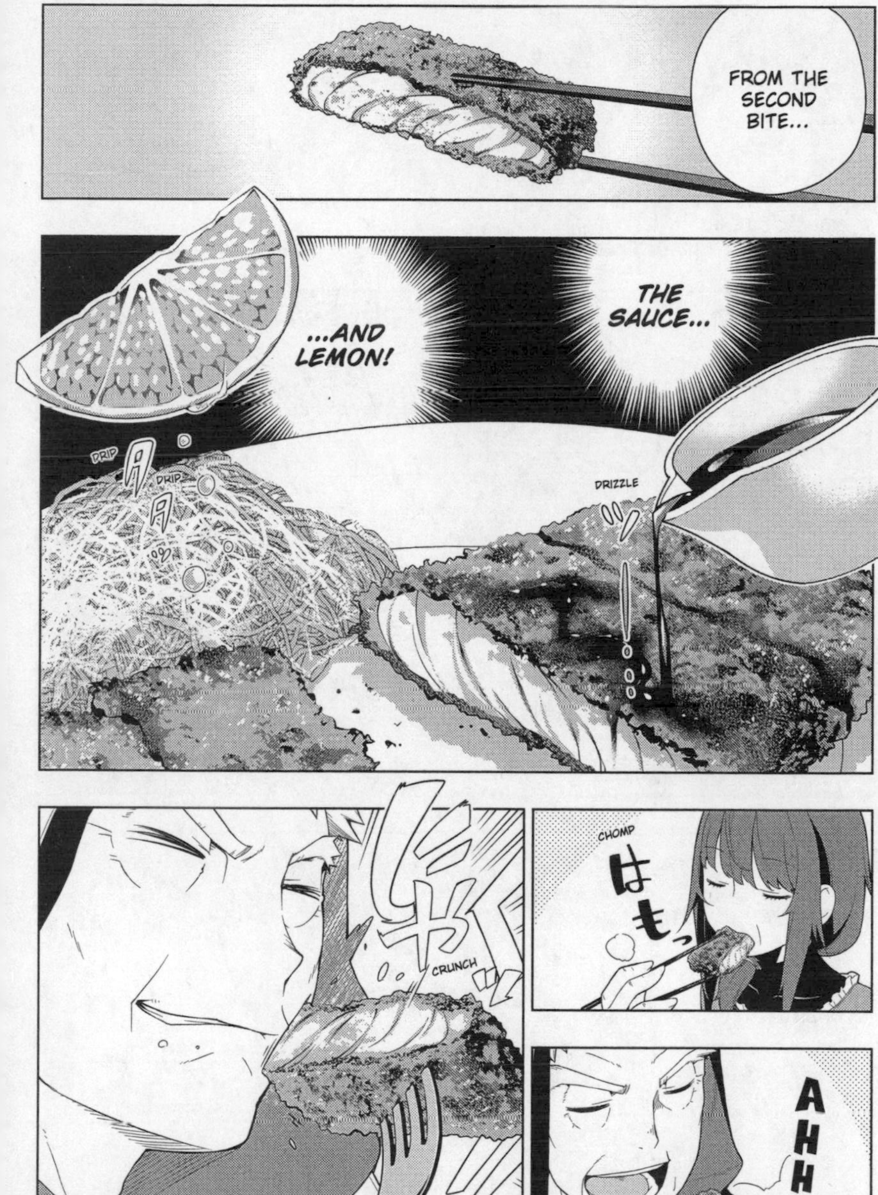
FROM THE SECOND BITE...
THE SAUCE...
...AND LEMON!
DRIZZLE
DRIP
DRIP
CHOMP
はもっ
AHHH...
CRUNCH

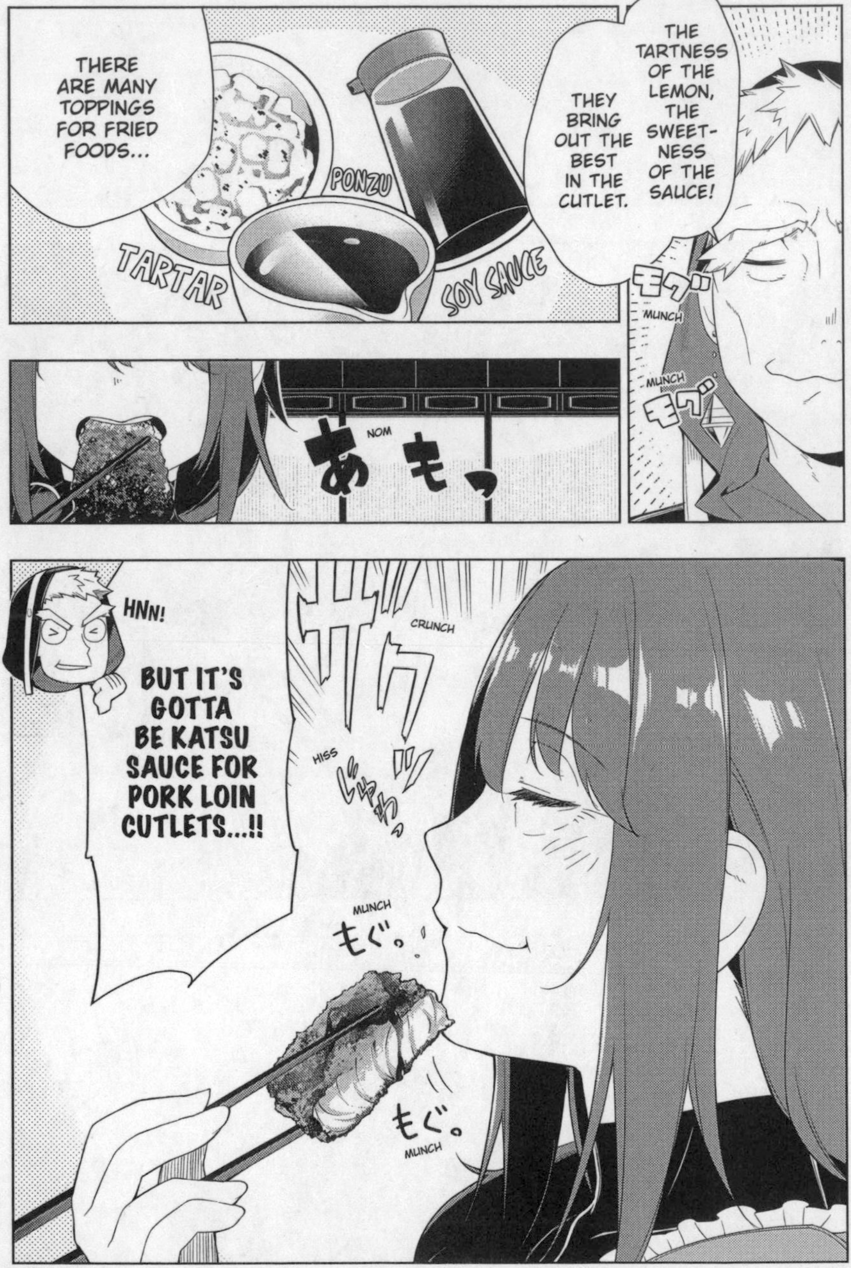
THE TARTNESS OF THE LEMON, THE SWEETNESS OF THE SAUCE!
THEY BRING OUT THE BEST IN THE CUTLET.
モグ
MUNCH
MUNCH
モグ
THERE ARE MANY TOPPINGS FOR FRIED FOODS...
PONZU
TARTAR
SOY SAUCE
NOM
あもっ
HNN!
BUT IT'S GOTTA BE KATSU SAUCE FOR PORK LOIN CUTLETS...!!
CRUNCH
ザクッ
HISS
じゅわっ
MUNCH
もぐ。
もぐ。
MUNCH

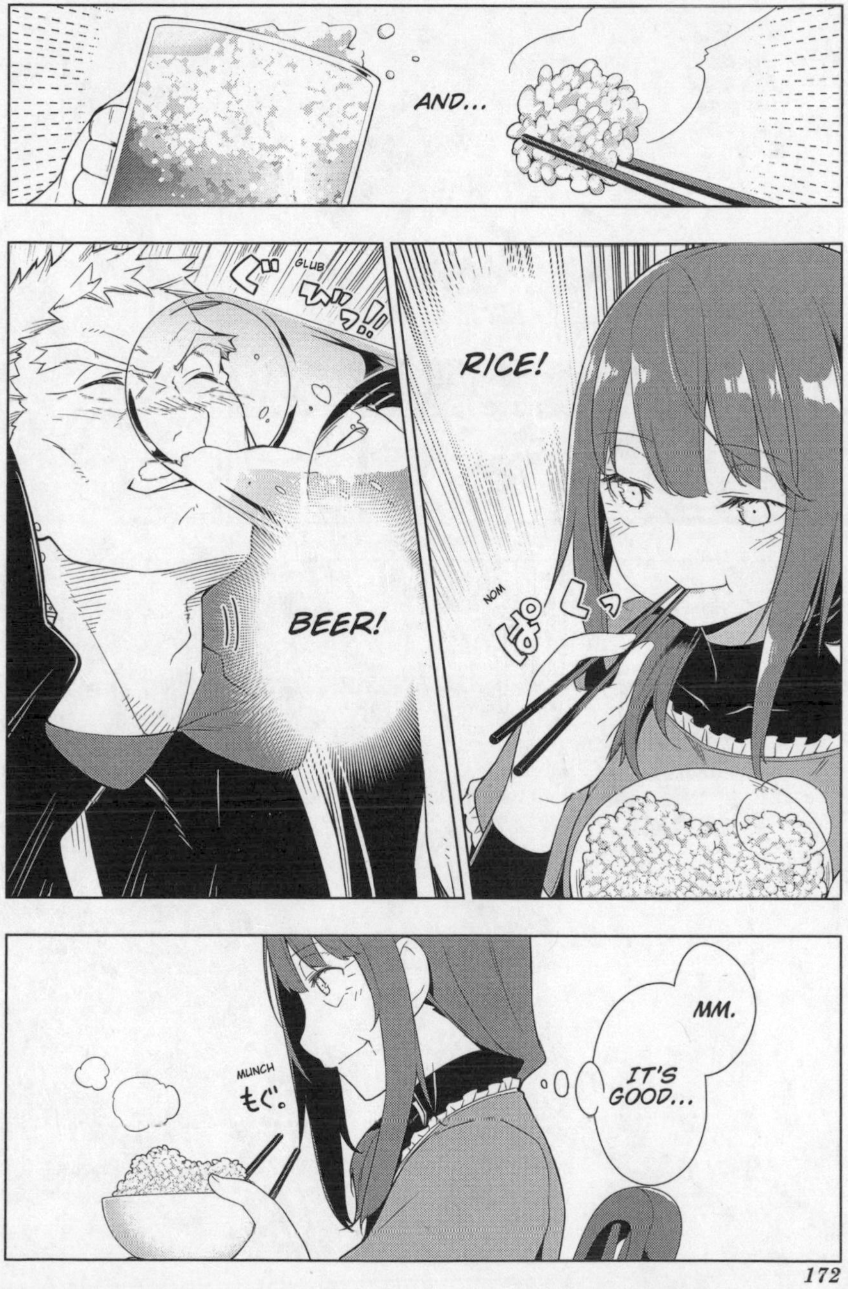
AND...
RICE!
NOM
ぱくっ
BEER!
GLUB
MM.
IT'S GOOD...
MUNCH
もぐ。

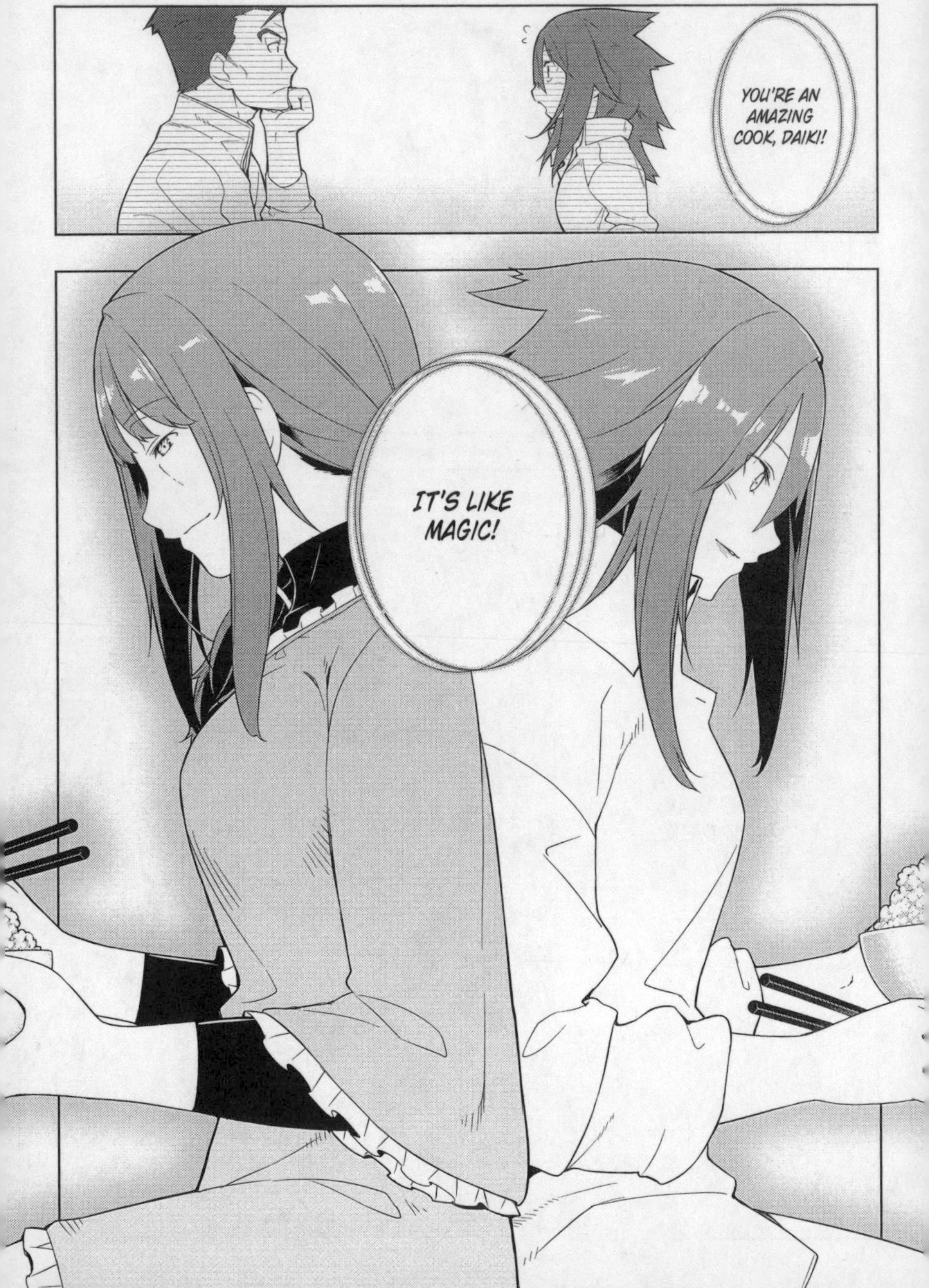
YOU'RE AN AMAZING COOK, DAIKI!
IT'S LIKE MAGIC!

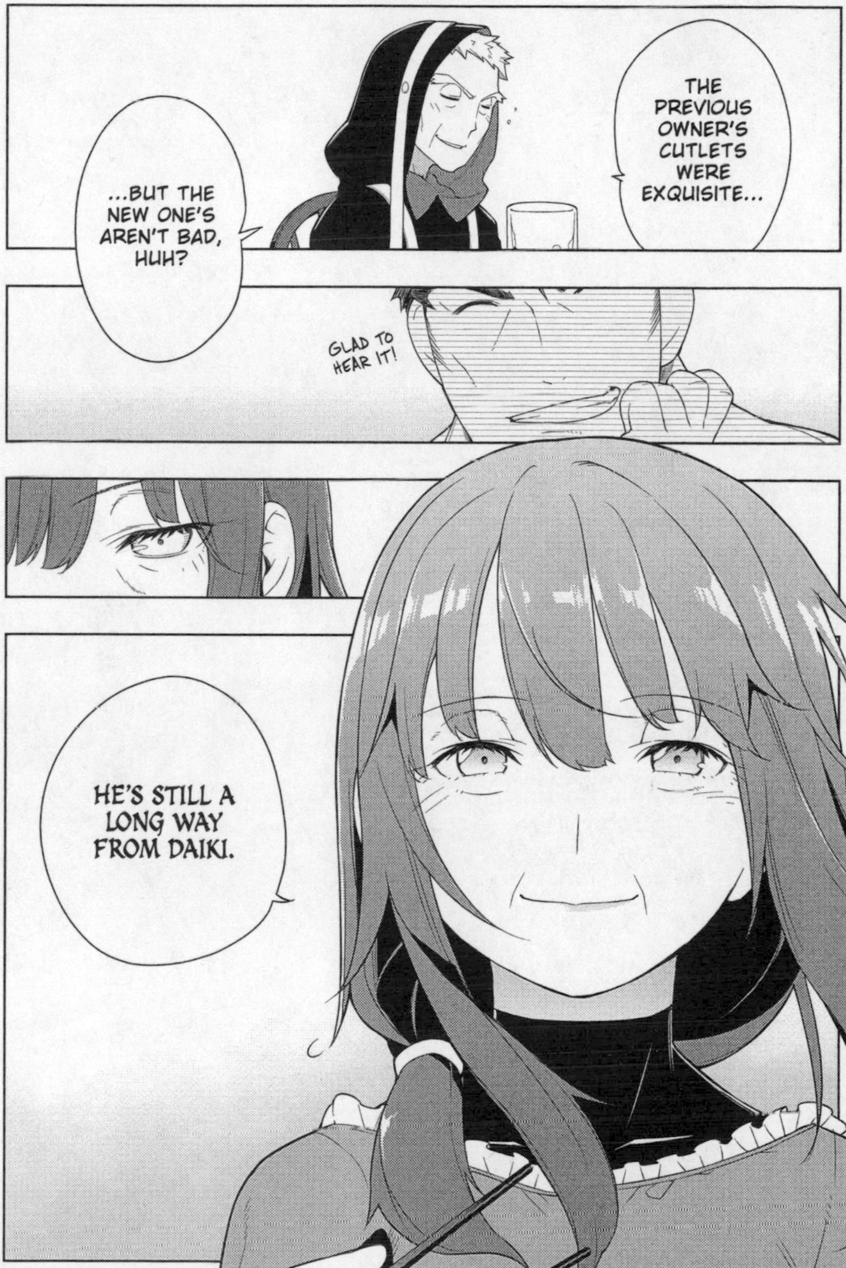
THE PREVIOUS OWNER'S CUTLETS WERE EXQUISITE...
...BUT THE NEW ONE'S AREN'T BAD, HUH?
GLAD TO HEAR IT!
HE'S STILL A LONG WAY FROM DAIKI.

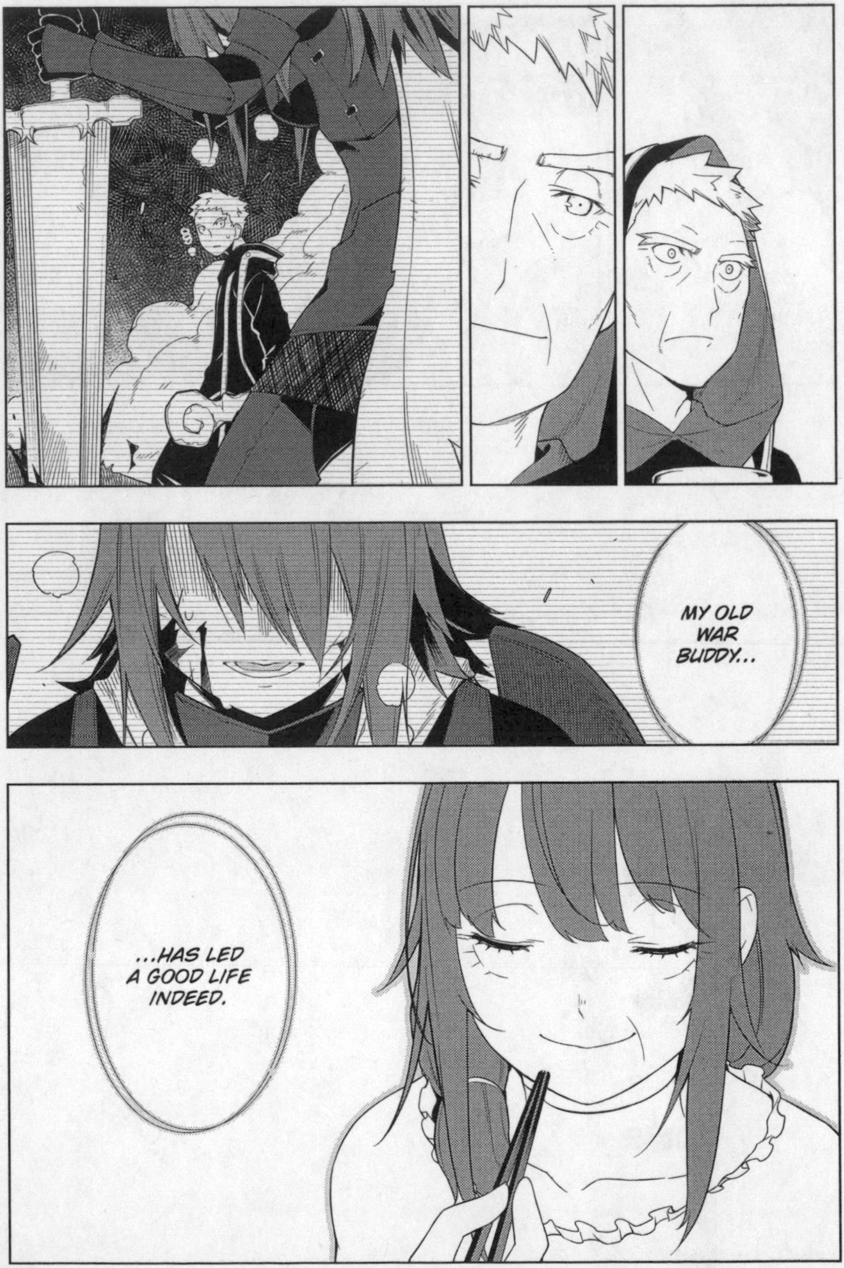
MY OLD WAR BUDDY...
...HAS LED A GOOD LIFE INDEED.

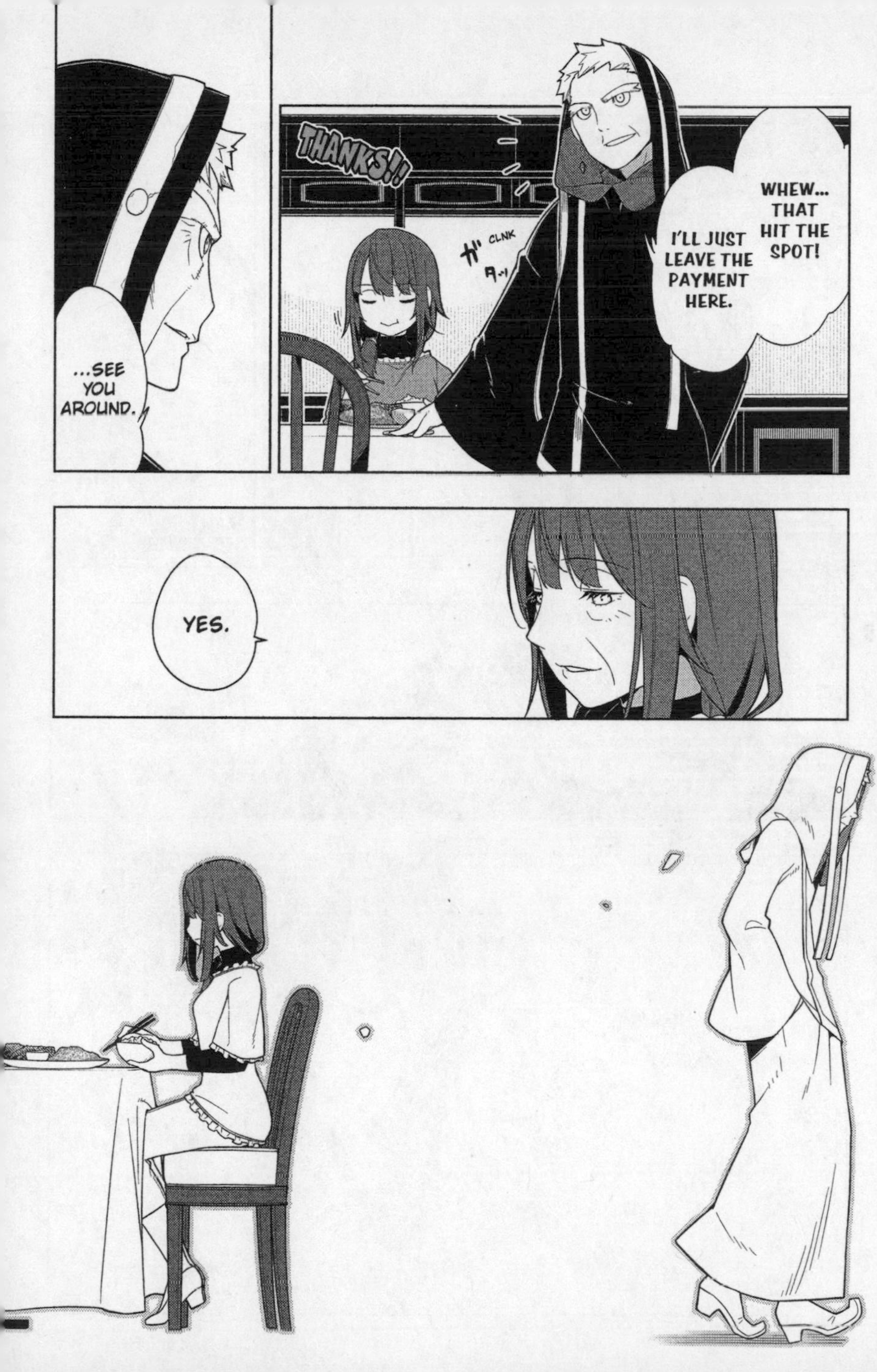
WHEW... THAT HIT THE SPOT!
I'LL JUST LEAVE THE PAYMENT HERE.
THANKS!!
CLNK
...SEE YOU AROUND.
YES.

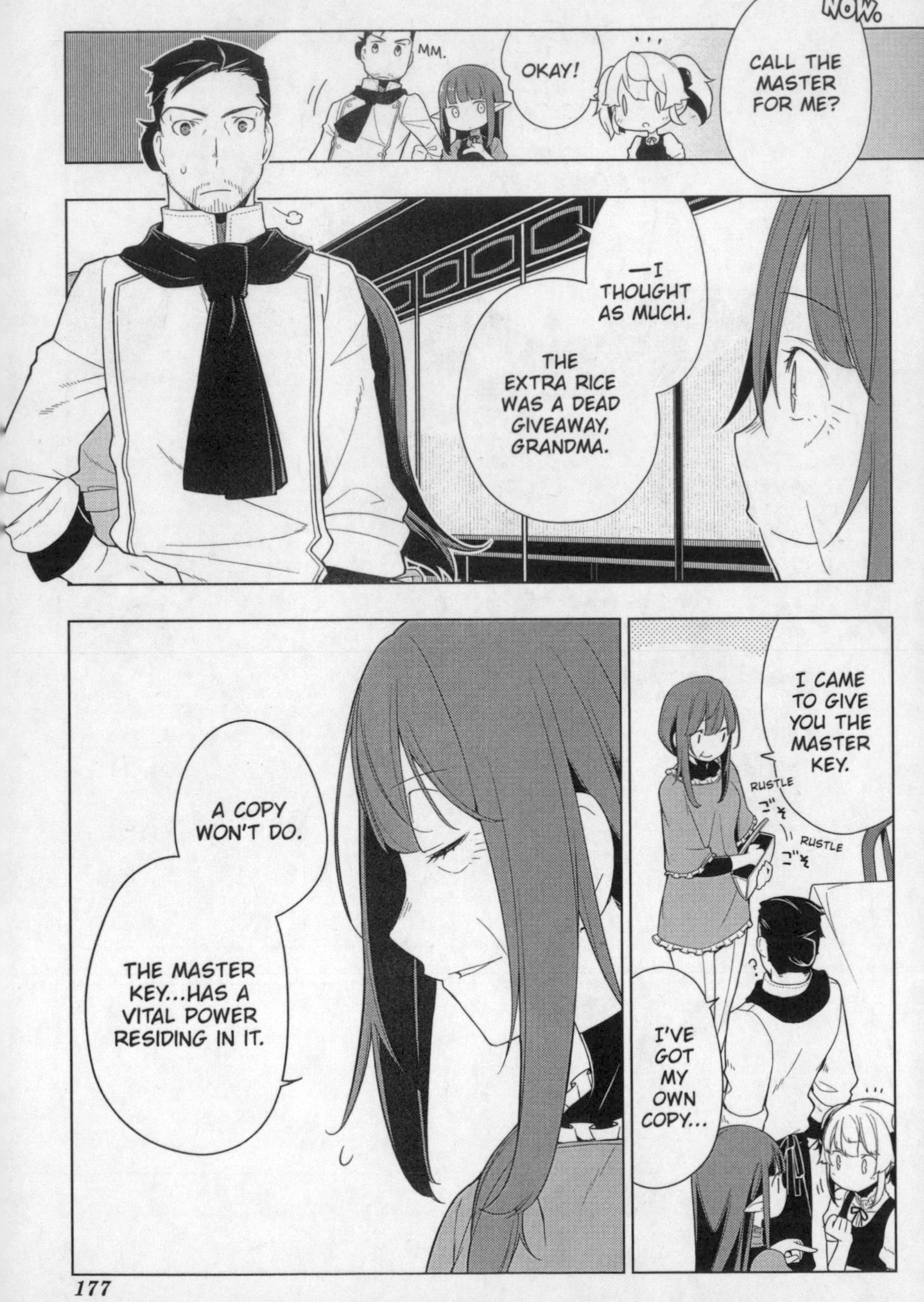
NOW.
CALL THE MASTER FOR ME?
...
OKAY!
MM.
—I THOUGHT AS MUCH.
THE EXTRA RICE WAS A DEAD GIVEAWAY, GRANDMA.
I CAME TO GIVE YOU THE MASTER KEY.
RUSTLE
RUSTLE
I'VE GOT MY OWN COPY...
...
A COPY WON'T DO.
THE MASTER KEY...HAS A VITAL POWER RESIDING IN IT.

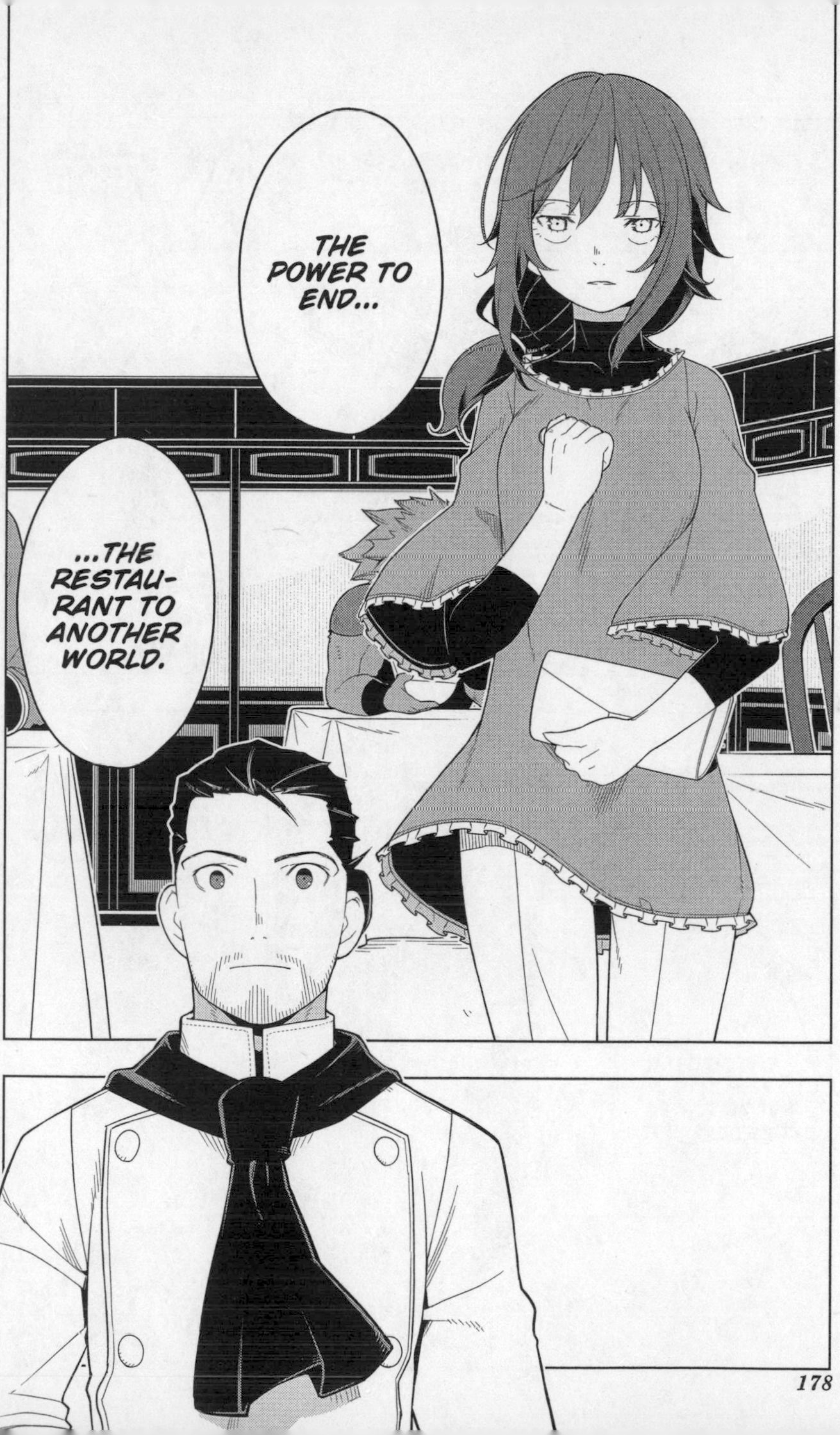
THE POWER TO END...
...THE RESTAU-RANT TO ANOTHER WORLD.

EVEN WITH DAIKI GONE...
...YOU'VE KEPT THIS PLACE GOING.
SO...
...I'M NOT THE ONE WHO SHOULD HOLD THE KEY.

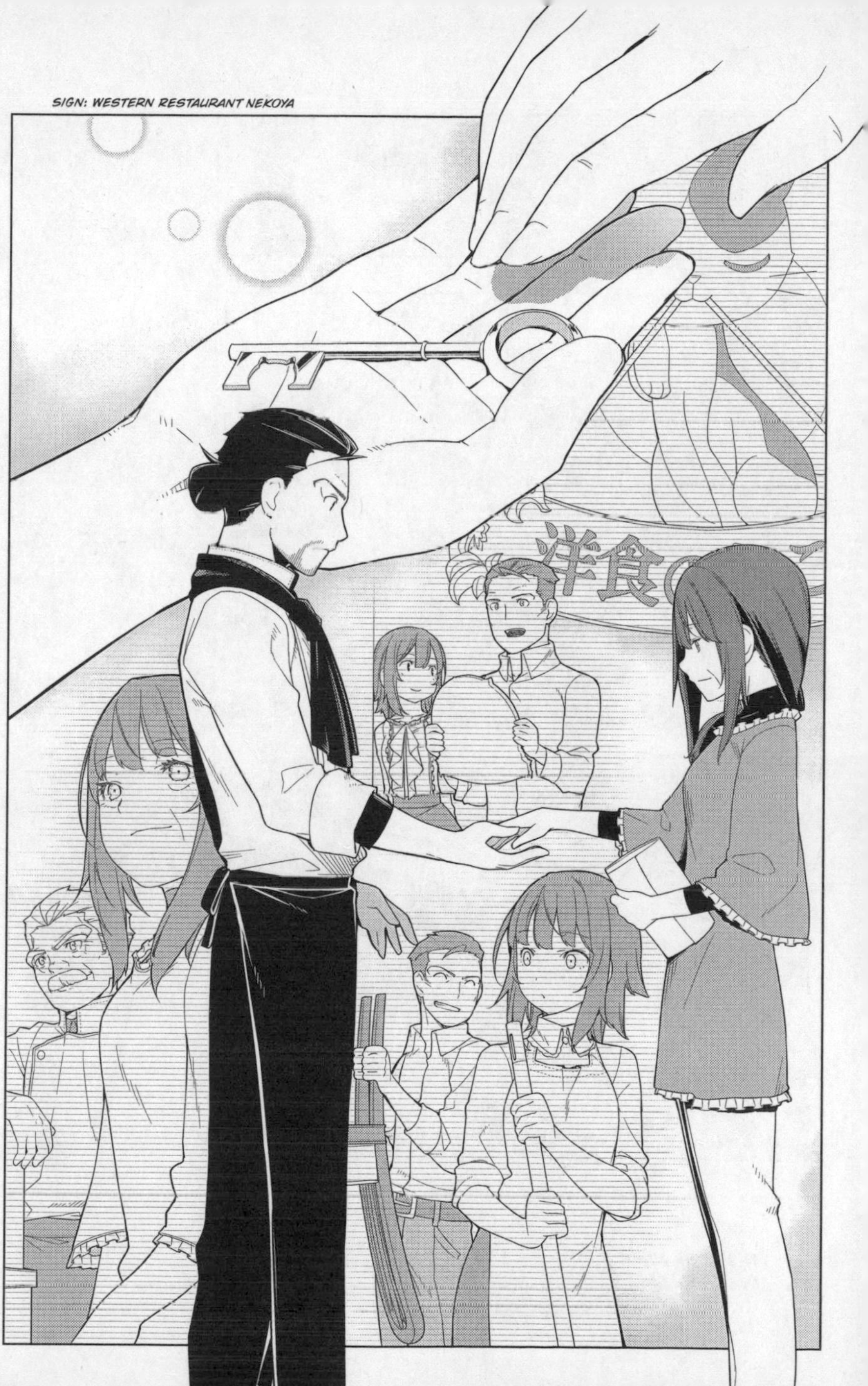
SIGN: WESTERN RESTAURANT NEKOYA

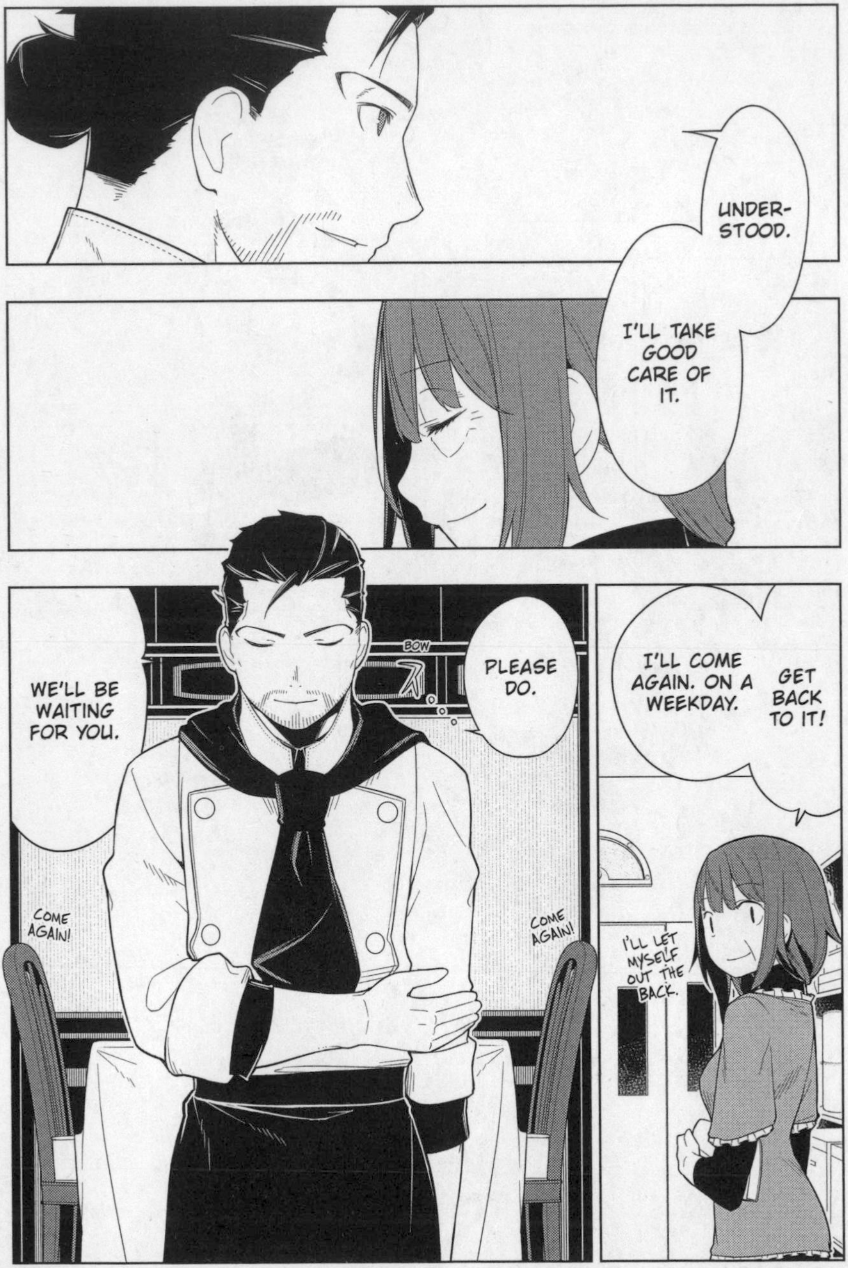
UNDER-STOOD.
I'LL TAKE GOOD CARE OF IT.
I'LL COME AGAIN. ON A WEEKDAY.
GET BACK TO IT!
I'LL LET MYSELF OUT THE BACK.
PLEASE DO.
BOW
WE'LL BE WAITING FOR YOU.
COME AGAIN!
COME AGAIN!

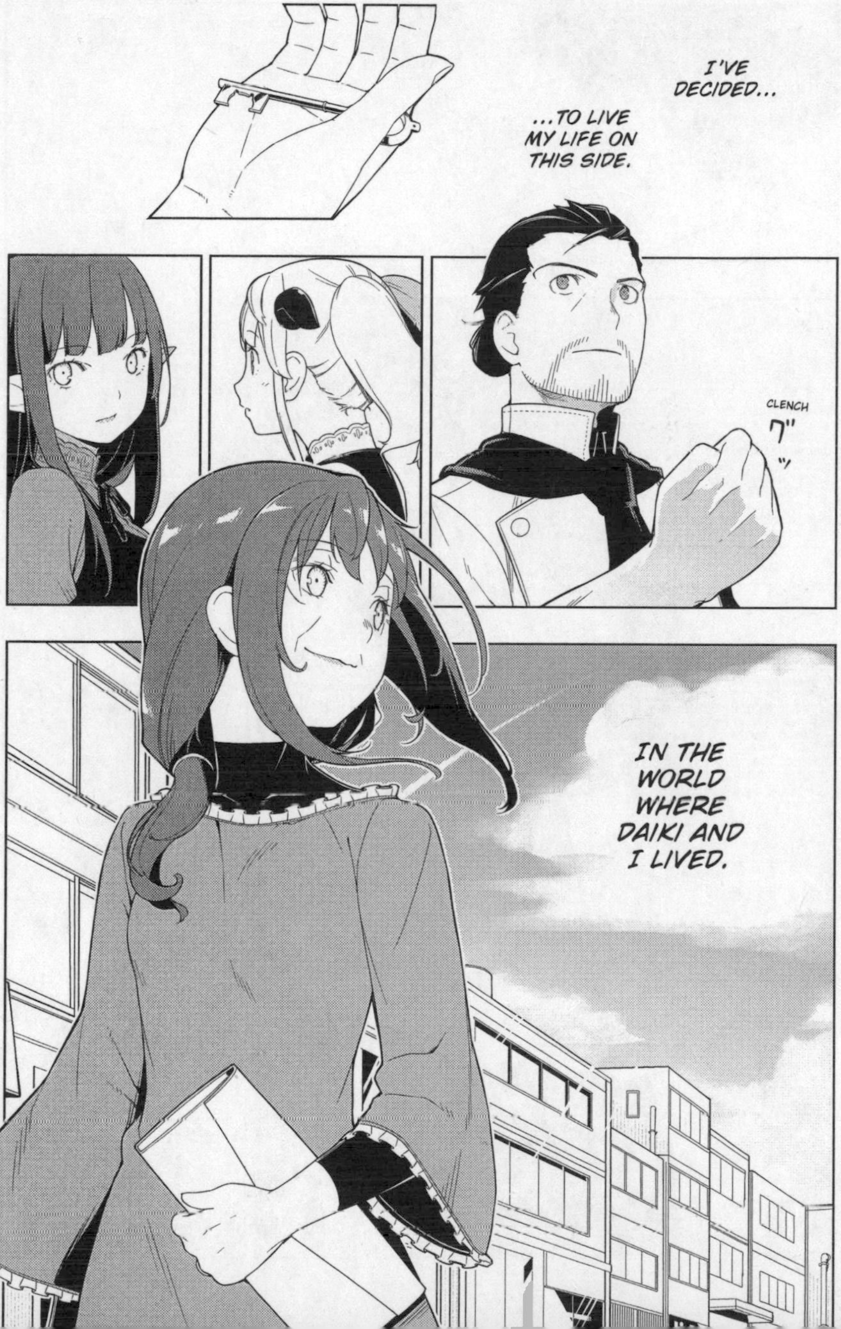
I'VE DECIDED...
...TO LIVE MY LIFE ON THIS SIDE.
CLENCH
グッ
IN THE WORLD WHERE DAIKI AND I LIVED.

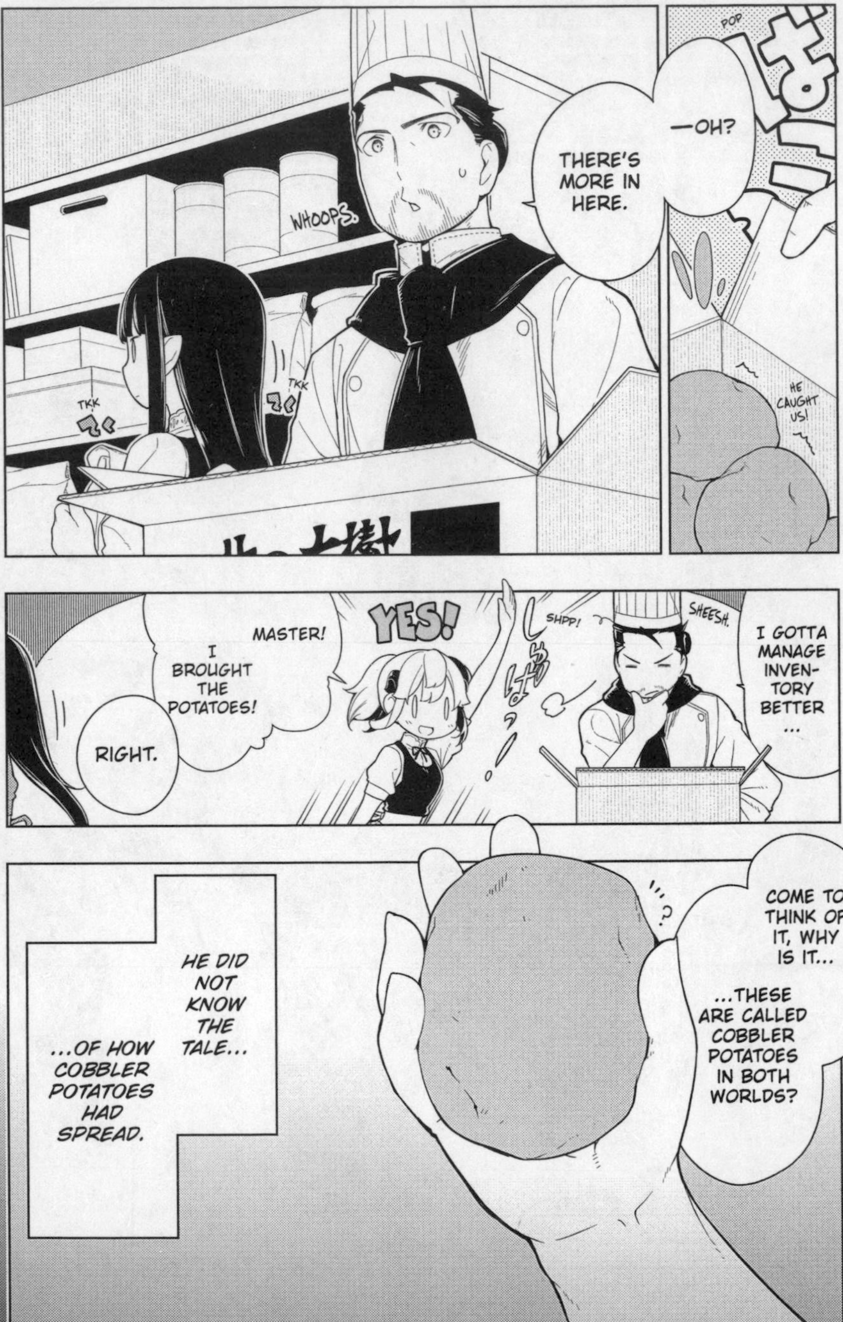
POP
—OH?
THERE'S MORE IN HERE.
HE CAUGHT US!
WHOOPS.
TKK
TKK
I GOTTA MANAGE INVENTORY BETTER...
SHEESH.
SHPP!
YES!
MASTER! I BROUGHT THE POTATOES!
RIGHT.
COME TO THINK OF IT, WHY IS IT...
...THESE ARE CALLED COBBLER POTATOES IN BOTH WORLDS?
HE DID NOT KNOW THE TALE...
...OF HOW COBBLER POTATOES HAD SPREAD.

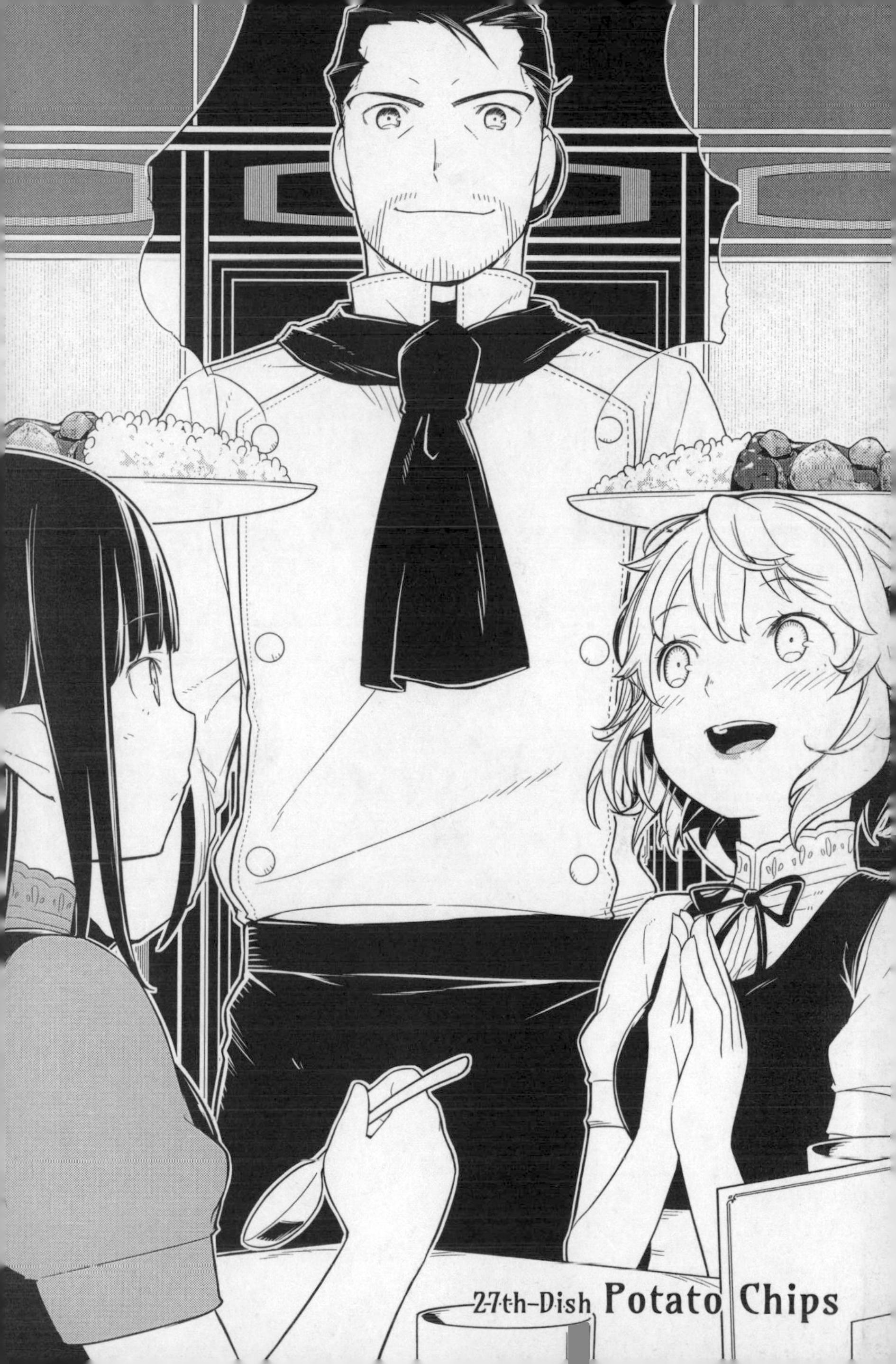
27th-Dish Potato Chips

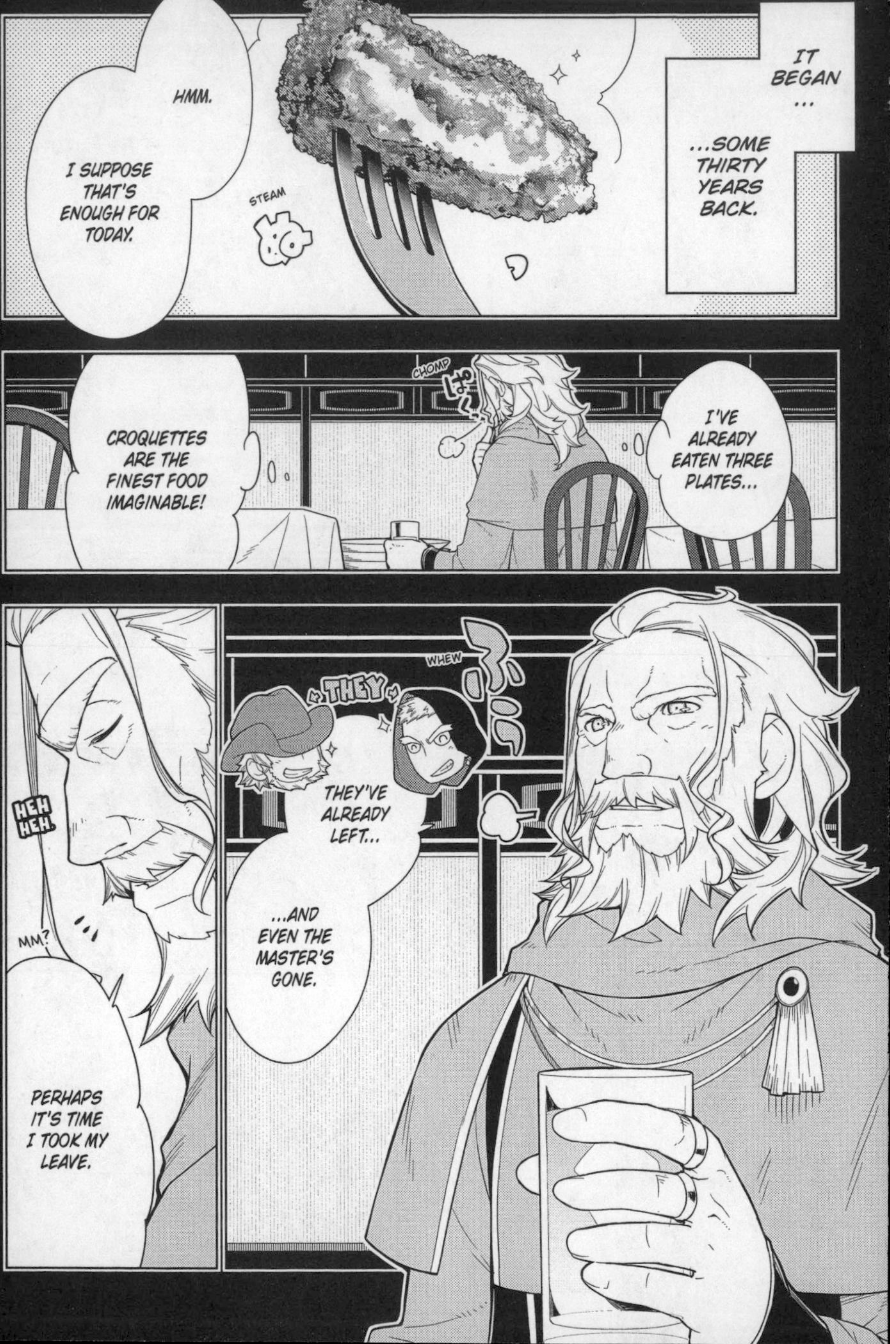

IT BEGAN ...
...SOME THIRTY YEARS BACK.
HMM.
I SUPPOSE THAT'S ENOUGH FOR TODAY.
STEAM
CHOMP
I'VE ALREADY EATEN THREE PLATES...
CROQUETTES ARE THE FINEST FOOD IMAGINABLE!
WHEW
THEY
THEY'VE ALREADY LEFT...
...AND EVEN THE MASTER'S GONE.
HEH HEH.
MM?
PERHAPS IT'S TIME I TOOK MY LEAVE.

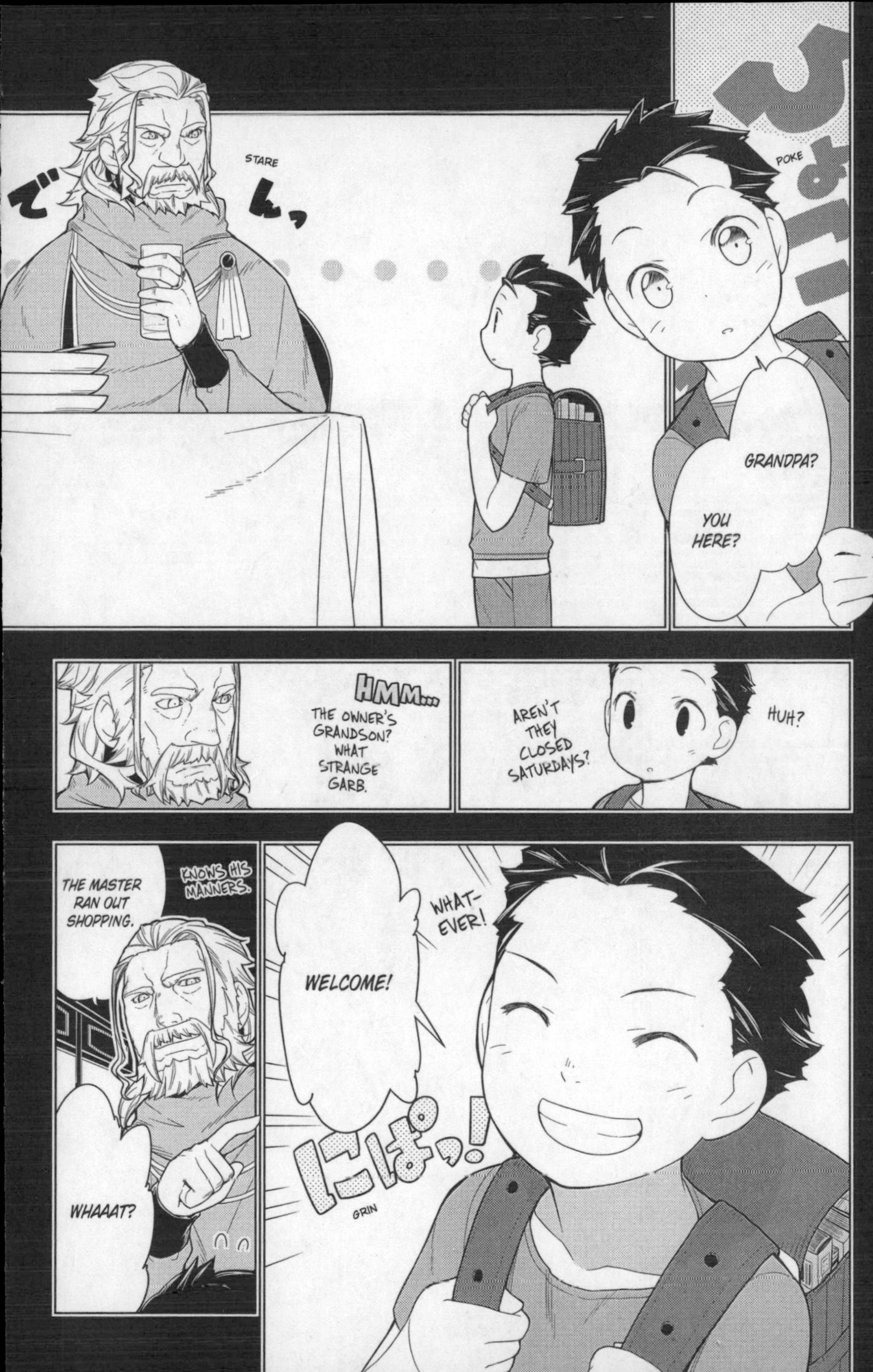
POKE
GRANDPA?
YOU HERE?
STARE
HUH?
AREN'T THEY CLOSED SATURDAYS?
HMM...
THE OWNER'S GRANDSON? WHAT STRANGE GARB.
WELCOME!
WHAT-EVER!
にぱっ!
GRIN
KNOWS HIS MANNERS.
THE MASTER RAN OUT SHOPPING.
WHAAAT?

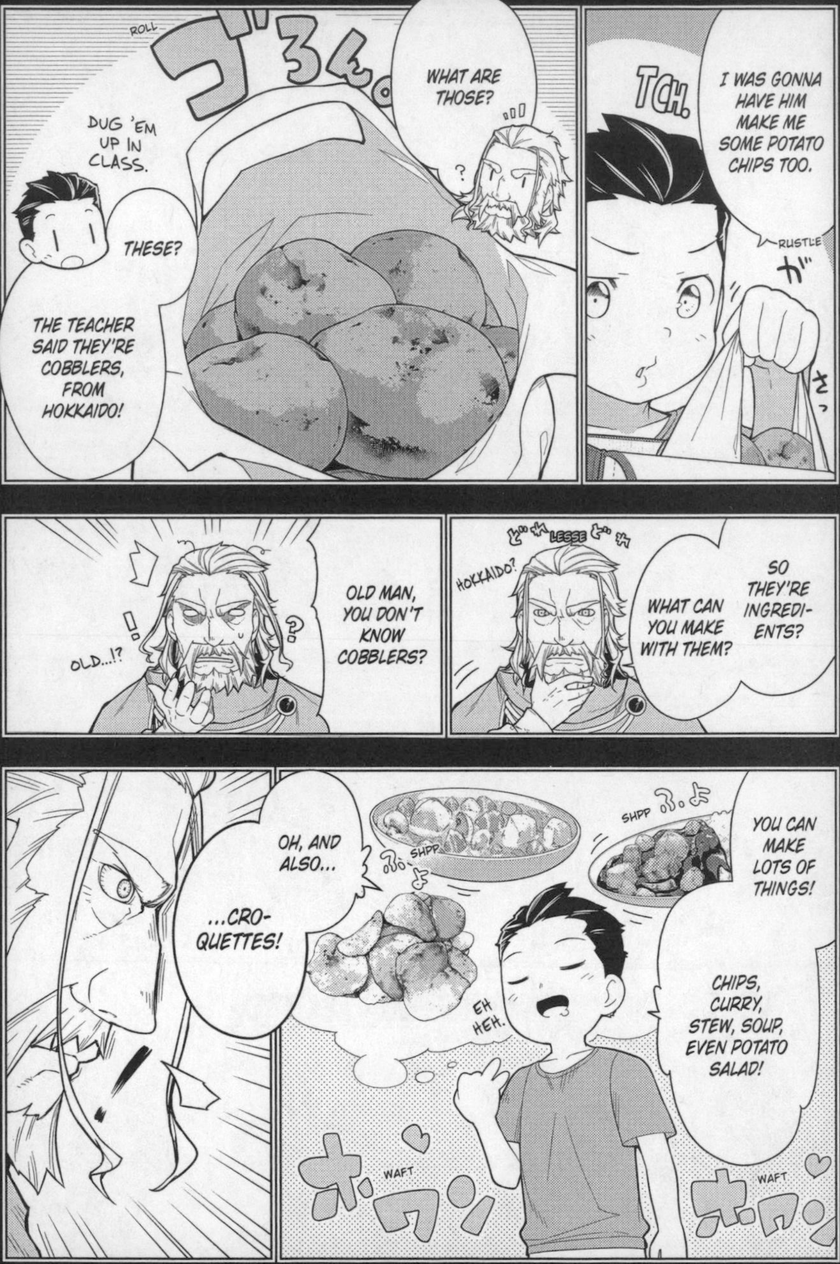
TCH.
I WAS GONNA HAVE HIM MAKE ME SOME POTATO CHIPS TOO.
RUSTLE
ROLL
WHAT ARE THOSE?
?
DUG 'EM UP IN CLASS.
THESE?
THE TEACHER SAID THEY'RE COBBLERS, FROM HOKKAIDO!
LESSE
SO THEY'RE INGREDI-ENTS?
WHAT CAN YOU MAKE WITH THEM?
HOKKAIDO?
OLD MAN, YOU DON'T KNOW COBBLERS?
!
?
OLD...!?
YOU CAN MAKE LOTS OF THINGS!
SHPP
CHIPS, CURRY, STEW, SOUP, EVEN POTATO SALAD!
SHPP
OH, AND ALSO...
...CRO-QUETTES!
EH HEH.
WAFT
WAFT

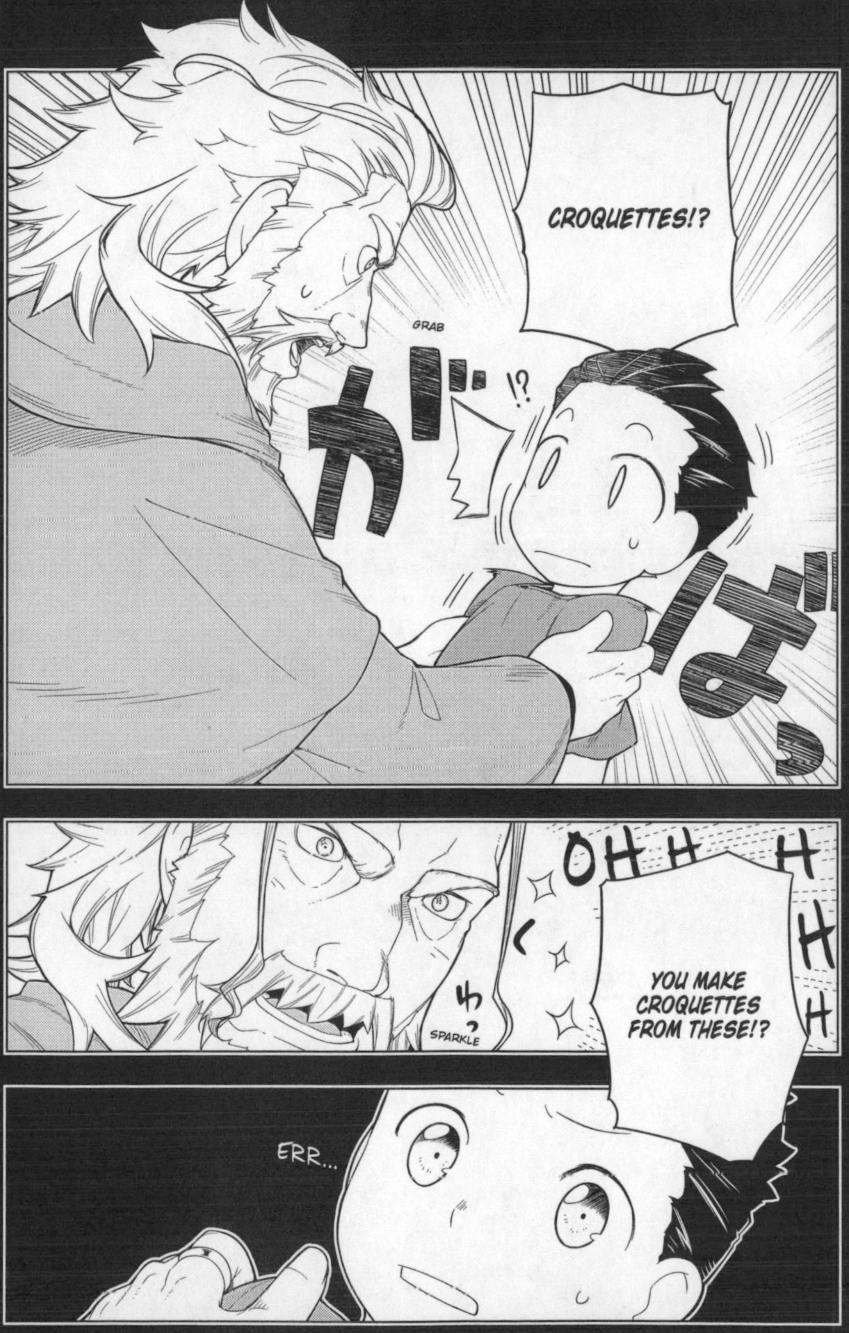
CROQUETTES!?
GRAB
!?
OHHHHHH
YOU MAKE CROQUETTES FROM THESE!?
SPARKLE
ERR...

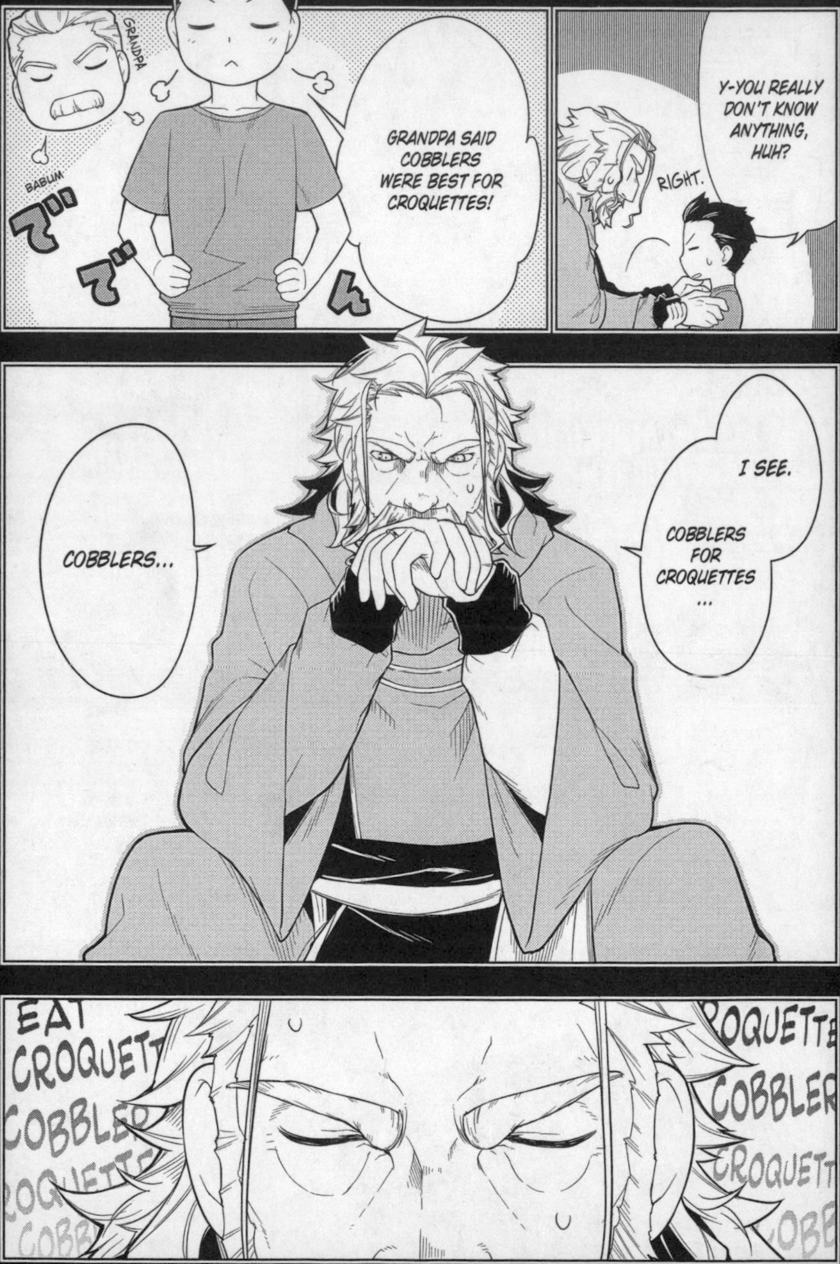
Y-YOU REALLY DON'T KNOW ANYTHING, HUH?
RIGHT.
GRANDPA SAID COBBLERS WERE BEST FOR CROQUETTES!
GRANDPA
BABUM
I SEE.
COBBLERS FOR CROQUETTES ...
COBBLERS...
EAT

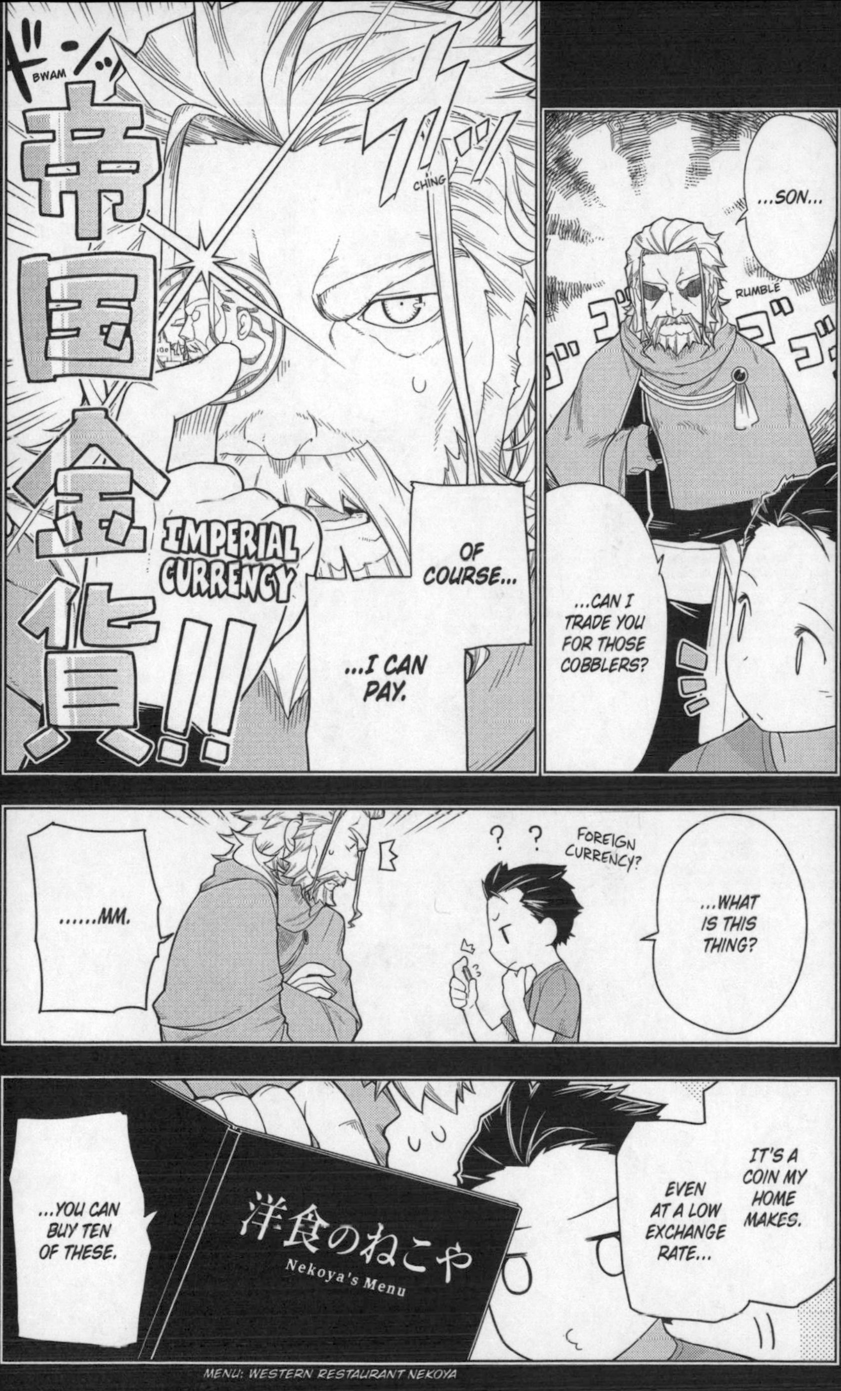
...SON...
RUMBLE
...CAN I TRADE YOU FOR THOSE COBBLERS?
BWAM
CHING
帝国金貨!!
IMPERIAL CURRENCY
OF COURSE...
...I CAN PAY.
...WHAT IS THIS THING?
FOREIGN CURRENCY?
? ?
......MM.
IT'S A COIN MY HOME MAKES.
EVEN AT A LOW EXCHANGE RATE...
洋食のねこや
Nekoya's Menu
...YOU CAN BUY TEN OF THESE.

MENU: WESTERN RESTAURANT NEKOYA

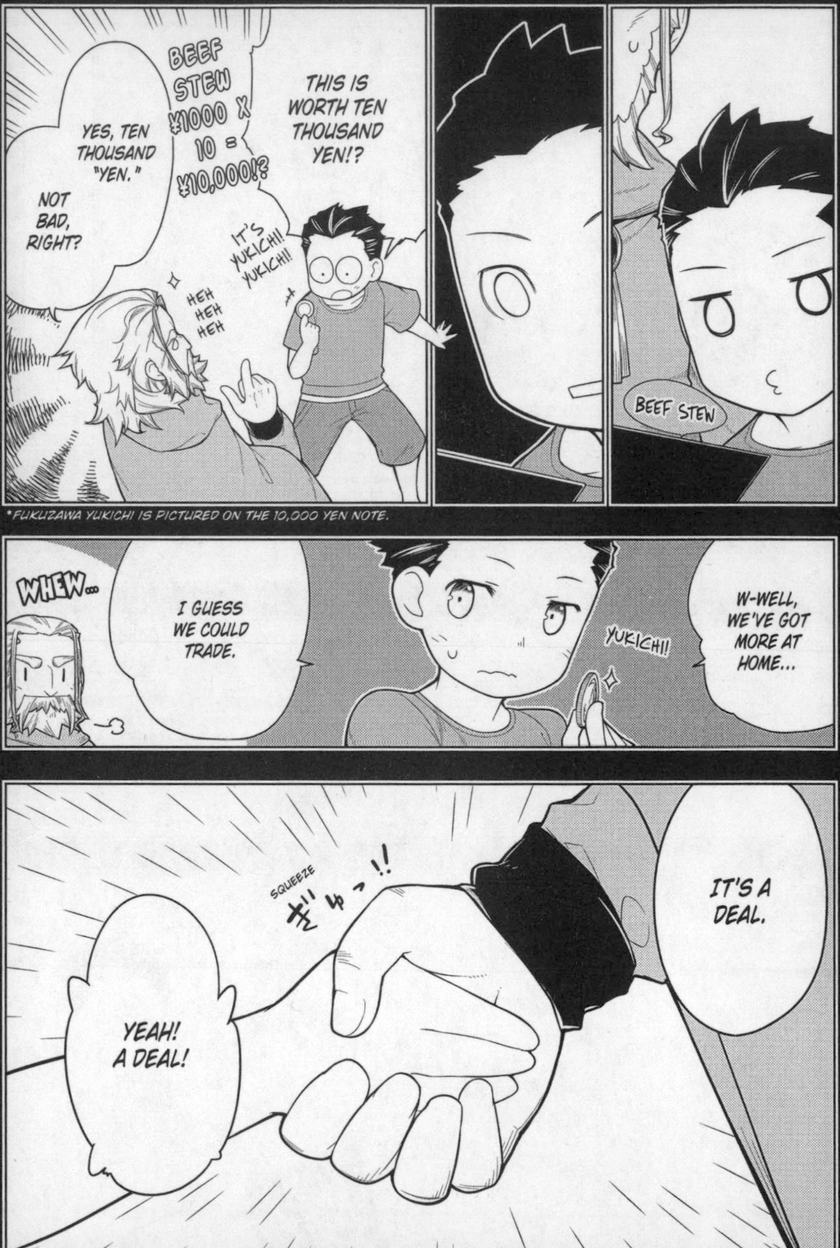
BEEF STEW
THIS IS WORTH TEN THOUSAND YEN!?
BEEF STEW ¥1000 X 10 = ¥10,000!?
YES, TEN THOUSAND "YEN."
NOT BAD, RIGHT?
IT'S YUKICHI! YUKICHI!
HEH HEH HEH
W-WELL, WE'VE GOT MORE AT HOME...
YUKICHI!
I GUESS WE COULD TRADE.
WHEW...
IT'S A DEAL.
SQUEEZE
YEAH! A DEAL!

*FUKUZAWA YUKICHI IS PICTURED ON THE 10,000 YEN NOTE.

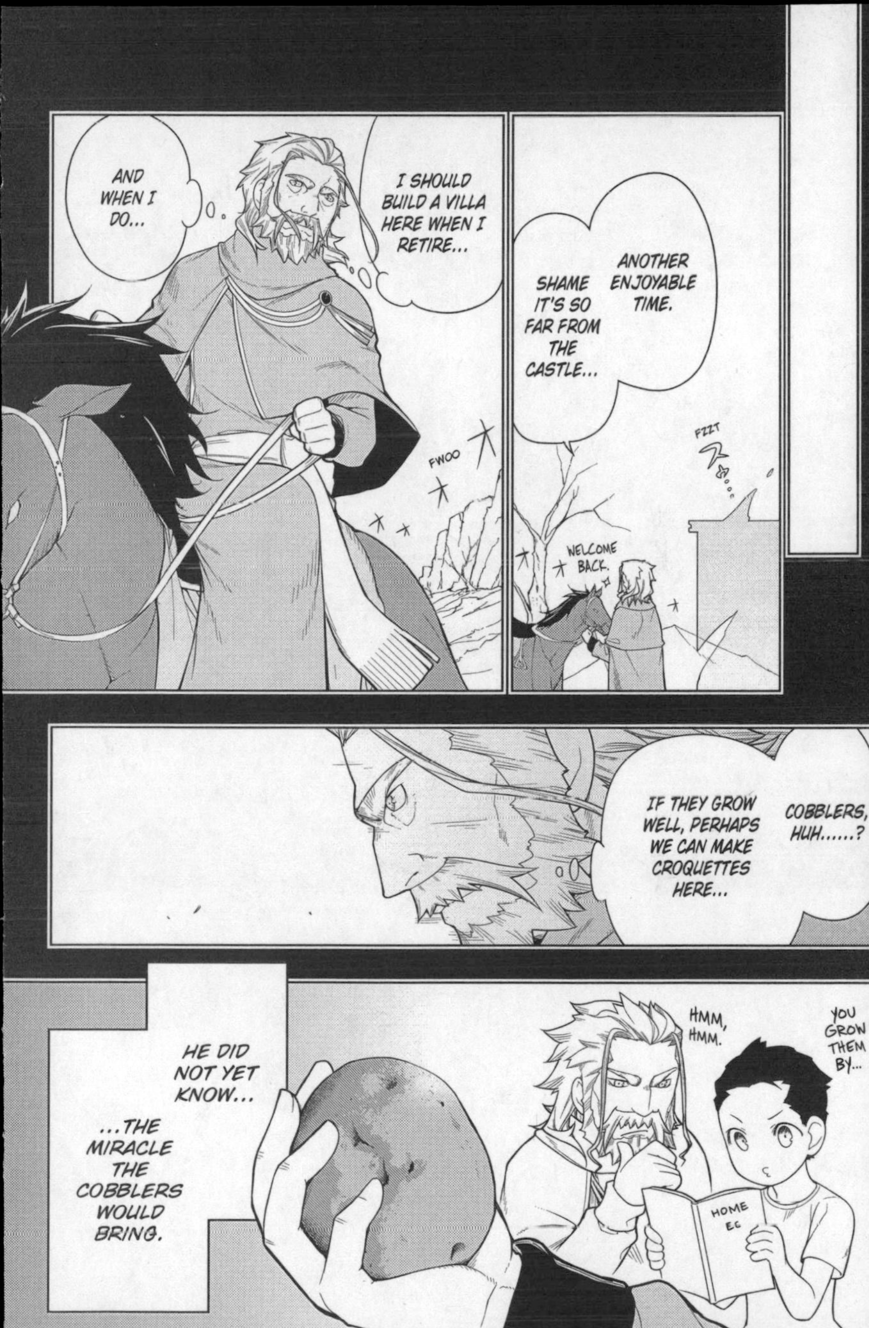
ANOTHER ENJOYABLE TIME.
SHAME IT'S SO FAR FROM THE CASTLE...
FZZT
WELCOME BACK.
I SHOULD BUILD A VILLA HERE WHEN I RETIRE...
AND WHEN I DO...
FWOO
COBBLERS, HUH......?
IF THEY GROW WELL, PERHAPS WE CAN MAKE CROQUETTES HERE...
YOU GROW THEM BY...
HMM, HMM.
HOME EC
HE DID NOT YET KNOW...
...THE MIRACLE THE COBBLERS WOULD BRING.

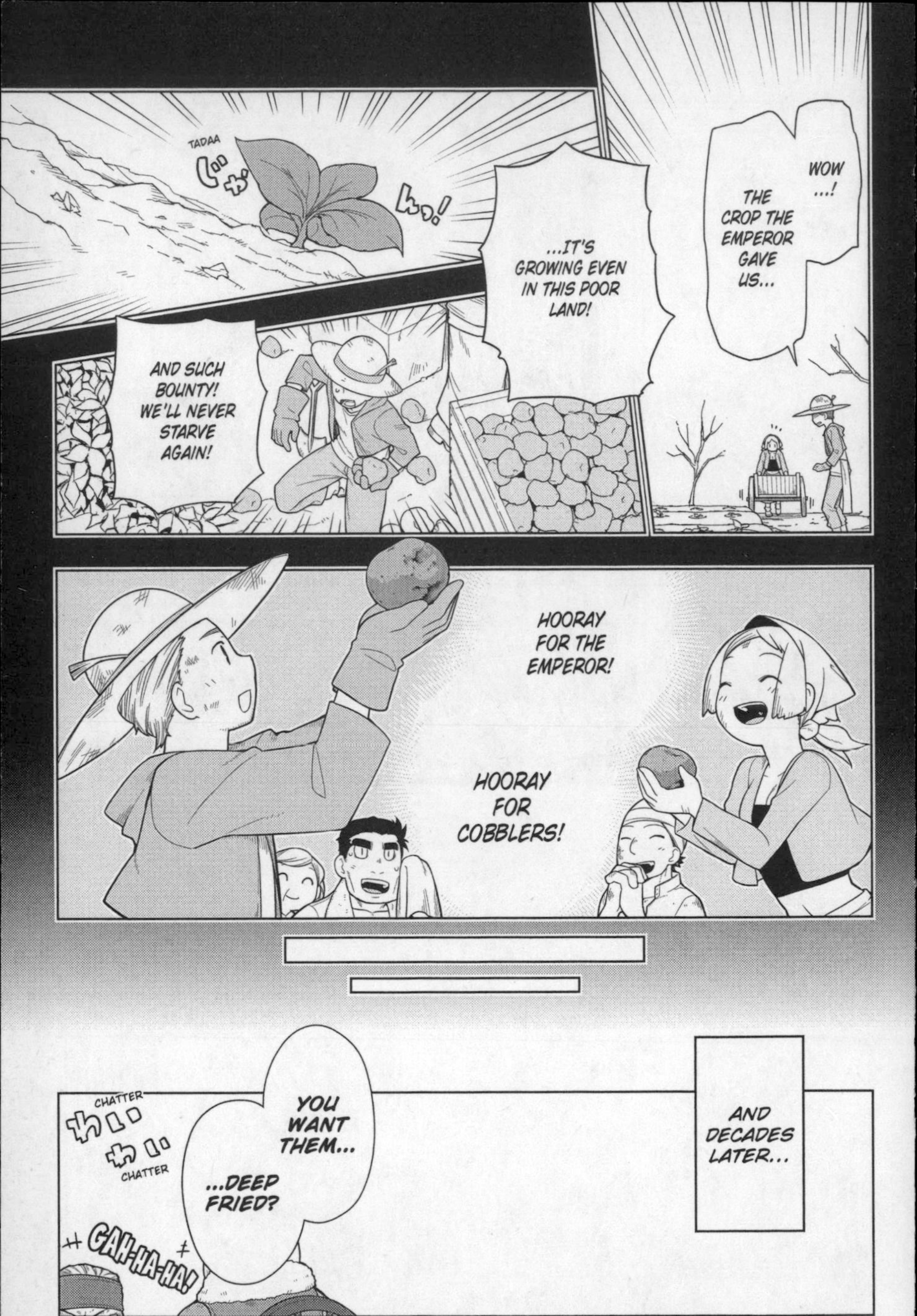
WOW ...!
THE CROP THE EMPEROR GAVE US...
TADAA
...IT'S GROWING EVEN IN THIS POOR LAND!
AND SUCH BOUNTY! WE'LL NEVER STARVE AGAIN!
HOORAY FOR THE EMPEROR!
HOORAY FOR COBBLERS!
AND DECADES LATER...
YOU WANT THEM...
...DEEP FRIED?
CHATTER
CHATTER
GAH-HA-HA!

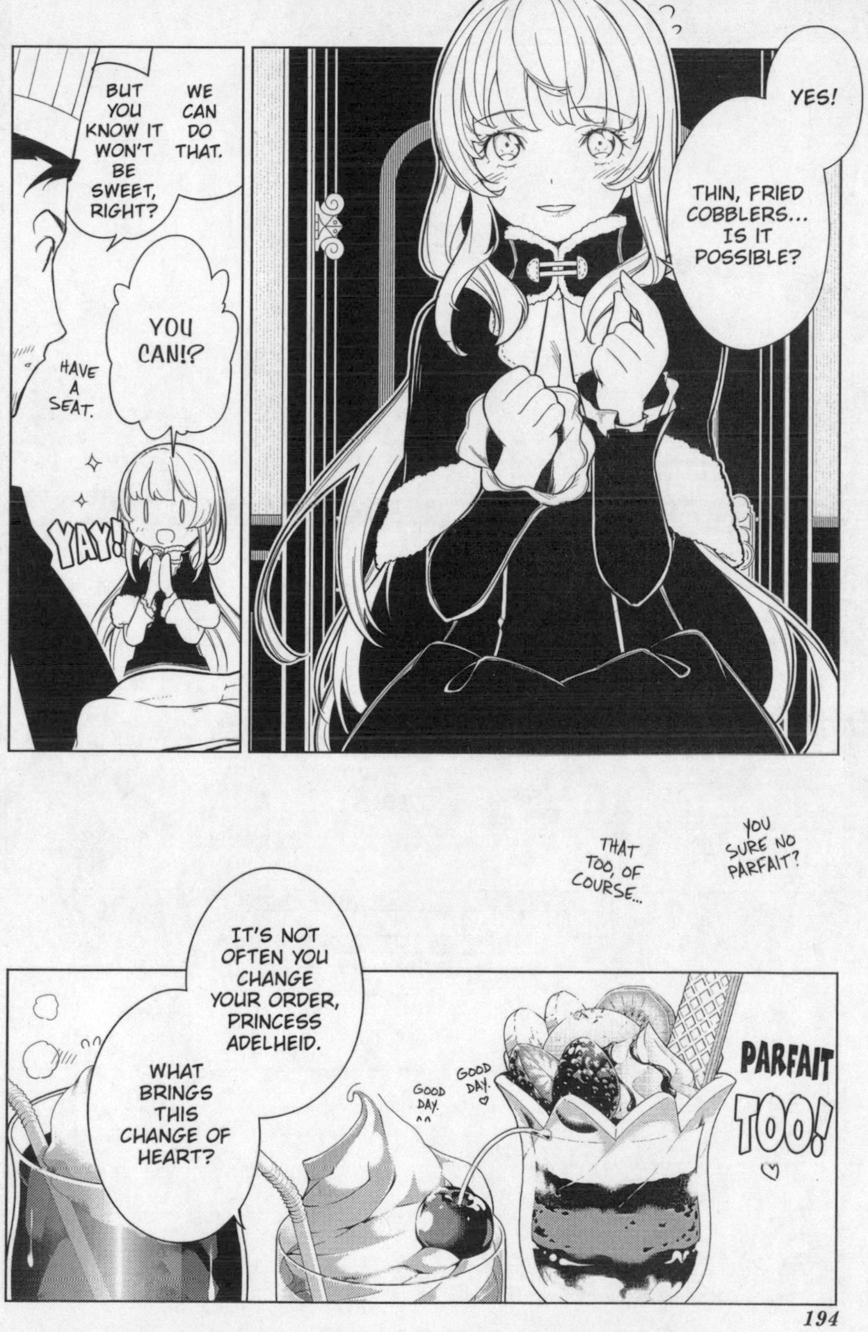
YES!
THIN, FRIED COBBLERS... IS IT POSSIBLE?
WE CAN DO THAT.
BUT YOU KNOW IT WON'T BE SWEET, RIGHT?
YOU CAN!?
HAVE A SEAT.
YAY!
YOU SURE NO PARFAIT?
THAT TOO, OF COURSE...
IT'S NOT OFTEN YOU CHANGE YOUR ORDER, PRINCESS ADELHEID.
WHAT BRINGS THIS CHANGE OF HEART?
PARFAIT TOO!
GOOD DAY.
GOOD DAY.

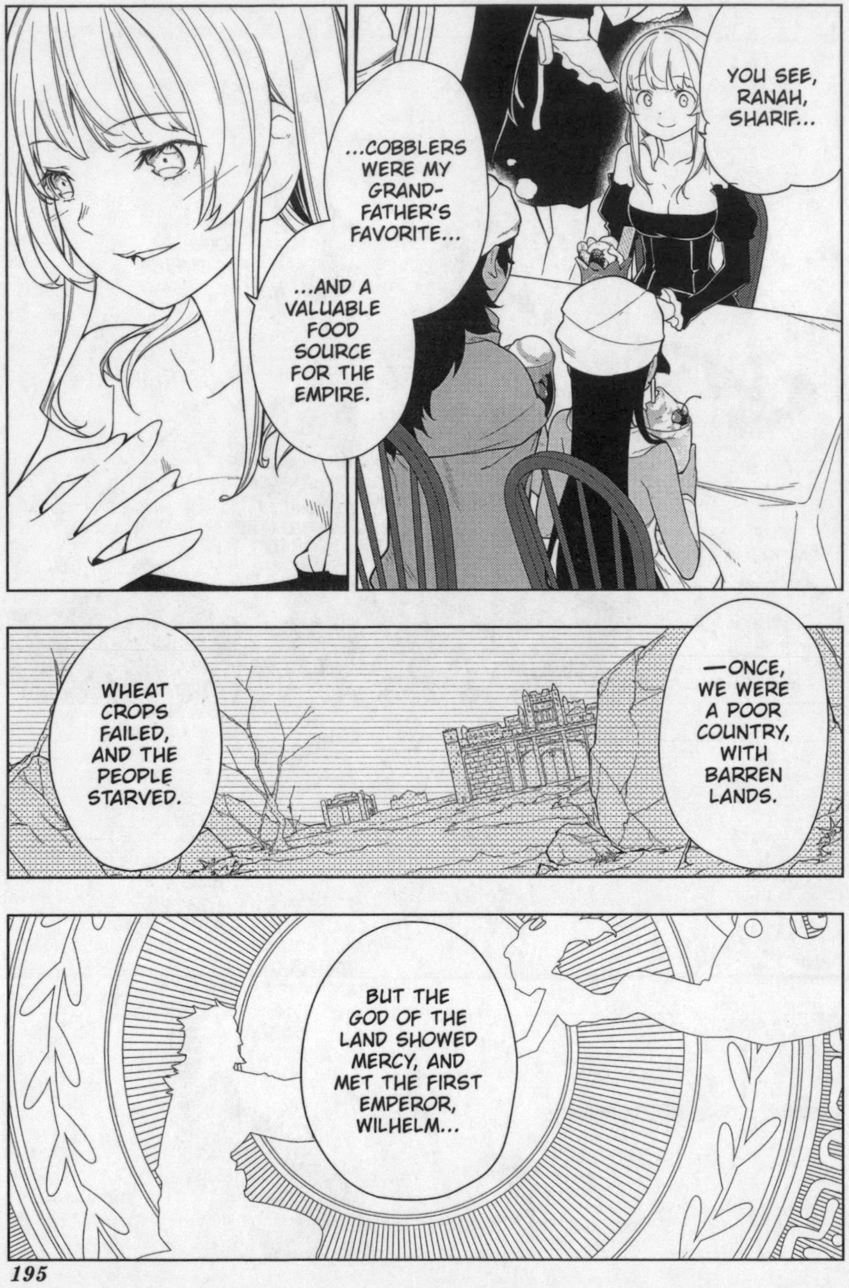
YOU SEE, RANAH, SHARIF...
...COBBLERS WERE MY GRAND-FATHER'S FAVORITE...
...AND A VALUABLE FOOD SOURCE FOR THE EMPIRE.
—ONCE, WE WERE A POOR COUNTRY, WITH BARREN LANDS.
WHEAT CROPS FAILED, AND THE PEOPLE STARVED.
BUT THE GOD OF THE LAND SHOWED MERCY, AND MET THE FIRST EMPEROR, WILHELM...

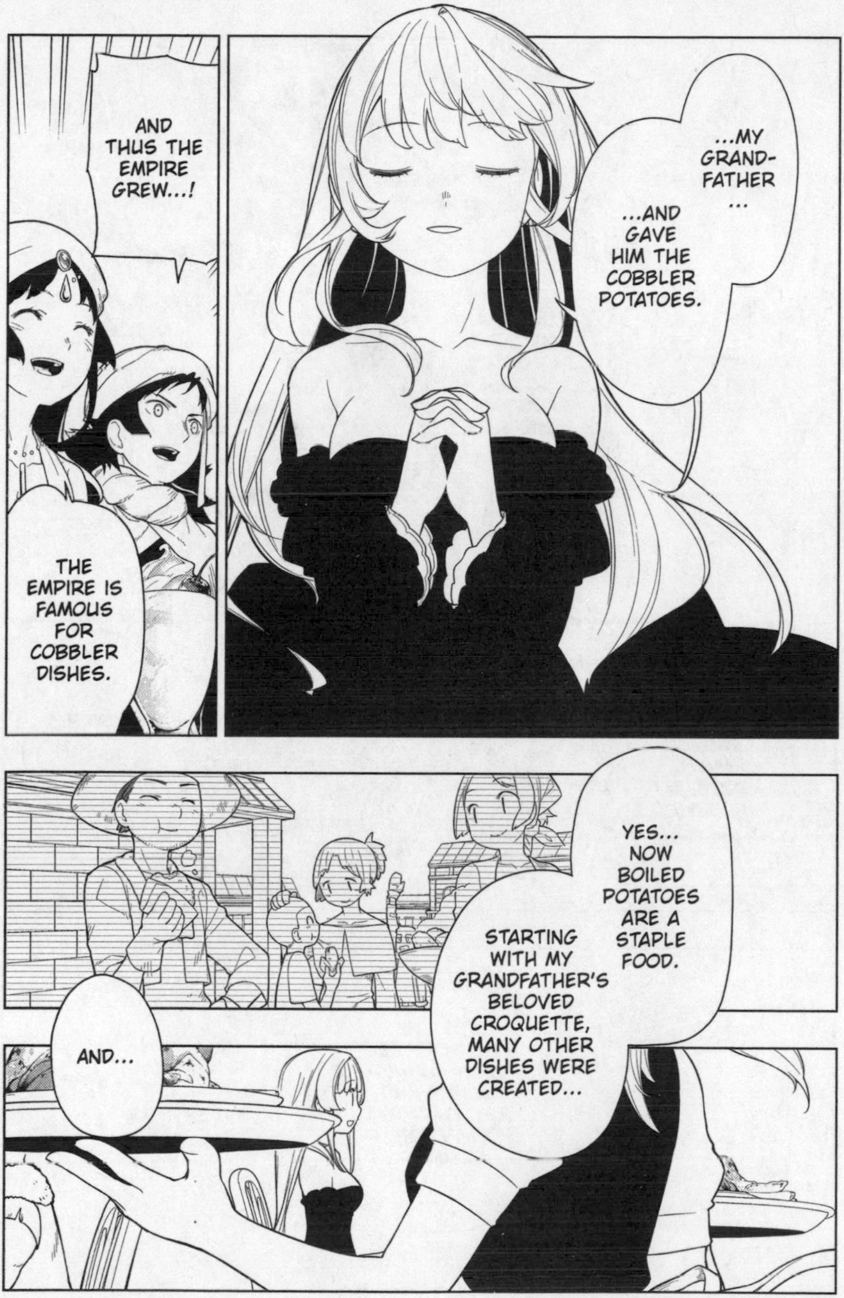
...MY GRANDFATHER ...
...AND GAVE HIM THE COBBLER POTATOES.
AND THUS THE EMPIRE GREW...!
THE EMPIRE IS FAMOUS FOR COBBLER DISHES.
YES... NOW BOILED POTATOES ARE A STAPLE FOOD.
STARTING WITH MY GRANDFATHER'S BELOVED CROQUETTE, MANY OTHER DISHES WERE CREATED...
AND...

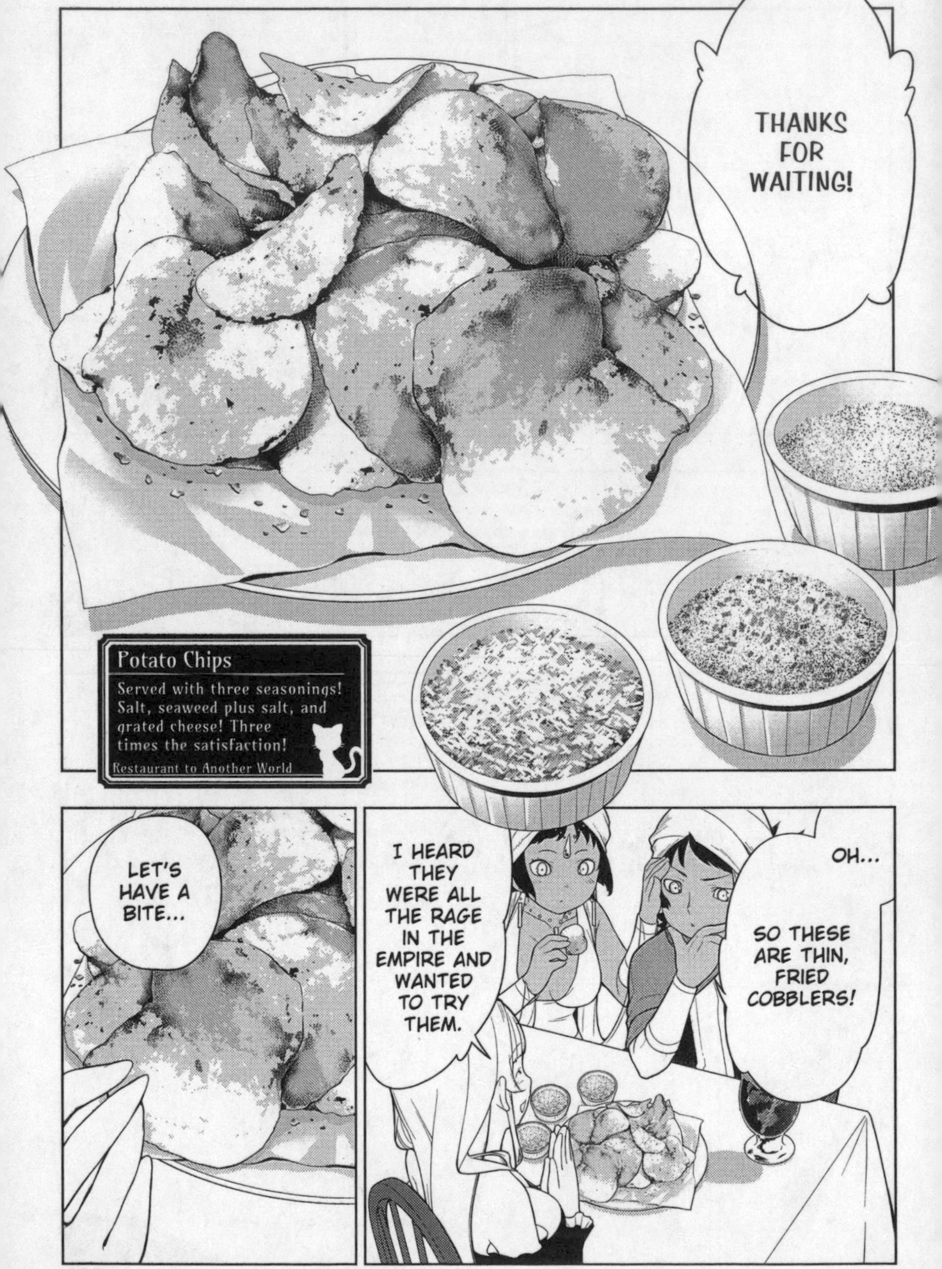
THANKS FOR WAITING!
Potato Chips
Served with three seasonings! Salt, seaweed plus salt, and grated cheese! Three times the satisfaction!
Restaurant to Another World
OH...
SO THESE ARE THIN, FRIED COBBLERS!
I HEARD THEY WERE ALL THE RAGE IN THE EMPIRE AND WANTED TO TRY THEM.
LET'S HAVE A BITE...

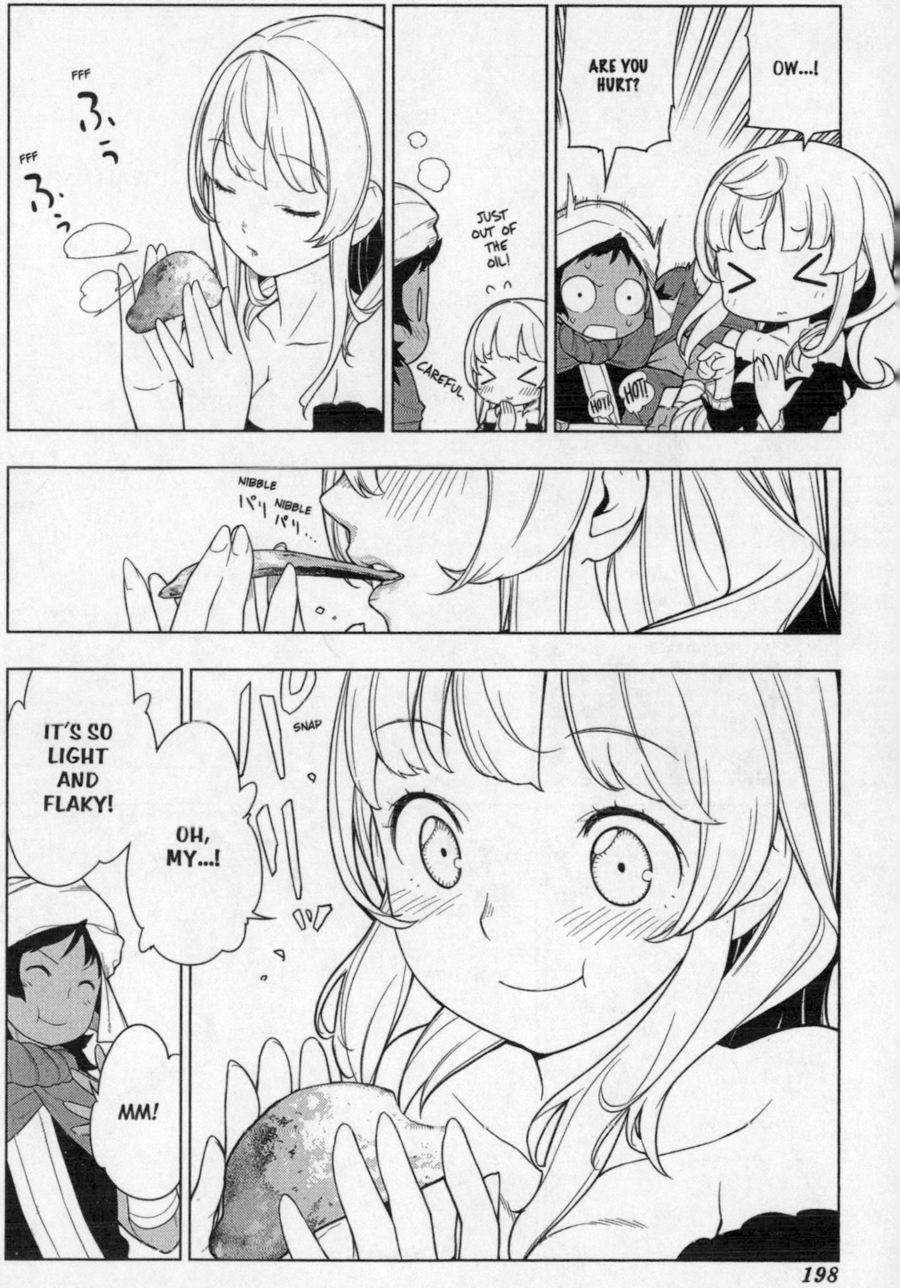
OW...!
ARE YOU HURT?
HOT!
HOT!
JUST OUT OF THE OIL!
CAREFUL.
FFF
ふぅ
FFF
ふぅ
NIBBLE
パリ
NIBBLE
パリ...
SNAP
OH, MY...!
IT'S SO LIGHT AND FLAKY!
MM!

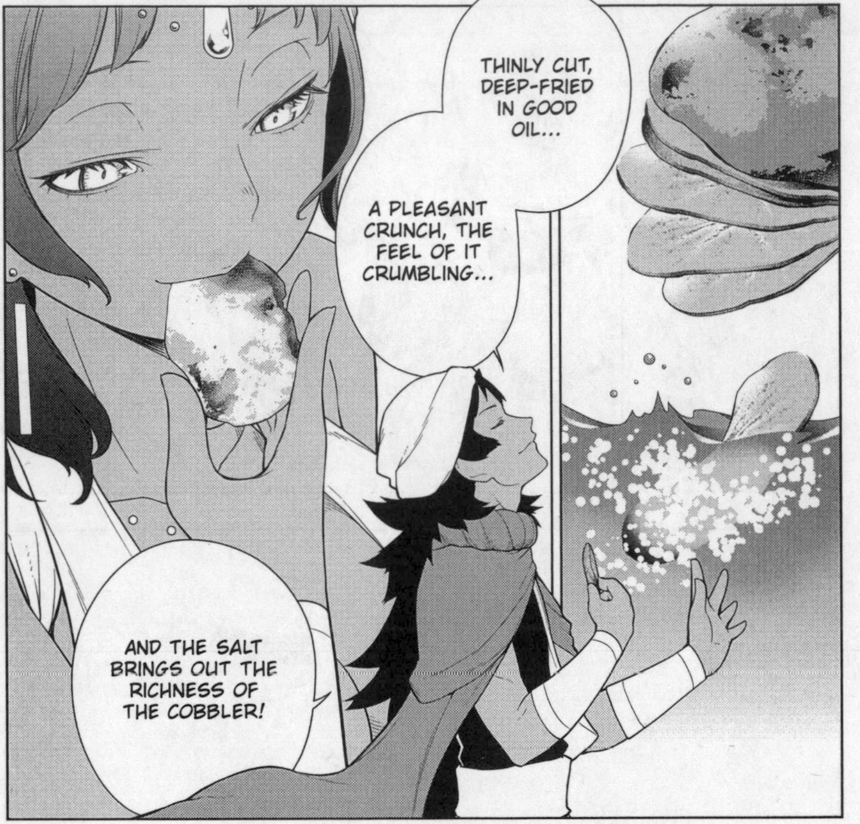
THINLY CUT, DEEP-FRIED IN GOOD OIL...
A PLEASANT CRUNCH, THE FEEL OF IT CRUMBLING...
AND THE SALT BRINGS OUT THE RICHNESS OF THE COBBLER!

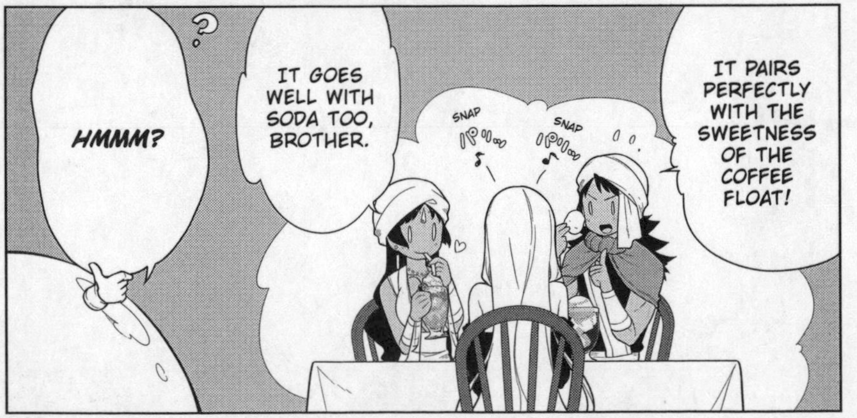
IT PAIRS PERFECTLY WITH THE SWEETNESS OF THE COFFEE FLOAT!
SNAP
SNAP
IT GOES WELL WITH SODA TOO, BROTHER.
?
HMMM?

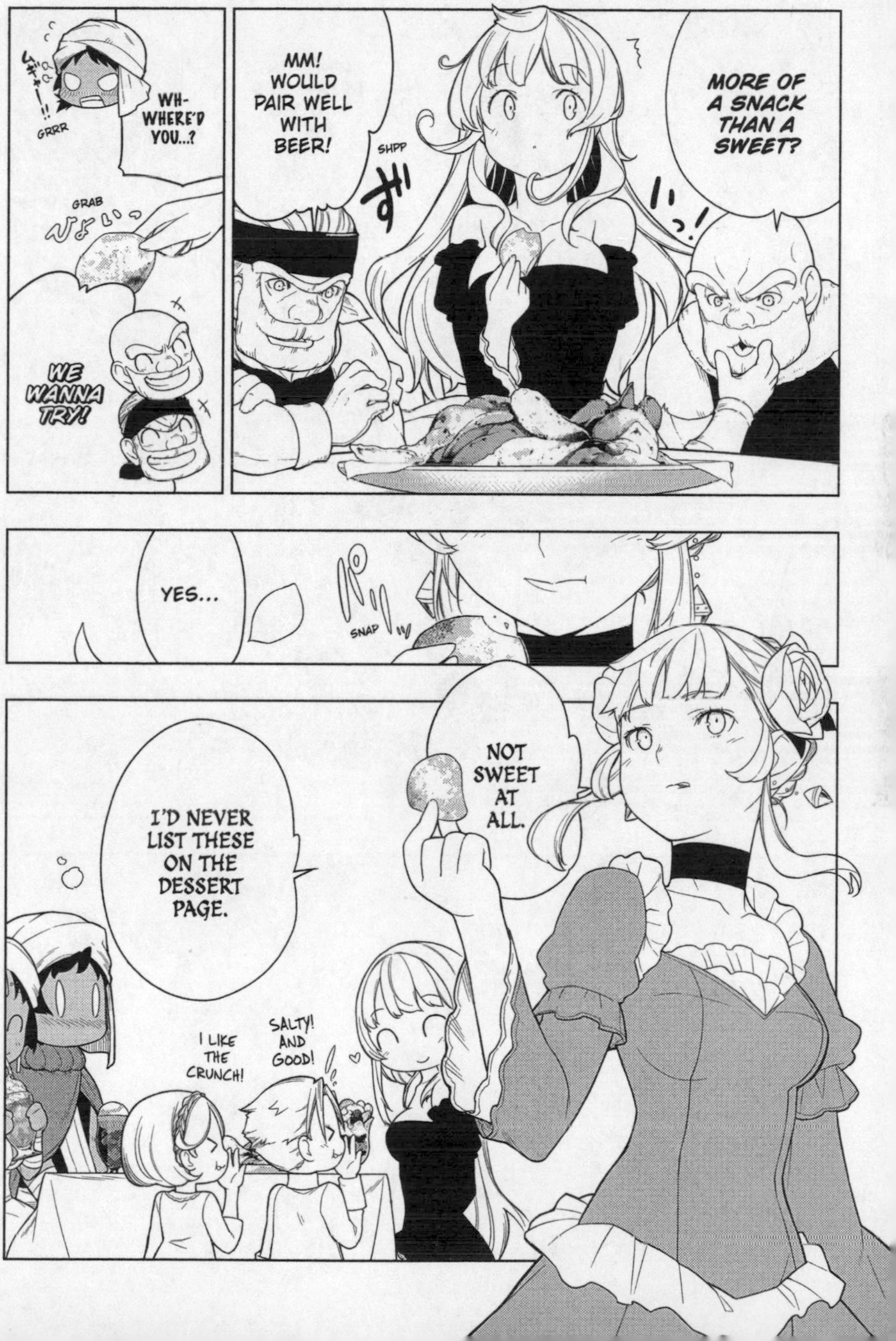
MORE OF A SNACK THAN A SWEET?
MM! WOULD PAIR WELL WITH BEER!
SHPP
ず
WH-WHERE'D YOU...?
ムぎゃー!!
GRRR
GRAB
ぴょいっ
WE WANNA TRY!
YES...
パリッ
SNAP
NOT SWEET AT ALL.
I'D NEVER LIST THESE ON THE DESSERT PAGE.
SALTY! AND GOOD!
I LIKE THE CRUNCH!

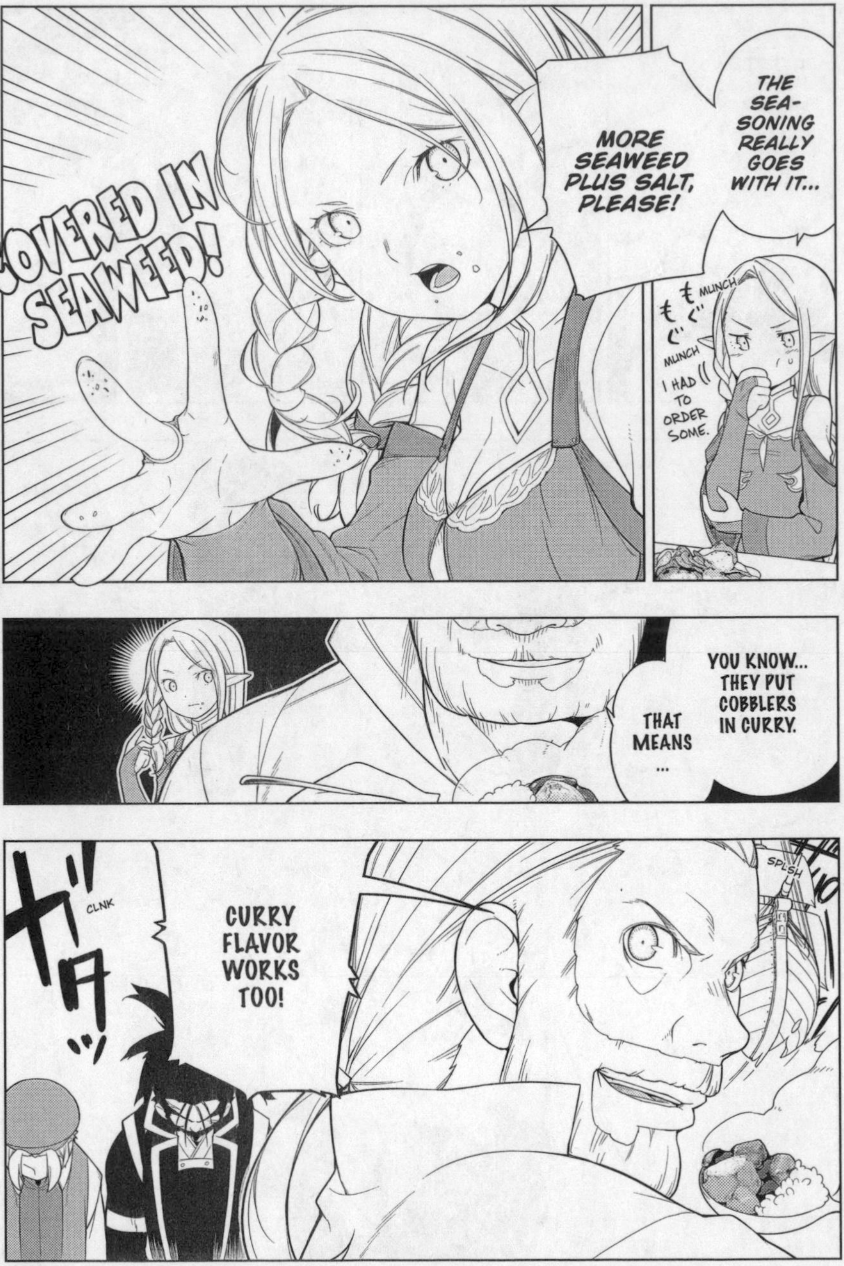
THE SEA-SONING REALLY GOES WITH IT...
もぐもぐ
MUNCH
MUNCH
I HAD TO ORDER SOME.
MORE SEAWEED PLUS SALT, PLEASE!
COVERED IN SEAWEED!
YOU KNOW... THEY PUT COBBLERS IN CURRY.
THAT MEANS ...
SPLSH
CURRY FLAVOR WORKS TOO!
ガタッ
CLNK

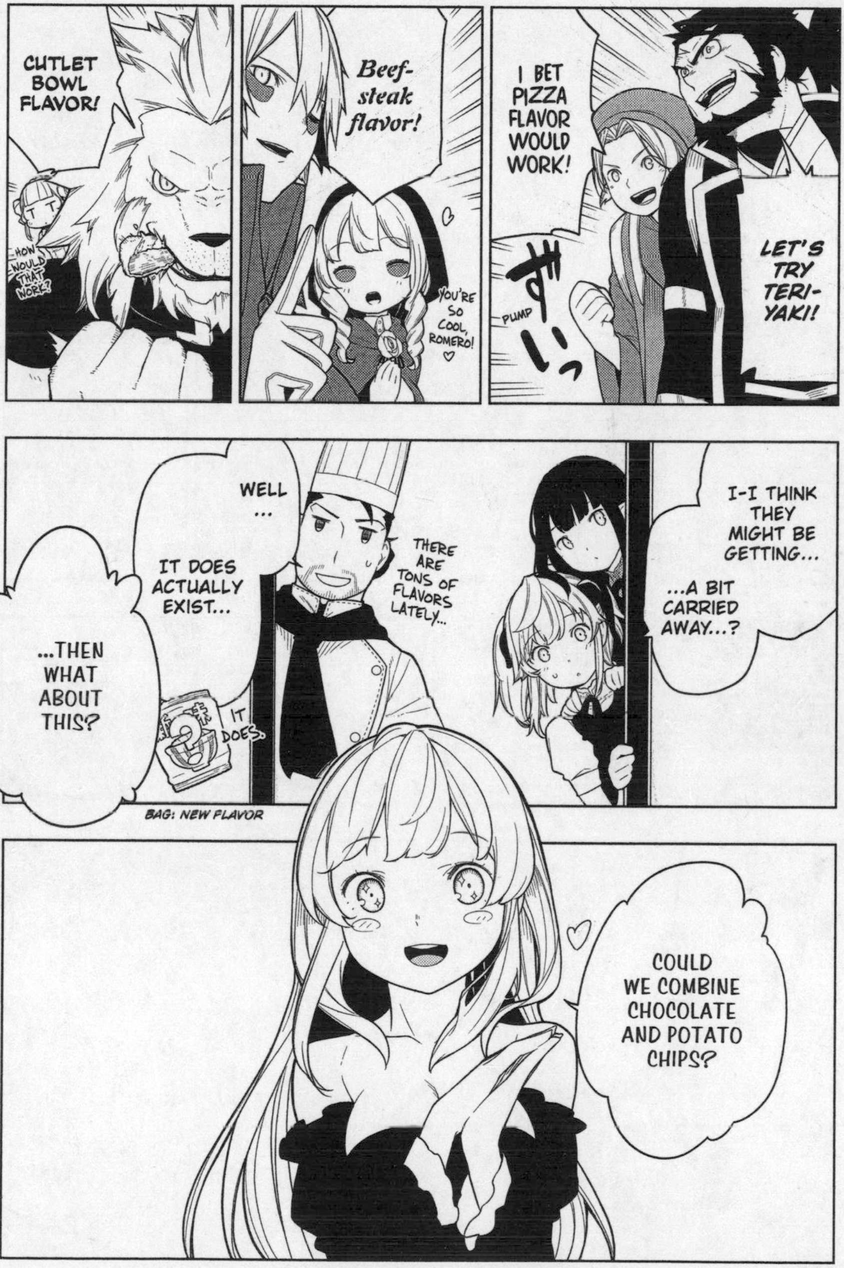
I BET PIZZA FLAVOR WOULD WORK!
LET'S TRY TERI-YAKI!
PUMP
Beef-steak flavor!
YOU'RE SO COOL, ROMERO! ♡
CUTLET BOWL FLAVOR!
HOW WOULD THAT WORK?
I-I THINK THEY MIGHT BE GETTING...
...A BIT CARRIED AWAY...?
WELL ...
IT DOES ACTUALLY EXIST...
THERE ARE TONS OF FLAVORS LATELY...
IT DOES.
...THEN WHAT ABOUT THIS?
BAG: NEW FLAVOR
COULD WE COMBINE CHOCOLATE AND POTATO CHIPS?

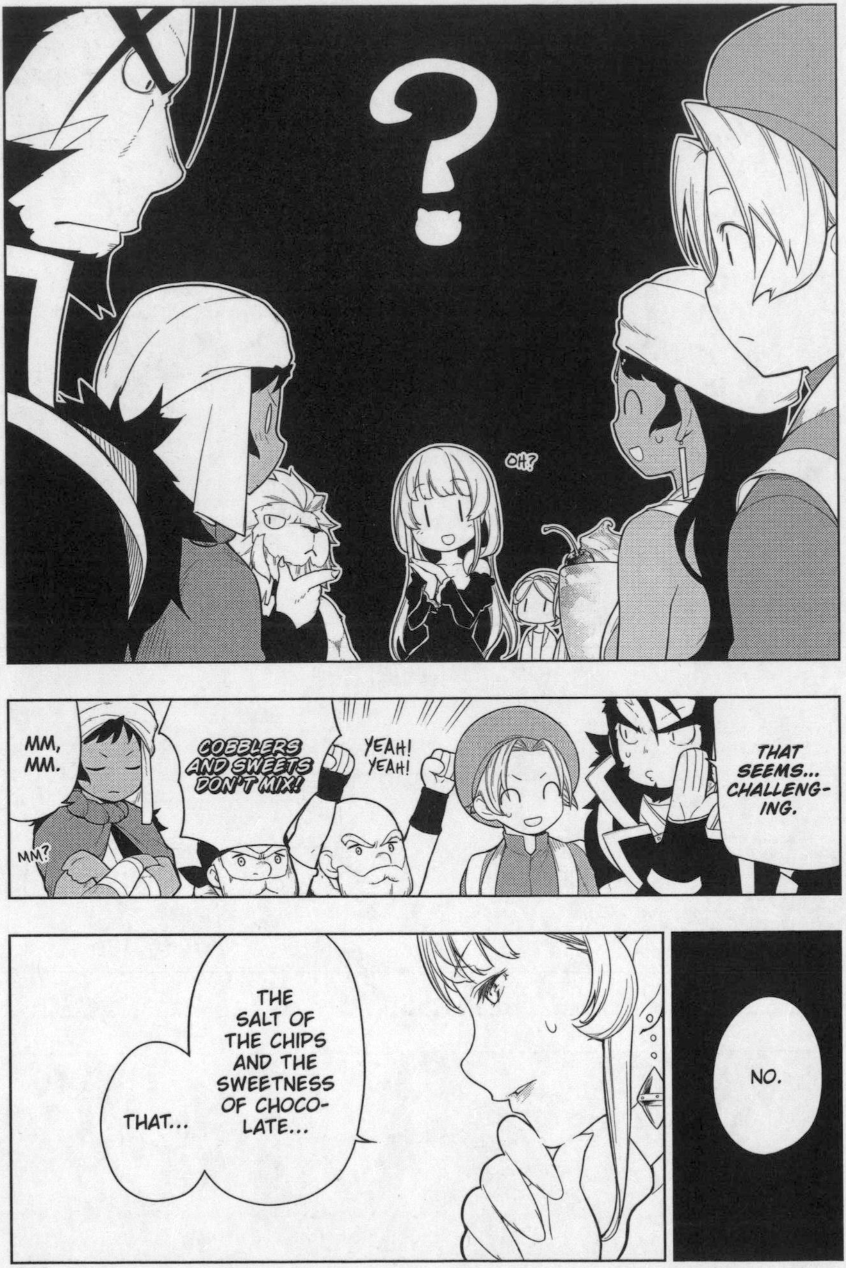
?
OH?
THAT SEEMS... CHALLENG-ING.
YEAH! YEAH!
COBBLERS AND SWEETS DON'T MIX!!
MM, MM.
MM?
NO.
THE SALT OF THE CHIPS AND THE SWEETNESS OF CHOCO-LATE...
THAT...

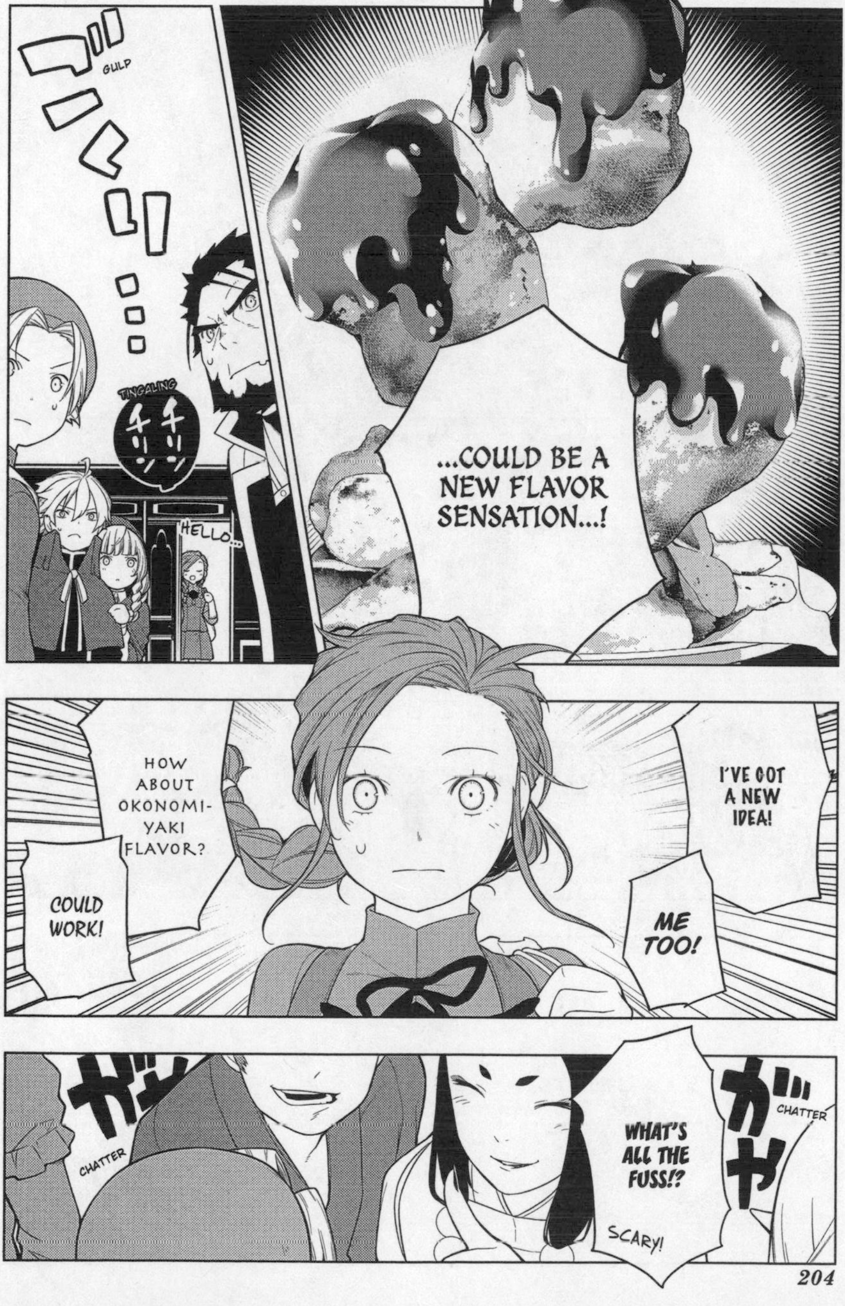

...COULD BE A NEW FLAVOR SENSATION...!
GULP
TINGALING
HELLO...
I'VE GOT A NEW IDEA!
ME TOO!
HOW ABOUT OKONOMI-YAKI FLAVOR?
COULD WORK!
CHATTER
WHAT'S ALL THE FUSS!?
SCARY!
CHATTER

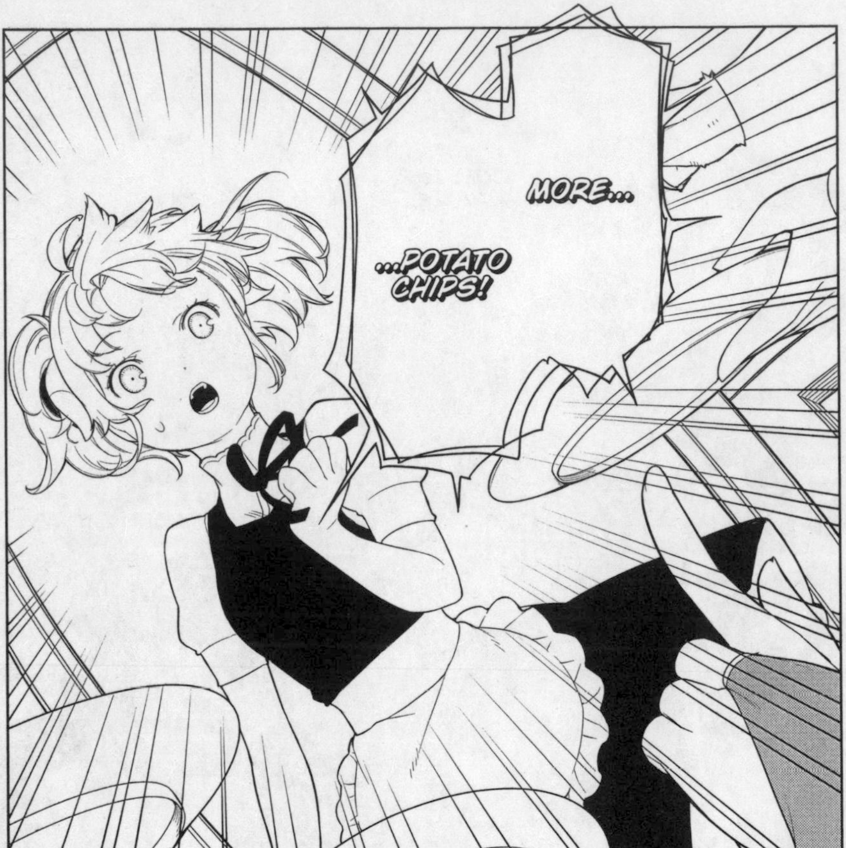
MORE...
...POTATO CHIPS!
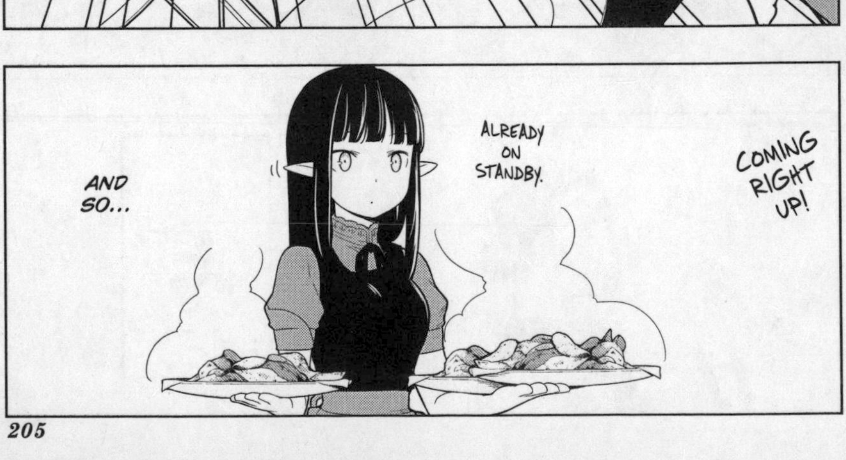
COMING RIGHT UP!
ALREADY ON STANDBY.
AND SO...

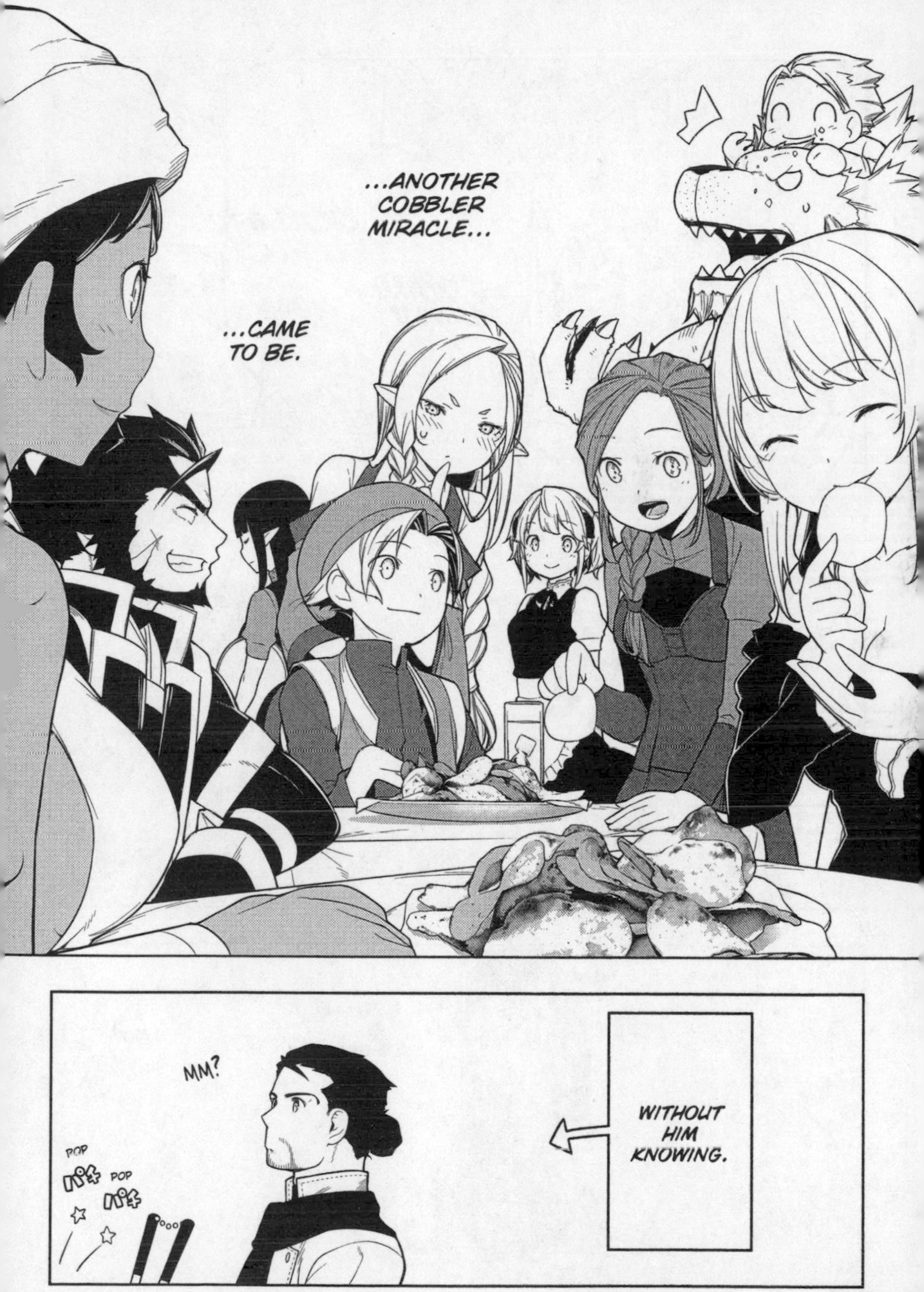
...ANOTHER COBBLER MIRACLE...
...CAME TO BE.
WITHOUT HIM KNOWING.
MM?
POP
パチ
POP
パチ

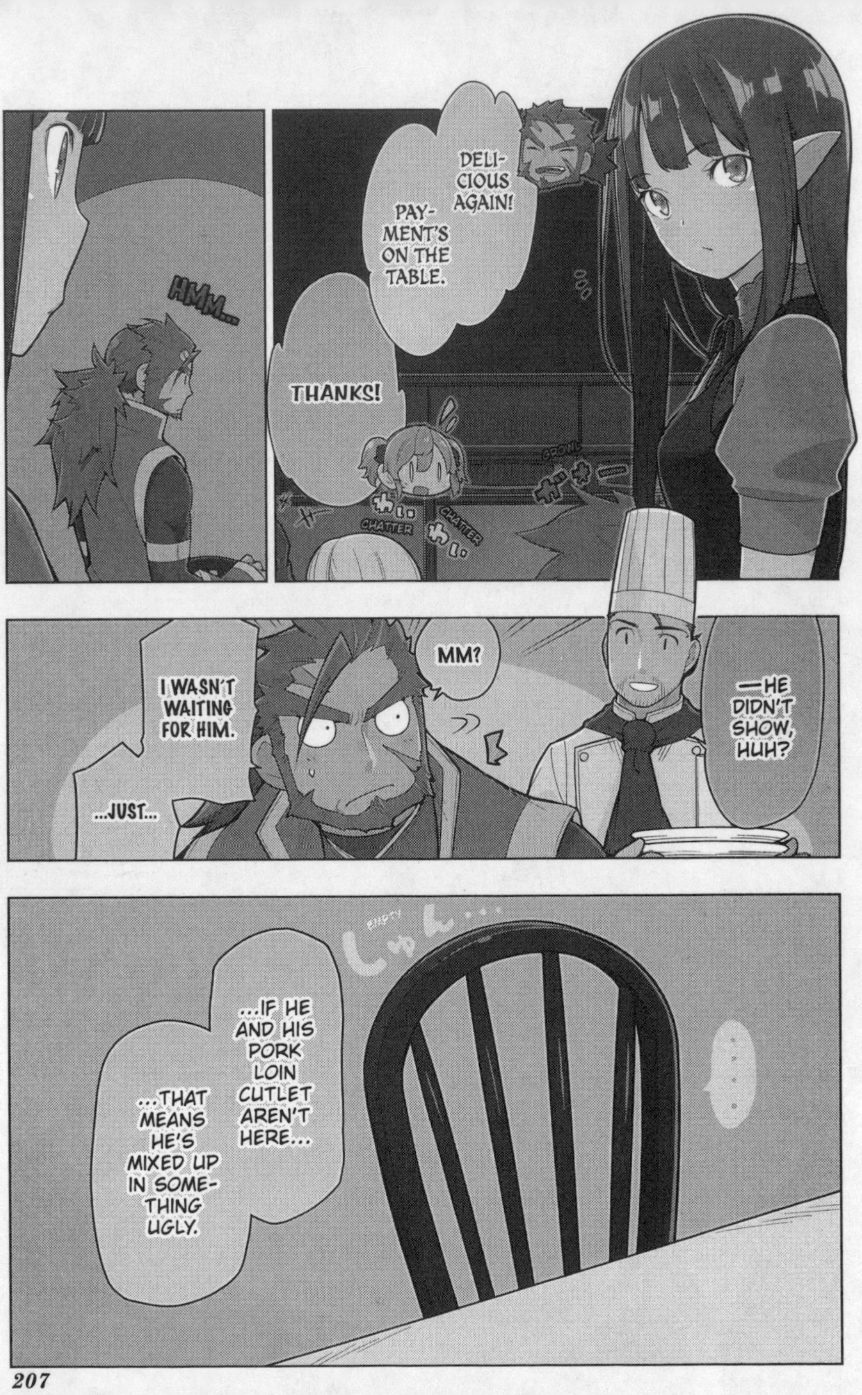
DELI-CIOUS AGAIN!
PAY-MENT'S ON THE TABLE.
THANKS!
GROWL
CHATTER
CHATTER
HMM...
—HE DIDN'T SHOW, HUH?
MM?
I WASN'T WAITING FOR HIM.
...JUST...
EMPTY
...
...IF HE AND HIS PORK LOIN CUTLET AREN'T HERE...
...THAT MEANS HE'S MIXED UP IN SOME-THING UGLY.

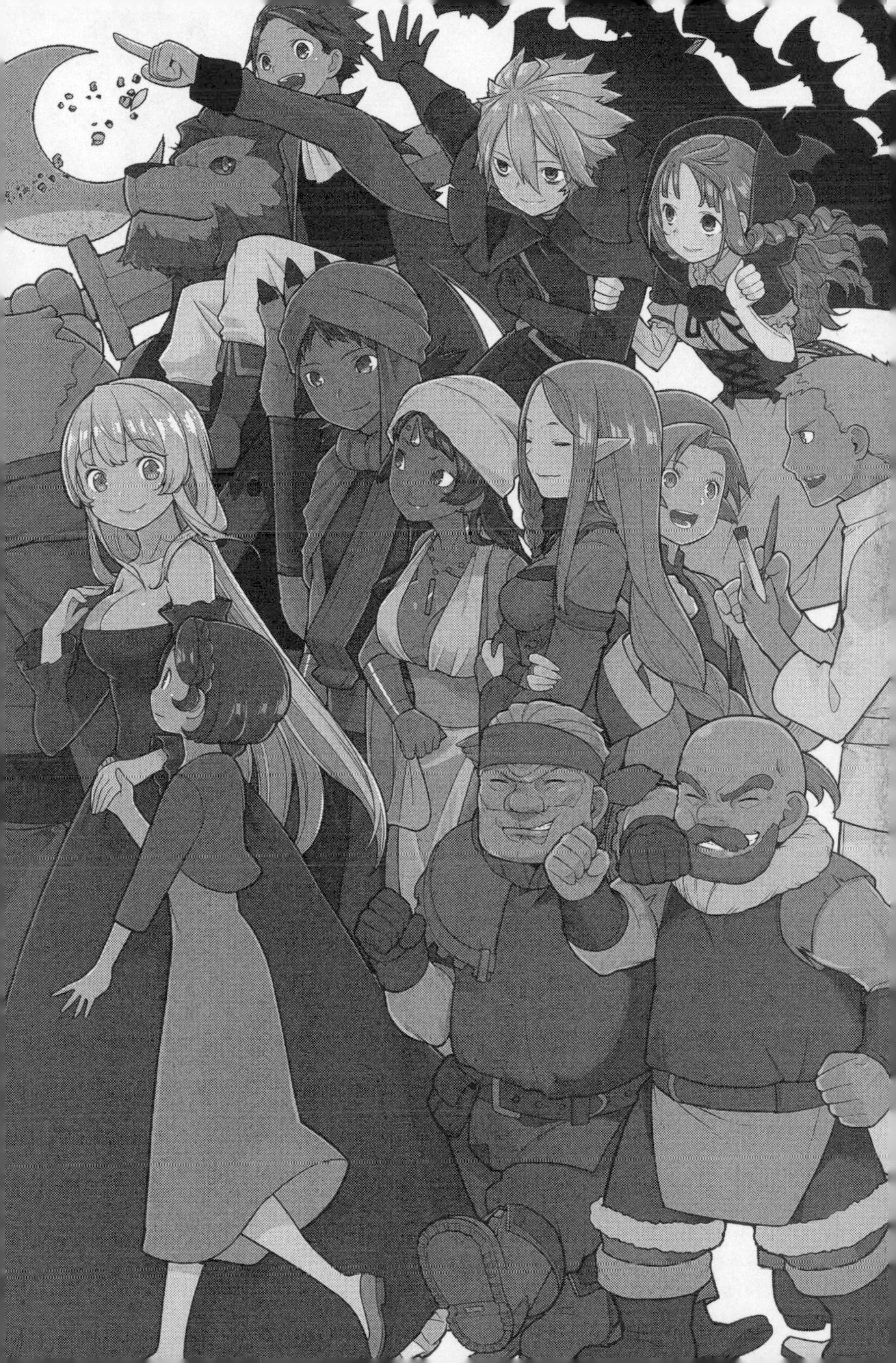

28th Dish Croquette

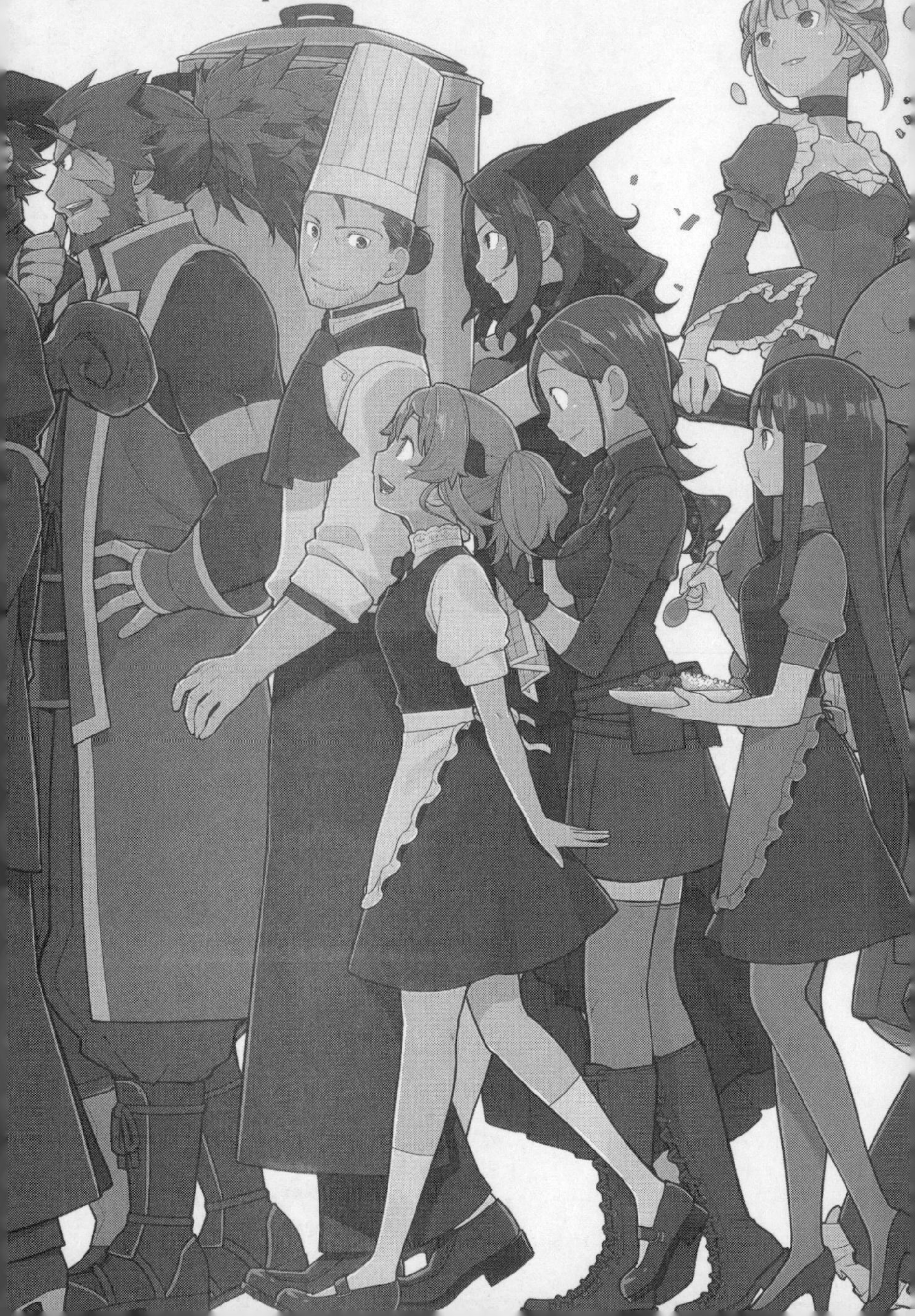

RESTAURANT TO Another World

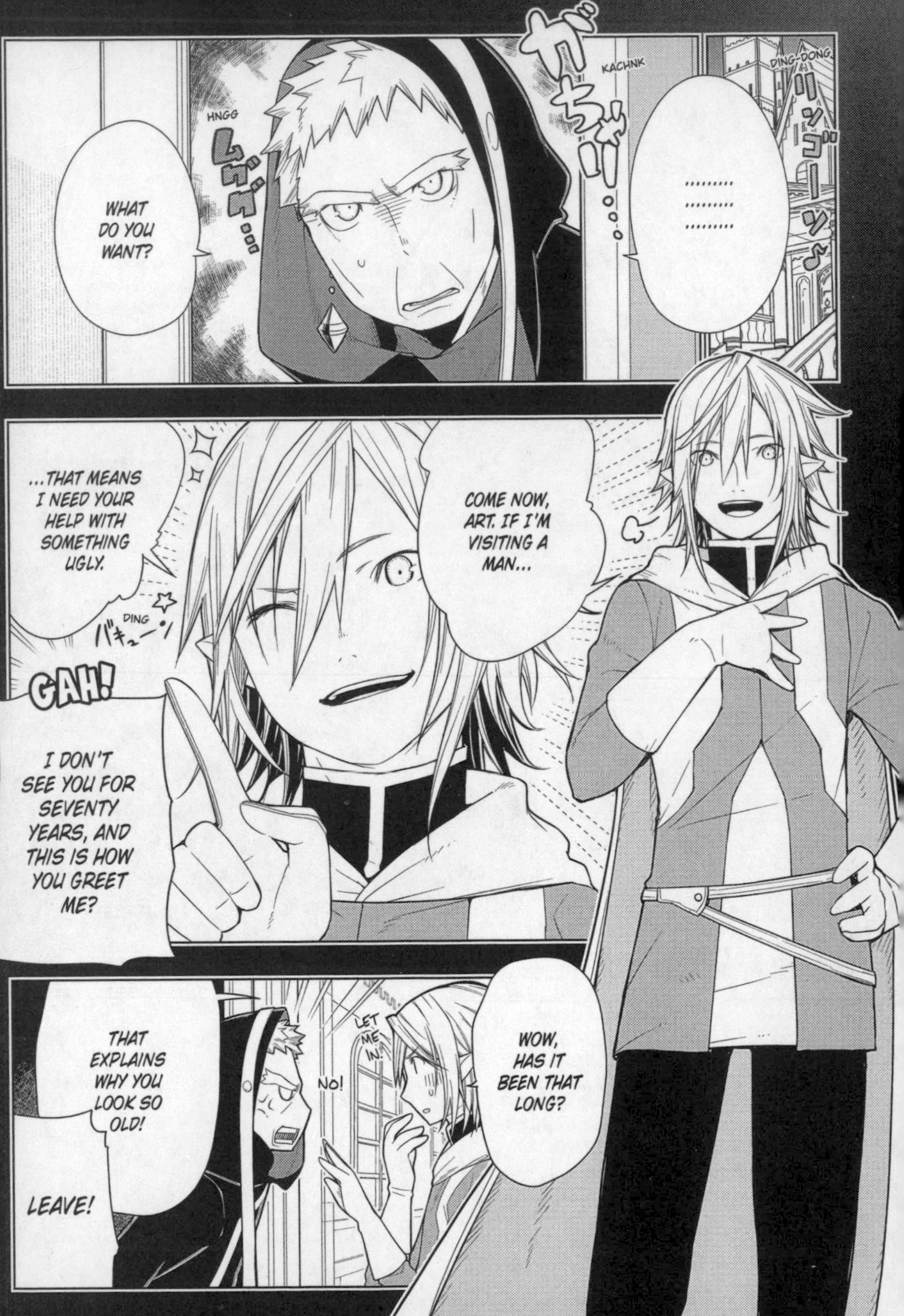
DING-DONG
......
......
......
KACHNK
HNGG
WHAT DO YOU WANT?
COME NOW, ART. IF I'M VISITING A MAN...
...THAT MEANS I NEED YOUR HELP WITH SOMETHING UGLY.
DING
GAH!
I DON'T SEE YOU FOR SEVENTY YEARS, AND THIS IS HOW YOU GREET ME?
WOW, HAS IT BEEN THAT LONG?
LET ME IN!
NO!
THAT EXPLAINS WHY YOU LOOK SO OLD!
LEAVE!

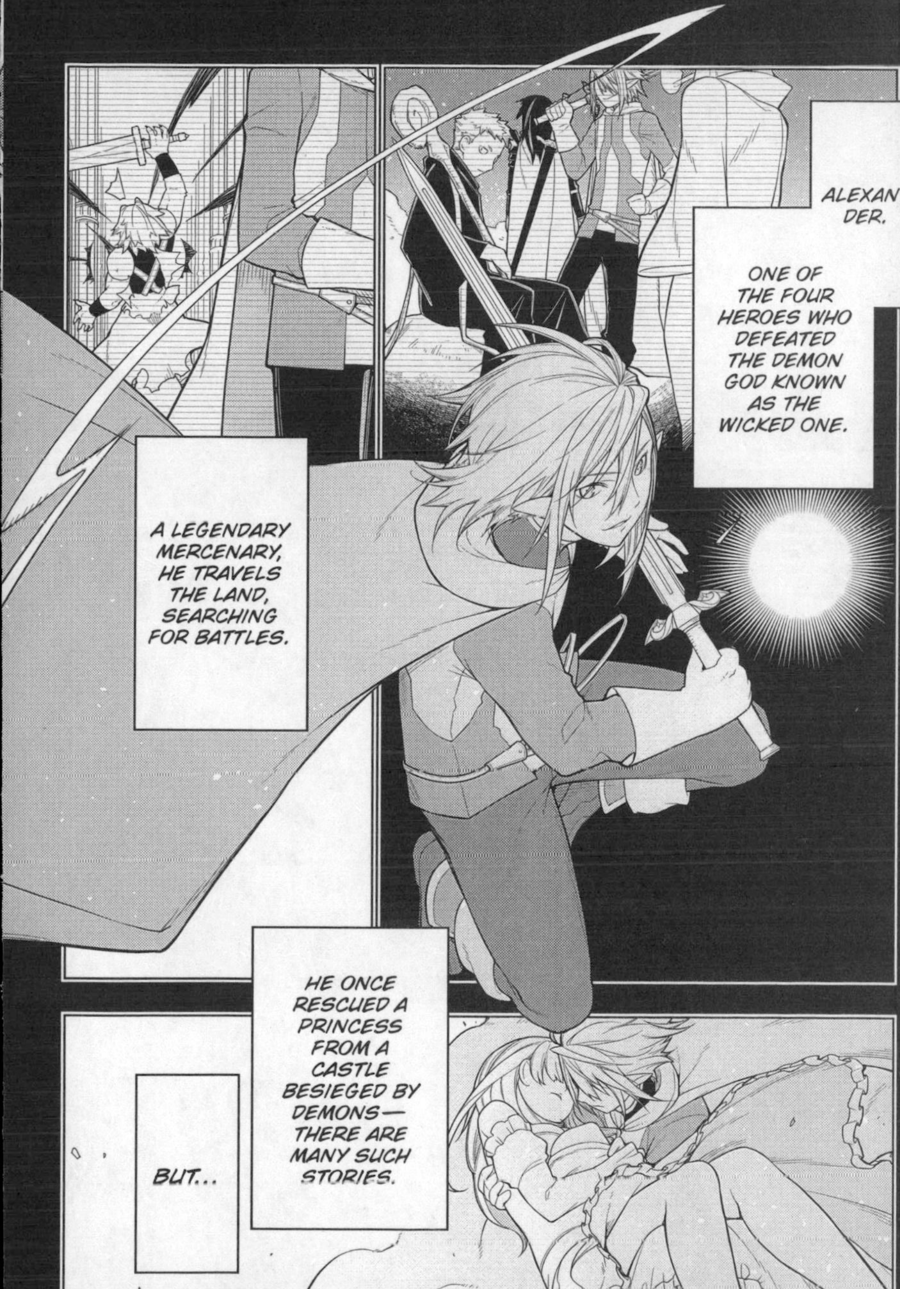
ALEXAN-
DER.
ONE OF THE FOUR HEROES WHO DEFEATED THE DEMON GOD KNOWN AS THE WICKED ONE.
A LEGENDARY MERCENARY, HE TRAVELS THE LAND, SEARCHING FOR BATTLES.
HE ONCE RESCUED A PRINCESS FROM A CASTLE BESIEGED BY DEMONS—THERE ARE MANY SUCH STORIES.
BUT...

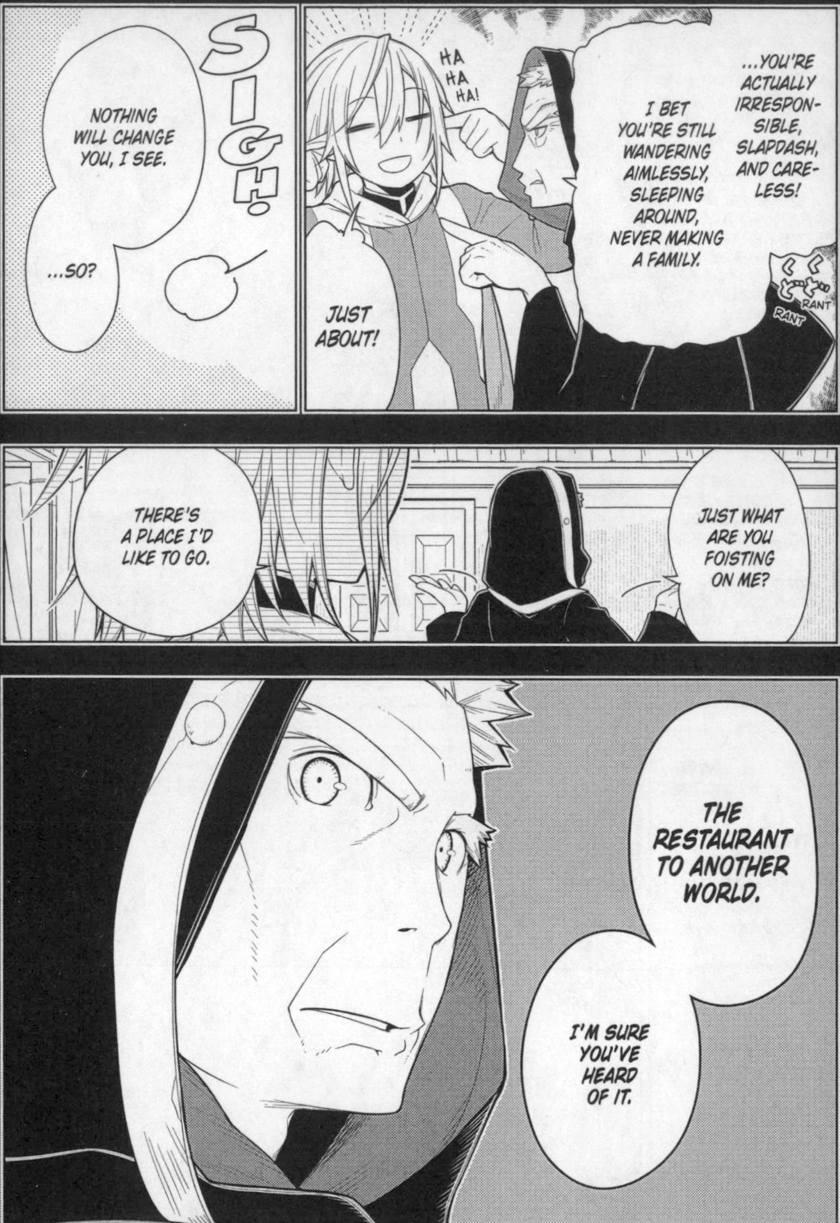
...YOU'RE ACTUALLY IRRESPONSIBLE, SLAPDASH, AND CARELESS!
I BET YOU'RE STILL WANDERING AIMLESSLY, SLEEPING AROUND, NEVER MAKING A FAMILY.
RANT RANT
HA HA HA!
JUST ABOUT!
SIGH!
NOTHING WILL CHANGE YOU, I SEE.
...SO?
JUST WHAT ARE YOU FOISTING ON ME?
THERE'S A PLACE I'D LIKE TO GO.
THE RESTAURANT TO ANOTHER WORLD.
I'M SURE YOU'VE HEARD OF IT.

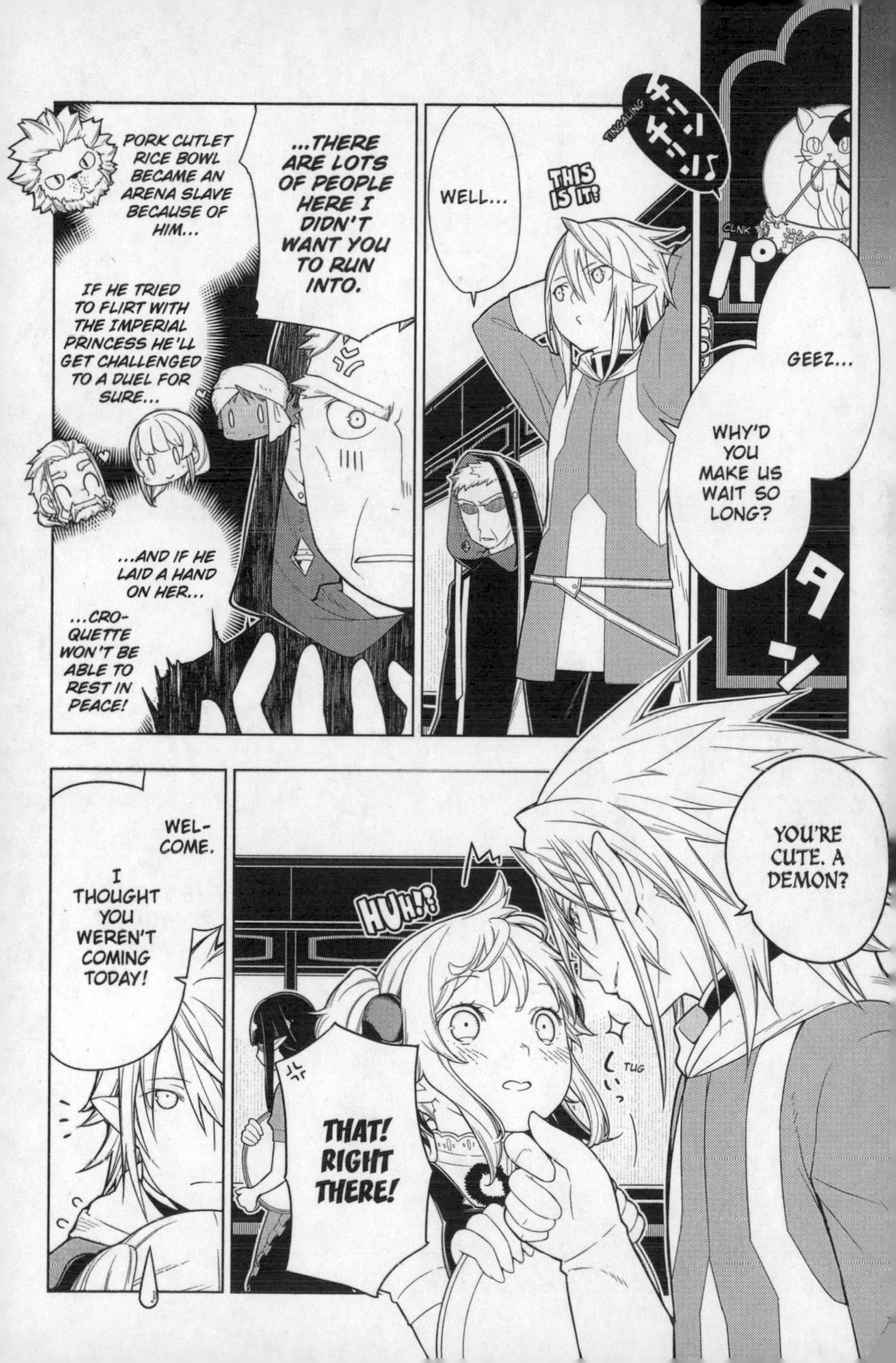
TINGALING
CLINK
GEEZ...
WHY'D YOU MAKE US WAIT SO LONG?
THIS IS IT!
WELL...
...THERE ARE LOTS OF PEOPLE HERE I DIDN'T WANT YOU TO RUN INTO.
PORK CUTLET RICE BOWL BECAME AN ARENA SLAVE BECAUSE OF HIM...
IF HE TRIED TO FLIRT WITH THE IMPERIAL PRINCESS HE'LL GET CHALLENGED TO A DUEL FOR SURE...
...AND IF HE LAID A HAND ON HER...
...CROQUETTE WON'T BE ABLE TO REST IN PEACE!
YOU'RE CUTE. A DEMON?
HUH!?
TUG
THAT! RIGHT THERE!
WELCOME.
I THOUGHT YOU WEREN'T COMING TODAY!

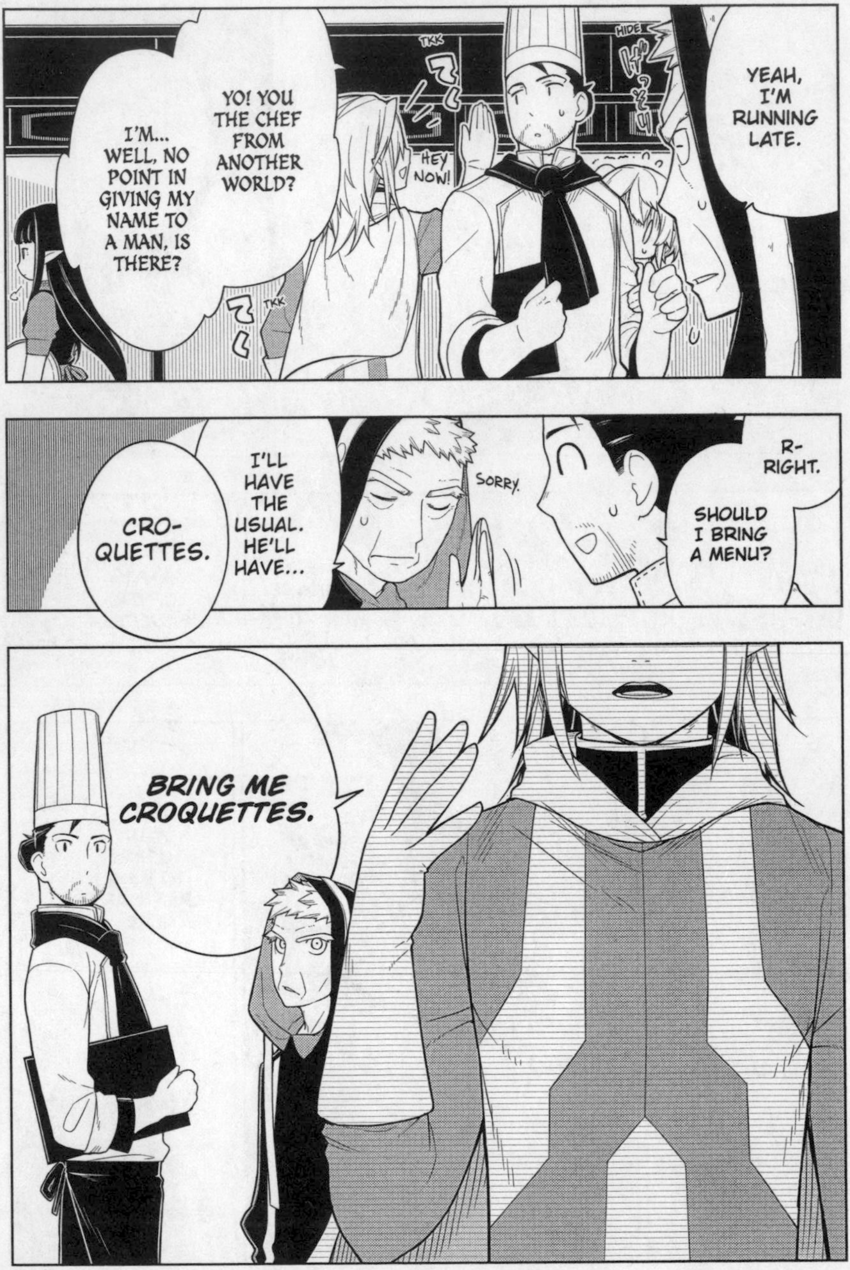
YEAH, I'M RUNNING LATE.
HIDE
TKK
YO! YOU THE CHEF FROM ANOTHER WORLD?
HEY NOW!
I'M... WELL, NO POINT IN GIVING MY NAME TO A MAN, IS THERE?
TKK
R-RIGHT.
SHOULD I BRING A MENU?
SORRY.
I'LL HAVE THE USUAL. HE'LL HAVE...
CRO-QUETTES.
BRING ME CROQUETTES.

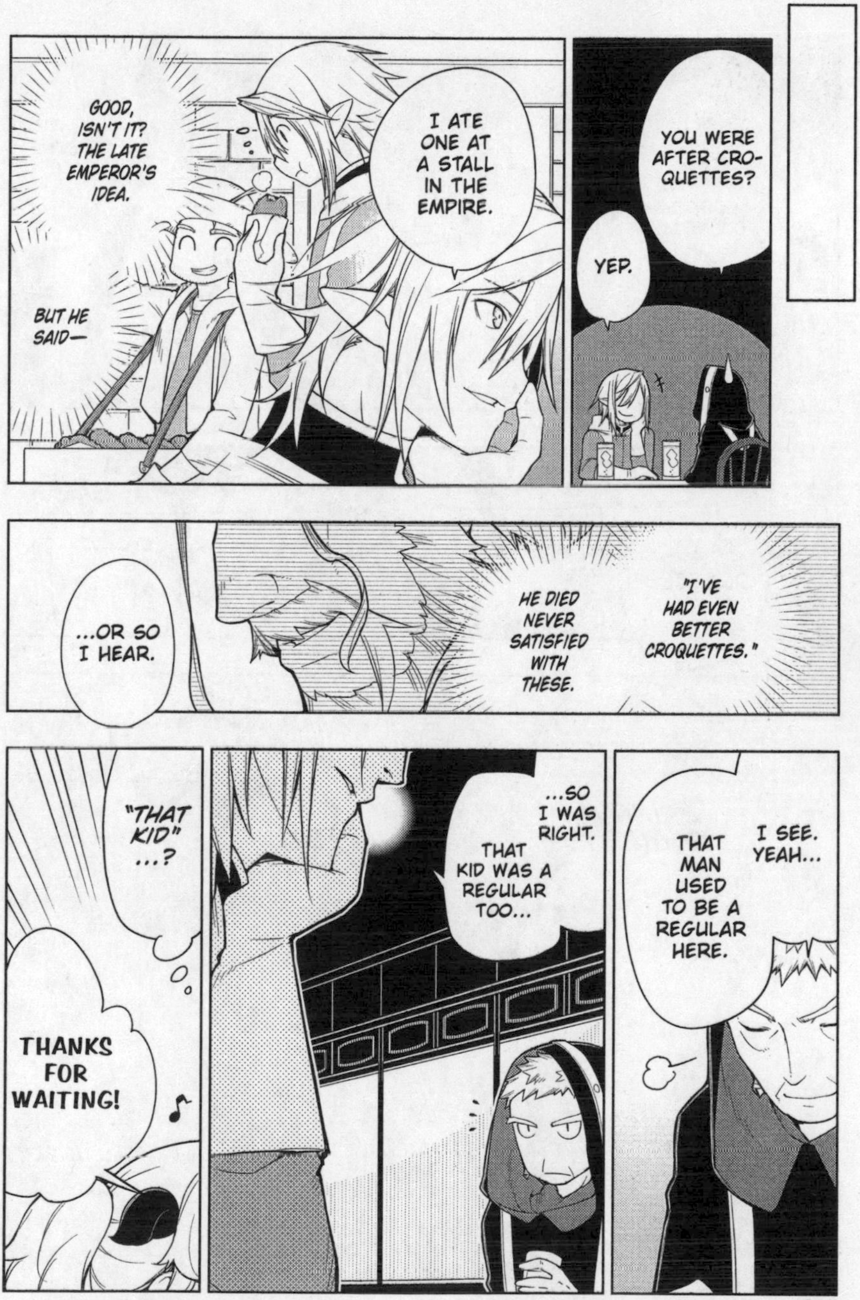
YOU WERE AFTER CRO-QUETTES?
YEP.
I ATE ONE AT A STALL IN THE EMPIRE.
GOOD, ISN'T IT? THE LATE EMPEROR'S IDEA.
BUT HE SAID—
"I'VE HAD EVEN BETTER CROQUETTES."
HE DIED NEVER SATISFIED WITH THESE.
...OR SO I HEAR.
I SEE. YEAH...
THAT MAN USED TO BE A REGULAR HERE.
...SO I WAS RIGHT.
THAT KID WAS A REGULAR TOO...
"THAT KID" ...?
THANKS FOR WAITING!

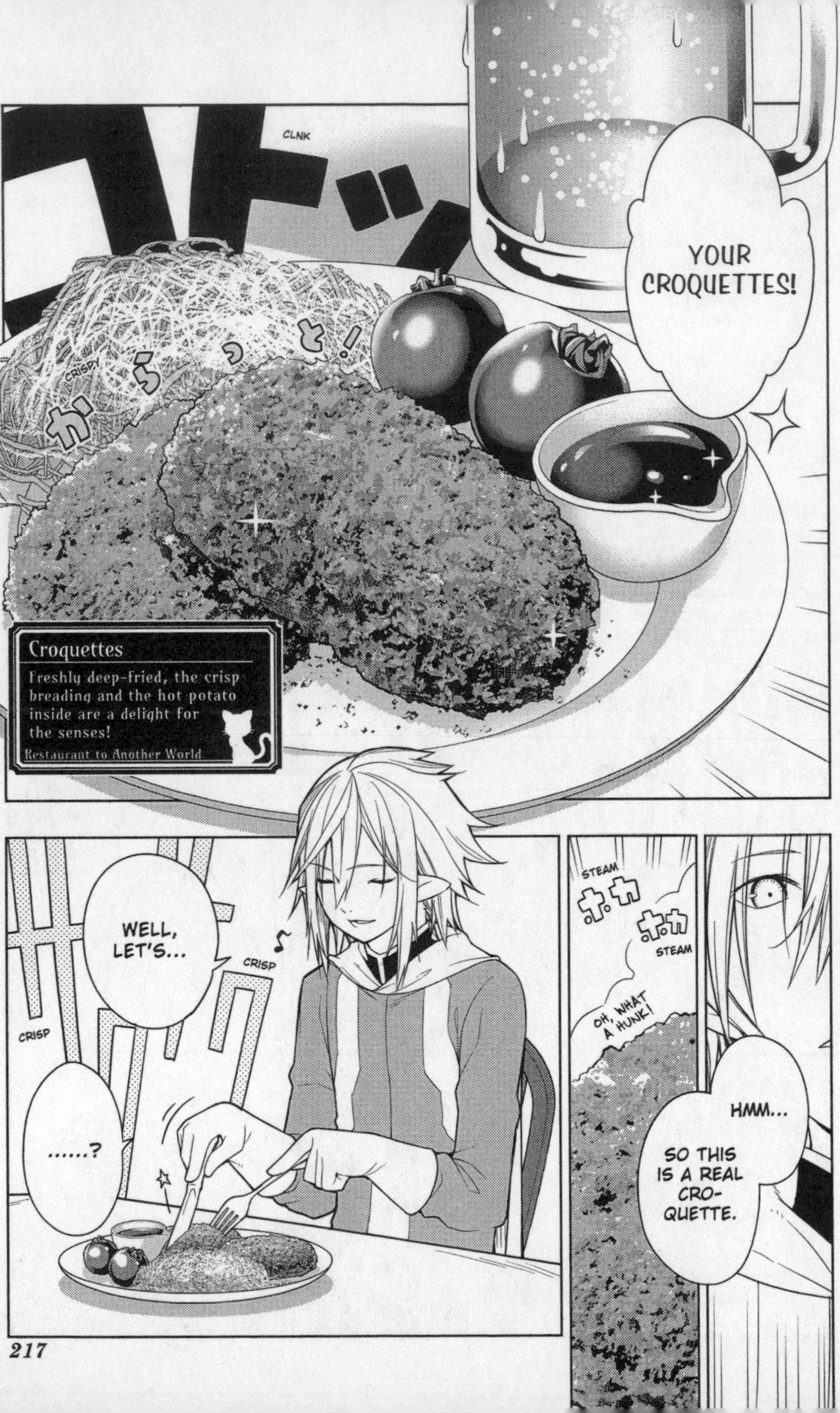
YOUR CROQUETTES!
CLNK
CRISPY
Croquettes
Freshly deep-fried, the crisp breading and the hot potato inside are a delight for the senses!
Restaurant to Another World
STEAM
STEAM
OH, WHAT A HUNK!
HMM...
SO THIS IS A REAL CRO-QUETTE.
WELL, LET'S...
CRISP
CRISP
......?

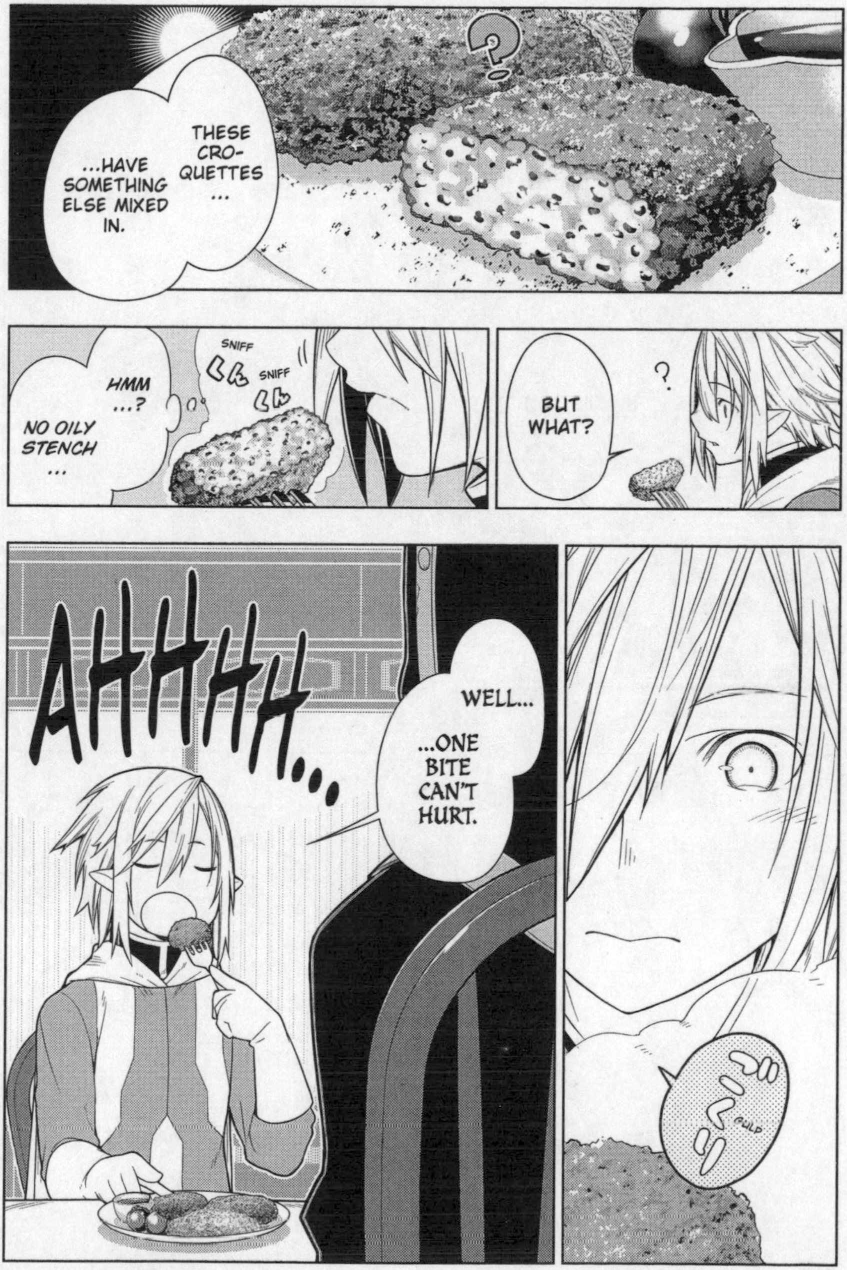
THESE CRO-QUETTES...
...HAVE SOMETHING ELSE MIXED IN.
BUT WHAT?
SNIFF
SNIFF
HMM...?
NO OILY STENCH...
GULP
AHHHH...
WELL...
...ONE BITE CAN'T HURT.

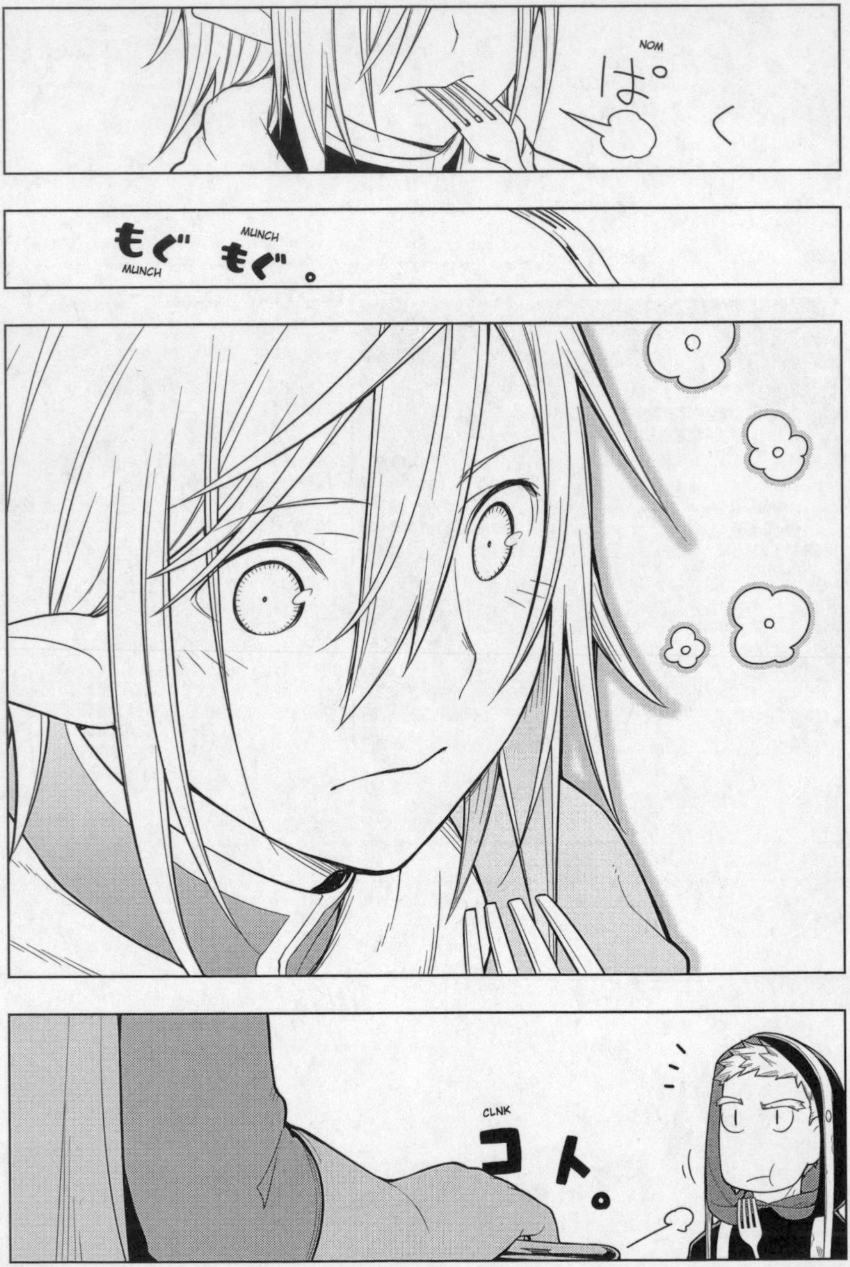

NOM
ぱく
MUNCH
もぐ
MUNCH
もぐ。
CLNK
コト。

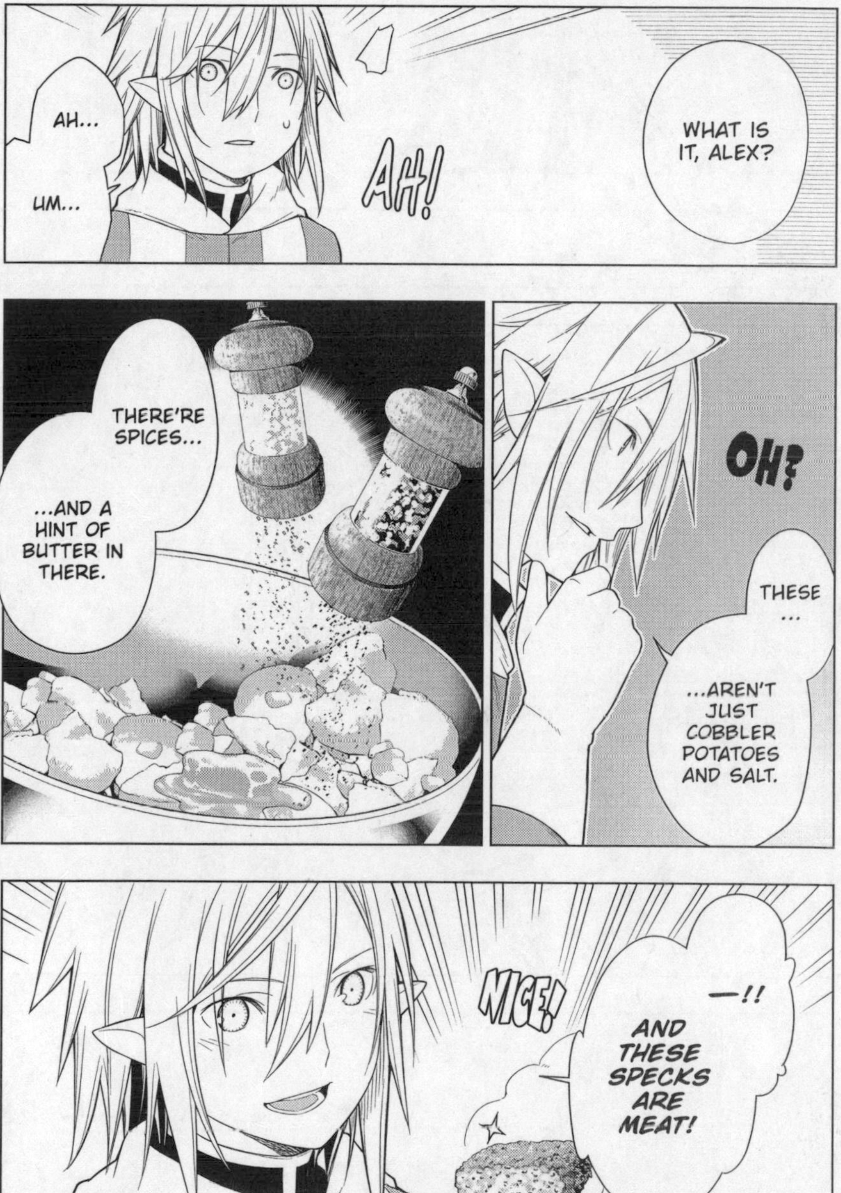
WHAT IS IT, ALEX?
AH!
AH...
UM...
OH?
THESE ...
...AREN'T JUST COBBLER POTATOES AND SALT.
THERE'RE SPICES...
...AND A HINT OF BUTTER IN THERE.
—!!
AND THESE SPECKS ARE MEAT!
NICE!

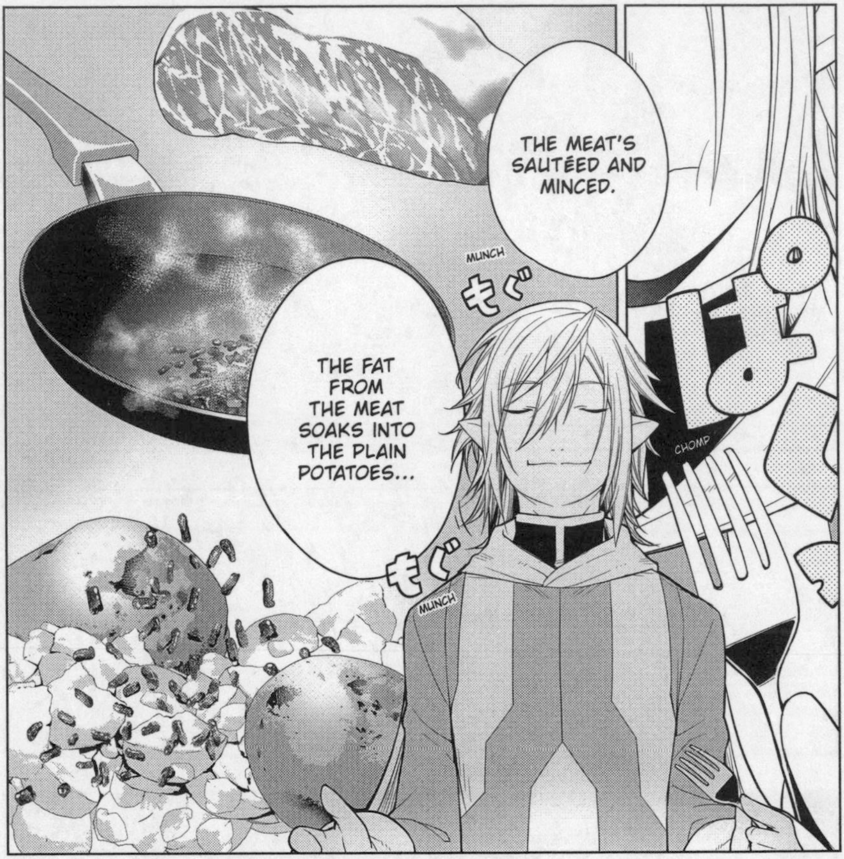
THE MEAT'S SAUTÉED AND MINCED.
CHOMP
もぐ
MUNCH
THE FAT FROM THE MEAT SOAKS INTO THE PLAIN POTATOES...
もぐ
MUNCH

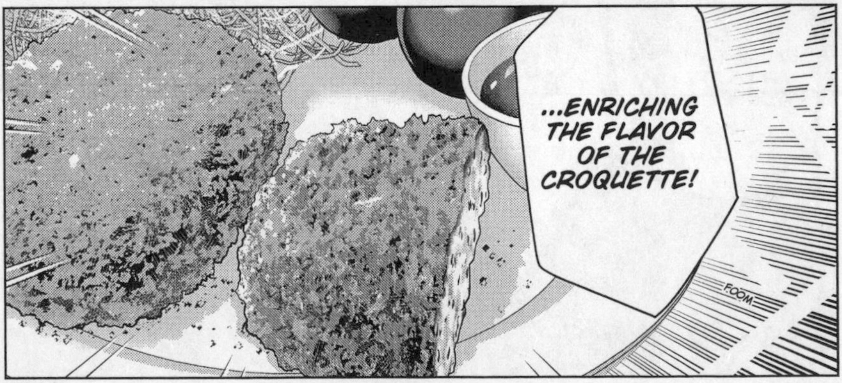
...ENRICHING THE FLAVOR OF THE CROQUETTE!
FOOM

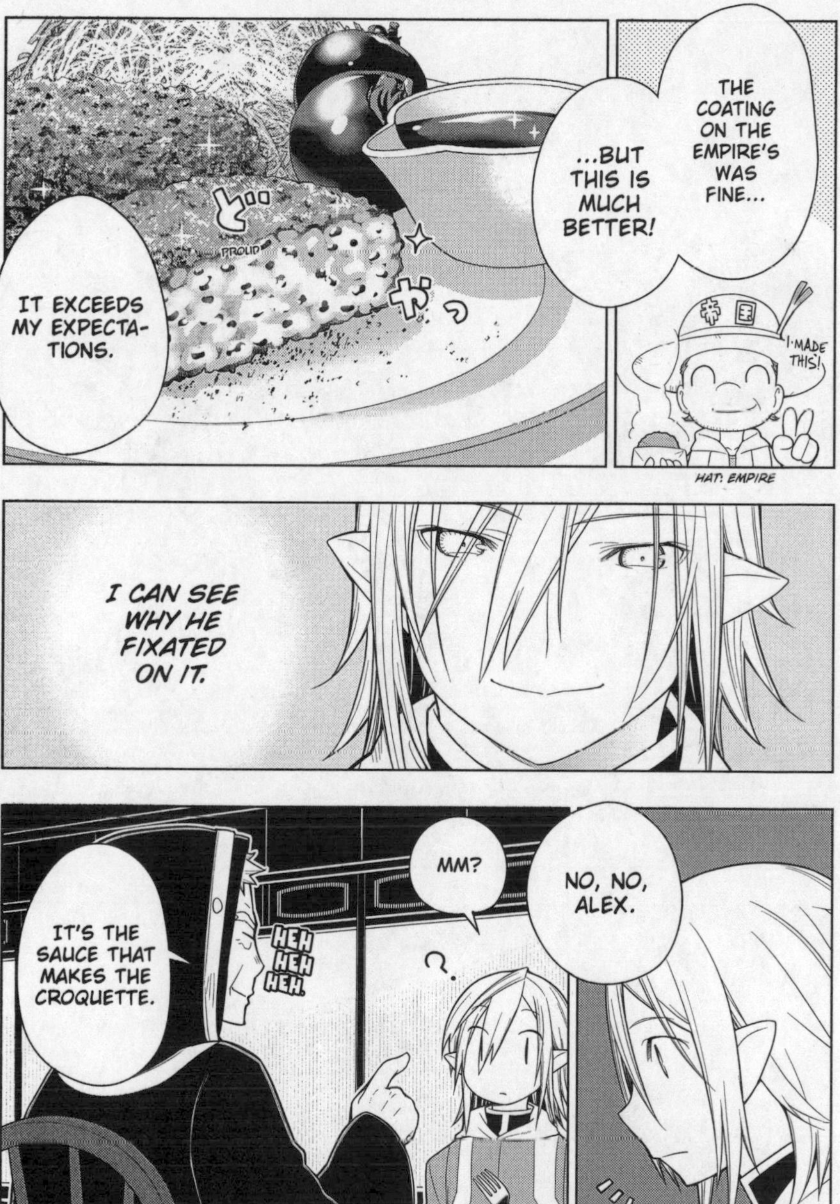
THE COATING ON THE EMPIRE'S WAS FINE...
...BUT THIS IS MUCH BETTER!
I·MADE THIS!
HAT: EMPIRE
PROUD
IT EXCEEDS MY EXPECTATIONS.
I CAN SEE WHY HE FIXATED ON IT.
NO, NO, ALEX.
MM?
HEH HEH HEH.
IT'S THE SAUCE THAT MAKES THE CROQUETTE.

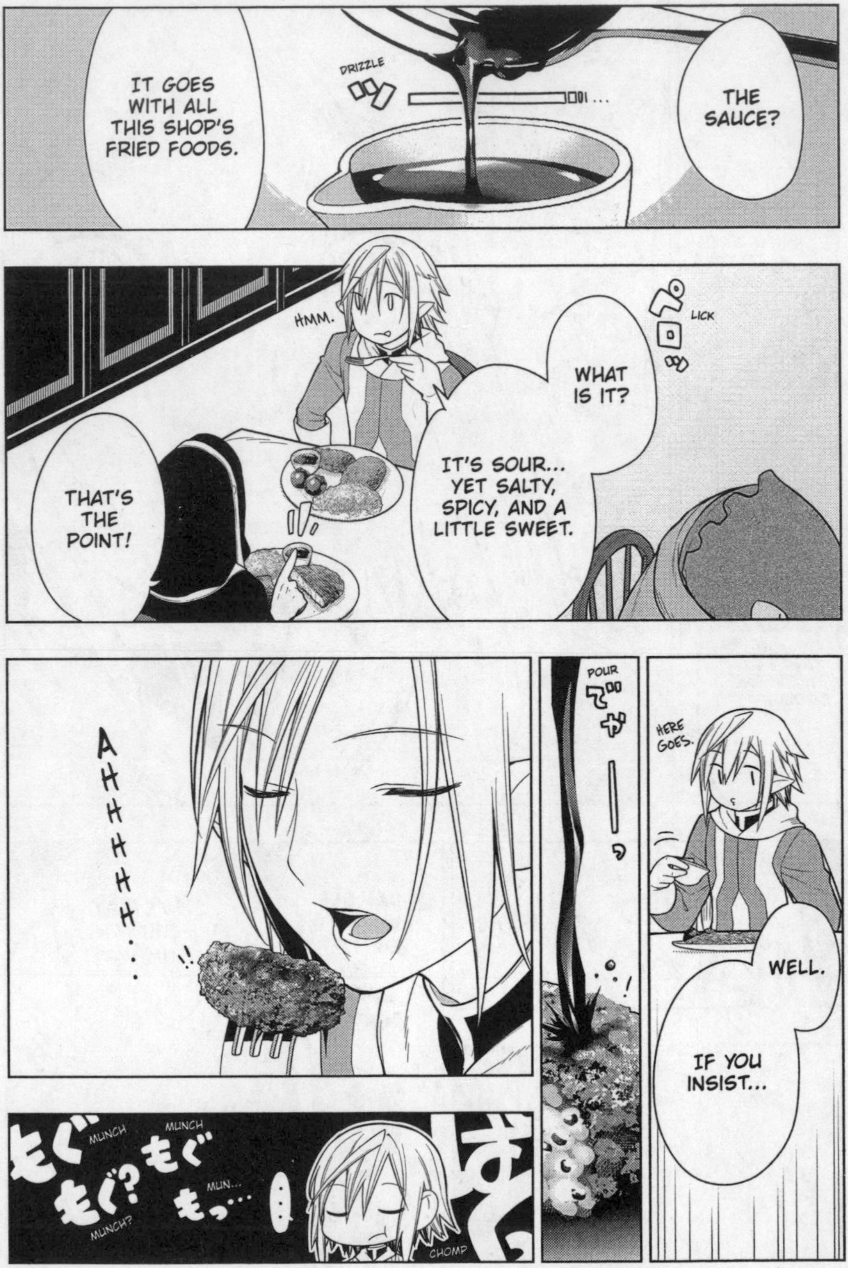
THE SAUCE?
DRIZZLE
IT GOES WITH ALL THIS SHOP'S FRIED FOODS.
LICK
WHAT IS IT?
HMM.
IT'S SOUR... YET SALTY, SPICY, AND A LITTLE SWEET.
THAT'S THE POINT!
HERE GOES.
WELL.
IF YOU INSIST...
POUR
AHHHHHH...
MUNCH
MUNCH
MUNCH?
MUN...
CHOMP

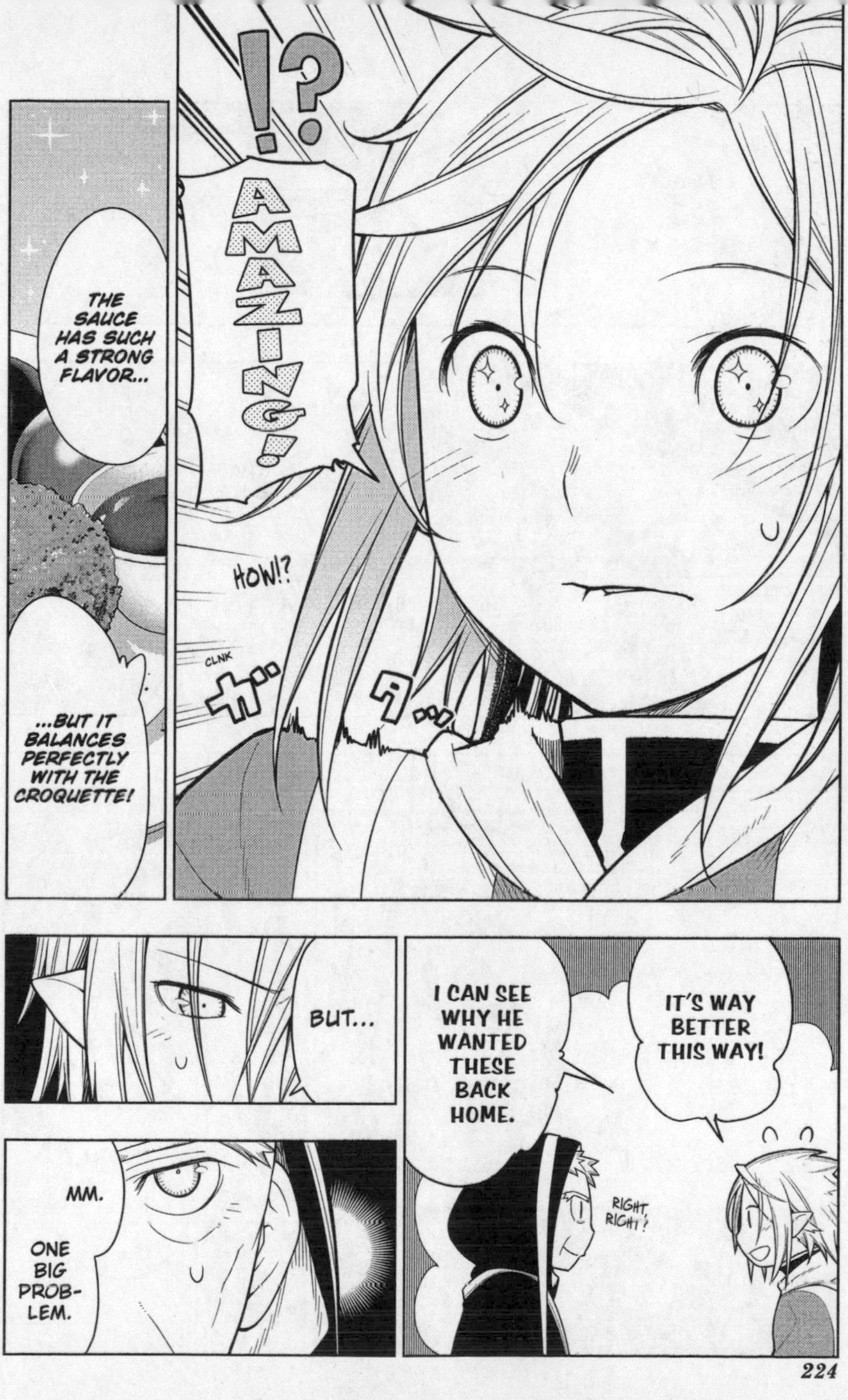
!?
AMAZING!
HOW!?
CLNK
THE SAUCE HAS SUCH A STRONG FLAVOR...
...BUT IT BALANCES PERFECTLY WITH THE CROQUETTE!
IT'S WAY BETTER THIS WAY!
I CAN SEE WHY HE WANTED THESE BACK HOME.
RIGHT, RIGHT?
BUT...
MM.
ONE BIG PROB-LEM.

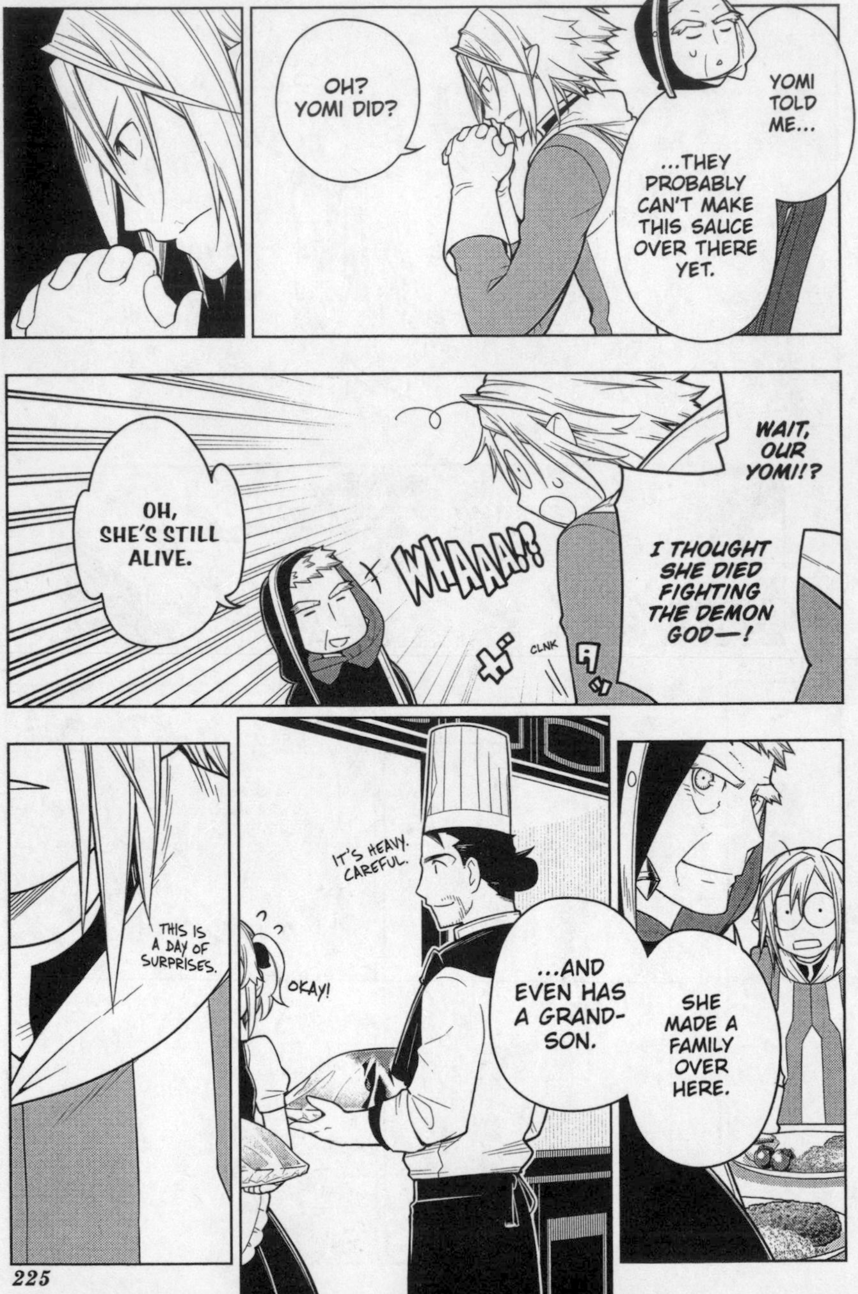
YOMI TOLD ME...
...THEY PROBABLY CAN'T MAKE THIS SAUCE OVER THERE YET.
OH? YOMI DID?
WAIT, OUR YOMI!?
I THOUGHT SHE DIED FIGHTING THE DEMON GOD—!
WHAAA!?
CLNK
OH, SHE'S STILL ALIVE.
SHE MADE A FAMILY OVER HERE.
...AND EVEN HAS A GRANDSON.
IT'S HEAVY. CAREFUL.
OKAY!
THIS IS A DAY OF SURPRISES.

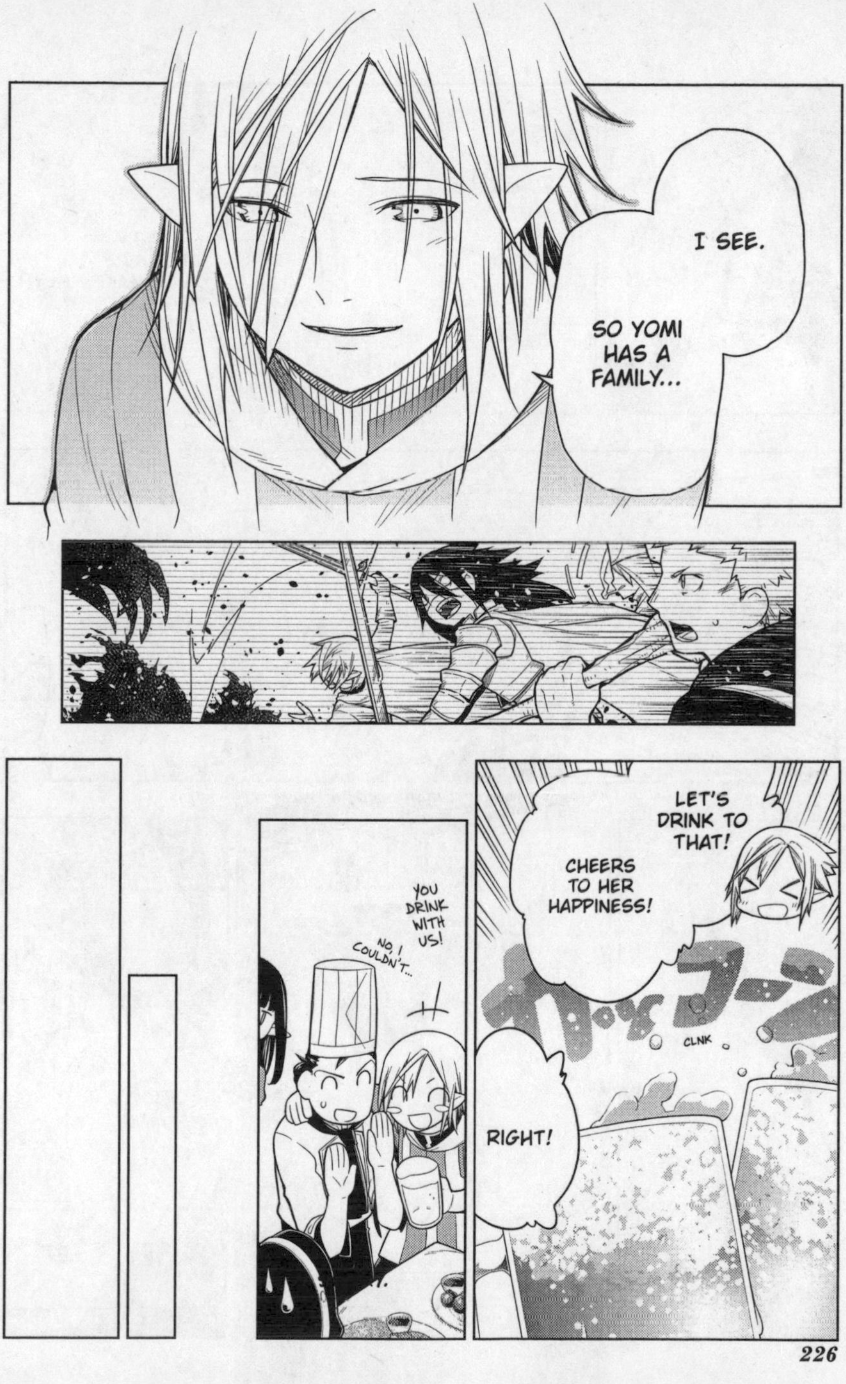
I SEE.
SO YOMI HAS A FAMILY...
LET'S DRINK TO THAT!
CHEERS TO HER HAPPINESS!
CLNK
RIGHT!
YOU DRINK WITH US!
NO, I COULDN'T...

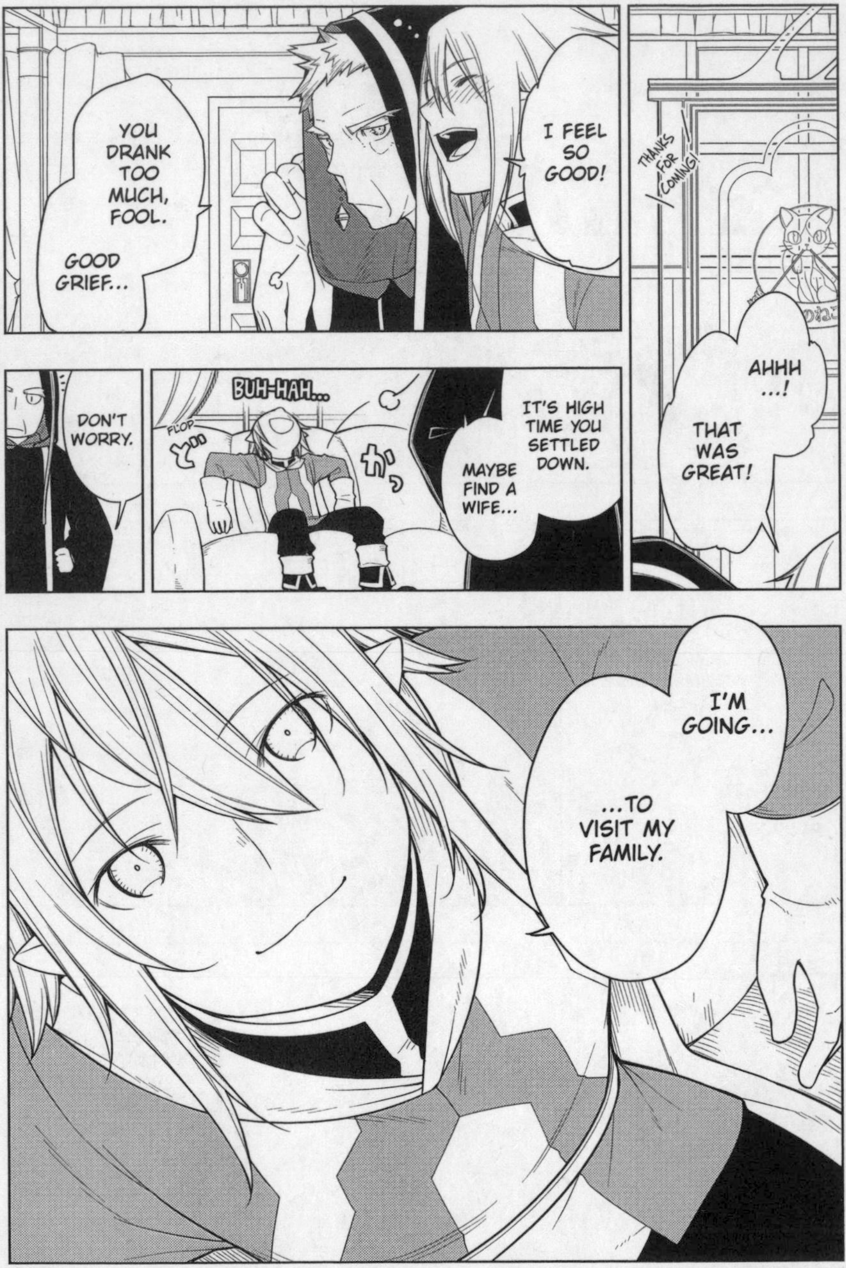
THANKS FOR COMING!
AHHH...! THAT WAS GREAT!
I FEEL SO GOOD!
YOU DRANK TOO MUCH, FOOL.
GOOD GRIEF...
IT'S HIGH TIME YOU SETTLED DOWN.
BUH-HAH...
MAYBE FIND A WIFE...
FLOP
DON'T WORRY.
I'M GOING...
...TO VISIT MY FAMILY.

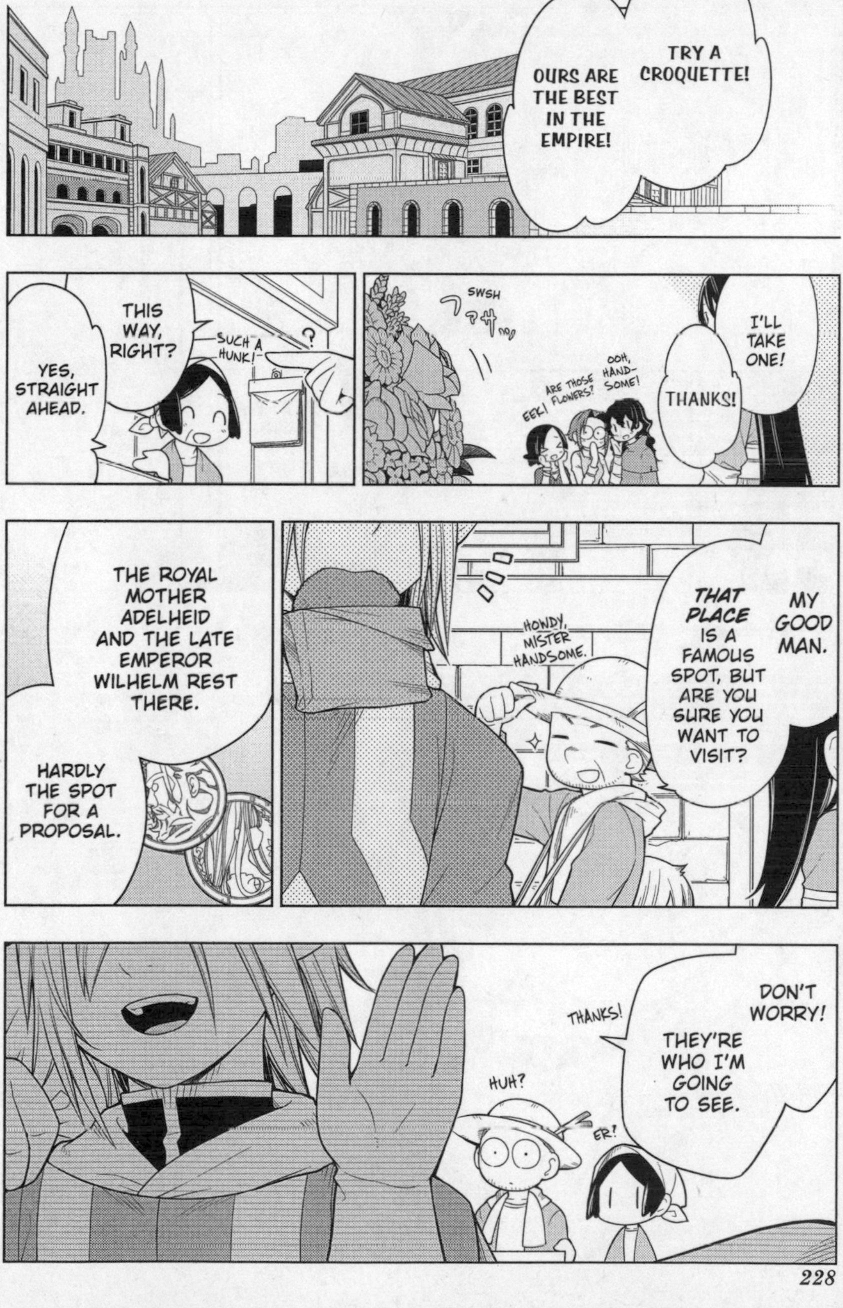
TRY A CROQUETTE!
OURS ARE THE BEST IN THE EMPIRE!
I'LL TAKE ONE!
THANKS!
OOH, HANDSOME!
ARE THOSE FLOWERS?
EEK!
SWSH
THIS WAY, RIGHT?
SUCH A HUNK!
YES, STRAIGHT AHEAD.
MY GOOD MAN.
THAT PLACE IS A FAMOUS SPOT, BUT ARE YOU SURE YOU WANT TO VISIT?
HOWDY, MISTER HANDSOME.
THE ROYAL MOTHER ADELHEID AND THE LATE EMPEROR WILHELM REST THERE.
HARDLY THE SPOT FOR A PROPOSAL.
DON'T WORRY!
THEY'RE WHO I'M GOING TO SEE.
THANKS!
HUH?
ER?

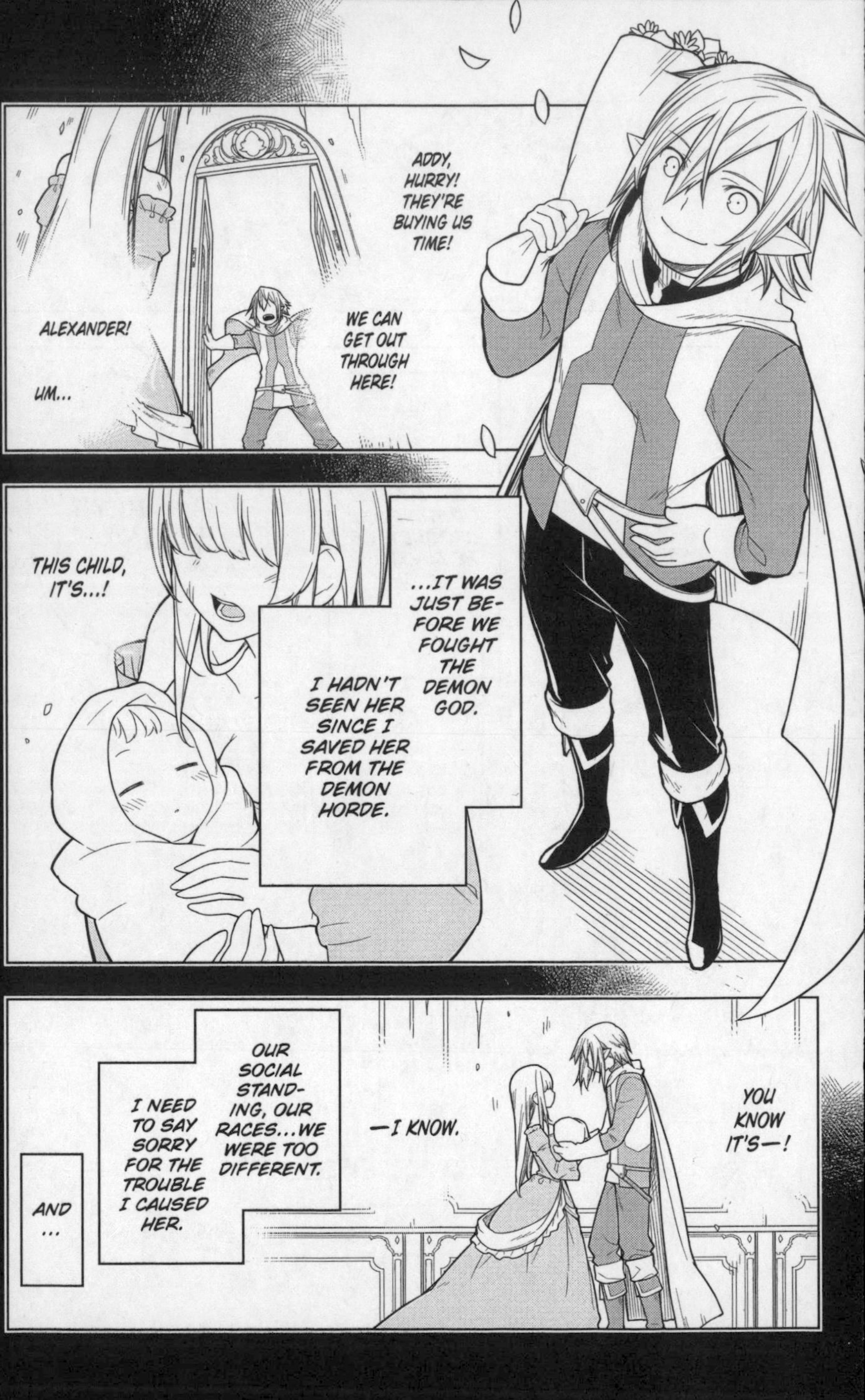
ADDY, HURRY! THEY'RE BUYING US TIME!
WE CAN GET OUT THROUGH HERE!
ALEXANDER!
UM...
...IT WAS JUST BEFORE WE FOUGHT THE DEMON GOD.
I HADN'T SEEN HER SINCE I SAVED HER FROM THE DEMON HORDE.
THIS CHILD, IT'S...!
YOU KNOW IT'S—!
—I KNOW.
OUR SOCIAL STANDING, OUR RACES...WE WERE TOO DIFFERENT.
I NEED TO SAY SORRY FOR THE TROUBLE I CAUSED HER.
AND ...

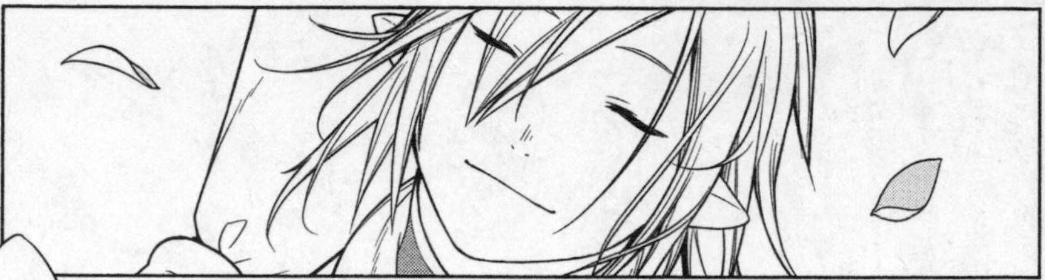

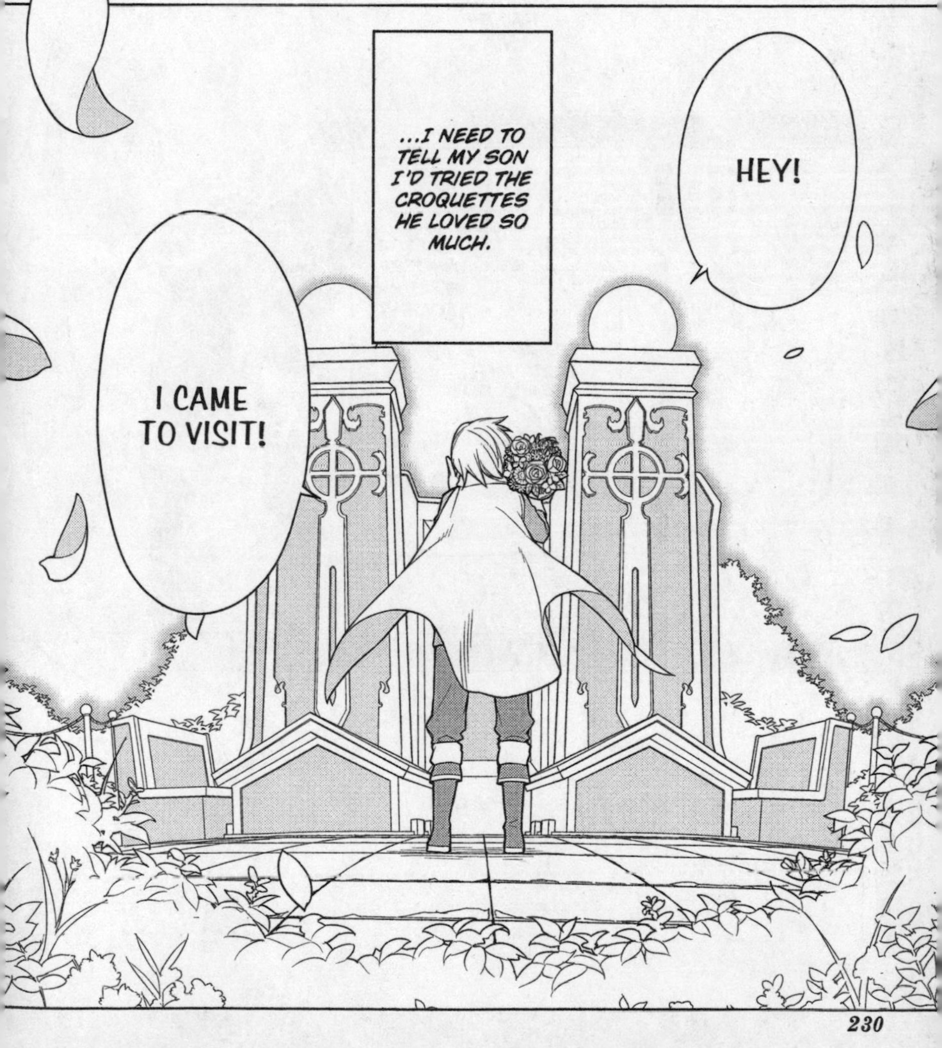
...I NEED TO TELL MY SON I'D TRIED THE CROQUETTES HE LOVED SO MUCH.
HEY!
I CAME TO VISIT!

29th Dish Pork Miso Soup

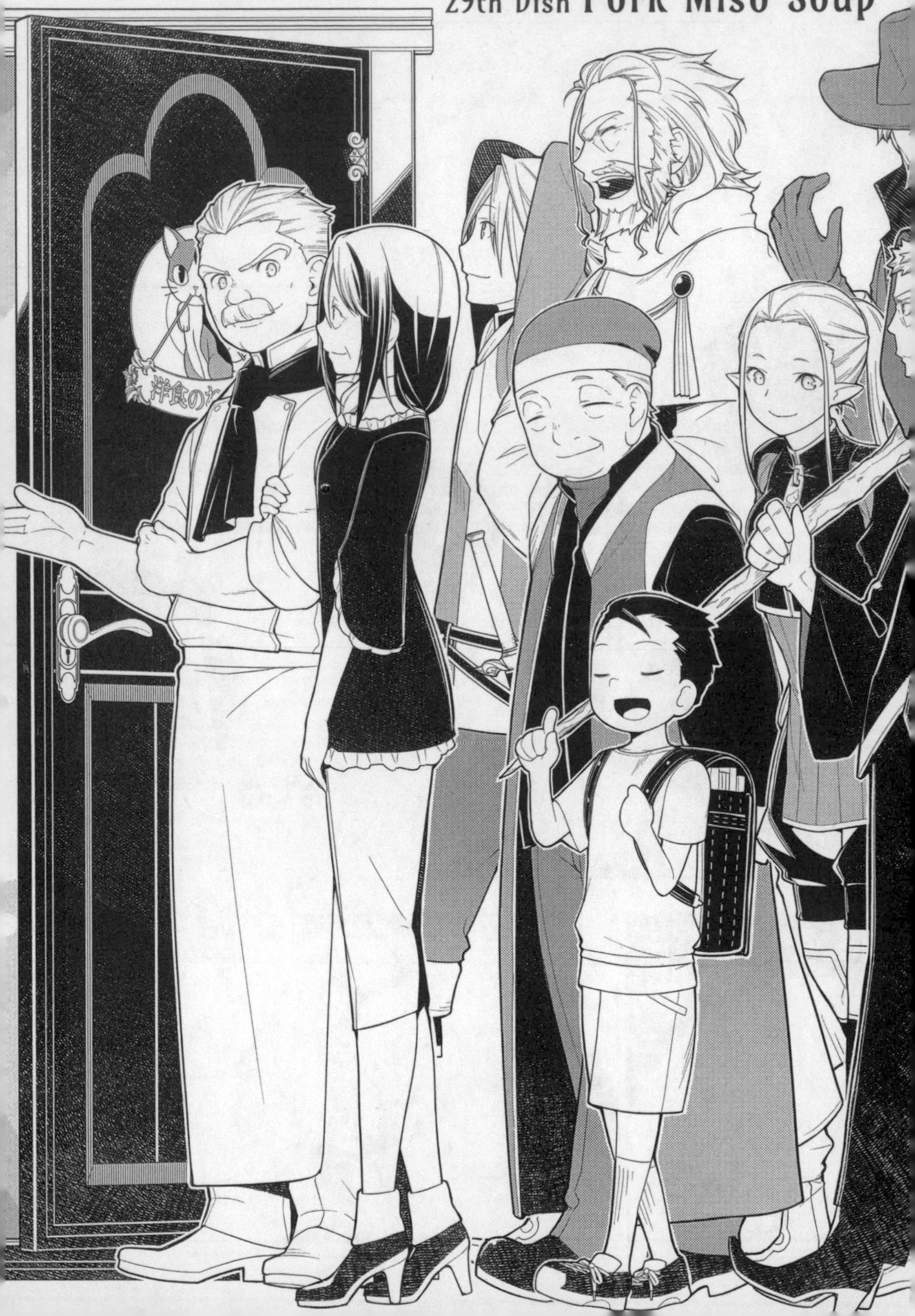

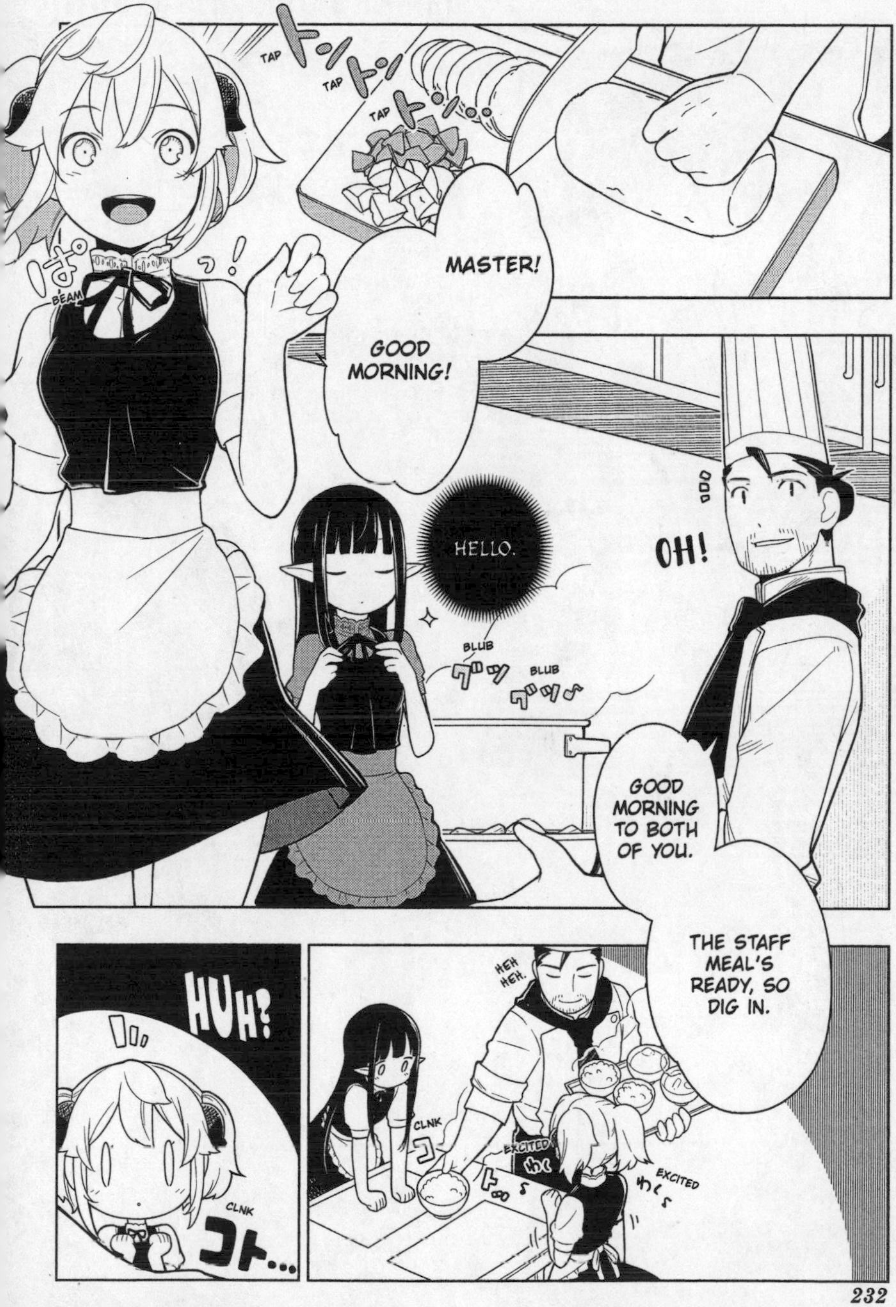

TAP
TAP
TAP
BEAM
MASTER!
GOOD MORNING!
OH!
HELLO.
BLUB
BLUB
GOOD MORNING TO BOTH OF YOU.
THE STAFF MEAL'S READY, SO DIG IN.
HEH HEH.
CLNK
EXCITED
EXCITED
HUH?
CLNK

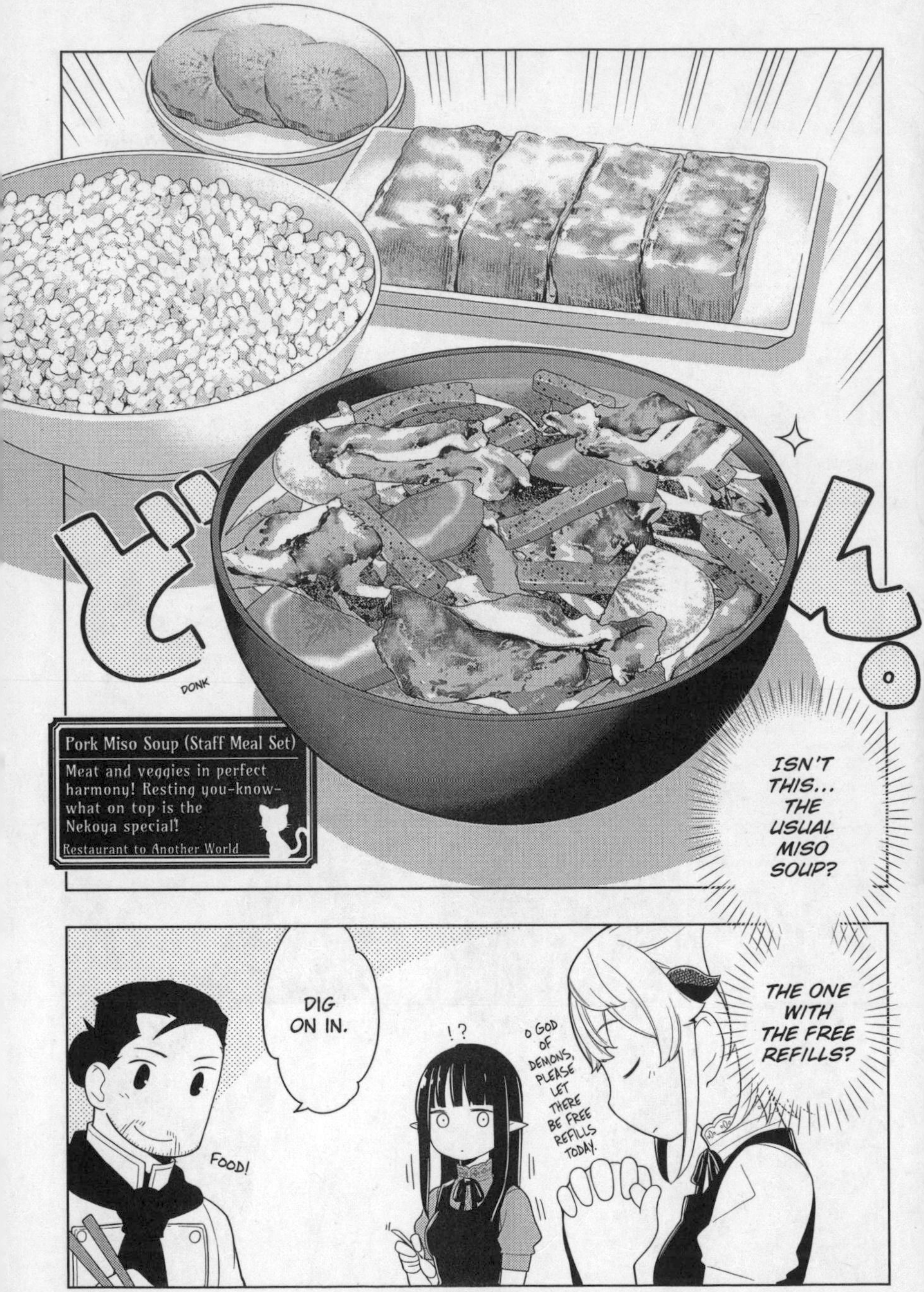

DONK
Pork Miso Soup (Staff Meal Set)
Meat and veggies in perfect harmony! Resting you-know-what on top is the Nekoya special!
Restaurant to Another World
ISN'T THIS... THE USUAL MISO SOUP?
THE ONE WITH THE FREE REFILLS?
O GOD OF DEMONS, PLEASE LET THERE BE FREE REFILLS TODAY.
!?
DIG ON IN.
FOOD!

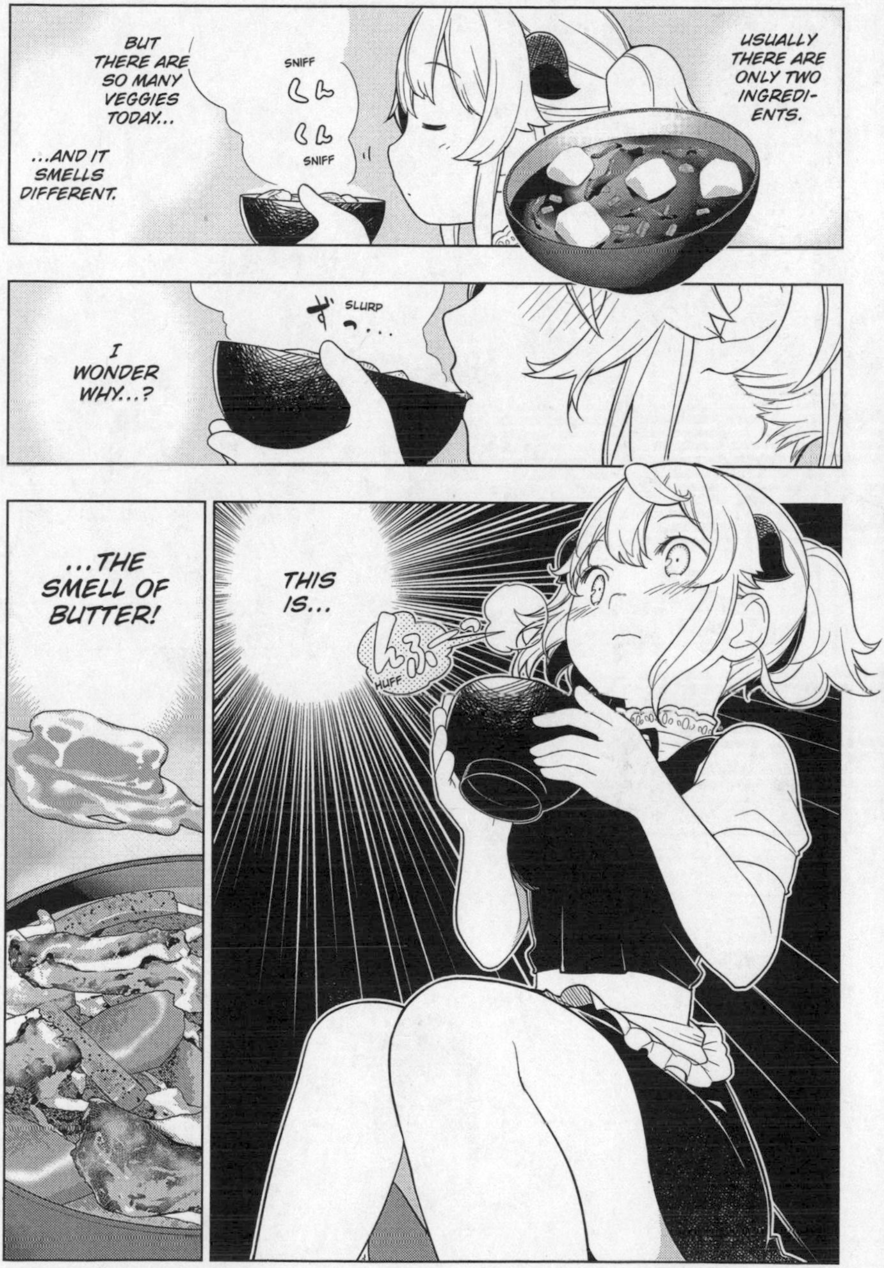
USUALLY THERE ARE ONLY TWO INGREDI-ENTS.
BUT THERE ARE SO MANY VEGGIES TODAY...
SNIFF
SNIFF
...AND IT SMELLS DIFFERENT.
SLURP
I WONDER WHY...?
THIS IS...
HUFF
...THE SMELL OF BUTTER!

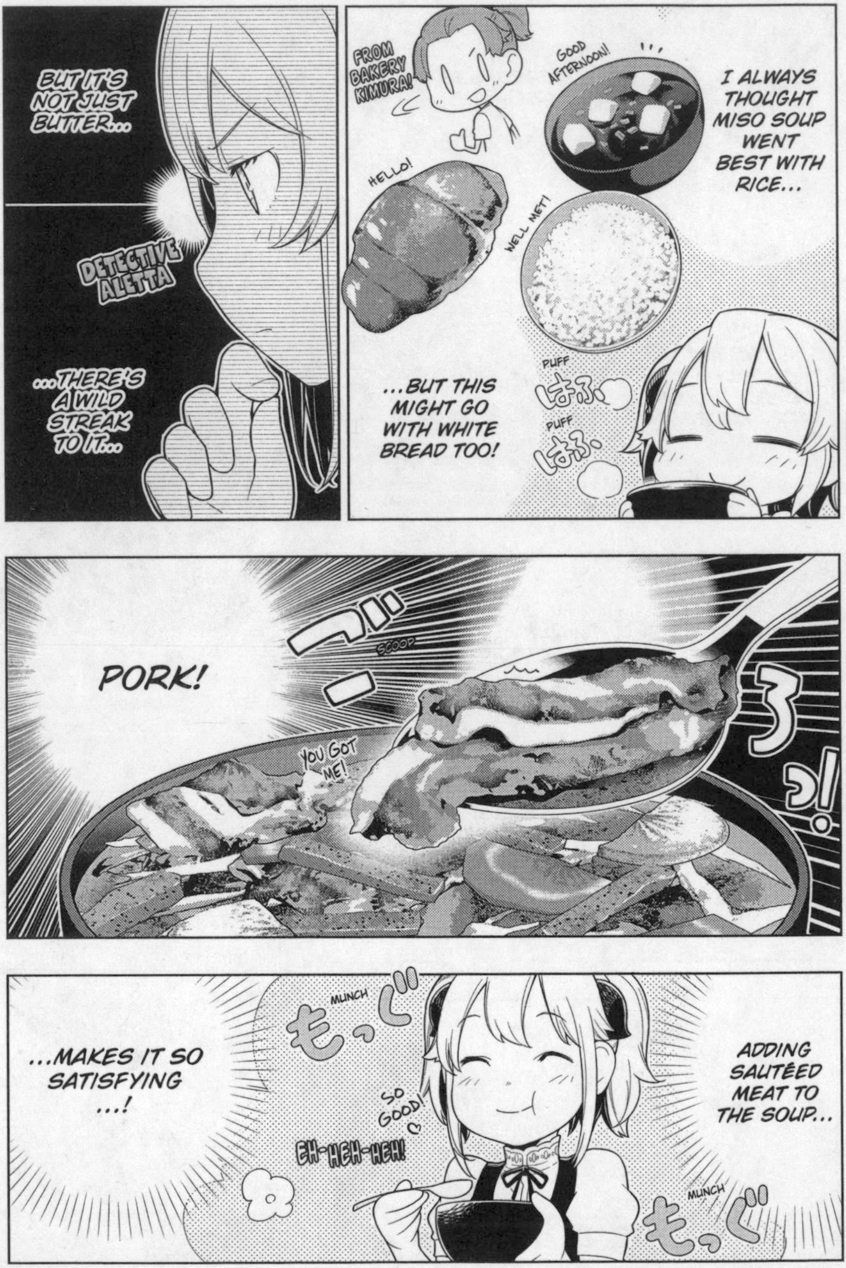
I ALWAYS THOUGHT MISO SOUP WENT BEST WITH RICE...
GOOD AFTERNOON!
FROM BAKERY KIMURA!
HELLO!
WELL MET!
...BUT THIS MIGHT GO WITH WHITE BREAD TOO!
PUFF
はふ
PUFF
はふ
BUT IT'S NOT JUST BUTTER...
DETECTIVE ALETTA
...THERE'S A WILD STREAK TO IT...
SCOOP
PORK!
YOU GOT ME!
ADDING SAUTÉED MEAT TO THE SOUP...
MUNCH
もっぐ
SO GOOD!
EH-HEH-HEH!
...MAKES IT SO SATISFYING ...!
MUNCH
もっぐ

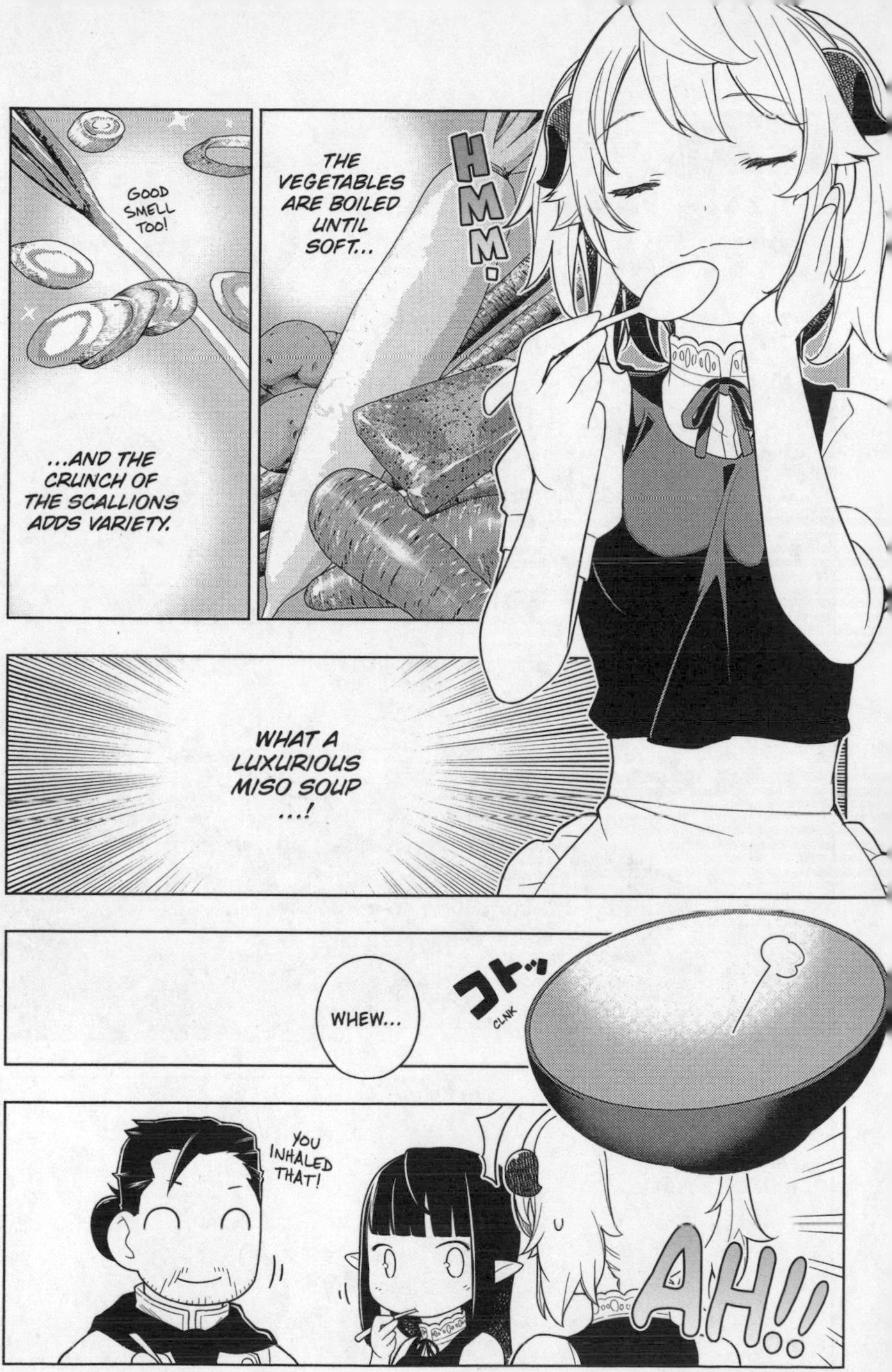
HMM.
THE VEGETABLES ARE BOILED UNTIL SOFT...
GOOD SMELL TOO!
...AND THE CRUNCH OF THE SCALLIONS ADDS VARIETY.
WHAT A LUXURIOUS MISO SOUP ...!
コトッ
CLNK
WHEW...
AH!!
YOU INHALED THAT!

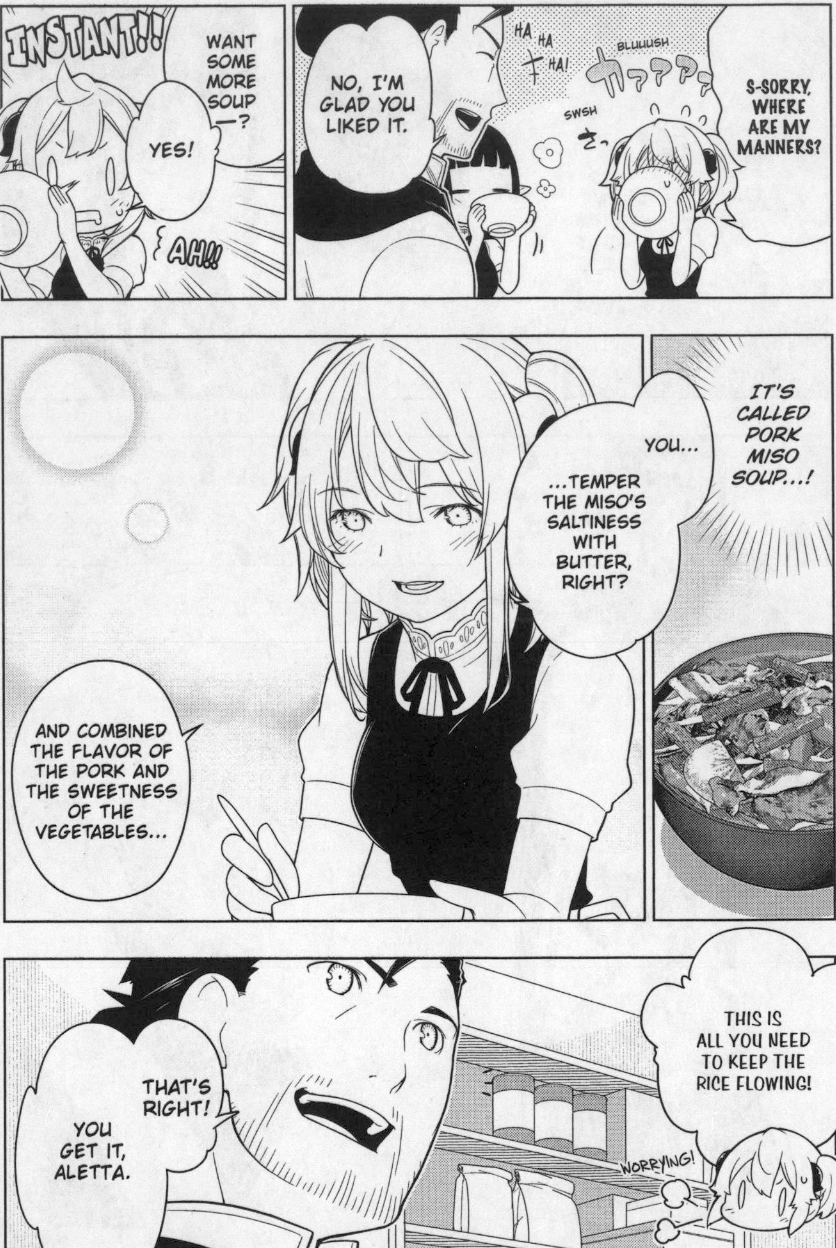
S-SORRY, WHERE ARE MY MANNERS?
BLUUUSH
SWSH
HA HA HA!
NO, I'M GLAD YOU LIKED IT.
WANT SOME MORE SOUP—?
INSTANT!!
YES!
AH!!
IT'S CALLED PORK MISO SOUP...!
YOU...
...TEMPER THE MISO'S SALTINESS WITH BUTTER, RIGHT?
AND COMBINED THE FLAVOR OF THE PORK AND THE SWEETNESS OF THE VEGETABLES...
THIS IS ALL YOU NEED TO KEEP THE RICE FLOWING!
WORRYING!
THAT'S RIGHT!
YOU GET IT, ALETTA.

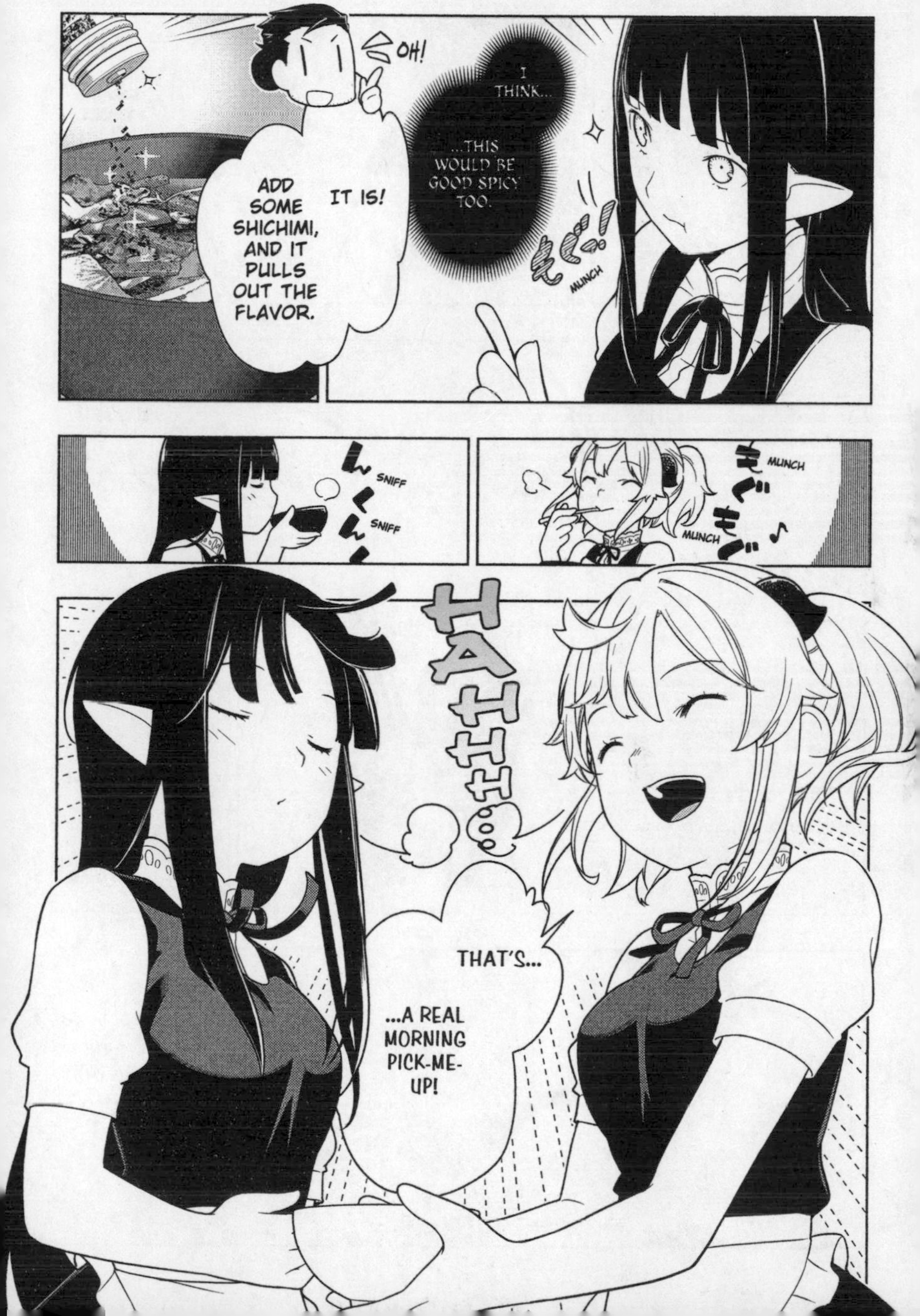

I THINK...
...THIS WOULD BE GOOD SPICY TOO.
もぐっ!
MUNCH
OH!
IT IS!
ADD SOME SHICHIMI, AND IT PULLS OUT THE FLAVOR.
MUNCH
MUNCH
SNIFF
SNIFF
HAHHH...
THAT'S...
...A REAL MORNING PICK-ME-UP!

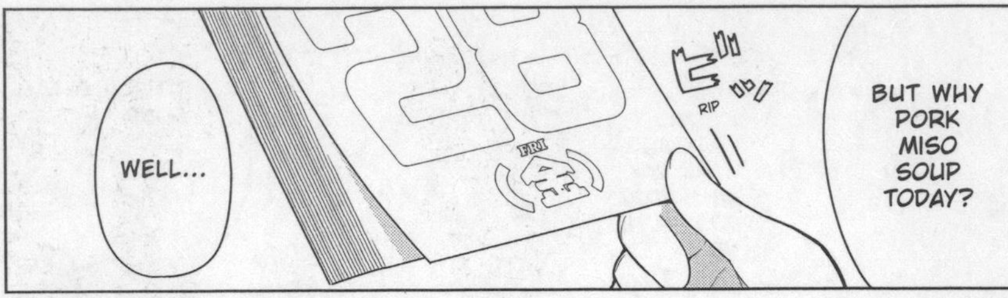
BUT WHY PORK MISO SOUP TODAY?
RIP
28
FRI
WELL...

* "29" IN JAPANESE CAN BE PRONOUNCED AS "NIKU," OR "MEAT"

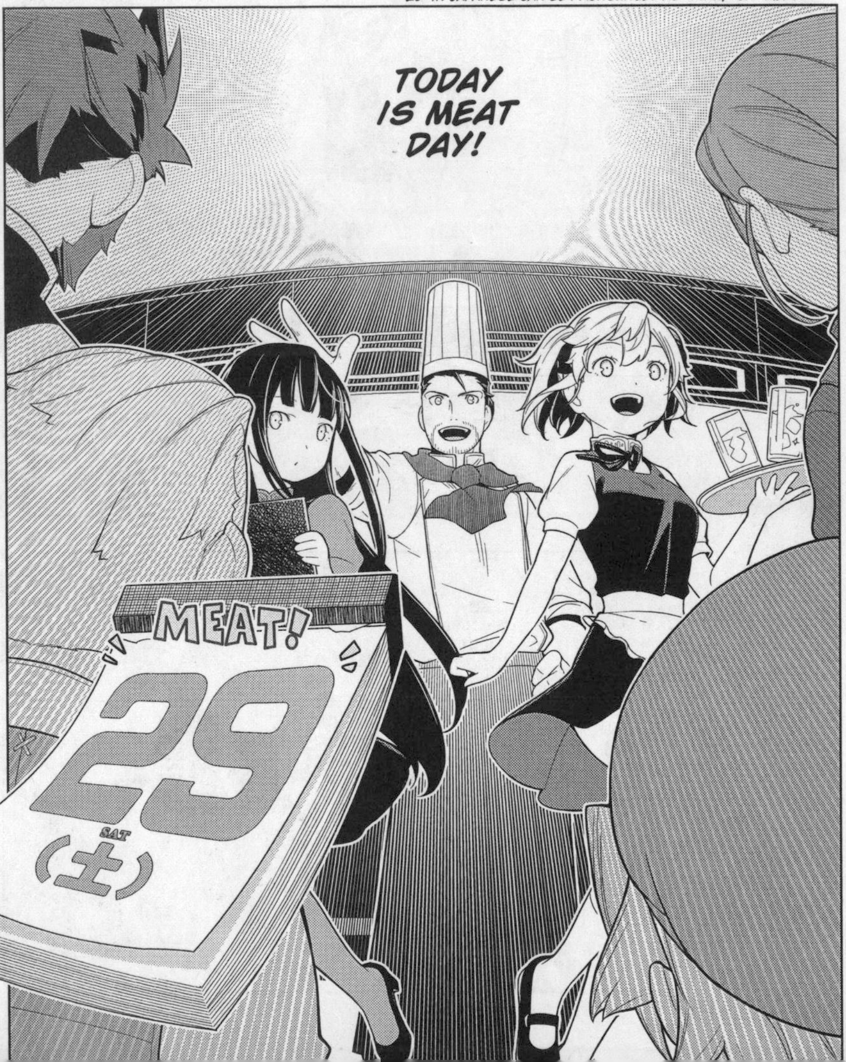
TODAY IS MEAT DAY!
MEAT!
29
SAT

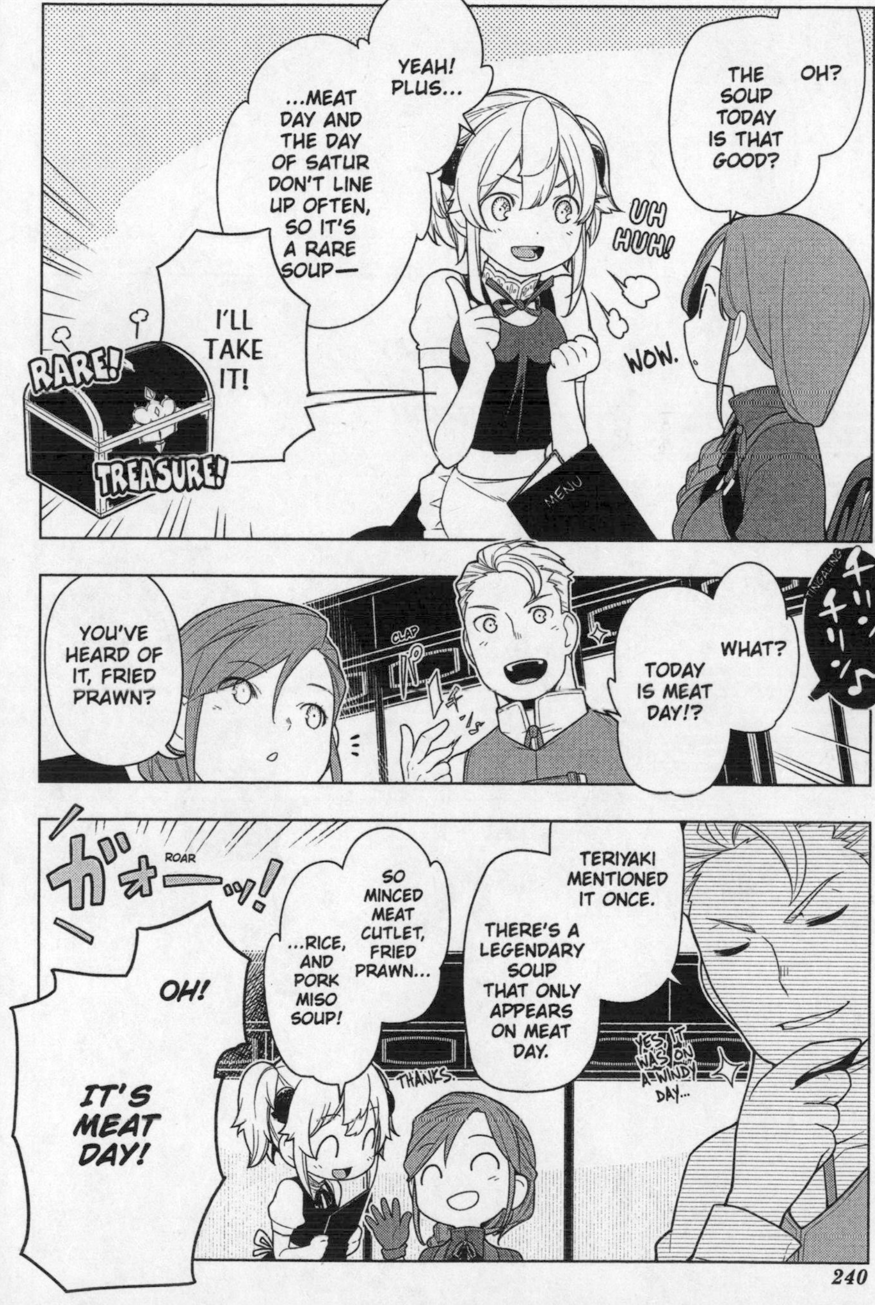
OH?
THE SOUP TODAY IS THAT GOOD?
UH HUH!
WOW.
YEAH! PLUS...
...MEAT DAY AND THE DAY OF SATUR DON'T LINE UP OFTEN, SO IT'S A RARE SOUP—
I'LL TAKE IT!
RARE!
TREASURE!
MENU
TINGALING
WHAT?
TODAY IS MEAT DAY!?
CLAP
YOU'VE HEARD OF IT, FRIED PRAWN?
TERIYAKI MENTIONED IT ONCE.
THERE'S A LEGENDARY SOUP THAT ONLY APPEARS ON MEAT DAY.
YES, IT WAS ON A WINDY DAY...
SO MINCED MEAT CUTLET, FRIED PRAWN...
...RICE, AND PORK MISO SOUP!
THANKS.
ROAR
OH!
IT'S MEAT DAY!

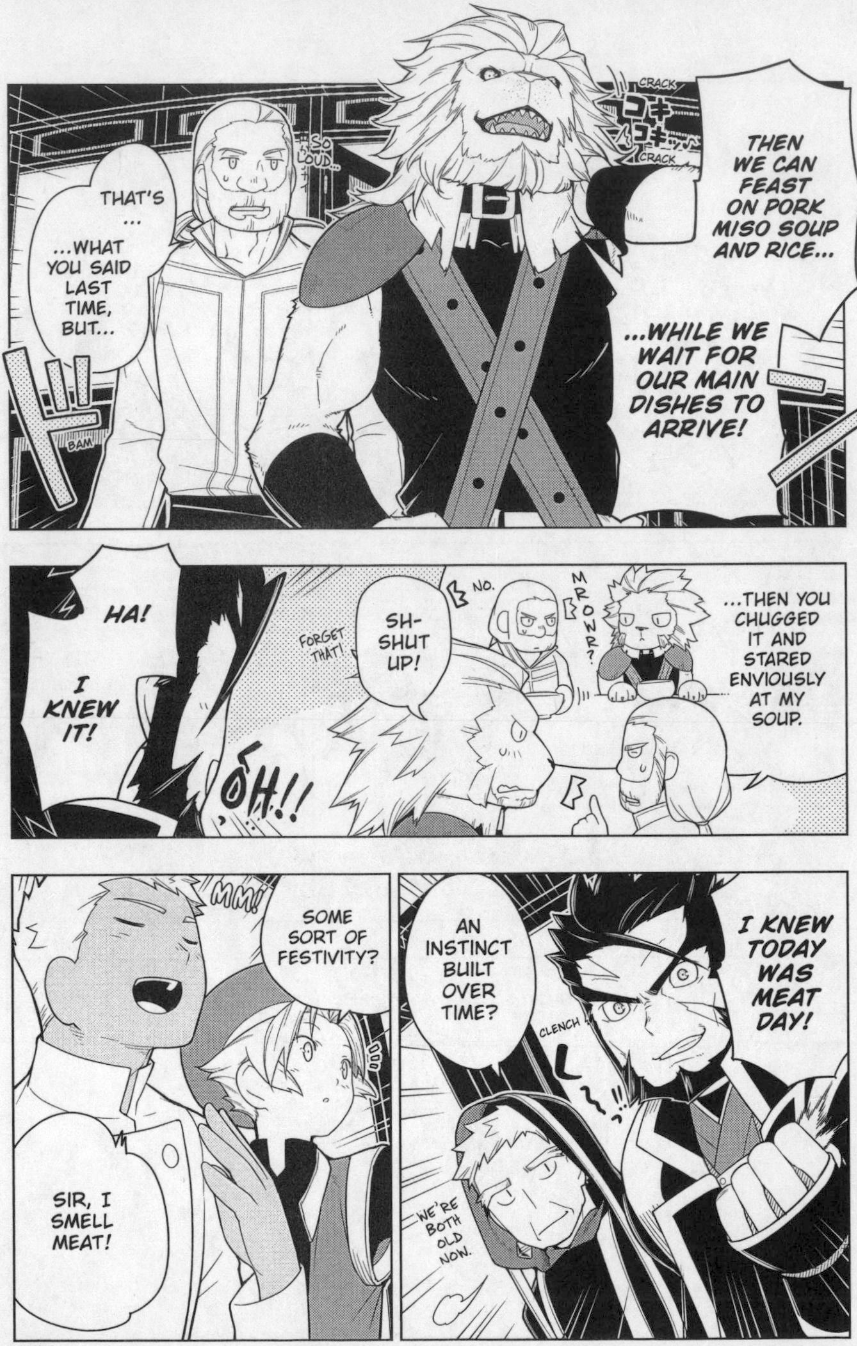
CRACK
CRACK
THEN WE CAN FEAST ON PORK MISO SOUP AND RICE...
...WHILE WE WAIT FOR OUR MAIN DISHES TO ARRIVE!
SO LOUD...
THAT'S...
...WHAT YOU SAID LAST TIME, BUT...
BAM
...THEN YOU CHUGGED IT AND STARED ENVIOUSLY AT MY SOUP.
MROWR?
NO.
SH- SHUT UP!
FORGET THAT!
OH!!
HA!
I KNEW IT!
I KNEW TODAY WAS MEAT DAY!
CLENCH
AN INSTINCT BUILT OVER TIME?
WE'RE BOTH OLD NOW.
MM!
SOME SORT OF FESTIVITY?
SIR, I SMELL MEAT!

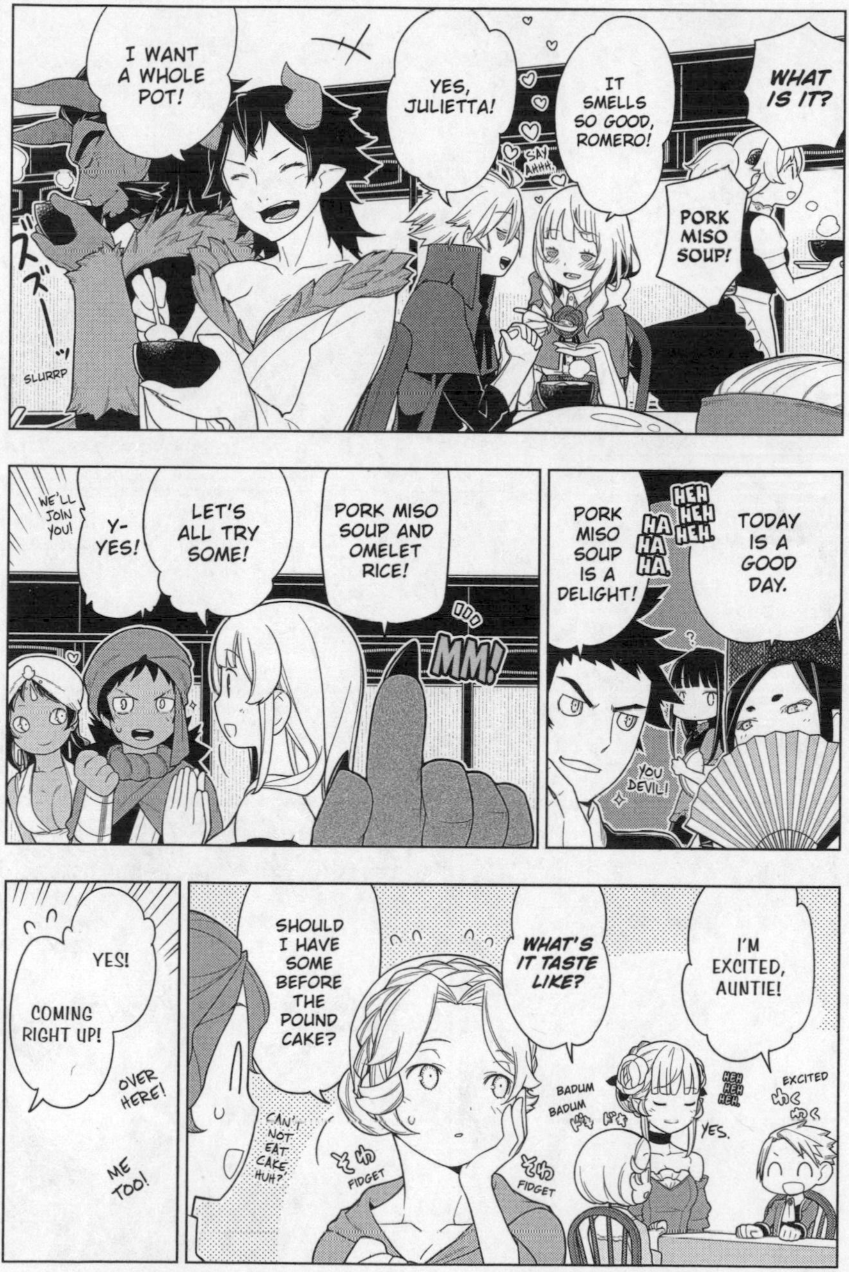
WHAT IS IT?
PORK MISO SOUP!
IT SMELLS SO GOOD, ROMERO!
SAY AHHH.
YES, JULIETTA!
I WANT A WHOLE POT!
SLURRP
TODAY IS A GOOD DAY.
HEH HEH HEH.
HA HA HA.
PORK MISO SOUP IS A DELIGHT!
YOU DEVIL!
MM!
PORK MISO SOUP AND OMELET RICE!
LET'S ALL TRY SOME!
Y-YES!
WE'LL JOIN YOU!
I'M EXCITED, AUNTIE!
EXCITED
HEH HEH HEH.
YES.
BADUM BADUM
WHAT'S IT TASTE LIKE?
FIDGET
SHOULD I HAVE SOME BEFORE THE POUND CAKE?
FIDGET
CAN'T NOT EAT CAKE, HUH?
YES!
COMING RIGHT UP!
OVER HERE!
ME TOO!

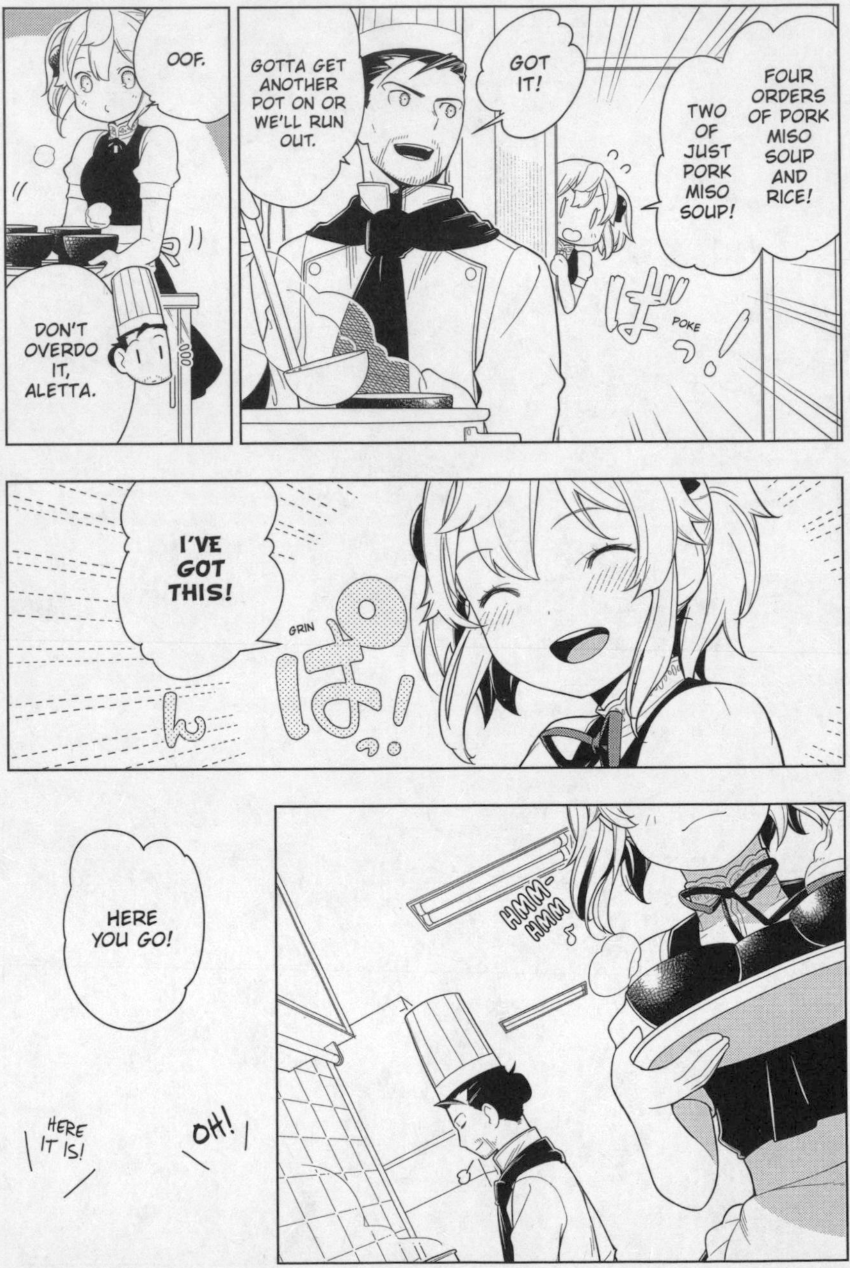
FOUR ORDERS OF PORK MISO SOUP AND RICE!
TWO OF JUST PORK MISO SOUP!
ばっ!
POKE
GOT IT!
GOTTA GET ANOTHER POT ON OR WE'LL RUN OUT.
OOF.
DON'T OVERDO IT, ALETTA.
I'VE GOT THIS!
ぱっ!
GRIN
ん
HMM-HMM
HERE YOU GO!
OH!
HERE IT IS!

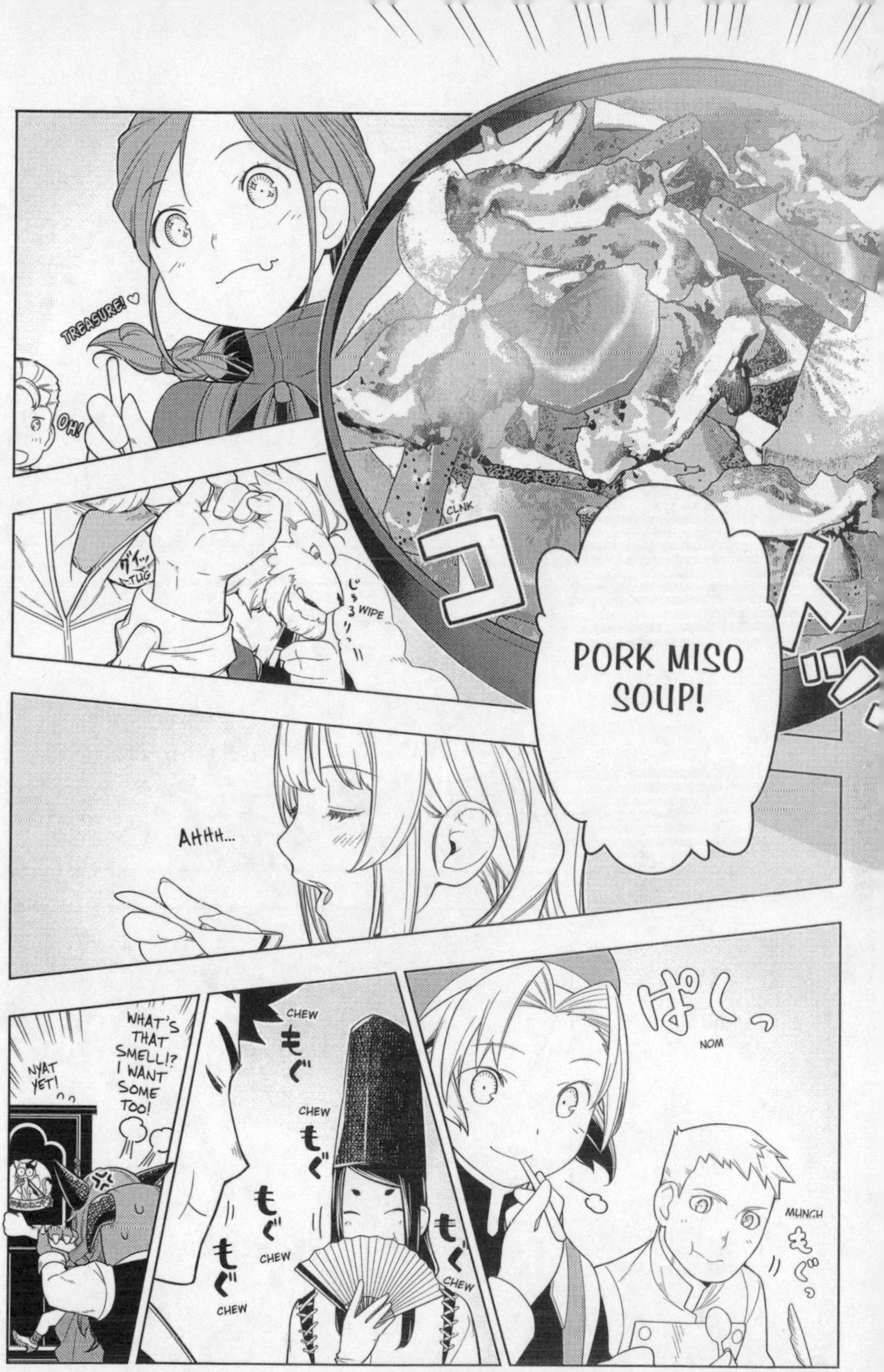
CLNK
コト
PORK MISO SOUP!
TREASURE! ♡
OH!
グイッ
TUG
じゅるりっ
WIPE
AHHH...
ぱくっ
NOM
MUNCH
もぐっ
CHEW
もぐ
CHEW
もぐ
CHEW
もぐ
CHEW
もぐ
CHEW
もぐ
WHAT'S THAT SMELL!? I WANT SOME TOO!
NYAT YET!

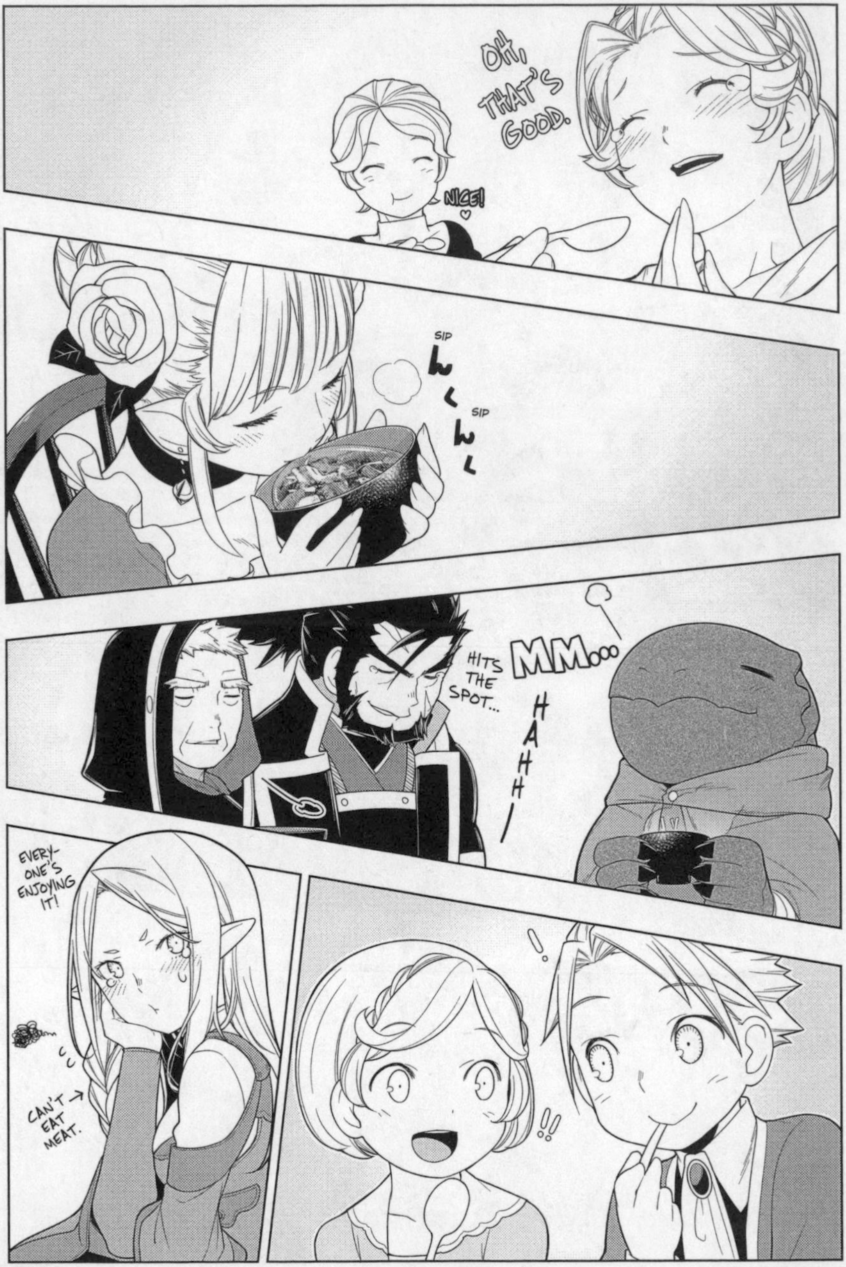
OH, THAT'S GOOD.
NICE!
SIP
SIP
MM...
HAHH!
HITS THE SPOT...
!
!!
EVERY-ONE'S ENJOYING IT!
CAN'T EAT MEAT.

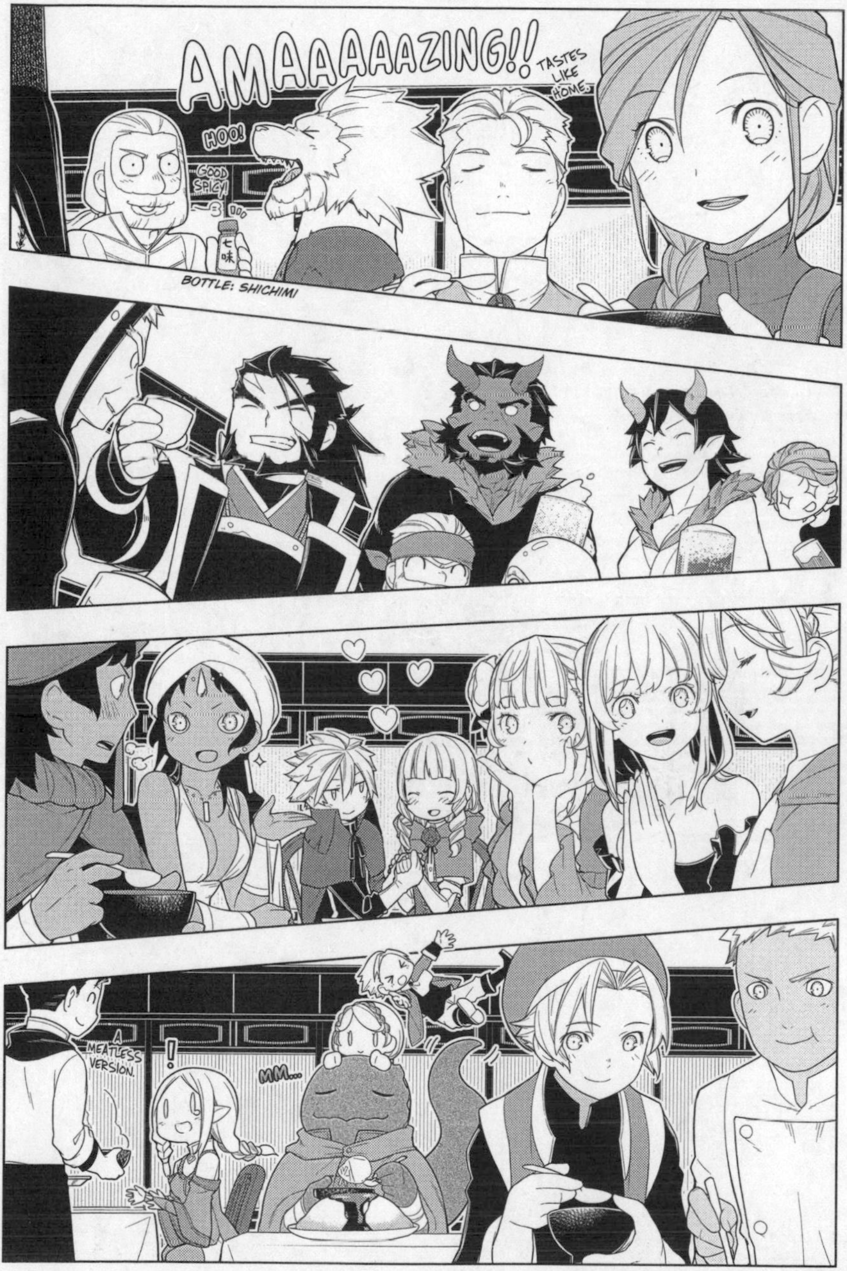
TASTES LIKE HOME.
AMAAAAAZING!!
HOO!
GOOD SPICY!
七味
BOTTLE: SHICHIMI
MM...
!
A MEATLESS VERSION.

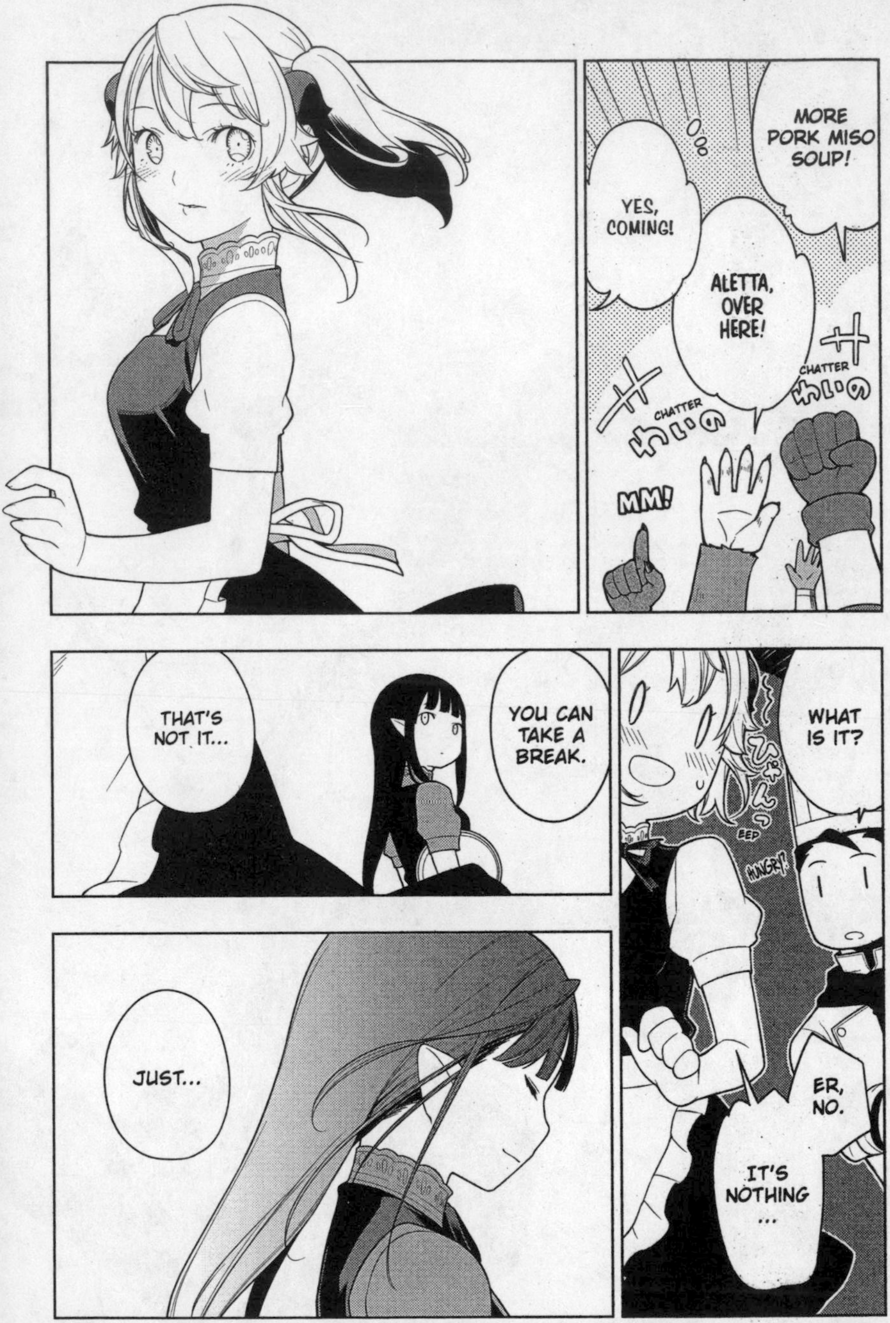
MORE PORK MISO SOUP!
ALETTA, OVER HERE!
YES, COMING!
CHATTER
CHATTER
MM!
WHAT IS IT?
EEP
HUNGRY!
ER, NO.
IT'S NOTHING ...
YOU CAN TAKE A BREAK.
THAT'S NOT IT...
JUST...

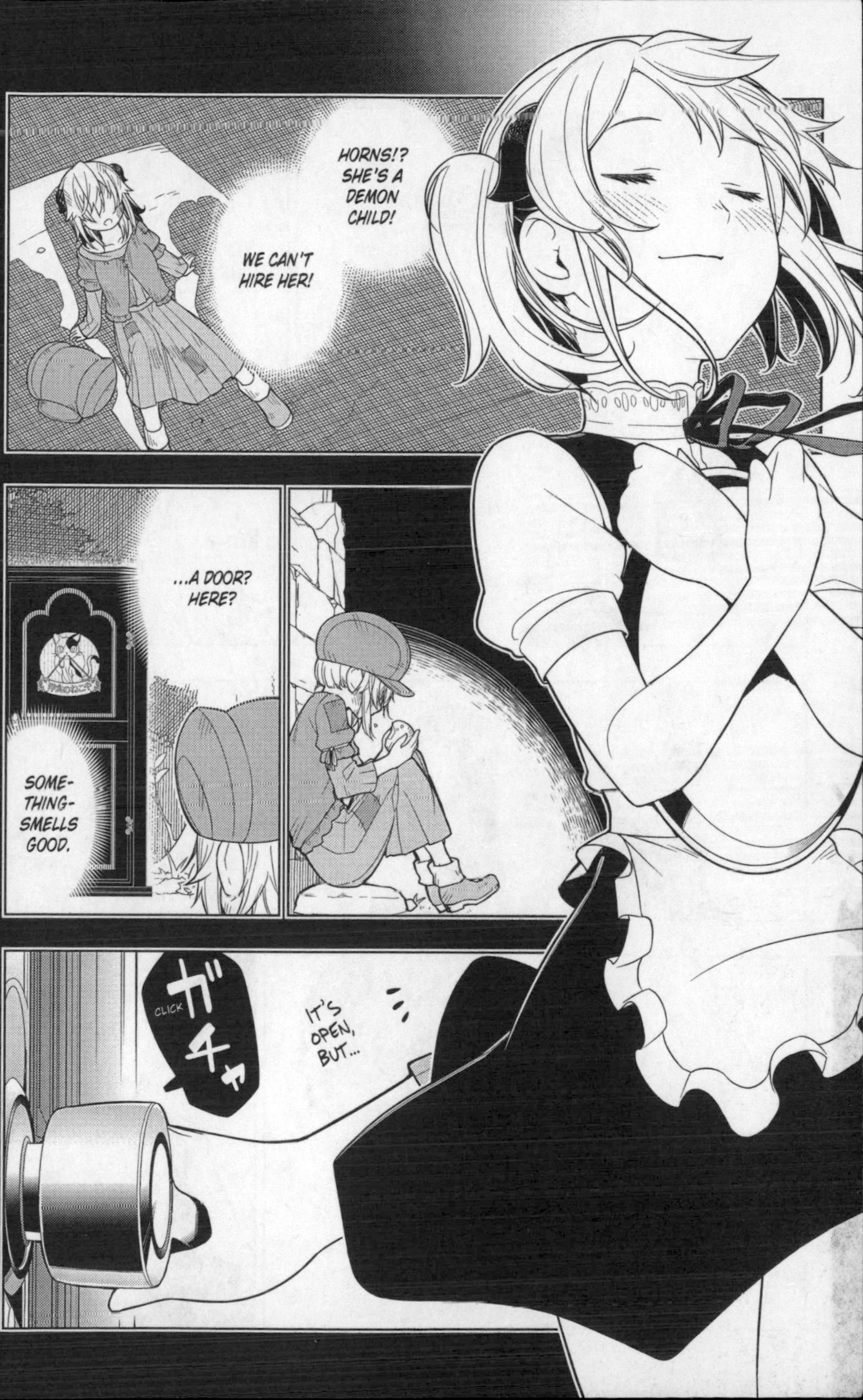
HORNS!? SHE'S A DEMON CHILD!
WE CAN'T HIRE HER!
...A DOOR? HERE?
SOME-THING-SMELLS GOOD.
IT'S OPEN, BUT...
ガチャ
CLICK

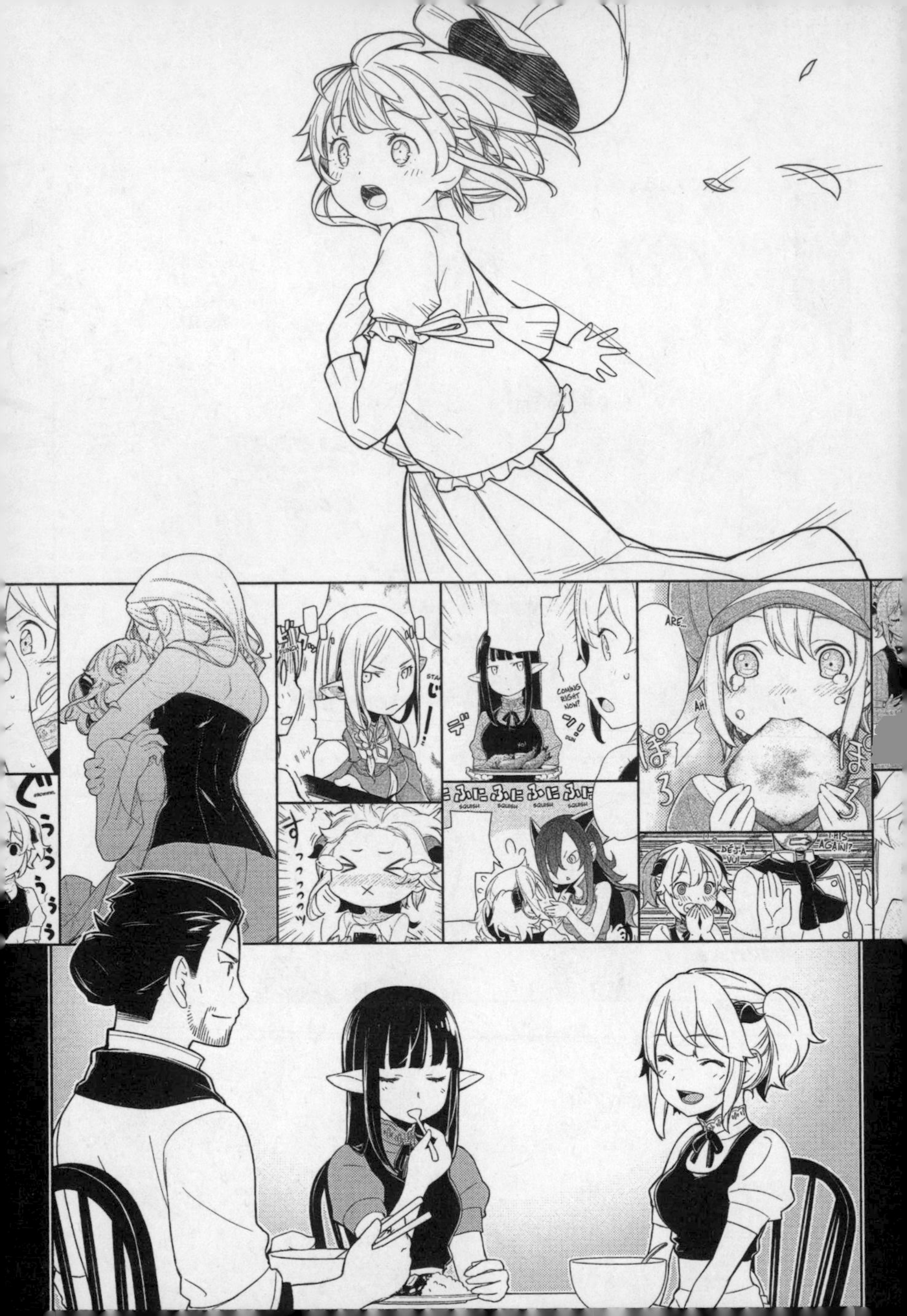
ARE...
AH!
ぽろ
ぽろ
THIS AGAIN!?
DÉJÀ VU!
COMING RIGHT NOW?
デ
ふにふにふにふに
SQUISH SQUISH SQUISH SQUISH
FLINCH
じー!!
す
ぐううう

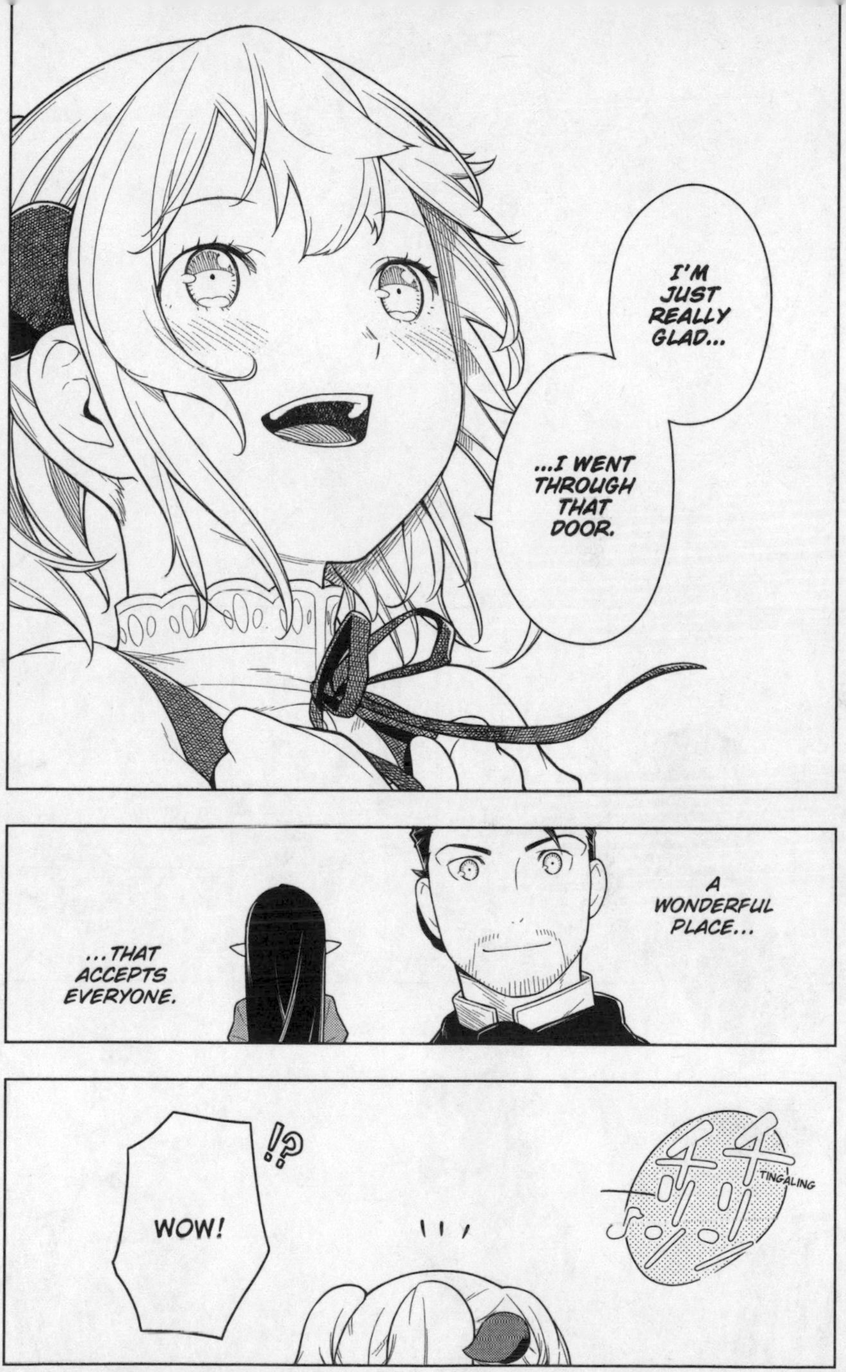
I'M JUST REALLY GLAD...
...I WENT THROUGH THAT DOOR.
A WONDERFUL PLACE...
...THAT ACCEPTS EVERYONE.
TINGALING
!?
WOW!

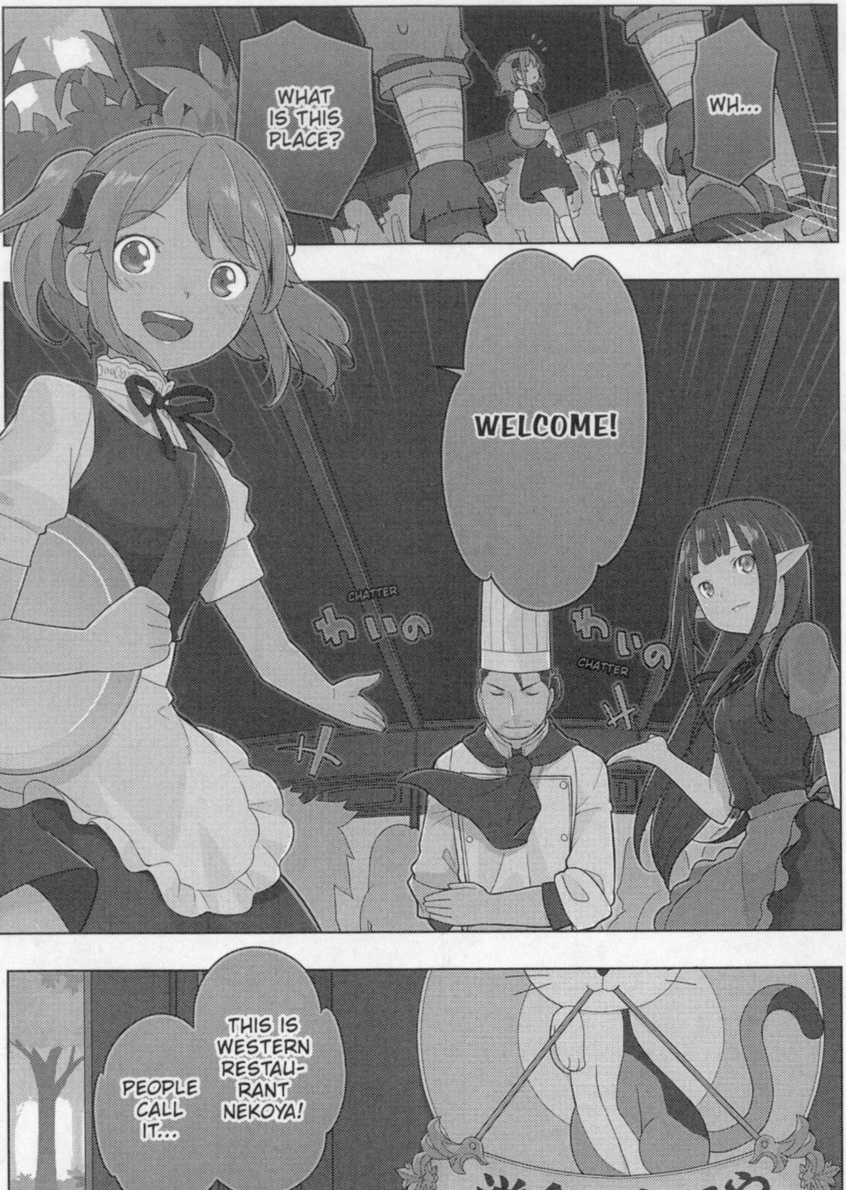
WH...
WHAT IS THIS PLACE?
WELCOME!
CHATTER
わいの
CHATTER
わいの
THIS IS WESTERN RESTAU-RANT NEKOYA!
PEOPLE CALL IT...
洋食のねこや

SIGN: WESTERN RESTAURANT NEKOYA

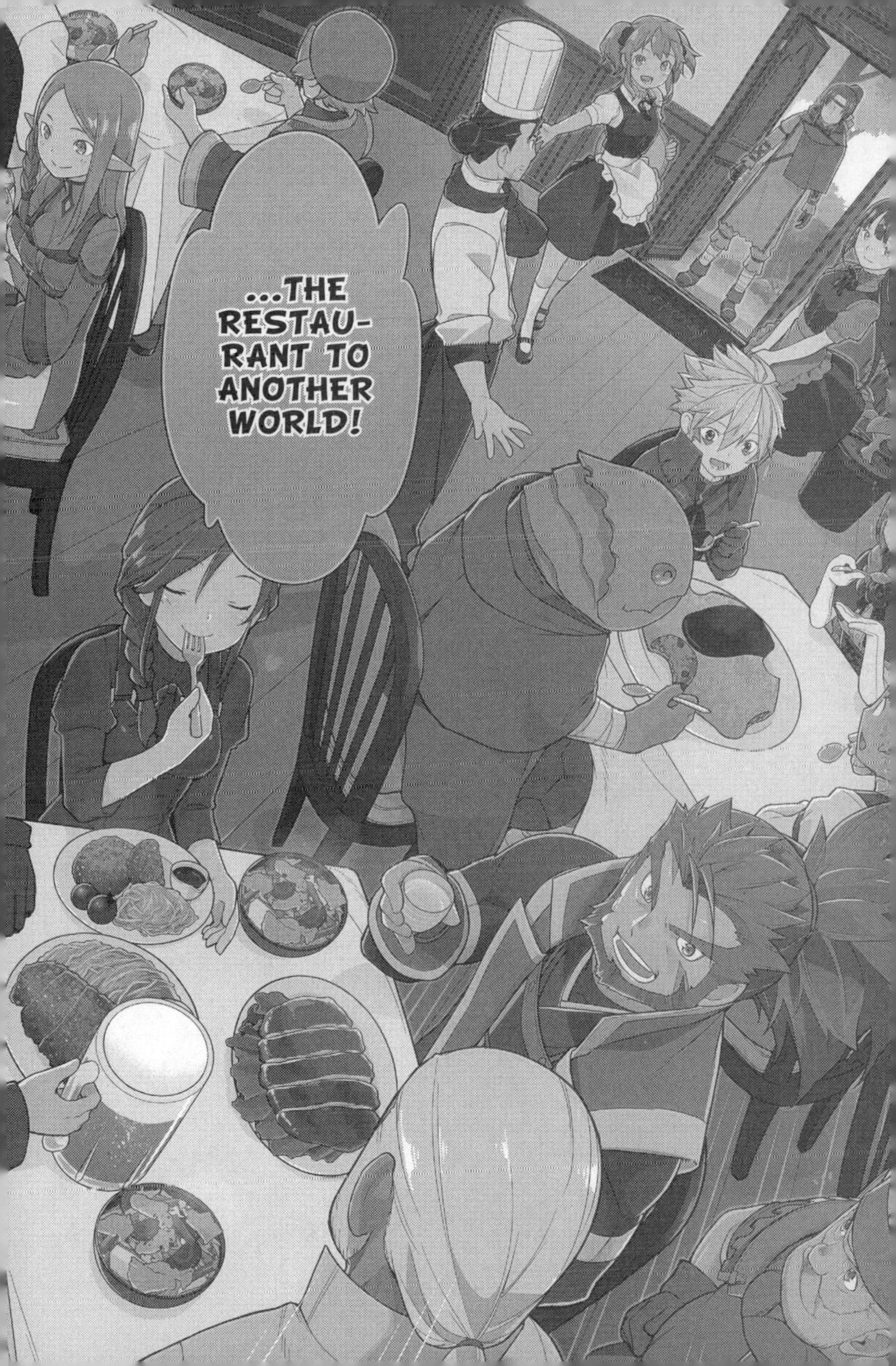
...THE RESTAU-RANT TO ANOTHER WORLD!

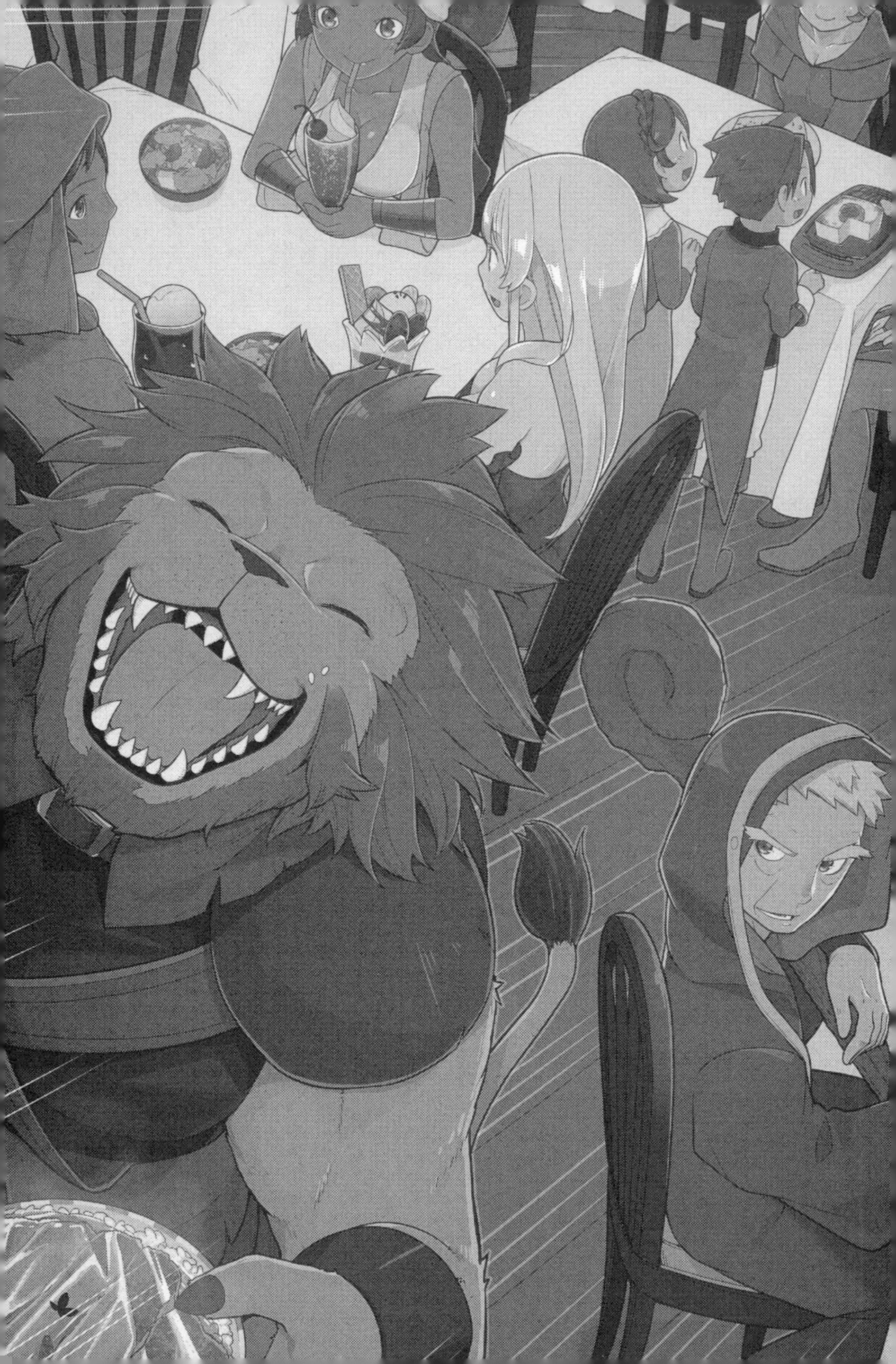

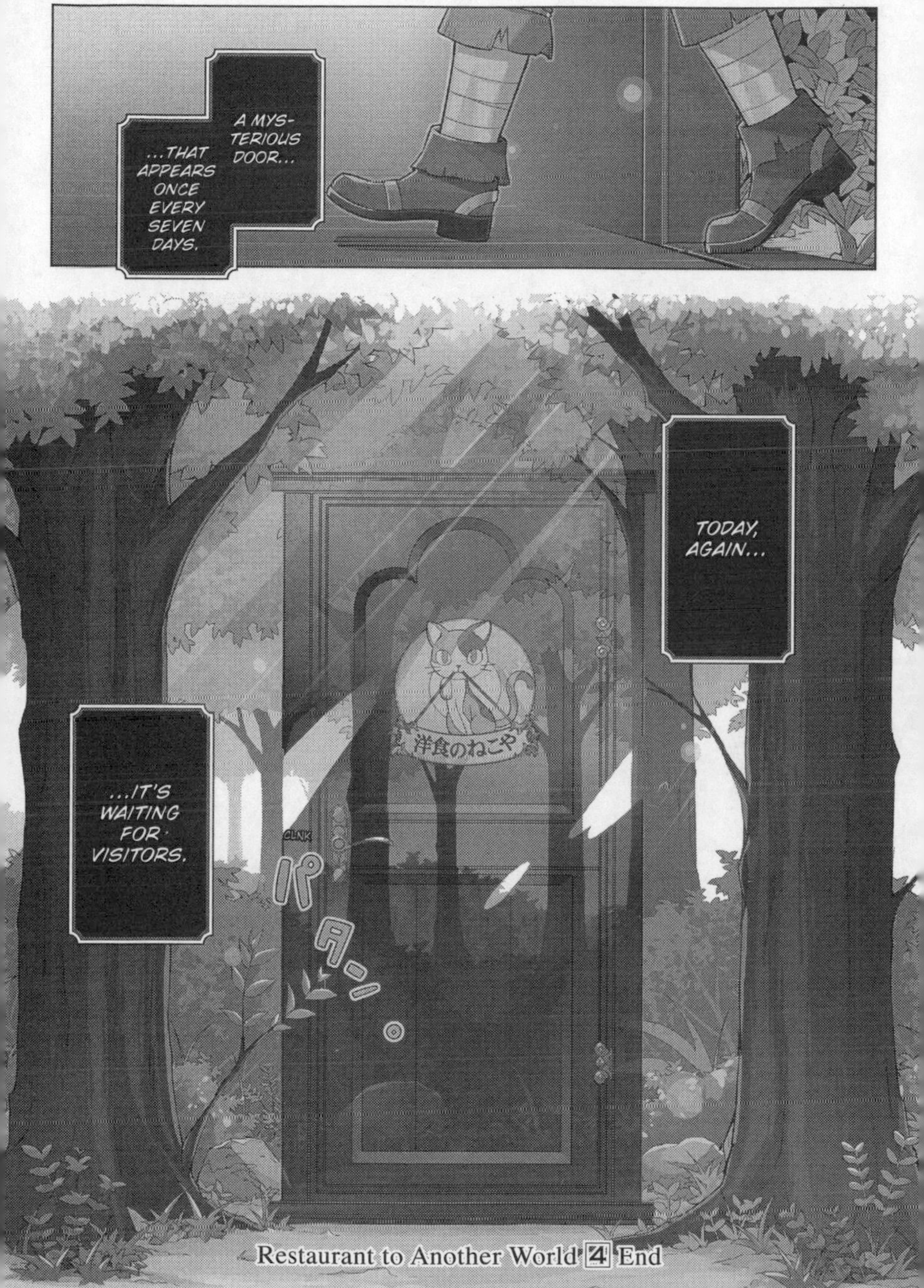
A MYSTERIOUS DOOR...
...THAT APPEARS ONCE EVERY SEVEN DAYS.
TODAY, AGAIN...
洋食のねこや
CLNK
パタン。
...IT'S WAITING FOR VISITORS.
Restaurant to Another World 4 End

AFTERWORD

Thank you for reading *Restaurant to Another World* 4! There were hard times and plenty of problems during serialization (and plenty of delights as well!), but thanks to everyone, I was able to complete it! Thanks! The manga version wraps up here, but the original novels still exist, and the anime DVD and BD are on sale now, so please continue supporting *Restaurant to Another World*! I hope we can meet again some Saturday, through a door that opens somewhere.

Takaaki Kugatsu

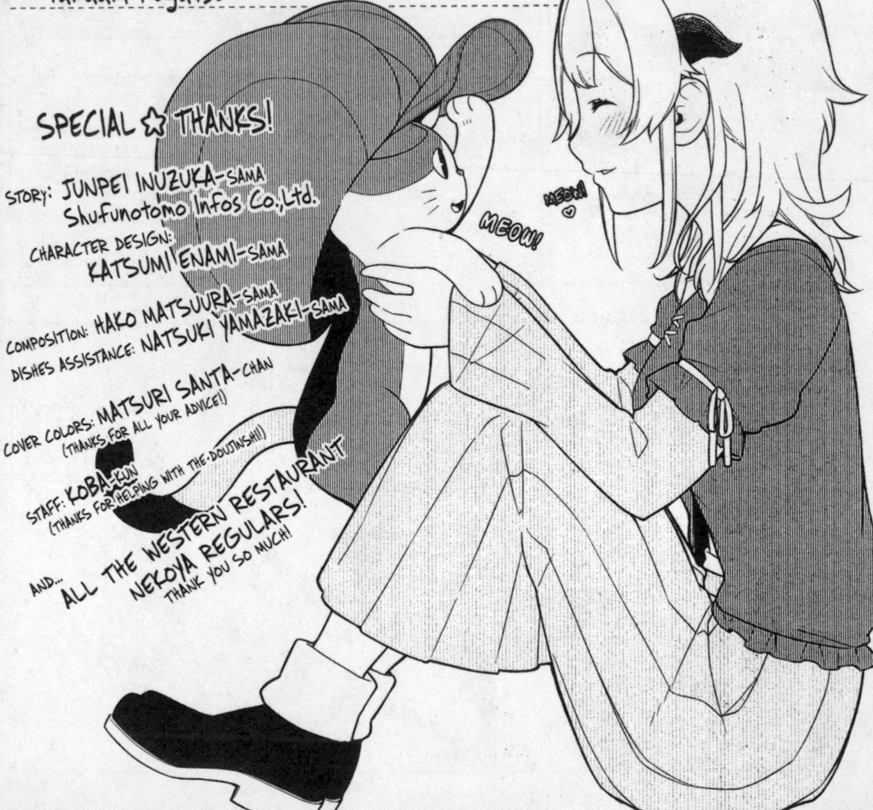
SPECIAL ☆ THANKS!
STORY: JUNPEI INUZUKA-SAMA
Shufunotomo Infos Co.,Ltd.
CHARACTER DESIGN:
KATSUMI ENAMI-SAMA
COMPOSITION: HAKO MATSUURA-SAMA
DISHES ASSISTANCE: NATSUKI YAMAZAKI-SAMA
COVER COLORS: MATSURI SANTA-CHAN
(THANKS FOR ALL YOUR ADVICE!)
STAFF: KOBA-KUN
(THANKS FOR HELPING WITH THE DOUJINSHI!)
AND... ALL THE WESTERN RESTAURANT
NEKOYA REGULARS!
THANK YOU SO MUCH!
MEOW!
MEOW!

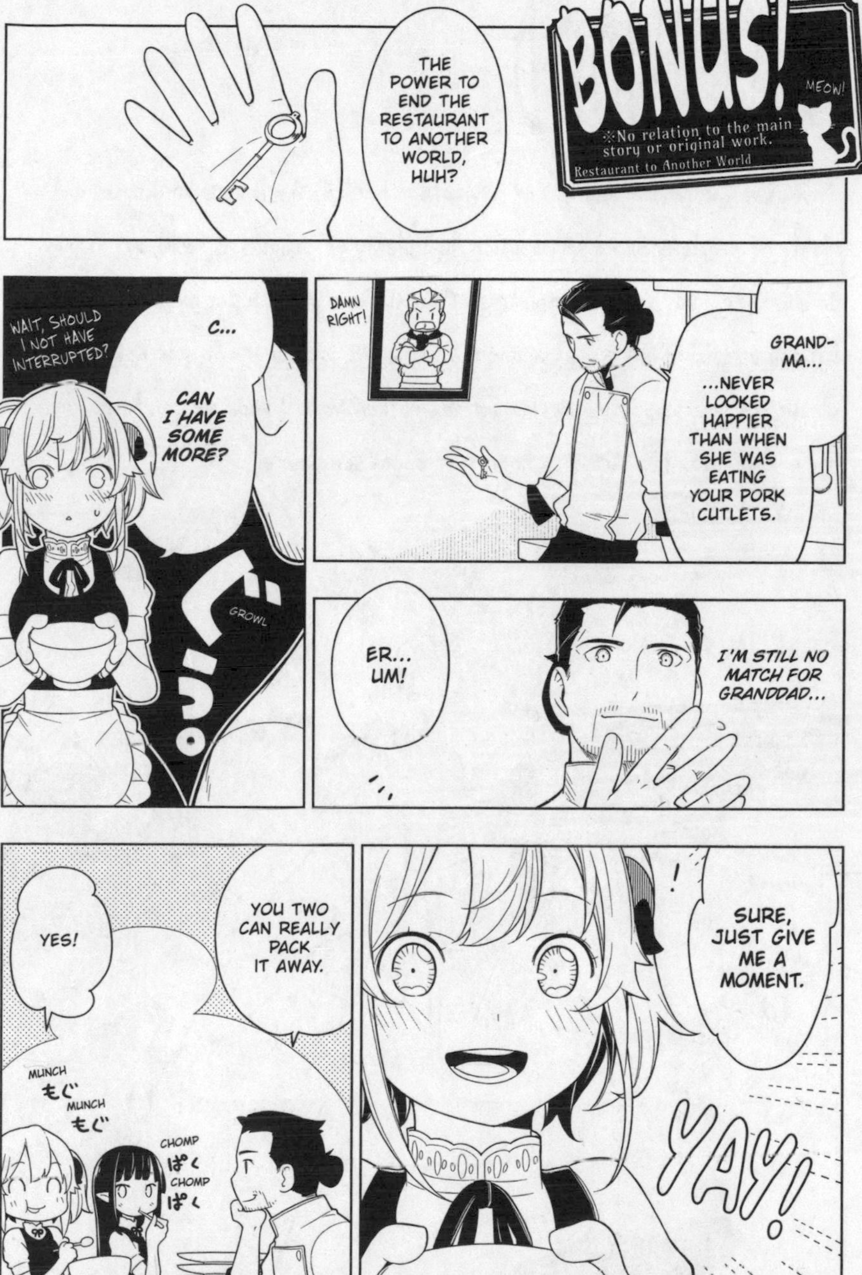
BONUS!
MEOW!
※No relation to the main story or original work.
Restaurant to Another World
THE POWER TO END THE RESTAURANT TO ANOTHER WORLD, HUH?
GRAND-MA...
...NEVER LOOKED HAPPIER THAN WHEN SHE WAS EATING YOUR PORK CUTLETS.
DAMN RIGHT!
I'M STILL NO MATCH FOR GRANDDAD...
ER... UM!
C...
CAN I HAVE SOME MORE?
WAIT, SHOULD I NOT HAVE INTERRUPTED?
GROWL
!
SURE, JUST GIVE ME A MOMENT.
YAY!
YOU TWO CAN REALLY PACK IT AWAY.
YES!
MUNCH もぐ MUNCH もぐ
CHOMP ぱく CHOMP ぱく

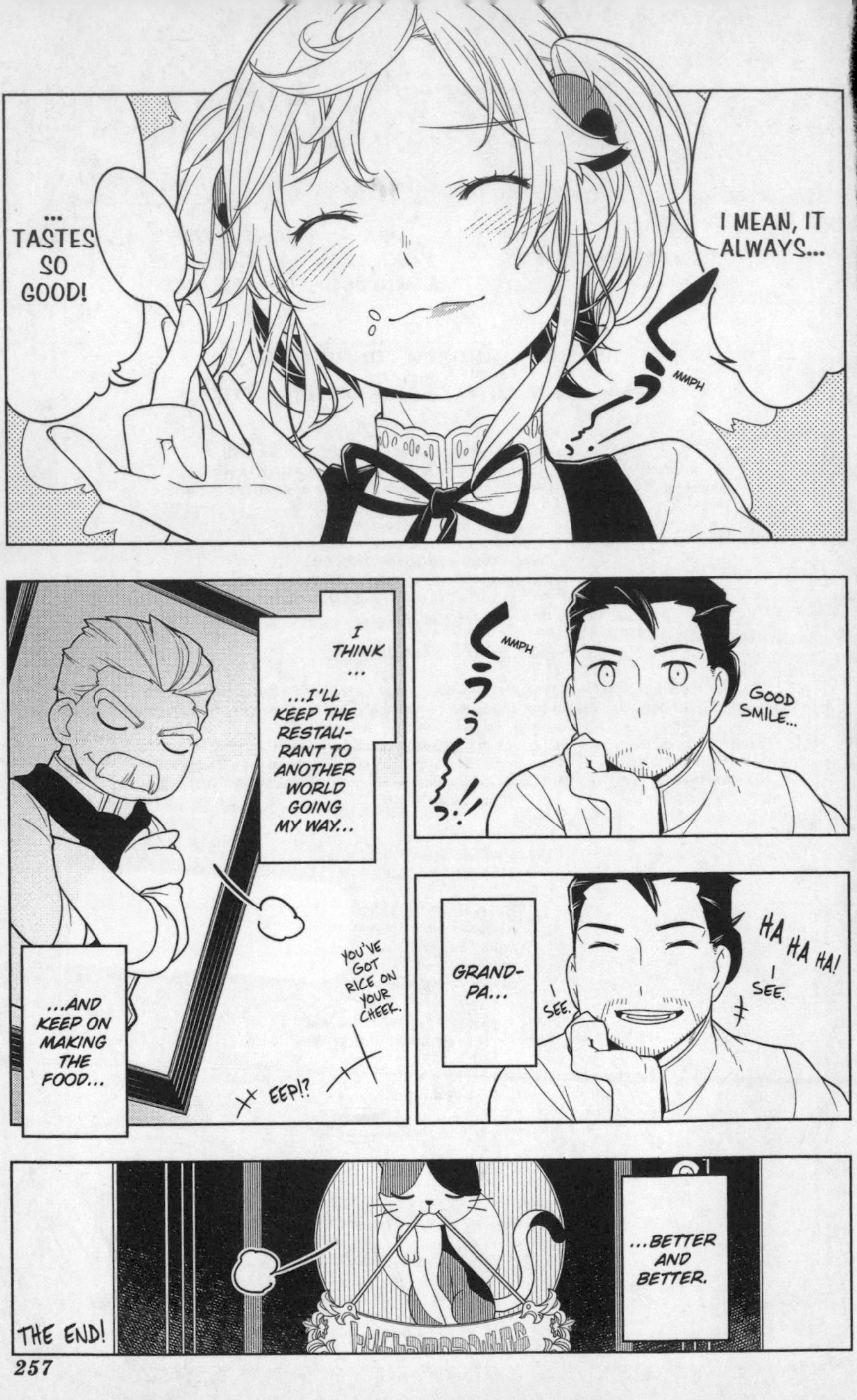
I MEAN, IT ALWAYS...
MMPH
...TASTES SO GOOD!
MMPH
GOOD SMILE...
HA HA HA!
I SEE.
I SEE.
GRANDPA...
I THINK...
...I'LL KEEP THE RESTAURANT TO ANOTHER WORLD GOING MY WAY...
YOU'VE GOT RICE ON YOUR CHEEK.
EEP!?
...AND KEEP ON MAKING THE FOOD...
...BETTER AND BETTER.
THE END!

RESTAURANT to Another World

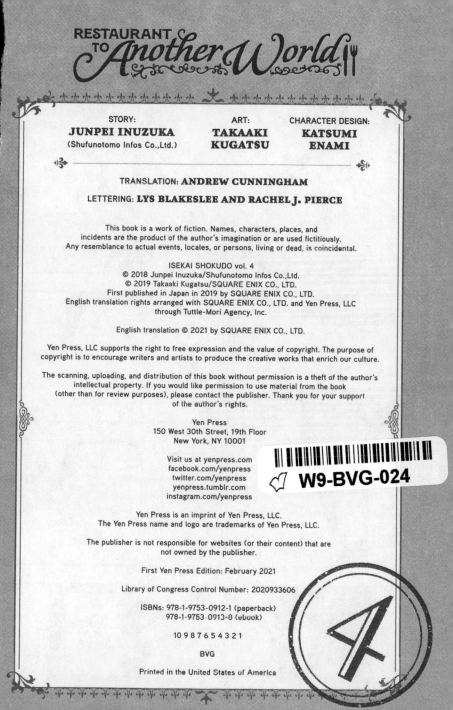

STORY:
JUNPEI INUZUKA
(Shufunotomo Infos Co.,Ltd.)

ART:
TAKAAKI KUGATSU

CHARACTER DESIGN:
KATSUMI ENAMI

TRANSLATION: **ANDREW CUNNINGHAM**

LETTERING: **LYS BLAKESLEE AND RACHEL J. PIERCE**

ISEKAI SHOKUDO vol. 4
© 2018 Junpei Inuzuka/Shufunotomo Infos Co.,Ltd.
© 2019 Takaaki Kugatsu/SQUARE ENIX CO., LTD.
First published in Japan in 2019 by SQUARE ENIX CO., LTD.
English translation rights arranged with SQUARE ENIX CO., LTD. and Yen Press, LLC through Tuttle-Mori Agency, Inc.

English translation © 2021 by SQUARE ENIX CO., LTD.

Yen Press
150 West 30th Street, 19th Floor
New York, NY 10001

Visit us at yenpress.com
facebook.com/yenpress
twitter.com/yenpress
yenpress.tumblr.com
instagram.com/yenpress

Yen Press is an imprint of Yen Press, LLC.
The Yen Press name and logo are trademarks of Yen Press, LLC.

The publisher is not responsible for websites (or their content) that are not owned by the publisher.

First Yen Press Edition: February 2021

Library of Congress Control Number: 2020933606

ISBNs: 978-1-9753-0912-1 (paperback)
978-1-9753-0913-8 (ebook)

10 9 8 7 6 5 4 3 2 1

BVG

Printed in the United States of America

W9-BVG-024